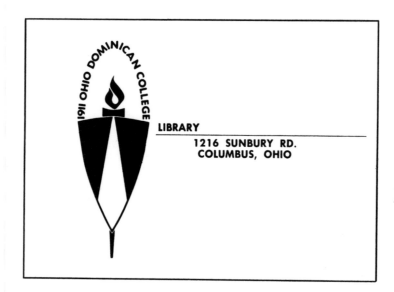

HISTORY
AND ITS
IMAGES

HISTORY
AND ITS
IMAGES

ART AND THE
INTERPRETATION OF THE PAST

Francis Haskell

YALE UNIVERSITY PRESS
New Haven & London

Frontispiece: Joachim von Sandrart, frontispiece to his
Iconologia Deorum of 1680. This plate (which has been loosely adapted
from the title-page designed by Rubens in 1645 for a new edition,
published by the Plantin press, of the complete works
of the antiquarian Hubert Goltz) shows, on the left,
Time hurling the ancient world into the abyss, while on the right
its relics are being recovered by the arts of painting and sculpture, and
by Hercules, Mercury and Minerva.

Endpapers: Alexandre Lenoir, *Musée des Monuments Français,
Salle du 13ème siècle*, plate 18 of the Album de Lenoir
(Paris, Louvre; photo: RMN)

Copyright © 1993 by Yale University

Second printing, with corrections, 1993

Designed by Gillian Malpass
Set in Linotron Bembo by Best-set Typesetter Ltd, Hong Kong
Printed and bound in Great Britain by the Bath Press

Library of Congress Cataloging-in-Publication Data

Haskell, Francis, 1928–
History and its images: art and the interpretation of the past /
by Francis Haskell.
p.   cm.
Includes bibliographical references and index.
ISBN 0-300-05540-4 (hbk)
0-300-05949-3 (pbk)
1. Art and history.   2. History—Sources.   I. Title.
D5.H25   1993   909—dc20   92-41145 CIP

A catalogue record for this book is available from
The British Library

To Nick,
who will recognise the origin of many of the ideas in
this book which began to take shape in my mind while
we were working together on an earlier one.

Contents

Acknowledgements

I am most grateful to the large number of people who, over many years, have helped me with the writing of this book, and I am indebted to the following for answering questions, giving me ideas and information, allowing me access to material under their control and facilitating the increasingly difficult business of obtaining illustrations: the late Jean Adhémar; David Alexander; Jonathan Alexander; Gerald Aylmer; Janet Backhouse; A. Balis; B.C. Barker-Benfield; Martin Brooke; Patricia Fortini Brown; Kevin Butcher; Andrea Buzzoni; Lorne Campbell; Antoine Caron; John Cherry; Timothy Clayton; Richard Cooper; Paul Culot; John Cunnally; Carol Dowd; John Fleming; Jonathan Franklin; Lodovico Franzoni; Burton Frederickson; Carlo Ginzburg; Pascal Griener; Enriqueta Harris; Colin Harrison; Anne Holly; Hugh Honour; Christopher Howgego; Michael Inwood; André Jammes; Mark Jones; Martin Kauffmann; Michael Kauffmann; Bram Kempers; Cathy King; Marion Koninck; Thomas Kren; Peter Krückmann; Sheila Lee; Anton van der Lem; Willy de Loup; Claire Lyons; Elizabeth McGrath; Neil McWilliam; Elly Miller; Bertrand Meyrab; Christian Michel; Sir Oliver Millar; Jennifer Montagu; George Painter; Renan Pollès; Krzystof Pomian; Dominique Ponnau; Alex Potts; the late Menna Prestwich; Marcia Reed; Marianne Roland Michel; Ruth Rubinstein; Antoine Schnapper; Salvatore Settis; François Souchal; Andrew Stewart; Franco Strazzullo; Dirk de Vos; Lucy Whitaker; Jon Whiteley; Linda Whiteley; Marek Zgorniak; Zdzislaw Zygulski. I am certain to have omitted many names, and I sincerely apologise to those concerned. Moreover, it has regrettably not been possible for me to record those members of audiences at lectures given by me who have raised pertinent, and sometimes crucial, points about the theme of this book.

Some institutions and individuals have been so important to me that I wish to single them out for special thanks. An unexpected invitation from the Getty Museum to spend three months there as a visiting scholar arrived at exactly the right moment: without the ideal working conditions (depending as much on the good-natured assistance of the staff as on the resources of the library) which I enjoyed in Santa Monica I would not have been able to complete this book. In Oxford the libraries of the Ashmolean Museum, of the Department of the History of Art and of Duke Humfrey in the Bodleian have, of course, been invaluable – as, too, has been the tireless help given to me from those who work in them. My debt to the Library of the Warburg Institute and to the London Library is equally great, and, in the case of the latter, has been vastly increased by the index made for this book by the Librarian, Douglas Matthews.

A superb article by the late Arnaldo Momigliano (to which, directly or indirectly, I often allude in the following pages) played a major role in stimulating me to explore further some of the ideas raised in it – I deeply regret the fact that I had so very few opportunities to discuss them with him; Ernst Gombrich attended the earliest set I gave of (three) lectures which constituted the nucleus of what has developed into this long book – he gave me much encouragement and advice, but his impact on my work has been incomparably greater than can be suggested by these few words; Nicholas Penny (to whom the book is dedicated) read the whole of it in typescript and proposed a large number of improvements – remaining weaknesses and errors are entirely my own; Linda Klinger most generously allowed me to read (and plunder) her thesis on Paolo Giovio which will not, I trust, remain unpublished for long; the friendliness, patience and efficiency with which Sheila Ballard produced order out of a long series of chaotic drafts gave me the spirit to continue writing at times when I felt like abandoning the project altogether; the constant friendship and encouragement I have received from John Nicoll and Gillian Malpass (who has designed this book with such imagination and skill) have, once again, made it a pleasure, as well as a cause of intense satisfaction, to be published by Yale University Press. What I owe to my wife is too deep to express.

Introduction

i

For much of recorded history men and women have lived in close proximity to images created by earlier generations – images recognisable enough in general appearance, though sometimes disturbingly strange in their particular features. Cave paintings and incised obelisks, temple sculptures and frescoed palaces, gigantic stone statues and tiny figurines of bronze or clay, decorated pottery, coins, altarpieces, funerary monuments – these and other artefacts have long been familiar throughout the inhabited, or once-inhabited, areas of the globe and have attracted varying responses, ranging from awe to greed, from nostalgia to simple curiosity – or indifference. And sometimes the historian has turned to them when seeking to verify or challenge some legend or fable or well-attested narrative handed down from the past by word of mouth or in written texts. Thus when, in the fifth century BC, Herodotus learnt of the existence in the temple of Taenerum of 'a small bronze figure of a man on a dolphin' which had been an offering made by Arion, he felt more confident about the truth of a story, told by the Corinthians and the Lesbians, concerning the escape of that famous singer and composer from the murderous intentions of his ship's crew and his rescue from the sea by a music-loving dolphin. On the other hand, when he was in Egypt, he rejected the tradition that (some two thousand years earlier) Mycerinus, son of Cheops, had raped his own daughter – partly because, when he was shown the 'twenty naked wooden figures of great size' believed to represent servants whose hands had been cut off as a punishment for their negligence in allowing the king access to the girl, he saw that the hands had, in fact, 'simply dropped off through age. They are still there, plainly visible – lying on the ground near the statues' feet.'[1]

A thousand or so years later another Greek historian, Procopius of Caesarea, vividly characterised the Romans of his day who, even as their world was disintegrating around them, were 'eager to protect all their ancestral treasures and to preserve them, so that nothing of the ancient glory of Rome may be obliterated', and as evidence of their great traditions he described, at length and with awe, 'the ship of Aeneas, the founder of the city,' which was still kept on the bank of the Tiber, 'intact throughout, just as if newly constructed by the hand of the builder'.[2]

Yet, with the passing of time, serious historians showed themselves to be increasingly reluctant to use the evidence offered by art or artefacts when trying to interpret the past. And after nearly another thousand years, following the recovery in the fifteenth century of so much ancient literature, written records came to monopolise the sources on which they drew. Moreover, historians were concerned not with evoking the past but with deriving moral and intellectual lessons from it, and (as has been frequently pointed out[3]) the study of figured monuments was left to 'antiquarians', whose often imaginative and sometimes brilliant investigations at first made little impact on historical writing. However, although these antiquarians and also connoisseurs (scholars who could claim expertise in the study of images) eschewed theoretical issues, they always insisted on the historical significance of their researches. And many of their claims, though often extravagantly expressed and unconvincingly argued, were to win recognition when, for various reasons, historians broadened the nature of their own interests in the past and it became clear how important the labours of their despised colleagues had been for a new, broader approach to be made feasible. For before the historian can try to make valid use of a visual source, however undemanding, however simple, he has to know what he is looking at, whether it is authentic, when and for what purpose it was made, even whether it was considered to be beautiful. He also has to have some awareness of the circumstances, conventions and constraints that always govern what can be represented in art at any given time and of the technical means that are available to the figurative artist for expressing his vision. The present book is therefore concerned with the course of a long dialogue, sometimes a dialogue of the deaf, sometimes acrimonious, but occasionally punctuated by moments of reckless *détente* – a dialogue that has been stimulated by the claims of those who have tried to insist that an image can be seen as a valuable historical source.

There is no doubt that this issue can arouse deep hostility. Everyone who is moved by art must frequently have felt that the experience of looking constitutes its own, sufficient, reward – a reward that is only desecrated by analysis. The historian has (often justifiably) been accused of a crude, insensitive reliance on iconography – of having ignored delicacy of touch, subtlety of drawing, harmony or discord of colour, the imaginative transformation of reality and all those elements of virtuosity that can fundamentally affect the nature of the image that he is trying to interpret: at best he is granted a licence to concern himself with the battered, the fragmentary, the remote, the mass-produced and the second-rate. Indeed, in a later chapter we shall see how this attitude has in itself been of significance for his research. But although it is natural enough to sympathise with the distaste expressed by art lovers, and even art historians, for those who use great works of sculpture or painting as 'historical documents', we are liable to forget that such images have often been created to serve that very purpose, and have survived (or, sometimes, been destroyed) just because of it. Contemplating the devastation that had followed the collapse of the Roman Empire, Vasari wrote that 'even the memory of painting and sculpture would soon have disappeared had they not represented before the eyes of the generations that gradually succeeded each other those people who had been honoured through such means so as to render them immortal. Images and inscriptions to preserve their fame were placed on public and private buildings, such as amphitheatres, theatres, baths, aqueducts, temples, obelisks, colossi, pyramids, arches, reservoirs and treasuries, and finally in their very burial places.'[4] Moreover, an awareness of their importance for us as history, rather than of their significance for contemporaries as political and social documents, can sometimes be the price that we must expect to pay in order to appreciate fully some of the greatest works of art – the frescoes by Ambrogio Lorenzetti devoted to Good and Bad Government in the Palazzo Pubblico in Siena, for instance. And even if we turn to paintings of a very different kind – such as the genre scenes produced by Dutch masters in the seventeenth century – is it wholly unreasonable to imagine that Ostade, Teniers and Steen could themselves have had in mind some of the ambitions that Hegel was later to attribute to their art with such sympathy and acumen?[5] 'Here we have, riveted and brought before our eyes, changing nature in its fleeting expressions, a burn, a waterfall, the foaming waves of the ocean, still life with casual flashes of glass, cutlery, etc., the external shape of spiritual reality in the most detailed situations, a woman threading a needle by candlelight, a halt of robbers in a casual foray, the most momentary aspect of a look which quickly changes again, the laughing and jeering of a peasant . . . It is a triumph of art over the transitory, a triumph in which the substantial is as it were cheated of its power over the contingent and the fleeting.'

A refusal to try to recover that memory and that contingency – to look at a fine bust of Nero or at Van Eyck's portrait of Arnolfini and his wife without some awareness of the access that such works seem to provide to distant epochs – may actually diminish the intensity of our perception, for while it is true that many images of historical interest are devoid of artistic quality, it does not follow that the reverse of this proposition is equally valid. Variations of style raise their own, different, questions about the past, and to admire the delicate porcelain pinks and blues of Pontormo's *Deposition of Christ* (which to our eyes appear to jar so provocatively with the crazed expressions of those who are enveloped in them) without wondering what, if anything, is revealed of the religious convictions of the artist and his Florentine patrons would surely require us to impose an unnatural curb on the limits of our aesthetic responses. And yet the practice of scrutinising images in the hope of making contact with the past has been a discontinuous and difficult one, full of traps and false turnings. All too often a visual approach, which appears to be spontaneous and immediate, has been adopted merely to supplement what is already known from the written word. There have, of course, been many civilisations that have left no records to later generations other than those that can be seen and felt and measured, and, even where this is not the case, there have been times when seeing has appeared to provide a more useful way of understanding the past than reading: but it is often forgotten how erratic and potentially misleading a process has been the survival of most visual evidence. Moreover, seeing can itself be learned only by complex stages, and this book will be much concerned with trying to examine these.

The difficulties (as well as the pleasures) of such learning, and of profiting from the experience, have certainly been obscured by the unquestioning deference that has been inspired by visual evidence ever since the widespread use of photography, cinema and television in the recording of contemporary life.[6] That the camera *can* lie was recognised and exploited within some thirty years of its invention;[7] but despite the exposure of countless photographic distortions of reality turned to account by propagandists during the course of the present century,[8] and despite the ambiguities that are as inherent in photographic as in other images,[9] it is doubtful whether these limitations have been generally accepted even now, in relation either to our own times or, still less, to earlier ages. 'The idea of the camera', it has recently been pointed out,[10] 'has so implanted itself that our very imagination of the past takes the snapshot as its notion of adequacy, the equivalent of *having been there*. Photographs are the popular historicism of our era; they confer nothing less than reality itself . . . historical knowledge declares its true value by its photographability'.

It has, therefore, been too readily assumed that much of the imagery surviving from earlier epochs aimed to serve a documentary purpose of a similar kind. Indeed, although artists once feared that photography would kill painting, and although it certainly did usurp many of the functions of painting as far as the recording of contemporary events was concerned, for the historian it had the paradoxical effect of strengthening the authority of all images, including those made long before its invention. Techniques for recording the present by means of photography coincided almost precisely with an increasing readiness to visualise the past through the eyes of painters, sculptors and print-makers.

Even images wholly unrelated to specific events have made the past more generally accessible. The brightly illustrated dust-jackets within which publishers insist on disguising the most obscure and abstruse historical texts provide a telling, if frivolous, acknowledgement of the view that any authentic painting surviving from the period under discussion can, like Proust's *madeleine*, bring it magically to life. The evocative appeal of historical illustrations can, in fact, be traced back to the seventeenth and eighteenth centuries. It was not, however, until the second half of the nineteenth that theories adumbrated by Hegel and others to the effect that 'the arts, taken as a whole, are the truest expression of society' first reached a wide public. The claim was made in 1871 by Paul Lacroix, a pioneer in the production of lavishly illustrated volumes devoted to social life in earlier ages. 'Of all that an epoch can leave to succeeding ages,' he asserted, 'it is art that represents it most vividly . . . the arts of an epoch bring it to life and reveal it to us'.[11] The continuing, indeed the rapidly growing, success of his formula can be verified in any serious bookshop.

Commercial considerations are perhaps not alone responsible for the handsome reproductions now so prevalent in historical surveys, textbooks and even monographs. It has become increasingly fashionable to challenge the very concept of a past that can be understood – let alone explained or judged: in its place we are asked to contemplate a fiction invented by interested parties to suit their current preoccupations. The theory is not a new one and, in an essay to which my debt is immeasurable, the late Arnaldo Momigliano demonstrated that an earlier version of it was combated by antiquarians who turned to coins and monuments for tangible proof that the accounts of the past that they had read in their books were right – or, very occasionally, wrong.[12] If present-day scepticism has played a similar role in encouraging historians to look more sympathetically at the arts, the times have been propitious. Easy travel, the growth of museums and exhibitions, the opening of private houses and collections and, above all, improved techniques of photographic reproduction have made the visual arts more accessible than ever before.

Yet the potential dangers inherent in too visual an approach to the past have also become more apparent in recent years, and have been frequently stressed. In his superb essay, *Dutch Civilisation in the Seventeenth Century*, written in the last decade of his life and published in 1941, Johan Huizinga found himself deploring the intellectual deformation that had been brought about by 'the one-sided aesthetic view' of history.[13] It is true that even in *The Waning of the Middle Ages* of a generation earlier he had had his reservations about such a view, but it was none the less he who had been more responsible than any other serious historian for its propagation. Thus his disenchantment, which will be discussed in the last chapter of this book, must have made a significant impact on those fascinated by his achievements. More disturbing, perhaps, have been many hints by art historians, which have not yet been widely disseminated, that it may be not so much the past that is a fiction as these very arts to which recourse has been made in an attempt to establish the existence of the past. Many investigations over the last few years have, with varying degrees of tendentiousness and success, sought to demonstrate that even images formerly assumed to depict only what could have been seen by an 'innocent eye' were in fact the products of conscious or unconscious manipulation: Dutch genre scenes and still lives, for instance; or the landscapes of Constable and the Impressionists; or even, indeed especially, photographs. Nor has there been any lack of historians impatient to underline a point, the implications of which – it must be admitted – had not, until recently, been given adequate weight: most of the great art that has come down to us was created for a comparatively limited number of privileged patrons, whose aspirations it was designed to satisfy. On a more fundamental, psychological, level Ernst Gombrich has warned of the risks involved in what he has called the 'physiognomic fallacy'.[14] 'Who', he asks, 'would find it easy, after a visit to Ravenna and its solemn mosaics, to think of noisy children in Byzantium, or who thinks of haggard peasants in the Flanders of Rubens?' This would be a 'harmless fallacy, if it did not strengthen the illusion that mankind changed as dramatically and thoroughly as did art'.

The fallacy is, we have seen, a comparatively new one. When one reads the comments made by contemporary observers on the astonishing diversity of artistic styles that could already be seen jumbled together in countless European towns of the seventeenth or eighteenth centuries – a classical portico adjoining a Gothic church, a Baroque fresco obscuring a Byzantine mosaic, tombs of the most varied forms confined within a family chapel – it is chastening to discover how very rarely such changes (which were, of course, often noted and sometimes recorded) spoke to the historical imagination. Arbiters of taste and moralists might approve or disapprove, but the question whether differing styles might reflect differing beliefs or aspirations or achievements was raised by relatively few people. Among these was Daniel Defoe, who visited Winchester cathedral some time before 1724 and commented that 'the Outside of the Church is as plain and Course, as if the Founders had abhor'd Ornaments, or that William of Wickham had been a Quaker, or at least a Quietist';[15] at much the same time Roger North suggested rather more whimsically that the columns of Durham cathedral were notable for an air of grandeur, strength and reasonableness, 'such as an extraordinarily high-spirited judicious Barbarian, might be supposed originally to invent'.[16]

One type of architecture has, however, long been associated with evoking a vivid sense of the past: the ruin. The literature on this is extensive, and a fine recent study has emphasised the impact on English historical writing and antiquarianism of the destruction of monastic buildings and libraries during the Reformation;[17] but among all the poignant lamentations inspired by this vandalism, not one appears to look to the surviving visual evidence provided by the ruins in order to point out, whether with praise or reproach, even such obvious features as the wealth or grandeur of the monks who had once inhabited them or the skills of the craftsmen whom they had employed.

The past evoked by ruins is a generalised one, deeply imbued with meditations on the transitoriness of earthly powers and the fragility of human achievements. Only when confronted with the vast expanse of the walls and crumbling buildings of Rome – so much greater in extent than the half-deserted city lived in during the Middle Ages and early Renaissance – did the moralising and nostalgia of some visitors combine to make the 'historical' point that the one-time inhabitants of the city must surely have belonged to a wholly different breed of men from the population that inhabited it during their own times. And although it may have been the ruins themselves that inspired such reflections, it was the fame of Rome, as it had been transmitted through literary sources, that gave them substance.

It need hardly be pointed out that, even within the course of the Renaissance itself, archaeological investigations could be made to yield far more revealing insights into the past than commonplaces of this kind, and that since then – and especially in very recent years – such investigations have played an over-whelmingly important role in deciphering those aspects of earlier societies for which written documentary evidence is lacking or inadequate or apparently misleading.

This book, however, is concerned essentially with the figurative arts and, to a slight extent, with architecture; very little with archaeology. It is true that the frontier between art and archaeology is not always clear, but it is recognisable above all through the acknowledgement that it pays to the notion of quality. Aesthetic discrimination must always lie at the heart of any serious discussion involving the arts,[18] even in an inquiry (such as the present one) that is not intended to make a contribution to art history as the term is generally understood. And yet, when we turn to one fundamental issue arising out of the potential significance of the arts as an historical source, no such discrimination is possible. For some two and a half thousand years the mere existence of art (or, at least, of what we now classify as art) has been acknowledged to be an important historical fact. Roman emperors were sometimes praised for the magnitude of the buildings they caused to be erected, without any reference being made to their quality, and, as soon as Christianity emerged from persecution, patronage of the arts becomes a central theme of history and biography. The example was set by Eusebius, 'the father of church history', in his life of Constantine, and was taken up with well-informed enthusiasm by Procopius in his detailed account of the buildings commissioned by Justinian. Moreover, in much more meagre sources, such as the *Liber Pontificalis*, the construction and decoration of churches is often presented as the most significant (sometimes the only) feature of a pope's reign. So influential has this concept been that it has continued almost without interruption until the most recent lives of the popes, such as those by Ludwig von Pastor, to an extent that is only rarely matched in the biographies of secular rulers. Similarly, mediaeval chronicles often list great artists, such as Giotto, among the most important citizens of the towns they glorify,[19] and the presence in these towns of celebrated paintings, sculptures or buildings is recorded as a significant fact in itself, even when no attention is paid to specific examples. This tradition, too, has proved to be long-lived – one need think only of Voltaire's *Le Siècle de Louis XIV* and countless modern textbooks – and by the nineteenth century the very existence (almost as much as the quality) of a distinctive school of art had come to be accepted as the most telling gauge of the significance of a nation's past.

ii

I have so far touched on the background to this book and on some of the problems that are raised in it. Because these are so many and so various, so controversial and so formidable, I must briefly explain a few of the more general ways in which I have tried to engage with them.

   In a study devoted to the impact of the image on the historical imagination I have aimed, above all, to indicate the nature of the images available and the approaches of those historians whose imaginations were struck by them. This concern has affected the structure of the book both as a whole and in detail. Thus the first four chapters, all subsumed under the comprehensive title of 'The Discovery of the Image', consider some of the pagan and Christian antiquities and mediaeval artefacts brought by proselytising antiquarians to the attention of historians – and largely ignored by them; but in subsequent chapters on 'The Use of the Image', which discuss the achievements of individual historians who did indeed respond with insight and enthusiasm to the visual arts (such as Michelet and Huizinga), I have also described at some length the precise collections (the Musée des Monuments Français and the exhibition of Flemish primitives held in Bruges in 1902) that first inspired those responses. I am, of course, aware that significant theoretical issues are at stake, and I hope that I have not unduly neglected them; but I am convinced that to try to follow the emotions and reasoning of particular historians looking at specific works of art offers by far the most rewarding way of coming to terms even with the more abstract ideas that are discussed in this book. Indeed, I would claim that if we are not aware of just which pictures or sculptures or buildings were accessible to these and other historians, we shall often fail to understand the substance of their conclusions and hence the more valid theories that may be deduced from them.

Ambitious though the aims of this book already are, they would have been even more so had I tried to confine its scope to a consideration of those few figures and artistic schools about which I have some serious first-hand knowledge. The essence of the underlying theme summed up in its title can be appreciated only if we see it being applied, or misapplied, in different places at different times and on the basis of different sources. The antiquarians with whom the book opens in the late Middle Ages and the Renaissance were aware of belonging to an international community which cut across all conventional frontiers imposed by nationality, religion or social class; the historians with whom it closes in the nineteenth and twentieth centuries were equally aware that they had at their disposal a range of art and artefacts that cut across all conventional classifications imposed by nationality, period and status. Any attempt to cope adequately with so much material would be impossible for this (or any other) writer – and intolerable for his readers. I have, however, tried to mitigate a few of the more tiresome consequences that have arisen from my decision to cover too much ground. Thus, in order to give an element of cohesion, or even of narrative interest, I have, when offered a choice from among a number of works of art or historians who could be cited to exemplify some particular approach, often selected names that have already been referred to in some other context earlier in the book, and omitted others whose contributions may have been just as considerable.[20] Moreover, of those historians' works I have discussed only such passages as bear directly on the problem that concerns me: admirers of Montesquieu and Gibbon must expect to be surprised, and perhaps dismayed, by the emphasis given to what amounts to a secondary aspect of their achievements as a whole. And in certain chapters, such as the fifth, 'Problems of Interpretation', I have provided little more than signposts to fundamental themes which would quickly take over the whole book if treated in detail. But neither these nor other expedients can help me with the most important difficulty I have had to confront.

At what point to conclude this survey worried me even before I had begun to embark on it. The opening caused no problems: Petrarch chose himself, as he has chosen himself for so many authors interested in tracing the origins of some new approach to the humanities. But thereafter I could find no historians who had either made so decisive a contribution to the issues raised by that approach or who had so effectively demolished the various kinds of assumption that lay behind it that their verdicts could be drawn on by me in order to bring my own speculations to an end. On the contrary. As I write this book, calls for new forms of co-operation between the historian and the art historian echo all around me.[21] Calls they usually remain – but a few responses to them of real interest can also be detected, although I do not know of many that are concerned with the issues raised in these pages.[22] I have read some of this literature with great profit and have occasionally written about it elsewhere;[23] but to begin my exploration with Petrarch and end it *in medias res* with what would amount to a series of artificially amalgamated book reviews could give only a misleading impression of its purpose. And so although I am aware of how much has been written on the subject since the death of Johan Huizinga, I have decided to end this book with a consideration of his great achievement. The reasons for this will become apparent in my final chapter. Here I need say only that Huizinga strikes me as a having been both the first writer of real stature to have produced a major work of history based on a perception of the visual arts which pays due attention to issues raised by style and quality, and at the same time, the last to have discussed with such insight the problems that faced him as he did so – problems that remain as acute as ever for other historians wishing to embark on a similar task.

iii

The historian of medicine is not expected to be able to cure a stomach ache: should the historian of a particular historical method be required to solve the problems raised by its use? When I gave a lecture on the theme of this book in Paris a few years ago a student in the audience commented that I had spent much of my time implicitly criticising some great historians for not having paid enough attention to the arts and the rest of it explicitly criticising others for having done so in an unconvincing manner. I would like to fall back on this entirely legitimate observation in an attempt to answer my question. The aim of the chapters that follow is to explore how, when and why historians have tried to recapture the past, or at least a sense of the past, by adopting the infinitely seductive course of looking at the image that the past has left of itself. This has led me to conduct a sustained debate – the notion of debate is more congenial to me than that of criticism – with many of the most brilliant and imaginative writers to have considered, sometimes with sympathy, at others with indifference or disdain, the principal issues involved. From that debate, and also from the few words I have devoted earlier in this introduction to the little recognised but often valuable researches of the antiquarians of the sixteenth and seventeenth centuries, some sort of indication will, I hope, emerge as to how those issues can most validly be approached – but it does not worry me unduly that the book ends both abruptly and on a note of interrogation. One or two points are surely incontrovertible and are comforting to those who, in scholarship as in most other branches of human activity, believe that wisdom is to be found in the mean between two extremes. On the one hand, the ambitions of the inexperienced Hippolyte Taine to write 'a history making use of paintings rather than literary sources as documents' are unrealisable: the documents offered by the visual arts may, as Ruskin claimed, be 'irrefragable', but (as will become clear again and again in these pages) they are by no means easily decipherable. On the other hand, the theory that the arts invariably 'reflect' some belief or state of mind or political event that is more easily apprehended by reading the written sources is almost equally untenable. What we choose to call art is indeed best interpreted by the historian when it is studied in conjunction with other available testimony, but it does have a 'language' of its own which can be understood only

by those who seek to fathom its varying purposes, conventions, styles and techniques. Fruitful cooperation between the historian and the art historian can be
based only on a full recognition of the necessary differences between their approaches, not, as is so often implied, on the pretence that these approaches are
basically the same.

To talk of caution in a work whose inaccuracies are bound to reveal how little
that concept has here been adopted is itself foolhardy. None the less, it seems to
me worthwhile admitting that when I began this book I planned to call it 'The
Arts and the Historian'; that when I was about half-way through, it occurred to
me that the title of 'The Arts and the Historical Imagination' would offer a more
accurate and, paradoxically, less challenging impression of its contents;[24] and that
only after it had been completed did its present title strike me as the one that could
best hint at that balance between artistic creation and historical research that lies at
the heart of my inquiry.

1

The Discovery of the Image

1

The Early Numismatists

When reading the biographies of the later Roman emperors, Petrarch one day came across the statement that Gordian the Younger (who ruled AD 238–44) had been a man of handsome features. 'If that is true,' he wrote in the margin of his copy of the *Historia Augusta*, 'he employed a feeble sculptor [*sic hoc verum fuit, malum habuit sculptorem*]'.[1] This apparently trivial comment marks a milestone of real significance in the development of historical thought, for Petrarch is here not only giving almost equal weight to a figured and a literary source, but recognising that they are not in agreement.

Though this type of reference to what was probably a coin (pl. 1) (or, perhaps, a bust wrongly inscribed) is exceedingly unusual, Petrarch frequently annotated his books with observations inspired by his keen interest in coins.[2] In general he looked to them to confirm what he had already read (about the appearance of some emperor, for instance), but sometimes he amended the written text in the light of the differing evidence that they provided – though in almost every case so far recorded he drew on the inscription rather than on the image for this purpose.

The fifteenth century witnessed the formation of many important collections of Roman coins, but it was only very rarely that commentators made use of them in order to solve literary or historical problems.[3] Petrarch's casual researches in this field did not become known for many centuries (though his enthusiasm for coins and medals did attract much attention), and thus his timid doubts about the beauty of Gordian's features were not followed up. The discovery, editing and publication of so many dispersed written sources relating to the events of the ancient world led to Roman historians being credited with a formidable authority which lasted – with only the occasional challenge[4] – for nearly two centuries. Although scholars acquired increasing skills in identifying the images that they found on coins, and sometimes made use of such images to illustrate manuscript, and later printed, editions of Livy, Suetonius, Plutarch and other writers, they did so for decorative or evocative purposes rather than to supplement (let alone correct) these authors. Similarly, the penetrating attention paid by Flavio Biondo and his followers to the physical remains of

1 (above). *Aureus* of the Emperor Gordian III (AD 238–44).

ancient Rome did not seriously alter the fact that, as far as the study of the past was concerned, the triumph of humanism implied the triumph of the word. The image was relegated to a wholly subordinate position as a potential source of evidence.

During the first decades of the sixteenth century books were published in Italy, Germany and elsewhere about the ancient emperors and other famous personages which were fully illustrated with what purported to be authentic portraits taken from their coins. It was not, however, until at least a generation later that extravagant claims began to be made for the historical importance of images, because it was only then that the study of coins came to be recognised as a serious branch of learning. For despite the great impact that had long been made by the excavated statues as well as by the triumphal arches and columns to be seen in Rome and a few other cities, it was naturally coins that provided by far the most accessible supply of figured images to survive from the ancient world – images, moreover, that were securely datable. They existed in huge quantities, and (although varying much in price) they could reach collectors not only in Italy but in the remotest parts of Europe. In fact, the care devoted to numismatics in the sixteenth and seventeenth centuries constitutes one of the greatest (but most neglected) achievements of Renaissance scholarship, equalled only by contemporary developments in the editing of ancient texts.

For reasons that cannot easily be explained, the mid-1550s saw the sudden and almost simultaneous publication in France, Germany, Italy and Flanders of a number of very important books devoted to this new science. It proved to be a branch of learning that transcended national frontiers, ideological differences and barriers of class – indeed, the point was frequently made that the study of coins and medals was an occupation worthy of being pursued by gentlemen.[5] The fame and influence of these pioneering works survived the appearance, during the next century and a half, of hundreds more such studies, and they constantly reappeared in revised editions. Some impression of the general scope of the movement can best be conveyed by referring to a few of the principal figures involved in it.

Guillaume Rouillé's *Promptuaire des médailles* was first published in Lyon in 1553 with a dedication to Marguerite of Savoy, sister of King Henri II and patroness of Ronsard. Three editions – in French, Italian and Latin – appeared simultaneously, and all were written by Rouillé himself, who was one of the two leading publishers in the city and who often worked in collaboration with partners in Italy and Spain. For his books, which included works on jurisprudence, medicine and theology as well as on history and archaeology, he was able to employ the finest printers and artists in Lyon, Corneille de La Haye among them.[6]

In the same year, 1553, and in the same city, Lyon, Jacopo Strada, the courtier and amateur architect, art dealer, antiquarian and collector, who had been born in Mantua some forty-six years earlier and who in the following decade was to be immortalised in one of Titian's finest portraits (pl. 2), published at his own expense French and Latin editions of his *Epitome du Thrésor des Antiquitez*; a German edition followed in Zurich in 1557.[7] This very elegant book – in which the heads and surrounding inscriptions stand out in white against a deep black

2. Titian, *Jacopo Strada* (Vienna, Kunsthistorisches Museum).

3. Jacopo Strada, *Epitome Thesauri Antiquitatum*, (Lyon 1553; reprinted Zurich 1557).

ground (pl. 3) – reproduced a selection from the thirty volumes of numismatical drawings (ranging in time between Julius Caesar and the Emperor Charles V) which he had compiled while working for Hans Jakob Fugger, a member of the Augsburg banking family. Strada explained that he had intended to produce a far more extensive work which would have included a long life of each emperor followed by descriptions of all the coins and medals associated with him, but that he had hesitated before publishing this because he had heard that similar projects were already under way in Rome and Venice. As these had not yet appeared, he had decided to print his own summary without further delay. Unlike some other authors, he had not merely copied out material from existing books, nor had he invented images when he had been unable to find authentic ones – on the contrary, he had left blanks – and he had personally supervised his engraver with great care. Although his book contained only the obverses, he was already working on another that would include the reverses. In fact, Strada never had the chance to publish this or most of the other material he assembled throughout his life in preparation for his extremely ambitious plans for the scholarly investigation of coins: and he does not seem to have got very far with another proposed book in which 'je rapporte les Medailles à la vérité de l'histoire'. In the *Epitome* his descriptions are as sober as are his illustrations (and rather more informative), and the work is valuable partly for the inclusion of many coins of the late Empire and early mediaeval periods which were of greater interest to Habsburgs eager to establish their imperial ancestry than to Italian collectors and connoisseurs brought up on ancient history.

In Lyon Strada was in close touch with Guillaume du Choul, for whose 'magnificent' house with its collection of gold, silver and bronze medals he expressed great admiration; and two or three years later, in 1555–6, Rouillé published the first, French, edition of Du Choul's *La Religion des anciens romains*, which was followed by an Italian translation in 1558–9.[8] Little more is known about Du Choul than what he tells us in this and in his other works. He was descended from a noble family and held official posts under the king. He had visited Italy and was clearly a man of means, and many of the coins he illustrated were found and brought to him by the peasants working on his estates. He was certainly an experienced numismatist, and the aim of his book was to make use of coins (and other figurative sources) to throw light on all the gods and religious ceremonies discussed in ancient literature. The large-scale study of Roman antiquities that was commissioned from him by François Ier was never published, and only the first volume appears to be extant, in the form of a superbly illustrated manuscript (pl. 4).[9] This shows us that Du Choul planned to draw on the evidence supplied by 'médailles Pompes Triumphes Edifices'[10] so as to combine, in a most original spirit, a history of the Roman emperors arranged chronologically with a thematic treatment of specific topics (such as circuses and temples) as they emerged during the course of his narrative. Two such excursuses – on military fortifications and on baths – were published, and the former became well known.[11] Other projects that he had in mind were to be carried out by other antiquarians only long after his death. None the less, enough of Du Choul's researches survive to show that, as we shall see later, his was probably the most ambitious, interesting and imaginative contribution to this early phase of numismatic scholarship.

It was not, however, the most influential. That distinction must be granted to Enea Vico's *Discorsi sopra le medaglie de gli antichi* (pl. 5), which was also first published in 1555, seven years after an illustrated anthology of ancient coins that he had produced in collaboration with Antonio Zantani.[12] Vico had been born of a noble family in Parma and had become an excellent and prolific engraver. He then turned to the study of antiquity – by which was meant primarily coins and medals – and became enough of an authority to be put in charge of the medal cabinet of the Estes in Ferrara. He is reported to have died of apoplexy while carrying an ancient vase to the duke. But that was in 1567, by which year he had, fortunately, completed a number of beautiful and interesting treatises.[13]

The year 1557 saw the publication in Antwerp of the three separate editions, in Latin, Italian and German, of a superb set of portraits of the emperors from Julius Caesar to the still-living Ferdinand I, freely adapted from their coins by the Dutch artist Hubert Goltz,[14] who latinised his name as Goltzius and was uncle of the

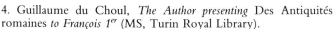

4. Guillaume du Choul, *The Author presenting* Des Antiquités romaines *to François 1ᵉʳ* (MS, Turin Royal Library).

5. Enea Vico, *Discorsi sopra le medaglie de gli antichi*, Venice 1555: dedicatory page to Cosimo I of Florence.

much more famous Hendrick. Goltz had trained as a painter under Lambert Lombard in Liège and the precise technique that he used for printing his plates is still a matter of controversy. The effect is overwhelming. Each page of his folio volumes reproduces only one greatly enlarged coin (about eighteen centimetres in diameter) in the colour of a tawny lion, while the rim, around which runs the inscription, is lighter in tone and some of the highlights are picked out in white (pl. 6). Prototypes of the coins can, for the most part, still be identified, although he sometimes combined features taken from separate issues and he depicted only specimens in perfect condition. The characterisation is bold and sharp, and few images of the sixteenth century convey quite so vividly the impact made by the majesty of the ancient world and the survival of imperial power into later ages. Most of the coins in this first publication were copied by Goltz from ones in local collections, notably that of the great geographer Ortelius, but the success of the book – it was translated into French in 1559 and into Spanish in 1560 – led to his visiting many hundreds of medal cabinets in France, Italy, Germany and the Low Countries in search of new material; and in subsequent years he published a succession of fine volumes which often broke new ground and which were enormously admired. Antonis Mor was so pleased with a copy of the volume on Augustus which Goltz presented to him in 1574 that he painted a portrait of him

PRIAMVS MIRVM IN MODVM BEATVS FVIT, QVOD PATRIAM SIMVL CVM REGNO PERDITAM VIDIT.

Poſtquam annos .xxxii. vixiſſet, .xiiii. verò Imperium adminiſtraſſet, ſibi ipſi manum intulit.

B

6. Hubert Goltz, *Vivae Omnium fere Imperatorum Imagines*, Antwerp 1557: Nero.

(in less than an hour) (pl. 7). In the seventeenth century Goltz's works were to be handsomely republished by the Plantin press, but by then he had long since died, apparently in poverty, after a series of accidents and business failures.

Among the collectors visited by Goltz was Sebastiano Erizzo, a member of one of the leading patrician families of Venice.[15] Erizzo was to enjoy an active public life and also to produce a volume of *novelle*, but his principal claim to attention, in his own time as today, lies in his study of numismatics. In his splendidly decorated house in the parish of S. Moisè he had (by the time of his death in 1585) assembled nearly two thousand coins and medals and over a thousand books, and these collections were well known to most scholars interested in the field. In 1559, at the age of thirty-four, Erizzo published his *Discorso sopra le medaglie* which was to appear in three further, amended, editions during the next fourteen years.

7. Hubert Goltz, *Sicilia, et Magna Graecia*, Bruges 1576: engraving of the painted portrait of Goltz by Antonis Mor, now in the Musée des Beaux-Arts, Brussels.

This list of early treatises and anthologies could be vastly expanded – and many major numismatic works projected at just this time by such renowned figures as Annibale Caro, Pirro Ligorio (who was familiar with Erizzo's collections) and others never saw the light.[16] Thus in 1558 the Austrian doctor and antiquarian Wolfgang Lazius, who, twelve years earlier at the age of thirty-two, had won fame for his history of Vienna and who, some years later, was to write a strikingly illustrated book on the migrations that followed the collapse of the Roman Empire, became involved in a project to catalogue the coins in the imperial collection. His qualifications for this were dismissed as inadequate by Jacopo Strada, but this did not discourage him from announcing in the same year an astonishingly ambitious proposal to compile a complete repertoire of all surviving types of ancient coins. He estimated their number to be some 700,000, and although his plan came to nothing, it attracted much attention, if only because it provided a stimulating example to scholars and collectors working on similar lines but on a smaller scale throughout Europe.[17]

Even this brief glance at some of the more important publications and proposals to appear within the space of a mere five years makes it clear that noblemen and artists, Northerners and Italians, amateurs and professionals were all involved in this new form of research which brought to light a vast number of hitherto unknown visual sources. Moreover, all seemed to be in contact, aware of each others' contributions and usually ready to work in surprising harmony even when voicing disagreements. However, the flood of serious studies that continued to flow from the presses in France, Italy and the Low Countries soon began to show a certain narrowing in the social background of the scholars responsible for it. It was not long before physicians assumed a dominant role,[18] and although most invalids of the period would have received far sounder advice from their doctors about their coins than about their digestions, it is tempting to speculate whether the medical training of so many numismatists of the sixteenth and seventeenth centuries may not have been at least partly responsible for the high standard of technical competence attained by this branch of scholarship.

Almost without exception these many and varied authors stressed that the principal reason for studying coins was the value that they had for the historian. Were it not for the existence of coins, inscriptions and 'wonderful ruins', wrote Enea Vico, we might find ourselves doubting the veracity of the great events narrated by the historians of Rome.[19] A knowledge of history, asserted the states-man Sebastiano Erizzo, was the most necessary of all human accomplishments, particularly for princes and politicians; but written histories were often defective or biased, and this made the study of buildings, inscriptions and ancient medals in gold, silver and other metals particularly important.[20] His complete corpus of ancient coins, claimed Lazius, in the small preliminary fraction of it that was all that he published, would – when finished – provide a key to the most complicated histories.[21]

But the obstacles that stood in the way of such ambitions were formidable. In the first place, it was not exactly clear what was the nature of the evidence. Enea Vico was convinced that the objects he collected and engraved had been used as currency; but Sebastiano Erizzo disagreed and argued that most of what was considered in his day to be ordinary coinage had, in imperial times, been minted as commemorative medals. Other authors joined the debate, and by the end of the century it was generally agreed that Vico had been correct. However, Vico's awareness of the true purpose of Roman coins in no way diminished his great respect for them; he was, for instance, keen to emphasise that in antiquity the dignity attaching to the imperial likeness forbade their being taken into brothels.[22] Indeed, the whole discussion is of interest not only for the light it throws on scholarly methods, but also because it emphasises the reverence that was felt for such relics from the past – 'ces pièces immortelles, ces petits aziles de la mèmoire des Grans-hommes, ces depôts sacrez de la vertu et de la gloire', as they were to be described a century later.[23] We shall see that it was partly this very veneration for ancient coins that was to be responsible for their sometimes being so misleading.

Another issue that attracted attention was the origin of coinage. One theory claimed that coins had been invented by Tubalcain, son of Zilla, who is recorded in the Book of Genesis as having been 'an instructor of every artificer in brass and iron'.[24] In the light of this, it was not wholly unreasonable for Erasmus to have believed that he had seen a coin that portrayed on one side Noah and his

8 and 9. Gold *stater*, Olbia, last third of first century BC, showing, on the obverse, three men in Roman togas, and, on the reverse, an eagle standing on a sceptre with a wreath in one claw, copied from a Roman coin representing Lucius Junius Brutus and his lictors.

sons leaving the ark and on the other the dove with the olive branch, when, in fact, what was represented was Brutus and his lictors, and the Roman eagle (pls 8, 9).[25]

That sixteenth- and seventeenth-century numismatists were frequently deceived by deliberate forgeries is well enough known and was much pointed out by succeeding generations. It is less often emphasised that the remarkable quality of many of those forgeries that have come down to us provides telling evidence of the skill and scholarship both of the craftsmen who made them and of the scholars who were taken in by them: and many forgers were warmly admired for their talents by leading writers of the time. In any case, this issue (which has loomed so large in discussions of Renaissance numismatics) is insignificant when compared with the fact that with very rare exceptions these students of coins were not, despite the boldness of their claims, interested in making use of them as evidence for their investigations of the past, as Petrarch and a few other scholars had occasionally been. They wished rather to explore what was to be seen on coins in the light of what they already knew about the past; and some of them also wished to assemble a store of visual references that would be of use to the artists of their own day. In this latter aim they were eminently successful. The illustrations of ancient coins published and interpreted by Enea Vico and his successors became the most important source used by painters for the depiction of such abstract virtues as Liberality or Clemency or Charity, and the language of allegorical art was radically and permanently altered. In the following generation, a host of antiquarians played their part in working out such identifications, and they corresponded with each other throughout Europe. Indeed, the deciphering of the symbols and allegories to be found on the reverses of coins and medals eclipsed nearly all other considerations. Theories concerning their meanings fill the correspondence, which extended over a period of nearly twenty-five years from 1559 to 1583, between Don Antonio Agustín, the great Spanish jurist and Archbishop of Tarragona, and Fulvio Orsini, librarian of the Farnese family in Rome.[26] Well before ways of representing such symbols had been codified into iconographical dictionaries in the seventeenth century, their significance had been worked out by men such as these.

And yet, paradoxically, the methods by which these results were achieved led to the appearance, and sometimes even the existence, of the image being played down by the more learned numismatists, for in almost every case identifications were made on the basis of written texts or of the inscriptions to be seen on the reverses. The most striking example of this attitude is provided by Costantino Landi, yet another scholar of the generation of Vico, Du Choul and Erizzo, who offered his explanations of the symbolism of Roman coins in a book published in 1560 without any illustrations at all. Yet even Agustín, whose learned and lively dialogues on ancient medals first appeared in 1590 and soon rendered easily accessible (in many editions and translations) the researches of all his predecessors, was far less interested in the image than in the text. It is true that he, too, stressed the value of seeking inspiration from the portraits of virtuous men and even the interest of looking at the features of the villainous Nero or of so strange a creature as the crocodile. He went so far as to express some awareness of the variations in artistic quality of the medals he was examining, and he recognised how many important and still surviving statues and other monuments were represented on them. But when he proclaimed that greater trust should be put in medals and carved inscriptions than in books, he was referring not to otherwise unknown historical information that was to be obtained only from such sources, but merely to matters of spelling and script.[27]

Looking back on issues of this kind nearly a hundred years later, the French traveller and antiquarian Jacob Spon, who had a real feeling for natural beauty, for art and for its changing styles, none the less made what was essentially the same point. When defending his pursuits against those who objected that there could be no purpose in searching for ancient history on broken pieces of marble or half-erased stones if one could do so far more easily by studying the books in one's library, he argued that the great scholars of the sixteenth century had not mastered their studies by relying only on books. They had made use of inscriptions, medals, manuscripts, 'les Grâvures antiques, et enfin tous les Moyens dont l'Antiquité s'est servy pour faire connoître son Histoire à la Posterité'.[28] This sounds remarkable, but in fact what Spon had in mind was the search for textual accuracy.

The magnetic and potentially corrupting appeal of sheer erudition increasingly stifled the ambitious and imaginative claims that continued to be repeated about the importance of coins for the historian. In matters affecting the transmission of an ancient text the scholar was prepared to acknowledge that there might be significant differences between what was to be seen on a coin dating from antiquity itself and what was to be found in manuscripts or printed books issued well over a thousand years later. But beyond that he was rarely prepared to venture. For we can now see that the overwhelming difficulty faced by the students of the sixteenth and seventeenth centuries was that they could not accept that the kinds of history offered by writers and medallists might be different – and even incompatible. Whatever reservations these students may have suggested in the prefaces to their treatises, when it came to the main body of their works they accepted the authority of the ancient historians as sacrosanct. On the other hand, coins, too, were primary sources whose evidence could not be disputed. Somehow the two had to be reconciled, for (as will become apparent later) no one could appreciate that one or both might be false or that both – because of the very different purposes they had been called upon to serve – might have been trying to make entirely different points.[29]

And so images themselves came to be used less and less as a form of evidence that might challenge, or substantiate, or even modify those more usual forms of history that had been passed down in books: at best they might supplement it or help to unravel some minor problem. Thus we are told that had Polydore Vergil, later to become historian of England, bothered to examine Roman coins he would not, in his enormously popular *De inventoribus rerum*, have had to confess himself so puzzled about the number of wheels to be found on ancient chariots.[30] In fact, Enea Vico, who made this point, did offer many precise examples (as distinct from general allusions) of the valuable hints that historians might have derived from the study of medallic images. But such matters were rarely pursued, and those antiquarians who did not confine themselves to abstruse explanations of the language of symbolism, were concerned essentially with details of dress or weapons or ceremonies – matters of little interest to the historians of their day (though fortunately of great fascination to artists, as is demonstrated by the supreme example of Rubens). Disputes there were in plenty, but to those not involved they appeared to be trivial and pedantic, quite without intellectual substance.

Coins – and monuments of all kinds – nevertheless remained pre-eminently important for the reassurance they could offer that the past recorded in books really had existed and was not a mere series of fictions wrangled over by partisan historians. In the words of Charles Patin (published in 1665, two years before he had to flee into foreign exile after being sentenced to the galleys for trafficking in subversive books), 'one can say that without medals History would be stripped of all proof and would be considered by many people to be either a product of the strong feelings of historians writing about what had happened in their own times or a mere description of past records which might be either false or biased'.[31] And yet to those who raised wider historical issues the information offered by coins and medals appeared to be becoming thinner.

Indeed, by the 1680s we can begin to discern, in differing parts of Europe, an increasing number of indications that – as far as the historian was concerned – all was not well. Scepticism developed not so much as regards the importance of the coins themselves but out of dissatisfaction with the manner in which they had hitherto been interpreted. It was not just ridiculous mistakes that were worrying: more serious concerns were involved. The point was best made by Ezekiel Spanheim (pl. 10), greatest of German numismatists, but also a sophisticated observer of the current European scene and a diplomat, who, as representative of the Elector of Brandenburg, was to spend the last years of his life in London and to be buried in Westminster Abbey. There are, he warned in 1683, professional students of medals who devote to them all their time and all their resources.[32] They are ignorant of almost everything else, and do not even know to what use they can put their researches.

As for me, I have always believed that it is just as dangerous and reprehensible to attach oneself only to medals as to despise them: the one attitude is a

10. Ezekiel Spanheim, *Dissertationes de praestantia, et usu numismatum Antiquorum*, London 1706: portrait of Spanheim.

consequence of lack of sense, the other of pure ignorance or ridiculous prejudice. Let us say quite openly that it is unfortunate that until now the greatest and most learned critics have paid no attention to medals while the majority of medallists and antiquarians have not been scholars: the former through lack of opportunity, through lack of appreciating all the benefit that could be derived from this study, or finally through lack of leisure; the latter, on the contrary, though being satisfied with making of their work a profession or a commercial enterprise. I naturally exclude Antonio Agustín and Fulvio Orsini from these categories – but only a very few others.

Spanheim was right to emphasise that the high hopes with which the study of coins had been launched well over a century earlier had not really been fulfilled because it had become an end in itself divorced from wider historical interests; and although (as we shall see) a great deal of brilliance (as well as some absurdity) was applied to deciphering the meanings of reverses, no one explicitly raised the fundamental question of what had been the purpose intended to be served by these images.[33] And, finally, while it is true that the beauty of design to be found in medals was often greatly admired, ultimately it was not the art that was proving to be of use to the historian, but the inscription. Adapting a formula that was often applied to emblems, the French numismatist Louis Jobert (an enthusiastic admirer of Spanheim) wrote at the end of the seventeenth century in a treatise that was to be frequently translated that: 'Ainsi l'on doit regarder la légende comme l'âme de la médaille, et les Figures comme le corps'[34] – and in practice this had been accepted from the first. In the influential claims he made for the study of coins a few years later, Joseph Addison was justified in claiming that they constituted 'a kind of Printing', before the art was invented. It was thanks to this that Monsieur Vaillant 'has disembroiled a history that was lost to the world before his time, and out of a short collection of Medals has given us a chronicle of the Kings of Syria . . .',[35] for, like all numismatists, Vaillant had essentially relied on the inscriptions rather than on the images for his important historical researches. Medals were considered essentially as texts – texts that could be much more reliable than surviving histories, but texts none the less. It is for this reason that numismatic studies cannot in themselves play as weighty a role in this book as might have been expected.

And yet their indirect importance can hardly be exaggerated. It was through the study of coins that antiquarians and historians first became familiar with the notion that figurative sources could bring them into close and exhilarating contact with aspects of the past that were not apparently accessible in any other way. Thus it was usually through the study of coins that they learned to investigate the significance of marble sculptures and of many other visual records whose decipherment was so much more complicated because of the frequent absence of written inscriptions. Numismatic research was also inseparable from the pursuit of quite different sources no less attractive to scholars and amateurs, whose methods provide helpful guidance as to how we can best survey this wider field; for even the briefest examination of the huge literature (and illustrative material) inspired by coins and medals will show that the books concerned tend to divide themselves, on the one hand, into anthologies of portraits and, on the other, into treatises which pay primary attention to the religious, historical, allegorical and topographical information to be derived from the reverses. It is therefore not unduly misleading to adopt this principle when approaching the figurative material available to sixteenth- and seventeenth-century historians.

Portraits from the Past

i Medals and Pseudo-Medallic Anthologies

For many centuries portraiture remained by far the most important, and often the only, figurative evidence of the past that was regularly accessible to readers – and writers – of history. In antiquity historians had very occasionally referred to the evidence of statues when trying to describe the appearance of important characters who had lived before themselves;[1] but during the later Middle Ages, when an interest in reconstructing the ancient world first became sustained and articulate, it was naturally coins and medals that provided a uniquely rich – and (so it was believed) authentic – fund of information about the features of the emperors and other figures who were already familiar from written accounts. Even before the example of Petrarch had begun to stimulate enthusiasm and research, Roman coins had been used as sources for the adornment, and hence for the imaginative interpretation, of works of history. In about 1320 the Veronese cleric Giovanni Mansionario illustrated his *Historia Imperialis* with portraits of the Roman emperors.[2] Only the later part of his manuscript has survived, but from it we can see that, although the identification of coins dating form the third and fourth centuries was subsequently to present difficulties to many generations of numismatists, Mansionario went to some pains to make use of the most accurate sources available to him (pl. 11). Naturally he was by no means always successful, and as well as making a number of mistakes, he was often quite ready to substitute one emperor for another, presumably when unable to get hold of some coin he needed. Mansionario, and probably other scribes also, were in turn used as sources by painters and sculptors who portrayed the heads of the Caesars on a much larger scale during the fourteenth and fifteenth centuries.

Such works were essentially designed to be evocative, and a more interesting example of the figurative representation of the past is provided by the drawings of an unknown artist that survive at Fermo and which are believed to date from about 1350.[3] They were made to illustrate a manuscript of the *Lives of the Caesars* by Suetonius, and they appear to constitute the first recorded instance of the use of authentic material for this purpose; but although the heads have been copied with great care (and a considerable degree of accuracy) from the relevant coins, this is not immediately apparent, because the emperors are represented as half-length figures and have been supplied with attributes (pl. 12) – attributes that are not

11a and b (above). Giovanni Mansionario, *Historia Imperialis*, *c*.1320: head of the Emperor Aurelian (270–5) derived from coin.

12a and b. Suetonius, *De Vita Caesarum*, *c*.1350: half-length 'portrait' of the Emperor Galba, adapted from coin.

always derived from surviving coins but that have been chosen to correspond with information available from the textual sources. We shall see that when coins and medals acquired greater prestige, this process was usually reversed so that portraits derived from the most varied sources (including the imagination) were given a medallic format as a suggestion of authenticity.

Later it became quite common to decorate manuscripts of Suetonius (and sometimes other ancient writers) with illustrations derived from coins. The Paduan scribe (and friend of Bembo) Bartolomeo Sanvito produced a particularly fine version in the 1470s (pl. 13);[4] but although medal cabinets were by then already plentiful and fashionable, it was not always possible to locate accurate likenesses of famous men, and this shortage of true originals led to an extensive supply of what can be described as creative or imaginative forgeries. For us the significance of these lies partly in what they tell us about the interest of Renaissance collectors, artists and scholars in the physiognomic representation of character; or, rather, the lack of interest. Only much later did it become a popular pastime to interpret historical portraiture in the light of literary descriptions: in the seventeenth century, for instance, an English traveller to Rome could write of a (conspicuously feeble) marble group believed to represent Nero's nurse with her infant charge that Nero 'though very young yet did represent a kind of fierce looke with him'.[5] However, when artists first began to make portraits of the young Caracalla – devised apparently by themselves and not based on antique prototypes – they produced boys who can surely never have been thought of as anything other than charming.[6] In fact, the notion that a man's true character was reflected in his features had been firmly established in antiquity, but we shall find that it played little part in discussions of portraiture until well into the sixteenth century.

Despite the examples hitherto discussed, and many others that have been omitted, it was not until 1517 that there was published the first extensive set of 'images of the illustrious' ostensibly based on ancient medals.[7] The chief compiler and scholar responsible for this elegantly designed book was almost certainly Andrea Fulvio, best known for his collaboration with Raphael on the antiquities of Rome. There were more than two hundred portraits in all, and the chronological span ranged between Alexander the Great (whose portrait, however, was preceded by that of the double-headed Roman deity, Janus) and the Holy Roman Emperor Conrad, who ruled between AD 911 and 918.

The vast majority of the portraits were of the Roman emperors and (in the early period) their womenfolk and other members of their families. There were also a few eminent non-rulers, such as Cicero; and there were some very strange omissions, among them Charlemagne – despite the fact that a few years before the publication of the book a convincing medal portraying him had been made.[8] It is these arbitrary touches that give the impression (and were perhaps designed to do so) that Fulvio had chosen to illustrate only those historical figures of whom authentic portraits were available. This impression is strengthened by the use of a device that (as we have seen) was later imitated by other writers. From time to time a blank space was left under the account of some personage (such as Cossutia, the first wife of Julius Caesar) implying that no true likeness of her had yet been found. Elsewhere an image was reproduced (of Antonia Augusta, mother of the Emperor Claudius (pl. 14), although nothing was written about her in the place available for the text – as though the coin were being illustrated because it was obviously genuine, even though the figure represented was of no interest to history. In fact, many of the medals – such as that of Cicero – were pure inventions, and the number of fantastic creations increased decisively in the later part of the book devoted to the period following the end of the Roman Empire in the West. Nevertheless, Fulvio had produced the first comprehensive (and

VITELLII·IMP·VITA·ITELLIORVM·ORIGINEM·ALII·ALIAM·ET QVIDEM·DIVERSIS

simam tradunt: partim ueterem, & nobilem: partim uero
nouam, & obscuram atq; & sordidam. Quod ego per adu
latores, obtrectatoresq; Imperatoris Vitelly euenisse opi
narer: nisi aliquanto prius de familiæ conditione uaria
tum est. Extatq; elogij ad Q. Vitellum Diui Aug. Quæ
storem libellus: quo continetur Vitellios Fauno Aborigi
num Rege: & Vitellia Quæ multis locis pro numine cole
retur: ortos Toto Latio imperasse. Horũ residuam stirpe
ex Sabinis Transisse Romam: atq; inter patricios allecta.
ndicia stirpis mansisse diu viam Vitelliam ab Ianiculo,
ad mare usq;. Item Coloniam eiusdem nominis: qua Gen
tili copia aduersus Equicolos tutandam olim depoposcisse.
empore deinde Samnitici belli, presidio in Apuliam mis
so: quosdam ex Vitellijs subsedisse Nuceriæ: eoɾ̃q; pro
geniem longo post interuallo repetisse Vrbem atq; ordine
Senatoriũm. Contra plures autorem generis libertinũ
prodiderunt. Cassius Seuerus nec minus alij, eundem

Vitellia numeɾ̃

Vitellia via.

Gentilis copia.

Cassius Seuerus

13. Suetonius, *De Vita Caesarum*, *c*.1470, MS by Bartolomeo Sanvito: Emperor Vitellius.

14. Andrea Fulvio, *Illustrium Imagines*, Rome 1517: Antonia Augusta.

apparently plausible) gallery of rulers whose achievements were familiar to all educated people, and his book was much plagiarised and imitated, despite the fact that the features of those portrayed in it were nearly always characterless and sometimes almost indistinguishable from each other.

The most famous (or notorious) of such compilations has already been mentioned – Guillaume Rouillé's *Promptuaire des médailles des plus renommées personnes qui ont esté depuis le commencement du monde, avec une briève description de leurs vies et faicts, receuillie des bons auteurs*, first published in Lyon in French, Latin and Italian in 1553.[9] Its range was even greater than that of Fulvio's *Illustrium Imagines*, for the first portrait illustrated was of Adam (pl. 15) and the last was of the still-living Henri II, King of France; and among the many hundreds of figures represented were not only rulers, but also artists (such as Raphael and Michelangelo) and philosophers (such as Diogenes and Marsilio Ficino), as well as Noah, Jesus Christ, Judas Iscariot and Mahomet. In his dedicatory letter to the reader Rouillé explained that he had taken the best advice possible and had gone to great trouble to obtain authentic images, so that where several different medals survived of the same emperor he had chosen the truest one. Illustrated portraits as unconvincing as some of those to be found in Rouillé had been published often enough before, but his are distinguished from mediaeval precedents by an attempt to indicate variations in costume and gesture between different figures and different periods; whereas in some German publications of the last years of the

INSEGNACI la sacra scrittura, come Dio nel principio creò il cielo & la terra, & dipoi, nel sesto dì, formato l'huomo (cioè Adamo & Eua) à la imagine, & similitudine sua, & collocatolo nel paradiso terrestre, lo prohibì con minacci della morte, dal mangiar del frutto dell'albero della scienza del bene & del male: & come poi ingannata dal serpente la prima donna Eua, ne mangiò & indusse il marito à mangiarne contro al diuin precetto: & che subito cascati sotto il giogo del peccato & della morte, furno discacciati di quel paradiso sempre virente, & che tutto spontanamète produce, nella terra maladetta, doue in fatiche, & sudori infiniti tirassino lor vita: & che Adà esercitò la terra, & cognobbe sua cösorte Eua, che gli partorì Caino, & appresso, Abello, poi da Caino per inuidia vcciso. Vedi nel Gen. cap. 1. 2. 3. & 4. & Iosef. lib. 1. cap. 1. 2. 3. & 4.

ADAM, d'anni 130. generò Seth, dalqual tirorno l'origine i santi padri. Seth sendo d'anni 105. generò Enos, che cominciò à inuocare il nome di Dio. Enos, d'anni 90. generò Cainam, qual d'anni 70. generò Malaleel: & questo d'anni 65. generò Iared: qual d'anni 162. generò Enoch. Enoch d'anni 65. generò Mathusalem. Enoch, vissuto anni 365. fù tolto via da Dio, ne più apparue. Mathusalè, dopo anni 187. generò Lamech: & Lamech d'anni 182. generò Noe, & Noe d'anni 500. generò Sem, Cham & Iafet, anni 100. prima che venissi il diluuio. Perche Noe haueua anni 600. al tempo del diluuio. Gen. cap. 5. & 7.

EL SIGNOR nostro IESV Christo, vero Dio, & vero huomo, nato di vergine, fatto sotto la legge, per ricomperare quegli che erano sotto la legge, patì & morì in Croce per la nostra salute & vita, l'anno della sua età 33. & del mondo 3994. & dell'Imperio di Tiberio, 18. Dopo tre dì, risuscitò da morte: acciò quello che morendo haueua destrutta la nostra morte: resurgèdo anchora, reparasi la nostra resurrettione. Imperò che el morì per i peccati nostri: & risuscitò per la nostra iustificatione, acciò che morti à i peccati, viuiamo alla iustitia, faccendo certa la nostra vocatione per l'opere buone. Il quadragesimo dì della sua morte, montò in Cielo, & il quinquagesimo, mãdò lo Spirito Säto, come a i suoi haueua promesso, & hà à venire à giudicare i viui, & i morti nel fine de secoli, & beati quei serui, i quali venendo trouerrà vigilanti & parati. Gl'euangeli, l'epistole, di san Paulo, Pietro, Giouäni, Iacopo, ci metteno innanzi à gl'occhi tutte queste cose, la vita di Christo, la morte, l'ascensione, la missione dello Spirito santo, il bruciamento & incendio del mondo, l'vltimo giudicio anchora di esso Christo, & la vita eterna, & el supplicio eterno.

AA 5

15. Guillaume Rouillé, *Prontuario de le Medaglie*, 2nd edition, Lyon 1577: 'portraits' of Adam and Eve.

16 (above right). Guillaume Rouillé, *Prontuario de le Medaglie*, 2nd edition, Lyon 1577: 'portrait' of Jesus Christ.

17 (right). *Solidus* of the Byzantine Emperor Justinian II (AD 685–95), with head of Christ as obverse (Oxford, Ashmolean Museum).

fifteenth century, standard types in contemporary dress had been repeated even for Roman emperors.[10]

Indeed, Rouillé acknowledged that when it came to Adam, Abraham and the patriarchs, he had had to rely on written sources and then resort to creative imagination, just as Phidias had sought inspiration from Homer in order to divine the form of the 'invisible Jupiter'. But if many of the medals reproduced were pure fabrications (as was soon recognised),[11] a few of even the most improbable celebrities whose features were recorded in the *Promptuaire* and similar publications could claim a certain degree of respectability which may escape those who look at them today. Thus, as was also soon recognised, the head of Christ had first appeared on Byzantine coins of the seventh century and continued to do so until five years before the fall of the Eastern Empire (pls 16, 17).[12] Du Choul obtained one from Constantinople (of a rather different kind from Rouillé's) 'par le moyen dung mien amy',[13] and it is quite possible that both men believed that these images were much older than in fact they were and might therefore be true likenesses. It is hardly surprising that Hellenistic medallions which showed the head of Homer were thought to date from the poet's own lifetime; and although sixteenth-century numismatists readily acknowledged that coins representing the portraits of prominent Romans who had lived before Julius Caesar could only have been minted posthumously, it was not at all unreasonable to suggest that they might have been copied from the wax ancestral portraits which Roman families were known to cherish.[14] In the case of modern figures Rouillé could often make use of genuine likenesses drawn from the life by Georges Reverdy and Corneille de La Haye which were then printed for him in the form of medals.[15] Thus for all the many doubts about authenticity raised by the *Promptuaire*, Rouillé was an important pioneer in the publishing of portraits. He relied on different kinds of evidence and he included a more adventurous range of characters than was usual at the time – for Paolo Giovio's great collection of portrait paintings in Como (which will be discussed later in this chapter) had not yet appeared in print, and even sets of copies taken from it were relatively inaccessible.

Rouillé's formula of publishing copies of genuine coins and medals – or, sometimes, of pseudo-medallic images – in order to convey an illusion of authenticity provided a popular and much-imitated source for many of the countless volumes devoted to historical portraits accompanied by texts of varying lengths that were issued throughout Europe during the sixteenth and seventeenth centuries. A high proportion of these concentrated on rulers and their immediate families, but there were also collections of warriors, Church leaders, reformers, writers and other categories of distinguished figures. The *raison d'être* for most of these richly illustrated publications was similar to that also proposed for most books of conventional written history at this period: the features, like the actions, of great men could prove an inspiration to later generations.[16] To that extent, a portrait was as much a historical fact as was an account of a military victory. None of the compilers of these books seems to have felt that it might be wrong to record for posterity the countenance of so wicked a man as Nero, 'detestable, pernicieux à la republique, et flambeau et perdition des hommes'.[17] In any case, the natural desire to own a complete set of portraits – perhaps also a certain fascination with wickedness – would have led to such protests being ignored. Good and bad alike were, therefore, immortalised in countless illustrations whose quality depended more on the talents of the engraver than on the morality of the subject. Moreover, Enea Vico had (rightly) pointed out that Nero's coins were among the most beautiful of all those minted during the course of the Roman Empire.[18]

The impression that specific medals had been used as the source for the portraits to be seen in illustrated anthologies was not always conveyed as strongly as in Rouillé's *Promptuaire*. A profile, or sometimes a full-facing head, surrounded by a circular border, could be sufficient to make the general allusion clear, and portraits were often displayed in this way even when there could have been no question of a true medal ever having existed. The stricter convention was more current in Italy,

18. Padre Torsellino, *Ristretto dell'historie del mondo*, Rome 1634: Moses.

19. [Jean de Bussières], *Flosculi historici delibati*, Cologne 1656: Moses and other figures from the Old Testament and ancient history and myth.

as is apparent from a comparison between two historical manuals illustrated with portraits of all the great men (and often women) in the world from Adam until the author's own day which remained sought after throughout much of the seventeenth century and later. Both were the work of Jesuits. Although the prolific Orazio Torsellino, who taught for many years at the Collegio Romano, died in 1598, posthumous editions of his *Ristretto dell'historie del mondo*, which first appeared in that year, continued to be published in constantly updated versions. In one of these, brought out in Rome in 1634, the 'prudent reader' was told that he would find 'the effigies of the greatest men whom the bountiful centuries have produced'.[19] The images that follow include Abraham, Moses, Samson, Solomon, Caesar, Brutus, Trajan, Dante and very many more, all deliberately presented as though copied, or at least adapted, from ancient coins (pl. 18) – as in some cases (such as that of Nero) they genuinely were. On the other hand, an edition published some twenty years later in Cologne of Jean de Bussières's *Flosculi historici delibati* (which had first appeared in Lyon in 1649) embraced an even greater range of 'portraits', but represented the protagonists of world history in a far more exotic manner.[20] It is true that here too the heads were enclosed in circular rimmed borders, but with the exception of the ancient Romans, no serious attempt was made to imply that medals had ever existed, and numismatists would have seen at once that even for the Romans there had often been no original prototype (pl. 19). Neither book was intended for a popular market (the one published in Cologne is written in Latin), and the reader interested in the appearance of Moses would have been somewhat baffled by comparing the two 'portraits' available to him (pls 18, 19); but neither publisher made any attempt to explain what were the sources on which he had drawn for these or any other images to appear in his anthology.

Other writers, both earlier and later, were more forthcoming. Thus Antoine du Verdier adopted a vaguely medallic format, including neatly designed Latin inscriptions, for the portraits included in his *Prosographie ou description des personnes insignes* of 1573. However, like Rouillé before him, he made it clear that they could not have been drawn from life, but had been designed by him and his collaborators to correspond with the literary evidence. Indeed, they had been chosen partly because they were not to be found in published collections of medals: this was not very surprising as, besides Marsilio Ficino and various conventional figures, they included the Devil, as well as Adam and Eve – although not, as Verdier complained, Messalina and Pope Sylvester who had been promised by the engraver but had not yet arrived.[21]

Other writers were more exigent – at least in theory – and explained that they were relying on 'medals diligently sought for in all the most excellent cabinets of the Kingdom of France and elsewhere';[22] and in the seventeenth century we occasionally come across editors of the classical historians going to some lengths to justify their use of particular medals. The Daciers did so when discussing the handsome (but hardly convincing) illustrations for their Plutarch of 1695; but they did so chiefly because they had been ridiculed for confusing a head of the wicked Commodus with one of the virtuous Marcus Aurelius when editing that emperor's *Meditations*. 'I do not know whether that is true, and it really worries me very little,' they blustered, 'I am only amazed that so learned a man who could do better things should amuse himself by making a criticism that, even if correct, would be unworthy of him.'[23]

The Daciers' need to dismiss the significance of their unfortunate mistake is, of course, understandable enough; but their comments were unusual. Most educated people, and not only antiquarians, were keen to uphold in public the convention that authentic likenesses of great men were desirable, however curious were the means by which they set about obtaining, or manufacturing, them in private. Illustrations from earlier publications were constantly plagiarised and adapted to serve new purposes, many medals were forged, and many others were newly created to commemorate figures who had never been so honoured in their own times. It is, however, rare for us to be provided with first-hand information about such procedures, and this gives particular interest to the evidence of the Flemish engraver Jacques de Bie who in 1636 published *La France métallique* containing portraits of all the kings of France – a book that, as we shall see, proved to be of

20. Jacques de Bie, *La France métallique*, 1636: reverses of coins supposedly minted by Pharamond and other early French monarchs.

notable interest to historians. De Bie was a keen admirer of the 'incomparable Goltzius', whose works he re-edited,[24] and he went out of his way to emphasise that he aimed to follow Goltz's example by leaving blank spaces whenever he had been unable to find genuine coins so as not to 'show contempt for art lovers by reproducing frivolous and capricious images'.[25] In a rather convoluted preface to *La France métallique* he explained that because it was clear that the French were now capable of rivalling the Romans in every field, he had conceived the idea of telling their history through the images to be seen on their medals (which were of surpassing beauty), 'in the same way that antiquarians have treated the history of Rome'. He added, however, that the further he went back in time, the harder it was to find authentic medals, and that none was obtainable dating from before the reign of Charlemagne. At this point he decided, with the help of friends, to design appropriate reverses (conforming to the antique pattern) for imaginary medals of the first twelve kings of France (pl. 20). These he did not apparently intend to publish, deeply though he regretted that 'so many noble actions had been described in different ways according to the commitment or flattery of writers, and had not achieved the solid steadfastness of true and incorruptible metal'. But he then had the unexpected good fortune to meet Claude Frémy, 'an excellent craftsman and modeller in wax', who, quite independently, had already made medallic portraits of these first kings of France, basing himself on ancient tombs and sculptures. Eventually they agreed to collaborate and the results of their joint labours were published in *La France métallique*. De Bie was very careful to stress that as these particular medals were not available to the public, there was a risk that people would think that the later ones were not based on originals, 'as for the most part they have been';[26] and besides leaving some blank spaces, he also indicated the whereabouts of the authentic medals that he did publish. Yet his apparently frank policy of acknowledging the source of his models (designed probably to bolster the claims of other fabrications, which may or may not have been deliberate) did not succeed for long in appeasing the more informed scholars of the day, and he was severely criticised by Peiresc among others.[27]

When Charles Patin went to Germany in the late 1660s, he found in Ulm a certain M. Schermeier, who was preparing a Universal History to be illustrated with medals; as he could not obtain examples for all periods of history he was proposing to rely extensively on Rouillé's *Promptuaire* and De Bie's *La France métallique*. 'I made use of my French freedom of expression', Patin informs us, 'to tell him that these two books enjoyed no reputation, and that scholars, and especially collectors, disliked the fakes with which they were filled . . . he appeared somewhat amazed to hear such news of two books that he greatly esteemed'.[28]

ii *The Medal as a Source for Other Forms of Portraiture*

Antique coins and medals could naturally be used for more important purposes than the provision of illustrations for portrait anthologies or editions of classical texts. From at least as far back as the middle of the fifteenth century it had been recognised, first perhaps by Flavio Biondo, that such coins, which were invariably inscribed with the name of the figure represented on them, were indispensable for identifying the countless marble or bronze statues and busts that survived – either more or less intact or in a fragmentary state – without any clear identification.[29] It would be interesting to know when guides in Rome first began the practice (of which we hear only very much later) of carrying ancient coins with them when conducting visitors around the collections of unlabelled busts and statues to be seen in the city.[30] And it is certainly very tempting to suggest that Jacopo Strada (whose numismatic interests and publications have already been touched on) may have been the first scholar in the field to make extensive use of his expertise in coins and medals in order to identify and acquire specific Roman heads, and forgeries of them, on a systematic scale. There is absolutely no proof of this, and even the evidence to sustain it is inadequate, but we do know that Strada was intimately involved in all the early stages of the first comprehensive collection of portrait sculpture to be formed in sixteenth-century Europe: the busts and statues acquired

21. Munich, Antiquarium.

CONSPANTIA
FINIS ET
CONSVMMATIO
VIRTVTVM

LEX
OMNIVM
ARTIVM
IPSA
VERITAS

M·AVRELI·
VS·ANTONINVS·IMP·
CAESAR

M·AELIVS·AVRE
LIVS·COMODVS·
IMP·CAESAR

ANNIVS·VERVS
MARCI·AVRELII
ANTONIN·PATER

P·AELIVS·PERTI
NAX·HELVII·F·
IMP·CAESAR

L·SEPTIMVS·
SEVER·PERTI
NAX·IMP·CAES·

22. Munich, Antiquarium.

from a number of Italian cabinets by Duke Albrecht V of Bavaria from 1566 onwards for the purpose-built Antiquarium in the Residenz of Munich, his capital. This formed the ground floor of a two-storey building, the upper part of which was given over to the Library – an association between the written and the visual of great cultural significance.[31]

Strada was the duke's principal agent in searching out and buying up antiquities; he also produced drawings for the design of the magnificent hall that was used for their display, and he was almost certainly responsible for the planning of their original arrangement.[32] Portraits played a prominent, though not exclusive, role in the duke's collection from the first,[33] but it was only long after Strada had left his service that the heads of the emperors and their families were arranged in approximately chronological order on a series of marble slabs, on which their names were carefully incised.[34] The inspiration for an arrangement of this kind naturally came from the prototypes to be found in contemporary medal books (Strada's, but not only his, among them); and one consequence that inevitably follows from this is that – as in coin cabinets – it was essential to obtain as complete a sequence as possible of all the imperial portraits between Caesar and Gratian, with whom the series closed. Unfortunately, it is not clear whether Strada himself had conceived of anything quite so well ordered, and because so many of the busts that were to be seen in the Antiquarium in his own day (and even much later) have since disappeared or can no longer be identified, it is impossible to determine how far they really did correspond to those to be found in contemporary publications.[35] But we do know that Strada was closely involved in the restoration of the sculptures before they reached Munich[36] and that this was carried out in Vienna, where he kept his incomparable collection of drawings of Roman coins. There would have been no lack of opportunities for instructing his craftsmen to make just those discreet alterations to some battered bust that would turn it into a portrait hitherto missing from the ducal collection. Be that as it may, the fact remains that before the end of the sixteenth century it was only as guests of the Wittelsbach dukes of Bavaria that lovers of history, and of the inspiration to be derived from it, would have been able to see an apparently complete set of marble heads of those emperors and their families about whom they had read so much in Suetonius, Tacitus and other writers. The order still seems to have been very haphazard,[37] but the effect must have been overwhelmingly evocative. Beneath a vault richly decorated in the Italian style the busts, which were raised on high socles, faced each other across the hall (pl. 22). Each was elegantly clad in coloured marbles, and groups were arranged symmetrically between the ribbing of the long walls by fitting the busts into niches and on to bases set at different levels (pl. 21).[38] On these bases were inscriptions, in Roman lettering, which allowed the visitor to identify the features of Julius Caesar and Caligula, Trajan and Julian the Apostate. Nowhere outside Rome itself (and perhaps not even in Rome) was the Empire presented in such powerfully visual terms – and this achievement could have been made possible only by a careful study of numismatics.

Among the contacts that Strada established in Italy was one with the circle of Fulvio Orsini, the scholar who was to make the first serious attempt to produce a major repertoire of ancient portraits, based partly, but not only, on coins.[39] He was born in Rome in 1529, an illegitimate son of a member of the noble and powerful Orsini family, and he spent much of his life in the household of Cardinal Farnese, the most cultivated patron in Rome during the middle years of the sixteenth century. Orsini was involved in diplomacy and also acted as one of Farnese's artistic advisers, but he is best remembered as a great collector of antiquities of all kinds (he owned some 900 engraved gems, 58 marble busts and bas-reliefs and 2,500 coins and medals)[40] and of books (his library was considered to be finer than that of the Vatican),[41] and for the use he made of them. Orsini was in touch with many of the leading scholars in Europe, but although a great scholar himself, he was reluctant to publish his researches. However, in his *Imagines et Elogia Virorum Illustrium*, which first appeared in 1570 and then in subsequent, amended, editions both before and after his death, he produced a far more systematic study of ancient portraiture than any that had yet been composed.

The illustrations in this book stand out with stark immediacy from among most of those to be found in the antiquarian literature of the sixteenth century. After leafing through so many publications in which flawlessly complete coins had been arranged into neat symmetrical patterns and surrounded by pedimented frames decorated with elaborate strapwork and allegorical figures, gryphons or garlands, collectors must have been dismayed by the brutal simplicity of many of Orsini's plates: a battered and headless herm; a statue with the arms broken off; a fragmented relief; a bust (the eyeballs unpierced) set on a base inscribed in Greek; a few

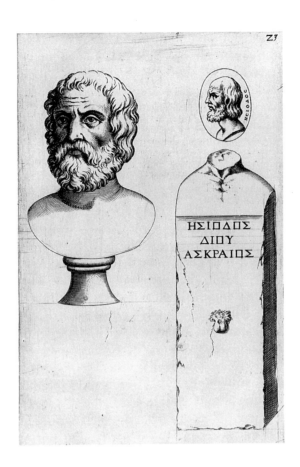

23. Fulvio Orsini, *Imagines et
Elogia Virorum Illustrium*, Rome
1570: Hesiod.

coins and gems of differing sizes – and, occasionally, combinations of these on the
same page.

Indeed, the novelty of Orsini's approach lay above all in his reliance on so many
different sources. Almost each one of these had been explored separately by earlier
writers, but it was he who pioneered the notion of combining the study of
epigraphy with that of coins, statues, busts and other types of image in order to
discover true likenesses of the illustrious ancients. He thus often reproduces more
than one portrait of the individual whom he is discussing – in the case of Socrates,
for instance, he publishes three different marble heads and a seated statue. Collections of imperial portraits had naturally included many examples of each emperor,
but this had never been done (as it was here by Orsini) for purposes of comparison. And Orsini was also ready to include portraits of the same man in a
variety of media. Of Hesiod we are told what is known from the literary sources
of the likenesses made of him in antiquity, and we are then shown a marble bust,
an engraved gem, and the base of an inscribed herm (pl. 23). It is true that the
mutilated genitals on the latter are hardly of much use for identifying Hesiod, but
Orsini was, rightly, very conscious of the fact that in many cases incorrect heads
had been placed on such inscribed bases.

What made Orsini's achievement – and that of the many scholars who collaborated with him – even more remarkable is that his energies were devoted primarily to just those spheres (Greece and Republican Rome) that had generally been neglected by numismatists who tended to concentrate on the more accessible field of imperial portraiture. Moreover, unlike most of his predecessors and contemporaries, Orsini explored the social background and origins of portraits, and also their use in private libraries, public commemoration and so on.

Yet looking at Orsini's book and its later editions, as well as the correspondence stimulated by them, it is impossible not to feel that what we have are merely the fragmented remains of a far more ambitious scheme – which is hardly surprising as he is said to have spent only twenty days on preparing the 1570 edition for the press.[42] He continued to explore (and to collect) ancient portraits of all kinds long after the publication of the *Imagines et Elogia*, but although he intended to write a full-scale study of the subject, he never did so, and it was only when he was approached by the Flemish artist Dirk Galle that the question of making use of this new material once again came to the fore. Galle made a series of 246 drawings of the portraits belonging to Orsini, Cardinal Farnese and other collectors, and then returned to his native city of Antwerp to engrave them.[43] In 1598 he published 151 of these – somewhat to the dismay of Orsini, who had wanted all the drawings to be published and who had also wanted his own notes to be added to them. But the real weakness of the new edition is due to just the feature in it that Galle had particularly insisted on. In only three cases is more than one portrait reproduced of any individual, although the use of such different sources as busts, coins, gems and statues is still retained. Galle was alarmed that some of the varied portraits claimed to be of the same man would undermine faith in the authenticity of the project as a whole[44] – and it is true that the discrepancies are sometimes too conspicuous for it to be possible to accept specific identifications. None the less, it was the very variety of the portraiture to be found in the first edition that made Orsini's book so important for future study of the subject, and the new editions, while containing more illustrations of better quality and justifying their reputation as the fullest and most seriously researched iconographical collections seen to date, are in many ways of less interest than that of 1570.

iii   Beyond the Medal: Portrait Anthologies

Coins and busts were the essential sources for the appearance of the ancients, but prominent figures from late antiquity and the early Middle Ages could also have been seen represented in mosaic, in fresco and in other media. However, at a time when interest in Roman coins was already highly developed, such cruder figures attracted little attention. Naturally enough, the popes were often depicted, either in complete sets or in small groups or individually, throughout the Middle Ages and the Renaissance, but – unlike the analogous case of the emperors – little if any attempt was made to imply that these were true likenesses derived from authentic images. Thus the powerfully expressive terracotta heads of 170 popes from Christ

24. Siena cathedral, details of wall of nave with terracotta busts of the popes made in the late fifteenth century.

until Lucius (who ruled from 1181 to 1185), which were manufactured for Siena cathedral towards the end of the fifteenth century – perhaps as part of what had been intended as a complete set – and which are to be seen high up on the walls of the nave (pl. 24), included until 1600 one of the legendary Pope Joan. In that year, at the request of the ruling pope, Clement VIII, she was transformed into Pope Zaccarias, who reigned between 741 and 752 and who had perhaps been omitted from the original series.[45]

During the period of the Counter-Reformation attempts were made to return to such battered and repainted original sources as still survived, and to have faithful copies made of them. The most significant of these sources was a series of inscribed bust-length effigies of the early popes which had been painted in fresco along the walls of the naves of the ancient basilica of S. Paolo Fuori le Mura. The series, which began with St Peter, is believed to have been inaugurated in the fifth century and to have continued until the end of the seventh.[46]

These heads attracted some attention from theologians, but they hardly conformed to notions of educated taste. One of the leading scholars and Christian

25. Giovanni Battista de' Cavalieri, *Omnium Romanorum Pontificum Icones*, Rome 1595: St Marcellus.

antiquarians of the age, Onofrio Panvinio, had a few of them engraved and painted in small versions,[47] but it was not until 1634 that the effigies in S. Paolo were copied in a systematic way. Nevertheless, well before then, in 1580, a number of them had been drawn on for the publication of what was claimed to be a complete set of authentic portraits of all the popes. The moving spirit behind this was once again Panvinio, who provided the biographical entries. The plates, which were derived from a wide variety of sources, were supplied by Giovanni Battista de' Cavalieri (pl. 25).[48] Many years earlier Cavalieri, who had been born near Trent in about 1525 and who had probably settled in Rome when a very young man, had produced major anthologies of the most important ancient monuments and sculptures in the city, and in 1583 he was to publish a complete set of portraits of the Roman emperors.[49] Thus he was probably the single most significant figure of the whole sixteenth century to make visually accessible to a wide public throughout Europe the past personalities and glories of his adopted city.

However, the principal stimulus for the publication of collections of effigies of all kinds came from the huge international reputation enjoyed by the approximately

26. Francesco da
Sangallo, medal of
Paolo Giovio.

four hundred portraits that had been assembled by Paolo Giovio and that hung, for
the most part, in his lakeside villa just outside Como, on land that had once
belonged to Pliny the Younger.[50] Giovio – physician, historian, courtier and
bishop (pl. 26) – had been born in the town in 1483, and he was to be present at
some of the most dramatic events of Italian history to occur during his lifetime,
such as the Sack of Rome in 1527 and the coronation of the Emperor Charles V in
Bologna two years later. He was a man of wit and also of great social ambition,
and, since early youth, he seems to have shown an interest in the arts.[51] It is not,
however, until 1521 that we first hear of his intention, which was by then being
put into effect, to build up a collection of paintings. He wished to decorate the
rooms in which he was living in Florence in the service of Cardinal Giulio de'
Medici (soon to become Pope Clement VII) with portraits of Italian writers, most
(if not all) of whom had long since died: he already owned pictures of Dante,
Petrarch, Boccaccio, Pico della Mirandola, Marsilio Ficino and several others.[52]
There was nothing particularly new about seeking inspiration from moral teachers
in this way – Federico da Montefeltre's *studiolo* at Urbino provides an obvious
precedent – or of honouring great men in general by commissioning paintings of
them, as is shown by many cycles of ancient and later heroes produced in the
Middle Ages. But although such examples must have played a part in stimulating
Giovio, as too must others recorded from antiquity, his own collection was very
different.

It was not built up on systematic lines to conform to some predetermined
programme, and the fact that Giovio specially mentions that he had been unable to
obtain a large number of portraits that he was looking for (those of Guarino,
Polydore Vergil, Reuchlin and many more[53]) appears to confirm that, unlike so
many of his rivals and imitators, he was not prepared to have 'likenesses' fabricated
to suit his imagination or, at best, to conform to literary sources. On the contrary.
Giovio told the Grand Duke of Tuscany that, as he wanted to show the world that
the portraits were 'true and faithfully taken from the originals, I shall give the

necessary evidence by describing what each one had been copied from, so that anyone who wants confirmation can go to see them for himself'.[54] With extremely few exceptions, which Giovio claimed had been made directly from life, all the portraits in his collection were indeed replicas of existing images. But those images were of the most varied kind. They included coins and medals; drawings, wood-cuts and paintings, in miniature, on canvas or in fresco; and sculptures in wood and in marble, either busts or standing figures. Each portrait derived from these sources was inscribed with the name of the sitter, and some standardisation of size was imposed, although this was not carried through with much rigour.[55]

The more portraits that Giovio obtained – by purchase, by direct commission (from copyists and only very rarely indeed from celebrated artists), by soliciting his friends – the more ambitious he became: his thoroughness, he wrote, was 'so costly as to be almost mad'.[56] He changed the nature of his original collection by giving increasing attention to the living and by no longer confining himself to literary figures. He now became determined to obtain depictions of rulers and of men of war, especially of the Sultans and their entourage. This longing was triumphantly satisfied, first in about 1535 when he somehow got hold of a 'concorso nobile' of leading members of the Turkish court (probably painted in Italy from drawings made in Istanbul), and then, a decade later, when he was able to buy from Virginio Orsini an ebony and ivory box, containing eleven miniatures of the Sultans. These had been brought to Marseille by Grand Admiral Haireddin 'Barbarossa', who was one of the men portrayed in the picture of the 'concorso' that Giovio already owned. The miniatures were then copied for him on to canvas so as to conform to the standard format he had adopted for his collection.[57]

By 1535 Giovio was sending his portraits from Rome and Florence to the family house in Como. Two years later he began to have a villa specially constructed outside that city in order to have sufficient room in which to hang them, although he appears to have retained a certain number in the town palazzo he had inherited and in another house adjacent to it which he bought in 1543.[58] International interest in his project was already sufficiently great for the building and decoration of the villa to be subsidised in part by François Ier of France, Cosimo I of Florence, Alfonso d'Avalos and other notable princes. It was wholly completed by 1543, by which time it had already been in regular use for two years.

The villa appears to have consisted of a two-storey building disposed rather loosely around a courtyard. Most of the rooms were dedicated to particular motifs – Fame, Honour, the Sirens, Minerva, Mercury and other pagan deities – and were adorned with appropriate frescoes.[59] The portraits were probably distributed (not very systematically) quite widely throughout the complex, but by far the greatest number were kept in one large hall with a terrace overlooking the lake. It was decorated with depictions of Apollo and the Muses, and it constituted what was at once described by Giovio and his contemporaries as the 'Museum'. To visitors it appeared 'miraculous'.[60]

The rhythm of Giovio's collecting now increased, and so, too, did the size of the portraits.[61] Below each one hung a small parchment with a brief biography of the sitter,[62] and four general categories were established, although these did not necessarily correspond exactly to the arrangement on the walls. In the first place there were men noted for their 'productive genius' and already dead; then came those who were still living; artists and wits ('faceti'); and, finally, popes, kings and captains, who had distinguished themselves in peace and war.[63]

The quality of the portraits to be seen in the collection varied widely, although both the owner and his visitors were much too interested in the personalities on view to be unduly concerned. Giovio owned a few portraits from the life (or, at least, versions of such portraits) made by artists of the calibre of Bronzino and Titian. The overwhelming majority, however, had been copied by second-rate painters, whose names have not been recorded, from prototypes which were themselves of indifferent quality. From the pictures that have survived we can see that the level of distinction must in general have been low.

The reliability of the portraits (which soon achieved canonical status) was much more erratic. We have seen that Giovio refused to have them fabricated when no apparently authentic example could be traced, and a number of instances have been recorded of his making very serious attempts to locate such examples. When, for instance, he claims that his painting of Hannibal was derived from a bronze original of Hannibal on an elephant which he had seen in the collection of Isabella d'Este before the Sack of 1527,[64] he was evidently referring to a medal representing a man riding an elephant which probably did indeed date from the Carthaginian advance into Italy in about 216 BC (pl. 33); and he verified the identification by comparing the figure to a marble bust on the façade of Messina cathedral which was also believed to represent Hannibal.[65] Sometimes he relied on obvious and trustworthy sources – Uccello's fresco in Florence cathedral for Sir John Hawkwood, and Melozzo da Forlì's fresco (now in the Vatican) of Sixtus IV appointing Platina as his librarian (pls 27, 29), on which he drew both for Bartolomeo Platina himself (pl. 28) and for Pietro Riario, the pope's nephew.[66] At other times he went to locations that seemed likely to yield satisfactory results, such as the Campo Santo in Pisa, in order to make his own identifications – with varying degrees of plausibility.[67] He was also perfectly prepared to accept 'likenesses' that had been made very much later than the figures whom they were supposed to represent. His Farinata degli Uberti (pl. 31), who had been head of the Ghibelline faction in Florence and who had lived between 1201 and 1266, was adapted from the fresco of famous men painted by Andrea del Castagno in the late 1440s (pls 30, 32).[68] It was always possible to argue that later images of historical personages, including some of those depicted in frescoes in the Vatican by his own friends and contemporaries, such as Raphael and his followers, had themselves been based on genuine coins and medals.[69] Medallic authority carried considerable weight and overruled considerations of chronology. The portrait of Attila in Giovio's museum was derived from a medal (which showed him with horns and elongated ears) that had been made in the fifteenth century.[70]

Although Giovio is less forthcoming about the originals that he used for the portraits of writers in his collection than for those of rulers, he does usually indicate the burial-place of those portrayed,[71] and he often compares the literary and visual sources at his disposal and draws conclusions from them about the

27 (above left). Detail of pl. 29, showing Bartolomeo Platina.

28 (above right). Paolo Giovio, *Elogia Virorum literis illustrium*, Basle 1577: Bartolomeo Platina.

29. Melozzo da Forlì, *Pope Sixtus IV with his four nephews, and his librarian Bartolomeo Platina kneeling, c.*1480, fresco transferred to canvas (Vatican, Pinacoteca).

appearance of some famous man. Nevertheless, despite the diligence of his researches and his refusal to countenance outright fabrications, Giovio must clearly have known that many of his 'portraits' were not exact likenesses but were images that had been made to correspond to impressions derived from knowledge of the sitter's life and actions. It is not at all certain that all his contemporaries reacted to them with the same prudence.

The museum at Como attracted great attention both north and south of the Alps. Its contents were copied, and copies were made from these copies, to meet the demands of other collectors who were inspired by Giovio's achievement; and it seems possible that his portrait of Admiral Haireddin 'Barbarossa' may have reached Rouillé through just such a second- or third-hand route.[72] Giovio himself was very keen that all his portraits, or at least those of the famous warriors, should be engraved in a format a little larger than that of ancient medals, and if possible in colour: such a book, he thought, would be more attractive than any that had appeared since antiquity.[73] He had coloured drawings made of the Visconti rulers of Milan, and these were engraved by Geoffroy Tory and published, with Giovio's accompanying eulogies, in Paris in 1549;[74] but only a few of his other portraits were reproduced (except through the medium of painted copies for important personages) in his lifetime.[75]

It was, in fact, not until 1575 and 1577, some twenty-five years after Giovio's death, that a selection of his pictures became widely available. The initiative was taken by Pietro Perna, a Protestant from Lucca, who had settled in Basle and had established there one of the most important printing presses for the diffusion of humanist texts.[76] Perna was a keen admirer of Giovio, and in about 1570 he decided to reproduce the portraits that had belonged to him and that now faced an uncertain future.[77] He sent Tobias Stimmer to make drawings of them, and from these wood-blocks were cut. The plates were printed in two folio volumes together with the eulogies which – much to his regret – Giovio had had to publish many years earlier without illustrations.[78] The first of Perna's volumes contained 128 (out of 150) rulers; the second 62 (out of 200) writers.[79] Adaptations and later editions of these books (sometimes with previously unpublished plates) appeared not long afterwards,[80] but Perna himself paid no attention to the portraits of artists that had belonged to Giovio: as we shall shortly see, he probably considered that their inclusion would by now have been unnecessary. His volumes proved to be among the most influential of the century. They are also among the most misleading.

The problem is not so much that some of Stimmer's beautiful plates appear to be unreliable as copies of Giovio's paintings or that he occasionally had to resort to some quite different source for a portrait that he wished to include.[81] It is, rather, that Stimmer's very distinction as an artist obliterates both the confusion and the mediocrity that must have characterised the actual collection – and also, perhaps, the rare work of excellence and singularity that was to be found in it. The volumes are surely more true to the spirit than to the reality of Giovio's enterprise, and it is not surprising that they have always appealed to historians, such as Burckhardt, who have conceived of the Italian Renaissance principally

30 (above left). Detail of pl. 32.

31 (above right). Paolo Giovio, *Elogia Virorum
bellica virtute illustrium*, Basle 1575: Farinata
degli Uberti.

32. Andrea del Castagno, *Farinata degli Uberti*,
c.1449, fresco transferred to plaster ground
(Florence, S. Apollonia).

33. Silver *tetradrachma*, Carthago
Nova, third century BC: man on an
elephant – believed, in the
Renaissance, to represent Hannibal.

34 (right). Paolo Giovio, *Elogia
Virorum bellica virtute illustrium*,
Basle 1575: Hannibal.

in terms of the glorification of a series of outstanding men. We are offered a series
of bust-length portraits, of the highest elegance and vitality, each of which is,
however, enclosed in a square frame of such size, splendour and elaboration that
the figure seems to be overwhelmed by the surrounding sumptuousness. Moreover, the repertoire of motifs used for the decoration of these frames is a limited
one and is applied apparently at random, irrespective of any relevance it may have
to the character of the dignitary portrayed: surmounted by projecting strapwork, a
bare-breasted Red Indian woman, holding a bow and a decapitated head, stands at
one side of the frame and a royal warrior at the other, and they gaze at each other,
indifferent to Alexander the Great, Scipio, Bartolomeo Colleoni, Amurath
Emperor of Turkey, Giuliano de Medici, Flavio Biondo, the Byzantine scholar
Janos Angyropoulos and many another figure renowned in history and literature
who finds himself rigidly enclosed between them; heraldic beasts lunge at each
other, and half-naked Oriental slaves writhe in torment beneath the heroes;
helmeted and scantily dressed figures twist their lithe bodies into elegant curves
and try to join hands across the garlands that separate them. Within, Hannibal,
rather oddly provided by Stimmer with a horse rather than an elephant (pl. 34),
and Saladin seem to bury their differences and to merge into the anonymity of
distant grandeur.

It was surely Giovio's collection that inspired one of the more original and
ambitious attempts made in these years to reproduce a convincing set of portraits
of men who, for the most part, had lived at a much earlier date than their
biographer. Giorgio Vasari was a friend and protégé of Giovio, and his *Lives of the*

Most Excellent Italian Architects, Painters and Sculptors had, so he claimed, been written at Giovio's suggestion after they had been discussing the museum of celebrities at Borgo Vico.[82] For the second edition of this book which appeared in 1568, Vasari added a portrait of each artist to the relevant Life. It seems reasonable to assume that he must, to some extent, have drawn on those that had been assembled by Giovio, who was by now dead; and, if he did so, Perna would naturally not have wished to include them in his own anthology of portraits from Giovio's museum which he was to publish only a few years later.[83] Certainly, Vasari used some of Giovio's methods to track down apparently original sources.[84] He would, for instance, often have copies made of what could plausibly be claimed (on grounds of documentation, inscription or local tradition) to be self-portraits or contemporary portraits, and, on other occasions, he maintained that he had been able to identify the likenesses of artists included in historical and religious scenes by comparing them with those, painted or in stucco, to be found in the collection of the sitter's descendants. There is good reason to believe that this was not always strictly true, but the claim is of considerable significance in the context of historical research. The portraits used by Vasari to illustrate his *Lives* are in fact important both because they are necessarily all of non-royal persons who lived after antiquity, and also because they made no pretence to having been based on medals.

Among the vast numbers of painted or engraved collections that were built up on the lines of Rouillé's and of Paolo Giovio's, André Thevet's *Pourtraits et vies des hommes illustres* of 1584 is of special interest because we are reasonably well informed by the author himself as to how he set about compiling it.[85] Thevet (who was prepared to criticise Giovio for inaccuracy) claims to have taken particular trouble to provide authentic likenesses of a very large number of illustrious personages from the entire history of the world ranging from antiquity to his own day, and he, too, left empty frames when he was unable to find a faithful likeness. He died in his eighties after an adventurous life, one year before the appearance of the book to which he devoted nearly thirty years. As cosmographer to the King of France he had travelled widely not only in Italy, Greece, Constantinople, Syria and Egypt, but also in Spain and South America which provided for his anthology some personages whose appearances were exotic but whose costumes were reproduced with surprising accuracy both from the life and from an Aztec manuscript in his possession.[86] His friends included Rabelais, Ronsard and Du Bellay as well as Du Choul (to whom he gave some of the medals he had collected in the East),[87] and he seems to have had access to all the most important private collections in France. It was in them that he found many of his sources: coins and medals, of course, but also family portraits and (above all) the drawings by François Clouet that belonged to the Queen Mother, Catherine de Médicis. He also spent much time visiting churches and religious institutions of all kinds: he had copies made of the figures on tombs, as well as of portraits in illuminated manuscripts and even of one in a tapestry, though in the book these sources are all reproduced in the same rectangular format. From all over France his friends sent him additional material: a portrait of an Arab ruler came from a former captive who had spent forty years in Morocco, and one of Joan of Arc was copied from a

35. André Thevet, *Pourtraits et vies des hommes illustres*, Paris 1584: Pliny the Younger.

36. Peter Stent, '*Thomas More*'.

monument in Orléans. He accompanied his illustrations with biographies of the figures represented.

Thevet's many enemies and critics – including the historian Jacques-Auguste de Thou – accused him of dishonesty, vanity, ignorance and credulity. However, his extraordinarily ambitious collection of portraits drew on a greater variety of accurate sources than any yet made and supplied an unrivalled repertoire of historical effigies, as well as some bizarre anomalies, such as the portrait of Pliny the Younger at work on his (well-illustrated) *Natural History* (pl. 35), copied from one 'that I saw and brought from Sicily, little different from one I saw in Crete'.[88]

Throughout the seventeenth century collections of engraved portraits that could lay no claim to the authority that came from the backing of a contemporary medal poured from the presses of most European countries: the features of past and also of living kings and cardinals, soldiers and statesmen, poets and scientists were recorded for an eager public which evidently derived much of its impression of earlier historical periods from such illustrations. Sometimes the sources for these can still be identified with ease. Famous court portraits of Titian, Pourbus, Van Dyck and other great masters were arbitrarily adapted to suit whatever format was required, and the editor might or might not acknowledge his debt to the originals.

But it is often by no means simple to verify the accuracy of what was claimed to be a true likeness, and opportunities for fraud were plentiful – and could be seized with great recklessness. Thus in the 1640s the London print-publisher Peter Stent arranged for a copy to be made of an etching by Rembrandt dating from only a few years earlier (believed to represent his father) and used it as a portrait of Thomas More (pl. 36), despite the fact that the features bore not even the faintest resemblance to those of More which were familiar enough through many versions of Holbein's portraits and even through medals.[89]

Stent was unusually unscrupulous – or unusually naïve – but when portraits from very distant epochs were illustrated, the inventions of publishers were obviously far less easy to detect; nor is it clear whether the images they produced were actually intended to deceive rather than to evoke a general impression (based on literary sources) of an unknown world. What, for instance, did contemporary readers make of the many collections of portraits of the kings of France from Pharamond to the present which were published in the sixteenth and seventeenth centuries in order to emphasise the antiquity and continuity of the monarchy? The more recent portraits were recognisable enough (and their sources present few serious problems even today). But what of Pharamond himself, who was believed to have ruled in the fifth century? Sometimes we know of some fifteenth- or sixteenth-century woodcut from which later versions were adapted,[90] but we cannot always be sure whether the artist was relying wholly on his imagination or whether he was adapting some source that he believed to be original or at least to record a genuine tradition. What is certain is that, although even Jacques de Bie prudently refrained from supplying a portrait of Pharamond,[91] by the early seventeenth century it would have been possible to have obtained at least two (and probably many more) representations of that king which differed so radically from each other that any readers interested in the history of France must have been baffled by them. Had their earliest king been pinched and anxious, with skin pressed tightly over his cheekbones and a vaguely Habsburg jaw lightly covered with stubble, and had he worn an Oriental turban on his head with a small crown perched precariously at the back of it (pl. 37)?[92] Or had he been a tough, thickly moustached and bearded figure with prominent ears and ferocious eyes, arrayed in a splendid suit of armour that was adorned with heavily embossed arabesque decoration (pl. 38)?[93] It is probable that in some cases of this kind, one portrait type drove out all the others and thus acquired the sort of authority that is derived from constant repetition. But this appears not to have happened with Pharamond, for by the later seventeenth century the image of the 'timid' king was still being propagated (pl. 39),[94] while in other publications of almost exactly the same date a quite new version was to be seen. Gone are the turban and moustache and beard, and also the rude iron crown, which is replaced by one that, though still essentially simple, is far more elegantly bejewelled; thick hair now covers the king's ears and straggles down almost to his neck; to the modern observer at least the eyes seem a little sad and the hint of a smile plays around his lips (pl. 40).[95]

Serious scholars, such as Peiresc, naturally knew how difficult it was to obtain true records even of kings who had reigned much later than Pharamond,[96] and it

PHARAMVNDVS.I.REX FRANCIÆ.FILIVSMARCÕ
                                    MIRI
Regnauit xi.annis et   Regno xi. anni et
obijt anno Dñi .430.   morse l'anno 430
                                        .L.

37. *Ordo et effigies regum Franciae*, n.pl., n.d. (c.1600): Pharamond.

38. *Cronica Breve de i fatti illustri de' Re di Francia*, Venice 1588: Pharamond.

may well be argued that it is anachronistic to comment in this way about images that can have aimed to do no more than hint at the fashions of a remote and barbarous past – images, therefore, that inevitably reflected the imaginations of different artists in different places at different times; just as it would be anachronistic to speculate why an Alexander the Great or a Scipio or a Caesar who appears in some picture of the period does not correspond precisely to the 'portraits' of these men found in the medallic compilations of Enea Vico or Rouillé. In fact, however, the issue is not so simple, for by the seventeenth century it was fully recognised that the conventions governing the production of historical portraiture and of narrative painting were quite different.[97] Moreover, the texts of these various volumes make it clear that they were aimed at an educated public of much the same kind that eagerly read the richly illustrated *Histoire de France depuis Faramond jusqu'à maintenant* published by François de Mézeray between 1643 and 1651: and Mézeray left a blank cartouche where the portrait of Pharamond should have appeared and wrote beneath it:

> Tu ne vois icy la naturelle Image
> De ce Roy, qui fonda l'Empire des François
> Mais tu peux voir par tout qu'il eust cet avantage
> D'avoir joint le premier les Armes et les Loix.[98]

39. *Der Könige in Frankreich, Leben, Regierung und Absterben*, Nuremberg 1671: Pharamond.

40. Nicolas de Larmessin, *Les Augustes Representations de tous les Roys de France*, Paris 1679: Pharamond.

It was not long before Pharamond had lost more than his features. In 1713 Père Daniel, Mézeray's successor as the leading historian of France, clearly implied that he had been a prince of whom only the name was known and virtually nothing else.[99] However, more than half a century after that, in 1778, his portrait reappears in a history of France, and this time with features that are quite different from any that have so far been mentioned.[100]

The somewhat mythical figure of Pharamond naturally presented problems of a very special kind. Most of the historical portraits published in seventeenth-century anthologies were based on what appeared to be far more trustworthy sources than those available for studying the earliest French kings; and even when such sources were not in fact genuine, considerable efforts could be made to create a convincing illusion of the past by paying conspicuous attention to costume, pose, gesture and stylistic conventions. In Jean-François Le Petit's *La Grande Chronique ancienne et moderne de Hollande...*,[101] published in 1600 at Dordrecht, it is clear that the illustrator Christoffel van Sichem had looked carefully at fifteenth-century Flemish stained glass (and perhaps also at tapestries) in order to produce his etchings of the early counts of Holland (pl. 41). The fact that most of these had ruled centuries before the appearance of the extravagant and mannered style that inspired him

41. Jean-François Le Petit, *La Grande Chronique ancienne et moderne de Hollande etc.*, Dordrecht 1601: 'Thierri, premier comte de Hollande et de Zeelande, l'an 863 regna 40 ans'.

42. [Etienne Tabourot], *Les Pourtraits des quatre derniers Ducs de Bourgogne*, Paris 1587: Philip the Bold.

would obviously not have worried those readers who looked at the portraits in question.

Sometimes, however, the sources themselves required to be newly constructed. Thus at least three illustrated books designed to glorify the Este rulers of Ferrara were published in that city between 1640 and 1646 – at a time when it had already been absorbed into the papal states for nearly half a century.[102] The year 1640 saw the appearance of the first five of twenty-four projected 'memorie' of the 'Heroes of the House of Este' written by Francesco Berni, who introduced them with a somewhat plaintive apology for the incomplete state of the volume. Accompanying each memoir (of some ten pages) was a half-length portrait of the ruler and eight lines of verse to celebrate his or her heroic qualities (pl. 43). In the following year a much shorter book was published by the printer Cattarino Doino. This contained thirteen plates, which showed twenty-six members of the family arranged in pairs, and short biographical notices by Antonio Cariola (pl. 44). Despite the very different formats of the two sets of portraits and the fact that some of them are reversed and modified in other ways, it is clear that (with one very curious exception[103]) they all derive from the same source. In a rather confused prefatory note Doino explained that he had begun by working on the plates of the 1641 volume (the second one to be published), had then collaborated on the incomplete one written by Berni, and had eventually turned back to his original project and had solicited Cariola for a text. And then in 1646 there appeared yet another volume, in which some of the illustrations are very close to those that had been published by Doino five years earlier although others differ markedly from them. Most of the text, however, had been written more than a century before by Gasparo Sardi, a Ferrarese historian much admired by Paolo Giovio.[104]

The rulers represented go back to the end of the tenth century and all the pairs in the volumes of 1641 and 1646 – of brothers, or cousins, or spouses – are standing. Sometimes they look at us, sometimes at each other; sometimes their relationships seem intimate, sometimes they appear to be unaware of each other's existence. Despite this lack of clarity or coherence in their gestures, some trouble has been taken over their costumes. The family likeness is often transmitted from generation to generation with such dedication that the artist must surely have been instructed to emphasise that genetic consistency that was held to be inseparable from dynastic continuity. Nevertheless, by making some of the figures bearded and some cleanshaven and by other touches of a similar kind, he has also tried to distinguish between different periods and, beneath an overall conformity of approach, to retain some indications of the artistic styles of earlier epochs: the image of Borso d'Este, in particular, makes a clear allusion to the many fifteenth-century portraits of that duke that were easily available. There seems every reason to believe that seventeenth-century readers would have accepted all these images as reliable historical portraits.

In fact, we know that the etchings in all three volumes were derived from large-scale frescoes depicting two hundred members of the Este family which had been painted by various local artists in the courtyard of Ferrara castle as recently as 1577.[105] These frescoes in turn had been taken from drawings by Pirro Ligorio which must have been made as exemplars (pl. 45), and the seventeenth-century etchers certainly had access to these drawings as well as to the frescoes. However, Ligorio had portrayed not only the Este rulers, as was later to be required for the books, but also other prominent members of the family. The etchers, therefore, had to pick and choose carefully which models to use, and they often had to split up pairs and consequently to alter the stances of the figures. Thus we have seen that in Berni's book of 1640 the portraits were shown down to the busts, while in the other two the rulers were represented standing – although they were cut down to knee length and the architectural settings in which Ligorio had placed them were eliminated.

Ligorio had entered the service of Alfonso II of Ferrara (who commissioned these frescoes) as ducal antiquary in succession to Enea Vico, and he was famous above all for his reconstructions in pen and ink of the topography and vanished monuments of ancient Rome. Here, however, when trying to interpret a world that was far less familiar to him and to convey a persuasive impression of it, he

Dagli Azzi, ond'hebbe Roma Illuftri fregi
Scese Almerico il giufto, il cui ualore
Con merauiglia inuidiando i Regi,
A lui crebbe la Fama, a' se l'honore.
Spira il nobil sembiante i chiari pregi
Di diuota pieta' che acceso il core;.
Cosi la prisca eta' uidd'esser uero,
Che Virtu ferma in Dio nasce all'Impero.

A

ALMERICO I. MARCH. | TEDALDO I. MARCH.
di Ferrara. 1. | di Ferrara. 2.

43 (above left). Francesco Berni, *De gli eroi della serenissima casa d'Este*, Ferrara 1640: Almerico I, Marquess of Ferrara.

44 (above right). Antonio Cariola, *Ritratti de Ser^mi Principi d'Este Sig^ri de Ferrara*, Ferrara 1641: Almerico I and Tebaldo I, Marquesses of Ferrara.

VVELFO. IX. VVELFONIS. VIII. F. | AZO. VII
M.CLXIII. | RAINALDI. FIL
MCLXXV.

45. Pirro Ligorio, drawing (pen, brown wash over black chalk) made for an illustrated genealogy of the house of Este (Oxford, Ashmolean Museum).

seems to have collaborated with court genealogists who could have shown him mediaeval manuscripts as well as fifteenth-century medals and frescoes – although some of the stranger costumes drawn by him were probably intended to look German in order to reinforce dynastic claims being made by the Estes, in which Ligorio was much interested.[106]

The duke's courtiers, and other readers in Ferrara or in the new Este capital of Modena, would probably have recognised the relationship of the illustrations to be seen in the volumes by Francesco Berni, Antonio Cariola and Gasparo Sardi to those painted, seventy years earlier, in the courtyard of Ferrara castle, although it is most unlikely that they would have been familiar with Ligorio's drawings. They may even have known that those frescoes had to some extent themselves been inspired by previous ones (more Roman in character), which could perhaps have reflected traditional, if not accurate, portraits of the early Estes.[107] But people outside Ferrara had no means of grasping the ideological implications of a long series of celebratory images. For them the illustrations in the three books probably appeared to be direct reproductions of authentic portraits.

In the sixteenth and seventeenth centuries many publishers of grandiose and apparently fanciful portrait collections went out of their way to emphasise the meticulous nature of their researches and to make clear that it was 'not without the expense of great labour, trouble and money' that they had explored 'seals, monuments, statues, paintings and books' in their determination to reproduce genuine likenesses.[108] Sometimes sources were indicated rather loosely: thus in his book devoted to the 'history of all the cardinals who were French by birth', François Duchesne wrote of one of his illustrations that 'the drawing of this portrait was sent to me by the late M. Camusat, who in his lifetime was a canon in the cathedral church of Saint-Pierre in Troyes, and a man of very great knowledge and erudition'.[109] But as early as the 1570s certain writers made a point of indicating as precisely as they possibly could the whereabouts of some or all the portraits they reproduced.

One of the most striking of such instances is both one of the earliest and also one of the smallest. Etienne Tabourot, who is more remembered for his comic verse than for his contributions to scholarship, published his duodecimo volume on 'les Pourtraits des quatre derniers Ducs de Bourgogne de la Royale Maison de Valois' in 1587.[110] In it he explained that the countless portraits to be seen of the dukes were so 'difformes et disproportionnez' that they looked as if they represented village clowns. Tabourot therefore took the remarkable step (which did not become at all current for some generations) of employing a painter, Nicolas d'Hoey, to copy a few absolutely certain portraits which he then had engraved. In each case he gives the source of the image reproduced. For Philip the Bold (pl. 42) he instructed the artist to make use both of the marble statue 'très-ingénieusement elabourée' on the duke's tomb in the Chartreuse de Champmol near Dijon, and of an indifferent picture hanging near the high altar; and he combined two images in a similar way for John the Fearless. He was equally precise when discussing the other two dukes, and he pointed out that a good wooden carving of 'Charles le Guerrier' had been destroyed by the Huguenots in 1575. Many of his prototypes can still be checked and it is evident that they were copied with considerable care.

iv Physiognomy

Great claims were made for the value to the historian of compilations of the kind we have been looking at. In 1699 Roger de Piles asserted that for those interested in history the most useful of all engravings would be portraits 'of the sovereigns who have ruled a country and the princes and princesses who are descended from him; of those who have held some high rank in the state, in the church, in the army or in the magistracy; of those who have acquired merit in the different professions, and of private individuals who have played some part in historical events. These portraits are accompanied by a few lines of text which give some indication of the person's character, rank, remarkable achievements and date of death'.[111]

But precisely why should the historically minded have been interested in portraits of this kind? Neither Roger de Piles nor many other theorists who wrote in the same vein provided any explanation that ventured much beyond the frequently repeated contention that portraits of great men, like the panegyrics that constituted so much of the biographical writing of the century, evoked their virtues and encouraged emulation of them. To some extent the precise configuration of the actual features was irrelevant because (as has already been said) the mere existence of the portrait was the historical fact. What is perhaps most characteristic of all these volumes of portraits accompanied by written lives is the lack of any correlation between the text and the image. Almost never does the biographer even refer to the likeness, let alone draw any inferences from it. Only very occasionally might his words seem to reflect some banal and half-remembered physiognomic treatise (much as his successors today may call on vague Freudian theory) in order to make a conventional point. Thus, when writing about the series of portraits that he added to his history of the Orsini family in 1565, Francesco Sansovino observed that 'in these pictures of such distinguished men, we must notice that in the Orsini dynasty greatness and majesty are to be found in the features and the faces, because as these men were full of spirit and military prowess, they have broad foreheads and, for the most part, very large mouths, which signifies men of great eloquence and truly royal appearance. So that even if we knew nothing else about them except these portraits, we would believe that they certainly descended from high and noble blood, because we can draw conclusions from their faces (which give a true indication of the mind) about the greatness of their noble and high aspirations.'[112]

The early numismatists, of course, realised that some of the Roman emperors had been very wicked and that their coins therefore conveyed a flattering impression of their morals. But these scholars never looked for evidence of such flattery in the nature of the portraits to be seen on those coins; if anywhere (for in most cases the image was treated as if largely irrelevant to the life) they tended to seek it on the allegorical versos where the emperor appeared to have been granted every virtue and to be compared with the gods.[113]

Du Choul once went a little further and briefly alluded to the problem that there could be a real conflict of evidence between what we know of the lives of the emperors and the images of themselves that they chose to have recorded[114] – a conflict that, had it been adequately explored, would have undermined his own conclusions and those of his fellow numismatists. He takes the case of Septimius Severus as a specific example of the grotesque flattery awarded the emperors by the oppressed people of Rome. He points out that although Severus was (among other things) 'a barbarous and bloodthirsty man', yet 'he received from the Senate – more out of fear and adulation than for his virtue or merits – those titles that it granted to good emperors'. But although Du Choul reproduces a coin of the emperor whose obverse does indeed make him look fairly bloodthirsty while the reverse (inscribed SPQR OPTIMI PRINCIPI) shows him majestic on horseback, he draws no conclusion from the contrasting image and inscription, and it seems clear that his comment on the flattery accorded to this emperor, as also to others, is derived essentially from literary, rather than figurative, sources.

Even Fulvio Orsini who, as we have seen, laid the foundations for the comparative study of portraiture by reproducing several images of the same person taken from differing prototypes, never makes use of these to draw conclusions about the character or life style of his protagonists. At the most he will point out that the portrait of Mark Antony to be seen on a cornelian in the collection of Cardinal Farnese (which had been identified through comparison with many coins of gold, silver and bronze) confirmed Plutarch's words that in adolescence he had had 'a beautiful and amiable appearance'.[115]

In 1586, however, the attention of biographers, historians and collectors could well have been drawn to the possibility of making use of portraiture as an indication of character on a far more ambitious scale than the timid efforts that had hitherto been current. For it was in that year that Giovanni Battista della Porta of Naples published what proved to be the first of a large number of editions, in Latin, French, Italian and other languages, of his *De Humana Physiognomia* (pl. 46). Many such treatises had appeared ever since antiquity, but Della Porta (who was extremely critical of most previous ventures into the field) acquired a reputation that eclipsed that of all his predecessors, even though much of his contribution to the subject was derived from earlier sources. Part of the success of the book must certainly have been owing to the great reputation that Della Porta was already winning for himself as poet, scholar and dramatist and as an authority on medicine, agriculture and cryptography with unmistakable leanings towards the occult;[116] but much of its appeal must also have depended on the fact that it was very fully – and very bizarrely – illustrated. And among the portraits to be seen in it were a certain number that must have appeared familiar, for they had been taken, or adapted, from some of the compilations that have been discussed in this chapter. The museum of Paolo Giovio, as published by Perna, was a particularly promising source.

Della Porta set out to demonstrate that the characters of human beings can best be interpreted by analysing the similarities of their features to those of the animals that most resemble them, because the appearance of every species of animal is determined by its nature.[117] His volume was therefore illustrated with engravings of an ass, a monkey, a lion, a dog, a chameleon, 'which we keep alive in the house

46. Giovanni Battista della
Porta, *De Humana
Physiognomia*, Vico
Equense 1586: frontispiece
with portrait of the
author.

for the purpose',[118] and various other creatures, all of which were juxtaposed to
portraits of famous men. These portraits were principally drawn from the collection of busts and medals that had been assembled by Della Porta's uncle and, above
all, by his brother Giovan Vincenzo, whose expertise in the study of antiquities
was held to be surpassed only by that of Fulvio Orsini and of Don Antonio
Agustín.[119] The brothers shared a house in a fashionable district off the Via
Toledo, and after Giovan Vincenzo's death in about 1603 two of the rooms in it
were set aside by Giovanni Battista for use as a combined study and museum.[120]
By the time of his death in 1615 his collection included among much else (such as
an astrolabe, many ancient vases and sets of his own books) five complete portrait
statues, seventeen heads arranged in niches – Alexander the Great, Cicero and

Della Fisonomia dell'Huomo

Vedasi nella sottogiacente figura l'imagine del Duca Valentino, e del Tamerlano, considera gl'occhi cani,e piccioli.

Della Fisonomia dell'Huomo

Contempla l'essempio dell'episcino sopra il naso del Can mastino, con l'imagine d'Azzolino tiranno di Padoua.

47. Giovanni Battista della Porta, *Della Fisionomia dell' Huomo*, Padua 1622: Cesare Borgia and Tamerlane.

48. Giovanni Battista della Porta, *Della Fisionomia dell' Huomo*, Padua 1622: Ezzelino, Tyrant of Padua.

Augustus among them – and thirty-three smaller figures and heads placed on a ledge running around one of the rooms. All these were of marble. Hanging on the walls were forty-two portraits of the kings of Spain and of various saints (all evidently of the same format) and a few more of some contemporary figures, including Galileo; there was also an assortment of medals kept in a large walnut desk.[121]

Della Porta's prototypes are not always easy to discern, because he drastically adapted them if necessary in order to make them conform to the animals with which they were to be compared. Moreover, in many cases both he and Giovio evidently drew on images that were widely diffused. It seems likely, however, that in his various treatises on physiognomy Della Porta took his portraits of Tamerlane (pl. 47), of the fourteenth-century tyrant Ezzelino (whose features were compared to those of a hunting dog) (pl. 48), of Cesare Borgia, of the ugly long-nosed Angelo Poliziano (who resembled a rhinoceros) and of Pico della Mirandola from illustrations that were easily accessible in the Giovio volumes (pls 49, 50).[122]

There appears to be no instance in which Della Porta published a portrait of some historical figure whose features conflicted with the characterisation of him that would have been accepted by contemporaries: no straightforward man was shown with small eyes like those of the mendacious Cesare Borgia; no villain had the beautiful features of the young Pico della Mirandola, who turns up on a number of occasions as the very model of purity and docility (pl. 51). Where – to a modern reader at least – the countenance appears to be at variance with what has been recorded about the character, it is the countenance that is interpreted to make it conform to traditional notions. The Empress Faustina, wife of Marcus Aurelius, will play a prominent part in a later chapter of this book.

In Della Porta we come across her in the company of Messalina (pl. 52). The two woman face each other in profile – the very image, one might imagine, of rectitude and domestication. But the thinness of their features and the abundance of their hair revealed their depravity – a depravity that was familiar enough in the case of Messalina, but that was also characteristic of Faustina who 'went so far as to sleep with gladiators and other people of low condition, as we know from all the history books'.[123]

The last phrase is significant. Della Porta was no more prepared than any of his contemporaries to propose that character can be understood on the basis of physiognomy alone; or even to acknowledge that a portrait might modify the impression to be derived from reading history. For him, too, the text and written tradition were paramount. And yet his treatises stand out with intense vividness from all other portrait books of the sixteenth and seventeenth centuries. For the first time we find the image being granted a guiding and not merely an exemplary role; for the first time we feel that the historian or the biographer or even the antiquarian might – for better or for worse – have been able to broaden the scope of his investigations by drawing on the tools with which Della Porta had provided him.

This did not happen. The territory was dangerous, uncomfortably close to magic at times, and Della Porta himself ran into trouble, although he vigorously defended himself against charges of unorthodoxy.[124] His books proved to be immensely fascinating – but they also caused some embarrassment. Jacob Spon

49. Paolo Giovio, *Elogia Virorum bellica virtute illustrium*, Basle 1575: Tamerlane.

50. Paolo Giovio, *Elogia Virorum bellica virtute illustrium*, Basle 1575: Ezzelino, Tyrant of Padua.

51. Giovanni Battista della Porta, *Della Fisionomia dell' Huomo*, Padua 1622: Pico della Mirandola.

52. Giovanni Battista della Porta, *Della Fisionomia dell' Huomo*, Padua 1622: Messalina and Faustina.

showed extreme caution when he wrote about the issue in an essay of 1683, promisingly entitled 'De l'utilité des médailles pour l'étude de la physionomie': 'I do not want to apply myself to proving the truth of the rules of physiognomy, which can sometimes be deceptive. I leave that to the experts in the profession. I want only to establish this general rule, that nature often draws the portrait of our soul on our face, and that certain expressions and structures have a tendency to echo man's temperament and signify his inclination'.[125] Spon did not pursue the matter, and he concluded that antiquarians had written nothing about physiognomy: certainly no case appears to be recorded of the identification of some unknown portrait being proposed, or rejected, on the grounds that the features conformed, or failed to conform, with the psychological traits believed to be characteristic of the man or woman in question.

In fact, as Spon makes clear, such little physiognomical analysis of the portraits of well-known people as we come across in the seventeenth century is of the simplest kind, and is hardly ever related to the theories of Della Porta. Thus when in 1635 the French writer Jean Tristan looked at a coin of the Empress Faustina he was as certain as had been Della Porta that it demonstrated her dissolute character – both men had, after all, read about her in the same Roman histories – but he found no need to bring hairiness and leanness into the discussion: 'Her medals portray her as very beautiful and with such a pert and lively expression that it would be easy to judge from her physiognomy that she was more lascivious than her mother, even if we had learned nothing about her from the historians.'[126]

It is at the very end of the seventeenth century that we come across the most sustained of all the many justifications that had yet been made for the publication over the previous 150 years of innumerable volumes of historical portraits. In his *Numismata* of 1697 John Evelyn once again points out how important medals could be for the historian, but he soon widens his coverage to include other forms of portraiture, and (fortified by a certain amount of physiognomic theory) he argues that from paintings, coins and engravings alike we can derive faithful and independent testimony of character. It must, however, be admitted that the examples he gives in support of his thesis would carry more weight were they not so wholly predictable. 'Let him that would write and read the History of the late Times, particularly that of the late Usurper Cromwell', he begins, 'but seriously contemplate the Falls, and Lines of his ambiguous and double Face (as accurately stamp'd in his Medal by Symmons, or engrav'd in Taille-Douce by Lombard, from a Picture of Walker's, the most resembling him) to read in it, without other Comment, Characters of the greatest Dissimulation, Boldness, Cruelty, Ambition in every touch and stroak . . .'; whereas 'in the Noble Earl of Strafford, painted by Van Dyke, and engraven by Lucas Vosterman, [we see] a steady, serious, and judicious Countenance. In Henry the Seventh, painted by Holbein, a close, dry, wise and careful Effigies, as in that of his Predecessor, Richard the Third, a twisted Face, and not a line but what bespeaks Hypocrisie, Craft and Cruelty.' And he continues in the same spirit, finding 'a stiff, bigotted, and formal look . . . in Philip the Second . . . in Erasmus [of Holbein] Quickness, with an easie, pleasant facetiousness, and honest Gravity', and so on.[127] Evelyn's attitude to portraiture is a fine example – surprising only in that it develops so late – of one that was to reach a climax in countless biographies of the nineteenth and twentieth centuries; but it hardly suggests that visual evidence can do any more than evocatively illustrate what is already known from written sources.

Indeed, it was probably only when those written sources did not exist that physiognomy could be drawn upon to provide possible answers to historical enquiry. Thus in a book published in 1740, but apparently completed much earlier, with the challenging title *Histoire de Carausius, Empereur de la Grande-Bretagne, collègue de Diocletian et de Maximien. Prouvée par les Médailles*, Claude Genebrier, a Frenchman and (predictably) a doctor, wrote of some coins of this little-documented figure (pl. 53) that

> he seems to have been aged barely about fifty or fifty-five, so that he was still of an age to undertake new expeditions. His medals show him with a sort of moustache as emperors had in those days. If we look at them, we can see that he had rather small eyes, a rather aquiline nose, a thick neck, broad shoulders, a full and rather long face, a double chin and a bold expression. All this is characteristic of a strong man with a robust temperament, used to work and the continual practice of navigation and war – just such a man, in fact, as one who had devoted himself to these two pursuits since his tenderest youth . . .[128]

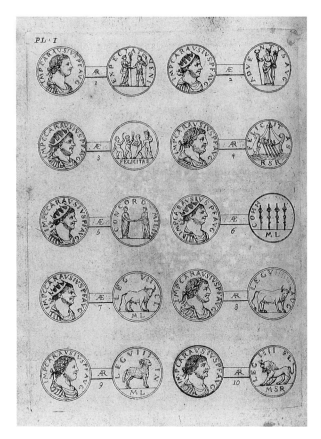

53. Claude Genebrier, *Histoire de Carausius . . . Prouvée par les Médailles*, Paris 1740: coins of the Emperor Carausius.

Even here, the writer is using the image to confirm a preconception. None the less, Genebrier's observation stands out with a quite startling freshness from the conventionality of almost all previous analyses of portraiture.

v   Historians and the Use of Portraiture

But what of the historians themselves – those historians for whose attention publishers, editors and antiquarians clamoured with so much diligence and so much energy, so much eloquence and so much fantasy? The pattern is everywhere similar.

Many of the great narrative historians of the sixteenth and seventeenth centuries were keenly aware of the evocative appeal of historical portraits, and they sometimes built up impressive collections of their own. But beyond that they refused to go.

Paolo Giovio himself provides the most telling example of such caution. He claimed that his *Elogia* (which were first published without illustrations) had been directly inspired by the portraits in his museum,[129] and for the most part this must surely be true. It can, however, be shown that on a significant number of occasions

Giovio described as real a picture that did not correspond to any that he actually owned:[130] there was, after all, a well-established convention of drawing on an imaginary portrait in order to create a character sketch in words. We also know that sometimes he wrote a eulogy before he was able to obtain a portrait of the sitter concerned,[131] and that once or twice he failed in all his attempts to remedy this omission – thus causing notable problems for Pietro Perna, when he decided to publish his illustrated volumes long after Giovio's death.[132] And sometimes his descriptions of the historical figures whom he sets out to memorialise are almost certainly derived from literary sources rather than from his painted portraits of them.[133] Nevertheless, in a large number of cases, what Giovio wrote was stimulated by what he saw.

However, as Duke Cosimo sharply reminded him, 'truth being the nerve of history, which your reverend lordship is expected to serve in the six [books of the Histories] that remain, it will be difficult to maintain credit if your lordship turns wholly to the *Elogia*, in which it is permitted in a certain manner to pass over and shade the truth'.[134] Giovio has frequently been accused of 'passing over and shading the truth' as much in his *Historiarum sui Temporis libri XLV*, which finally appeared in 1550, as in his *Elogia*. Yet it is clear that he, too, looked upon these two branches of writing as quite separate. The *History* covered the whole of Europe – indeed, 'the whole world' as Giovio boasted in his preface (a boast that is amply justified by the range of his narrative). Its long, haunting first phrase conforms to the elegiac tone common to Italian historians when they looked back on the recent past – and not only to them:

> The whole world was then at peace and living quietly, and no tremor of war could be heard anywhere; and Italy above all (which not long before had been disturbed by internal discords) flourished in peace and tranquillity, when there flared up a greater and much more terrible war than man had ever known; which war within a few years disturbed not only the whole of Europe, but also the remotest parts even of Asia and Africa, everywhere overturning or ruining the empires of even the most famous nations.[135]

Giovio's account of subsequent events included much lively psychological detail, and the richly pictorial style of his writing has been greatly admired;[136] but never did he draw directly on the evidence to be found in his portrait collection in order to describe the features or the expressions of the principal figures in his *History*. He must surely be thinking of his own museum when he describes with such eloquence the sacking of the Medici palace in 1512, with its accompanying sale of 'ancient statues, jewels, gems remarkable for the wonderful skill with which they had been incised by ancient craftsmen, vases made of precious stone, and gold, bronze and silver medals portraying the most illustrious captains',[137] and yet he never looks to his museum for material with which to enrich his narrative. It is certain that the historian in Giovio stimulated the collector, but it seems equally certain that the collector had little to say to the historian – however much he may have succeeded in inspiring the eulogist.

The case of Jacques-Auguste de Thou in France is somewhat similar. This exceptionally humane character and friend of Montaigne was born in 1553, the year after Giovio's death, and he began to compose what was to become his great *Historiarum sui temporis libri 138* in 1583.[138] Like Giovio he was a man very closely involved with the events he was describing, and as a politician and diplomat he knew many of the protagonists of his History. During the course of trying to negotiate between the warring religious factions of his country and while in the service of the future Henri IV, he travelled widely in Germany and Italy, as well as in France.[139] Wherever he went he admired the local monuments and art treasures for which, as he said of himself, he 'avoit un goût fort délicat'.[140] He was a skillful draughtsman who enjoyed watching painters at their work,[141] and he may have played some part in designing the mausoleum for his father which he commissioned from Barthélemy Prieur – 'Ouvrage où la beauté du travail renouvelle avec plaisir le souvenir d'un si bon Citoyen et l'excellence de l'Ouvrier'.[142] He climbed the principal tower of Strasbourg cathedral,[143] and he went to inspect Sebastiano del Piombo's altarpiece of *The Resurrection of Lazarus* at Narbonne.[144] In Florence he was guided round the city by Vasari. When they looked together at the portraits of the young boys Giovanni and Garzia de' Medici, De Thou asked Vasari whether there was any truth in the rumour that those princes had been assassinated by their father. Vasari remained silent, and this convinced De Thou that the rumour must indeed have been correct; he was, however, prevented by Henri IV from publishing this in his *History*.[145] In Rome he met Fulvio Orsini and his circle at the Palazzo Farnese,[146] and in Venice he may have met Erizzo, about whom he was later to write with enthusiasm.[147] In Bruges he asked after Hubert Goltz, who happened to be out of town,[148] and in Augsburg he was deeply impressed by the great palaces and medal collections of the Fuggers.[149] He himself owned copies of the treatises by Strada, Erizzo, Goltz, Augustín, Du Choul, Fulvio Orsini and the other principal numismatists of the time.

Indeed, De Thou was probably more imbued with antiquarian culture and artistic enthusiasm than any other historian of the century with the exception of Giovio. Moreover, he added to his library which was to become one of the greatest in private hands anywhere in Europe, a collection of 134 portrait paintings of different sizes.[150] While this was not nearly as ambitious in scope as that of Giovio's – and, as the pictures were not engraved and have all disappeared, we can have no idea of its quality – it included many of the sovereigns of his own and earlier periods, a large number of writers (ranging from Petrarch to Ronsard, and including Giovio himself), great men of the Church and other prominent figures. It was thus far more than a collection of portraits of friends, family and colleagues (although these were certainly included) – with some indication of loyalty to the reigning family – of the kind that was now becoming widespread. De Thou probably thought of his pictures, as he must certainly have thought of his books, as necessary adjuncts to the History he was writing. Yet no more than Giovio does he ever call upon them to supplement the lively account he frequently gives of the characters and activities of so many of those men whose portraits he could see hanging 'au dessus des tablettes de la Bibliothèque' at which he was working.

The spirit of De Thou's great saga – so vivid and so colourful, so tolerant and yet so committed – can surely be detected in the masterpiece of another historian who, half a century later, was to write an account of his own, equally turbulent, times, and who was to seek out representations of those who had participated in them. Although the future Lord Clarendon may have begun buying pictures during his exile in France and the Low Countries between 1648 and 1660, by far the largest proportion of his fine portrait gallery was acquired – by gift, purchase and commission – after the Restoration and was used to decorate his splendid mansion in Piccadilly during the short time that it was in his possession before his second exile in 1667.[151] The collection included portraits of Erasmus, Wolsey and figures from the age of Elizabeth and James I,[152] but the overwhelming majority were of the men of his own time – some now dead, such as Laud and Strafford – whom he had known personally. Like Giovio and probably De Thou, he was more interested in the features of the personages represented in his gallery than in the quality of the pictures; and although he owned some fine originals by Van Dyck and other masters, many of his pictures were only copies – and almost certainly acknowledged to be. Clarendon's magnificent *History of the Rebellion* was begun in 1646 and was then radically altered, amended and eventually completed after he left England in 1667.[153] For most readers it is memorable, above all, for the characterisations, both physical and psychological, of the protagonists of the Civil Wars, but – as with Giovio and De Thou – not once did Clarendon refer to any actual portraits of these men whom he described with such graphic intensity and such subtle perception. It is true that he was accumulating his portraits in London at the very time when he was at the centre of public affairs and had no time for writing his *History*, and that when he fled to France and resumed work on his book he was forced to leave his pictures behind in London. None the less, this refusal to make use of paintings was so common among serious historians (as distinct from antiquarians) that we cannot put it down merely to contingent circumstances.

There was, however, to be an important sequel to Clarendon's abstemiousness. The *True Historical Narrative of the Rebellion and Civil Wars in England* was published in 1702–4, nearly thirty years after his death, in three unillustrated volumes. The anomaly was quickly noted. '*Painting* gives us not only the Persons, but the Characters of Great Men', wrote Jonathan Richardson in 1715.[154] 'The Air of the Head and the Mien in general, gives strong Indications of the Mind and illustrates what the Historian says more expressly and particularly. Let a Man read a Character in my Lord *Clarendon* (and certainly never was there a better Painter in that kind), he will find it improv'd by seeing a Picture of the same Person by *Van Dyck*.' Three years later it was being reported that Clarendon himself had intended to include plates in his *History*, for in 1718 Thomas Hearne heard from an acquaintance of the existence of a set of the three volumes 'with the Heads of the Heroes mentioned in that work. Several of them are done by Hollar, and he believes all were taken from original Pictures. This Collection was begun by the Great Lord Clarendon, and finished by his son, who bequeathed it to the old Dutchess of Beaufort, and she bequeathed it to her Son, the present Possessor. Several of them are done in Indian Ink.'[155] Whatever the truth about Clarendon's own intentions, there can be no doubt that extra-illustrated editions of his *History* became extremely popular, and are indeed among the earliest examples of the genre. Within ten years Hearne wrote of a version for which Sir Thomas Seabright had paid sixty guineas.[156] Another antiquarian, the famous George Vertue, also heard of volumes of Clarendon being illustrated with prints and drawings and fetching high prices;[157] and in 1728 a catalogue could advertise 'a set of ten prints of the reign of King Charles the First' by claiming that they were 'most curiously engraved, the best by far of any relating to our English history; they are all contrived of one size – and will admit of glass, when used for furniture, or serve to be bound in my Lord Clarendon's history.'[158] When, much later, in the second half of the eighteenth century, James Granger launched the fashion for binding illustrations into historical and other volumes,[159] Clarendon was one of the most popular authors to be treated in this way, culminating in the magnificent set of thirty-one volumes containing 14,489 portraits, which was begun in 1795 by Alexander Hendras Sutherland and is now in the Ashmolean Museum in Oxford.[160]

However, one of the earliest works of serious history for which authentic illustrations were planned from the first had already appeared in France in the middle of the seventeenth century. Although the achievement suffered from some of the limitations that have been discussed earlier in this chapter and did not quite justify the high-sounding claims that its author made for it, the project was so ambitious in conception that it deserves attention. François Mézeray was born in 1610, the son of a surgeon.[161] He was educated at the University of Caen, and served in the army before being taken up by Richelieu and then writing his impressive *Histoire de France* which was completed in 1651. For much of his life thereafter he was concerned with preparing new, amended and abbreviated versions of this book. It won him fame – but also caused him problems. His scholarship and originality were attacked by the 'érudits', and it is true that he himself emphasised that he wished to make his *History* accessible to polite society and not only to other writers. His style was later to be criticised as inelegant and unpolished: but this was a fate he shared with many other authors who lived – or at least wrote – before the full flowering of 'the age of Louis XIV'; and, above all, he ran into trouble with the authorities, for his refreshing frankness conflicted with the orthodoxies being enforced by the king and Colbert.

Mézeray was very aware of the fact that although he was often drawing on conventional sources which had been used by historians before him, he was none the less approaching his subject in a spirit that was wholly original. 'Si la matière est vieille,' he writes in his preface, 'la force que je lui donne, la rend toute nouvelle',[162] and he argued that to know thoroughly the history of France, one should know first of all 'that of all Europe as a whole and in detail, the origins, the deeds and the customs of all the states, both ancient and modern, the genealogies of the most illustrious families', and, he continued in a remarkable passage that must surely have been read by Michelet, 'all its provinces, castles, forests, mountains, marshes, rivers, roads and other topographical details, without which knowledge one inevitably falls into precipices. From Europe as a whole one should move to study France and for that one should know, so to speak, the most insignificant castle, the smallest stream and the last gentleman's house . . .' Later, he drew up proposals for a journal which was 'to record the new discoveries and *lumières* which are to be found in the sciences and the arts, knowledge of which is not less useful to humanity than actions of war and politics . . . the sciences and the arts distinguish great states no less than do armies' – words that are far more surprising to find in the middle of the seventeenth century than in the pages of Voltaire.

It is in the context of these remarkably fresh approaches to history that we should look at Mézeray's attitude to illustration, even though the discussion will carry us somewhat beyond the limits of a chapter that has been concerned essentially with portraiture. On the first page of his preface he declares that both 'portraiture and narrative are almost the only means' whereby one can preserve the fame of great men, which is the true purpose of History. Portraiture

> traces the features and displays the exterior and majesty of the body, while narrative relates actions and depicts character. Similarly, the outlines of what is written can put on record the achievements of the prince, and at the same time the physiognomy of his face explains what he does by natural instinct. The History that I have undertaken is made up of these two parts: the pen and the etcher's needle are engaged in noble combat as to which will be the better at representing the objects being treated . . .

He then discusses 'the incredible expenses' caused by the etchings, which include portraits of the kings, and their queens (something no other author had ever yet touched on, as though, he adds, ladies were incapable of heroic actions), and also the dauphins, as it was unfortunately not possible to include also all the other royal children. 'As for the portraits, they are not of the kind that one sees in other books; they have not been constructed from the whim of an engraver, who has thought them up to entertain the ignorant. They are so authentic and drawn from such good originals that in order to enable even the most sceptical reader to check them for himself, the sources from which they have been drawn are indicated.'

Mézeray goes further than this. He announces that, in addition to the royal portraits, he is going to include eight hundred medals to illustrate the successive reigns – and these he is drawing from Jacques de Bie's *La France métallique*. He is less than generous about this compilation: he fails even to name the author and derides the 'muddled explanations' of the medals featured in it: he intends to replace them with much fuller and more satisfactory commentaries. Mézeray's reliance on this somewhat suspect source led to his work being slighted in later years, but it is nevertheless remarkable. Each reign is prefaced by a portrait in an elaborately framed roundel (pl. 54), and its source is indicated – often a church or Fontainebleau or the Louvre, sometimes a private collection. Within the text of the chapter devoted to each king is to be found one or more medals, always showing the reverse to illustrate his principal achievement or achievements (pl. 55). These reverses are explained in some detail and, however dubious their authenticity,

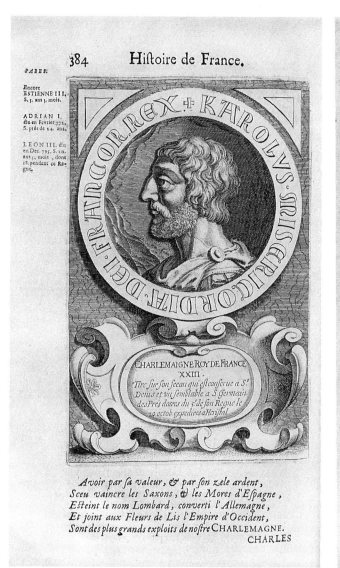

PAGES:
Encore
ESTIENNE III,
S. 5. ans 5. mois.

ADRIAN I,
élu en Fevriet 772,
S. pté de 24. ans.

LEON III, élu
en Dec. 795. S. 10.
ans 5, mois , dont
18. pendant ce Re-
gne.

CHARLEMAIGNE ROY DE FRANCE
XXIII.
Tiré fur fon fceau qui eftconferve a S.
Denis et vn femblable a S. Germain
des Prés datees du 5.e de fon Regne le
20 octob. expedieés a Herifal.

Avoir par fa valeur, & par fon zele ardent,
Sceu vaincre les Saxons, & les Mores d'Efpagne,
Efteint le nom Lombard, converti l'Allemagne,
Et joint aux Fleurs de Lis l'Empire d'Occident,
Sont des plus grands exploits de noftre CHARLEMAGNE.
CHARLES

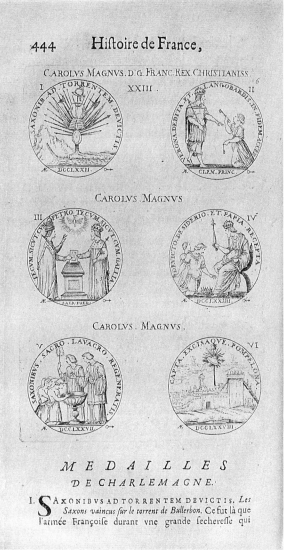

CAROLVS MAGNVS. D. G. FRANC. REX CHRISTIANISS
XXIII.

CAROLVS . MAGNVS

CAROLVS . MAGNVS .

MEDAILLES
DE CHARLEMAGNE.

I. **S** AXONIBVS AD TORRENTEM DEVICTIS, *Les*
Saxons vaincus fur le torrent de Bullerbon. Ce fut là que
l'armée Françoife durant vne grande fechereffe qui

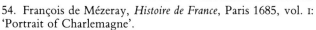

54. François de Mézeray, *Histoire de France*, Paris 1685, vol. I:
'Portrait of Charlemagne'.

55. François de Mézeray, *Histoire de France*, Paris 1685,
vol. I: 'Reverses of medals of Charlemagne'.

Mézeray is justified in claiming that his explanations are fuller than those to be found in previous works of the kind. Portraits are also included of the queen and of the heir to the throne, even if he died in childhood and was dauphin for only a few months. However, we have seen that the earliest kings, such as Pharamond or Clodion, have no portrait – merely a blank roundel with verses underneath; and occasionally Mézeray makes clear that he has not been able to find a portrait of one of some king's children.

In many ways the medallic reverses constitute the most interesting feature of the book, for, especially in the case of the earliest kings, they are intended to supplement the histories with authentic visual material dating from the period under discussion. It is true that, for the most part, these reverses are only used to illustrate some event that has already been discussed in words; but there are occasions when Mézeray comes very close indeed to making use of the image as essential evidence if no literary source is forthcoming. As the book proceeds – it is three volumes long – its character changes. Both portraits and medals of the later kings are far more authentic and accurate (and plentiful) than those of the first ones (thus Mézeray reproduces twelve reverses for Charles VI and fifty-eight for Henri III), and the historical narrative is also grounded on much more serious sources. And yet with growing availability and growing reliability, the medal reverses lose much of the intrinsic relationship they had once had with the text. They and the explanations of them are increasingly segregated at the end of each reign instead of constituting an integral part of it; and, because they are almost without exception allegorical rather than narrative in content, they can serve only a limited role in directly illuminating the written text. Despite this, Mézeray's very handsome volumes are probably the most important historical works of the seventeenth century to draw – however tentatively – on the evidence of visual sources.

vi   The Growth of Scepticism

By the end of the seventeenth century it was not only historians who were generally reluctant to draw conclusions from the evidence of portraiture – or even to make much use of it. A number of other writers, and even of antiquarians (especially in England), were themselves becoming sceptical about its value. In part, this may have been a perfectly logical response to the widely differing, and sometimes wholly incompatible, delineations of the same historical figure to be found in the anthologies of portraits issued by competitive publishers – publishers, moreover, who in their prefaces would openly ridicule the irresponsibility of their rivals. But there was probably another, even more compelling, reason for doubting the veracity of such portraits as became accessible, although (as we shall see) it was one that antiquarians have often been unwilling to accept. A glance at what was happening in their own day could well have alerted them to the possibility that similar practices might also have been current in the past. Thus Peter Stent, the inventive London publisher whom we have already come across, was by no means alone in commissioning from the engravers working for him a standard portrait type (often equestrian) in which the head could be altered as demand required: Richard Cromwell (pl. 57) could be transformed into Charles II (pl. 58) with only the slightest trouble and expense.[163]

When this technique was carried out at a yet further remove from the original the results could be very strange. Anyone even remotely familiar with the appearance of Charles I – and who in 1690 was not, for by then images of the martyred king had been very widely distributed? – would surely have been bewildered by the hardly recognisable portrait of him, standing in a suit of armour designed for a Habsburg prince a century earlier (pl. 56), which appeared that year in Gregorio Leti's *Teatro Belgico* published in Amsterdam – to be followed, in 1692, by the same author's *Historia, e Memorie recondite sopra alla vita di Oliviero Cromuele*

56. Gregorio Leti, *Teatro Belgico*, Amsterdam 1690: Charles I.

in which many of the illustrations bear no resemblance at all to the figures whom they are supposed to represent. It is unlikely that the unconvinced would have been much impressed by Leti's refutation of the charges of careless haste frequently brought against him: 'I sleep little, I rise early in the morning, make few visits, rarely go out, usually take only two cups of light chocolate in the morning and do not dine until the evening; on three days a week I do not go to sleep without having written for twelve hours, and on the others for at least six', and so on.[164]

Nearly twenty years later the antiquarian Thomas Hearne, when visiting the cathedral of Christ Church in Oxford, 'took the opportunity to view distinctly the statue just put up in one of the nitches within the College, by the Dean's lodgings, of Bp. Fell. The Statuary was at work. All people that knew the Bp agree 'tis not like him, he being a thin, grave man, whereas the Statue represents him plump and gay. I told the Statuary that it was unlike, and that he was made too plump. Oh,

Within the image:
Richard Lord Protector Of the Common Wealth of England Scotland & Ireland, with ye Dominions and Territories thereunto belonging.

WINDSOR

P. Stent excudit.

57. Peter Stent, *Richard Cromwell.*

Charles the 2.d Crowned King of England
Scotland France & Ireland natus May 29 A. 1630.
Ætatis Suæ 1660.

DIEV ET MON DROIT.

Sould by Iohn Ouerton at f   white horse without   Newgate neere f fountaine tavern

P. Stent exeudit.

58. Peter Stent, *Charles II*.

59. Statue of Bishop Fell in the
grounds of Nuneham Park,
Oxfordshire.

says he, we must make a handsome Man. Just as if it were to burlesque the Bp, who is put in Episcopal Robes, and yet by the Statue is not represented above 20' (pl. 59).[165]

How many purchasers of Peter Stent's prints or of Gregorio Leti's volumes or acquaintances of Bishop Fell would have projected their misgivings on to the past? Even John Evelyn, who believed that so much was to be learned by studying the portraits of Cromwell and other protagonists of the English civil wars (though not presumably those reproduced in the books of Gregorio Leti), could be struck by momentary doubts. Might it not be, he asked, that the portraits on imperial coins were far more flattering than the truth warranted – just as, he adds in a comparison that will appear strange (or very malicious) to anyone familiar with the pictures in question, Carlo Borromeo was flattered in the portraits of his own time?[166]

And although the arguments deployed are somewhat different, the reflexions that occurred to Daniel Defoe during his visit to Holyroodhouse in 1726 implicitly provide what is perhaps the most cogent case that had yet been made against the general class of imagery discussed in this chapter:

The North Side is taken up with one large Gallery, reaching the whole Length of the House, famous for having the Pictures of all the Kings of Scotland from King Fergus, who, they say, reign'd Anno ant. CHR 320. But, in my opinion, as these Pictures cannot be, and are not suppos'd to be Originals, but just a Face and Dress left to the Discretion of the Limner, and so are all Guess-work, I see no Rarity, or, indeed, any Thing valuable in it. As to their later Kings there may be some Pretence to have their Pictures from old preserv'd Draughts, or from their Coins or Medals, and such may be, indeed, worth preserving; and tho' they were but copy'd again, it would have been worth seeing; but, as it is, I must confess it seems a trifling Thing, rather than a Gallery fit for a Court.[167]

60. Peter Heymanns, tapestry (446 × 690 cm) showing Martin Luther preaching in the presence of princes of the houses of Saxony and Pomerania, 1554 (Greifswald, Ernst-Moritz-Arndt-Universität).

Historical Narrative and Reportage

The medal reverses from Jacques de Bie which François Mézeray used as illustrations for his history of France were essentially allegorical, although in a few cases allegory was applied so sparingly to the representation of some specific event that the image conveys an appearance of unadorned reality. In any case, by the time his book appeared there had been in existence a long, but discontinuous, tradition of contemporary visual records (made in a variety of techniques) of important public events which could be read as straightforward reportage. On the walls of Charlemagne's palace at Ingelheim, for instance, facing the valorous deeds of ancient kings and heroes were large paintings depicting King Pepin's conquest of Aquitaine as well as Charlemagne's own subjugation of the Saxons and his coronation.[1] Illustrated manuscripts recording the murder of Thomas à Becket were in circulation within ten years of the event itself in 1170 (pl. 61).[2] Splendidly illuminated volumes of the *Grandes Chroniques de France*, dating from the late thirteenth and the fourteenth centuries, showed incidents from contemporary history – the imprisonment of the Templars, the coronation of Charles V – as well as episodes from the lives of Charlemagne and his successors who now belonged to the distant past;[3] and, in a similar manner, past and present mingled in an extensively illustrated copy of the chronicles of Giovanni Villani of Florence which was made in the second half of the fourteenth century.[4] The Norman Conquest of England was recorded in detail on a great embroidery while many who had taken part in it were still alive;[5] and the preaching of Luther (pl. 60), the capture of François Ier at the battle of Pavia and the defeat of the Spanish Armada were all celebrated in magnificent sets of tapestry.[6] Velázquez painted Justin of Nassau's surrender of Breda to Ambrogio Spinola within ten years of the siege, and the assassination of Count Wallenstein was depicted in a lively picture by the little-known Pietro Paolini (pl. 62).[7] The execution of Mary Queen of Scots, the Massacre of St Bartholomew, the entry of Henri IV into Paris were all engraved by artists of varying abilities and thus became familiar to a wide international public.

It is true that not one of these contemporary representations of important public affairs was, however convincing in appearance, an 'eye-witness report', as some nineteenth-century historians liked to claim; moreover, many events of equal significance were not recorded by artists at all;[8] and, in any case, scenes such as the ones mentioned here were far out-numbered by long-established subjects chosen

61 (right). Earliest-known representation of the murder – in 1170 – of Thomas à Becket, *c.*1180 (British Library).

63 (facing page). *Reception [in ninth century] of the Relics of St Mark in Venice*, thirteenth-century mosaic above Porta di Sant' Alippio, basilica of S. Marco, Venice.

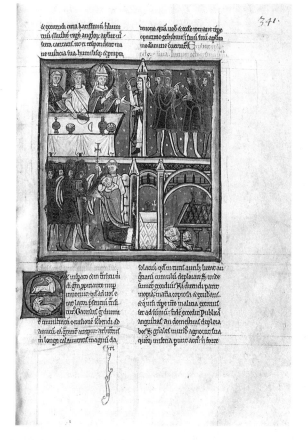

62. Pietro Paolini, *Murder [in 1634] of General Wallenstein*, *c.*1634 (Lucca, Palazzo Orsetti).

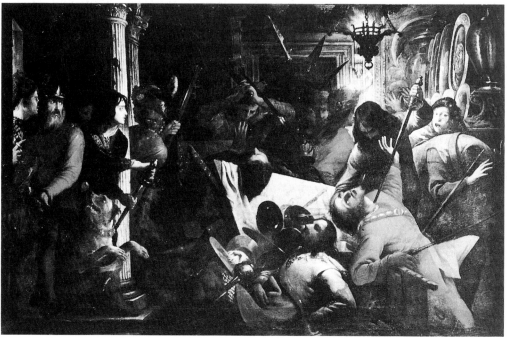

from the Scriptures, from the lives of the saints, or from Greek and Roman literature. None the less, some at least of the paintings of more local events to be seen in public places came to assume fundamental importance because they were granted a status as decisive (and sometimes more so) as that assigned to the written word in establishing the authenticity of matters open to historical debate. It was in Venice that this notion proved to be particularly influential.[9] Thus a chronicler writing in the city between 1267 and 1275 about the removal to it of relics from Alexandria nearly 450 years earlier concluded his account with the words: 'and if any of you wish to verify that these things happened just as I told you, come to see the beautiful church of San Marco in Venice, and look at it right in front, because the story is written there just as I have told you'. Despite his use of the word 'written', Martin da Canal is here alluding to scenes represented in mosaic in the lunettes above the four portals on each side of the main entrance of the basilica (pl. 63) – mosaics that were, in fact, being installed at much the same time as he was writing his own account.

It was, however, the controversy surrounding the 'peace of Venice' of 1177 that, more than anything else, demonstrated the importance that could be attached to

64. Illumination from Venetian manuscript of the mid-fourteenth century showing the emperor and the pope making peace in front of St Mark's in 1177 (Venice, Museo Correr).

visual sources as historical evidence. In that year, claimed the Venetians, they had to all intents and purposes saved the papacy from catastrophe by mediating from a position of strength between Pope Alexander III and the Emperor Frederick Barbarossa; moreover, the pope himself had acknowledged the momentousness of their intervention by presenting Doge Ziani with a number of symbolic gifts. Selected episodes from this legendary achievement were extensively recorded in paintings and illuminated manuscripts (pl. 64) as well as in chronicles – which, so it was claimed in Rome, were tendentious and misleading. And as late as 1584 Fra Girolamo Bardi, a champion of the Venetian cause, referred in support of it not only to some fifty written sources in German, French, Spanish, Italian and Latin, but also (as previous authors had already done) to an 'ancient' fresco in Siena and, above all, to the paintings by Bellini, Carpaccio and other artists which, until the devastating fire of some years earlier, were to be seen in the Sala del Maggior Consiglio in the Palazzo Ducale. To the objection that these pictures had been painted 300 years after the events that they purported to record he answered that an examination of the charred walls of the Council Hall revealed that they had replaced earlier, and exactly similar, paintings in the *maniera greca* which could be dated, from a faded inscription, to the year 1226.

In Rome representations of these twelfth-century events could still cause trouble.[10] In the 1560s Pope Pius IV had commissioned a series of frescoes to decorate the Sala Regia in the Vatican Palace. The subjects were chosen from the more triumphal moments of papal history, and among them was the submission of Frederick Barbarossa to Pope Alexander III in the presence of Doge Ziani outside the church of St Mark's. This was entrusted to Giuseppe Porta (Salviati) who spent most of his life in Venice and who was thus able to render with special forcefulness the grand exoticism of the architecture in front of which the humiliation of the emperor was played out (pl. 65). This particular outcome of the Venetian saga was

65. Giuseppe Porta (Salviati): '*The Peace of Venice*', fresco in Sala Regia of Vatican Palace.

in no way controversial: when, twenty years or so later, Federico Zuccaro was required to paint the same episode in the Sala del Maggior Consiglio of the Palazzo Ducale, the emphasis he gave to the various figures was not significantly different from that to be found in Salviati's treatment of the story, in which the emperor, seen from behind, kneels at the feet of the pope, who looks down upon him from the steps on which he stands with the doge at his side, while the crowd mills around to witness this glorious consummation of Roman diplomacy.

However, the message conveyed by Salviati's fresco was entirely undermined by the inscription beneath it which ended with the amazing words: 'Thus the restoration of authority to the pope was due to the good offices of the Venetian Republic.' The Venetians were later to claim – in a statement that shows that as late as the middle of the seventeenth century they still retained a certain trust in the value of visual evidence as historical source – that the inscription had been chosen with particular care by a committee of cardinals and learned men who had relied on 'very ancient documents, the common consent of authors, inscriptions, paintings, marbles and countless records'. Pope Urban VIII was less impressed. In the 1630s he ordered the inscription to be painted over and then replaced with one that certainly conformed more to the spirit of what was to be seen in the fresco above it. This in turn led to a diplomatic incident, and the Venetians withdrew their ambassador. It was not until the following papacy that the original inscription was restored. The fresco itself had not been touched.

It is hardly surprising that a certain scepticism about the reliability of written history became particularly intense in the sixteenth and seventeenth centuries. The accusations of tampering with, or misinterpreting, documents which pole-micists hurled at each other during the period following the Reformation must surely have encouraged the belief that figured sources were somehow more valu-able than written ones in describing events 'as they had actually happened'.[11] It is, however, curious that this idea should have gained currency at the very time that images were themselves being widely used in order to spread conflicting versions of contemporary events; but – as so often happens – it proved extremely difficult to assess the true character of evidence surviving from the past in the light of lessons learnt in the present. It was, in fact, during the second half of the sixteenth century, in the aftermath of Luther's secession from the Church, that the potential power of a new kind of visual propaganda first became fully appreciated. It is true that both sides resorted to much crude satire of an obviously allegorical nature, but some episodes of the terrible religious wars that afflicted France were recorded in paintings (and above all in prints) by Jean Perrissin and others (pl. 66), which were indeed designed to be tendentious but which were realistic enough in treatment to be able to convey – both to contemporaries and to later historians – an impression of absolute, observed authenticity.

Closely related to the faith placed in images of the past was the concept (which has proved so influential ever since) that great or extraordinary events will nec-essarily be recorded as much through the medium of the visual arts as they are in written histories, and that if they are not so recorded they not only lose some of their power to move later generations but also some of their actuality. Thus John Evelyn, who was enthusiastic about Wenceslaus Hollar's engravings of a few of the most important events of his own day, maintained that 'had we a perfect and uninterrupted series of medals, we should need almost no other History'.[12] He was therefore very concerned about the lack of any visual evidence for many of the greatest episodes in English history. He writes of 'the defeat of that *Invincible Armada in Eighty-Eight* . . . in danger of being quite forgotten, as to any such durable Monument among us, when ever those Incomparable *Tapestries* that now Adorn the House of *Peers* (so lively Representing to the Eye both the Persons, and Circumstances of that Glorious and Renowned Action) shall be quite worn-out; or by other fatal Accident, miscarry'.[13] And, after describing paintings to be seen in Whitehall which had some claim to be contemporary records of the events they depicted (and which often still survive), such as the expedition of Henry VIII to Boulogne and the cavalcade of Queen Elizabeth to Tilbury, he continues, without any sense of incongruity: 'And ah! what an Illustrious *Table* would the Conflict of *Agincourt*, fought by our *Henry the Fifth* against the whole Power of *France*, in the

Reign of the *Sixth Charles* . . . produce painted by the hand of *Rubens*, or *Verrio*.'
These comments suggest that Evelyn is not merely regretting the absence of what
might have been great artistic masterpieces, but is also implying that the lack of
such visual representations (which, unlike those he had previously discussed, could
have had no claim to being thought of as contemporary records) in some way
subtracted from the validity of the historical events themselves. A similar fear was
to be expressed not long afterwards in Paris where it was pointed out that 'the
most brilliant actions, the most memorable achievements [of the early years of the
reign of Louis XIV] were forgotten or ran the risk of being forgotten, because no
steps had been taken to preserve the memory of them in marble and in bronze'.[14]
And when this neglect had been remedied Evelyn showed himself to be deeply
envious of the great 'medallic histories' that were being issued in France and the
Low Countries. Although medals had, of course, always been designed to convey
messages, it was not until the last part of the seventeenth century that rulers began

66. Jean Perrissin, *Premier volume contenant quarante tableaux ou histoires diverses qui sont memorables touchant les guerres,
massacres, & troubles advenus en France en ces dernières années*, [Geneva] 1570: massacre at Tours in 1562.

to commission complete sets which were then reproduced in superbly produced volumes. The experiences of two centuries of antiquarian research were fully present to the minds of those responsible for organising such enterprises. 'Just as the Romans were so careful to strike medals to perpetuate for all time the memory of the constellation under which the Emperor Augustus was born,' commented the author of the *Médailles sur les principaux évènements du règne de Louis le Grand*, published in 1702, 'so here the aim has been to transmit to posterity (without conceding anything to the chimaeras of Astrology) the memory of the position of the sky at the moment that God gave to France the Prince who has made her the most flourishing monarchy in the world.'[15] The appeal to future historians is characteristic – but so too, in the case of this and of nearly all the other medals in the series, is the use of allegorical rather than strictly factual illustration (pl. 74).

Enough has been said about visual records of contemporary events, and the importance attached to them, in the Middle Ages and the Renaissance for it to be apparent that antiquarians and historians might well have expected, and must certainly have hoped, to find similar records in the figured remains that most attracted their attention – those dating from antiquity. Yet whatever might once have been the case (and the writings of Pliny do not suggest that many such records had been made in Greece), the fact remained that no obvious representation of the conspiracy of Catiline, or the assassination of Julius Caesar, or the suicide of Nero, or any of the most familiar episodes from Roman history was to be seen on any known coin or sculpture – although in 1457 Cardinal Barbo owned a coin whose reverse was believed to represent Brutus and his friends setting out to kill Caesar.[16]

In these circumstances sixteenth-century numismatists were sometimes driven to suggest the most reckless interpretations in order to make the images they were looking at conform to what they might have expected from written texts. Thus the reverse of a rare coin (or medal) of Nero displayed a fish, a river prawn, a cuttle fish and a polyp (pl. 67); there was no inscription. Erizzo was so puzzled by this that he thought at first that it might be a modern fake, because all these creatures could be interpreted only as insults to the emperor: the fish, for instance, was looked upon by Egyptian priests as an emblem of 'someone abominable and hateful'; and the prawn, the cuttle fish and the polyp concealed similar meanings. It was inconceivable, concluded Erizzo, that such a medal could have been struck in Rome, but it was also undeniable that a reading of Suetonius made clear that all the vices symbolised on it had indeed been exemplified by Nero. The only explanation must be that it had been struck in some city subject to Rome in order to demonstrate the horror felt for Nero, represented in a manner that would be accessible exclusively to the educated classes and not to ordinary people. Even Erizzo himself was a little doubtful about this interpretation, and he acknowledged that Pirro Ligorio thought it more likely that the water creatures shown were symbols of Reggio and Squillace on the straits of Messina, both of which were provided with an abundance of fish: in that case the mysterious medal might have originated in one of those cities.[17]

67. Sebastiano Erizzo, *Discorso sopra le Medaglie*, 4th edition, n.d.: 'Reverse of a medal of Nero'.

68 (centre and right). Roman spintria (Oxford, Ashmolean Museum).

On the other hand, Erizzo felt that no problem at all was presented by the obscene 'medals' (later known as spintriae) that represented 'all the different modes of lascivious couplings, both male and female' (pl. 68). These, he asserted, had been designed by the Emperor Tiberius in order 'to transmit to posterity all his shameful and criminal activities' – lusts that were, of course, fully documented in Suetonius.[18] It is ironical that many scholars now believe that these 'medals' were in fact tokens intended to be used in brothels just because ordinary coins which carried the head of the emperor could not – as Vico reminded his readers – be taken into such places; but explanations of the kind suggested by Erizzo are hardly surprising in view of the fact that, on the very rare occasions when Roman historians themselves mentioned the design of coins, they were (according to modern historians) liable to be misleading in a precisely similar way. Thus Suetonius had claimed, whether through error or on purpose, that the Apollo playing a lyre to be seen on a coin of Nero, which was probably intended to flatter the emperor's pride in his musical performances by associating him with the god, had in fact been specifically commissioned by him as a portrait of himself – a claim that was, naturally enough, repeated in the sixteenth century.[19]

Only the great triumphal arches and columns provided any extensive examples of historical narrative, but it so happened that, in almost every case, the episodes recorded on these monuments were ones that had left little if any trace in the surviving literature. The reliefs on these arches and columns were naturally studied by everyone interested in the history and art of Rome, but they were not easy to elucidate. This was certainly the experience of the mysterious (and possibly English) 'Master Gregory' who visited Rome probably at the beginning of the thirteenth century. 'Master Gregory' stands out from his predecessors and contemporaries both for his interest in secular history and for the independence and care with which he struggled to understand the carved stories to be seen on a number of the principal monuments in the city. Some of those that he described have subsequently disappeared, but his interpretations of them have seemed reasonable enough to have convinced modern scholars of their essential accuracy. And, on other occasions, where it is possible to show that he was mistaken, we can to some extent follow the processes by which he tried to reach his conclusions.

Unlike so many later observers who knew in advance what they expected to discover and interpreted the material accordingly, 'Master Gregory' – who found difficulty in reading and accurately copying Latin inscriptions – often ridicules the stories repeated by his contemporaries and is sometimes ready to admit that he does not know what he is looking at. He therefore recorded what he saw and reminded himself to consult literary sources on his return home so as to be able to locate in them a suitable explanation for what he had noted. However, he was able to satisfy himself on the spot that the column of Marcus Aurelius (or perhaps of Trajan) must have been erected to commemorate the noble consul Gaius Luscinus Fabricius who (as reported by many ancient writers) had refused to accept the offer made by the doctor of Pyrrhus, the great enemy of Rome, to murder his master in return for a handsome reward. Evidently the scenes on the column showing captives being brought before the emperor (pl. 69) recalled to 'Master Gregory's' memory the freeing by Pyrrhus of all his Roman prisoners as a gesture of gratitude to Fabricius.[20]

'Master Gregory's' response to this monument reveals the discriminating spirit with which he treated his sources: he must have rejected the identification (which was current well before his arrival in Rome) of the column with that of Marcus Aurelius because he believed that the reliefs on it portrayed historical events with which he was familiar. And even though the name of Fabricius may perhaps have been suggested to him by another tradition (of which, however, we hear only in the following century), his readiness to submit to his own impression before the original was exceptional. Contemporary and later visitors to Rome usually went out of their way to reject evidence of this kind. 'Triumphal arches', wrote John of Salisbury, 'make their contribution to the fame of celebrated men, because the inscriptions explain the reasons for which they have been erected. Thus only when the inscription indicates that the triumph (on his arch) is that of Constantine (to whom our Britain gave birth) does the observer recognise the liberator of the fatherland, the founder of peace. Only the written word can give lasting glory'. And, not long afterwards, Boncompagno da Signa complained that 'the Romans aimed to make use of reliefs and the Greeks of statues to enable posterity to recall their great deeds. But it is more praiseworthy to transmit the memory of these events through books than through reliefs and statues. Indeed, since the beginning of the world such deeds have been entrusted by most people to writing in order that the memory of the ancients should not be lost.'[21] This widely shared and long-lasting distrust of images is ironical in view of the fact that we now know that Roman historians themselves were sometimes required to rely partly on pictorial sources for their literary works.[22]

However, in 1411 Manuel Chrysoloras, the Byzantine scholar who, since his arrival in Italy some fifteen years earlier, had played an influential role in spreading a knowledge of Greek, wrote an exceptionally vivid letter in which, for the first time, he pointed out the full significance of the carved reliefs to be seen on the triumphal arches of Rome and even made a specific analogy between them and the work of Herodotus, one of the greatest of ancient historians.[23] And yet even as he did so, he hesitated because (in an insight of extraordinary lucidity) he appreciated

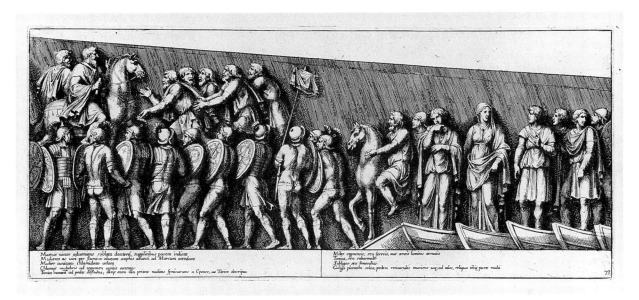

69. Pietro Santi Bartoli, engraving (in G.P. Bellori, *Columna Antoniniana Marci Aurelii*, Rome n.d.) of a relief from the column of Marcus Aurelius in Rome in which high-ranking barbarian men and women are shown giving themselves up to the emperor.

70. Pietro Santi Bartoli, engraving (in G.P. Bellori, *Colonna Traiana*, Rome n.d.) of a scene from Trajan's Column, in which the head of Decebalus, king of the Dacians, is being displayed by the victorious Roman army to Roman and Dacian soldiers.

how widely separated the realms of narrative history and antiquarianism had already become. After listing some of the reliefs – 'battles and captives and spoils, fortresses taken by storm, and also sacrifices and victims, altars and offerings' – and adding that 'it is possible to know what each is through the inscription there', he concludes that 'Herodotus and other writers of history are thought to have done something of great value when they describe these things (what arms and what costume people used in ancient times, what insignia magistrates had, how an army was arrayed, a battle fought, a city besieged or a camp laid out, what ornaments and garments people used); but in these sculptures one can *see* all that existed in those days among the different races, so that it is a complete and accurate history – or rather not a history so much as an exhibition, so to speak, and manifestation of everything that existed anywhere at that time.'

Chrysolaras's observations are of interest not only for their freshness – elsewhere he describes himself 'clambering up palace walls, even up to their windows, on the chance of seeing something of the beauties inside' – but also because of the qualifications with which he limits the value of the reliefs as narrative sources: after all, as he well knew, inscriptions by no means explained everything that was to be seen on the triumphal arches, nor even did the surviving works of Roman (or Greek) historians. And so to the twentieth-century reader this brilliant scholar, who was writing at a time when serious historical study had barely begun to make an impact on the post-classical world, appears as if he stands on the very brink of inaugurating an approach that might have transformed the whole subject. Be that as it may, later writers followed Chrysolaras's essentially cautious 'antiquarian' approach even to the most obviously revealing narrative sequences.

To this general rule there is at least one noteworthy exception. In the first years of the sixteenth century the Bolognese artist Jacopo Ripanda was commissioned to paint, in 'the first great hall' of the palace in Rome belonging to Cardinal Fazio Santoro, a series of frescoes which were to represent scenes from the life of the Emperor Trajan.[24] The seventeen scenes chosen by him and his adviser concentrated mainly on the emperor's campaigns against the Dacians, and below each one was placed a Latin explanation of its content.[25] These inscriptions were recorded by a visitor to the palace towards the end of the sixteenth century (the frescoes have long since disappeared), and – as is to be expected – they were mostly based on the summary (which alone has survived) of the account of Trajan's wars written by the Romanised Greek historian Dio Cassius some hundred years after the event. However, it is clear from one or two of these inscriptions that the scenes chosen for Ripanda did not look back to this, or to any other written source, but rather to the reliefs to be seen on Trajan's column. Thus one of them showed the head of Decebalus, the king of the Dacians who had committed suicide, being displayed to the Roman army. This episode is not recorded in any of those sections of Dio's history that have survived (though it may well have appeared in the work as originally written), but it does occur on the column (pl. 70). There can, of course, be no doubt that these reliefs must have proved invaluable as models for Ripanda's compositions in general – he had, at great personal risk, been lowered in a basket to make copies of them, and he was renowned for his battle scenes 'in the manner in which the ancient Romans used to fight'.[26] However, to rely on scenes carved on the column as primary historical sources, despite the fact that there was no literary warrant for doing so, makes what may be a small, but is none the less a significant, stage in the interpretation of visual material.

So imaginative a response was not shared by writers of the time or even of much later – it is certainly not to be found in the commentary provided by Alfonso Chacon to accompany the publication in 1576 of the first full set of engravings, loosely based on the drawings by Ripanda, of the reliefs on Trajan's column. Indeed, interest moved in a quite different direction, and in a preface, written in 1665 to a handsome volume of entirely new illustrations which had just been made of the reliefs, its publisher, Giovanni de' Rossi, lays all his emphasis on their use as a fund of antiquarian lore.[27] He echoes the sentiments of Chrysolaras 250 years earlier, but without any of that writer's awareness that he might have been erring on the cautious side: 'In this book you have the history of the first and second Dacian wars conducted by Trajan against King Decebalus; indeed, you are presented with a universal store of information concerning antiquity, especially ancient Roman customs and those of the barbarians, the clothes, the weapons, the standards, the military discipline, the auguries, the living quarters, the buildings, the ships, the bridges, the castles, the military meetings, the assaults, the battering rams, *testudines* and machines, attacks, battles, booty, victories, killings, captives and trophies. In addition, you have constantly before your eyes the religious ceremonies, the displays, the sacrifices and many other splendid rituals'.

It was just this antiquarian emphasis in the treatment of visual narrative that, a generation earlier, had already attracted the attention, though not the approval, of Agostino Mascardi, author of some of the most remarkable reflections on history to be published in the seventeenth century.[28]

Mascardi was a Jesuit (apparently of dissolute morals) who had been born at Sarzana, south of Genoa, in 1590 but who quickly made his name in Rome. He was taken up by Pope Urban VIII and appointed Professor of Eloquence at the Sapienza in 1628. He was in touch with the leading talents who circulated round the papal court, and, besides a number of orations and literary compositions, he wrote some works of history, the most famous being an account of the conspiracy of Count Giovan Luigi de' Fieschi, which had taken place in 1547. Mascardi was also keenly interested in painting, and in 1629 he translated, with a long commentary, a Greek dialogue called *The Table*, which at the time was attributed to a Theban disciple of Socrates called Cebes and which purported to describe a picture, representing an allegory of human life, found by two travellers in front of the temple of Kronos. By far his most interesting work, *Dell'Arte Istorica*, which appeared in 1636, also contains many allusions to painting: at one point, for instance, in his discussion of literary style, he follows what was by now a common convention in singling out a number of artists (in this case the Cavaliere d'Arpino, Guido Reni, Lanfranco and Pietro da Cortona) in order to make the point that each has all the essential qualities of a great painter while yet possessing an individual manner of his own.[29] And his feeling for the visual is demonstrated again in some impressive pages in which he strongly defends the right of the historian to set the action he is discussing against a vividly described background (such, for instance, as the city of Venice), as long as this contributes to, rather than detracts from, the main action.[30] Nevertheless, despite his perceptive attitude to the arts, which is also revealed on a number of other occasions, Mascardi goes out of his way to dismiss the value, for the true historian of his own day, of monuments surviving from the past. He recognises that there have been times when 'pictures, sculptures, arches, columns and similar public monuments constituted a silent narration of great and noble actions from which it was possible to learn of the deeds of valiant men'; and he gives examples of how the earliest Romans, 'who had no history of any kind', had used such means 'to transmit to posterity the memory of ancient things'.[31] He also agrees that children, like the common people, 'have no books other than painting, which by representing past events in colour can, as a sort of mute history, insinuate into simple minds these examples of good and evil that others, better educated, would read in the form of written records'.[32] It is just this issue of the moral significance of history that concerned him when he considered the claims that had been made by antiquarians over the preceding hundred years:

> The relics of the arches of Constantine and Septimius in Rome, the last relics of the voracity of time and the pride of the barbarians, the two columns of Trajan and Antoninus, entirely figured in bas-reliefs, contain records that are so beautiful that antiquarians have copied many things from them to enrich their very learned books: many military costumes, many weapons of war, many adornments of triumphs, and much else [che so io] have been taken from these marble books and transferred to paper books to teach us all. But records of this kind I have not proposed for the purpose of the art of history which I am composing.[33]

And, later, he writes:

> Others take tireless trouble to collect all customs and rites, both sacred and profane: the ceremonies used in sacrifices, the procedures observed at funerals, the distinctive dress of magistrates, the ranks of soldiers, the pomp of triumphs, the institutions of magistrates, the differing laws: the augurs, the prophecies and the thousand other curiosities that combine to make up erudition.

But, claims Mascardi, all this, useful though it is for elucidating difficult points in ancient writers, had already been done sufficiently for it to be no longer necessary. It must be distinguished from true history which should educate the mind and teach us how to organise our lives by comparing the past with the present.[34]

It was partly, no doubt, to remedy just such deficiencies that so many scholars were determined to discern in any ancient sculpture that did not offer opportunities for research of the kind promoted by the antiquarians (as well as in many that did) illustrations of some of the more spectacular episodes of Roman history. As has already been pointed out, while there was no lack of such visual records for modern times, ancient art seemed, on the surface, to provide few (if any) examples

71. Marble statue believed in the Renaissance to represent the Emperor Commodus as Hercules (Vatican Museum).

to set beside them. On the surface – but might not more thorough investigation prove rewarding?

It is very rare to be able to witness the origins of some of the more ambitious attempts to do this, but at least one is well documented. On 15 May 1507 a statue was excavated in the garden of a house in the Campo de' Fiori in Rome (pl. 71).[35] It was at once identified (correctly) as a Hercules, but the learned were puzzled by the child whom he held in his left arm. Within a few days Tommaso Inghirami suggested that the statue represented not Hercules himself, but the Roman Emperor Commodus who was reported by ancient historians to have identified himself with Hercules. Inghirami, who was soon to be in charge of the Vatican library and to become one of the leading figures at the court of Pope Leo X (although he is now chiefly remembered through Raphael's fine portrait[36]), would, of course, have known these literary sources, but it is also possible that he had come across one or more of the various coins on which Commodus was actually portrayed as Hercules. In any case, the identification was accepted, partly – so it seems – because the expression of the face struck people as being so ferocious; but the addition of the child (who is not found on coins) remained mysterious. It was not until 1597 that the antiquarian Jean-Jacques Boissard explained that his presence also could be accounted for by the authors of the 'Augustan History', for he must be the 'little boy who tossed out of his bedroom a tablet on which were written the names of those who were to be put to death' by the emperor.

72a and b. Roman *as* of Faustina II with reverse, inscribed *Veneri Victrici*, portraying Mars and Venus.

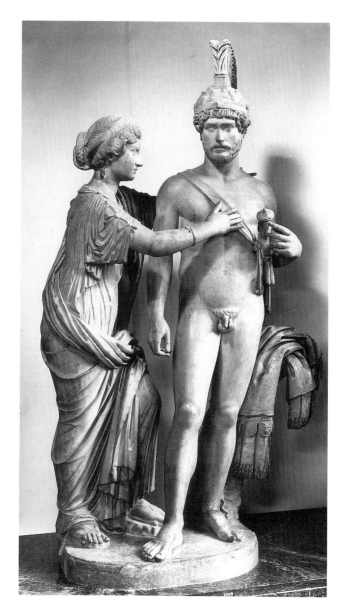

73. Marble group of Mars and Venus in the guise of an imperial couple, formerly known as 'Faustina and the Gladiator' (Paris, Louvre).

The successive interpretations are characteristic of much early iconographical research. In the first stage a mythological figure is replaced by one taken from Roman history – this change is not intrinsically absurd, but it is not actually required by the nature of the image. In the second stage a precise and dramatic moment is substituted for an official effigy – and (in this instance, at least) one cannot but be amazed that no one seems to have wondered under what circumstances a statue representing so grotesque a scene could actually have been commissioned.

Even more remarkable is the case of 'Faustina and the Gladiator', whose story can tell us much about the minds of early antiquarians and historians. Among the coins (or medals, as he believed them to be) owned by Sebastiano Erizzo was one that displayed, on the obverse, a female head in profile inscribed FAUSTINA AUGUSTA and, on the reverse, the inscription VENERI VICTRICI S.C. surrounding a nude warrior with a helmet and shield and a half-draped woman holding his arm (pl. 72).[37] Erizzo (who showed no particular interest in Faustina) very reasonably assumed that the figures on the reverse were intended to represent an allegory of Venus trying to tame or mitigate the fury of Mars.

However, to students of history the Empress Faustina was a notorious woman.[38] The writers of the 'Augustan History' had attributed to her a disreputable liaison with a lowborn gladiator, doubtless so as to be able to account for the depraved character of the Emperor Commodus which was so different from that of his putative father, the virtuous Marcus Aurelius, husband of Faustina. We have already seen that Giovanni Battista della Porta had detected signs of immorality in her features and that in 1635 Jean Tristan was to reiterate this when looking at a coin similar to the one owned by Erizzo. Tristan was not wholly convinced by the story of the gladiator, but he had no doubt about Faustina's sexual voracity, and for him the reverse of the coin indicated that she was prepared to use all her feminine guile – including nudity and feigned tears – in order to keep the emperor from his dangerous military campaigns so that she would be able to indulge with him in 'la douceur des combats amoureux'. And might not this 'most affected courtesan of her time' also be hinting that if he refused to stay with her or at least take her with him, she would be able to show him on his helmet ('sur son armet') that she would be ready to manage without him? There was another possibility: perhaps Marcus Aurelius was trying to persuade her to accompany him, partly because he could not bear to be away from her for so long, but partly also because he realised that it might be dangerous to leave behind so seductive and so capricious a woman.[39]

At much the same time a different idea was gaining ground. Two marble groups were known of the 'Mars and Venus', both of which were very similar in composition to the reverse of the Faustina coin. In his anthology of the best statues to be seen in Rome, which appeared in 1638, the French artist François Perrier illustrated the one that belonged to the Borghese family (pl. 73) and explained that 'some people' thought that it represented Faustina not with her husband but with her gladiator lover, though others believed the figures to be 'Volumnia pleading with Coriolanus her husband for the fatherland'.[40] It was the first of these theories that carried the day, and we next come across it (now with reference to the medallic version) three years later in 1641 when Francesco Angeloni, then aged about eighty-three, published his *Historia Augusta da Giulio Cesare infino a Costantino il Magno illustrata con la verità delle antiche medaglie*. Angeloni is well known to students of seventeenth-century Rome for his important art collection, which was particularly rich in drawings by Annibale Carracci, and it was through the mediation of Poussin that he was able to dedicate his book to Louis XIII.[41] There are, however, moments when his early career as an author of 'novelle piacevoli' seems more relevant than his artistic sensibility to the history that he wrote based on the 'truth' of Roman medals. Looking at the reverse of the medal, he commented that 'some people claim that the figures represent Mars and Venus, and that she is given the title of "victrice" because of her power to restrain Mars . . . but I would say that the scene represents the wild passion of Faustina for the young gladiator expressed under the guise of Venus and Mars'.[42]

No one seems to have challenged this interpretation (at least in print) for two generations, and it is not until 1685 that we come across the first objections to it. Angeloni's nephew, the very distinguished scholar, connoisseur and theorist, Giovan Pietro Bellori, was always anxious to defend the reputation of the uncle to whom he owed so much of his culture and whom he looked upon as a second father. Nevertheless, he could not accept his interpretation of this medal when he published a revised edition, with a commentary of his own, of Angeloni's *Historia Augusta*. Like all the scholars of his time, he believed that the reverse of the coin alluded directly to Faustina and Marcus Aurelius, but for him the Senate had portrayed Venus restraining Mars in order to hint that the empress should restrain her husband from constant wars in Germany and persuade him to return to Rome. When offering this suggestion Bellori cautiously, but explicitly, made the point (which now seems so obvious, but which then was quite novel) that it was unlikely ('non è probabile') that the Senate would disgrace Marcus Aurelius and his son Commodus by representing on a coin issued under its authority the scandalous love affair between Faustina and the gladiator. In other words, Bellori was groping his way towards uncovering the flaw that had marked so much numismatic scholarship of all kinds – the notion, that is, that the same sort of information was likely to be found on an official source (such as a coin) as in the texts of scandal-mongering Roman historians, usually writing much later than the events they described.

None the less, it was some years after Bellori's intervention in the debate that there was published the most remarkable of all the descriptions of the (by now very celebrated) marble statue in the Villa Borghese, so evidently related to the coin that had caused such extensive discussion. 'One cannot look at this group', wrote an admirer in 1700,

> without believing that one sees Faustina herself trembling for the life of the gladiator with whom she was so desperately in love, trying to hold him back when he is on the point of going to fight in the amphitheatre. One can discern among her feelings the infatuation with which she has been gripped; the passion which burns to achieve satisfaction; her aristocratic birth which she can well see that she is dishonouring; the distinction of her rank which she is degrading – all the tensions, timid and shameless, feeble and bold, of a woman in love who yet knows that she is sinning; the fear she feels that her lover will die; the efforts she is making to stop him – for all these passions are expressed with such naturalness in her expression and her gestures that one cannot bring oneself to look at her without entering into her feelings: and one would feel pity for the distress of so great an empress if one did not feel shame for her weakness.[43]

It is perhaps the identity of the author of this description that should surprise us at least as much as that of the statue he is describing. The Abbé Raguenet was aged about forty when he saw it in Rome – he had gone there in the service of Cardinal de Bouillon, whose nephews he tutored. Nine years earlier he had published a well-received book on Cromwell, which in fact remained the standard French work on the subject until the nineteenth century. Despite its dedication to Bossuet and its obvious sympathy with the plight of Charles I, the book is reasonably impartial in tone, and it is well documented from published and unpublished primary sources (in French and Latin translations) which are carefully recorded. And – most important of all from our point of view – Raguenet goes out of his way to emphasise to his readers that he has carried out much research into the medals celebrating Cromwell's deeds and has consulted the leading experts on the matter (including Pierre Bizot, the numismatist responsible for the *Histoire médallique de la République d'Hollande*). He reproduces – accurately enough[44] – a number of these medals in his book and explains them carefully. So sophisticated, so knowledgeable a historian would have derided the notion that marble statues could have been carved of any of the rulers of his own day in the arms of a prostitute or a guardsman; and yet he would also have been perfectly well aware of the fact that there was nothing inherently unlikely in such behaviour. However, Raguenet had no hesitation in believing that the Romans might have made works of just this kind. Curiously enough, neither he nor any other advocate of the Gladiator theory ever refers to the one antique precedent that might have strengthened their case: the story told by Pliny of a picture painted by Ktesikles which showed Queen Stratonice in the arms of the fisherman she loved – a picture that the queen so much admired for the excellence of the likenesses that she refused permission for it to be removed from the port of Ephesus where it was on view.[45]

The readiness shown by Boissard, Raguenet and other writers to interpret coins and marble statues as being deliberately offensive to the imperial figures they were believed to represent is analogous to the use of medals for hostile propaganda which flourished in many European countries during the second half of the seventeenth century. The Dutch were particular masters of the genre, and the ingenuity with which they manipulated the flattering and conventional imagery to be seen on the medallic reverses designed for the leading monarchs of the period aroused considerable indignation in the courts of England[46] and France. It is true that such images were almost invariably of an allegorical nature, but, as with the visual propaganda used in the religious wars of a century or so earlier, some of the most effective medallic blows were struck when allegory merged with realism in order to give at least some illusion of genuine reportage. Thus among the many cunning alterations made by the Dutch to the bombastic imagery devised for Louis XIV's mint by the Académie des Inscriptions et Belles-Lettres was the 'operation' performed in Amsterdam on a French medal which showed the king triumphantly driving his chariot to victory (pl. 74). Soon afterwards a version was minted in Holland which portrayed the king on a wheelbarrow being tugged by women, while the inscription read VENIT VIDIT SED NON VICIT (pl. 75): but in both cases the obverse showed similar portraits of Louis.[47] The parallel between medals of this kind and coins that appeared to many scholars of the seventeenth century to combine a sober portrait of Faustina Augusta on one side with evidence of her

74a and b. Bronze medal issued to celebrate Louis XIV's second conquest of the Franche-Comté in 1674.

75a and b. Dutch medal, dated 1693, parodying the victorious issues of Louis XIV.

dissolute way of life on the other is a striking one, but it is surely coincidental. Both examples, however, certainly give a new context to the repeated claim that 'truthful and incorruptible metal' was somehow of greater historical value than 'the differing accounts of committed or flattering writers'.

The misdeeds of Faustina and Commodus are only two among innumerable episodes of Roman history (such as loyal slaves rewarded or victims of tyranny driven to suicide) which antiquarians claimed to be able to detect in surviving monuments of all kinds – and not only of Roman history. While the Abbé Raguenet was identifying the precise emotions of a woman who had loved and sinned, other visitors to Italy were working out the relationship between Calvin, Luther and Luther's wife in a scene of domestic music-making in a picture that was then believed to be by Giorgione but is now more prosaically described as 'A Concert' by Titian (pl. 76). The identification of all three protagonists was complete by the 1690s – though hints of it were current well before then – and so enthusiastically was it accepted (despite the fact that Luther's true features were very well known) that when, as late as 1818, it was first pointed out that Giorgione had died only two years after the birth of Calvin, the distinguished scholar who noted this went out of his way to explain that, as the identification of the figures was correct, the picture should be attributed to 'Venetian School' rather than to Giorgione.[48] As late as 1844–5 the young Theodor Mommsen had no qualms in acknowledging the presence of Luther and his wife, though he called the third figure Melanchthon.[49] And by then many of the more notorious protagonists of European history such as Machiavelli and assorted members of the Borgia family had been detected in Renaissance pictures.

This kind of approach to individual coins, sculpture and paintings was certainly important, but there was one field of historical enquiry in which the very existence of art itself, irrespective (at first) of content or quality, radically transformed the whole nature of the problems under discussion. Despite the cult of relics, visual evidence of the earliest tribulations and triumphs of the Christian Church was even more deficient than that recording the more spectacular events of Roman history. The accidental discovery by some labourers in June 1578 of a group of richly decorated Christian tombs beneath an estate two miles outside the gates of Rome near the Via Salaria Nova was therefore greeted by Catholic polemicists with an immediate awareness of its crucial significance for the study of the past.[50] 'One can now see with one's own eyes,' said a report within two months of the event, 'how, in the days of the pagan idolaters, those holy and pious friends of Our Lord, when they were forbidden public meetings, painted and worshipped their sacred images in these caves and subterranean places: those images that blinded Christians today seek, with sacrilegious zeal, to remove from the churches'.[51]

The question of whether or not the early Christians had made use of the visual arts was one of the liveliest points at issue between Protestant and Catholic historians. Even before Luther's break with Rome the role of images in the Church

76. Titian, *A Concert* (Florence, Palazzo Pitti).

had been much debated, and thereafter discussion of it led to bitter divisions and active iconoclasm.[52] Arguments of many kinds were deployed by Catholics and the different Protestant sects, but among the issues raised the only one that concerns us here is that which looked back to historical sources. Had the decoration of churches been sanctioned by Christ Himself (to whom the Mosaic commandment, 'Thou shalt not make to thyself any graven image', would no longer be relevant once He had chosen to become Man) and by his earliest followers? It seemed that the existing texts could be understood in different ways while to the more austere and bellicose Protestants, the well-known affirmation of Pope Gregory the Great (590–604) that 'Pictures are used in churches so that those who are ignorant of letters may at least read by seeing on the walls what they cannot read in books' carried no weight because such words were exactly what they would have expected of a pope. But now the mere existence of paintings was a decisive historical fact which proved that the first Christians – for no one as yet doubted that the decoration of the catacombs must date from soon after the death of Christ Himself – had indeed made use of images in their holiest places.

Cardinal Baronius, by far the greatest and most influential of the Catholic historians, was just completing the first volume of his *Annales Ecclesiastici* at the time of the discovery of the catacombs, and he naturally went to see them.[53] Recalling their impact, he wrote that 'all Rome was filled with wonder, for it had had no idea that in its neighbourhood there was a hidden city, filled with tombs from the days of the persecution of the Christians. That which we knew before from written accounts and from a few cemeteries which were only partially opened out, we can now realise fully, and, filled with wonder, see with our own eyes the confirmation of the accounts of St. Jerome and Prudentius.'[54] Even here the claim is characteristic of traditional history in the homage it pays to the supremacy of the written word, for while it is true that the fourth-century Spanish poet Prudentius had revelled in descriptions of the richness of the tombs of the martyrs,[55] St Jerome had referred to the catacombs only as places of infernal gloom.[56] Indeed, even to the sixteenth-century visitor – however devout, however exultant – miles of dank, subterranean corridors, lined with rows of empty *loculi* (tomb slots) of all sizes, carved out of the porous rock, must have presented an alarming, as well as an exhilarating spectacle. But as he stumbled, or even crawled, head bent carefully down, into the unknown, he would suddenly find the space widening out into a rectangular 'cubicle', and his flaming torch would illuminate broken, but elegantly inscribed, marble slabs on the floor, and crude painted figures – now dim and faded, now garish – flaking from the reddish or grey background of the walls or low, overhanging vault, accompanied sometimes by exquisitely designed stucco reliefs. A whole new world of images opened up to the scholar. The arts of the past, which not many years earlier, had – in the form of pagan statues – seemed to constitute a threat to the Church, were gradually to become one of the most important weapons in the armoury of the Catholic historian. From one point of view the discovery, and intellectual exploitation, of the catacombs constitutes a starting point for any examination of that type of historical approach for which the visual element provided an essential ingredient.

And yet the process was slow and uncertain, for that visual element was of a very unfamiliar kind, and although its general significance was quickly appreciated, the tools with which to explore it had hardly yet been fashioned. Thus, as we have seen, Cardinal Baronius ecstatically welcomed the investigation of the catacombs and made one or more visits to them. But, although he was rare among the historians of his day in his readiness to draw freely on evidence supplied by visual sources, he seems to have preferred doing so when those sources were known to him only at second or third hand. Such was the case, for instance, of the bronze statue of Christ reported by Eusebius to have been commissioned by the woman whose issue of blood he had staunched – a statue that was not only to acquire great doctrinal significance, but also to attract a certain amount of art-historical interest. It was brought to the attention of the modern world by the famous theologian of Louvain, Jan Molanus.[57] Basing himself on early texts, he told how it had been removed from its pedestal by Julian the Apostate, who replaced it with a statue of himself. It had then been badly damaged by the avenging fire from Heaven that burnt down Julian's statue. Fortunately, the fragments had been reassembled by devout Christians, and this enabled its original appearance to be described, and derivations from it to be illustrated in antiquarian folios (pl. 77):[58] the woman who had been restored to health was shown kneeling

77. Giovanni Bottari, *Sculture e pitture sagre estratte dai cimiterj di Roma*, I, 1737: sarcophagus.

78. Detail of pl. 77, showing two figures once believed to reflect a bronze group commissioned by the woman whose issue of blood was staunched by Christ.

opposite the standing figure of Christ and stretching out her arms to him (pl. 78). Baronius deduced from the very existence of the statue that she must have been a Gentile rather than a Hebrew (because the Scriptures prohibited the making of such images).[59] In the eighteenth century there was some speculation among those less committed to religious inflexibility than he had been that the group might have represented a ruler receiving the homage of a local inhabitant in gratitude for his benefactions to the community, or perhaps an emperor celebrating his victory over a conquered city or province: Gibbon, for instance, thought that it had been erected to some 'temporal saviour'.[60] Other theories were also proposed, and Cicognara argued that, in any case, the sources must have been referring to a relief rather than to a free-standing statue.[61]

Conjectures of this kind were, it need hardly be added, utterly alien to the outlook of Baronius – and not merely for their unorthodox implications. As a historian he put far more trust in the word than in the image. Ritual clothes, jewelry, ceremonies and so on had to be described at great length, for they constituted a crucial feature of his reconstruction of the life of the early Church – but he always relied on written accounts for his discussions of them.[62] Nevertheless, he was himself one of the most notable and erudite promoters of church decoration in the Rome of his day, and it seems likely that he must have experienced a special feeling of elation when he (like all ecclesiastical historians) found himself having to lay particular stress on the patronage of popes and emperors and to record the great Christian monuments that had been built thanks to their support.

Even in the use he made of such conventional sources as coins or medals, Baronius showed himself to be more systematic (and, at times, imaginative) than any writer before him, or, indeed, than most of those who followed him during the next century and a half. Of the twelve volumes of his *Annales* the earlier ones especially were illustrated with good engravings which were carefully inserted into the text not for decorative purposes but in order to further the argument. The copies were made from coins belonging to contemporary antiquarians, such as Fulvio Orsini, Pirro Ligorio and, above all, Lelio Pasqualino, a scholarly canon of Santa Maria Maggiore, whose house near the Campidoglio was said to contain the finest antiquities in the whole of Rome.[63] Baronius frequently drew on coins and other monuments to solve or to challenge (in his highly selective way) controversial issues in Roman history. He reproduced, for instance, the astonishing scene on the column of Marcus Aurelius which showed Jupiter, as the god of rain, assuaging the thirst of the Roman army and destroying its enemies by flooding their camp (pl. 79); but, basing himself on a later legend, he claimed that the

79. Baronius, *Annales*, II: relief from column of Marcus Aurelius showing Jupiter as the god of rain assuaging the thirst of Roman army.

impression given by the frieze was deliberately misleading because, in fact, a letter from the emperor proved that it was the Christians who had prayed for rain on his behalf: it was thus only fair that the column should subsequently have been badly damaged by the barbarians and struck by lightning, and that after its restoration by Pope Sixtus V it should have been crowned with a statue of St Paul.[64] More usually Baronius relied on medals to demonstrate the gradual adoption by Constantine and subsequent emperors of specifically Christian symbols. He could approach this sort of issue with some sophistication – thus he pointed out that 'a certain antiquarian who believes himself to be very knowledgeable' had claimed that the reverse of a coin of Julian the Apostate represented the Virgin and Child, chosen because the emperor was at that time pretending to believe in Christ; in fact, however, comparison with a coin of Hadrian proved beyond doubt that the figures were of Isis with a child at her breast: 'God forbid that we should rely on fictions in our endeavours to illustrate the Christian religion!'[65] And although Baronius referred only very occasionally indeed to aesthetic quality – despite the fact that the range of his interest in images extended far beyond those medals and sculptures that had hitherto attracted the enthusiasm of collectors and writers – we shall see that when he did so, his suggestions were decidedly imaginative.

All this should make clear that Baronius was well placed among contemporary scholars and polemicists to take advantage of the new visual material that was coming to light as he worked on the *Annales*. But although he did, once or twice, refer to them in order to settle specific historical controversies,[66] for Baronius the paintings in the catacombs constituted only a relatively small addition – however awe-inspiring – to a whole mass of more tractable visual evidence already at hand for the study of the early Church.

To Protestant historians the catacombs were an embarrassment. Much scorn was poured on the Catholics for the superstitious adulation that they attracted (and superstition aroused anxiety also among the more discriminating Catholic historians); there was mockery of the 'relics' found in them ('if they chaunce to find a bone . . . whether it be a Dog, a Hog, a Sheepe, or any Beast, they can tell presentlie what Saint's bone it was'); and it was repeatedly pointed out that the darkness was such that it was difficult to see anything at all. In fact, of course, few serious Protestant historians had much of an opportunity to inspect the catacombs carefully, and it was not until 1685–6 that one of them found himself able to propose an apparently plausible explanation of their appearance. Visiting Rome at that time, Gilbert Burnet, now chiefly remembered for his *History of the Reformation in England* and the posthumously published *History of his Own Time*, came to the conclusion that the catacombs had not, in fact, been the work of the primitive Christians but had been heathen burial-grounds where the ancient Romans deposited the remains of their slaves and 'meaner sort of people'. Only after the era of Constantine had they been used by the Christians,[67] and as the bas-reliefs on sarcophagi in the catacombs appeared later in style than Roman work and as the inscriptions also were 'more *Gothick* than Roman', it had to be assumed that the contents generally were the work of mediaeval monks hoping to make a profit out of the trade in relics.[68] The theory that the decoration of the catacombs had been a late development was enthusiastically adopted by other Protestant polemicists.[69]

Fortunately, the task of identifying the actual images on the walls and ceilings of the catacombs was carried out in a less controversial spirit. For the most part the problem was not difficult, though the scenes were only very rarely inscribed and though the style in which they were painted must have been surprising, indeed disconcerting, to those familiar with the elaborate compositions beloved of contemporary artists in Italy. The convention for treating each subject was one of such ruthless simplification that only its absolute essentials were represented. Thus a man with one reclining lion on each side of him symbolised Daniel in the den of lions, while the story of Jonah was told through a series of similarly abbreviated scenes. Once this principle was understood it became clear to students that the repertory of images chosen had been a very limited one – confined for the most part to the Old Testament and to a few episodes from the life of Christ – of a kind that (disappointingly perhaps?) need not have offended the most bigoted Protestant.

A certain number of the paintings did, however, pose real problems of interpretation, and in his erudite and handsome *Roma Sotterranea* (whose first edition appeared posthumously in 1634) (pl. 80), Antonio Bosio, the great archaeologist, published these with an acknowledgement that he was unable to determine the subjects. But although Bosio had probably seen all these for himself – his accounts of discovering the various underground tombs discussed by him are extraordinarily fresh and vivid – he, and other historians and antiquarians of the time, inevitably had often to rely for their researches on the pen-and-ink drawings made for them by a series of copyists. That the quality of these drawings was extremely weak and made almost no attempt to convey the style of the originals was less important than the fact that, when in doubt, copyists were inclined to produce images of what they expected – and, no doubt, hoped – to see. In this way, we find (admittedly very unusual) depictions of the Adoration of the Magi (pl. 81) and of the Infant Christ being bathed by Midwives being converted into (the more familiar) martyrdoms of saints (pl. 82), while a Noah in the Ark (pl. 83) is transformed into a Pope Marcellus preaching (pl. 84).[70] Thus, without deliberate fraud, did the embattled historians of the sixteenth century compensate for some of the more regrettable omissions of early Christian artists. There were, however, a few other stumbling blocks. The most distressing of these was the discovery of at least two, and possibly more, scenes representing figures who could only be Orpheus and the animals. The importance of the catacombs for Catholic historians rested largely on the assumption that only Christians had been buried in them and that they had not, as asserted by the Protestants, been contaminated by the presence of pagans or Jews. It was therefore essential to demonstrate – as was done with much learning and some embarrassment – that the choice of Orpheus as a kind of prefiguration of Christ had received perfectly reputable (though perhaps unfortunate) backing in the works of the Church Fathers.[71]

This sort of issue was not, of course, wholly new: Protestants frequently

ROMA SVBTERRANEA

80. Antonio Bosio, title-page of *Roma Sotterranea*.

81 and 82. Painting in the catacomb of Domitilla in Rome depicting the Adoration of the (four) Magi, and the late sixteenth-century copy of the painting, interpreted as the martyrdom of a saint.

83 and 84. Painting in the catacomb in the cemetery of Novella (Via Salaria) in Rome depicting Noah in the Ark, and the late sixteenth-century copy of a similar painting, interpreted as St Marcellus preaching.

charged their Catholic opponents with taking part in rituals that were riddled with pagan superstition; but when the practices of the early Christians were at stake, the question of spiritual confusion assumed particular significance.

One of the earliest antiquarians to be faced with trying to cope with this dilemma was Guillaume du Choul of Lyon whose investigation of Roman religion, based largely on the study of ancient coins, has already been referred to. Du Choul was unusual among his contemporaries in taking as his starting point a great theme rather than discussing historical scenes or symbols or portraits primarily as a convenient means of classifying an already existing collection of coins. As he pursued his researches he became increasingly fascinated by the analogies to be found between certain ancient customs and those of his own day. Thus when reproducing a Roman bas-relief which represented Faith by showing two figures clasping hands, he commented that this was 'almost as is still done by our goldsmiths in certain gold rings'.[72] Or again, when discussing how the Romans mourned the deaths of their emperors, he mentioned that on one side of the elevated bed of rich ivory on which lay a wax figure of the dead emperor, sat 'all the Roman ladies, each according to the dignity and rank of their fathers and husbands with no ornaments such as rings, bracelets or gold chains, but only lightly dressed in white – almost in the same way as the ladies of France dress themselves in such circumstances'.[73] Other examples could be quoted, and by the end of his book Du Choul found himself confronted by an alarming (and possibly dangerous) hypothesis – of the very kind that, two centuries later, was to delight the *philosophes* of the Enlightenment: 'In conclusion,' he writes in the last lines of the last page, 'we find and see that the procedures of our religion are in many ways similar to those of the ancient Egyptians and Romans – such as, for instance, the shirts of the priests, the stoles, the chasubles, the shaved tonsures which the French call crowns, the bowing of the head when facing the altar, the beginning and end of the sacrifice, the prayers, the oaths, the orations, the hymns, the sung music, sounds like those of the organs, processions and many other things, which a shrewd man could easily decipher after a careful consideration of our ceremonies and theirs; except,' he ends with lame forcefulness, 'that those of the pagans were false and superstitious, whereas ours are Christian and Catholic, and are devised in honour of God the Father Omnipotent and of his Son Jesus Christ to whom let there be eternal glory.'[74]

Du Choul's words indicate that at the heart of the historian's investigation of the artefacts and visual images of earlier times there had often been a certain ambiguity of response: from one point of view, such apparently direct contact with the surviving relics of a vanished age seemed to bring that age to vivid, autonomous life; but from another point of view, the remarkable feeling of spiritual and cultural kinship between past and present established in this way threatened to distort the evidence available and make of it something absurd or dangerous.

New techniques – notably consideration of stylistic change – and the development of new conceptual frameworks were soon to enable historians to cope more fruitfully with the vast increase in material that had now become available.

The Issue of Quality

We have seen that during the fifteenth and sixteenth centuries coins and medals were extensively collected and attracted much attention from numismatists who aimed to decipher the images shown on them and to emphasise how important the interpretation of those images could be for the understanding of written history. Comments on the beauty, as distinct from the utility, of these artefacts were, however, only made sporadically.

It was the ambition of all collectors to acquire – at the very least – sets of coins (in gold, silver or bronze) representing each of the Roman emperors between Augustus and Constantine, and often later.[1] The coinage of some of these emperors, such as Otho who had reigned only briefly, was known to be particularly rare and valuable, and it was this consideration that especially encouraged the production of forgeries. But the very skills needed for this purpose reveal how carefully originals were scrutinised, and imitations were often highly regarded in their own right.[2] It is therefore surprising that changing standards of artistic quality seem to have aroused very little specific comment from early connoisseurs. It is true that Enea Vico, who was himself an artist of great distinction, wrote in 1555 that, while the finest imperial coins were those of Nerva, Caligula, Claudius and Nero, all were good 'until Pertinax and [Septimius] Severus [i.e., until the end of the second century], after which the art went into a steep decline'[3] – a comment that, as we shall see, was to be of some historiographical importance. But Vico himself did not pursue the matter, nor did he try to account for the decadence he had noticed. Few, if any, of the acutely observant numismatists at work in the generation or so following his publications raised the matter again until the last years of the century when the great Spanish antiquarian Don Antonio Agustín wrote, in one of the most influential of all manuals, that high standards prevailed until the decline that set in after the reign of Gallienus (252–60), and that by the time of Justinian (527–65) such an abyss had been reached that thereafter coins could scarcely be looked at.[4]

Chronological disagreements of this kind are hardly surprising, for the juxtapositions that can now be made so easily in huge collections available to students render it more evident to us than it could have been to the sixteenth-century connoisseur that no easy pattern is detectable in the stylistic changes undergone by Roman coinage. A crude, harsh, unmodelled portrait of almost caricatural simplicity may well be followed by the neat, sophisticated creation of a 'classical revival'. The varying qualities of coins issued within even the most limited timespan often depend on the types of metal used or the mints at which they were produced – not to mention the conditions under which they have survived for nearly two thousand years. Moreover, certain categories, such as the larger bronze 'medallions', maintained the high, traditional elegance of an earlier age long after declining standards of technique and design had become clearly apparent elsewhere – and not only in coinage. For the inevitably conventional, not to say conservative, demands imposed on design by the very function of coins (still so evident today), combined with the fact that such enormous numbers, covering so long a period, had survived, made it difficult to discern changes of style, despite the practice of arranging them in chronological order. For this reason the impact made by some of the other figurative arts surviving from the ancient world can reveal more to us about the interest shown by historians in the sixteenth and seventeenth centuries in the phenomena of progress and decline.

By the early fifteenth century it had become commonplace to assert that Giotto had brought the art of painting back to light after it had been buried for many centuries, and similar claims were to be made about admired architects and sculptors.[5] But for how many centuries had the arts been buried, and why had this happened? A number of artists began to consider the problem and to propose solutions to it.

When Lorenzo Ghiberti raised the issue in the 1440s,[6] he had almost completed many years' work on the bronze 'Gates of Paradise' for the Baptistery of Florence cathedral;[7] and in order to design his reliefs in the 'antique' style, which was then becoming fashionable, he had had to give much attention to finding suitable models. What could he have seen? We have to imagine an Italy in which, on the one hand, far more of the great buildings and ruins of antiquity than survive today were still visible (though usually half buried), while, on the other hand, almost none of the celebrated marbles – the *Apollo*, the *Laocoön*, the *Antinous* and many others later to serve as touchstones of quality for generations of artists – had been uncovered. Even far inferior works of a similar kind were exceedingly rare and lay, battered, limbless and featureless, among the ruins, waiting to be smashed completely by building workers and burned for lime. On his visit or visits to Rome[8] Ghiberti would have seen the huge *Horsetamers* on the Quirinal, 'signed' on their bases by Phidias and Praxiteles – masters whose towering reputations in antiquity were familiar to him through his reading of Pliny – and also a group of bronze statues (notably the *Wolf*, the *Spinario* and the equestrian portrait generally believed to represent the Emperor Constantine) raised high on columns outside the Lateran Palace. He also witnessed the excavation of a marble hermaphrodite whose beauty greatly struck him, and somewhere he was able to acquire for himself a Roman relief which was thought to portray Vulcan in a bed on which sat a naked Venus apparently about to join him.[9] It is true that this became very famous, but for the most part there was little more to be seen than dismantled sarcophagi which had been re-used for burial and for altars,[10] and such coins, gems, medals and small bronzes as had recently entered the collections of those Florentine writers

85. Maso di Banco, *St Sylvester Performing Miracles in the Roman Forum*, fresco, *c*.1335–40, in the Bardi di Vernio chapel in Santa Croce, Florence.

with whom he was in touch. For a man who had carefully read Pliny and Vitruvius and who was much concerned with his own relationship to the ancient artists about whom they had written, the awareness of irredeemable loss, of mere fragmentary survival, must have been not only overwhelming in itself but also seriously inhibiting in his attempts to emulate his great predecessors. For Ghiberti was well placed to appreciate the fact that the apparent disappearance of almost all ancient sculpture had meant that with it had disappeared also those rules and skills that had formerly made possible the very existence of good art. He had no doubt where the blame was to be laid. Although he must certainly have known of the long-held legend that in the sixth century Pope Gregory the Great had ordered the utter destruction of all surviving 'heathen idols' – a legend that had hitherto been handed down with little evident disapproval[11] – he nevertheless attributed the devastation to the Emperor Constantine and his contemporary Pope Sylvester.[12] As early as the fourth century Eusebius had praised Constantine for his destruction of the cult statues of the pagans, but the idea may have been suggested to Ghiberti by an image: the fresco cycle (with which we know him to have been familiar) showing events from the life of that pope (and saint) painted in about 1340 by Maso di Bianco in the church of Santa Croce in Florence (pl. 85); for the scene of

86. Filarete, bronze reduction, dated 1465, of the equestrian statue of Marcus Aurelius, at that time installed in front of the Lateran palace; on the top surface of the base, Filarete identifies the emperor as Commodus.

one of St Sylvester's miracles, which takes place in the presence of Constantine, is set in a Rome consisting of shattered pagan fragments in the foreground, while the new, Christian, city rises behind it.[13] Whatever his source, Ghiberti declares unequivocally that Constantine and Sylvester had 'destroyed all pagan statues and paintings – works of such nobility and such ancient and perfect dignity' – and that it was through them that severe rules had been imposed to prohibit the making of new ones. Once art was finished, 'the sanctuaries remained bare for six hundred years'.[14] In other words, the triumph of the Christians had meant the end of art, and the absence of so many masterpieces celebrated by Pliny was almost as visible a proof of that triumph as was the presence of so many churches.

About fifteen years later the architect and sculptor Antonio Filarete touched once again on the problem of why Roman art had come to such an ignominious end.[15] Though he, too, came from Florence – and perhaps from Ghiberti's studio[16] – he spent most of his active life in Rome and Milan, and he also travelled widely elsewhere in Italy, notably to Venice. The twelve years he devoted to working for the papacy on a bronze door for St Peter's may have dissuaded him from visualising that institution as having been responsible for the ruins he daily saw around him. He also made a small bronze version (the first of its kind since antiquity) of the statue, which had been set up in front of the Lateran Palace, of an emperor on horseback representing, so he believed in defiance of prevailing opinion, the outstandingly wicked Commodus (pl. 86).[17] He therefore knew of at least one pagan monument of the highest quality that had been preserved (rather than destroyed) by successive popes. Moreover, if – as has often been suggested[18] – he looked back self-consciously to early Christian art as inspira-

87. Venice, façade of St
Mark's (detail).

tion for his bronze door, it would hardly have been possible for him to accept
Ghiberti's notion that the activities of Constantine and Sylvester had had an
entirely negative impact on sculpture. Be that as it may, Filarete, who was more
interested in the history of architecture than in that of the other arts, laid the
blame for what had happened not on Christian iconoclasm but on the barbarian
invaders.[19] And as evidence of this he cited the kind of buildings that had been put
up in place of the once-great monuments destroyed by them. Looking presumably
at such intricate and apparently capricious churches and palaces as Milan cathedral
or St Mark's (pl. 87) and even the Palazzo Ducale in Venice, Filarete deduced from
them that the barbarians had had no real architects of their own. They had
therefore had to make use of painters, stonemasons and particularly goldsmiths
who 'used the fashions they knew and what seemed [best] to them in the modern
tradition. The goldsmiths built their [buildings] like tabernacles and thuribles.
They made buildings in this same manner, because these forms seemed beautiful in
their own work, but they also have more to do with their own work than with
architecture. These modes and customs they have received, as I said, from across
the mountains, from the Germans and the French.'[20]

   After another interval of some twenty years or so, Filippo Brunelleschi's biographer, Antonio Manetti, came to an almost identical conclusion in the 1480s: 'As

88. Florence, S. Miniato al Monte, façade.

had happened in other places . . . with the decline of the empire, architecture and architects declined. Barbarian tribes of Vandals, Goths, Lombards, Huns and others arrived, bringing their architects with them, and built in their manner in those lands where for hundreds of years they ruled.'[21] But Brunelleschi and Manetti were as familiar with Florence as Filarete had been with Rome and Milan, and looking around them they noted something that was to confuse other observers for centuries to come: certain churches – Santi Apostoli, for instance, and S. Piero Scheraggio – did not fit into the pattern of decay that their theory demanded, for they appeared to be relatively classical in style (as also did S. Miniato (pl. 88)), and yet they had been built well before 'the revival of ancient architecture' which had been inaugurated by Brunelleschi himself. Only one explanation seemed possible: after he had rooted out the Lombards from Italy, Charlemagne had brought in architects from Rome, and this had led to a slight improvement in style – slight because these architects had had too little practice to know how to build really well. But Charlemagne's empire had soon fallen apart, and 'the German style' had gained strength once more.[22]

Fifteenth-century writers thus all attributed the decline of art to sudden political changes: the destruction of ancient models of perfection inflicted either by the Christians or by foreign invaders. There is no evidence that they had noted any progressive loss in quality in such remains of antiquity as had survived into their own times. The delicate mosaics in the church of Santa Costanza, for instance, attracted their unconditional enthusiasm. It is, however, true that the vines and clusters of grapes that feature so prominently in the decoration (pl. 89) suggested to most of them that the church had once been a temple of Bacchus, and that it was not until the period of the Counter-Reformation that the imagery of some of the mosaics which, until 1620, were to be seen in the vault, was recognised as having Christian significance and hence as belonging to a late phase of Roman civilisation.[23]

89. Rome, Santa Costanza, detail of mosaic decoration of mid-fourth century AD, showing scenes of wine harvesting and bust of an unknown figure.

A decisively new step was, however, taken in the sixteenth century when Raphael, with the help of Castiglione, composed his famous letter to Pope Leo X on the antiquities of Rome and their preservation.[24]

Raphael agreed that the ancient architecture of Rome, which he had studied with extreme care,[25] had indeed fallen victim first to the ravages and then to the barbaric taste of the German invaders. But although he forcefully reminded the pope of the terrible responsibility that must be borne by His Holiness's predecessors for so much neglect and casual destruction of what had survived the 'Goths, Vandals, and other treacherous enemies of Latin civilisation [del nome latino]', he did not suggest – as had Ghiberti – that deliberate Christian iconoclasm had played any part in the demolition of the monuments of antiquity. He then put the whole issue of the decline of these monuments on to a new footing by implying that what was truly surprising was that the excellence of ancient architecture had survived so long, for 'literature, sculpture, painting and nearly all the other arts went into a lengthy period of decline, getting worse and worse by the time of the last emperors'. Indeed, Raphael seems to be challenging the development of a new theory (of whose existence at this date we should otherwise know

90. Rome, Arch of Constantine, AD 315.

91 (below). Rome, Arch of Constantine, detail showing the horizontal relief of the emperor addressing the citizens, carved in the early fourth century, and, above it, circular medallions showing a hunting scene and the sacrifice to Diana after the hunt, dating from the period of Hadrian (117–38).

nothing) when he declares that it was simply not true to claim that 'among ancient buildings, those that were less old were less beautiful, or less well-composed or designed in some other style'. In other words, there had been no decline in the quality of architecture before the arrival of the Goths, because although many earlier buildings had been restored, or even replaced by the Romans themselves, the work had always been carried out in traditional styles. To demonstrate how long and successfully the standards of Roman architecture had been maintained, Raphael singled out one of the last great monuments in the city, the Arch of Constantine, which 'was well composed and well made' (pl. 90). However, the sculptured decorations on the surface told a very different story (pl. 91). Immediately above the two smaller arches on both the main façades and, at the same level, on the sides of the monument were six narrow rectangular friezes which Raphael recognised as being contemporary with the arch: they were 'quite ridiculous, without art or any sense of good design'.[26] Nevertheless, just above these were roundels, and in the passageway and on the attic there were some far more elegant friezes which, noted Raphael, had been removed from monuments dedicated to Trajan and Antoninus Pius (who had lived two centuries earlier), and these were 'absolutely excellent and of the most perfect style'.

Although previous artists seem to have been well aware of the change that had occurred between the earlier and the later decorations – for among the surviving drawings made of various parts of the arch there are none of the Constantinian reliefs[27] – Raphael was the first to comment in writing on the evidently drastic decline in sculptural quality which had taken place between the second and the fourth centuries. He may even have anticipated most of the conclusions that were reached by archaeologists only three or four hundred years after his researches.[28] In any case, the implications of Raphael's observations were clear enough: the 'end of art' had not been a uniform process as hitherto suggested, and – as regards sculpture and painting – it had not been brought about by either of the causes proposed: barbarian invasions or Christian iconoclasm. Indeed, he seems to have felt that Christianity had had no part in the process at all, for the two examples of sculptural decoration that he picks out for special contempt are those produced, on the one hand, for the persecuting Emperor Diocletian and on the other for Constantine – both of whom, however, he credits with having inspired fine architecture. The slow decline of the figurative arts was virtually complete by the time of Constantine[29] – the much admired equestrian monument once said to represent that emperor was now believed by scholars to portray Marcus Aurelius or one of the other Antonines[30] – and although Raphael gave no specific reason for this decline, it is clear that he (and those later writers who shared his analysis of late Roman art) would have thought of it as a natural consequence of the decline of the empire itself.

In 1550, and then more elaborately in 1568, Vasari who, directly or indirectly, was familiar with all the theories so far mentioned, tried to combine them into a single embracing explanation. It is true that for Vasari the problem was not exclusively an historical one. He took over from many philosophers of history, both ancient and modern, the very influential concept that there was a close analogy between the development of the arts and the successive stages of human life – childhood, adolescence, maturity and decrepitude.[31] Thus decay had been inevitable and did not require the intervention of any external force to explain it. But, like most writers who accepted this general approach, he was not prepared to leave the matter there, and although his more strictly historical arguments were deployed somewhat confusingly, he backed them up with far more specific examples than had been presented by earlier authors. It was therefore through his preface to the second edition of his *Lives* that the most widely held theories became available to historians of all kinds.[32]

Vasari agreed that Roman sculpture and painting, which were designed primarily for pleasure, had begun to decay well before architecture, which was necessary for humanity. New buildings had usually been constructed out of the fragments of older ones whose examples were thus kept alive – though even in these there was some decline in quality.[33] He follows Raphael, but goes further than him, in contrasting those 'very clumsy' narratives and *Victories* on the Arch of Constantine, which dated from the emperor's own lifetime, with the 'excellently carved' reliefs of the period of Trajan and 'the spoils taken to Rome from various places' – among them the figures of the prisoners which crowned the façade. It had been necessary to incorporate these earlier works into the arch, he explains, because of 'the lack of good craftsmen' in Constantine's day, and he supports this theory by referring to the additional evidence supplied by other statues of the period, and also by coins and medals. This last reference was almost certainly inspired by the observations of Enea Vico, whom he greatly admired, for he had not mentioned coinage in the first edition of his *Lives*. But although Vasari repeatedly stresses that 'sculpture had greatly declined well before the arrival of the Goths in Italy', he does not give any historical explanation for this early stage in the process; he somehow combines a determinist belief in the inevitability of general decay with a conviction that the weaknesses of individual artists could be held responsible for it even when outward circumstances improved.[34] However, he makes clear in the most vigorous language that by far the most devastating blows to the arts had come later and that they had had three causes: Christian iconoclasm, the displacement of the capital of the Empire to Constantinople and the barbarian invasions. It was not hatred of the arts, Vasari finds it necessary to explain, that had inspired the Christians to spend such energy on removing and utterly eliminating anything, however small, that could lead the beholder into error: 'not only were all the marvellous statues, as well as the sculptures, paintings, mosaics and ornaments of the false gods of the pagans disfigured and pulled down, but also the memorials and honours that had been paid to countless excellent persons to whose distinguished merits statues and other memorials had been set up in public by the most noble [laws of] antiquity'.[35] The transfer of the capital had led to the departure from Rome of her best citizens, and then to the looting by the Byzantine Emperor Constans II ('that Greek scoundrel') of her remaining monuments;[36] as for the Byzantine style itself (as seen in the adornment of various churches in Rome and Ravenna), it represented the absolute nadir in the fortunes of Italian art. Meanwhile, the various waves of barbarian hordes had not only brought devastation to Italy and thus completed the destruction of models for future artists, who were thereby compelled to rely for inspiration exclusively on their own instincts ('la qualità degli ingegni loro'),[37] but had also introduced the detestable German style of architecture.

Ever since the time of Petrarch it had been natural for writers and artists as well as their patrons, secular and clerical alike, to look upon the forms handed down from pagan antiquity as stylistic exemplars to which they should all aspire. Subsequent deviations from those forms were deplorable and were to be avoided, and the highest praise that could be given to a sculptor or a poet was that his work equalled (or, very occasionally, surpassed) that of antiquity. It was rare for this notion to be seriously challenged in the sixteenth and seventeenth centuries, but when the spirit of the Counter-Reformation was at its most intense, new thought was given to the matter, and many assumptions that had hitherto been taken for granted began to be treated with greater circumspection. The exceptional voice could once again be heard praising the 'noble action' of Pope Gregory for having supposedly organised the destruction of pagan monuments.[38] Such an attitude was hardly acceptable to cultivated opinion, however devout; but it was embarrassing to have to admit that, even though the decline of art was by now widely agreed to have been a gradual process, the actual sculptures particularly singled out as examples of degeneracy should have been the reliefs on the arch which had been built to commemorate the triumphs of the Emperor Constantine who had brought about the peace of the Church. In the last years of the sixteenth century a solution to this difficulty as reckless as it was ingenious was offered by Cardinal Baronius, the greatest Catholic historian of the time.[39] When discussing the arch in the third volume, published in 1594, of his *Annales Ecclesiastici*, he produced a completely new explanation to account for the incorporation into it ('which it is easy for even the novice to see') of excellent sculptures taken from buildings that had been erected by Marcus Aurelius and other earlier emperors, and he implicitly rejected Vasari's suggestion that this had been made necessary by the feeble state of the arts in the time of Constantine. The presence of these fine reliefs, he claimed, dem-onstrated the marvellous and quite incredible enthusiasm for Constantine displayed by the Senate which, in order to honour him, had not demurred from demolishing the works of those previous emperors whom it held most dear. And Constantine had welcomed this step, even though he, too, greatly respected Marcus Aurelius, because it made clear 'how far the majesty of a Christian emperor towered over the most renowned [pagan] emperors, because those images of pagan superstition that had been placed there [on the arch] were like spoils of victory to show that superstition had been conquered, since it was the custom that conquered enemies were displayed on triumphal monuments to do them honour'. In reaching this impressive insight Baronius was surely stimulated by the policy of Pope Sixtus V (which was being put into effect just as this section of the *Annales* was being written) of surmounting famous pagan monuments, such as Trajan's column, with statues of the Apostles. However, when Baronius tried to account for what he was forced to acknowledge as 'the crude, rough and unpolished' style of the reliefs dating from Constantine's lifetime, he came up with a solution of the most extravagant and perverse ingenuity: all the outstanding Christian artists had, he suggested, been swept away in the great persecution [of Diocletian], with the result that sculpture had apparently come to a complete end.[40] Thus the poor quality of the reliefs on the Arch of Constantine demonstrated to the historian that pagan civilisation had decayed, while the Christians (who alone had been able to maintain traditional standards of artistic quality) had been massacred. This conclusion proved to be so totally unconvincing that no credence seems to have been give to it even by Baronius's close followers. Silence constituted the most prudent course both as regards the quality of the Arch of Constantine and – still more – that of the paintings that came to light in the catacombs.

The discovery of these made accessible a range of art of a new kind, for with the exception of the 'grotesques' in Nero's Domus Aurea, which had been studied during the Renaissance, Roman painting remained little known before the eighteenth century. As has already been mentioned, Baronius and other Catholic historians greeted the wall paintings with enthusiasm because the evidence that they offered about early Christian practices appeared to contradict the arguments of Protestant iconoclasts. Thus they studied the iconography and symbolism with great care; but there was little that they could say about the quality which, to cultivated scholars brought up to respect (perhaps with some unease) the antique sculptures by now partly hidden away in the pope's garden-museum of the Belvedere, must have appeared crude, indeed abysmal.

In a curious way the paintings of the catacombs may seem – to a reader of our own day – to have been described before they had ever been seen. While the Counter-Reformation was at its height many tracts were written to denounce the cults of sophisticated beauty and of nudity which were associated with Michelangelo and which were corrupting contemporary religious art; and in 1564 one writer urged a return to primitive simplicity, 'which to our moderns appears mean, clumsy, plebeian, old-fashioned and lacking in talent or skill'.[41] But such exhortations, as also occasional expressions of interest in the symbolism of mediaeval mosaics, referred to content rather than to style, and, despite all the raptures inspired by the discovery of the paintings in the catacombs, there was no one to recommend them as examples to be followed. Indeed, in the more than 600 pages of Antonio Bosio's great illustrated folio, *Roma Sotterranea*, all of which are devoted to celebrating – sometimes with notable eloquence – the achievements of the early Christians, there is hardly a single word that can be interpreted as expressing any reaction to the artistic merit of the works described at such length.

None the less, Bosio's illustrations, many of which were in circulation well before their complete publication in the posthumous volume of 1634, did encourage some of those who perused them to try to appraise (for the first time) the aesthetic quality of the frescoes that had been so crudely reproduced for him. Among the connoisseurs who raised the matter was Giulio Mancini, doctor to Pope Urban VIII and one of the most perceptive of early seventeenth-century commentators on the arts. Mancini's allegiance to orthodoxy was by no means as unconditional as Bosio's,[42] but his notes (which have been published only recently) show that he, too, expressed surprise at the presence of Orpheus among the figures to be found in Christian cemeteries. It was amazing, commented this 'grand et parfait Athée', perhaps with irony, that 'sacred things should have been mixed with profane ones, true things with false and fabulous ones, by those Christians who were so religious, observant and zealous that, for the sake of their faith, they had – at great risk to themselves – been prepared to go below ground'. However, 'astonishment and doubt must cease' as soon as one read Tertullian and the Fathers of the Church, for then 'it seems to me, deferring, of course, to better judges, that

Orpheus signifies Christ our Saviour'. Mancini observed that the frescoes in the catacombs must date from different periods, and then made a cautious attempt to answer his own carefully worded question as to why 'those paintings, even though they were created in a good century, are nevertheless not really perfect'. This must be because

> those Holy Fathers had been very poor and could not spend money, and also because the paintings had been produced below ground by candle light in conditions of great danger to life and health, and hence by masters who were not of the first order; also it was dangerous for them to work for the Christians who were in trouble with the government, and besides they were more interested in devotion and piety than in decoration; none the less, one can see in them that element of quality and that common seed to be found in all painting of the time. And indeed, we owe much to Signor Bosio, who out of Christian piety has had them nearly all copied and engraved.[43]

Rubens faced the same problem when he looked at Bosio's volume which, as he noted in a letter to Peiresc, was 'a great and devout work', but he confined himself to referring non-committally to the 'simplicity of the primitive Church, which though it surpassed all the world in piety and true religion, remained far behind paganism in grace and excellence'.[44]

There is something impressive (as well as devious) about the attempts made by that subtle art lover Giulio Mancini and that great religious painter Rubens to reconcile what clearly struck them as abysmally feeble works of art with the obligations they owed to the Christian tradition. However, it was not until much later, in the early eighteenth century, that a really bold and satisfying solution was proposed to what had hitherto been an embarrassing problem. It appeared, almost casually, in a somewhat dry and scholarly catalogue of Christian artefacts compiled by the antiquarian Filippo Buonarroti, whose observations on this and on many of the other issues that have been discussed in these chapters deserve to be remembered.[45]

Buonarroti, the great-nephew of Michelangelo the Younger who was himself the great-nephew of the artist, was born in 1661 and at the age of twenty left his native Florence to go to Rome, where he spent the next eighteen years or so devoting himself largely to antiquarian studies.[46] He filled notebook after notebook with sketches, some rapid and some very careful, of coins, medals and other small objects, and he quickly earned the reputation of being one of the greatest antiquarians of his day – 'profound, weighty and reflective; taciturn in company though open enough in genial company; a lover of natural philosophy . . . very cautious and reserved and never one to pursue extravagant or chimerical fantasies', as he was to be described by Scipione Maffei, a particular admirer.[47] Through his membership of Queen Christina's circle and later of the Arcadian Academy, he met many of the leading figures of the intellectual community and became closely involved in some of the most important scholarly enterprises of the time, above all the editing (towards the end of his life) of Thomas Dempster's *De Etruria Regalia*, which had been written a hundred years earlier.[48]

In 1698 Buonarroti published his first book, which was devoted to medals belonging to Cardinal Carpegna, his principal patron. This follows the conventional pattern of identifying subjects and symbols, but – as might be expected from an author coming from such a cultivated background – he shows a greater feeling for quality than was usual among numismatists. It was, in fact, his spontaneous response to aesthetic distinction that led him to look at works of art of all kinds without any of the usual preconceptions of his colleagues and thereby to formulate some insights of genuine significance. Thus, because he had seen some extremely good sculptures carved by the Egyptians, he refused to believe that the crudeness (*rozzezza*) of their idols was due to lack of skill: on the contrary, it must have been the result of a deliberate policy to imitate the still greater crudeness of much earlier idols so as to encourage feelings of devotion. Above all, Buonarroti was not prepared to accept without question current notions concerning the inevitable decline of later Roman art: the excellence of design and sheer beauty of a medallion of the short-lived Emperor Trebonianus Gallus of the middle of the third century struck him as being at least as fine as anything made by the Greeks themselves, and this proved to him that a good artist can rise high above the standard of his times; and he looked with equal freshness on other coins.[49]

Soon afterwards Buonarroti returned to Florence, and there in 1716 he published his *Osservazioni sopra alcuni frammenti di vasi antichi di vetro ornati di figure trovati ne' cimiteri di Roma*. He had visited the catacombs in the company of other scholars interested in Christian archaeology, and he had also acquired an impressive familiarity with ivories, mosaics and wall paintings. To a man of his taste most of these appeared hideous, a depressing contrast to the medals of Hadrian which had so appealed to him in the Carpegna collection. Like his earlier book, this one also was dedicated to the cultivated but extremely bigoted Grand Duke Cosimo III of Tuscany, and Buonarroti went to extravagant lengths to demonstrate the extent of his piety. It was just this combination of genuine (or perhaps contrived) religious devotion and true sensitivity to beauty that led him to make his remarkably original appraisal of early Christian art. Stimulated perhaps by what he himself had written nearly twenty years before about the greater veneration likely to have been felt for the crudely carved gods of ancient Egypt than for the much more refined representations which could certainly have been made by later artists, he now carried this line of thought much further. Confronted by figures of the Apostles Peter and Paul painted on glass (pl. 92), which had been found in a catacomb and which struck him as being of even lower quality than the other fragments he was forced to reproduce in his book, he claimed that this very feebleness was

a clear argument and certain proof of the great piety of the early Christians. Inasmuch as they were so jealous and so careful of the purity of their religion that they did not want to stain it with even the slightest blemish, we learn from Tertullian that they always refrained from those arts through which they might have run the risk of contaminating themselves with idolatry. And so it was that few or none of them took up painting and sculpture, whose principal aim was to

92. Filippo Buonarroti,
*Osservazioni sopra alcuni
frammenti di vasi antichi*, 1716:
bases of glass bowls of fourth
century AD showing the
Apostles Peter and Paul.

represent the gods and fables of the pagans; so that when the faithful wished to
decorate their vases with symbols of devotion they were for the most part
compelled to make use of unskilled craftsmen who were employed on quite
different tasks. These men who had no experience of good design fashioned
figures guided only by their own natural talents and a crude observation of
nature which – as had occurred at the birth of painting and sculpture – presented
only its material aspects to them. They were, in fact, unable to distinguish the
components of nature or their arrangement and beauty. However, it is impossible to deny that the very crudity of the artists did much to achieve the true
purpose of sacred images – that is, to give fruitful instruction to the faithful. For
as these figures are entirely lacking in any beauty or decoration, which usually
distracts the spirit and the mind from contemplation, and as they are made with
natural simplicity and no admixture of external things, they strengthened the
feelings of devotion in those who looked at them.[50]

Buonarroti brought his argument to an end by claiming that the lack of grace and
design led to a certain reverential fear and majesty which were well suited to

religious art. In other words, that crudity, which must hitherto have struck educated connoisseurs as a shameful falling off (requiring explanation or apology) from the standards of the arts that they were accustomed to admire and collect, was now affirmed to be its greatest merit. Of course, we can come across many previous examples – even in antiquity – of both connoisseurs and theorists standing up for archaic simplicity in reaction against too much sophistication,[51] and we have seen that such notions had been pressed by champions of the Counter Reformation writing a century and a half before Buonarroti. None the less, Buonarroti's claims for the edifying value of clumsy artefacts produced by unskilled amateurs (claims backed up – to his own satisfaction and to that of his contemporaries – by specific examples carefully reproduced) do open a new chapter in the historian's understanding of art. From now on it became increasingly accepted that weakness itself could be the best guarantee of purity and devotion. It was agreed, for instance, that paintings by the angels were likely to be particularly ungainly so that there could be no risk of the faithful being won round by their beauty.[52] And when, in the middle of the eighteenth century, Giovanni Gaetano Bottari, who was a convinced Jansenist, produced a new, revised edition of Bosio's *Roma Sotterranea*, he combined a heartfelt devotion for the remains of early Christianity with a carefree readiness to dismiss them as coarse and feeble.[53] The impact on the interpretation of images of Buonarroti's attitude to hallowed relics was, in fact, to be profound and long-lasting.

2

The Use of the Image

93. J.-B. Oudry, *Composition aux livres* (Montpellier, Musée Fabre).

---------------------------------————— *5* —————----------------------------------

Problems of Interpretation

i

In 1719 there appeared in Paris the first volume of a most impressive enterprise that was to continue over the next six years and that was eventually to include more than thirty thousand illustrations. *L'Antiquité expliquée et représentée en figures* was written and edited by the Abbé Bernard de Montfaucon of the Benedictine congregation of Saint-Maur established at Saint-Germain-des-Prés. His aim was to produce as complete an illustrated record as possible of everything that could throw any light on antiquity. The material was arranged thematically – by religion, by warfare, by transport, by dress and so on, and it ran to ten volumes (pl. 93). It proved to be an enormous success and was followed by a supplement of five volumes to the original ten and then by a second edition.

Montfaucon was one of the greatest textual critics of the age. His editions of the works of St Anastasius and St John Chrysostom had already made him famous, and he had revolutionised the study of Greek palaeography. None the less, he was to claim, in a provocative phrase, that in order to recover the world of antiquity the study of etymology was 'rarely necessary and usually frivolous'.[1] His own explanation of the intellectual voyage that led him to this conclusion is of the greatest interest.

Montfaucon emphasised that, having been instructed by his Superiors to prepare editions of the works of the Greek Fathers of the Church, he quickly realised that a sound knowledge of pagan literature was essential for his purpose: how otherwise, for instance, could one expound the metaphors and allusions to Homer to be found in the works of St Gregory Nazianzen?[2] But he soon discovered that even this was not enough: objects of classical antiquity, and drawings of them, were also essential for an understanding of the texts, and so 'I spent my days between studying Scripture and the Holy Fathers, on the one hand, and antiquities on the other' – even though he was at first alarmed (understandably enough) by the excessive length of the treatises devoted to them. The years between 1698 and 1701 were spent in Italy, and although it is the notes he made there on the manuscripts to be found in countless unexplored libraries that were to prove of fundamental, immediate and lasting importance, Montfaucon pointed out that 'the most fruitful part of my time was spent visiting ancient monuments and the large numbers of private collections': some of his investigations were recorded in an influential and

controversial travel book, published in 1702 on his return to France.[3] At much the
same time he decided, after some hesitation, to compile his visual record of the art
and artefacts of the ancient world.

He was prompted to take this step partly by dissatisfaction at the existing state
of antiquarian literature which he found to be both too long-winded and too
specialised, too pedantic and yet too erratic in its conclusions.[4] He himself aimed
to produce a corpus of material that would be as uncontroversial as possible and
compact enough to be mastered by the reader in two years at most; and by
publishing his text both in Latin and in French he hoped to attract an international
as well as a native public, and also (though he does not specifically make the point)
an educated, in addition to a learned, readership.

Montfaucon acknowledged his debts to many predecessors, but he emphasised
that (unlike some of them) in only three or four cases at most had he had drawings
made for his book on the basis of written descriptions, and that all the other
illustrations were taken directly or indirectly from antique monuments. He
naturally had to rely on the help of friends, colleagues and collectors in many
parts of Europe – we learn that the pope was rather offended not to be included in
the list of those whose collaboration was acknowledged and decided to have one of
his antiquities copied so as to remedy the situation[5] – but Montfaucon made it clear
that he was imposing some limitations on his compendium. Essentially he was
interested only in 'la belle antiquité' which ended, at the very latest, with the
column of Theodosius in Constantinople,[6] and he thought that the figures of the
Egyptian divinities were too 'bizarre' to be included in the opening volume of
the series. It was doubtless partly for this reason that he accepted the recommen-
dation of one of his colleagues not to call the book 'Théâtre d'Antiquités', because
such a title was both 'trop commun et trop emphatique'.[7] Montfaucon's *L'Antiquité
expliquée* – both the illustrations, which were drawn from published and unpublished sources and varied considerably in their degrees of accuracy, and the
text, which was sensible, balanced and unpedantic – represented antiquarianism at
its most accessible. For all its weaknesses it proved to be invaluable for scholars
and art lovers, artists and all who were enthralled by the past (it seems fitting that
in January 1824, nine years after his publication of *The Antiquary*, Sir Walter Scott
should have been sent by George IV a set of the fifteen folio volumes richly bound
in scarlet morocco[8]). But, although Montfaucon rightly claimed that 'on verra
souvent dans les images des histoires muettes que les anciens auteurs n'apprennent
pas',[9] it was not itself a work of history: there is little sense of chronology, and
little recognition of changing styles or of differing functions.

To some extent Montfaucon seems to have appreciated this himself. His
cautious empiricism and avoidance of futile (because insoluble) controversies were
not prompted only by consideration for the general reader. He wanted to steer
clear of certain dangerously sensitive problems which were becoming popular and
which (as we have seen) had aroused the curiosity of Du Choul as early as the
middle of the sixteenth century. Although Montfaucon could no longer brush these
aside as airily as had once been possible, and although he expressed himself with

characteristic courtesy, his brief dismissal of them is all the more devastating on account of the tone of weary scepticism in which it is phrased:

> Other scholars of the first rank have gone to some trouble to uncover relationships between the Holy Scriptures and mythology: they have claimed that many of the features of the sacred books were imitated by the mythologers; that many gods and heroes were the same men of the earliest times about whom we read in the Old Testament. I respect the great men who have dazzled us in this field of literature, but I confess that I have no taste for this kind of erudition. All we get from it are conjectures deduced with varying degrees of skill, and in my view they are of little interest; it is, for instance, of very little consequence to us to known whether those who say that Vulcan was the same as Tubalcain have produced a more plausible hypothesis than those who claim that he was the same as Moses.[10]

It was partly the lack of originality, and the intellectual prudence, to be found in the *Antiquité* that Montfaucon set out to remedy in a new, far more extraordinary undertaking which he seems to have projected as early as about 1710.[11] In his preface to the second edition of the *Antiquité* he described at some length the form that he thought should be given to a possible continuation covering the period between the barbarian invasions of the fifth century and the Renaissance (though he does not use the term) of the fifteenth century.[12] Although he implied that this would be the work of other scholars, it was he himself who between 1729 and 1733 published the five volumes of *Les Monumens de la Monarchie françoise* – a work that, because it inspired so little interest at the time, was unfortunately never completed. The most important novelty of Montfaucon's new venture lies in the subtitle he gave to it – 'qui comprennent l'Histoire de France'. With this in mind he arranged the illustrations in chronological sequence, with the intention that they would throw light on his narrative. He had, he tells us,[13] originally planned that these illustrations of kings and princes and their accoutrements and battles would be kept isolated, but he had then changed his mind and had decided to insert the relevant plates to follow his account of each reign, thus enabling the student to consult them after having read about the events described. Montfaucon acknowledged that many of the works he was reproducing would shock by their crudity of style, but he claimed (in a comment with implications of extraordinary importance) that this crudity itself needed to be taken into account: 'ce different goût de sculpture & de peinture en divers siecles peut même être compté parmi les faits historiques'.[14]

Montfaucon gathered his illustrations for this book, as for his book devoted to antiquity, from a wide variety of sources, but three-quarters of all the drawings he used had been assembled by one remarkable man, whose collections he himself had helped to form without realising their later significance for his own work.[15]

Roger de Gaignières, who was born in 1642, was closely involved throughout his life with the nobility and monarchy – as tutor, royal governor and equerry.[16] Such connections and support long remained essential for the study of mediaeval

TABLEAU qui eſt au deſſus de la porte de la Sacriſtie dans la Sᵗᵉ Chapelle
du Palais a Paris, ou eſt repreſente JEAN Roy de France .

imagery, as was to be indicated in the wry comment, made well over a hundred
years later, about one royal visit to just such a collection: 'Eh! comme les Grands
aiment à se voir perpétuer de Siècle en siècle: les Portraits de leurs ayeux sembloient
leur faire verser des larmes d'attendrissement.'[17] As a young man Gaignières
developed an insatiable urge to collect all available visual records that could throw
light on the manners and customs of past ages, but he broke with the example of
most earlier antiquarians by showing almost no interest in the ancient world.
Although not a rich man, he was able to acquire a huge collection of engraved
portraits as well as pictures attributed to Holbein, Titian and Van Dyck among
other painters. And – much more important – what he could not buy for himself
he arranged to have copied by two retainers who travelled with him throughout
France. His sources included portraits, inscriptions, illuminated manuscripts,
armour, seals and, above all, church monuments. In the first place a rapid sketch
would be made on the spot and this would then be worked up into a standard
format; sometimes a seated figure was copied from some painting and later
adapted to a standing position (pls 94, 95).

It was these drawings, already differing in varying degrees from the original
sources, that were in turn copied by Montfaucon's draughtsmen. It is therefore

ROY DE FRANCE.

JEAN Roy de France, surnommé le Bon, fut sacré à Rheims le 26. Septembre 1350. mourut à Londres en Angleterre le 8.ᵉ Avril 1364.

Ce portrait est tiré d'un tableau qui est au dessus de la porte de la Sacristie à gauche de l'Autel de la S.ᵗᵉ Chapelle du Palais à Paris.

94 (facing page). Roger de Gaignières, copy of wall painting in Sainte-Chapelle showing an artist presenting a diptych to Pope Innocent VI in the presence of Jean II, King of France (Paris, Bibliothèque Nationale).

95. Roger de Gaignières, *Jean le Bon, Roy de France* (Paris, Bibliothèque Nationale); the figure has been adapted from the seated king in plate 94.

hardly surprising that his stylistic analyses were by no means always reliable: what is remarkable is the self-confidence with which he tackled the problem of dating works of art that were so foreign to his sympathies and so unreliably recorded. We shall shortly see that Montesquieu was, at much the same time, adopting a somewhat similar approach when trying to establish a chronological framework for the development of ancient sculpture; but investigations along these lines were still very rare.

For Montfaucon the essential change that had occurred in what would now be described as early mediaeval art was from the flat to the more rounded: this change could be dated between the fifth and the ninth centuries – that is, between the time of Clovis and that of Charlemagne.[18] This analysis led him to make some serious mistakes which, because of his prestige, were to confuse the study of French mediaeval art for many decades to come.

It had long been held that the sculptured figures, many of them crowned, to be seen in the porches of French cathedrals represented the earliest kings of France, and in 1703 Jean Mabillon (Montfaucon's great mentor at Saint-Germain-des-Prés) had reaffirmed this traditional view, in part because it lent strong support to the authenticity and antiquity of the charters that had established Benedictine abbeys

96. Montfaucon, *Monumens*, vol. I, Paris 1729, pl. vii: porch of Saint-Germain-des-Prés, Paris (now destroyed) showing 'Clovis et ses fils'.

(pl. 96).[19] Mabillon had also claimed that the statues in question must actually have been carved during the age of the Merovingian kings whom they were supposed to represent. However, in 1724 another scholar had provided very persuasive reasons for thinking that the figures could only have been produced much later – not before Charlemagne at the earliest (for he claimed to recognise Charlemagne among the kings portrayed) and probably not before the eleventh century. Montfaucon ignored this new evidence and satisfied himself that the 'flatness' of the sculpted figures proved that they must have been made several centuries earlier: it seems that his conclusions were not based exclusively on stylistic observation and that he deliberately suppressed inconvenient evidence so as to able to support Mabillon's assertions and the Benedictine claims that rested on them.[20]

The incorrect dating was perhaps no more than a regrettable mistake, though a number of writers, of far less distinction than Montfaucon, realised that there was no reason for believing that a portrait had necessarily to be contemporary with the subject portrayed. On the other hand, the identification of the figures in cathedrals as French monarchs (of whatever date) – an identification that was not seriously disputed until 1751 – proved to be one of the most catastrophic errors in the history of art because it was to lead to their wholesale destruction during the anti-royal vandalism that accompanied the French revolution.

Montfaucon showed himself to be genuinely interested in historical method and – in principle, at least – he challenged the orthodox view that written texts must prevail above all else. Let us suppose, he writes, that someone should deny the existence of the siege of La Rochelle.[21] There would be no need to turn to the historians: many hundreds of people were still alive whose fathers had taken part in it, his own among them. Similarly, oral tradition, as much as written histories, could testify to the flight from Paris of Henri III in 1585. But when, towards the end of the book, he repeats the claim that we have already heard so often that 'Le lecteur remarquera que souvent ces Estampes nous apprennent bien des particularitez, que les Historiens ne disent pas . . .',[22] we have to confess to some disappointment. For in fact, Montfaucon showed himself as reluctant as any of his predecessors to make use of visual records in order to elucidate historical problems. He did not fulfil his declared intention of integrating the 'monuments' into the 'history', and the long passages of narrative were mostly transcribed directly from Gregory of Tours and other well-known sources. Discussion of the illustrations is limited and is confined mostly to describing armour, coronation rituals and so on, with no deductions being drawn from these to throw light on what had been written in the text. However, while Montfaucon was already at work he was suddenly faced with a problem of great importance, and, in trying to cope with it, he found himself – almost against his will and almost without realising what was at stake – making a contribution of real significance to historical interpretation.

In 1724 Antoine Lancelot, an antiquarian who had for some time been studying the sources of French mediaeval history, came across a coloured, but evidently incomplete, copy of a series of illustrations which, as was apparent from Latin inscriptions, depicted scenes relating to William the Conqueror (pl. 97). The copy was found among the papers of Nicolas-Joseph Foucault, who had died three years earlier at the age of nearly eighty after a very distinguished career in the royal administration.[23] This had included fifteen years service as Intendant at Caen, where he was remembered both for the extreme brutality he had shown to the Protestants and for his discerning encouragement of archaeological excavations. Among the seventeen thousand medals he acquired were those that had been used by Francesco Angeloni for his *Historia Augusta* and others that had belonged to Charles Patin; and some of the copies made for him of ancient artefacts in his own collection had been drawn upon by Montfaucon for his *Antiquité expliquée*. For some (as yet unexplained) reason, Foucault sold all his ancient medals during the last decade of his life, though his interest in the Middle Ages seems to have led him to retain the illuminated manuscripts that, like Roger de Gaignières, he keenly collected, as also the copies of the exploits of William the Conqueror which attracted the attention of Lancelot.

Lancelot could not determine whether the original had been a bas-relief, a set of sculptures round the choir of a church, a tomb, a frieze, a fresco, a stained-glass window or a tapestry. Nor did he have any idea when the copy had been made. On the whole he thought it likely that the scenes came from the tomb of William the Conqueror which had been in a church in Caen before being destroyed by the Huguenots in 1562, or, alternatively, from a set of stained-glass windows in the same church. He published these speculations, as well as some very perceptive observations on the significance of his discovery, in the *Memoires de l'Académie des Inscriptions et Belles-Lettres* (the main forum for antiquarian research), and, being a man of exceptional 'sweetness and cordiality', he also informed Montfaucon of the problems raised by it.[24]

Montfaucon was far better placed than Lancelot to investigate these problems. He had the copy copied and published large details to make it more legible, and he alerted his network of Benedictine colleagues in Normandy to track down the original. From their reports he concluded that this was a tapestry kept in the cathedral at Bayeux, where it was exhibited on certain days each year, as was remembered by an elderly priest who, however, 'not knowing that it contained the exploits of William the Conqueror, did not have the curiosity to go and look at it closely'.[25] As the tapestry was as long as the church itself, Montfaucon deduced that the copy owned by Foucault must have been incomplete, and he arranged for a new, full and accurate copy to be made. He instructed the draughtsman, Antoine Benoît, not to change the style in any way, even though it was 'extremely vulgar and barbarous [*goût des plus grossiers et des plus barbares*]', because 'in my opinion the decadence and the revival of the arts constitute an important historical fact'.[26] Benoît's careful copies were indeed remarkably faithful (pl. 98), and those scenes of the tapestry that had not yet been reproduced were published in the second volume of Montfaucon's *Monumens* along with an extended commentary. For this reason he has always been credited with having introduced the Bayeux Tapestry to the world. In fact, however, as Montfaucon generously acknowledged, most of the more interesting points about it had already been made by Lancelot (on the basis of inadequate and distorted drawings), who also supplemented Montfaucon's account with additional information. The two men collaborated in the most amicable way, and their contributions to the history of the tapestry should be thought of as complementary, although in the following pages I shall, for the sake of convenience, follow the conventional practice of referring primarily to Montfaucon.

A crucial point concerned the dating of the tapestry. Montfaucon felt confident enough of his expertise in the stylistic analysis of mediaeval art to declare summarily that 'what is quite certain is that the tapestry is of that period [i.e., the Conquest itself]. The style, the type of weaponry and everything that can be seen in the picture leaves one in no doubt about that':[27] Lancelot had claimed no more than that everything – clothes, ornaments, style – 'reflects the age [*siècle*] of William the Conqueror or that of his children'.

97. Montfaucon, *Monumens*, vol. I, Paris 1729, pl. xxxv: reproduction of a part of the painted copy, made for M. Foucault, of the Bayeux Tapestry.

98. Montfaucon, *Monumens*, vol. II, Paris 1730, pl. i: reproduction of a part of the drawing, made for Montfaucon, of the Bayeux Tapestry.

Montfaucon was now faced with the difficulty of interpreting a long narrative in an unfamiliar, uncongenial style, which was only partially inscribed. With great ingenuity he referred back to the principal comparable works that were familiar to him – the historiated columns of Trajan and Marcus Aurelius in Rome – and he pointed out that, as in these antique monuments, trees were used in the Bayeux Tapestry to separate the various episodes of the story.[28] This insight has been upheld by some recent historians who have claimed that the mediaeval artist may himself have been directly inspired by these Roman columns.[29] And Montfaucon recognised that despite the scene that shows Harold and one of his companions half kneeling outside the church at Bosham (pl. 99), 'no doubt they actually went into the church to say their prayers. But the artist placed them outside as otherwise he would not have been able to let them be seen.'[30]

Such an understanding of the conventions of mediaeval art was remarkable, and – as we shall see – it allowed Montfaucon to draw some very important conclusions about what was actually represented in the tapestry. None the less, for him as for Lancelot, the narrative was the least interesting aspect of the images they were studying. Like their predecessors of the fifteenth, sixteenth and seventeenth centuries observing the triumphal arches and columns of ancient Rome, Lancelot and Montfaucon were fascinated above all by the information that was provided about customs and ceremonies, weapons and costumes and furniture. But when they made what was by now the almost obligatory, almost ritual, reference to the fact that images 'teach us about circumstances that were not known to contemporary historians',[31] they found themselves taking a step beyond that of any of their predecessors and making use of their antiquarian interests in an attempt to decipher the story. For the history of the Norman conquest of England was still controversial and, unlike Trajan's Dacian wars, difficulties over interpreting it derived more from a surfeit than from a lack of materials.

Lancelot pointed out that writers disagreed as to whether Harold had landed in Normandy because he had been accidentally shipwrecked there after setting out on a fishing expedition; or because (having first obtained the reluctant permission of Edward the Confessor) he had gone there to rescue his brother and nephew who were hostages of the duke – and in this version also he had been shipwrecked in the wrong place; or because he had been specifically sent by Edward the Confessor to assure William that he would be next in succession to the crown. And the matter is still controversial.[32] Lancelot acknowledged that the problem was not settled by the scenes shown on the tapestry, but he pointed out that in the first of these (pl. 100) Edward the Confessor is shown on his throne, the arms of which end in heads of dogs ('a common animal which has at all times been much esteemed in England') and appears to be giving an order to Harold and a courtier ('ce qui est exprimé par le geste de la main droite'). This suggested that the third of these hypotheses was correct, and Lancelot proposed that the defective inscription REX RD should be amended to read REX EDWARDUS MITTIT HAROLDUM AD WILLHELMUM. Lancelot proceeded carefully stage by stage, but the implications of his theory were remarkable. For the very first time it appeared that a historical problem of real importance had been solved on the basis of an image, and that the visual had

99. Montfaucon, *Monumens*, vol. I, Paris 1729, pl. xxxviii: Harold and a courtier in the church at Bosham (from the reproduction of the painted copy, made for M. Foucault, of the Bayeux Tapestry).

100. Montfaucon, *Monumens*, vol. I, Paris 1729, pl. xxxvi: Edward the Confessor with Harold and a courtier (from the reproduction of the painted copy, made for M. Foucault, of the Bayeux Tapestry).

taken precedence over the literary. Montfaucon summed up briskly: 'Le Roi Edouard dans son Trône donne ses ordres à Harold.'[33]

Lancelot and Montfaucon strengthened their interpretation of the narrative depicted in the Bayeux Tapestry by drawing on their antiquarian researches (which remained the principal focus of their interests). Thus Lancelot discussed the nature of the vessel on which Harold and his companions embark from Bosham and pointed out that it could not, in fact, be a fishing-boat. This provided further evidence that the expedition to France must (whatever its motive) have been deliberate and not the result of an accident. On the other hand, the fact that Harold and his entourage were shipwrecked on the territory of Guy Comte de Ponthieu – instead of proceeding directly to the Duke of Normandy as planned – and were humiliatingly arrested by him was indicated not only by the inscription but also by the 'étonnement [qui] est marqué sur leurs visages'[34] and by the way that Harold, who follows Guy on horseback, holds his falcon facing towards him – thus preventing its flying – as opposed to Guy, whose bird faces ahead. At other times Montfaucon pointed out specific events that were to be found in the tapestry and not in written accounts – for instance, the attack by Duke William on the town of Dinant (which was indicated by the inscription) when his troops set fire to the defenders' barricades.[35]

Acute though Montfaucon's interpretations often were, it never occurred to him that the images he was trying to interpret might – just as easily as written records – have been manufactured as political propaganda (the issue that concerns most historians today). Because he was convinced that the images had been made at the same time as the events they depicted had taken place, he was certain that the record they gave of those events must be true. In the words of Lancelot, those who had commissioned or woven the embroidery must have been 'témoins oculaires des évènemens qui y sont rapportez'.[36]

A good deal of the later discussion of the tapestry was to centre on just this point,[37] and it seems worth pursuing the matter here, even though it will carry us well beyond the time of Montfaucon. Thus in 1767 'the good Lord Lyttelton', so keenly admired by Pope, Thomson, Fielding and other authors, was the first historian of England to give serious attention to the matter.[38] Lyttelton, a scrupulous writer, dismissed the evidence about the nature of Harold's mission to the Duke of Normandy which appears to be indicated in the first scene, partly on the grounds that he did not accept Montfaucon's claim that the Tapestry had been commissioned by 'Matilda, the wife of William the Conqueror, and [was] therefore . . . an authentic evidence of the facts therein represented' – though the significant use of the word 'therefore' demonstrates that even those who were sceptical about the historical value of images were prepared to acknowledge their testimony provided that they could be shown to be contemporary. Lyttelton argued that because the tapestry portrayed certain events (such as the attack on Dinant) that were not recorded in the written sources, it could only have been composed much later on the basis of 'vulgar tradition' and was not at all reliable. In other words, he made use of just those claims that Montfaucon had put forward as indicating its special value (that it supplemented, as well as confirmed, written accounts) in order to demolish the historical foundations of the tapestry. And he rubbed home the point by boldly asserting that 'Tapestry-makers are bad historians: and it is a common fault in antiquaries to lay more stress upon a discovery of this kind than is really due to it, as Montfaucon seems to have done in the present instance.'[39]

It was, however, not until Napoleon brought the tapestry to Paris in order to whip up public enthusiasm for a second conquest that the problems of its dating and significance came to be discussed with real scholarship by writers on both sides of the Channel whose courteous, indeed cordial, relations were not interrupted either by war or even, with the arrival of peace, by differences of opinion.[40]

What emerges with particular force from their continuing debates is the fact that – as had been the case ever since Montfaucon – every one of them accepted the argument that if the tapestry could be shown to be contemporary with the Conquest, then it followed quite logically that its portrayal of events could be accepted as historically accurate: the central – almost the only – issue at stake was thus one of dating. 'It should be remembered', wrote the English antiquary Thomas Amyot in 1819,[41]

> that monuments of this kind derive much of their importance from antiquity, and are never exalted to the rank of historical documents until time has mouldered away most of those which have had a better claim to that title. Wace [the twelfth-century chronicler] and his contemporaries probably admired the Tapestry for what *they* deemed the skill of its workmanship, and the brilliancy of its colours, the beauty of its design, and the truth of its delineations: qualities which call less loudly for admiration at the end of seven centuries; – but they little dreamed that, when that period should arrive, learned historians would be found gravely citing as a document what they considered only as a pleasing picture.

Amyot's appraisal is of particular interest because although he accepted the tradition that the tapestry did in fact date from the time of the Conquest itself, he none the less asserted that 'It is perhaps a characteristic of the literature of the present age to deduce history from sources of second-rate authority; – from ballads and pictures, rather than from graver and severer records. Unquestionably this is the preferable course, if amusement, not truth, be the object sought for';[42] and he concluded that even 'if the Bayeux Tapestry be not history of the first class, it is perhaps something better. It exhibits genuine traits, elsewhere sought in vain, of the costume and manners of that age . . . in courts and camps – in pastime and in battle – at feasts and on the bed of sickness'. In fact, however, such old-style antiquarianism failed to put an end to attempts being made to decipher the narrative of the Conquest at its most sensitive and controversial points. No historian of England could afford to neglect it, and after the extensive use of photography to record the Crimean War and the American Civil War had led people to look for equivalent reportage of the momentous events of earlier centuries, the tapestry was scrutinised as though it were the work of a highly qualified war correspondent. Edward Augustus Freeman, the greatest nineteenth-century historian of the Conquest, felt, when looking at the tapestry in 1867, that he was 'in the presence of a work traced out by one who had himself seen the scenes which he thus handed down to later ages',[43] and he based his famous account of the Battle of Hastings on what he claimed to detect in it.

Nevertheless, Freeman admitted that the story 'is told from the Norman point of view',[44] even though the tapestry had 'hardly any of the inventions, exaggerations, and insinuations of the other Norman authorities' – and this recognition (for which there were only a few tentative precedents) that an image, even when contemporary, can 'pervert' history in much the same way (though perhaps not to the same extent) as can a written account marks a crucial stage in our exploration of the role played by visual sources.

So, too, do the rare acknowledgements to be found in studies of the tapestry that the gestures and expressions of the figures in it were not necessarily as easy to interpret as had always been (silently) assumed. Thus Amyot pointed out in 1818 that the theory (originally proposed by Lancelot nearly a century earlier) that, in the first scene, 'Edward is represented as *giving orders* to Harold to depart on his embassy' need not be correct, and that 'the King may with equal justness be supposed to be in the act of addressing Harold in the manner in which Eadmer asserts he did address him, namely, by permitting his journey, but expressing the strongest doubts of its success'.[45] Similarly, nearly sixty years later, even Freeman felt that it was rather over-confident to write, as had another historian, of Harold's second encounter with the king, that 'Harold comes into the presence of the Confessor like a guilty person, deploring his misdeeds and craving pardon . . . The King is evidently reproving him sharply.'[46]

ii

The issues raised by controversies of this kind were, although not always recognised, of fundamental importance for the understanding of narrative art, and in an unsystematic way they had been discussed frequently enough ever since the Renaissance. We hear about the problems involved chiefly from comments by artists themselves (or their biographers), and as they were of particular interest to Leonardo, it is not surprising that it should have been one of Leonardo's keenest admirers who first tried to classify the ways in which differing emotions or thoughts or passions or characters should be represented through differing kinds of bodily movement. The section devoted to this topic by the Milanese artist Giovanni Paolo Lomazzo in his long theoretical and unillustrated *Trattato dell'Arte della Pittura*, published in 1584, when he had already been blind for fourteen years, is pedantic and unimaginative. Prudent figures, he explains, must not be shown with their arms and legs all over the place but, like the ancient philosophers and priests of Polidoro da Caravaggio, looking grave, carrying books and with hands thrust into their beards; pain must be indicated by twisting of the body, tightening of the lips and raising of the eyebrows; the limbs of the dead must be depicted as in a state of complete collapse, like those of Christ in Daniele da Volterra's *Deposition*, and not as vigorous and capable of supporting the body . . .[47]

However, despite instructions of this kind, people concerned with the expressive possibilities of painting had long recognised that ambiguity was not easily avoided. In a well-known passage in his *Della Pittura* Leon Battista Alberti asked 'who, unless he has tried, would believe it was such a difficult thing, when you want to represent laughing faces, to avoid their appearing tearful rather than happy?'[48] Much later Vasari recorded that the members of the Signoria of Bologna had been uncertain whether Michelangelo's statue of Julius II in that city portrayed the pope as blessing or as cursing,[49] and even Lomazzo acknowledged that it was almost impossible to distinguish between the movements of a madman and those of a figure dancing if one was too far away to hear the music.[50] In the eighteenth century Sir Joshua Reynolds carried the discussion on to a higher level by pointing out that in a drawing of the *Descent from the Cross* Baccio Bandinelli had made use of an antique Bacchante, 'intended to express an enthusiastick frantick kind of joy', in order to represent one of the Marys in a 'frantick agony of grief', and Reynolds commented that 'the extremes of contrary passions are with very little variation expressed by the same action'.[51]

Points like this were, as a rule, of great concern to artists themselves, but of little significance for the interpretation of art, for the context almost invariably made clear whether a figure had been represented as laughing or weeping, blessing or cursing, joyful or grieving. But we have seen that where style and subject-matter were unfamiliar, as was the case with some of the paintings discovered in the catacombs or with the Bayeux Tapestry, ambiguities were not so easily resolved.

Some guidance might have been found by studying the illustrations to various treatises on gesture and expression that became popular in the middle of the seventeenth century, although these were for the most part stimulated by an interest in oratory and the theatre and certainly showed no curiosity about the conventions governing narrative art. Thus in John Bulwer's *Chirologia or the Natural Language of the Hand* (pl. 101) and *Chironomia or the Art of Manual Rhetoric* (pl. 102) published in London in 1644 there is not a single direct reference to painting or sculpture; but a few plates have been included, each containing twenty-four small drawings, to indicate the different meanings that could be expressed by only slight differences in the movement of an outstretched hand – irony, diffidence, approval and so on. Bulwer was a physician, who was particularly keen to invent a sign language that would make communication possible for the deaf and dumb. As the subtitles of his two books (which were published simultaneously) make clear, each one served a different, but related, purpose. In the *Chirologia* he analysed those gestures that, so he claimed, were entirely spontaneous, and indeed beyond our control. Thus he pointed out that 'the smiting of the hand upon the thigh, in the practise and conversation of common life, was ever frequent, and is so deeply imprinted in the manners of men, that you shall in vaine perswade a man *angry* and *inraged with griefe* to contain his Hand from this passion'.[52]

In the *Chironomia*, by contrast, Bulwer was mainly concerned with those more conventional or contrived gestures by which we seek to persuade others; but, like

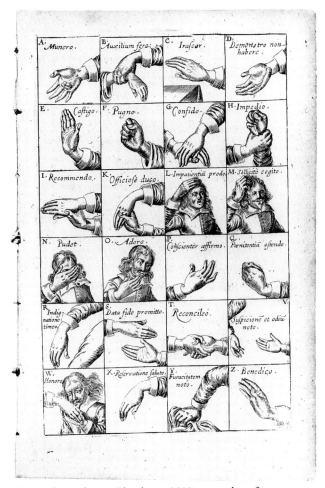

101. John Bulwer, *Chirologia*, 1644: examples of gestures illustrating 'the natural language of the hand'.

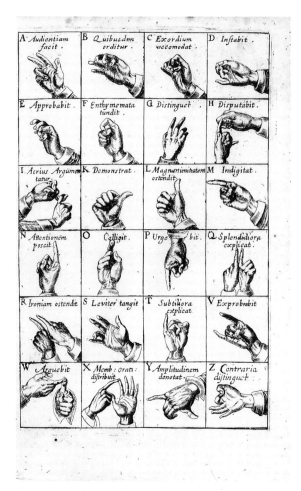

102. John Bulwer, *Chironomia*, 1644: examples of gestures illustrating 'the art of manual rhetoric'.

the ancients to whom he constantly refers, he insists that these, too, are most effective when they have 'some similitude with the truth of Nature'.[53] As one example of this he emphasises that the reason why 'the Middle Finger put forth, and brandish'd in extente, is an action fit to *brand* and *upbraide men with sloth, effeminacie, and notorious vices*' is that 'this action is Magistrall in Rhetorique, but grounded upon Nature; for this Finger, as some Chiro-crittiques [contend] was for its sloath and unactivenesse placed in the middest, as seeming to stand in need of the defence of the other neighbouring *Fingers*, and being longer than the rest, length and lazinesse going usually Hand in Hand, it may helpe to relate in a more open way of expression the notoriousnesse of their vices, who exceed others in vildnesse as far as this idle Finger appears eminent above the rest'.[54]

The implication of the researches of Bulwer and of many other writers at the time was that there did indeed exist a universal language of gesture and expression (based on natural appearances but of necessity much more stylised and schematic) and that it could be deciphered; and this issue, which excited keen interest among theorists of all kinds during the eighteenth and nineteenth centuries, has continued to attract attention until our own day.[55] It was obviously of great significance to artists, and whether or not that is exactly the point that Charles Le Brun was trying to make in his Lecture on Physionomies and his extremely influential drawings related to it, this was one of the conclusions that was drawn from them.

Towards the end of the seventeenth century we first come across some indications that critics and antiquarians were becoming aware of the importance of these issues for the interpretation of earlier art. Thus by 1698 Filippo Buonarroti seems to have envisaged the possibility of establishing a repertory of gestures that would help him to elucidate the meaning of some of the medallions in Cardinal Carpegna's collection. We find him concluding, for instance, that the 'pose of the foot placed on a base or rock with the elbow set down above the knee and the head resting on it seems to have been used by the ancients to depict certain kinds of people carefully listening to others who are speaking or taking part in some sort of activity'.[56]

Artists themselves were, however, aware of the difficulties raised by such an approach, as is shown by the exceptionally interesting chapters devoted to these issues in the *Groot Schilderboek* by the Dutch painter Gerard de Lairesse which was begun after he became blind in 1690 (the same affliction that had stimulated Lomazzo's treatment a hundred years earlier)[57] and was first published in 1707, four years before his death. Lairesse believed that our inner emotions and personalities are clearly revealed in our outward bodily movements and that it was therefore particularly important for a good painter to render those movements as comprehensibly as possible. Among the engravings made from his drawings for the book is one that strikingly recalls the illustrations to be found in manuals of etiquette. A number of hands are outstretched, each one of which is holding a glass in a different way, thereby revealing the social status of each of the figures (pl. 103).[58] And yet Lairesse repeatedly stresses how difficult it is to demonstrate the meaning of an action by relying on gesture alone, and this, too, emerges very

103. Gerard de Lairesse, *Het Groot Schilderboek*, Amsterdam 1707: illustration of variations in social status revealed by gestures of hands.

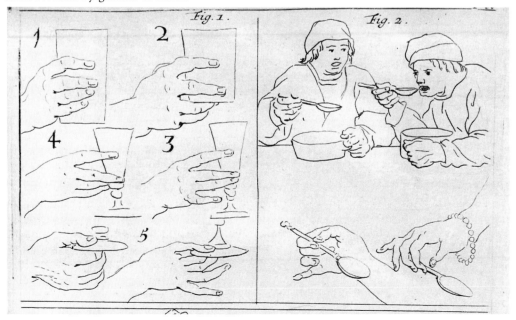

104. Gerard de Lairesse, *Het Groot Schilderboek*, Amsterdam 1707: illustrations of 'Liberality' (no. 3) and 'Voluntary Submission' (no. 2).

105. Gerard de Lairesse, *Het Groot Schilderboek*, Amsterdam 1707: nos 4, 5, 6 illustrate gestures representing different ways of giving.

forcefully from the diagrammatic engravings that accompany his text. Thus the juxtaposition of a drawing of 'Voluntary Submission' (in which a pusillanimous coward surrenders his sword to a man of courage) to one of 'Liberality' (in which a respectable man gives a handful of money to a poor man, who 'looks on the Gift with Joy, Eyes staring, open Mouth, as if he were saying, – *O ho!*') shows how similar are the gestures of the two figures in each scene (pl. 104) – although Lairesse does not actually comment on this.[59] He does, however, compare three illustrations, each of which represents the act of giving (pl. 105).[60] In the first, a young man presents an apple to another; in the second, a young man offers his friend a fine flower; in the third, a young man presents a ring to a virgin, as a token of fidelity or friendship. Lairesse then explains that 'as the Gifts in all the Examples are different, so the sentiments are often very various as well in giving as receiving', and yet 'whether it be done in *Sincerity*, out of *Hypocrisy*, or for the sake of *Decency*, the *Motions* in either Case *differ very little*'. For this reason the artist can eliminate all doubt and uncertainty only by 'Recourse to emblematic Figures, which will clear the Meaning, and point out Hypocrisy, Falsehood, Deceit, etc. by proper Images, Beasts, or hieroglyphic Figures'.

Lairesse very much admired Le Brun,[61] and one of the remarkable points he made (although it does not seem to have attracted much attention from the readers of his book) was that as the artists of antiquity had themselves been 'well-skilled in physiognomy', it was likely that in their portraits of the twelve Roman emperors they had been far more concerned with representing 'their innate Faculties than their outward Appearances'; it was therefore most improbable that these portraits provided accurate representations of their features.[62]

Whether directly or indirectly, many of the themes raised by Lairesse were absorbed into the artistic literature of the early eighteenth century, and it soon became clear that some of them had important implications for the interpretation of images. In the 1720s and 1730s writers both in England and in France emphasised how extraordinarily difficult it was for a painter or sculptor to convey the meaning of expression and action if the onlooker did not already know what to expect from his familiarity with the subject represented. The Abbé Du Bos, who was particularly keen on pointing out the subtleties of emotional conflicts represented in the features of antique statues once he was confident of their identity,[63] stressed that if painters wished to be understood, they should choose only well-known stories; and he went so far as to praise mediaeval artists, despite all the badness of their Gothic taste, for their custom of showing words issuing from the mouths of their figures. In a passage that was familiar to Lessing he pointed out how different were the resources available to the painter and the poet, and he discussed just what Poussin had been unable to show in his famous painting of the *Death of Germanicus* (pl. 106).[64]

Jonathan Richardson, who frequently gave examples of how to 'read' the Old Masters, turned to the same picture in order to make the point that 'here is an Instance amongst a thousand others of the Necessity of knowing the Story; and then the Painter may carry the Imagination beyond what the Historian can, Otherwise he will come Short, or be Unintelligible. For as *Germanicus* is pointing towards *Agrippina*, and the Little ones, and with an Air rather of Sorrow than of Indignation, one that remembers not the Story exactly, will certainly imagine him desiring his Friends to take care of them after his Death; which besides it being so subject to be Mistaken, is a Low, Common Thought, and Debases the Picture'. In fact, '*Poussin* has chosen the Instant in which *Germanicus* intreats his Friends to excite the People to Compassion, and Revenge by the sight of *Agrippina* and the Children'.[65]

However, just when Du Bos and Richardson were stressing the risks of ambiguity inherent in the choice of an unknown subject, Hogarth began to challenge their axioms by painting and engraving sequences of 'modern moral stories' for which there was no written source. His narratives were much more complex than such humourous topics as those involving dishonest fortune-tellers or grasping procuresses which had long been popular. They were consequently far less accessible to the public than an episode from Tacitus chosen by Poussin. Although Hogarth tried every possible method – including use of the 'hieroglyphic figures' recommended by Lairesse – to clarify his narratives, and although Horace Walpole insisted that they were in fact always comprehensible,[66] it was not long before some at least of his engravings were being scrutinised for their meanings with far greater care than had yet been given to the Bayeux Tapestry. And when in the

106. Poussin, *Death of Germanicus* (Minneapolis Institute of Arts).

1780s and 1790s Georg Christoph Lichtenberg came to write his commentaries on them, he had to point out that of one of the scenes in *Marriage à la Mode* (which dated from two years after his own birth) (pl. 107) there existed no less than five different interpretations.[67]

Lichtenberg was one of the most trenchant critics of the new 'science' of physiognomy which was being promoted at this very time by the Swiss clergyman Johann Caspar Lavater and which appeared to provide essential tools for the elucidation of problems of the kind raised by Hogarth's prints and by unfamiliar narratives of every sort. It is true that the prolific and repetitive Lavater devoted only very limited space to a discussion of poses and gestures and movements – but if (as he tried to demonstrate with innumerable illustrations) the facial traits of human beings offered a reliable and easily decipherable guide not only to their fundamental characters and emotions, but also to their more fleeting aspirations and states of mind, then those ambiguities that had, admittedly, failed to disconcert Montfaucon but that certainly confused Lichtenberg would obviously diminish greatly in number and importance.

When he died in 1801 Lavater was described in one English journal as 'for many

107. Hogarth, *Marriage à la Mode: Visit to the Doctor*.

years one of the most famous men in Europe', while in another it was claimed that
'a servant would, at one time, scarcely be hired till the descriptions and engravings
of Lavater had been consulted, in *careful* comparison with the lines and features of
the young man's or woman's countenance'.[68] Dozens of editions of his *Physiognomical Fragments* appeared in the principal European languages during his own
lifetime,[69] and a number of these (such as the one published in four volumes at
Leipzig and Winterthur in 1775–8[70] and the French version of it which appeared in
The Hague between 1781 and 1803[71]) were illustrated with plates of outstanding
brilliance, wit and charm. His reputation long survived him and his followers were
numerous.

Nevertheless, the tone of Lavater's prose, which is often as defensive as it is
cloying or over-assertive, reveals how great and how telling were the objections to
his theories, which were novel for their detail and pretensions rather than for their
substance. Like so many of his predecessors, Lavater tended to make use of images
to demonstrate what he already knew from other sources: Cicero's features show
him to have been 'intelligent and luminous', Caesar's that he was enterprising, and
so on.[72] When portraiture conflicted with personality, as it did with Socrates, at

once the ugliest and the wisest of men, Lavater became evasive[73] – Jesuitical, it is tempting to say of the man who discovered in the physiognomy of Ignatius Loyola 'cet esprit de cagoterie & d'intrigue qu'on a toujours reproché & au Fondateur & à tous les Membres de l'Ordre des Jésuites'.[74] Contemporary readers of differing versions of his books will quickly have realised how disingenuous he could be. Thus he would, on occasion, claim to be relying on an unfamiliar portrait in order to interpret the character of an unknown man, even though he had earlier published the same portrait elsewhere under its correct name.[75] And when, in a discussion of an illustration taken from Rubens of one of the most famous portrait-types to have survived from antiquity, he asserts with forthright and apparently defiant self-confidence that 'never could this head have been that of Seneca, if he is the author of the works that bear his name',[76] he quite fails to point out that many years earlier Winckelmann had also expressed doubts about this identification – although on different grounds. Lavater even retained a cautious belief in the value of deciphering human personalities by comparing their features with those of animals – although he reproached Della Porta with having sometimes exaggerated such similarities and although he himself preferred to examine the skulls or bones of elephants and monkeys, lions and horses for the light that they could throw on the nature of those beasts themselves without reference to man.[77]

Despite these limitations, however, and many more, the impact of Lavater must surely have been as overwhelming on students of the past as it was on employers on the look-out for a reliable servant. Doubts about the value of portraiture for the historian – of a kind that (as we shall see) had, some years earlier, assailed Gibbon in the medal cabinet at Modena – were now swept away; and it became common-place to 'read' busts and paintings for the information that they could provide about character, and hence about wider aspects of history. Length of nose and forehead, breadth and curvature of eyebrows, the shape of the hands and much else could be called upon as evidence. The great portraitists were appraised for their reliability – Mignard and Rigaud, for instance, were liable to be more trustworthy in this respect than Van Dyck, who was more interested in the 'broad generalities and spirit of physiognomy than in details'.[78] And, especially in the splendid edition published in The Hague, the illustrations supplied by Chodowiecki and a number of other artists are often so eloquent that they were able to create conviction at the time and are able to carry it into our own days even when portraying such complex expressions as that of a woman who listens 'attentively but without interest'.[79] Above all, the reader's powers of observation are constantly being presented with a series of challenges, almost of examinations. How much can be learned from this portrait or caricature or silhouette of an unknown man? What are the differences between these sets of portraits of the Roman emperors or Milton or Newton or Locke? How can one tell that this is the head of someone who is talented but incapable of depth, or of someone who is capable of gaiety but not of great joy?[80] Identify the attitudes and characters depicted in the little genre scenes represented on the following pages (pls 108, 109, 110, 111)?[81]

Although the *Physiognomical Fragments* were primarily designed to 'further the knowledge and love of man', we have seen that they were necessarily of interest

108. J.G. Lavater, *Essai sur la Physiognomie*, vol. III, The Hague 1786: 'Laquelle de ces deux attitudes préférez-vous? laquelle trouvez-vous la plus décente, la plus noble, la plus digne d'un caractère mâle et résolu, la plus propre à vous inspirer de l'intérêt et de la confiance?'

109. J.G. Lavater, *Essai sur la Physiognomie*, vol. III, The Hague 1786: 'Deux femmes qui ont toute la foiblesse de leur sexe. La première a l'air d'être aux écoutes, ou plutôt de s'être égarée dans quelque réverie; la seconde est nonchalam-mant assise, pour se délasser à son aise . . .'.

110. J.G. Lavater, *Essai sur la Physiognomie*, vol. III, The Hague 1786: 'Cette attitude indique une prétention ridicule, qui exerce son empire sur un caractère humble et timide'.

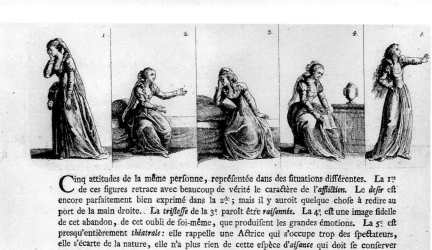

Cinq attitudes de la même personne, représentée dans des situations différentes. La 1re de ces figures retrace avec beaucoup de vérité le caractère de l'*affliction*. Le *defir* est encore parfaitement bien exprimé dans la 2de; mais il y auroit quelque chofe à redire au port de la main droite.. La *triftefte* de la 3e paroît être *raifonnée*. La 4e eft une image fidelle de cet abandon, de cet oubli de foi-même, que produifent les grandes émotions. La 5e eft presqu'entièrement *théatrale*: elle rappelle une Actrice qui s'occupe trop des fpectateurs, elle s'écarte de la nature, elle n'a plus rien de cette efpèce d'*aifance* qui doit fe conferver jufques dans les affections les plus violentes. Jettez un regard de comparaifon fur la vignette ci-deffous; le deuil de cette femme vous touchera bien davantage.

111. J.G. Lavater, *Essai sur la Physiognomie*, vol. III, The Hague 1786: 'Cinq attitudes de la même personne, représentée dans des situations différentes'.

also to anyone concerned with deciphering images of the past. It was, however, not until more than a generation after their first appearance that sustained investigation into a little-explored and puzzling branch of ancient art led to the publication of a book that was indeed partly inspired by 'the great work of Lavater',[82] but that was intended principally to 'take away the wrinkles from the face of antiquity'[83] and to enable archaeologists to understand the images from it that came their way.

The paintings on Greek (or, as they were sometimes believed to be, Etruscan) vases could no longer be thought of as depicting scenes from ancient history, once Winckelmann and his followers had ridiculed such fanciful identifications as 'Faustina and the Gladiator' being given to sculptures and medals. But, although it was everywhere acknowledged that myth played the preponderant role in ancient imagery, many of the episodes to be seen on recently excavated ceramics defied straightforward interpretation. It was these that the Canonico Andrea de Jorio had in mind when in 1832 he published his important book *La mimica degli antichi investigata nel gestire napolitano*.

Andrea de Jorio was born of a good family on the island of Procida in 1769, and after the death of his father twelve years later he was launched by an uncle on his successful career in the church.[84] In 1810, when Murat was still King of Naples, he was appointed Inspector of Public Education, but he must already have shown some interest in antiquities, for only a year later he was put in charge of the principal room in the Naples museum, that devoted to ceramic vases. From then on he produced monographs on this and related subjects and also a number of archaeological guides to Herculaneum, Pompeii, Pozzuoli and other ancient sites in southern Italy. These (and what seems to have been a very attractive personality) won him a European reputation which ranged beyond that of fellow scholars in England, France and Germany to include Byron as well as the kings of Prussia and Bavaria.[85] His guides are indeed lively and informative, but his approach remained essentially conventional – except in one respect: while preparing them, De Jorio (like Du Choul and a great number of other scholars since the sixteenth century) showed himself to be fascinated by certain analogies between the customs of antiquity and those of his own day. 'You can say, reader,' he comments during the course of his description of Roman paintings in the Naples museum, 'that two thousand years ago, these people were doing just what you are doing now'.[86] Nowhere were these analogies so apparent as in the region of Naples, where the excavations at Herculaneum and Pompeii had brought to light an ancient world that seemed more down to earth, more familiar, than any that could have been envisaged from the daunting monuments of Rome. It was De Jorio's imaginative development of this insight that formed the basis of his masterpiece.

Many observers of the Neapolitan scene, particularly foreigners, had been fascinated by the highly expressive gestures used by the inhabitants of the city to supplement – and sometimes to replace – the spoken language, and some of them had recorded examples of these in travel books and monographs. De Jorio went further, and, because he was so acutely aware of the close ties that bound together the social customs of his own day with those of antiquity, he argued that the

112 (right). Andrea de Jorio,
Mimica, Naples 1832: gestures
indicating silence (fig. 1),
contempt for a dupe or a coarse
figure (fig. 5) or for an imbecile
(fig. 7), etc. etc.

113 (facing page). Andrea de
Jorio, *Mimica*, Naples 1832: 'Nè?
Ch'aggio da scrivere?'

gestures still current among the local populace (which was certainly not lacking in 'natural philosophy, talent and spirit'[87]) provided living testimony of those that had been general among the Greeks and the Romans: if properly investigated, therefore, they could explain many of the baffling and controversial scenes that had been painted on the Greek vases in his charge.

De Jorio collected and classified, through a highly elaborate system of indexing, every possible gesture used by the common people and had many of them carefully engraved. He demonstrated, for instance, how to insult one's enemies (pl. 112) – and even to ward off the evil eye, a subject in which he must have had some expertise, as he was reputed to suffer from it himself. It was, indeed, said that the King of the Two Sicilies for long refused to grant an audience to his antiquarian for this reason, and that the morning after he had been finally persuaded to relent he was found dead of an apoplectic fit.[88]

De Jorio also commissioned another series of illustrations for his book. These were devised by himself in collaboration with the painter Gaetano Gigante, who had made his name as a large-scale decorator in fresco, but who had recently, in late middle age, turned to scenes of picturesque genre, of a kind that were being churned out more and more for foreign visitors. De Jorio was concerned that too many of these were devoid of vitality and narrative.[89] Gigante was therefore required to take special care to make every gesture absolutely comprehensible, and painstaking explanations were provided of each one. A respectably dressed letter-writer sits at a table (pl. 113)[90] – for it was quite wrong to show such men as shabby and half naked as some old-fashioned artists continued to do; from his spectacles it could be seen that he was someone who had written and read too much; in the chair that he has placed next to his table sits a married woman who asks him to write on her behalf to her husband; he, not knowing what she wants him to say, raises his left hand and brings together his thumb and second finger – as is explained on page 85, number 4, this denotes a sign of interrogation; she puts her right hand on her heart – see page 43, note 1, where it is shown that this means love; the fact that she wishes to express these feelings for her husband is further emphasised by the inclination of her body and the downward glance of her features; her left hand is opened, and this implies that she is asking a question – see page 84; she wishes to be sure that her husband loves her as much as she does him. The other woman is perhaps her sister, and she thinks that all this is absurd; she shows disapproval – see 'Negative', page 224, number 8; her right hand is out-stretched to denote money – see page 126. She is arguing that her sister should be asking for more cash rather than for love.

Nè? Ch'aggio da scrivere?

114. Andrea de Jorio, *Mimica*, Naples 1832: painting on a Greek vase interpreted by De Jorio as Minerva holding a council of war.

De Jorio's detailed explanations of this and more than a dozen other plates in the book might, he feared, lead readers to think that he was much too concerned with the modern and was in some way demeaning antiquity. But this, he insisted, was not the case.[91] It was by studying the gestures of common people and the use made of them by painters of contemporary scenes that archaeologists could learn to solve some of the difficult points to be found in the narratives of the ancients. In his commentary he gives many examples of how helpful his method could be, and he also analyses illustrations of two Greek vases (pl. 114) in exactly the same way as he does the genre scenes of Gaetano Gigante:[92] Minerva is in the middle, and must therefore be the protagonist – see page 19; the armed men on each side of her appear to be deliberating; she looks to her right, but holds up her left arm and her lance to her left, in which direction she also seems to be stepping; the old man seated on her right could be either contemplating motion or expressing surprise – see page 12 and page 299, note 2 . . . A long series of alternative suggestions are then made, and each is backed up by reference to the 'ABC of Gestures' with which the book opens. Eventually De Jorio concludes that the figures on the right are cautious about the great enterprise being proposed by Minerva, while those on her left are responding to it with unqualified enthusiasm.

De Jorio's book was widely acclaimed – Sir Walter Scott was a particular admirer[93] – and it is indeed a work of great fascination and ingenuity that does attempt to throw fresh light on the nature of some of the problems that might (or should) have faced Lancelot and Montfaucon when they tried to decipher the meaning of the Bayeux Tapestry. Nevertheless, it is not wholly surprising that the *Mimica degli antichi* has proved to be more useful to students of folklore and 'non-verbal communication' than to archaeologists.

The Dialogue between Antiquarians and Historians

i

The relative failure of Montfaucon's *Monumens de la Monarchie françoise* (which was never completed) was due not to any qualms about his interpretation of mediaeval narrative: it was caused by a lack of wide public interest in the obscure ceremonies and quarrels of barbarous princes expressed through the medium of crude imagery. None the less, there can be no doubt that Montfaucon had made 'the republic of letters' far more aware than it had ever been of the part that could be played by authentic images in the illustrating of books devoted to national histories (of the Middle Ages and later, as well as to those of antiquity).

One example – of the many that could be mentioned[1] – demonstrates this with particular clarity. In 1719 Jacques Lelong, a French priest, had produced a very well-informed volume which listed the most important charters, chronicles and other sources (both printed and manuscript) needed for studying the history of France. It was re-issued in five folios between 1768 and 1778, and the new edition augmented the greatly expanded textual matter with an unusual appendix. This was an inventory of the thousands of prints and drawings that had been assembled by Charles-Marie Fevret de Fontette (a learned bibliophile and an influential member of the Parlement of Dijon)[2] and that would, so it was pointed out, furnish to men of letters who undertook to write about French history 'help of a kind that was not available to others previously engaged on this task'.[3]

Not all 'men of letters' were interested and, of those who were, only a very few were able to make use of images to productive effect. But one, at least, had already glimpsed with remarkable insight an approach to the historical value of images that did indeed open up a whole new range of possible developments, although they were not to be pursued until well after his death.

Jean-Baptiste de La Curne de Sainte-Palaye, who became the greatest mediaevalist of the middle years of the eighteenth century,[4] quickly understood that the issue of sources was fundamental to his researches, and he was keen to pursue a rational course that involved neither the uncritical acceptance nor the uncritical rejection of the chronicles of those early and unfamiliar writers on whom he was compelled to rely. As early as 1727 he claimed, in a declaration of method that reads as if it had been written in our own day, that

> History is based only on the testimony of those authors who have passed it down to us. It is therefore of the utmost importance to know just who those authors were, and nothing should be neglected in our attempts to find out all about them: the times in which they lived, their birth, their station in life, their country, the part that they played in public affairs, the means by which they acquired their information and the interest that they had in it. All these are essential facts which should on no account be ignored, because on them depends the extent of the authority that we should entrust to them . . .[5]

La Curne de Sainte-Palaye also wished to break with the narrow, antiquarian study of the Middle Ages, exemplified in the work of Montfaucon, and to adopt a more 'philosophical' approach which would enable him to embrace every aspect of the life and culture of the times. For these reasons he turned for material not only to the chronicles, but also (as did some other writers of the day) to the arts and to chivalric romances, and the centre of his intellectual activities was always the Académie des Inscriptions et Belles-Lettres. Sainte-Palaye was enthusiastic and well informed about the painting, sculpture and architecture of the sixteenth and seventeenth centuries and of his own day: clearly, mediaeval styles could not inspire the same sort of feelings, although it is possible that he may have associated the Gothic with those feudal or, at least, anti-despotic principles that appealed to many political theorists at the time.[6] Whether or not this is the case, it is certain that he soon began to be more and more attracted by the 'great beauty' of the miniatures to be seen in the mediaeval manuscripts that he explored and classified with real care.[7] However, these fascinated him above all because they could provide useful information about the ceremonies, costumes and armour of the Middle Ages. But how reliable was this? The problem seems to have struck him for the first time in 1735. It was then that he examined in the Royal Library a manuscript of Froissart illustrated with miniatures which have been attributed by modern scholars to a Flemish artist, working perhaps for the court of Burgundy, soon after the middle years of the fifteenth century. Two of the scenes represented – the arrival in Paris in the year 1324 of Isabella, Queen of England (pl. 115), and the capture in 1356 of the King of Navarre on the orders of Jean le Bon of France (pl. 116) – had recently come to the attention of Montfaucon who, despite some doubts about their strict factual accuracy, had published engravings of them in his *Monumens de la Monarchie françoise* because of the importance of the costumes. Sainte-Palaye, however, pointed out that 'the painter had confused the costumes of his own century with those of the times whose history he was painting'.[8] This he regretted. But, three years later, when he came to discuss how useful it was for the antiquarian to study mediaeval romances as well as conventional works of history, for they could supply invaluable information about wars, the administration of justice, tournaments and so on, he reached quite different conclusions about the anachronisms to be found in such works. It is fortunate, he commented, that

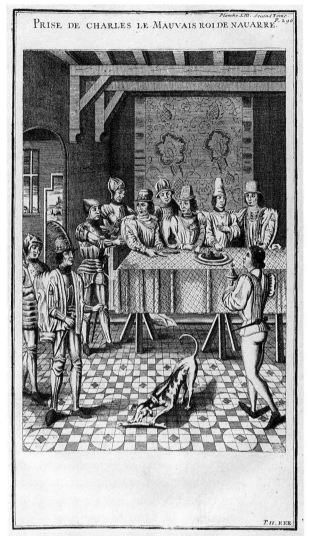

115. Montfaucon, *Monumens*, vol. II, Paris 1730: reproduction of miniature illustrating a mid-fifteenth-century manuscript of Froissart, showing the arrival in Paris in 1324 of Isabelle, Queen of England.

116. Montfaucon, *Monumens*, vol. II, Paris 1730: reproduction of miniature illustrating a mid-fifteenth-century manuscript of Froissart, showing the capture in 1356 of the King of Navarre on the orders of Jean le Bon, King of France.

those who composed these romances were not skillful enough to know and to observe what painters call 'le *costume*' [local colour]: they nearly always assigned to those stories of the past – whether true histories or fables – about which they used to write the customs of the times in which they themselves lived. In this they were like painters of the old days who came after the invention of gunpowder and who almost never depicted the siege of Troy in their miniatures without adding some piece of our own artillery . . .[9]

This casual comment amends in a very striking way Montfaucon's central belief – enunciated most clearly a generation earlier, in 1719 – that 'nothing is more instructive than paintings dating from the same period [as the events that they portray]'.[10] It is true that ever since the middle of the fifteenth century textual critics had relied on an insight similar to that of Sainte-Palaye when exposing the pious frauds of mediaeval monks who had composed documents that professed to date from much earlier periods. And in the seventeenth century men of letters had appreciated the fact that fictional accounts of the past were of value for the light that they could throw on the world of those who had devised them.[11] But La Curne de Sainte-Palaye seems to have been among the first scholars to welcome the principle as a useful guide to the historian and – even if only in passing – to have extended it to the visual arts. He travelled widely and was in touch with (or at least known to) many of the antiquarians and historians who will be mentioned in this chapter – Muratori, Maffei, Caylus and, above all, Gibbon. Moreover, his influence survived well into the age of Walter Scott. And his intuition into the true significance of pictorial anachronisms was, before long, to become a commonplace in mediaeval studies.

ii

It was not, however, only through the increasing availability of reproductions, or even through fresh insights as to how these might be exploited, that historians in the first half of the eighteenth century became much more aware of the possible significance for their researches of the visual arts. Nor – despite their growing importance – were mediaeval architecture, sculpture and painting the only means by which this awareness was communicated to them. New ways of displaying some of the more important Italian collections of antiquities also attracted attention, and behind at least one of these ventures, we can almost certainly detect the influence of Montfaucon himself.

In Turin the king's cabinet of curiosities, which was housed in a room on the ground floor of the university,[12] made a great impression on Gibbon when he visited it in 1764, only a year after its opening.[13] He and later 'persons of rank and men of letters' – women were not admitted without special permission[14] – were struck both by the objects themselves and by the manner in which they were arranged.

The pieces were placed in eight large glass-fronted cases, each of which was dedicated, in whole or in part, to one of the gods, around whose figure (or figures) were gathered any available articles associated with his cult and any representation depicting it: in the case assigned to Bacchus, for instance, were to be seen antiquities related to theatrical performances, actors, masks and so on. The gods were followed by Hercules, and a bas-relief showing his rescue of the daughter of the King of Troy led on logically to the display of Trojan and Roman objects. Gibbon, who was also struck by the presence of Sardinian bronzes, 'which revealed the beginnings of art and a taste far older than that of the Greeks and Romans', and of Egyptian paintings, 'which showed that the earliest artists . . . made legs, arms and bodies exaggeratedly long', felt that the coverage of mythology and of religious cults in the museum was extremely rich, almost complete, but that that of Roman history was very defective.

The management of the museum was the responsibility of the very learned – though 'un peu Charlatan'[15] – Giuseppe Bartoli, and Bartoli had been a (not very esteemed) disciple of Scipione Maffei.[16] Maffei had some years earlier reorganised the collection of antiquities belonging to the University of Turin according to the same principles that he had already established in his native Verona.[17] He had placed inscriptions 'and a mountain of statues, busts, heads, stones and reliefs' under the porticos of the courtyard, because he was convinced that such objects, which were in grave danger of being broken up, constituted primary sources for historians who were far too ready to take their materials at second hand. As Maffei in turn had been a protégé of Montfaucon, for whose learning he retained a profound, though sometimes critical, respect,[18] the links between the *Antiquité expliquée* and the new museum seem clear enough, even though they were by no means direct and even though it opened more than twenty years after Montfaucon's death.[19]

Far earlier, and far more influential, than the installation of the collection of antiquities in Turin, was the arrangement of those in the galleries of the Grand Duke of Tuscany in the Uffizi. It is not quite certain when this was completed, but it first began to attract the attention of foreign visitors in the early 1720s,[20] though the work had probably been carried on over a long period before that. Thus although Addison, who was in Florence in 1701, does not record being struck by the rational display of the sculptures, we do know that as early as 1680[21] (and possibly well before) some of its main features were in place, though a good deal of confusion certainly remained. This system, like the one later adopted in Turin, was based on thematic principles – with the essential difference that in this case an arrangement by subject-matter necessarily raised issues of style and change. For by 1722 at the latest, as complete a series as possible of busts and statues of Roman rulers from Julius Caesar to Gallienus had been placed in approximately chronological order, interspersed by a rather more arbitrary selection of gods and goddesses (including Michelangelo's *Bacchus*), writers, hunters and so on.[22]

It thus became possible for the visitor to obtain a remarkable impression of the sculpted portraits of familiar figures, ranging from before the time of Christ until the third century AD, of a kind that was no more than partially conveyed by the idiosyncratic grouping in the Munich Antiquarium and that was otherwise only available through the far less telling medium of medal cabinets and illustrated coin books (which, of course, had provided a direct precedent for the arrangement).

Montesquieu and Gibbon, the two most celebrated eighteenth-century historians of Rome, visited the sequence of busts and statues in the Uffizi and were much impressed, but when composing their masterpieces neither made any direct use of the evidence that could perhaps have been drawn from it.

Montesquieu was in Florence in 1728–9, and he studied painting, sculpture and architecture in the city, as elsewhere, with great care, consulting artists and scholars and making brief but perceptive notes. And the questions that he asked of the experts were – like those he raised concerning commerce, law or social life – far more penetrating than those of previous visitors to Italy. Thus he seems to have been the first historian to touch on the problem (so significant for the theme of the present book) of whether impressions concerning the ancient Romans that had been derived from reading and thinking about them were confirmed or falsified by looking at their busts and statues. He soon decided that their features must have been wholly different from those of his own contemporaries – 'il n'y a plus dans le monde de visage grec ni romain'[23] – as was to be expected in view of the huge changes that had come over Italy as a result of the barbarian invasions and of the fact that 'each nation has, so to speak, its own shape and physiognomy'. Moreover, the height of their statues shows that we must be taller than the Romans, although 'because we know them to have been a victorious and dominating people', we always imagine them to have been of great size ('d'une grande stature'). It is, in fact, possible that Montesquieu had reached these conclusions even before his visit to Italy,[24] but later we find him responding directly to what was to be seen in the Uffizi.

Curiously enough, despite his fascination with the quirks of human personality (especially the personalities of powerful rulers), so strikingly evident in his notebooks, Montesquieu pays almost no attention at all to the appearance of the emperors. When studying their busts he did not compare their features with the descriptions of them that he had read in the works of the Roman historians, but concentrated almost exclusively on social customs and artistic styles. Thus, stimulated as always by the issue of luxury, Montesquieu was struck by the far wider range of hairstyles apparently available to Roman empresses than to women in his own day, and he wondered whether fashions had changed with changing reigns or whether each individual empress had made special arrangements to suit her own particular looks. In any case, he pointed out, matters of this kind were best discussed by studying these busts rather than by concentrating only on written sources, as had been done some years earlier in a paper read to the Académie des Inscriptions et Belles-Lettres.[25]

Montesquieu himself could have gone a long way towards answering his apparently trivial question, for – in what was by far his most significant observation on the arrangement of the antiquities in the Uffizi – he noted that the sequence of portraits of the various emperors (whose dates were well known) made it possible to establish chronological guidelines for understanding the development of ancient artistic styles: indeed, Montesquieu's brief and scattered comments (which were not adequately published until the present century) can now be seen as having constituted the most important analysis of such problems before the appearance of Winckelmann's far more systematic investigation. It was, concluded Montesquieu, the treatment of the hair, the beard and the ears that most clearly indicated the age of a statue: in the earlier periods there was far greater variety than was the case later. Equally important were the folds of draperies. The earliest sculptors carved these in great number and made them very light so as to convey the nude figure beneath; later they became ill-fitting and coarse.[26] On the basis of such observations Montesquieu was in no doubt that the greatest pleasure to be derived from the Grand Duke's collection of busts and statues was that of following the decline of art – a decline that first became apparent during the brief reign of Didius Julianus at the very end of the second century, shortly after that of Commodus, and that proved to be inexorable. None the less, despite the evidence of his eyes, Montesquieu believed that the actual decline must have begun significantly earlier, at the time of Trajan or Hadrian, because he held it as axiomatic that arts and letters flourished and decayed with the changes in power and prosperity of a state.[27] On another occasion, however, he proposed a much more pragmatic reason for the fall in artistic standards. As Christians increased in numbers, fewer pagan statues were acquired, consequently competition diminished and craftsmen became interested only in earning their livelihood as quickly as possible.[28] But, whatever the reason for it, Montesquieu

117. *Raccolta degli Imperatori Romani*, 1780: bust of the Emperor Gallienus in the Uffizi.

was so certain of the fatal law of decay that the mere fact that a bust was of good quality was proof for him that it could not – as was claimed by those in charge of the museum – represent Gallienus who ruled in the middle of the third century (pl. 117). By the time of Constantine, art was 'entirely and completely' Gothic, and this convinced him that 'the Gothic style did not come from the Goths and other Northern peoples: they did not introduce it, but, by establishing the reign of ignorance, they did enforce it'.[29] Montesquieu's eye was a good one, but the conclusions he drew from what he had seen were often incorrect.[30] His theory of decline did not allow for short periods of 'intermission', and it was during one of these that – so it is now believed – the classicising bust of Gallienus was carved.

Less than three years after his visits to the Uffizi Montesquieu was at work on his *Considérations sur les causes de la grandeur des romains et de leur décadence*, which was first published in 1734. Much of this remarkable historical essay was devoted to the rule of the emperors whose busts he had looked at with such care and discrimination. Not one of these busts is mentioned by him, nor is any other work of ancient art or archaeology. It may, however, not be altogether fanciful to suggest that his observations on Roman sculpture had played some small part in at least confirming the conclusions he reached in his *Considérations*. In that book Montesquieu agreed with most historians that the fall of the Roman Empire had been caused not so much by pressures from outside its frontiers as by its own internal failings – which he summed up as the corruption of its military spirit; loss of prudence, wisdom and constancy; and the relapse into meaningless cruelty. To that extent the decline of Roman art from the middle of the third century matched the decline of Roman civilisation as a whole.

iii

When Montesquieu examined the sculptures in the Grand Duke's gallery it had long been accepted that Roman art had begun to decline well before the barbarian invasions; but while a few antiquarians had been prepared to exalt the devout spirit that emanated from the ugly artefacts of the early Christians, it was virtually impossible to come across any apologists within Italy for the artistic creations inspired by those Germanic and other tribes that had swarmed over the Alps into the peninsula. And yet early in the eighteenth century a number of great Italian historians began to reject the notion that the supremacy of Rome had always been desirable and that once it had been lost total barbarism had prevailed. Often in conflict with the pretensions of the papacy, and always in real danger from the Inquisition, these men (of whom Pietro Giannone and Lodovico Antonio Muratori were the most prominent) looked with some sympathy at the 'barbarian' invasions of both the Goths and the Lombards. Neither Giannone nor Muratori was by nature responsive to the appeal of architecture, painting or sculpture, but we shall see that Muratori certainly acknowledged in theory that his case would be much strengthened if it could be shown that the distinctive civilisation of mediaeval Italy had been marked by a flowering of the arts, sciences and letters. And Giannone and Muratori both realised that the obscure and defective chronicles concerning forgotten events which they were bringing to light required far more substantiation than did the familiar and authoritative histories of a Suetonius or Tacitus. Every additional piece of confirming evidence was desirable, and what had once been a luxury now became a necessity.

Years later, when composing his autobiography in prison, Giannone still remembered the complaints made by his teacher, the antiquarian and professor of civil law Domenico d'Aulisio, about the antiquarians of his day. These men, he said, carried out

> wonderful researches into the most ancient Greek and Roman medals; they understood, wonderfully well, those coins that had been found, and were still being excavated, of the ancient inhabitants of Asia and Greece and the Greek cities of Italy; they knew their Roman medals, which ones were consular and minted for the tribunes, and which imperial, and everything that belonged to the most remote and recondite antiquity; but as soon as they drew near to the years of the late Empire which were less remote from us, they became silent and utterly ignorant.[31]

Giannnone was by far the most subversive historian of his time, and in the preface to his *Istoria Civile del Regno di Napoli* he rightly boasted that the undertaking on which he had embarked 'will, if I am not mistaken, be entirely new'.[32] It was this book, first published in three volumes in 1723, that was eventually to lead to his passing the last years of his life in prison at the instigation of the papacy, for it was his aim to demonstrate how successfully clerical power had usurped what should by rights have belonged to the sphere of the civic authorities. Giannone made it clear that it was not his intention to discuss 'the magnificence of the spacious and noble buildings of the city',[33] but ironically he does find himself referring to these again and again – though nearly always in a tone that is (by implication) a pejorative one.[34] Wherever he went in the city he came across splendid churches and convents – Santa Maria di Dio,[35] for instance, or the Gerolimini[36] – their altar fronts gleaming with richly coloured marbles cut into the most intricate decorative patterns, their pictures and frescoes commissioned from the leading painters of the day, their statues and balustrades and climbing putti carved by the most skilled masters. And, he insists, these new churches had either come into being through the transformation of some palace belonging to one of the great noble families, that of the Prince of Tarsia, to take one example, or, when such a palace had turned out to be not on the scale needed – as had been the case of that bought from Carlo Seripando – it had been pulled down to make way

for a newly built church, such as that of S. Filippo Neri (the Gerolimini), 'the richest and most majestic ever put up in Naples, and one that now rivals the proudest and most magnificent palace of any prince' (pl. 118).[37] Palatial churches – there were many of them and they were much noted by foreign visitors – provided material proof of the main thrust of Giannone's claim that the Church was, so to speak, taking over the State under his very eyes.

The expanding role played by clerics and monks in the life of Italy was thus palpable enough, but it had been pursued unremittingly, long before evidence of it became so directly visible in the form of luxurious monasteries and churches competing with, and sometimes replacing, palaces in and around Naples. One had to go back as far as the seventh and eighth centuries to find rulers of Italy – the Lombard kings – who had been able to withstand the designs of ambitious popes. For this reason the popes had spread the legend that the Lombards were 'cruel, inhumane and barbarous'. In fact, after a rough beginning, Lombard rule had been so peaceful and productive that for two

118. Naples, façade of the church of the Gerolimini.

hundred years it was the envy of all other nations – a sort of golden age to be contrasted with that of the 'century of the monks, in which the ignorance and superstition of laymen and clergy alike plumbed the depths'.[38]

It was in connection with his researches into this almost unknown period of Italian history that Giannone was keen to examine Lombard coins, and he commented that even twenty years after the death of his teacher d'Aulisio the situation had scarcely improved, and that antiquarians were not yet able to elucidate coins of the Lombard kings.[39] Indeed, the only existing set of illustrations purporting to record such coins (two folio sheets devoted to a family tree of the Lombard kings of Italy) carried a warning by the author Angelo Breventano that the features shown were not in fact derived from actual Lombard coins, but from what were rather vaguely described as 'the coins of other peoples who had lived at the same time'.[40]

That had been as long ago as 1593. Giannone acknowledged, however, that some recent investigations had at last been carried out into the Byzantine and late phases of the Empire, and he singled out the works of Filippo Paruta and especially Matteo Bandur, the scholar-monk from Dubrovnik. Bandur did indeed make a considerable impact on literary and historical studies of many kinds.[41] When Montfaucon came to Florence in 1700 Bandur became one of his closest companions, and at Montfaucon's invitation he then went to Paris where he settled for the remaining forty-one years of his life. At first his researches were spectacular. Within a few months of his arrival in 1702 he had discovered 140 unpublished letters of Petrarch in the Royal Library, as well as an eleventh-century guide to Constantinople. The critical edition of this which he published some years later, enriched with ample notes and a commentary, under the title of *Imperium Orientale*... constitutes his major contribution to scholarship. It brought him fame and, with fame, a luxurious style of living which aroused the indignation of Montfaucon and his Maurine colleagues from whom he became wholly alienated.

Alongside his corpus of all existing literary sources on the 'antiquities' of Constantinople, Bandur had planned to include illustrations of two thousand unpublished coins and medals; but, for technical reasons, the two handsomely produced folios containing these, which were subsidised by Louis XIV, appeared separately in 1718.[42] In an age when public museums were unknown, numismatists naturally depended on the co-operation of private collectors. Although such collectors were themselves usually more concerned with historical significance than aesthetic quality, there were clearly limits as to what they were prepared to place in their cabinets. Giannone's complaint about the lack of investigation of Lombard coins was doubtless shared by other scholars, but it is hardly surprising that such ungainly images of a period that attracted little interest failed to appeal to even the most imaginative collectors. For his late imperial and Byzantine coins, however, Bandur was able to draw on the magnificent collection of Louis XIV and also on that of Nicolas-Joseph Foucault, the Intendant at Caen, whose copy of the Bayeux Tapestry was later to be drawn to the notice of Montfaucon. Perhaps even more important was the collection that had been assembled in Milan by Francesco Mezzabarba who, despite his death in 1697 at the age of only fifty-two, had won a

European reputation as a scholar, and had been awarded the title of count by the Holy Roman Emperor.[43]

Thus, when preparing the second edition of his Neapolitan history (which appeared posthumously), Giannone was able to include a few illustrations of coins and medals (some of which he was able to study in the fine cabinets to be found in Vienna, where he lived for nearly ten years under the protection of the Holy Roman Emperor) thanks to the expertise of Bandur and the handful of scholars of the time who shared his interest and enterprise.[44]

Lodovico Antonio Muratori, who was for a short time suspected – wrongly – of endeavouring to protect Giannone from his enemies,[45] had already been trying for some years to get hold of medallic images of the Lombard kings. He was compelled to draw on Breventano's inadequate compilation of 1593, and he asked his correspondents to put him in touch with any other publications they knew of.[46] As a young man he had had contacts with Mezzabarba,[47] and after Mezzabarba's death he continued for some years to seek numismatic information from his son Gian Antonio,[48] who had inherited the collection and who, despite his death in 1705 at the age of thirty-five, acquired an even greater reputation as a scholar both in Paris, where he spent two or three years, and in Milan. Both for Giannone and Muratori the inscriptions, and occasionally the figures, on early mediaeval coins could provide important evidence about such much-debated issues as the obligations of various Italian towns to the pope or the Holy Roman Emperor and the relationship between Byzantium and the West. They served as political documents, but were not used as a gauge of the prevailing civilisation, the nature of individual rulers or of any matter that can be described as social.

Indeed, we will see that Muratori's attitude to figurative sources was a complex one that makes of him at once the most typical historian of his time and, to students of today, the most puzzling. His reluctance, when he was already famous as one of the most learned and prolific of writers, to have his portrait engraved, on the grounds that 'people who want to know me will be satisfied with the little I have written',[49] should alert us to the fact that he was not only personally modest but also sceptical concerning the value of visual evidence.

Muratori was four years older than Giannone, and, like him, he began his career by studying law. In 1694–5, at the age of twenty-two, he moved from Modena to Milan, where he stayed for five years and embarked on a life of scholarship that was to make him one of the most renowned Italians of the eighteenth century. Like Giannone, Muratori was critical of papal pretensions and he deplored the extreme partisanship of historians such as Baronius:[50] he remained, none the less, a devout believer, albeit one with a mission to purge his faith of superstitious accretions. He was acutely aware of the restraints imposed by censorship: 'We Catholics constantly complain of the too many brakes which, to tell the truth, are sometimes imposed on us by those who have power,' he wrote warily to a friend, 'so that one can no longer talk or print anything about physics, astronomy, medicine, ecclesiastical history and other matters, without running the danger of our books being prohibited, or even greater misfortunes.'[51] To write dispassionately about late antique and early mediaeval Italian history was almost as hazardous as it had been at the height of the Counter-Reformation 150 years earlier when Carlo Sigonio had exclaimed 'O rem duram scribere historiam'.[52] Even an enquiry about the Lombards was likely to arouse suspicion,[53] and in seeking permission to consult official archives Muratori found it necessary to make clear that he did not intend to pursue his researches beyond the year 1200.[54] For the cautious Muratori, who went to considerable lengths to avoid charges of heresy or insubordination, had his troubles with the Inquisition[55] and was working in a potentially dangerous field. As Giannone and he well knew, the Middle Ages were far more intimately related to the actualities of Italian political life than Roman antiquity had ever been, for all the rhetoric that surrounded it. He was, for instance, commissioned by his sovereign, Rinaldo d'Este, Duke of Modena, to provide documentary justification for the seizure by the Holy Roman Emperor in 1708 of the papal fief of Comacchio and also to investigate the origins of the Este family itself[56] – the same issue that had engaged the attention of Pirro Ligorio and the book illustrators who followed in his wake. It was partly in pursuit of these researches that Muratori made a thorough exploration of the Este archives and engaged in a vast correspondence with scholars in Italy and elsewhere. And basing himself on these experiences he was to put the study of mediaeval history on to an entirely new footing. For he insisted that absolute primacy must always be given to original sources, and he recognised that such sources need not consist only of written documents.

Even before embarking on these enquiries, Muratori claimed that 'everything concerning customs, religion, clothes, buildings' and so on belonged to the province of history, and he was fully aware of the importance of visual sources for the understanding of periods whose written records were at best patchy.[57] He was in touch with many antiquarians and was always interested in looking at drawings of the artefacts in their possession: on one single day in 1728 he was to write to correspondents in Florence, Siena and Venice to ask for information about the earliest coins minted in those cities.[58] He also professed himself to be very impressed by the attempts of his friend (though later antagonist) Francesco Bianchini to make use of bas-reliefs and other images to demonstrate 'the truth of history'. This he thought, was a 'huge and noble idea'[59] – his choice of words may have been carefully considered, for a modern reader is likely to feel that Bianchini's confused execution of his project hardly matches the boldness of his ambition.[60] He encouraged young artists[61] and corresponded with painters such as Nicolas Vleughels and Giuseppe Maria Crespi (who claimed that he had 'learned what it is to be Christian' by reading Muratori's La Carità Cristiana);[62] and that he was interested in the history of painting is shown also by his protracted exchange of letters with the combative artist Lodovico Antonio David about the life and works of Correggio.[63] Above all, he was almost as aware as Montesquieu of the influence that images can exert on our perception of the past. Writing about the Lombards, for instance, he deplored the fact that most peoples' impressions of them had been derived from the crude woodcuts which, 150 years earlier, had been used to illustrate a book by Wolfgang Lazius (a writer whom he particularly despised) on the migrant peoples of the Dark Ages.[64] One of these illustrations showed 'a man of surly countenance and frightening appearance with beard and moustaches

119. Wolfgang Lazius, *De aliquot gentium migrationibus*, Basle, 1572: a Lombard and an Herulian.

spreading down over his chest, the back of his head shaved bare, dressed in patchwork, armed with spurs on his knees and a two-handed sword, a man, in fact, who looks capable of eating people' (pl. 119).[65]

The eight folio volumes of Muratori's *Dissertazioni sopra le antichità italiane* were designed to put into effect a programme of what would today be described as cultural history. He had drawn this up some years before beginning his actual researches, and he proposed to discuss the arts along with every other aspect of mediaeval life. In the preface he compares himself to a guide showing a visitor round some great palace: first the overall plan, then the rooms and staircases, followed by galleries, and the pictures and statues to be seen in them.[66] Yet when he embarks on the dissertations themselves, he seems to us to be surprisingly reluctant to look directly at just those pictures and statues, not to mention palaces, that would have helped to buttress his arguments. And when he does so, his allusions are of a vagueness that would have been wholly unacceptable to him if applied to a literary text. How much, he tells us, he would have like to see those large buildings which, though not beautiful in style, continued to be raised under the Lombards but which had long since been swallowed up by time.[67] But such actual buildings and objects from the period as did still survive are barely ever mentioned by him. He expresses the hope that the various 'noble memories of the barbarian age that remain standing' will not be pulled down, because 'although they lack Greek and Roman subtlety yet they do not fail to express venerable majesty and magnificence'.[68] Yet he does not mention what these buildings are. Again and again he insists that the arts constitute essential historical records of the mediaeval world, but what he tells us of late antique and mediaeval art is derived almost entirely from written mediaeval sources. This is all the more surprising because Muratori, like so many historians of his time, was acutely aware of the fallibility of literary evidence of this kind. Thus he points out that when an eighth-century chronicler such as Paul the Deacon refers to buildings erected by the Lombards as having been noble, you, the reader, may well say that *he* may have thought them noble, but that *we* should find them hideous. That, replies Muratori to his imaginary challenger – and he seems to be echoing a comment by Vasari on the Goths – is unlikely, for after all, Paul the Deacon had been to Rome and had seen the noble buildings there, and was therefore in a position to judge quality.[69]

Muratori's reliance on literary sources is also surprising because, soon after he began to embark on his historical researches, he had got in touch with the man who was then doing more than anyone else to reproduce, as well as comment on, some of the principal monuments of early Christian, Byzantine and 'barbarian' artists.[70] Monsignor Giovanni Giustino Ciampini was (despite his very close connections with the papacy) in the forefront of the intellectual revival that marked Roman culture in the last two decades of the seventeenth century through his direction of the *Giornale de' Letterati* and the *Accademia Fisico-matematica*.[71] He was also a Christian archaeologist of the highest distinction. He shared many of the preoccupations of Giovanni Bosio and the early investigators of the catacombs, and he often relied on drawings that had been made shortly after their pioneering researches. His own approach, however, was incomparably more sophisticated than theirs had been. In his discussions of mosaics, for instance, or of the bronze doors of mediaeval cathedrals, or of church furnishings, he did not refrain from commenting on their quality or on the degree to which they could be trusted as accurate historical sources. His careful observations of bricks and building patterns enabled him to establish a chronological framework for the architecture of the early centuries of the Christian era, and when looking at figured monuments he always tried to determine at what period they had been made, by examining relevant portraits and inscriptions and (occasionally) by judging the style. He was even prepared to conclude that in one scene an artist of the fifth or sixth century had tried to represent Rome not as it was then but as it had been hundreds of years earlier when the Apostles Peter and Paul were still alive (pl. 120).[72]

Ciampini was in touch with bishops and ecclesiastical officials in many parts of Italy who sent him detailed drawings of local antiquities of the early mediaeval period which were then engraved – crudely, schematically and sometimes inaccurately, it is true, but also legibly – and used to illustrate his various volumes. Thus Muratori could have had access to considerable visual documentation of those very arts that he chose to discuss in his books on the early Christian centuries – but he failed to use it. When discussing the mosaics of Rome and Ravenna, for instance, he refers exclusively to written accounts of their existence, despite the fact that Ciampini had enthusiastically reproduced those that were to be seen in the churches of S. Vitale (pl. 121) and S. Apollinare in Classe.[73]

The art of Ravenna was, in fact, a central issue for all those concerned with the fate of Italian culture at the hands of the barbarian invaders. It was there that Theodoric, King of the Goths, had made his capital, and ancient sources, particularly Cassiodorus, spoke very highly of the magnificent buildings he had erected. This tradition was, of course, kept alive in Ravenna itself, but the main stream of Italian art criticism which was based on 'Tuscan' principles had little time for it.[74] Vasari, for instance, had nothing but contempt for the Goths and the Lombards and was in no doubt that the deplorable quality of their civilisation could be gauged by the nature of the buildings they had left behind them in Ravenna. It was true that these might be 'great and magnificent', but he emphasised that their architecture was 'childishly clumsy' (goffissima) and that the effect made by them was owing to their size and the richness of their decoration rather than to any aesthetic quality.[75]

There was, however, one church, S. Maria Rotonda, just outside the city, that posed a real problem. Two storeys high and designed to a handsome circular plan, which was somewhat obscured by a cluster of mediaeval buildings attached to it, this church was covered by a massive vault made up of a single block of Istrian

120. Ciampini, *Vetera Monimenta*, vol. I, Rome 1690: mosaics, said to date from the fifth or sixth century AD, in the Basilica Siciniana, Rome, depicting the martyrdoms of Saints Peter and Paul.

121. Ciampini, *Vetera Monimenta*, vol. II, Rome 1699: mosaics in S. Vitale, Ravenna.

stone, and it obviously (and, according to the ancient sources, self-consciously), echoed the architecture of the Roman Empire (pls 122, 123). Vasari was extremely impressed by this 'very noble and marvellous' vault, and as he spent two months in Ravenna, it is almost inconceivable that he had not heard of the generally accepted view that the church had originally been the mausoleum that Theodoric, King of the Goths, had built for himself or that had been built for him by his daughter.[76] However, it would have been difficult for him to acknowledge that that barbaric and ignorant tribe could have managed such an astonishingly skilful feat of engineering: 'it seems almost impossible that a block of stone of that kind, weighing more than two hundred thousand pounds, could have been placed so high'; and he claimed, rather vaguely, that the building had been raised 'after the Lombards had been expelled from Italy'.[77]

Other writers also found it difficult to account for the grandeur of S. Maria Rotonda. Whether Vasari had avoided mentioning the connection with the Goths out of ignorance or out of self-deception, or even out of real conviction, is not absolutely clear, but there can be no doubt at all that when Scipione Maffei came to write about the church in 1730 its status as the former mausoleum of Theodoric had been firmly established. Yet Maffei also refrains from acknowledging this – indeed he specifically ridicules the notion: 'a fine job it would have been for the Lombards or the Goths to carve, transport and to place so high a block of this kind'.[78] Like Vasari, Maffei profoundly admired the church, but – in conscious opposition to Vasari – he refused to believe that the Goths had been responsible for the corrupting of architecture in Italy. Such a notion derived from 'our pride, according to which we have considered everything bad to be foreign'.[79] On the contrary, argued Maffei with great ingenuity, neither the Goths nor the Lombards had made much impact of any kind on Italy, and the Italians themselves must bear responsibility – or claim the credit – for the buildings to be found on their territory. Indeed, despite many deplorably designed monuments, a grandiose mastery of construction had survived almost uninterruptedly from Roman times, and feats fully comparable to raising the dome of S. Maria Rotonda could be matched in many mediaeval buildings, not least in Maffei's own Verona.

Of the three contemporary Italian scholar-antiquarians who made so great a contribution to the study of history during the first half of the eighteenth century, Maffei was by far the most sensitive to the visual arts (modern as well as ancient),[80] although he, too, always gave primacy to the written word; and despite the fact that his relationship with his rival Muratori was always uneasy (though marked with respect on both sides) and that he was prepared to be ironical about Giannone,[81] his career has many features in common with theirs. Like Muratori, he had been much influenced by Montfaucon, Bacchini and Bianchini; and, like both Muratori and Giannone, he, too, had trouble with the Inquisition – he was even imprisoned for a short time. His decisive transformation of the study of Greek palaeography and his contributions to Italian literature and political theory need not concern us directly here. What is, however, of importance to us is his noble birth. Unlike so many antiquarians of the two previous centuries the Marchese Scipione Maffei was a cosmopolitan who could travel widely and speak

122 (above). G.B. Piranesi, 'Tempio di
Ravenna', pen and bistre (London,
Courtauld Institute Galleries).

123. Ravenna, mausoleum of
Theodoric.

on equal terms with the leading figures of his age. He could cope with the arduous drudgery of detailed research, but he was also an adviser to princes. His pamphlets did not fall only into the hands of jealous and pedantic rivals, and his tragedy *Merope* was performed to great acclaim in the leading theatres of Europe.

Maffei was not the only scholar and antiquarian of the eighteenth century to enjoy such advantages. Jean-Baptiste de La Curne de Sainte-Palaye, the comte de Caylus, Jean-Baptiste-Louis-George Seroux d'Agincourt, Conte Leopoldo Cicognara: a mere recital of the names gives some indication of the fact that social eminence did not, at this period, necessarily exclude a genuine commitment to erudition. This was of real significance. The dialogue between historical writing, on the one hand, and the pursuit of new kinds of historical evidence (including the image), on the other, did not become very intimate; but it might not have developed at all had its protagonists not enjoyed at least a few of the attractions – of birth, wealth, charm and looks – that, in most societies, have allowed mere learning to extend its influence beyond the circles to which it is usually confined.

Maffei came to history from antiquarianism, but (less trammelled by the demands of powerful patrons than was the humble Muratori) he was able to apply his study of the past not merely to contingent problems but also to a wide range of more general issues – issues that were of interest to thinkers and statesmen, who would surely have dismissed as pedantry his enthusiasm for measuring the stone blocks out of which the Colosseum had been built. When discussing the Romans, for instance, he emphasised how different from the sectarianism of the Greeks had been their policy of extending citizenship to subject peoples, but he then pointed out that, despite this, their lack of representative government on the English pattern had led to corruption and eventual collapse.[82] Like that of Giannone and Muratori, Scipione Maffei's history – as exemplified in his masterpiece, *Verona Illustrata*, published in 1732 – broke with the traditions of the annalists and straight-forward writers of political and military narrative to cover a huge spectrum of human behaviour ranging from the political and military to the intellectual and cultural. His devotion to Verona occasionally amounted to petty parochialism, but his history of the city was to some extent also a history of Italy. It was, as he rightly wrote to a friend when the book was still in its early stages, 'as far removed from a history of Verona as you can possibly imagine, and you will be horrified by my audacity'.[83]

Unlike Giannone and Muratori, however, Maffei had no desire to sever the continuity between the Italy of his own day and that of the Roman past. Invasions by the Goths, the Lombards and the Byzantines had been purely negative interruptions to the progress of civilisation, and, as he repeatedly emphasised, they had left no lasting impact whatsoever: on language or on morals, on clothes or on architecture, on religion or on customs. In one of those sudden references to the present that tend to enliven his pages, he commented that at the very moment he was writing there were some eighty thousand German soldiers – not to mention their servants, their wives and their children – in those parts of Italy ruled by Austria: this was certainly no fewer than the Lombards who had once dominated much of the peninsula. 'Yet do we now find that the Italians are giving up their own jobs and that the Germans are busy building, painting, practising penmanship or taking up other employments of the kind? Or that the style of the arts is changing and that the language is undergoing alteration and that the manner of writing is being transformed? Not in the slightest'.[84]

Maffei was so keen on the need for historians to rely on primary sources rather than on literary traditions that he was largely responsible for creating the museum of sculptures and inscriptions in Verona (though its origins date back to well before his intervention),[85] and that (as we have seen) he installed a similar museum in the University of Turin. For Verona Maffei collected many pieces of antiquity from local churches, some of which had been known and described in the sixteenth century, but he also ranged further afield: the Greek sculptures, for instance (mainly Hellenistic funerary monuments), probably came from Venice and formed an exceptional group in eighteenth-century Europe. In addition, he obtained Etruscan tombs, and Hebrew and Arab inscriptions (the latter from a cemetery in Palermo); and among the mediaeval objects was the magnificent twelfth-century stone sarcophagus of Saints Sergius and Bacchus, which has been taken to the Museo di Castelvecchio.

It was no doubt Maffei's insistence on the need for absolute authenticity that made him refrain from having his sculptures restored in any way, and this, too, distinguished the collection at Verona from nearly all others formed in the eighteenth century; indeed, it is the reliefs and statues acquired in Rome (where they had been restored as a matter of course) that stand out as exceptional.

Maffei was in close touch with the architect Conte Alessandro Pompei about the design of the very simple single-storey Doric portico (since drastically enlarged) which was to run around the courtyard – in front of the Teatro Filarmonico – under whose arcades most of the objects were displayed, though the reliefs were fitted into the walls usually within specially constructed marble frames. The arrangement was rigorously thematic: Etruscan, Greek, Latin, Fake, Christian; and within the class of Latin inscriptions and objects (which was naturally by far the most numerous) subdivisions followed the principles established in Montfaucon's *Antiquité*: the sacred, the imperial, matters relating to the senate, the magistracy and so on.[86]

Towards the end of his life Maffei wrote that 'nothing would be more useful for scholarship than a general study of the visual remains of antiquity and an examination of the most important prints relating to them. A very long time ago I applied myself to this task, and I collected a vast amount of material with just such an aim in mind; but I never set my hand to it, because I wanted to complete my researches into the written sources of antiquity which I had already begun and which had made good progress.'[87] Nevertheless, in his scholarly writings he does draw constantly on evidence provided by the visual arts to support his arguments – coins and medals, of course, and architecture; but also 'Christian antiquities' such as a sarcophagus 'which speaks more than a book',[88] or a font. He did not usually think very highly of the aesthetic quality of these sources,[89] but he insisted that it was a great mistake to neglect them on that account, and he was keen to show how, for instance, early Christian sculptors had borrowed figures from pagan monuments.[90] He also turned to Renaissance painting in order to examine the customs of the sixteenth century just as keenly (but also just as uncritically) as his sixteenth-century predecessors had examined the bas-reliefs of antiquity: a frieze by Domenico Brusasorzi depicting the procession of Pope Clement VII and the Emperor Charles V in Bologna was 'more expressive than any book, showing what people took part, the order in which they proceeded, the clothes, the manner and the real features and portraits of the most worthy people there . . . What will our descendants learn of our customs and clothes, our ceremonies and spectacles from the painters of today?'[91] Above all – and in this respect he made a radical break with antiquarian tradition – he looked carefully at the arts of his own day in order to understand what had happened in the past and to confront the question that had to be tackled by all cultural historians: why had the arts declined with the decline of the Roman Empire? In one of the earliest, most eloquent (and least known) denunciations of the extravagances of the late Baroque he pours scorn on the designs to be seen all around him: in picture frames, altarpieces and saddles as much as in architecture; in the profusion of crystal, mirrors and stucco; in the decoration of libraries which hurts the eye even before one has begun to read. All this, claims Maffei, is due to a frantic craving for novelty.[92] Exactly such a craving had been responsible for the collapse of architecture at the end of the Roman Empire:[93] the barbarians had played no part in it, nor, he argues silently, had the Christian destruction of pagan monuments. Maffei does not discuss why such a frantic pursuit of fashion is likely to occur at some moments in history rather than at others, but he refers ominously to Plato's conclusion that the corruption of music can lead to the corruption of behaviour, and he points to the need for an academy to control architectural excess.

In 1732, soon after the publication of his *Verona Illustrata*, Maffei went to France. Within a year he was in Paris where he remained until 1736 (when he moved on to London) and where at first he enjoyed a great social success.[94] However, it was not long before he disconcerted some of his *confrères* by devoting too much time to writing a long treatise on the attitude of the early Christians to free will, and he was later to antagonise others by interfering in what the French felt should be a matter of exclusively French concern: the arrangement and the study of antiquities in French collections. Shocked by the neglect and inaccessibility of the material, and by the presence among it of some fakes, and proud (perhaps rather too ostentatiously so) of his own achievements in Turin and Verona, he outraged members of the Académie des Inscriptions et Belles-Lettres by implying that the absolute control they had been granted over the inscribed and figured monuments belonging to the king had not been exerted entirely in the interests of scholarship. He proposed that all such pieces – and others scattered throughout Paris – should be safeguarded by being placed in a secure but public museum, perhaps in the courtyard of the Tuileries. In this way they could be studied so as to yield 'certainty and truth about the customs, the opinions and the learning of ancient times'. As a demonstration of what he had in mind Maffei published his views on a horizontal marble relief which portrayed a reclining bare-breasted woman evidently on her death-bed who is being watched over by musicians and grieving

124. 'Conclamatio' – Italian marble relief of the fifteenth century (Paris, Louvre).

figures (pl. 124). He had, he explained, come across this in the Louvre just before his departure from Paris, and it had been surrounded by casts from Trajan's column, by busts and by pieces of modern French sculpture.

Maffei took the relief to be the front of a sarcophagus, and he commissioned from Natoire a drawing of it to be given to an engraver. He then wrote with feeling and some eloquence about its beauty and perfect state of conservation (it is, in fact, now believed to have been carved in the Renaissance rather than in antiquity), but he pointed out that 'the monument is much more precious for what it can teach us' about the religious customs observed by pagans on their death-beds – customs that were not recorded anywhere in literature – and he proceeded to describe at some length (but very tentatively) what he thought could be learned about these: the three figures standing to the left of the dying woman were priests, in togas and crowned with laurel wreaths, and the two musicians playing the horn behind her were presumably doing so in order to drive away evil spirits. Maffei backed up his views by referring both to other works of art and to literary sources.

Maffei's views were quickly misrepresented and derided, but nearly a quarter of a century later, just four years after his death, they were (as has been shown in an important study by Krzystof Pomian) reconsidered in a far more sympathetic light by the comte de Caylus, an aristocratic *amateur*, man of letters and antiquarian of similar tastes to his own, although the two had never actually met when this might have been possible, either in Verona or, later, in Paris. Caylus entirely agreed with Maffei that the antiquities belonging to the king needed to be thoroughly reorganised, and he also agreed with some, but not all, of the salient points of his interpretation of the relief. However, he thought that the musicians were more likely to be trying to soothe the dying woman and that the so-called priests were in fact servants waiting to prepare the body for burial. He rather sententiously reproved both Maffei and his critics for not having given the measurements of the relief and for not having paid enough attention to the quality of the carving.

iv

The reputation of Caylus has suffered through his having been despised by one genius (Diderot), patronised by another (Winckelmann) and heartily disliked by almost every contemporary who wrote about him. But however much he may have used his social power to bully his acquaintances and to try (like both Diderot and Winckelmann) to direct the course of modern art, readers today are likely to find the repeated charges of dry pedantry and tyrannical dogmatism surprising, for the antiquarian studies of Caylus are marked by a wholly new spirit of modesty and free enquiry.[95] Again and again he stresses the tentative nature of his conclusions. 'How frequently', he comments, 'is the antiquarian obliged to make use of "I don't know" – that phrase that is so damaging to his self-esteem; that phrase that is not only honest in itself, but flattering for anyone who considers the truth to have a place in the highest circle of the deities.'[96] He emphasises the fact that antiquarian research should be compared to that of the scientist: one new fact can dispose of a whole elaborate hypothesis.[97] Even more striking is an almost imprecedented sensitivity to the material object itself (as distinct from literary reflections of it) and, above all, an enthusiasm for his work which is often conveyed in memorable tones: 'when his treasures arrive, the antiquarian opens with a mixed feeling of sweet anxiety and hope the cases in which they have been packed: he flatters himself that he will find there rare and unknown objects. The moment of discovery is one of pleasurable thrill [*jouissance vive*].'[98]

Caylus was born into the highest nobility in 1692, and after serving in the army he travelled both in Italy and in Turkey. He became an accomplished etcher and was always to remain scornful of those antiquarians who were ignorant of artistic techniques or arbitrary restorations and thus liable to construct fanciful theories on the basis of untenable evidence.[99] His wealth and social connections brought him into contact with many of the leading figures of his day, most notably the extremely rich collector Pierre Crozat with whom (and another friend, the connoisseur Pierre-Jean Mariette) he became associated in an ambitious project to reproduce the most important paintings to be found in French collections.[100] This enterprise left him with an acute awareness of the need for accuracy when illustrating his own antiquities – 'la querelle des Antiquaires et des Graveurs n'est pas prête à finir'[101] – though it must be admitted that the copyists he employed were often of the dimmest quality. Caylus was also closely involved with the artists of his own day – as a young man he used to draw with Watteau and later he was to 'discover' Bouchardon – but he had no doubt that, with a few exceptions, the ancients were vastly superior to the moderns.[102]

Caylus's contributions to antiquarianism, which began when he was already middle-aged, were divided between thirty-seven papers he read to the Académie des Inscriptions et Belles-Lettres, by then the leading institution devoted to study-ing the artefacts of early civilisations,[103] and the seven thick volumes of his *Recueil d'Antiquités* which appeared at irregular intervals between 1752 and 1767 (the last one posthumously). These concentrated on Egyptian, Etruscan, Greek, Roman and (from 1759) Gaulish objects, the vast majority of which were in his own collections and those of his friends. As he candidly explained, the arrangement was quite unsystematic, for he would often acquire some piece after he had published related material, and this meant that an engraving of it would be introduced into an unsuitable context.[104] The many thousands of illustrations constitute one of the most valuable features of the *Recueil*, as Caylus himself appreciated;[105] but not much pleasure is to be derived from most of the dryly reproduced statuettes and vases and lamps and medals and coins and fragments of furniture. Moreover, the very timidity (rather than arrogance) of an approach based almost entirely on the publication of small objects derived from a few specialised collections was soon to appear old-fashioned and absurdly limited in scope. Nevertheless, despite basing himself on unpromising material unpromisingly presented, Caylus was able to propose (though not to develop, for he had no talent for synthesis) a great number of fresh and stimulating ideas which are of central importance to the theme of the present book. It is these only, and not his many contributions to the study of the technical aspects of the arts and other important issues, that will be discussed here.

Thus Caylus claimed that the arts 'present a picture of the morals and spirit of a century and of a nation; it is possible to deduce from them, if not actual proof, at least solid conjectures regarding history, the character of rulers, and changing systems of government'; and that a people's spirit, sometimes its very temper ('caractère de ses moeurs') can be gauged from the number, the taste or the barbarism of its artefacts.[106] In Caylus's eyes the essential aesthetic qualities of simplicity and good craftsmanship – in ancient and in modern art alike – carried with it a distinctly moral connotation: of some Greek pottery which he published he wrote that 'if these people drew such dazzling attention [*ont fait briller*] to that noble simplicity that elevates the spirit on their vases destined for ordinary day-to-day usage, what care would they not have devoted to workmanship in more precious materials?'[107] This was published in 1752, three years before Winckelmann had begun to write on the arts; but Caylus was unable to make good his more ambitious claims for the historical use of antiquarianism partly because, unlike Winckelmann, he was never able to work out a satisfying chronological frame-work within which to fit his stylistic observations, though he sometimes implied that he had done so.[108] Like everyone who had thought about the problem, he believed that very old implied very bad,[109] and that thereafter progress was a law of nature, which applied to the arts of all those civilisations whose artefacts he was collecting and trying to interpret. He also agreed with the general view that the arts had declined towards the end of the Western Empire, and to illustrate this he chose a small ivory which he believed to portray one of the later Roman emperors or proconsuls, but which is today recognised as a piece from a twelfth-century chess set which was probably made in Southern Italy (pl. 125). The causes of

125. Caylus, *Recueil*, vol. VI, Paris 1764: piece   126. Caylus, *Recueil*, vol. II, Paris 1756: gold
from a twelfth-century chess set from southern   plaque (late antique?) of figure holding a
Italy (Paris, Bibliothèque Nationale).   cornucopia.

degeneration were to be sought in a 'hectic desire for novelty . . . which makes
men attribute merit to the continuous alteration of the best things that have been
handed down', and, hence, remain blind to 'the sublime works with which Greece
and Rome itself were then still filled'.[110] This moral view was certainly inspired by
his campaign against the 'frivolous' (and very different) taste and fashions of his
own day and also by the remarkably similar notions of Scipione Maffei, which
have been mentioned earlier. But Caylus then proceeds to give a historical dimension to this moral judgement: the Romans, who had no natural gift for the arts,
had long since dominated Greece, and this had led to the destruction without trace
of the Greek schools of art, thus removing any obstacle to the depravation of taste.
He acknowledged that the 'century of Alexander the Great' had been unsurpassed
in the realm of the arts until the papacy of Leo X,[111] but he never made any
attempt to characterise its qualities, and his proposal that there had been a revival
of quality under Trajan suffers from the extreme vagueness of his one brief allusion
to the weakness of the arts that had preceded that age.[112] In fact, he gives only two
more or less precise indications of specific artistic developments: at some stage in
their history the Egyptians made a division between the two legs, hitherto joined
in rigid unity, of their statues;[113] and in the works of the later Romans feebleness
of composition precedes weakness of execution.[114]

But if Caylus was unable to determine the chronological sequence of styles and
unwilling to advance any overriding theory – 'the antiquarian should shun every

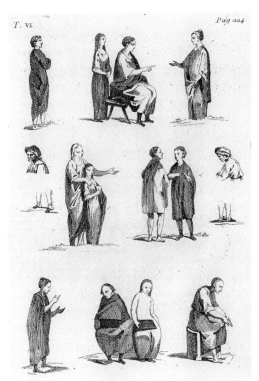

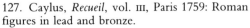

127. Caylus, *Recueil*, vol. III, Paris 1759: Roman figures in lead and bronze.

128. Caylus, *Recueil*, vol. VI, Paris 1764: reproduction of details from the frescoes found in Herculaneum.

kind of system: I look upon them as an illness of the spirit'[115] – he did, none the less, open up many avenues to attentive cultural historians.

By concentrating on the visual, Caylus was able to avoid the prevailing tendency of trying to interpret all art in the light of literary sources, often of the most recondite kind. 'The ancients', writes this passionate champion of the ancients, 'were not always great, austere, noble and serious', and he stresses that some of their small ornamental figures were much more likely to have been intended as humorous playthings than as elaborate allegories.[116] 'The arts have always been submitted to the whim of powerful patrons', writes this would-be reformer of contemporary patronage, and he uses such whims to account for the appearance of an agate vase 'lacking subtlety of design or beauty of detail'.[117] Artists, he pointed out on another occasion, when discussing an idiosyncratic Etruscan representation of Achilles engraved in intaglio on to a cornelian, are perfectly capable of interpreting subjects in their own way and they are often right to do so.[118] He acknowledged, however, that in some societies, such as that of ancient Egypt 'full of superstitions and dominated by priests', it is most unlikely that they would have been granted such freedom.[119] Elsewhere he suggests that a bronze figure of a naked woman apparently emerging from a bath was likely to be exactly that rather than a Venus, as usually assumed (pl. 127).[120]

In the later volumes of his *Receuil* Caylus increasingly recognised the novel and important truth that artistic and literary sources might well be in conflict or, rather, might well provide the historian with quite different kinds of evidence, for the artist does not (and should not) always produce merely a faithful record of what he sees:[121] Tertullian ridicules the womens' hairstyles of his day – but we do not find them carved in contemporary portrait busts; Domitian we know to have been bald – but he is not shown as such on his coins. Similarly, the artistic sources themselves needed to be carefully collated: thus the recently discovered frescoes in Herculaneum (pl. 128) made it clear that in ordinary life the Romans did not clothe themselves in the stylised draperies to be seen on their monumental sculptures, while the Greeks obviously represented their figures in a greater state of nudity than would have been usual in reality.[122] On the other hand, despite the importance he gives to stylistic analysis, Caylus does occasionally fall back on the traditional practice of allowing subject-matter alone to determine an interpretation despite stylistic evidence to the contrary. Looking at a gold plaque, representing a half-draped female figure holding a cornucopia and a sword, which he felt instinctively was 'of the late Empire, that is to say a work that dates from after the reign of Constantine' (pl. 126), he nevertheless finds himself forced by the apparently pagan subject-matter to conclude that 'despite the indications provided by the workmanship and the taste' it must have been made as far back as the time of Domitian in the late first century. He presumably chose this date because it was the last possible one before the cultural revival that he believed to have taken place before the rule of Trajan. From it he deduced that 'the Gothic taste – that taste that plunged the arts into barbarism – arose in Rome earlier than is generally believed'.[123]

From the standpoint of later historians, Caylus's most interesting contribution to the study of antique objects may well consist in the importance he assigned to trade and cultural relationships. He was particularly fascinated by works of art that revealed a mixture of national features, for they 'recall those happy or unhappy revolutions that have changed the face of the universe; those famous epochs when empires have been destroyed by other more powerful or more unjust empires and the inhabitants of differing countries been made to submit to the same domination'.[124] And as he was convinced of the overriding importance of the Egyptians as the true source of art and wisdom he continually reproached the Greeks – who were none the less 'the most agreeable nation to have inhabited the earth' – for their ingratitude in failing to acknowledge their debt to Egypt. They had even, so he claimed, gone so far as to destroy their own early artefacts in order to convey an impression of national autonomy.[125] Again and again he would detect in the style of some fragment of pottery, some terracotta figurine or bronze statuette, characteristics that demonstrated trading relations between different parts of Gaul or between Egypt and the Etruscans, Egypt and India, Egypt and China.[126]

One further example may be given of the way in which Caylus used his artistic researches to throw light on historical change. He insisted on the value of studying simple household objects as well as great and unusual monuments because they could give special insight into 'the progress and resources of the human spirit'. They illustrated, for instance, the stages whereby men had attained to those conveniences that they now enjoyed without reflexion.[127] But, as he was to point out later, observation as to how the process had taken place could lead only to a somewhat pessimistic view of history. The inventive capacity of human beings was feeble and their ability to develop such inventions as they had accidentally made were tardy in the extreme. Man himself has often tried to conceal these limitations, but the antiquarian with his ability to compare objects from many different parts of the world has been able to unmask him: what was thought to be a new invention can be shown to have been in use well before in some other society.[128]

The study of apparently insignificant objects served another purpose. By confining himself to works of great art, which were nearly always works of religious significance, the antiquarian is misled into believing that artistic styles changed only very slowly among the Greeks and Romans. Were we able to look at more of their domestic furnishings – lamps, for instance – we should discover 'a reality that is consoling to the French nation': the ancients were just as prone as we are to the lure of rapidly changing fashions.[129]

Caylus's literary style is monotonous, and although his flashes of insight are remarkable, he did not have the breadth of vision required to form them into a coherent synthesis. Moreover, too much concentration on small collectors' items leads him almost to forget the standards set by those great buildings and statues that, as a young man, he had once enthusiastically admired in Rome and amid the Greek ruins of Asia Minor. Nevertheless, from the unmethodical researches of this lonely and embittered old aristocrat opening his packing-cases with such passion and then poring with such concentration over the artefacts that had been crammed into them – artefacts, for the most part of insignificant quality, often forged and sometimes bearing no relation to what he believed them to be; artefacts that had been presented to him by friends or acquired from petty dealers or smuggled from forbidden sites – the sympathetic reader can derive a remarkably vivid impression of the ancient civilisations of the Mediterranean: their migrations and commerce and conquests; their exotic rites, customs and superstitions; their mechanical ingenuity and striving for beauty. No historian had yet conveyed these phenomena with such power; and it is only rarely that we find more than the feeblest reflections of them in the works of earlier antiquarians, even those of Montfaucon, with whose invaluable but erratic volumes Caylus was, of course, thoroughly familiar, although his own insights were almost entirely derived from the scrupulous and first-hand observation of countless specific objects. It is this observation that encouraged Caylus to make the remarkable claim (which he himself was never fully able to justify) that 'the genius of these peoples, their customs, their mentality [*la tournure de leur esprit*], if I may be allowed to use that expression, is to be understood as much in the works of sculpture and painting that have come down to us as in the books that they have left us'.[130] And it is this lesson that Caylus tried to pass on to his disciple Seroux d'Agincourt who, years later, remembered that 'he often used to repeat to me that the forms, the style and the details that can be found on tombs and mausolea can tell us about the general well-being of art at any given time and also about the condition of contemporary life'.[131]

v

In 1761, when he was already aged sixty-nine, Caylus 'devoured' the *Essai sur l'étude de la littérature*, the earliest publication of Edward Gibbon,[132] which contained a flattering reference to him and which had been shrewdly sent to him by the author on the advice of his father and friends.[133] Gibbon was then twenty-four, and he had come across the works of Caylus three or four years earlier when, in a step that was to prove crucial for his intellectual development, he had 'exchanged a bank-note of twenty pounds for the twenty volumes of the Memoirs of the Academy of Inscriptions'.[134] He was not altogether impressed by what he read – Caylus's observations were 'without any plan, too minute, and sometimes, when stripped of their technical dress, injudicious'[135] – but when he went to Paris in 1763, he called on Caylus three or four times and was warmly received. Nevertheless, despite the kindness with which he was welcomed, he was again somewhat disappointed. He had hoped to find in the comte de Caylus 'a combination of man of letters and gentleman of quality', but 'he gets up late in the morning, spends the whole day visiting artists' studios, then gets back home at six in the evening, puts on his dressing gown and shuts himself up in his study. What a way of seeing one's friends!'[136]

Gibbon's attitude to most of the antiquarians who have been mentioned in these pages was somewhat guarded, but he studied them carefully,[137] and the reservations he felt about their work taught him how to break free from the intellectual caution that had so restricted their contributions to the interpretation of history as a dynamic process. Of Muratori he made the pertinent comment that although he was more than a 'simple Erudit', he had failed to draw from his own researches the fullest conclusions possible for illuminating the history, geography and economic conditions of the century he was investigating.[138] Later, when discussing the rule of the Goths in Italy, Gibbon noted that, as an Italian noble, Maffei exaggerated their injustice, while 'the plebeian Muratori crouches under their oppression'.[139] Of all the Italians who had renewed the study of the Middle Ages, only Giannone won his whole-hearted enthusiasm. He was to claim, towards the end of his life, that the *Civil History of Naples* had been one of the 'particular books [that] . . . may have remotely contributed to form the historian of the Roman Empire' and that from it he had learned of 'the progress and abuse of sacerdotal power'.[140] It also seems likely that he intuitively understood the part that may have been played by artistic monuments in giving substance to Giannone's theories in this respect. As a young man of eighteen Gibbon, who had been sent by his father to Lausanne to be 'cured' of his Catholicism, went on a tour of Switzerland. During the course of this he visited the great Benedictine abbey of Einsiedeln not far from Zurich which was one of the most important centres of Catholic pilgrimage and which not long before had been rebuilt by Caspar Moosbrugger and very lavishly (but rather heavy-handedly) decorated by a succession of sculptors, painters and stuccoists. Gibbon – who had never seen any example of Central European Baroque – recorded how powerful was the effect it made on him.[141] More than thirty years later, when writing his *Memoirs*, he still recalled the 'deep and lasting impression' of his visit, and it is surely significant that the page on which he discussed Einsiedeln follows immediately his reference to Giannone and the 'progress and abuse of sacerdotal power'. Moreover, he now recorded, as he had not done in his original account, that 'I was astonished by the profuse ostentation of riches in the poorest corner of Europe: amidst a savage scene of woods and mountains, a palace appears to have been erected by magic and it *was* erected by the potent magic of religion'.[142]

After gazing at the *Venus de' Medici* in the Tribuna of the Uffizi in July 1764, Gibbon noted that he had heard it spoken of 'ever since my cradle: books, conversations, engravings, copies had placed it before my eyes a thousand times'.[143] Indeed, although he was a conscientious sightseer in France and Switzerland, there is little doubt that it was in Italy that his enthusiasm for painting and sculpture became insatiable:[144] he visited the Uffizi fourteen times, and he made very extensive notes on what he saw in most of the towns he passed through. His taste was orthodox enough – Correggio, Guido Reni, the principal antiquities – but his approach differed significantly from that of most previous travellers, some of whose accounts of Italy he carried with him. He became more and more interested in the possibilities available to the artist for expressing the emotions, and this inevitably led to his thinking hard about the conventions of narrative painting. To the modern reader (as perhaps to the eighteenth-century connoisseur) Gibbon's obsession with these issues may sometimes appear insensitive and unduly 'literary', but it is most unlikely that artists themselves would have misunderstood or even resented the attention he paid to the communication of feelings. Should not, he asked, the figures fleeing in a picture of *The Flood* attributed to Domenichino show a variety of different emotions rather than merely that of fear, represented in a variety of different ways? Would not Veronese have done better in his *Judith with the Head of Holofernes* to have depicted his heroine accompanied not by a negro slave, capable of revealing only 'stupid amazement' at what had happened, but by a Jewish confidante who 'would have shared Judith's joy at the same time as fear and horror, while some remains of pity would have made a contrast with the obstinate and inflexible zeal of her mistress'?[145]

Occasionally Gibbon also tried to relate the varied architectural monuments he saw to the nature of the societies in which they had been created; thus he found the style of Pisa cathedral to be that of a business community on account of its curious jumble of misunderstood features.[146] But it was, inevitably, in the field of antique art that his speculations were most fruitful, even though he had probably not yet conceived his *History of the Decline and Fall of the Roman Empire*.

Gibbon was as fascinated as Montesquieu had been by the sequence of busts and statues of the Roman emperors and other great figures of antiquity to be seen in the galleries of the Uffizi, and he, too, experienced there 'a very lively pleasure' at following the 'progress and decadence of the arts'.[147] He was, in fact, already familiar with this pleasure (though he had then admitted that it might better be described as sadness) through having been shown a year earlier the medal cabinet of the King of France by the Abbé Barthélemy, the most famous numismatist of the day.[148] And, like Montesquieu, Gibbon was so convinced of the inexorable laws that governed 'the progress and decadence of the arts' that he was prepared to challenge those attributions and identifications that did not comply with them. Thus of a bust in the Uffizi said to represent Sappho, which had been accepted without demur by the French connoisseur Cochin (whose *Voyage en Italie* he carried with him), Gibbon noted that 'sculpture was in too imperfect a state in the 6th century before Christ for us to be able to consider the head of this celebrated woman as an original. I am inclined to believe this even less because Sappho, who sparkled more on account of her wit than her beauty, certainly did not have the beautiful oval face, slightly rounded by plumpness, which this sculptor has given her.'[149]

This combination of literal-mindedness and sophistication appears again and again during the course of Gibbon's close study of the arts in Italy. It is a combination that makes it evident that he could have used some of his observations to telling effect had he decided to call on them when writing his history a few years later; and yet it also helps to explain why he did not do so and why the figurative arts do not play much more of a role in the *Decline and Fall of the Roman Empire* than they do in Montesquieu's *Considérations sur la grandeur des romains et de leur décadence*. For the more Gibbon looked at the arts the more sceptical he became about their value as historical evidence.

Although he realised that on grounds of style the bust of 'Sappho' he was shown in the Uffizi could not be an original or authentic portrait of the Greek poetess – it is now believed to be a late and feeble derivation from the *Aphrodite* of Phidias[150] – Gibbon was, very reasonably, as unsure of his own judgment as he was of that of most of his contemporaries concerning the physical condition of the ancient sculptures he saw in Italy. Towards the end of his eleventh visit to the Grand Duke's gallery he found himself forced to admit that not only were most of the statues of indifferent quality, but that 'one does not even have the pure satisfaction of living with the ancients', for the majority of pieces had been broken or mutilated and then so drastically restored that 'one can boldly say that of all the attributes which appear to characterise the gods or men only very few are not modern'.[151] As a result, 'the writer is always afraid of building whole systems based on the caprice of some modern sculptor'. This is a risk to which he may have been alerted by Caylus, but he was in any case being too generous. Most writers had no such inhibitions, and he himself pointed out that even the antiquarian Anton Francesco Gori, whose illustrated volumes on the Grand Duke's collections he had once so admired but which he now thought not to have been written in good faith, often squandered his erudition on explaining or justifying the wild imagination of some Florentine artisan.[152]

It was not only style and fanciful restoration that presented problems to the historian. Gibbon understood that the identification of portrait busts had necessarily to be based on the study of inscribed coins and medals. He himself had devoted

130 (above). Head of Agrippa on bronze *as* issued by Caligula.

129. Raphael, *Pope Julius II* (London, National Gallery).

many hours to reading Addison and especially Spanheim before embarking on his Italian journey,[153] and, once in Italy, he made the ingenious suggestion that a drawer containing relevant coins should be inserted into the pedestal of each bust so as to enable the visitor to come to his own conclusions concerning the reliability of the identification proposed.[154] But a far more vexing question remained. Even supposing that a portrait did present a true likeness – as could be assumed in the case of those to be seen on coins and medals – what, if anything, could this tell one about the character of the man or woman whose features were recorded? The question had first struck him in Modena, a month or so before he began to visit the Uffizi with such assiduity. Looking at a bronze coin which portrayed Marcus Agrippa (pl. 130), the powerful collaborator of Augustus in establishing the Roman Empire, Gibbon noted: 'I believed that I could read in the features of Agrippa those qualities of frankness, grandeur and simplicity which characterised this respectable man: but observations of this kind, although they have been sanctioned by Addison, strike me as very hollow. Is it so common for a man's soul to be legible in his features? I would like to hear of some ignorant person who, on being shown a head of Nero, would exclaim "There's a scoundrel!" It is so easy for the scholar who already knows that he was one.'[155] In this case, the issue was made more complicated by the fact that Gibbon was by no means convinced that Nero had been such a scoundrel as was usually claimed.[156]

Gibbon did not find it easy to abandon the more simplistic methods used in the investigation of character, but few of his predecessors, since the days of Addison, and almost none of his successors, have even made the attempt. Very soon after his sudden insight in the medal cabinet of Modena, he commented on the portrait of Julius II in the Uffizi, which was then believed to be by Raphael himself, that 'the soul of this proud and ambitious pope is painted on the canvas (pl. 129). I see there all the brusque violence of the patron of Michelangelo and the inflexible grandeur of the old man who dared to drive the victorious French from Italy'. And then he pulled himself up short: 'I contradict my own maxim – but this seems to be an exception.'[157] Some of the Roman heads in the Grand Duke's gallery also tempted him along this direction: had he not 'already known' of the merits of Vespasian, would he have found his expression 'cheerful, tranquil and majestic. His is really a human face and though he is more ugly than handsome, he is good and interesting. I am convinced that the resemblance is a striking one'[158] On the whole, however, Gibbon was cautious in making such judgments: the 'mocking smile' that he detected in the bust of Trajan[159] does not appear to correspond to any trait derived from literary sources, and when he came to the bust of Caracalla, by which most visitors claimed to be terrified,[160] he noted only that it was 'good, but it strikes me as a little dry', for by now sculpture was declining alongside architecture.[161]

Thus in his personal notes (for these comments were not intended for publication) Gibbon showed himself to be extremely well informed about the visual arts, but very doubtful about their value for the historian, even though he had once thought of Etruscan monuments and those of Herculaneum as 'two new methods of erudition'.[162] It is the scepticism that is chiefly apparent to the reader of the *Decline and Fall of the Roman Empire*.

In a celebrated phrase Gibbon was to claim that the initial inspiration for that book – whose original scope was to be circumscribed to the decay of the City, rather than of the Empire – had sprung in part from a visual experience,[163] and in his final chapter he evoked an even more powerful vision when he recalled how 'in the last days of Pope Eugenius the Fourth, two of his servants, the learned Poggius and a friend, ascended the Capitoline hill; reposed themselves among the ruins of columns and temples; and viewed from that commanding spot the wide and various prospect of desolation'.[164] In seeking to account for that desolation, Gibbon turned primarily to an essay he had read before visiting the city which laid the blame far more on the popes than on the 'barbarian invaders',[165] and he then proceeded to castigate the modern Romans for their equally culpable neglect or desecration of what had still remained intact even in Poggio's day. As an example of this deplorable state of affairs Gibbon repeated a story, which was by then well known,[166] concerning a statue said to be of Pompey, ten feet in length, which had been found (in the middle of the sixteenth century) 'under a partition-wall; the equitable judge had pronounced, that the head should be separated from the body to satisfy the claims of the contiguous owners; and the sentence would have been executed, if the intercession of a cardinal, and the liberality of a pope, had not rescued the Roman hero from the hands of his barbarous countrymen'.[167]

In retelling this story, however, Gibbon fails to note that when, many years earlier, he had been to the Palazzo Spada to see this gigantic nude statue, with one arm outstretched and the other holding an orb, he had concluded that it was most unlikely that it represented Pompey.[168] And on the very rare occasions that he draws on the evidence of the visual arts to substantiate his history, he invariably relies on written sources (as he was to do when referring to the sculptures on the Arch of Constantine); and where the implications of such sources seem to conflict with the point that he wants to make, it is the visual evidence that is sacrificed. A striking instance in which both these approaches are combined concerns his treatment of the palace of Diocletian at Spalato. Gibbon, who had never seen this, describes it in some detail, basing his account on that of 'an ingenious artist of our own time and country whom a very liberal curiosity carried into the heart of Dalmatia'.[169] This was Robert Adam who, after several days of rough sea journey from Venice, had arrived at Spalato on 22 July 1757, accompanied by Charles-Louis Clérisseau and two other draughtsmen, in order to be able to record a private Roman residence which would complement all the public monuments – temples, amphitheatres and baths – being published during these years. As they entered the grand bay and sailed slowly towards the harbour they were faced with a spectacle that was 'not only pictoresque but magnificent'.[170] The huge fortified country residence, some nine and a half acres in extent,[171] which had been prepared for Diocletian's retirement at the beginning of the fourth century had, some eight hundred years later, been gradually converted into a mediaeval trading city and was now under Venetian rule. Towering over its massive bulwarks and long colonnaded sea wall was an elegant campanile adjoining the cathedral which had once been the mausoleum of the last great persecutor of the Christians; houses had been built upon the old foundations, 'and modern works are so intermingled with the ancient, as to be scarcely distinguishable';[172] huge blocks of fallen masonry and bas-reliefs formed convenient supports for inhabitants and visitors – in tasselled fez or turban – who assembled there to barter goods or to lounge in the shade.

Adam and his companions spent five weeks in Spalato, drawing and measuring those extensive remains that had survived more or less intact and reconstructing in their imaginations those that were in ruins or that had totally disappeared. The general appearance of the palace had long been vaguely familiar to interested scholars; it was – as Adam pointed out – not necessary 'to traverse desarts or to expose [oneself] to the insults of barbarians' in order to see it;[173] but – as he also emphasised – it had never been properly recorded, and the fact that his own work was interrupted because he was suspected of spying demonstrates that his project was not without difficulties.

It was not until 1764 that Adam, who had long since returned to England, was able (through the support of several hundred subscribers, headed by the king and queen) to publish what Gibbon described as a 'magnificent work', the splendidly illustrated *Ruins of the Palace of the Emperor Diocletian at Spalatro in Dalmatia*. In his preface he referred to the objections that were likely to be raised against the volume, by acknowledging that before the reign of Diocletian there had been a 'visible decline of Architecture, as well as of the other arts'. None the less, he continued, Diocletian's 'munificence had revived a taste in Architecture superior to that of his own times, and had formed artists capable of imitating, with no inconsiderable success, the stile and manner of a purer age'.[174]

Winckelmann, who had seen the manuscript of the book and had discussed the preface with Robert's brother James, agreed with this conclusion and may even have inspired it.[175] In his own *History of the Art of Antiquity*, which appeared just before the *Ruins*, he referred to Adam's book and went out of his way to point out that architecture had escaped the degeneration that had afflicted painting and sculpture towards the end of the third century AD.[176] Gibbon, however, had devoted some of his most eloquent pages to emphasising the new 'ostentation of splendour and luxury' that had been introduced by Diocletian and that was based on 'the stately magnificence of the court of Persia': sumptuous robes of silk and gold, shoes studded with the most precious gems, the jealous vigilance of

131. Robert Adam, *Ruins of the Palace of the Emperor Diocletian*, 1764: view of the peristyle of the palace.

eunuchs . . . It was not easy to reconcile this with Diocletian's supposed encourage-ment of 'the stile and manner of a purer age', and Gibbon therefore found it necessary to discredit the evidence provided by Adam's reproductions and his text. To counter the first he slyly suggested that 'there is room to suspect, that the elegance of his designs and engraving has somewhat flattered the objects which it was their purpose to represent' (pl. 131); while to refute Adam's written claims, Gibbon declared that 'we are informed by a more recent and very judicious traveller, that the awful ruins of Spalato are not less expressive of the decline of the arts, than of the greatness of the Roman empire in the time of Diocletian'.[177] The traveller in question was the Abate Alberto Fortis, a Venetian polymath whose interests lay above all in geology and botany. In his *Viaggio in Dalmatia*, which attracted attention throughout Europe principally through its rhapsodic account, clearly written under the influence of Rousseau, of the customs of the wild, nomadic Morlachs, Fortis went out of his way to disclaim any specific interest in art. When describing Spalato, he did no more than refer to 'the work of Mr Adams, who has bestowed much on these proud ruins through the usual elegance of his pencil and burin'. But he could not refrain from insisting that, although the palace was among the most respectable monuments to survive from antiquity and that he did not want to detract from its merits, too close a study of it would none the less be damaging to architects and sculptors because 'in general the crudity of the carving and the bad taste of the times rival the magnificence of the building'.[178] It was by making very selective use of this passage that Gibbon set out to negate the evidence of Robert Adam, who had spent five weeks inspecting and illustrating the palace (but who, of course, had his own motives for exaggerating its qualities and who was at times prepared to adjust the visual evidence accordingly), in order to create a more consistent image of Diocletian.

vi

Many years later Gibbon's insinuations about the misleading nature of Adam's plates were repeated by two of the most important and influential writers to discuss the decline of the arts during the late Roman Empire and early Middle Ages. The illustrations of the volume devoted to the palace of Diocletian, wrote the French antiquarian Seroux d'Agincourt, 'give a fine, but perhaps too fine, idea of this architecture', and he proceeded to turn Adam's claims upside down by discussing the palace – which he had never seen for himself and which was known to him only through the plates whose accuracy he was belittling – as an example of the very degeneration that Adam (and Winckelmann) had denied. 'It is thus evident,' he wrote, 'that the corruption of art must be dated from before the time of Constantine. The vices we have just noted in the construction of Spalato can leave us in no doubt about this. This building presents dissonances of all kinds – a discordant mixture of columns of granite, porphyry and marble; of columns, whose shafts are of these materials and whose bases of something different; and finally of bas-reliefs whose subjects have been chosen without judgement or taste.

If artistic incompetence is to be seen in the execution of the decoration of the Arch of Constantine, it is just as apparent in the excess and the ponderousness of accessories to be found in architecture before the reign of that prince.'[179]

At much the same time Count Leopoldo Cicognara, the Italian historian of sculpture, wrote that

> the arts do not make progress or go into decline by leaps and bounds: they would not have been in such a ruinous state during the rule of Constantine had they not already shown signs of significant decay under Diocletian. By this I mean to propose that the work by Mr Adams on the ruins of Spalato ought to make this decadence rather more evident, since it fully and faithfully bears witness to the grandeur and magnificence of Diocletian's palace. Everyone seems to see in this work a great deal of better taste than there should be in a building of this period, and it may be that the modern artist who made the drawings of it has not been able to free himself from this impression.[180]

Both Seroux d'Agincourt, whose ambition it was to continue Winckelmann's history of art into the Middle Ages and beyond, and Cicognara, who aimed to produce a sequel to Winckelmann and Seroux alike by writing an account of sculpture from 'its resurgence in Italy until the century of Napoleon', were greatly affected by the narrative (as well as the erudition) of Gibbon. It was Gibbon who helped them to overcome the 'minutiae and lack of plan' by which he himself had been so dispirited in the researches of Caylus – the other figure who (with Winckelmann) stands behind both of them. Thus, just as Gibbon's *Decline and Fall* had been nourished by the works of antiquarians such as Maffei and Muratori, so now he in turn was able to provide the intellectual framework for a new generation of antiquarians who, partly under his inspiration, succeeded in becoming true historians. But it is also very tempting to trace in Seroux's *Histoire de l'art par les monumens, depuis sa décadence au IVe siècle jusqu'à son renouvellement au XVIe* some indication of the sort of material that Gibbon himself might have explored had he not felt inhibited by a well-justified reluctance to trust his own judgement when looking at painting or sculpture.

Such reluctance was quite alien to Seroux who had absorbed from Caylus the notion (which was then almost surprising) that when studying the history of art it was essential to give absolute primacy to the work of art itself: 'the productions of the arts of design,' he declares at the beginning of his six giant folio volumes, 'that is of Architecture, Sculpture and Painting, consist of objects . . . that are perceived through the sense of sight, and it is only through that organ that they make their impact on the soul; and this means that one must write of these arts or study their history only if one has their varied productions under one's eyes.'[181] In fact, such an aim was far too ambitious. Most of Seroux's observations were based not on the objects themselves (or, at best, only on distant memories of some of them) but on the thousands of drawings he commissioned from copyists in many different parts of Europe. He had these drawings engraved, and he tried, as far as possible, to ensure that the style of the original work of art was reflected in his reproduction of it.

It was as a repertoire of images – images not just of small terracottas or vases or figurines, but of mosaics, fresco cycles and cathedrals – that Seroux's book was chiefly valuable, and this not only was recognised by himself and his contemporaries but was also responsible for its retaining its importance for mediaeval historians of all kinds for at least a century. Until the illustrations published by him, much of the period covered by his volumes had been, in Seroux's own words, 'like an immense desert, in which one sees only disfigured objects, scattered fragments'.[182]

Seroux's route to that desert was a strange and surprising one.[183] Born into a noble family in 1730, he had become a successful *fermier général* of wide interests and had forged contacts with Voltaire, Buffon, Rousseau, Marmontel and many other leading writers and *philosophes*. He was an *habitué* of Mme Geoffrin's salon and a lover of the arts – the art of Boucher (by whom he owned a superb collection of drawings) and of Fragonard and Hubert Robert (with whom he was to be on friendly terms). In England he visited the celebrated collection of antiquities that had been assembled by Charles Townley at his London house, and he was warmly received at Strawberry Hill by Horace Walpole who encouraged him to look at Gothic cathedrals. Could this have been the turning point? He certainly took Walpole's advice when he went to the Low Countries and Northern Germany, but it is by no means clear whether he had already decided to devote himself to the study of late antique and mediaeval art before he embarked on what he had intended to be a conventional tour of Italy in 1778.[184] However, by the time he got to Bologna he had apparently formed the project in his mind. In November 1779 he reached Rome, and he never left the city thereafter except for short visits to the surroundings and to Naples, Pompeii and Paestum. He died in 1814 at the age of eighty-four.

The first volume of the *History of the Decline and Fall of the Roman Empire* appeared in 1776 and the second and third followed in 1781. Seroux d'Agincourt could have met Gibbon, who was seven years younger but already famous, either in London or in Paris. It is, however, unlikely that he did so because he never mentions such a meeting, despite the fact that he often alludes to historians, men of letters and artists who were personally known to him and despite the fact that there are many references to Gibbon's *Decline and Fall* in his own volumes. In one of his first chapters he announces that 'two men of great distinction have written about the decadence of the Roman Empire: Montesquieu and Gibbon . . . It is with the aid of these guides that I shall try to discern which, among the general causes of that decadence, are those particularly relevant to the arts'.[185] Seroux relies on both men (and also on Muratori) very heavily indeed – sometimes to the point of paraphrasing them – in the historical narrative embracing the political, civil and religious background with which he thought it essential to introduce his subject if the reader was not to be 'bored and even disgusted'.[186] Towards the end of his long life, however, when his book was at last on the point of appearing, after having been delayed for more than twenty years because of the impact on his finances of the French Revolution, Seroux was dismayed to discover that many younger people were not at all bored or disgusted. They were positively enthusiastic about the 'primitive' art to which he had introduced them.

Although Seroux had written his book partly as a warning against the prospect of a new decline and fall, it is not entirely surprising that this part of his intention was misunderstood, because the introductory political narrative was badly conceived. It was too detached both from the general chapters on the arts and from his analyses of individual works. Much of the text conveys the impression that, unlike his mentor Caylus, Seroux based his ideas of artistic decadence not on the works of art themselves but on some preconceived schema, derived. from Montesquieu, Winckelmann, Gibbon and other earlier writers. This impression is misleading. Seroux sought to have careful illustrations made of each single development in the history of art which he discussed in his text. In particular, he went out of his way to provide comparative material of a kind that was new to art history, so that we may find on the same plate a mediaeval mosaic and a Roman bas-relief or a series of architectural details arranged in sequence in order to represent the gradual stages of decay.[187] Moreover, he often rejected notions that had been, and sometimes still were, current: he did not, for instance, share the enthusiasm of Winckelmann for the patronage of the Emperor Hadrian whose eclectic tastes, he thought, led him dangerously close to decadence, despite occasional successes in restoring the arts to their earlier grandeur.[188] Above all, in challenging the theory that the general decay of the arts had been brought about either by the Christians or by the barbarians ('nos grands ancêtres'), he insists, with proud and self-conscious pedantry, that judgements can be guided only by a scrupulous regard to chronology.[189] From this he appears to conclude that the earlier phases of decadence had been prompted by the bad taste of individual emperors, and that by the time of the barbarian invasions the process had acquired such momentum that not even the cultivated rule of the Goths and then the Lombards had been able to arrest it: such a proposal had, as he acknowledged,[190] already been suggested by Muratori, though not with any specific reference to the visual arts.

Seroux d'Agincourt was an assiduous frequenter of the catacombs – and a dangerous one, for he caused much damage by trying to remove frescoes from the walls.[191] He claimed to be the first observer to study them from an aesthetic, rather than an exclusively historical, point of view; seen in this way, the mural paintings could not appear other than grotesque: 'the standing figures, rigid and isolated, bear no relation to each other; all the objects are disconnected; the heads are shapeless; the drawing is devoid of all rules and has no expression – or ridiculous expression: everything demonstrates that art was destroying itself to its very foundations'.[192] And yet, as Seroux writes in some remarkable passages which are not unlike those of Chateaubriand (whose raptures he admired), the catacombs made a profound impression on him (pl. 132).[193] How could he reconcile his outraged taste with his genuine sense of reverence? Like others before him, he found the task a difficult one, and his ingenious proposals often seem to contradict each other. During the times of the persecutions, he writes,[194] the frightened and sheltering Christians were hardly in a position to pay much attention to the

132. Seroux d'Agincourt, *Histoire de l'art par les monumens*, Paris 1823, vol. III, pl. IX: Seroux d'Agincourt meditating in the catacombs.

arts, and this accounts for the wretched productions to be found in the catacombs; later, when Christianity was officially recognised by the State, the fervour that had earlier been responsible for so much care being taken to decorate the tombs of the first martyrs, grew feebler and feebler, 'so that although it cannot be clearly proved that the decadence of art gives a measure of the decadence of that zeal felt by the faithful for the embellishment of the catacombs, it cannot be denied that they did at least go hand in hand'.[195]

Gibbon might well have expressed himself with some irony about these cautious and confusing manoeuvres made by a scholar who claimed to look to him for guidance, but Seroux d'Agincourt had, in any case, made use of the *Decline and Fall* above all as a quarry for the facts he needed. Leopoldo Cicognara, on the other hand, was far more aware of the implications of Gibbon's ideas and general attitude.

Cicognara met Seroux soon after leaving his native Ferrara for Rome in 1788 as a young man of twenty one; he found him 'piuttosto vecchio',[196] but although Seroux was indeed thirty-seven years older, he acted as a guide to the studies that Cicognara pursued intermittently during a period of his life devoted primarily to painting and worldly pleasure. The Revolution precipitated him into politics. He sympathised with its early stages and, although horrified by the execution of Louis XVI, he collaborated actively with the various regimes established in Italy by the invading French armies. He himself spent much time in France where he met Bonaparte, to whom in 1808 he dedicated his treatise *Il Bello*. In that same year he was persuaded by his close friend, the man of letters Pietro Giordani, to embark on a history of sculpture (which eventually emerged as almost a joint work); and he then again came into close contact with 'quel buon vecchio di d'Agincourt',[197] many of whose ideas he was to incorporate directly into his own book. After the defeat of France he was treated with some suspicion and even occasional hostility by the Austrian authorities in Venice, where since 1808 he had mainly lived after being appointed President of the Venetian Academy. He was also viewed with considerable distrust by the rulers of those restored regimes that he had once wished to see overthrown. Because of this, the Gibbonian influences on his approach to art can most easily be detected in the first volume of his history which was published in 1813 under the comparatively liberal rule of Eugène de Beauharnais. Indeed, it is from Cicognara's troubles with the censorship over the preparation of a second edition in 1824 that we gain a particularly interesting insight into his whole attitude.

Censors are usually ultra-sensitive and not often intelligent, but the various officials who pointed to heresy and subversion in this apparently innocuous history of sculpture could be sharp enough. 'Is this Cicognara speaking or a new resuscitated Gibbon?', opens one typical comment which continues as follows: 'About this passage I must observe that the author nearly always speaks of the Christian religion in terms of fanaticism and superstition'.[198]

The ideas of three philosophically inclined historians particularly affected Cicognara's approach to art. From the baron d'Hancarville and Charles Dupuis he derived above all the notion that, far from being unique, both Christianity itself and the imagery it encouraged were intimately related to exotic Eastern cults and perhaps even stolen from them: the censors deplored his allusions to Indian pagodas and Persian beliefs as being 'as gratuitous as they are malicious'.[199] And from Gibbon he learned to treat the early Church with oblique but mocking contempt and to put the worst possible construction on all it motives. 'I would like to ask the author', commented the censor when he came across Cicognara's sceptical views on the sculpture of Christ said to have been commissioned by the woman who had been cured of the issue of blood (pl. 78), 'why he prefers the conjectures of Gibbon and Beausobre, whom he praises as profound philosophers, to the authority of Eusebius, father of the Church and of criticism, in order to deny the existence of a statue of our Saviour? Could it be because they are the enemies of Religion? And in any case what can be the logic for adopting the conjectures of authors who belong to our own times and omitting the narrative of a contemporary?'[200]

The very nature of these objections will have made it clear that Cicognara had undertaken what was in many ways a more ambitious project than that of Seroux: as he implied in his 'Preliminary Discourse', his was to be a cultural history as much as a history of styles, in which the intrinsic nature and varying purposes of sculpture were to be explored against the social background. Thus when Cicognara came to his chapters on Canova – who played the same role as culminating hero in his history as Michelangelo (about whose achievement he felt considerable hesitation) had done in Vasari's *Lives* – he wrote to the artist to ask him for his memories of early patrons and other influences on his younger days.[201] From these and from many different sources he eventually produced a remarkable survey of the European cultural scene during the second half of the eighteenth century, which led him to discuss the varying roles played by (among others) Alfieri and Sir William Hamilton, Haydn and Beethoven.

For all his wider interests Cicognara was, like Caylus and Seroux d'Agincourt, in no doubt about the crucial importance of direct personal contact with objects themselves and about the need to provide good and plentiful illustrations, difficult though this was. In the later sections of his book Cicognara did indeed show himself to be a most careful and sensitive observer, but before he reached works of art that appealed to him, he, too, had to account for the decline and fall of Roman art, and here he based himself on general principles more than on specific examples. Nevertheless, he introduced into his discussion many ideas drawn from the experiences of his own lifetime. Decline dated from some not very well defined period of the later Empire – for, despite all their admiration and occasional criticism of Winckelmann, neither Seroux nor Cicognara really grasped the full significance of stylistic analysis as an aid to chronology. The elevation of innumerable statues to figures wholly unworthy of the honour had degraded talent, and the inhabitants of the mild and delicious countryside of Campania had failed to provide sculptors with that 'excitement that springs from glory'.[202] And he returned to this issue when he came to consider what was evidently for him the similar decadence of the eighteenth century. The effects of war and the ambitions of speculative builders[203] (another cause about which Cicognara felt deeply in the wake of the French invasions) had done serious damage; but although 'it is enough to see a broken column or a mutilated statue or the fragments of a vase for even the little children in Rome to repeat, "That is what has been done by those Gothic barbarians"', it was quite misleading to put the blame for destruction mainly on foreign invaders.[204] Theodoric, for instance, had often gone out of his way to preserve the monuments of the past. And – to the indignation of the censors – Cicognara repeated Gibbon's 'odious and malicious' opinion that the sack of Rome by the Goths had been insignificant compared to that carried out by 'Charles V, a Catholic prince and Emperor of the Romans'.[205]

It is, however, when he comes to the part played by the Christians that Cicognara deploys the weapon of Gibbonian irony to most telling effect by congratulating the Emperor Constantine on his religious tolerance and his patronage of pagan art: 'the same hand that raised so many basilicas to the true God was also generous in beautifying and restoring the temples of the gods in Rome; and the medals that were issued by his imperial mint carried the images and attributes of Jove, Apollo, Mars and Hercules, while through the apotheosis of his father Constantius he added a new deity to Mount Olympus'.[206] It is true that by removing statues to his new capital in the East, Constantine was later to cause fatal damage to the patrimony of Rome, but the more serious decadence was due to his own absence from the city and to the privileges that he granted to the Christians, followed by the divisions that grew up between the Greek and Latin churches, invasions, sectarianism and endless civil strife. However, final destruction came long afterwards, and in another passage that irritated the censors[207] Cicognara returned to the old (and by now discredited) claim that

> St Gregory carried his zeal so far as to have thrown into the Tiber all [pagan] monuments against which he could inveigh, even those in private possession, and that same tolerance that the Christians had once implored for their own customs was now being denied by them to others. And thus it will hardly seem strange that the austere and strange morality of those times aimed to discourage the arts and to close the workshops (to whose fame idolatry had made so great a contribution), and that anyone who cultivated, or even merely owned, some object of this kind, was looked upon as sacrilegious.[208]

As evidence of this 'austere and strange morality' Cicognara alluded to (and, according to the censor, misinterpreted) that very same passage in Tertullian about the aversion of the early Christians to artistic excellence – because of its association with paganism – art that had been used nearly a century earlier by Filippo Buonarroti, when he had sought to explain the crudity of the glass objects found in the catacombs by stressing the piety that had driven the faithful to employ unskilled craftsmen.

Cicognara remained a figure from the Enlightenment and some of his best writing (produced during a time of reaction) was prompted by the irreverent vitality of his anti-clerical convictions. The indignation of the censors is easy enough to understand. What they could not grasp (or, naturally, care about) is the fact that it was his supreme achievement to combine antiquarianism of a very high order with great aesthetic sensitivity, and at the same time to produce a coherent narrative based on an understanding of the principles of up-to-date 'philosophical' history. He did not, as Winckelmann had done, establish the history of art on an entirely new basis, but he did demonstrate – more than anyone else before him – how much art history had to gain from a thoughtful understanding of 'conventional' history. This was, perhaps, a prerequisite for the recognition (which had not yet fully dawned) by 'conventional' historians of how much they might gain from an understanding of art history.

The Birth of Cultural History

i

A few years before beginning to work on the *Decline and Fall of the Roman Empire* Gibbon had toyed with the idea of writing about the age of the Medici, which had been singled out by Voltaire as one of the four great peaks of European civilisation. He soon gave up the idea, but it is interesting (although, in view of Voltaire's claims, not altogether surprising) that a very similar notion had in 1759 already occurred to William Robertson, who had preceded Gibbon as a British 'philosophical' historian with a European reputation. Robertson's *History of Scotland* had been a phenomenal success, and wondering what field to embark on next, he considered writing an account of the age of Leo X. He seems, however, to have been deterred by a letter from David Hume, who very pertinently asked 'how can you acquire knowledge of the great works of sculpture, architecture and painting, by which that age was chiefly distinguished?'[1] Pertinently, but surprisingly, for the age of Leo X had hitherto been more celebrated for the revival of letters than for the splendour of the visual arts that flourished during the course of it, and it is most unlikely that any earlier historian would have felt inhibited by an objection of this nature. Indeed, Robertson himself wrote his celebrated first volume of *The History of the Reign of Charles V* (on which he embarked instead) without including a single reference to the visual arts, despite the fact that he called it 'A view of the Progress of Society in Europe, from the subversion of the Roman Empire, to the beginning of the sixteenth century'.

The fact that Hume also managed to steer clear of the arts in his *History of England* is, of course, less remarkable; none the less, his few discouraging words to Robertson are of great significance for, by implying that there were certain periods that could not be adequately discussed without taking account of the visual arts, they indicate how decisively the concept of historical writing had changed in recent years. To a large extent – even if somewhat indirectly – this change was due to the ambitious claims staked out for history by Voltaire.

Voltaire's precept that the study of history could be of philosophical value only if it concentrated on the worthwhile achievements of humanity – its laws and arts and sciences, above all – rather than on the essentially trivial ambitions of kings and courtiers was to be very influential. However, his own actual practice as an historian can sometimes leave those who take that precept to heart feeling rather perplexed. In *Le Siècle de Louis XIV*, in the *Essai sur les moeurs* and elsewhere Voltaire makes clear his belief that, in principle, the visual arts, as much as literature and the sciences, constitute a gauge for testing the quality of a civilisation. If the ages of Alexander the Great, of the early Roman Empire and of the fifteenth and sixteenth centuries in Italy had preceded that of Louis XIV as the only three peaks attained by humanity, the credit was due – as he acknowledged – to Apelles, Phidias and Praxiteles, to Vitruvius, Michelangelo and Palladio, as well as to Plato, Virgil, Horace and the scholars employed by the Medici. Indeed, one of the reasons he gives for not honouring the age of François Ier as highly as the ones he singles out for special distinction is precisely the fact that the king had had to rely on Italian, rather than on French, architects and painters.[2] Yet it soon becomes apparent that what interests Voltaire the historian is merely the presence (or absence) of the arts at any given period and not the actual nature of those arts.

Such an attitude was not new. Biographers and local historians had, ever since the late Middle Ages, given credit to individual patrons and individual cities (sometimes the very ones singled out by Voltaire) for the arts that had flourished under their auspices; and some of them had done so with a more acute perception of what had been achieved than Voltaire was to show. Voltaire's innovation was to convert into a yardstick for the measurement of civilisation in general what had hitherto been looked upon as particular, even if highly desirable, additions to the more essential qualities of military prowess or efficient government or pious munificence or princely virtue.

We can appreciate this if we compare his views with those of two French historians of an older generation who both fascinated and irritated him. Charles Rollin, who taught and administered for many years at the University of Paris and elsewhere, was in 1712 compelled to withdraw from public life because of the antagonism aroused by his Jansenist beliefs.[3] Nevertheless, he continued to demonstrate his enthusiasm for education by turning, at the age of sixty-seven, to the writing of historical works intended for young people. By the time of his death thirteen years later (in 1741) he had published his *Histoire ancienne des Egyptiens, des Carthaginois, des Assyriens, des Babyloniens, des Medes et des Perses, des Macédoniens, des Grecs* which began to appear in 1730 and which, in 1740, was reprinted in a handsome edition of six stout volumes, each containing between some five and eight hundred pages and attractively illustrated with maps and fanciful plates in rococo style.[4] He had also produced a substantial fragment of its sequel, the *Histoire romaine*. In a private letter Voltaire dismissed him as a 'prolix and useless compiler' (although elsewhere he often acknowledged Rollin's great literary gifts),[5] but the histories went into so many editions and were so widely translated that it is hardly an exaggeration to claim that for nearly a hundred years most Europeans were introduced to the ancient world through Rollin: Michelet's extracts from Rollin constituted his first written work, and as late as 1852 Sainte-Beuve could recall that 'notre enfance a vécu là-dessus et s'y est laissée porter comme sur un courant plein, sûr et facile'.[6]

Although Rollin admitted that he had done little more than bring together and translate the ancient sources – whose most improbable stories he accepted in a wholly uncritical spirit – Voltaire's reproach that he lacked 'philosophy' was not exactly true. Indeed, the preface to the *Histoire ancienne* expressed a number of sentiments so close to those of Voltaire himself that much of it could almost have been written by him:

> It matters little to us to know that the world once contained an Alexander, a Caesar, an Aristides, a Cato, and that they lived at such or such a time; that the empire of the Assyrians made way for that of the Babylonians, and this latter to the empire of the Medes and the Persians, who were themselves later subjugated by the Macedonians, who in turn were conquered by the Romans. But it is of the greatest importance to know how these empires were established, by what stages and by what means they attained that peak of grandeur that constitutes their lasting glory and their true happiness, and what were the causes of their decadence and collapse.[7]

For Rollin the solution to these problems was relatively straightforward. All developments in world history served ultimately to demonstrate God's purposes for humanity. The creation of the Roman Empire, for instance, had enabled Christianity to spread throughout Europe far more rapidly than would otherwise have been the case.[8] Such views were hardly original – they had been expressed by the early Christians themselves, and Bossuet had in 1681 given them renewed authority in his *Discours sur l'histoire universelle*[9] – but the attention paid by Rollin to the arts and sciences really was new and must surely have helped to inspire Voltaire's far more sophisticated treatment of the theme some years later.

Rollin was not an antiquarian, although he was extremely proud of his membership of the Académie des Inscriptions et Belles-Lettres,[10] and he must, in fact, have been one of the first historians to emphasise, openly and without qualification, that a 'knowledge of medals is absolutely necessary for the study of history. For history is not be learnt only in books, which do not always tell the whole, or the truth, of things. Recourse must therefore be had to material that supports it; and that neither malice nor ignorance can injure or transform; and such are the monuments that we call medals.'[11] Though he himself did not give specific examples of such usage, he emphasised that, in his discussion of the kingdoms of Egypt and Syria, which had been established after the death of Alexander the Great, he had relied much on the recent numismatic researches of Jean Foy Vaillant;[12] and when writing about ancient Egypt, he drew on the reports of contemporary, as well as of Greek and Roman, travellers to give enthusiastic descriptions of the pyramids and other monuments.[13] But his greatest innovation lies in the last quarter of the *Histoire ancienne*, whose chapters are devoted to Agriculture, Commerce, Architecture, Sculpture, Painting, Music, Poetry, Philosophy and so on. Rollin expressed surprise at his own audacity: 'the treatment of the arts and sciences has carried me much further than I imagined'.[14] And the usefulness of his enterprise was recognised when these chapters were published separately in an English translation, which included a number of illustrations specially copied from Montfaucon and other sources used by Rollin.[15] Astonishingly enough, a new edition of the section on ancient Greek painting appeared in London as late as 1901

in a publication whose aim was to make known the portraits recently excavated
from Fayoum which belonged to the Viennese dealer Theodor Graf![16] Yet this
very usefulness gives us an indication of Rollin's limitations. Even when expressing apparently first-hand enthusiasm, he had, in fact, done little more than
summarise all the literary sources he could discover about the arts in antiquity and
add to them some banal comments of a moralising kind.[17] Only once does he
imply that he has actually looked at something for himself: some drawings (or
engravings) of the ruins of Persepolis, which left him unimpressed.[18] His general
lack of interest in art (or his ignorance concerning it) is revealed by the fact
that after quoting Pliny on the famous statue of Laocoön and his sons, he comments only that 'the work must have been admirable, if equal to the beautiful
description . . . in Virgil, or indeed if it came near it'.[19] He never mentions the fact
that what was believed to be the original of this sculpture was one of the most
widely admired and reproduced glories of the pope's collection in Rome.

Rollin was not, therefore, a man who made use of visual sources when thinking
about the past, nor did he measure the value of earlier societies according to the
quality of their arts, as was to become the aim of Voltaire: although he discussed
the beautifying of Athens by Pericles, he strongly disapproved of the 'waste' of
so much money that could have been spent to better purpose.[20] But his very
influential histories of the ancient world did devote unprecedented attention to
architecture, sculpture and painting and thus opened the way for later writers to
approach these themes in a more sympathetic manner.

The other historian of an earlier generation whose work throws light on
Voltaire's attitude to the use of art as an historical source was very different. Ever
since the last years of the seventeenth century the Abbé de Saint-Pierre had been
assiduously compiling materials for his *Annales politiques*, of which a first draft had
been completed by 1730. They were later extended, and eventually published –
after his death – in 1757.[21] As early as 1738 Voltaire (who had by then been
working for some years on his projected *Siècle de Louis XIV* [22]) was trying to get
hold of a manuscript of Saint-Pierre's *Annales*, and although it is not clear whether
or not he succeeded, he was later to be accused of having drawn the inspiration for
the nature of his book from that work – a charge that he vigorously denied.[23]

The works were, in fact, wholly dissimilar. Saint-Pierre's *Annales*, which run
from 1658 (the year of his birth) until the end of 1739, are dry and lacklustre. They
were also consistently hostile to Louis XIV who was, at best, worthy of being
designated *Louis le Puissant* or *Louis le Redoutable*, but certainly not *Louis le Grand*:
'la grande puissance seule ne fera jamais un grand homme'.[24] On the other hand,
although the narrative of the *Annales* is arranged mechanically on a year-by-year
basis, Saint-Pierre realised that history ought to consist of more than battles, royal
births and the signing of treaties. He discusses at some length issues such as trade,
education, domestic economy and fashion (we are told, for instance, that card-
playing at court began in 1648); and he approaches all these topics from the high-
minded but sometimes narrow standpoint of one who 'much preferred to be useful
than to please [*être agréable*]'.[25] Thus he criticises what is taught in school on the
grounds that we are in far greater need of 'arithmetic and practical geometry . . .

than of amusing ourselves in writing Greek verses'.[26] It is from this angle that he considers the arts. Colbert, he writes, was not content with strengthening the French economy:

> he saw that the Italians had perfected themselves in painting and sculpture by academies where beginners could make progress very quickly and could take advantage from the teaching of the best masters. This made him decide to establish a similar academy in Paris, and it met at the old Louvre.
>
> Painting, sculpture, music, poetry, the theatre and architecture demonstrate the existing riches of a nation. They do not prove that its happiness will increase and prove lasting... What is the present state of Italy where the arts have reached a high level of perfection? They are beggars, do-nothings, lazy, vain cowards who spend their time on trivialities. It is to this state that the wretched successors of the Romans – who were once so worthy of admiration – have gradually been reduced by the enfeeblement of their government ... .[27]

To this Voltaire answered, in the later editions of his *Siècle de Louis XIV*, that 'these observations are as wrong as they are vulgar ('grossières') and vulgarly written. When the Italians reached their greatest achievements in the arts, it was under the Medici, at a time when Venice was the most warlike and opulent of republics. This was the age when the Italians produced great men of war and artists who were illustrious in every field. Similarly, it was in the most flourishing years of the reign of Louis XIV that the arts reached their heights ....'.[28]

Yet despite Voltaire's claims for the significance of the visual arts, his actual treatment of them during the course of his historical studies shows that the issue was for him of purely theoretical interest. He had no real feeling for painting and sculpture, and compared to literature and the sciences they play a small role in his appraisal of either the past or the present, and his reliance on them is meagre and indirect. It goes without saying that he had nothing but contempt for the kind of antiquarian studies associated with Caylus, as can be seen from a letter to Mme Denis in which he referred to all 'those wretched [*vilains*] bas-reliefs dating from the decadence of the Roman Empire' which he saw around the tomb of Maurice of Nassau at Cleves.[29] Indeed, Caylus's insistence on the part played by Egypt in the creation of Greek art must surely have been encouraged by Voltaire's provocative (and ill-informed) jibe in 1742 that 'it is all very well puffing the beauty of the arts of ancient Egypt. What has survived consists only of shapeless masses. The finest statue of the ancient Egyptians gets nowhere near what can be made by the most second-rate of our craftsmen today. The Greeks had to teach the Egyptians sculpture; the only good works ever to be found in Egypt were made by Greeks.'[30]

At one point Voltaire gives us a hint as to why he believed that the visual arts had little to offer the historian in the way of evidence. In his interesting discussion as to why civilisations are born and perish, he makes a distinction between those aspects of a culture that become 'exhausted' after attaining perfection and those that can be sustained indefinitely. In the first category he places literature; in the second, painting. No one, he claims, will ever again be able to treat the themes of *Andromaque* or *Tartuffe* which have been given definitive status by Racine and

Molière; whereas, despite Raphael, artists continue to paint the *Holy Family*. For this reason, he implies, the visual arts can tell us less than literature about the state of civilisation.[31] It is striking to us today that it never occurs to him to draw any conclusions from the different styles of a sixteenth- and an eighteenth-century *Holy Family*, even though Montfaucon had already demonstrated the possibility of doing this for much earlier centuries – but Montfaucon's achievements are summed up by Voltaire in a line or two of civil, but wholly uninterested, acknowledgement.[32]

In fact, Voltaire does write at some length about the visual arts in *Le Siècle de Louis XIV* – certainly more than is to be found in any other work of general history that had yet appeared – but the arts, along with the sciences, are not incorporated into the main substance of his book. Nor do they form its climax, as he had originally intended.[33] He makes the occasional passing reference to medals, triumphal arches and statues designed to commemorate some victory, but explains that he does not wish to treat the arts in those chapters that are devoted to political, military and religious history. He will, instead, consider them at the end of the volume.[34] Only once does he examine the imagery of a monument in search of specific historical evidence. His conclusions are disingenuous, but the imagination with which he treats his figurative source marks a significant moment in the approach of an historian to the visual arts. Louis XIV has, he points out, been accused of intolerable pride because the base of the statue of him by Martin Desjardins (pls 133, 134) which dominates the Place des Victoires is surrounded by slaves in chains (pl. 135).[35] This, however, had not been commissioned by the king, and in fact its ostentatious grandeur had been designed not to glorify him so much as its patron, the maréchal de la Feuillade. Moreover, the slaves symbolised vices that had been crushed rather than nations that had been conquered, and, in any case, they were no more than an old convention which could be seen in many other statues, including the one in Livorno of Ferdinando de' Medici, 'who certainly never enchained any nation'.[36]

In general, however, Voltaire confined his discussion of artists and the arts of all kinds to a supplement. He compiled this with much enthusiasm, but with none of the insight or wit that he brought to bear on other themes. Nor does he seem to have been too much concerned with consistency in his selection of names to be honoured. 'The list would have been fuller and more detailed', he wrote to President Hénault, 'had I been able to work in Paris; I would have given more space to the arts – that was my main intention. But what could I do in Berlin?' And when Hénault wrote to complain of the absence from the list of Jules Hardouin-Mansart, architect of the Invalides, Marly and the chapel of Versailles, 'who was, besides, the grandfather of my wife and of Madame Arpajon', Voltaire answered imperturbably that 'I have just given a place to Hardouin-Mansart in whom you show an interest'.[37] In fact, the amputation of these supplementary chapters would hardly affect the general structure of Voltaire's study.

The situation regarding his far more ambitious *Essai sur les moeurs* of some years later is very similar. The arts (and especially the fine arts) occupy remarkably little space in this work designed to cover several thousand years of history and many

133. Paris, view of the Place des Victoires in the early eighteenth century with the marble statue by Martin Desjardins of Louis XIV. Engraving.

134 (below left). Desjardins's statue of Louis XIV, engraving from Northleigh, *Topographical Descriptions*, 1702.

135 (above right). Desjardins, bronze figure of a bound 'slave' representing Turkey, (now in the Place des Sceaux). This was removed in 1790 from the base of the marble statue of Louis XIV which was originally in the Place des Victoires and was subsequently destroyed.

widely differing civilisations, and in this book also they are confined to special chapters kept separate from the main narrative. Voltaire apparently claimed that he had lost a folio of documents dealing with art history,[38] and it is tempting to associate these with some thirty or forty rather disorganised pages – covering poetry, the drama, scientific inventions, music, philosophy and so on – that were not published until well over a hundred years after his death.[39] The fraction concerned with the visual arts deals very largely with Italy – the only non-Italian contribution acknowledged by Voltaire is Jan van Eyck's discovery of oil painting – and its string of names (Cimabue, Giotto, Masaccio, Bellini, Perugino, Mantegna, Leonardo, Michelangelo, Raphael, Titian, Correggio and Domenichino) is clearly not based on any first-hand visual experience. In fact, so haphazard are Voltaire's notes that it is by no means always clear what were the sources used (or misused) by him: it is, for instance, difficult to imagine where he could have come across the claim that 'Pisanello, also born in Florence, adorned Italy with his statues', though it is not difficult to see how the muddle arose.

For all the inadequacies of his own treatment of the arts, Voltaire's legacy was of decisive importance in determining the manner through which later historians would approach them – and it is a legacy that is still being drawn upon. All those innumerable books in every European language that, after devoting most of their space to political, social, religious and military history, end with a chapter entitled 'Art, Literature and Science', ultimately spring from *Le Siècle de Louis XIV*. Although none of them (not even *Le Siècle de Louis XIV* itself) really seems to fulfil Voltaire's ambitions for a 'history of the human spirit', it is certainly true that before the appearance of that flawed masterpiece such a chapter would not even have been considered necessary.

Thus when a few years after the publication of *Le Siècle de Louis XIV*, Hume discouraged Robertson from writing about the Medici, on the grounds that the historian of Scotland did not know enough about the art of Italy, he was surely thinking not of a project for some wide-ranging cultural survey, but rather of that last general chapter, which now seemed so desirable. An early example of precisely this sort of approach may be found in a book that was indeed devoted to the Medici, though to a rather later period of their rule than the one that had tempted Robertson. In 1775 Pietro Leopoldo, the reforming Grand Duke of Tuscany, commissioned from Riguccio Galluzzi, his literary censor and chief archivist, a history of the realm of which he was now sovereign.[40] Although Pietro Leopoldo was himself a prince of the house of Habsburg-Lorraine, the book was to be devoted to the period when Florence had been ruled by the family with which its fame still remains indelibly linked. Galluzzi's scholarship, revealed in his five volumes which appeared in 1781 was as well documented as Muratori's, and his standpoint was as anti-papal as Giannone's, but, in contrast to both, he paid consistent attention to the arts – those arts that had been so ardently promoted by the Medici both before and after the Grand Duchy had been created for Cosimo I in 1539. The contents of each of the 'books' into which the *History of the Grand Duchy of Tuscany* is divided are arranged on very similar (and very conventional) lines. Some eight or nine chapters are devoted to political, diplomatic and military narrative, and, where a biographical sketch requires it, there may also be a brief discussion of a particular building or example of town planning; there then follows a final chapter – very much on the lines indicated by Voltaire – to which are consigned the arts and sciences. It cannot be claimed that Galluzzi shows any feeling for specific works of art – many of which he must have seen every day of his life – and he certainly relies more on written sources, such as Vasari, than on personal observation; still less does he attempt to interpret paintings or monuments with a view to throwing light on the rule of the Medici or the lives of their subjects. None the less, the very sobriety of his accounts (combined with the authoritative nature of his excellent *History*) conveys the impression that some consideration of the arts was now recognised as necessary even in an essentially traditional narrative of political events.

ii

It was probably before Galluzzi had begun his history of the Grand Duchy that, in England, William Roscoe first conceived the idea of writing a life of Lorenzo de' Medici, conceived on wholly different lines, although the actual book, elegantly illustrated with engravings taken from medals, paintings and even wood-blocks of the fifteenth century, was not published until 1796.[41] Roscoe rejected as tedious and pedantic those studies of the Medici that were chiefly concerned with politics. 'It appeared to me', he explained 'that the mere historical events of the fifteenth century, so far as they regarded Italy, could not deeply interest my countrymen in the eighteenth; but I conceived that the progress of letters and of arts would be attended to with pleasure in every country where they were cultivated and protected.'[42]

Although Roscoe himself claimed that his works of history were 'tales of old times bearing but little relation to the momentous occurrences of the present day',[43] even in his own lifetime his interest in Lorenzo was ascribed to a form of self-identification with a man whom he perhaps looked upon as a spiritual ancestor.[44] He, too, was a banker (but he became one only after the publication of his biography – his father was a butler); a poet; the friend of writers and thinkers, painters and sculptors; and an important patron and collector of art and of literature. He had been born in Liverpool in 1753, and apart from a short period which he spent in London as a Member of Parliament, he lived in or near that city until his death in 1831. Despite his very early enthusiasm for Italian literature, he refused the opportunity to travel and later claimed that 'Providence had placed my lot beyond the limits of that favoured country [Italy]'.[45] He was, however, certain that this constituted no great problem when compiling his biography of Lorenzo, as he could draw on his own library and on the assistance and researches of a close friend, William Clarke, who spent some time in Florence. Such an attitude, as well as Roscoe's confinement to 'a remote part of this remote Kingdom', may suggest that he approached his subject in a spirit of narrow, antiquarian pedantry. In fact, Roscoe, who campaigned relentlessly against the press-gang and the slave trade[46] –

two of the mainstays of the Liverpool economy – and who, as one of the 'Liverpool Jacobins',[47] showed so much sympathy with the French Revolution that he attracted suspicion and hostility during the wars with France, was a man of great breadth of mind. Well before Michelet or Burckhardt, he singled out 'the close of the fifteenth and the beginning of the sixteenth century' as one of the turning points in history, partly on the grounds of its cultural achievements:

> Almost all the great events from which Europe derives its present advantages, are to be traced up to those times. The invention of the art of printing, the discovery of the great western continent, the schism from the church of Rome, . . . the degree of perfection attained in the fine arts, and the final introduction of true principles of criticism and taste, compose such an illustrious assemblage of luminous points as cannot fail of attracting for ages the curiosity and admiration of mankind.[48]

Roscoe disclaimed any intention of writing the 'complete history of these times [which] has long been a great desideratum in literature',[49] but he did, nevertheless, envisage a cultural history of a new kind, inspired in part by the ideals of Voltaire to whose *Essai sur les moeurs* he often referred in his footnotes. He went further than any writer before him (and many after him) in introducing references to literature, philosophy and scholarship into his narrative of political and biographical events, for he followed the prevailing opinion (which has now once again become widely accepted) that Lorenzo's patronage was principally and most profitably directed to the revival of letters. None the less, he also commented from time to time on individual works of painting, sculpture and architecture, and towards the end of the book he devoted to these arts a whole chapter, which opens with the assertion that 'those periods of time which have been most favourable to the progress of letters and science, have generally been distinguished by an equal proficiency in the arts'.[50]

Roscoe's Chapter IX, devoted to the 'Progress of the Arts in Italy', covers the period from Giotto to Raphael and the young Michelangelo. It constitutes by far the fullest account of the subject that had appeared in English or, indeed, in any other language, even Italian, if one excludes those books that were specifically devoted to the arts, such as Vasari's *Lives* and others in that tradition and Luigi Lanzi's recently published *Storia pittorica dell'Italia*.

The assumptions that lie behind Roscoe's survey are that 'under the auspices of the House of Medici, and particularly through the ardour and example of Lorenzo, the empire of science and true taste was again restored' (after the deaths of Dante, Boccaccio and Petrarch),[51] and that 'the patronage of the family of the Medici is almost contemporary with the commencement of the art [of painting]'.[52]

This was hardly a novel view. The extent of Medici patronage had been universally acknowledged and repeatedly celebrated ever since the sixteenth century. What was more unusual was for a scholar to be drawn to a historical figure of the first rank essentially out of enthusiasm for him as a patron and then to visualise all his other activities in the light of that enthusiasm. But for this, too, there was a precedent in the form of a very handsome book which had appeared half a century earlier – although, as Roscoe does not mention it and as it does not appear in the sale catalogue of his very extensive library,[53] he may not have known it. In 1741, when the Medici were on the verge of extinction, Giuseppe (Maria) Bianchini had dedicated to the last surviving member of the family, Anna Maria Ludovica, wife of the Elector Palatine, a folio entitled *Dei Granduchi di Toscana*. Purchasers of the volume must have expected some variant of any one of dozens of standard eulogies devoted to ruling dynasties which had been appearing throughout Europe for more than two centuries: noble ancestry, military prowess, devotion to the true religion, imposing marriage, honours received from the emperor . . . What they got was indeed a finely illustrated volume of hagiography, but this was combined, in a surprising manner, with short disquisitions on the cultural history of Florence. In a complete reversal of long-standing conventions Bianchini explained that it was his intention to concentrate above all on the patronage of art and letters displayed by the members of the family: 'Only at the end of each essay have I decided to refer to a few of their other activities so as to give at least some impression of their value in other respects also.'[54]

As the title of the book implies, Bianchini (like Galluzzi after him) was essentially concerned with the period following Cosimo I's assumption of power in 1537, but he opens with several pages devoted to Cosimo's forbears, including Lorenzo, who had been admired throughout the world 'as the first patron and protector of letters and of all fine arts'. Although he records the names of many of the individual writers supported by Lorenzo, when it comes to the arts he merely alludes rather vaguely to the many villas, palaces and churches that he had had built. Only one artist is singled out by name: Michelangelo.

In 1741 a serious interest in any Florentine artist earlier than Michelangelo might have appeared eccentric, but by the 1790s when Roscoe was devoting himself whole-heartedly to Lorenzo, the situation had changed decisively. A brief look at the sources potentially available to him will help to define the nature of his achievement.

It was in Florence itself that the change could have been appreciated most vividly. Under the impact of Grand Duke Leopoldo, who took over the government in 1765, the galleries of the Uffizi were radically reorganised.[55] Among the many innovations was the return to the ducal collection of a number of fourteenth- and fifteenth-century paintings which had been widely dispersed. These were for the most part hung in the 'Fourth Cabinet', where already in 1764 Gibbon had been able to see, with considerable interest, 'une suite de tableaux des plus anciens maîtres depuis la renaissance de la peinture', two Fra Angelicos among them. The pictures on display included Uccello's *Rout of San Romano*, Fra Angelico's Linaiuoli altarpiece, Botticelli's two small paintings of Judith and Filippo Lippi's *St Augustine*.[56] Within a few years this cabinet was greatly extended and visitors could see a large selection of works by early Christian, mediaeval and Renaissance artists.[57] The gallery also contained sculptures by Mino da Fiesole, Donatello and other contemporaries.

Roscoe did not visit Florence, and his collaborator, William Clarke, had no inclination or instructions to look at pictures, but, in 1782, one of those responsible for the arrangement, the great antiquarian (and, later, art historian) Luigi Lanzi, published an account of the Uffizi which included a report on the 'Fourth Cabinet'.[58] If his words were known to Roscoe, they may well have fired his imagination:

> If we read with pleasure in Pliny of the progress in painting made by the Greeks, and the names of those masters who, in succeeding ages, enriched it with new discoveries; and if we read with pleasure in Vasari a similar history of the masters of modern painting; how much more will lovers of the arts enjoy seeing – not in someone's written history, but in an actual gallery – these gradual stages whereby art progresses; not described, but truly drawn and painted; not burdened with someone else's opinion, but recognised with one's own eyes? I do not for the moment refer to the enlightenment that a museum of this kind can give to a student of documents [*Diplomatica*] or to an historian of the religious or secular life of the Middle Ages; or even to a scholar of the Tuscan language – to all of whom these pictures are as important as are the paintings of Herculaneum or Rome for scholars of antiquity.

But Lanzi did not actually describe any of the pictures concerned, and Roscoe (who, not long afterwards, was himself to build up a collection of early Italian paintings designed to illustrate the history of art[59]) was forced to rely on, and be 'burdened by', the descriptions of others – Vasari, above all. He could, however, turn to a more immediate source for guidance.

Ever since 1779–80, when he had settled in London, the Swiss painter Johann Heinrich Füssli (Fuseli) had been a client and close friend of Roscoe, and it seems possible that when in 1792 he offered to make for his patron 'a design of the Assassination – or any other Scene you may select',[60] he was hoping to be given a commission to illustrate the *Lorenzo*. If so, he must have been disappointed,[61] for the engravings in that book are confined to portraits, manuscripts, medals and other objects presumed to date from the period under discussion – although for its sequel, *The Life and Pontificate of Leo the Tenth*, Roscoe commissioned not only such 'authentic images' (whose authenticity was, however, sometimes doubted by Fuseli), but also a rather mediocre set of historical vignettes from the popular book-illustrator John Thurston. None the less, Fuseli could be of help in other ways.

Roscoe was constantly worried that his chapter on the Progress of the Arts was 'flat and insufficient;[62] and he asked his protégé to read it for him before publication,[63] as he was to do again some years afterwards with his *Leo the Tenth*, emphasising that 'in all points we may not exactly agree; you write as Artist – I as a historian'.[64] For this volume, which covered a later period, Fuseli proposed many emendations and corrections.[65] As the very intelligent and articulate Fuseli had spent eight years in Italy (during the course of which he had paid two brief visits to Florence), the idea of seeking his advice regarding the dawn of Renaissance art was logical enough, and it could have had important consequences for the book. But, at a time when many English artists and continental scholars were rediscovering the merits, as well as the interest, of those Italian painters who had

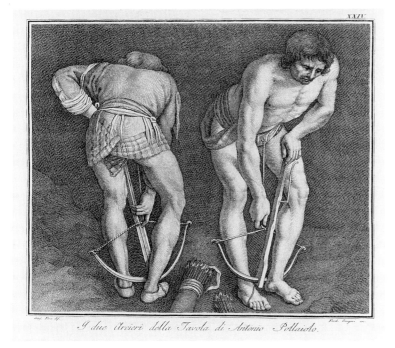

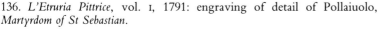

136. *L'Etruria Pittrice*, vol. I, 1791: engraving of detail of Pollaiuolo, *Martyrdom of St Sebastian*.

137. Antonio and Piero del Pollaiuolo (ascribed to), *Martyrdom of St Sebastian* (London, National Gallery).

worked before the golden age of the High Renaissance, Fuseli remained wholly impervious to their appeal. He seems to have made few, if any alterations to Roscoe's text, and any advice he may have given would probably have discouraged rather than stimulated the occasional glimpses of feeling that we find in the pages devoted to fifteenth-century art. After the book had appeared, Fuseli wrote an enthusiastic review of it[66] (which – it need hardly be said – did not wholly satisfy the author[67]), and he singled out for special admiration some of Roscoe's most dismissive comments. Of Pollaiuolo's *Martyrdom of St Sebastian* (pl. 137), which Vasari had warmly praised, Roscoe wrote that 'to everything great and elevated, the art was yet a stranger; even the celebrated picture of Pollajuolo exhibits only a group of half naked and vulgar wretches, discharging their arrows at a miserable fellow-creature, who, by changing places with one of his murderers, might with equal propriety become a murderer himself'.[68] To this Fuseli (whose work is hardly noted for its restraint) added a gloss of his own: 'It is the artist's fault if the right moment be missed. If you see only blood-tipt arrows, brain-dashed stones, excoriating knives, the artist, not the subject, is detestable'.[69]

Roscoe knew of the general appearance of the Pollaiuolo – and of some of the other pictures he chose to discuss – through a set of large engravings which, most conveniently, had been published in book form just as his *Life of Lorenzo* was nearing completion (pl. 136). *L'Etruria Pittrice*[70] (which Fuseli – reasonably enough – had found disappointing[71]) appeared in two volumes in 1791 and 1795: each contained sixty plates, which covered painting in Florence between the eleventh and the eighteenth centuries; indeed, it was the first illustrated work of the kind to be devoted to a national school.[72] The pictures had been chosen, and the commentary on them written, by Marco Lastri, a prolific and wide-ranging observer of Florentine history. He had also (in some way that is not quite clear[73]) been involved in the reorganisation of the Uffizi, but he drew on many different sources, including private collections, for his anthology. It appears to have been from Lastri's plates, and from them alone, that Roscoe was able to derive any idea at all – other than that obtainable from written descriptions – of those fine arts for whose development he felt Medici patronage to have been essential. Thus it is his reliance on *L'Etruria Pittrice* (leading him sometimes to take a rather eccentric view of Florentine paintings) that distinguishes him from those many historians discussed in this chapter, including Voltaire, for whom the mere existence of famous artists, rather than the actual nature of their achievements, constituted a gauge of civilisation. And although in the light not only of modern artistic scholarship, but even of that of his own contemporaries, his book appears as defective in execution as it was adventurous in conception, Roscoe surpassed all previous historians in integrating cultural history into a conventional biographical and political narrative.

Roscoe went out of his way to emphasise that he was just as concerned with Lorenzo as a statesman as he was with him as a patron. But he had approached Lorenzo through an interest in his role as a patron (of letters more than of the arts), and this naturally affected his treatment of him as a statesman. Despite the enthusiasm that greeted the book throughout Europe – and he was freely compared with Robertson and Gibbon[74] – there were those who felt that such an approach was unacceptable. Lorenzo's patronage was indeed admirable, it was universally agreed, but it had been an adjunct to less admirable activities, and not (as Roscoe appeared to think) the mainspring of his life.

Such was the response of Roscoe's most formidable opponent Simonde de Sismondi who could not make up his mind whether to laugh or to be angry (but decided to laugh) when trying to cope with Roscoe's excited defence of Lorenzo against the charge that 'il soutint par des exécutions sanglantes un pouvoir égöiste'.[75] Sismondi was a Swiss Protestant (whose family was of Italian origin) who travelled frequently to Italy, France and England, sometimes as a political refugee, for he was an outspoken liberal of high principles. His masterpiece, *Histoire des Républiques Italiennes du Moyen Âge*, was published in sixteen volumes between 1807 and 1818, but it had been conceived at almost exactly the time that the *Life of Lorenzo de' Medici* had appeared.[76] It was designed as a contribution to the history of freedom in Europe and was based partly on the premise that Italy's continuing misfortunes had originally sprung from the collapse of local communal governments at the hands of just such tyrants as the Medici. There is considerable irony in the fact that Roscoe and Sismondi, whose political views were so close, should have differed so strongly about the historical role of this family. Sismondi (somewhat reluctantly) acknowledged Lorenzo's services to literature, in which he himself was keenly interested, and also – in a very general way – to the arts, which did not inspire him with much feeling: when travelling in Italy in 1805 with Madame de Staël and August-Wilhelm Schlegel, he described the latter as 'the materialist of our group. It is he who gives most attention to exterior objects;

pictures, statues and fragments of ancient architecture attract him keenly, and he sometimes comes back from them full of enthusiasm.'[77]

None the less, Sismondi appreciated, perhaps more than any historian before him, how contact with the art and artefacts, as well as the physical terrain, of a nation can throw light on its history. On the (rather rare) occasions when he moves away from political or military narrative in order to sum up the general state of Italian civilisation at some given moment, he uses his direct visual experiences with an immediacy that makes a striking contrast with the second-hand information on the arts so laboriously collected by Roscoe. It is worth quoting one such passage at length, because although Sismondi has, ever since his own day, been thought of as a somewhat dry, 'philosophical' historian, he reveals here – almost despite himself – the change that came over historical writing at the dawn of the nineteenth century, a change that will be discussed in greater detail in the following chapters.

Thus the monuments with which Italy covered itself in the fifteenth century do not merely demonstrate that a refined sentiment of beauty guided the chisel, the brushes or the set square of her illustrious sculptors, painters and architects; seen as a whole these monuments once more bring before us a nation full of confidence in its strength, of hope in its future, of satisfaction for its past successes. Her temples are infinitely more solid and magnificent than the most famous ones in Greece; the palaces of her citizens surpass in extent and in the colossal thickness of their walls those of the Roman emperors; the simplest of her houses convey a feeling of strength, ease and comfort. When today one wanders through these cities of Italy, all half-deserted, all deprived of their former opulence; when one enters those temples that the crowd cannot fill even for the most solemn of ceremonies; when one visits those palaces in which the owners occupy barely one tenth of the rooms; when one sees the broken panes of those windows built with so much elegance, the grass growing at the foot of the walls, the silence of those huge dwellings, the poverty of the inhabitants whom one glimpses emerging from them, the slow gait, the vacant air of all those crossing the streets, and the beggars who alone seem to make up half the population; then one feels that towns like these were built by a different people from the one to be seen in them today, that they are the produce of life, but that death has inherited them; that they belonged to opulence and that destitution has followed; that they are the work of a great people, and that this great people can no longer be found anywhere.

The luxury of a king can sometimes create a magnificent capital, even when the nation over which he rules is still poverty-stricken or half barbarous and feels no desire to draw on the necessities of life in order to surround itself with a pomp that gives it no satisfaction. It is Louis XIV and not France, Frederick and not Prussia, Peter or Catherine and not Russia whom one sees in the palaces of Paris, Berlin, Petersburg; and, indeed, the distant provinces were, at the time when these palaces were being built, all the more wretched because of the sumptuousness of the capitals. But the richness and the elegance of Italian architecture are spontaneous; one finds the same quality in the villages as in the towns; everywhere it is on a higher level than the condition of the present owners, everywhere one finds larger and more comfortable buildings than those lived in by the same class of society in countries that are today thought of as very prosperous. If small, little-known townships such as Uzzano, Buggiano or Montecatini, situated on the slopes of the hills of the Val-de-Nievole, were to be transported entire to the centre of the oldest towns in France, Troyes or Sens or Bourges, they would constitute its best constructed districts; their temples could be an adornment for the greatest towns. Even when one ventures down the valleys of the Appenines, far from any important road or trading centre or human communications, one still finds villages where no new house has been built since the fifteenth century, where no old house has been repaired – villages such as Pontito, La Schiappa or Vellano – and which are, none the less, made up only of houses of stone and cement, several storeys high, and of elegant architectural proportions.

So it is that almost the whole of Italy – its agriculture, its roads, the shape given to the land by the hand of man, the architecture of its towns and its villages – retains records of its former wealth, of a prosperity that was enjoyed by all classes, of a spiritual vitality, of a zealous activity, which had been the effect, and once again became the cause, of the general well-being. This opulence, despite all the upheavals we have described, still existed at the end of the fifteenth century. It remains only to note the sequence of calamities that led to its destruction and the fetters that led to the crushing of the national spirit; so that, even after the wars had come to an end and even after the cessation of all the scourges that followed each other for half a century, the return of tranquillity, the enjoyment of a lasting peace which was envied by the other nations of Europe, could restore to Italy only a shadow of its earlier happiness.[78]

In these pages Sismondi moves far beyond that vein of poignant nostalgia that had affected historians ever since Petrarch had brooded over the ruins of Rome, and makes use of specific visual sources in order to evoke the economic and constitutional realities of a now-vanished society. Rarely if ever before had monuments played so discreet yet so telling a role in evoking the past.

8

The Arts as an Index of Society

i

During the last years of the eighteenth century and the early part of the nineteenth, historians, theorists and philosophers of differing convictions and in different countries frequently suggested that developments in the visual arts, as in music and in literature, were far more intimately linked to the political and social circumstances of their own, and of earlier, societies than was generally believed. Indeed, so organic were such links said to be that by the 1840s it had become almost conventional to assert that the arts of a country could give a more reliable impression of its true character at any given moment than those more usual yardsticks, such as military and economic success or failures, which had hitherto been made use of by historians. Although it is very difficult to follow the exact processes of thought that led to this conviction, there is no doubt that even in antiquity some observers realised that the arts could provide valuable information not only, as Herodotus noted, about specific events supposed to have taken place in earlier times but also about far-reaching issues to do with beliefs and social customs. Thus one of the speakers in Plato's *Laws* pointed out that in Egypt no painter or artist was allowed to innovate or to put traditional forms on one side so as to invent new ones: 'To this day, no alteration is allowed either in these arts or in music. And you will find that their works of art are painted or moulded in the same forms which they had ten thousand years ago; – this is literally true and no exaggeration, – their ancient paintings and sculptures are not a whit better or worse than the work of today, but are made with just the same skill.' From this uniformity of style and quality it could be deduced that, already thousands of years earlier, the Egyptians had recognised that their young citizens should be brought up according to unchanging standards of virtue.[1] And reasoning of a similar kind led most educated people during the Renaissance and the reign of Louis XIV to look upon the apparent irregularity and inconsistency of Gothic architecture as a true and revealing image of the general 'barbarism and ignorance' of the Middle Ages.[2] In the 1720s Giambattista Vico began to discuss the issues raised by interconnexions of this kind with a wholly new degree of imagination and profundity. However Vico (whose ideas were not to attract attention until very much later) was not interested in the visual arts, and his role, therefore, in establishing their new significance as a gauge by which to measure changing stages of civilisation was only an indirect one.

It is true that most discussions of these matters tended to refer in only a general way to 'the arts and sciences', but by the middle of the eighteenth century a few antiquarians had begun to make tentative but striking analogies between the quality of the painting, sculpture and architecture to be found in some particular nation or epoch and wider aspects of its life. Thus in his *Treatise on Ancient Painting* of 1740 George Turnbull wrote that 'the general or national Character of a People may be conjectured from the State of the Arts amongst them: and reciprocally, the State of the Arts amongst any People may be pretty certainly divined from the general, prevalent Temper and Humour of that People, as it discovers itself by other Symptoms in their Government, Laws, Language, Manners etc.'[3] And we have seen that in the following two decades Caylus could sometimes make use of precise examples (rather than of imaginative but unexplored suggestions) to illustrate notions of a similar kind. At much the same time the incomparably more influential Voltaire was laying the foundations for a new sort of history which should approach man's past from the vantage point of his culture. However, for Voltaire, as for most thinkers who were concerned to raise this 'philosophical' history far above the level of 'antiquarianism', it was the mere existence of great writers and artists that mattered rather than the actual nature of their achievements. Ultimately, the most important (although indirect) stimulus for the development of an approach to history that would be grounded in the interpretation of art came from an unexpected source: Winckelmann.

In his *History of the Art of Antiquity*, which was published in 1764, Winckelmann did not show himself much interested in the various theories that had hitherto been proposed to account for the decline of art: he hardly ever refers to the impact of the Christians, for instance, and he mentions the vandalism of the barbarians only at the very end of his book. He was in any case more concerned with a problem that had attracted much less attention: those circumstances that had encouraged the rise of Greek art, such as a warm but temperate climate which had beneficial effects on physical beauty and psychological vitality. None the less, he was eventually forced to tackle the issue of when and why art had declined, and in doing so he gave central importance to one political factor – that of freedom. Art flourished when free, declined when oppressed.

The idea was by no means new in itself, and early in the eighteenth century it had been discussed at some length by Lord Shaftesbury, whose works were carefully studied by Winckelmann. Shaftesbury wrote that

> 'Twas the fate of Rome to have scarce an intermediate age, or single period of time, between the rise of arts and fall of liberty. No sooner had that nation begun to lose the roughness and barbarity of their manners, and learn of Greece to form their heroes, their orators and poets on a right model, than by their unjust attempt upon the liberty of the world they justly lost their own. With their liberty they lost not only their force of eloquence, but even their style and language itself. The poets who afterwards arose among them were mere unnatural and forced plants.[4]

Acknowledging that he had 'fallen unawares into . . . profound reflections on the periods of government, and the flourishing and decay of Liberty and Letters', Shaftesbury continued that

> barbarity and Gothicism were already entered into arts ere the savages had made any impression on the empire. All the advantage which a fortuitous and almost miraculous succession of good princes could procure their highly favoured arts and sciences, was no more than to preserve during their own time those perishing remains, which had for awhile with difficulty subsisted after the decline of Liberty. Not a statue, not a medal, not a tolerable piece of architecture could show itself afterwards.[5]

Shaftesbury's optimistic conclusions that, because 'we are now in an age when Liberty is once again in its ascendant', the arts were bound to flourish in England with the return of peace proved popular with poets who like to contrast the artificial tyranny of the gardens of Versailles with the freedom of landscape gardening in England (while conveniently forgetting the formality of Dutch gardens). But Winckelmann was the first historian to make serious theoretical use of such very general impressions. For he alone was able to categorise clear stylistic differences between the varied arts of the ancient world and also to construct a chronological framework convincing enough to encompass the stages whereby they had developed and declined. His achievement was based on a critical study of all the ancient literary sources; on the lessons he drew from the development of the arts 'nearer our own times', in which style had been 'hard and dry' before the perfection attained by Raphael and Michelangelo – a perfection followed first by a period of bad taste and then by the 'eclecticism' of the Carracci and their followers;[6] and, above all, on his extraordinarily detailed and perceptive knowledge of the actual objects surviving from antiquity.

Thus for all his errors (many of which were quickly noted) Winckelmann carries more weight than his predecessors, even when he is making only the same sort of generalisations (usually based on circular arguments) as they had done – about the extravagant and monstrous art of the Egyptians, for instance, which reflects their fiery temperaments (the result of the climate in which they lived);[7] or about the bloody conflicts depicted on the urns of the Etruscans (as contrasted with the pleasant scenes shown on those of the Romans), which demonstrate the melancholy of their nature;[8] or about the similarity between the hardness of early Greek art, 'which gives their figures a certain grandeur and majesty', and the hard laws of those times, 'which punished every slight misdemeanour with death'.[9]

However, Winckelmann's serious discussion of the relationship between art and history involves far more subtle, complicated (and vulnerable) investigations than such simplistic analogies, as can be seen in his frequent references to the necessary connection between political freedom and artistic quality, most notably in that section of his book concerned with the 'History of the Art of the Greeks from its origins until Alexander the Great'. 'We shall begin by a consideration of the external circumstances of Greece,' he writes,[10]

> because these had a very great influence on the history of its art; for if the

sciences, and indeed wisdom itself, are affected by the times and by events, the dependence of art is even greater, maintained as it is by redundance rather than necessity and sustained by ambition. Thus reason demands that in this History I should indicate the changing circumstances in which the Greeks found themselves, although I will do this briefly and only when it is necessary for my purpose. From this it will emerge that it is to liberty above all that art is indebted for its progress and its perfection.

And yet, as Winckelmann's critics soon pointed out, he was by no means consistent in upholding this view.[11] It was obviously political opportunism that dictated his claim that 'under the clerical government of [contemporary] Rome, the people still seem to experience the liberty of the Republic so that it would be possible to raise an army of valiant warriors as ready as their ancestors to face death with scorn';[12] but he was unable, for all that, to put in a good word for the Italian artists of his day. Much more ambiguous (because much more sincere) was his attitude to the rule of Alexander the Great. Pliny and other early writers, unburdened by the need to assert the link between freedom and the arts, had considered the period as a sort of golden age for painting and sculpture.[13] So, too, did Winckelmann – and yet he could not deny that Philip of Macedon, and then his son Alexander, had put an end to the freedom of the Greek cities. He had therefore to accept Plutarch's view that the arts had flourished because of generous patronage and because of the taste of Alexander himself, to which benefits were added those of peace, perhaps in a somewhat degraded state, and the lack of internal feuding.[14] On many other occasions also Winckelmann found himself enthusiastically admiring sculptures which had been carved under autocratic governments or foreign domination. And yet from time to time he returned to a far more rigid, not to say pedantic, application of the theory he had proposed whereby supreme art could only flourish in conditions of freedom. The most notable instance of this occurs in his discussion of the *Torso Belvedere* in the Museo Pio-Clementino (pl. 138).[15]

The form of the letters in the inscription proved beyond doubt that it must be a late work dating from after the death of Alexander; yet its quality was of the highest: 'those who are able to penetrate the secrets of the arts will recognise in this statue, mutilated as it is, without head or hands or legs, a clear reflexion of the beauty of ancient times. In this Hercules the artist has fashioned the most sublime notion of a body that has been elevated above nature, and of a man of perfect years raised up to that freedom from need which is characteristic of the gods.' And Winckelmann concludes his rapturous description with the words: 'One could say that this Hercules is even closer than the Apollo [Belvedere] to the flourishing times of the "sublime style of art" – that is, the style that Winckelmann had dated to the period of Phidias and Polyclitus, when 'the age of philosophy and freedom had begun to thrive in Greece'.

To have dated the carving of such a masterpiece to a period that witnessed neither the political freedom (which Winckelmann regarded as essential for the creation of great art) nor even the generous patronage and peace within Greece itself provided by Alexander (which he was reluctantly prepared to accept as a

138. *Belvedere Torso*, marble (Vatican Museum).

substitute) would have severely damaged the theoretical foundations of his whole work. Yet the implications of the inscription were inexorable. Winckelmann was therefore driven to propose that Apollonius, son of Nestor, could have made the 'peaceful and deified Hercules', known as the *Torso Belvedere*, only during the short-lived restoration of Greek liberty following the victory in 194 BC (in fact 197) of the Roman consul Titus Quinctius Flaminius against Philip V of Macedon; for within half a century the Roman occupation of Greece had finally extinguished the freedom of its citizens and artists. Winckelmann was faced with a somewhat similar dilemma when he came to discuss a colossal head of Antinous which was then in the Villa Mondragone at Frascati and is now in the Louvre (pl. 139).[16] So great was his admiration that towards the end of his life he was prepared to describe it as 'the most beautiful monument of art to have survived apart from the *Apollo Belvedere* and the *Laocoön*'. In this case, the approximate date was not in doubt because portraits of the deified favourite of Hadrian were made only during the last few years of that emperor's rule, between AD 130 and 140. In order to account for the 'sublime beauty' of the bust – and the excellence of other Greek works which had so surprisingly been produced when the nation was only a province of the Roman Empire – Winckelmann found himself compelled to distort certain passages in the only surviving biography of Hadrian (the *Historia Augusta*) into implying that the emperor had not only lavishly patronised the arts in Greece, but had also 'planned to restore their original freedom to the Greeks and had begun by declaring Greece to be free'.[17]

The damaging chronological and other errors that critics soon noted in the work of Winckelmann were to make it impossible for serious historians to accept his simple equation between freedom and creative power – though it was to be seized upon again and again during the 1790s in order to justify the removal to a 'free' (and, hence, creative) Paris of works of art that had been appropriated from many parts of 'despotic' (and, hence, sterile) Europe.[18] But Winckelmann's beliefs did at least account, much more imaginatively than did rigid theories of inexorable decline, for some of the stylistic variations that could actually be detected in ancient architecture and sculpture. Some explanation was certainly needed, for no historian would have been prepared to affirm that the rise and fall of the arts had taken place in a spiritual vacuum, wholly subject to internal laws and quite without significance to anyone other than to connoisseurs or students of aesthetics. It is true that Winckelmann had not drawn the ultimate conclusion from his belief that great art could thrive only in conditions of freedom: he had not, that is, gone so far as to claim directly that the very existence of great art must of itself constitute proof that freedom, too, had once flourished. None the less, that is certainly the implication to be drawn from his observations on the *Torso Belvedere* and the bust of Antinous. Those observations and many similar ones, also based on the utmost sensitivity and precision of response combined with an intellectual discipline that was unparalleled but that did not exclude the imaginative, opened up a new road of historical enquiry. Thereafter it became increasingly tempting to scrutinise the nature of the arts surviving from earlier societies not necessarily for indications of the degree of freedom that they had enjoyed at any given time, but for evidence of

139. *Head of Antinous*, marble (Paris, Louvre).

the economic, social, political, moral, philosophical or racial changes to which they had been subjected.

It was, for instance, certainly as a result of reading Winckelmann (whom he much admired) that in 1786 the Scottish historian of Greece, John Gillies, put to his readers the remarkable question:

> Were it allowed to make the melancholy supposition, that all the monuments of Greek literature had perished in the general wreck of their nation and liberty, and that posterity could collect nothing further concerning that celebrated people, but what appeared from the Apollo Belvidere [*sic*], the groupes of the Laocoon and Niobé, and other statues, gems, or medals now scattered over Italy and Europe, what opinions would mankind form of the genius and character of the Greeks? Would it correspond with the impressions made by their poets, orators, and historians? which impression would be the most favourable? and what would be the most precise difference between them? The solution of these question will throw much light on the present subject.[19]

After discussing the vigour and emotionalism of the Greeks as recorded by their writers and describing (in words that echo those of Winckelmann but that utterly ignore Winckelmann's chronological distinctions) the three great statues he had chosen as exemplars of Greek art at its highest, Gillies suggested that 'Were we to deduce from these alone the character of the nation, it would seem at first sight, that the contemporaries of Pericles must have been a very superior people in point of fortitude, self command, and every branch of practical philosophy, to the Athenians who are described by poets and historians.' However, he had clearly put to good use the many years he had spent in Germany, for he then conceded that 'it is the business of history to describe men as they are; of poetry and painting, to represent them as may afford most pleasure and instruction to the reader or spectator', and he followed the 'admirable treatment of the subject by that great genius Lessing' in acknowledging that 'the aim of these imitative arts is the same, but they differ widely in the mode, the object, and extent, of their imitation'.

Gillies is exceptional among historians of his own time in raising the question so forthrightly and, among historians of later times, in answering it with such dismissive commonsense. Too dismissive, in fact, because he does not think it worth asking the further question of just why, when, where and how differing kinds of poetry and painting can afford more 'pleasure and instruction to the reader or spectator' than others. But Gillies was essentially concerned with political history (with a strong political message), and his few pages on Greek art constitute only an interlude in his general narrative. A far more systematic attempt to draw on the visual arts of a nation in order to illuminate the particular character of its way of life is to be found in the almost contemporary work of Johann Gottfried Herder – though in his case (as in so many others) it is often difficult to determine how far it is the arts themselves, rather than a preconceived notion of them, that have inspired the initial interest.

Herder was not only a great admirer of Winckelmann but also one of the first of his admirers to understand the nature of his thought and not just to respond to his eloquent enthusiasms. Moreover, Herder himself wrote with keen (but essentially theoretical) insight about Greek art (or what he believed to be Greek art) and fully accepted Winckelmann's views about its supreme quality. However, he could not endorse the intellectual background to Winckelmann's thought which owed so much to the ideas of the Enlightenment. For Herder hated the whole concept of universal standards, whether they had been imposed by force or merely by convention, and whether they applied to philosophy, to manners or to the arts. For him philosophy, manners and the arts should be judged only by the standards of the particular societies to which they belonged and to which they bore a relationship that was organic and that could not be modified by the tyranny of power or the whim of fashion.[20] And so in the youthful, sparkling and combative *Yet Another Philosophy of History*, which he published anonymously in 1774, he accused Winckelmann (who had died six years earlier) of having falsified the whole nature of Egyptian art because he had approached it from a Greek point of view. 'My dear Greek,' he wrote sarcastically,[21]

> those [Egyptian] statues were (as you can see from all their details) intended for anything other than to serve as models for artists according to your ideals, full of charm, of action, of movement – all things that were not known to the Egyptians or that were quite the opposite of what they were aiming to achieve. They had to be mummies [*Mumien sollten sie seyn!*] – memories of dead parents or of ancestors, completely accurate in their features and in their size, and made in accordance with a hundred rigid rules . . . Naturally they were without charm, without action, without movement, in that tomb-like posture with hands and feet full of calm and death. Eternal mummies of marble – that is what they had to be, and that is what they are, as perfect as the technique of art will allow, and according to the ideal that is their intention. So much for your fine critical dreams.

In a private letter written some years earlier, Herder had explained to Hamann that although he did not yet feel up to working his way through the volumes of Caylus's *Recueil*, which had been lying on his table for several weeks, he none the less realised that Caylus's travels had enabled him to approach the East at first hand. This experience was wholly lacking in Winckelmann, whose obsessive concentration on Greece and lack of interest in Egypt in his account of the origins of art left Herder with 'an empty heart'.[22]

Although the spirit of these words would doubtless find much support among Egyptologists, understandably determined to emphasise the intrinsic value of their field of study and understandably bored by the condescension of Winckelmann, it would be curious to know just how many Egyptian artefacts – or even prints of them (in Caylus or elsewhere) – Herder himself had actually seen before he chose to define, so very selectively, the particular characteristics of Egyptian art. But such a question is probably irrelevant. For him Egyptian art had to correspond to what he knew of Egyptian civilisation from the written sources – but one cannot help regretting that he did not live to see the excavation in the nineteenth century of those countless little wooden figures of industrious peasants and craftsmen and oarsmen who could have confirmed his impressions of a carefully ordered civilisation in which the development of agriculture, of private property, of well-policed laws and of industrial skills handed on from generation to generation, all derived from unalterable geographical circumstances. From the vantage point of the present day, he acknowledged, that civilisation (which could, it was true, be transmitted only by religion, fear, authority and despotism – for such are the means required to guide young men) may appear hard: but it was not a civilisation intended for our own day, and it is absurd to judge it as such, just as it is absurd to judge Egyptian art as if it is failed, or perverse, Greek art.

When, ten years or so later, Herder wrote his much more considered *Outlines of a Philosophy of the History of Man* he returned to the subject of Egyptian art and pointed out (quite correctly before the discoveries of Champollion) that 'the most authentic information we have respecting Egypt is derived from its antiquities; those vast pyramids, obelisks, and catacombs; those ruins of canals, cities, columns, and temples; which, with their hieroglyphics, are still the astonishment of travellers, as they were the wonder of the ancient World'.[23] They did not, however, astonish Herder, whose views on the Egyptians had not fundamentally changed, though he was by now somewhat impatient with them. He was still determined to demonstrate that they had been a temperate, hard-working and practical people, and he therefore played down all those bizarre indications of cults that had puzzled, and often dismayed, earlier antiquarians. The fact that the Egyptians had 'not only delineated and carved statues of animals, but interred them as sacred' is mentioned, but never discussed; and in a characteristic passage he writes that their 'catacombs, too, *setting aside the religious notions which the Egyptians connected with them* [my italics], unquestionably contributed to the healthiness of the air and prevented those diseases, which are the common pests of hot and humid climates'. As for pyramids – these had been erected on graves in all parts of the world, 'not so much as emblems of the immortality of the soul, as tokens of a lasting remembrance after death', and their inordinate size was due to the fact that the Egyptians possessed stone sufficient for these monuments and they had hands enough to build them. Hieroglyphs, it is true, were 'the first rude infantile essay of the human mind', and their long survival displayed a remarkable poverty of ideas and mental stagnation; but even they had served to contribute to the fundamental needs of the Egyptians, for 'is it to be wondered at that a nation so poor in writing, and yet not without capacity, should have been eminent in mechanic arts?'

By far the most remarkable instance of Herder's readiness to make use of evidence provided by the visual arts in order to characterise an earlier society occurs in his discussion of ancient Rome – that odious empire which 'destroyed Carthage, Corinth, Jerusalem, and many other flourishing cities of Greece and Asia; as it brought to a melancholy end everything civilised in the south of Europe, that lay within the reach of its sword'.[24] After long and eloquent descriptions of the tyrannical use of power by the Romans to crush all obstacles that stood in their way, Herder turns to their arts, in which they displayed themselves to the present World, and to posterity, as the sovereigns of the Earth, at whose nod were the materials of every country, and the hands of every conquered nation. From the beginning they were inspired with the desire of proclaiming the splendour of their victories by monuments of fame, and the majesty of their city by magnificent and durable structures; so that they very early thought of nothing less than the eternity of their proud existence. The temples that Romulus and Numa erected, and the places they assigned for public assemblies, already had victory in view, and a mighty popular government; till, soon after, Ancus and Tarquin laid the firm foundations of that architecture, which ultimately rose almost to immensity. The etruscan king built the walls of Rome of hewn stone. To supply his subjects with water, and keep the city clean, he erected those vast reservoirs, the ruins of which even now are among the wonders of the world; for modern Rome is unable even to clean them, and keep them in repair. In the same style were its galleries, its temples, its courts of justice, and that immense circus, which, erected for the amusement of the people merely, excites our veneration even now in its ruins. This path was pursued by the kings, the haughty Tarquin in particular; afterwards by the consuls and ediles; then by the conquerors of the World, and the dictators; but chiefly by Julius Caesar; and the emperors followed. Thus by degrees arose those gates and towers, theatres and amphitheatres, circuses and stadia, triumphal arches and honorary columns, splendid monuments and mausolea, roads and aqueducts, palaces and baths, which display the eternal footsteps of these lords of the World, in the provinces as well as in Rome and Italy. To contemplate many of these, even in their ruins, almost fatigues the eye; and the mind sinks under the conception of the vast idea, from which the artist generated these grand designs of solidity and magnificence. Still more little do we feel ourselves, when we reflect on the purposes of these structures, the way of life that was pursued in and among them, the people to whose use they were dedicated, and the persons, not infrequently private individuals, by whom they were erected. Then the mind feels, that the World never contained but one Rome; and that one genius prevailed, from the wooden amphitheatre of Curio, to the Coliseum of Vespasian; from the temple of Jupiter Stator, to the Pantheon of Agrippa, or the temple of Peace; from the first triumphal gate of a returning victor, to the triumphal arches, and honorary columns of Augustus, Titus, Trajan, Severus, and throughout every monument of public or private life. This genius was not the spirit of general liberty and comprehensive benevolence: for, when we reflect on the enormous toil of the labourers, who, as the slaves of war, were often obliged to procure these mountains of stone and marble from distant lands; when we consider the sums expended on these monsters of art, sums wrung from the blood and sweat of plundered and oppressed provinces; when we think of the barbarously proud and savage taste, which most of these edifices cherished, by their bloody combats of gladiators, their inhuman battles with wild beasts, their barbarous triumphal processions, &c., not to mention the luxury of their baths and palaces; we are compelled to think, that Rome was

140. G.B. Piranesi, *Vedute di Roma*: Campo Vaccino.

founded by some demon inimical to mankind, to exhibit to all human beings
traces of his supernatural demoniacal sovereignty.[25]

The tirade is a striking one; but, in fact, when Herder wrote it his eye had not
been fatigued by the ruins of Rome – for he had not yet been there: his short and
unhappy visit took place only after he had published this section of his *Outlines
of a Philosophy of the History of Man*,[26] but he must surely have relied for his
impressions of the city on the etchings of Piranesi (pl. 140) (who would, however,
have been horrified by such an interpretation being put upon them) as well as by
some of the accounts to be found in innumerable travel books and guides (none of
which, however, had described the Eternal City in this spirit).

Similarly, when Herder turned to the art of the Middle Ages in order to
emphasise the primary role played by cities in the economic and cultural life of
those times, he again referred, in passing, to buildings that he had never seen:

Gothic architecture would never have attained its flourishing state, had not
republics and wealthy commercial cities so eagerly rivalled each other in town
halls and cathedrals, as once the cities of Greece in temples and statues. In each
we can discern whence the models of its taste were derived, and the country to
which the stream of its commerce flowed: the most ancient edifices of Venice

and Pisa display a different style of architecture from those of Milan or Florence. The transalpine cities followed various models; but, on the whole, the better gothic architecture is most easily explicable from the constitutions of the cities, and the spirit of the times. For as men live and think, so they build and inhabit: foreign models they can copy only after their own manner, as every bird constructs her nest conformably to her figure, and mode of living. The boldest and most ornamental gothic architecture would never have taken place in convents, or in the castles of knights: it is the peculiar magnificence of public communities. In like manner, the most valuable works of art of the middle ages displayed the coats of arms of families, communities, and cities, on metals, ivory, glass, wood, tapestry, or vestments; on which account they have in general a permanent intrinsic worth, and are justly an inalienable property of cities and families.[27]

Herder's allegiance to Winckelmann's views of the art of the ancient world was still too powerful for him to view the Gothic with much sympathy, despite such demonstrations of theoretical respect; but although he has been criticised for his lack of appreciation,[28] it is precisely the fact that Herder did not respond to the visual arts with spontaneous feelings that renders so significant his evident need to include a discussion of them in his definition of the most important stages in man's development.

ii

The one-sidedness of Winckelmann's exaltation of the art of Greece at the expense of that of Egypt and of all other civilisations dismayed Herder and left even those among his readers who fully accepted this appraisal with a disturbing problem. Was there any hope at all that the arts could once again be raised to the level that they had attained in fifth-century Athens? Most of those who posed this problem were more concerned with aesthetics than with history and with the present than with the past. Nevertheless, the terms in which the issue was discussed were to exert a profound, if indirect, influence on historical thinking, which ranged far beyond any narrow consideration of the ancient world. For while it quickly became clear that Winckelmann had been mistaken in attributing the great flowering of Greek art to the effects of freedom, it proved perfectly possible to extend into other eras a suggestion which had been implicit in all his writing: the greatness of Greek art had been caused by a combination of social, political, religious, climatic and other conditions which were so particular to ancient Greece as to have been unique. Without a total transformation of the present world these conditions could never be revived; hence the arts had never reached their former level after the collapse of the ancient world, and almost certainly would never do so in future.[29]

The Gothic was soon to arouse just as much controversy and eventually almost as much pessimism. Gradually a style, which by the middle of the eighteenth century had become one among many to be adopted or rejected at will, was transformed into the symbol of a special way of life. In 1772, Goethe was aged twenty-three and, after living in Strasbourg for many months, he had recently fallen under the overwhelming influence of Herder (who had not yet written his *Yet Another Philosophy of History*). In a rapturous account of the cathedral and its putative architect, which was re-elaborated on a number of occasions, Goethe not only protested against the notion that the value of architecture should be measured by taste or by rules, but proclaimed that the Gothic had been brought about uniquely 'by the strong, rugged German soul on the narrow, gloomy, priest-ridden stage of the *medii aevi* . . . This is German architecture, our architecture. For the Italian has none he can call his own, still less the Frenchman.'[30] With what fruitful vitality taste changed in the wake of Goethe's reappraisal of a style that had hitherto been looked upon as 'undefined, disorganised, unnatural, patched together'! And yet how tragically scholarship was to be degraded by generations of nationalists trying to support or refute an absurd theory that was based on nothing more than ignorance or, at least, inexperience.[31] For the time being, it appeared only that the Gothic had been the exclusive and necessary produce of one particular civilisation.

Other writers saw the Gothic as having been the style of feudalism – and thus, by implication, as having been caused at a particular moment in history by a unique political development. But it was the essentially religious connotations of the style that received particular emphasis in Germany and in France, where in 1801 Chateaubriand made use of his incomparable eloquence to evoke images of mediaeval monasticism when referring to Gothic churches in general.[32] Thereafter the notion rapidly developed that, just as the supremacy of Greek art had been made possible only by a unique (and probably unrepeatable) combination of circumstances, so, too, Gothic, at its most serious, had been the product only of a genuine 'Age of Faith'. Despite all the pastiches that were erected in England and elsewhere in Europe, the true Gothic style could be revived only if true faith could be revived; correspondingly, true Gothic architecture provided an indication of the religious sincerity of earlier communities, whereas the classicising forms of the Renaissance were of themselves sufficient to demonstrate the amorality and 'pagan' leanings of European society between the fifteenth and the nineteenth centuries. So binding were the moral associations of these styles in the eyes of Pugin, fanatical Catholic and himself a Gothic architect, that in his *Contrasts* of 1836 he seems to have felt that he need do no more than juxtapose illustrations of buildings designed in the Gothic and classical manner, but intended to serve the same purpose, in order to establish the fact that ethics as well as taste had catastrophically decayed.[33] Fashions change, however, and associations fade. Later perusers of *Contrasts* might not have been as prepared as was Pugin to take it for granted that an inn or an ecclesiastical monument or a public fountain dating from the Middle Ages must necessarily be morally superior to their classically constructed analogues of subsequent centuries. Pugin, therefore, made his illustrations more explicit through the use of 'hieroglyphs', on the lines recommended by Lairesse and others concerned with the limitations of artistic communication. Thus bullying policemen or crude notice-boards or scrawled graffiti disfigure the modern scene so as to press home its iniquity. And in the second edition of *Contrasts* Pugin emphasises the point still

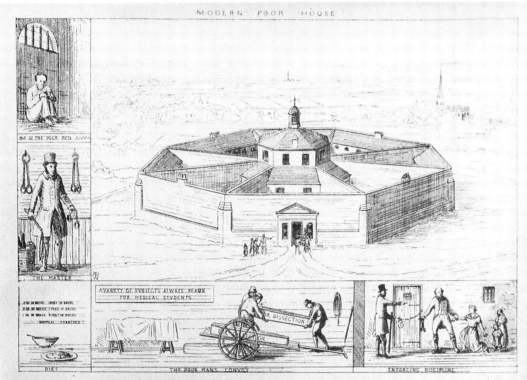

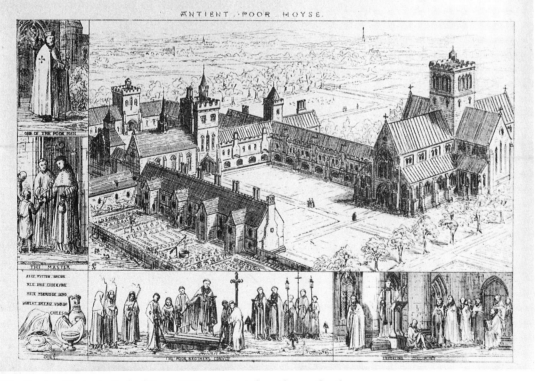

141. Pugin, *Contrasts*, 2nd edition, 1846: contrasted residences for the poor.

further by adding plates in which new types (as well as new styles) of buildings are introduced: the prison, the disciplinary poor house (pl. 141), the socialist hall of science.

No one had ever gone as far as Pugin in making use of images in order to evoke a change of spirit (and no one had yet shown visual wit of such mordant distinction), but he and the other writers who have been mentioned in this chapter were interested in such issues only because they wished to celebrate particular moments in the past or to propagate specific styles; and while their approaches can hardly be described as empirical, they were certainly far more haphazard than systematic. However, by now apparently incontrovertible principles had been established which – so it was believed – extended the relationship between the arts and every other human pursuit to the whole of recorded history.

iii

'This sense for the perfect plasticity of gods and men was pre-eminently at home in Greece.'[34] To the students who first heard these words in one of Hegel's lectures on aesthetics delivered in Berlin during the 1820s – as to the wider public which was not able to read them until they were posthumously published in 1835 – the sentiment was familiar enough. What followed, however, was more surprising.

In its poets and orators, historians and philosophers, Greece is not to be under-stood at its heart unless we bring with us as a key to our comprehension an insight into the ideals of sculpture and unless we consider from the point of view of their plasticity not only the heroic figures in epic and drama but also the actual statesmen and philosophers. After all, in the beautiful days of Greece, men of action, like poets and thinkers, had this same plastic and universal yet individual character both inwardly and outwardly. They are great and free, grown independently on the soil of their own inherently substantial personality, self-made, and developing into what they [essentially] were and wanted to be. The Periclean age was especially rich in such characters: Pericles himself, Phidias, Plato, Sophocles above all, Thucydides, too, Xenophon, Socrates – each of them of his own sort, unimpaired by another's; all of them are out-and-out artists by nature, ideal artists shaping themselves, individuals of a single cast, works of art standing there like immortal and deathless images of the gods, in which there is nothing temporal and doomed. The same plasticity is charac-teristic of the works of art which victors in the Olympic games made of their bodies, and indeed even of the appearance of Phryne, the most beautiful of women, who rose from the sea naked in the eyes of all Greece.

To claim that we cannot understand Pericles and Plato, Sophocles and Thucydides without 'an insight into the ideals of sculpture' – no historian or philosopher, not even an artist or antiquarian in his most missionary mood had even dared to suggest as much, and it is not surprising that Walter Pater was to seize on this passage with enthusiasm.[35] But John Gillies, who was aged eighty-eight and in excellent health, still had one year to live when Hegel's lectures were published; and although it is hardly conceivable that he came across them in Clapham, it is tempting to fancy him doing so and recalling that, half a century earlier, he had toyed with the notion that what he thought of as Greek statues might be able to throw some light on Pericles and his contemporaries – and had then dismissed the idea on the grounds that history and the arts were not close enough in their aims to make the matter worth pursuing.

Hegel himself rarely gave primacy to the arts in quite so forthright a manner as in this haunting evocation of sculptures about which he knew only at second or third hand. But that the arts constituted an integral element within a quasi-divine pattern which also embraced every other human activity was central to his thinking on historical development and was to have profound and lasting effects.

Even during Hegel's own lifetime and still more in the following decades so many students confessed to a failure to understand his philosophy while yet being intoxicated by it that, in the context of this book, it is fortunately of far greater interest to consider what was made of him – even by those who never in fact read him – than to examine the nature of what he was actually concerned to say. And what was made of him was the discoverer of a mystical but orderly scheme of things that eliminates those irritating accidents and exceptions that obstruct the path of historical research. Certain concepts – the childhood, adolescence, maturity and decrepitude of the arts, for instance, or what is loosely known as Freudianism – have at different times gained widespread currency and encouraged the pursuit of bold and imaginative ventures which would hardly have been possible had the premises behind them been subjected to sceptical analysis. Such has been the effect of Hegel's 'World Spirit' which encompasses every aspect of the progress of mankind and which unfolds itself inexorably through successive civilisations on the road to freedom, from the Oriental to the classical to the Germanic, developing itself as it does so. And in each civilisation it is, so to speak, incarnated in the activity or the art that is most appropriate to it – architecture, sculpture, painting or music – and expresses its essence within that form: thus Egyptian civilisation, which is riddled with contradictions, is characterised, above all, by symbolic memorials made up of a multitude of forms and images in which we recognise that the Spirit feels itself compressed and can express itself only in a sensuous mode. It is, in fact, the Sphinx, 'symbol of the symbolic itself', that best exemplifies the Egyptian spirit: half architectural and half sculpture; half animal and half man struggling to free himself.[36]

The range of Hegel's artistic interests still baffles the imagination; as does the fact that he could speak with such confidence about so much that he had never seen – not just the monuments of China and India and Egypt, but even the art of Greece and Italy. And yet his system had perforce to include the whole of human history if it was to be of relevance to any single part of it. The 'World Spirit' could not pick and choose which path it would follow and omit those regions of Europe and Asia that were not accessible to Hegel. But although Hegel's impressions of the visual arts were often necessarily derived from written accounts, he followed current researches with a sympathetic and creative imagination. He was as familiar with Belzoni's work on the pyramids of Egypt as he was with Von Rumohr's ideas concerning the stylistic development of Duccio and Cimabue.[37] He was indebted primarily to Winckelmann for his understanding of Greek art, but he was fully aware that the approach to that art had been radically affected by Lord Elgin's removal to London of the marbles from the Parthenon, which had saved 'those works of art for Europe and preserved them from complete destruction, and his enterprise deserves recognition through all time'.[38] He understood how vital had been the role played by the young Goethe in drawing the attention of the world to the specifically Germanic qualities of Gothic architecture, but he also knew that since then 'more and more efforts have been made to get to value in these grand works both a peculiar appropriateness to Christian worship and also a correspondence between architectural configuration and the inmost spirit of Christianity'.[39] And when Hegel, who regularly visited museums, refers to pictures he has actually seen – a 'Raphael' in the Louvre from which he can 'scarcely tear himself away', a Murillo in Munich,[40] the Dutch genre pictures that delighted him in the Netherlands[41] – he immediately conveys with what sensitivity he responds to the experience of looking.

The intrinsic fascination of these and many other passages should not, however, conceal the fact that the writings of Hegel would be of cardinal importance for those interested in the historical significance of art even if he had never written a word about painting. For the arts of a period or a country were as subject as were its laws and military and philosophical achievements to the working of the 'World Spirit', which once it reached a specific stage 'builds this principle into the entire wealth of the world, works it out into the many-sidedness of its existence, so that all the other specific characters of that world are dependent on this fundamental one'.[42] It was, therefore, pointless to try to understand the various strands that go to make up the essence of human development – such as religion or art or politics – by considering them in isolation. In a passage that Ernst Gombrich has described as 'all-important'[43] Hegel explained that

> World history represents . . . the evolution of the awareness of the spirit of its own freedom . . . Every step, being different from every other one, has its own determined and peculiar principle. In history such a principle becomes the determination of the spirit – a peculiar national spirit. It is here that it expresses concretely all aspects of its consciousness and will, its total reality; it is this that imparts a common stamp to its religion, its political constitution, its social ethics, its legal system, its customs but also to its science, its art and its technical skills. These particular individual qualities must be understood as deriving from that general peculiarity, the particular principle of a nation. Conversely, it is from the factual details present in history that the general character of this peculiarity has to be derived.

Hegel 'became his admirers'. His influence has been detected in many of the greatest art historians, and all the greatest cultural historians, of the nineteenth and twentieth centuries. It is an influence that derives not from precise examples or from a semi-theological system (both of which were probably familiar only to

those who had studied him carefully at first hand), but from the assumption –
demanded by his theory, even if not always insisted on by him personally – that
any artistic style or form or convention will necessarily coincide with every other
aspect of the civilisation in which it is found. Tentative steps in this direction had,
as we have seen, been taken long before: now they became giant, self-confident
strides. It came to seem axiomatic that the 'naïve' style of early Italian painters
must reflect an innocent and childish society, or that there must be an intrinsic and
determined (rather than plausible and spasmodic) relationship between the Baroque
style, Catholicism and authoritarianism.

Versions (or travesties) of Hegel's ideas spread quickly, and in France they were
successfully popularised by the highly admired writer and philosopher Victor
Cousin. It was also Cousin who in 1824 encouraged Edgar Quinet to translate
Herder's *Outlines of a Philosophy of the History of Man* (for which task Quinet relied
on the English translation which had appeared in 1802), and it was through Cousin
that Quinet met Jules Michelet.[44] Michelet professed to find nothing very much in
Herder that was not already familiar to him through his very close study of Vico;[45]
nor did he have much sympathy for the rigid theorising of Hegel whose works he
began to explore in 1827 and to which he returned at various moments in his life.[46]
None the less, it was their ideas, and the versions of them spread by other writers
in the first quarter of the nineteenth century, that enabled Michelet (and, following
him, very many subsequent historians) to make use of the evidence provided by
the arts in an incomparably richer and more imaginative spirit than had ever been
done before, and thus to give a serious historical dimension to the overwhelming
impression that, as we shall see, was made on him, when still only a child, by the
Musée des Monuments Français.

9

The Musée des Monuments Français

Early in 1800 Chateaubriand returned to Paris after having spent seven years in England. He found himself in a city where, we are told, one still seemed to hear on all sides 'the crumbling and collapse of temples blackened by the centuries, those old basilicas that had welcomed Charlemagne, Philippe-Auguste, Henri IV . . . No longer does the traveller see from afar those consecrated towers that rose up to the heavens like so many witnesses for posterity; and our towns, stripped of their memories, looked like towns newly built in the middle of a new world.'[1]

Chateaubriand and a friend walked at night through the Charterhouse of Paris, its roofs now smashed in, its window leads wrenched away, its doors closed only with upright planks. Black marble tomb stones had been strewn casually around, some totally broken up, some with faint traces of an inscription still just visible. In the inner cloister, wild plum trees grew among the uncut grass and the rubbish. And in the sanctuary, 'instead of hymns raised to honour the dead, one now heard the shriek of the labourer's saw cutting through the tombs'.[2]

The years of Chateaubriand's absence had coincided with the most systematic campaign that had been carried out in any country of modern Europe to eradicate its past: the names of its provinces and streets, the very calender it used, and (of course) many of its principal monuments. But, paradoxically, it was just this relentless destruction, and the subsequent reaction to it, that gave to the arts an historical (and, by implication, ideological) dimension hitherto lacking or, at best, taken for granted. 'Soon', wrote a journalist in 1793 (when that destruction was at its height), 'it will at last be possible for a republican to walk through the streets of Paris without running the risk of damaging his eyes by having to see all those emblems, all those degrading attributes of royalty, which have been carved or painted on almost every public building or private house'.[3] Some eyes, however – even some republican eyes – were to be just as afflicted by the savage eradication by the Jacobins of those very emblems. They were certainly ubiquitous but they only became offensive when attention was drawn to them.

Revolutionary 'vandalism' – the word was coined in 1794[4] – was complex in its origins and in its effects. It was openly discussed for the first time in June 1790 when plans were made to destroy, or at least dismantle, the four bronze slaves at the base of the marble statue of Louis XIV standing in his coronation robes in the Place des Victoires (pls 133–5) – those slaves whose cause had been ingeniously championed by Voltaire nearly half a century earlier.[5] Although it was hostility to the Church and aristocracy, as well as the monarchy, that had first stimulated action on both official and unofficial levels and that thereafter swamped half-hearted attempts to moderate the devastation, greed played almost as influential a role as ideology. The abbey of Cluny, one of the most celebrated of French sacred monuments, continued to be used as a profitable stone quarry long after the restoration of both Christianity and the Bourbon monarchy. It was the architecture and sculpture of the Middle Ages that suffered most at the hands of the revolutionaries and their heirs, because taste and politics often combined in condemning them; but the images that first attracted attention had been very different.

In November 1789 Church possessions were nationalised, and not long afterwards many convents were closed and their contents confiscated by the State, as had already happened some years earlier in the Habsburg Empire. And, as had been done there, it was decided to sell various works of art and other treasures from the buildings concerned. For this purpose depots were established at various places in Paris where the objects could be sorted out into those which were to be disposed of and those which were to be retained. By far the most important of these store-rooms was the convent of the Petits Augustins, on the left bank of the Seine, which had been among the first to be taken over. In September 1790 it was put under the charge of Gabriel-François Doyen,[6] who some twenty years earlier had established his name as one of the most impressive painters of the day with his huge Rubensian altarpiece *St Geneviève interceding for the Victims of the Plague ('Le Miracle des Ardens')*, commissioned for the fashionable church of Saint-Roch. Doyen, whose faith in the determination of the new authorities to preserve the heritage of the past was somewhat over-optimistic, drew up inventories of the possessions of many of the principal churches and organised the transport to the Petits Augustins of large numbers of the pictures, sculptures and silver objects that he recorded in them. But he had had very close contacts with the court and the nobility, and in December 1791 – a few months after the failed attempt of the royal family to flee the country – he found it prudent to accept a long-standing invitation from Catherine the Great to become Professor of the Imperial Academy of Arts at St Petersburg. Within little more than a year some of his own paintings were to be stacked up in the depot that he had controlled,[7] including his masterpiece, *Le Miracle des Ardens*, which was taken there in 1793 after the church of Saint-Roch had been turned into a 'Temple of Reason'.[8]

The pictures were received by Doyen's pupil and admirer, Alexandre Lenoir, who had worked in the depot since its foundation[9] and whose position there as *gardien* was officially recognised in June 1791.[10] In 1792, after his master's hurried departure to Russia, he took control.

Lenoir was now aged thirty-one, and the situation facing him was soon to become much more urgent and complicated than it had been in the early stages of the depot's existence. There had, it is true, been much sporadic vandalism directed against monuments in Paris and the provinces from the first, but the proclamation of the Republic in September 1792 and the abolition of Christianity in October 1793 stimulated a far more destructive policy than hitherto with regard to anything that could be associated with the Church and the monarchy. Some of the initiative may have come from below – 'we receive complaints from all sides', claimed a police report,[11] 'that the eyes of patriots are offended by various monuments raised by despotism in the era of slavery' – but much more was prompted by official and unofficial committees keen to harness popular energies for purposes of their own. Moreover, as had often happened in earlier centuries, it was quickly realised that melted-down bronze statues could be of great value to the army. And so coats of arms were chipped off from buildings and furniture and hacked out of tapestries; equestrian statues were hauled out of town squares and sent to the foundry (pl. 142); compromising portraits were thrown into huge bonfires; the heads of the 'first kings of France' around the porches of Notre-Dame and other churches (whose identifications had been confirmed by Montfaucon) were battered from their bodies; stained-glass windows were smashed for the sake of the lead frameworks surrounding them; jewels and precious ornaments were removed from the sacristies.

The devastation was huge, but by far the most arrogant and provocative of all relics were the great and often flamboyant tombs, ranging in date from the early mediaeval to the late eighteenth century, which could be found in most churches and abbeys – and nowhere more conspicuously than in the abbey of Saint-Denis (renamed Franciade) where the kings of France had been buried sporadically ever since the seventh century, and systematically since the end of the tenth. The desecration of these began on 6 August 1793 and continued without interruption and with astonishing zeal for seventy-two hours (pl. 143). Fifty-one tombs had been destroyed by then: in three days, commented one of the monks, the work of twelve centuries had been wiped out. Two months later began the more sinister job of removing the actual corpses. We are told that most of them were in a state of putrefaction: 'a thick, black, evil-smelling vapour emerged from them, and this was countered through the use of vinegar and burning powder, which did not, however, prevent the workmen getting diarrhoea and fever – though without serious consequences'.[12]

Bronze and lead seals from the tombs were seized immediately and were used for the manufacture of weapons, although some fragments survived. Marble was of less direct use for the war effort, and between November 1793 and the spring of 1796 cartloads of broken tombs were taken from Saint-Denis to the Petits Augustins. There they were carefully identified by Lenoir on the basis of the illustrations to be found in Montfaucon and other antiquarian volumes.[13] They then joined stacks of altarpieces, treasures seized from émigrés and many objects that still had to be sorted out.

Lenoir had no feeling for mediaeval art, and he probably approved of the Revolution – he certainly found it essential to claim that he did. He also agreed (though whether for reasons of conviction or of prudence is not clear) to various acts of destruction, such as the burning (in honour of Marat) of assorted 'feudal' portraits.[14] None the less, he and a few others realised that irreparable damage was being inflicted on French art – he may well have shared the views of the Abbé Grégoire whose use of the word 'vandalism' in his famous denunciation of 1794

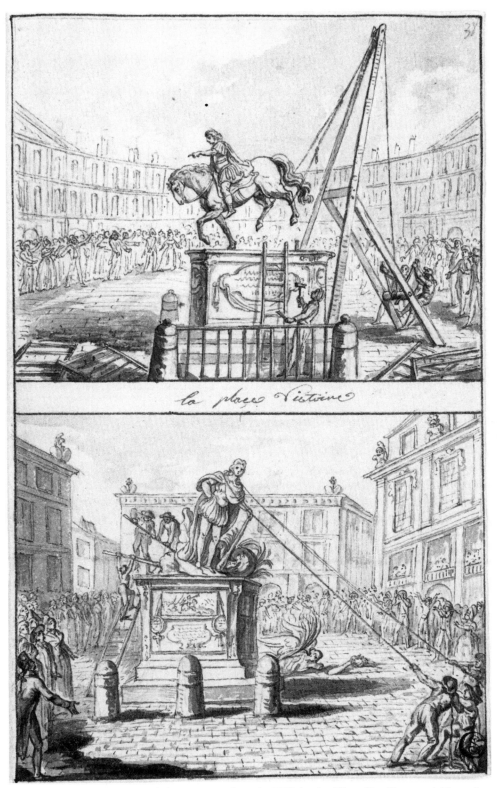

la place Victoire

142. Destruction in 1792 of the statues of Louis XIV in the Place Vendôme and Place des Victoires in Paris, pen and ink with wash, Soulavie Collection (Paris, Louvre: coll. Edmond de Rothschild).

143. Hubert Robert: *Desecration of the Tombs at St Denis* (Paris, Musée Carnavalet).

144. Alexandre Lenoir trying to prevent the destruction of the monuments in Saint-Denis, pen and ink with wash, Soulavie Collection (Paris Louvre: coll. Edmond de Rothschild).

makes it clear that he had in mind the 'collapse of art', lasting for a thousand years, that had followed the barbarian invasions of the Roman Empire. In any case, inspired probably by the preparations under way for the creation of a great museum in the Louvre, Lenoir seems to have come to the conclusion, as early as June 1793, first that he would try to preserve, and even restore, the objects under his control, and then that he would establish a museum of his own.[15] He was later to emphasise that the principal reason why he cherished 'that famous revolution . . . which has established a new order of things founded on reason and justice' was that it was to it 'that I owe the bringing together of the monuments that I have the privilege to exhibit to the friends of order and of the fine arts'.[16]

Although Lenoir produced the first of his many catalogues of the contents of the depot in June 1793 and was allowed to open it to the public for a short time in August,[17] it was not until August 1794, a few days after the execution of Robespierre, that he drew up a full account of the sculptures stored in the Petits Augustins. A little over a year later, on 1 September 1795, the Musée des Monuments Français was opened on a permanent basis,[18] although it was only granted official recognition towards the end of October.[19]

One of the problems facing Lenoir (and never solved by him) was how to reconcile two conflicting views which he constantly reiterated: on the one hand, he liked to project the image of himself as the solitary embattled saviour of the French heritage; on the other, he was anxious to stress that his every step was taken with the full accord of the authorities.[20] For he had to act very carefully. The material was in his charge just because it *was* 'counter-revolutionary', as was made painfully clear to him when he was wounded in the hand by a bayonet as he tried to prevent the total destruction of Girardon's fine allegorical tomb of Richelieu (cf. pl. 144). He was, therefore, eager to point out that it was only the cardinal's effigy, and not his body, that was of any interest: it was in neutral (perhaps even sympathetic) tones that he reported that 'one of the agents of the government of 1793, seeking in his revolutionary fury to avenge the victims of this cruel minister, cut Richelieu's head from the skeleton and showed it to those onlookers who happened to find themselves in the church of the Sorbonne'.[21] Although Grégoire was to make the ingenious point that the very act of conserving 'the monuments of despotism' involved 'condemning them to a sort of eternal pillory',[22] Lenoir, at least in the early stages of his project, had to convince the administration that preservation carried with it no ideological overtones[23] – and this was not easy in view of the fact that so much destruction clearly was motivated by ideology. 'Please believe me, Citizens,' he wrote in an application to the Committee of Public Instruction, 'that it is not in order to honour the memory of François Ier that I ask permission to rebuild the monument that I am about to describe to you. I forget his morals along with his ashes. I am concerned only with the progress of art and education.'[24]

Thus Lenoir was aspiring to reject all those associations between the image and history that, as we have seen, had attracted writers ever since Petrarch. The claims of art and (art) education were to be the passports that would allow the restored effigies of kings, noblemen and cardinals to be granted asylum in the Petits Augustins after they had been driven from their original resting places. Lenoir had therefore to devise an arrangement that would make clear that the arts had progressed from infancy under the Goths to perfection under François Ier and then, after declining through the bad examples set by Vouet and Lebrun,[25] had once again revived in his own day. To emphasise this he included a number of monuments whose only function was to serve as examples of the primitive and the decadent. His approach was strongly influenced by Winckelmann's *History of the Art of Antiquity*, and he acknowledged this both in his catalogue and through the unique tribute of a portrait bust which he specially commissioned for his museum.[26]

The progress and decline of art was demonstrated through the display, in the longest and best-lit gallery of the former convent (originally the chapel),[27] of a series of important monuments arranged in approximately chronological order: most of these appear to have dated from the sixteenth and seventeenth centuries, but there were also earlier works (ranging back to fragments of a Roman altar) and a few later ones.[28] It would seem, however, that as the Terror subsided, the nature of Lenoir's interest in the art of the past – or, perhaps, the claims that he felt able to make for that art – changed significantly, for he pointed out that 'wherever possible I have tried to collect for the museum everything that can give some idea of the costumes of the past . . . I hope that in time this collection will be useful for artists wanting to reproduce costumes that they would [otherwise] find it difficult to see.'[29] However, as Lenoir was convinced that for 'young people wishing to pursue a career in the arts a study of the antique is absolutely essential', it is hard to believe that he really thought that it could be of much use for them to learn about clothing between Clovis and Philippe II (1180–1223).[30] It is far more likely that it was he himself who became absorbed in the information that works of art could supply about the appearance and customs of earlier generations – such an interest would, after all, be natural for a man who revered the memory of Montfaucon, and whose last, most devoted and most uncritical follower he showed himself to be.

It was surely this antiquarian passion, combined with a strong feeling for the picturesque, that also guided Lenoir's extravagant and exotic decoration of the separate rooms of the Petits Augustins, each one of which was to be devoted to a separate century of French sculpture: 'in order to present to the lovers of the arts and of their history the spectacle of a century as distant [as the thirteenth], we have tried to take account of all those details that give the truest picture of the taste of those centuries preceding the one in which we live. Such researches are basically useful for our work, and we shall pursue them in all the rooms of the museum.'[31] So much for that simple demonstration of rise and fall that, he had once claimed, was the only benefit he wished to render to artists. Increasingly it was the creation of local colour and historical atmosphere that preoccupied Lenoir.

The 'Salle d'Introduction', with its selection of sculptures from all periods, led into the much smaller rectangular 'Salle du 13ème siècle', which had once been the sacristy of the convent (pl. 145). The vaults were painted blue with gold stars, and the illumination was deliberately kept low partly through the insertion of stained-glass windows removed from the abbey of Saint-Germain-des-Prés so as to create the impression of 'magic whereby the population which had been terrorised by superstition was kept in a state of perpetual feebleness'.[32] This notion (which Lenoir quietly suppressed when attacks on the Christian religion ceased to be in vogue)[33] had been promulgated in a recently published book which he much admired, Charles Dupuis's *L'Origine de tous les cultes*.[34] Indeed, the 'damp, gloomy, ruinous assemblage of monkish horror'[35] displayed in the 'Salle du 13ème siècle' made a powerful impact on visitors to the museum: the German dramatist August von Kotzebue found it 'impossible to walk through this dark place of tombs without being seized by secret terror'.[36]

Other reactions were, however, possible. On 27 December 1800 Bonaparte visited the museum accompanied by his wife Josephine, and when going through the 'Salle du 13ème siècle' he exclaimed, 'Lenoir, you transport me to Syria; I am very satisfied; continue your researches, and I shall always see the results with pleasure.'[37] The eastern accent was supposed to be given by the ogive arches of the doors and windows, specially fabricated from the debris of a vandalised church, and by the 'encrusted coloured glass, gilding and mystical colours', so as to illustrate Lenoir's theories about the Arab origins of Gothic architecture. In its final form this room contained some of the most evocative monuments and reclining figures from Saint-Denis as well as the 'tomb of the children of St Louis', built by Lenoir's craftsmen from two other tombs which had been removed from the Abbey of Royaumont.[38]

'Period rooms' were designed on similar principles for the sculpture of other centuries, but Lenoir's appeal to sentiment and the historical imagination was revealed at its most blatant in a feature of the museum that had had no part in his original concept of it and that, indeed, ran counter to all his declared intentions when planning it. As from 1799 the grounds of the convent were converted into an 'Elysée' (pl. 146) which was largely dedicated to the memory of the great figures of French history:[39] 'In this calm and peaceful garden', he wrote, 'are to be seen more than forty statues: tombs placed here and there on the green lawn rise with dignity amidst the silence and the tranquillity. Pines, cypresses and poplars keep them company, and masks and cinerary urns placed on the walls combine to give to this place of happiness the sweet melancholy that speaks to souls of sensibility' (pl. 147).[40] Among the monuments in the Elysée it was the one of Héloise and Abelard (later transferred to the cemetery of Père Lachaise, where it can be seen today) which appealed most to Lenoir himself – and to the public[41] – and he asked rhetorically whether there was to be found 'anywhere on the globe a soul capable of feeling who has not shed tears onto the pages of Pope and Colardeau'. Lucien Bonaparte gave special permission for their ashes to be brought from Nogent-sur-Seine to Paris,[42] and Lenoir designed for them an extraordinary 'mediaeval' sepulchre (pl. 148). This was partly made up of fragments of destroyed monuments, with a canopy surmounting a large rectangular block of elaborately carved marble. On this lay the two statues, the one of Héloise being 'the figure of a woman made about that time' to which was attached a head carved by the sculptor Louis-Pierre Deseine.[43]

Lenoir himself selected those figures from national (occasionally, European)

145. J.-L. Vauzelle (engraving after), 'Salle du 13ème siècle' in the Musée des Monuments Français (Paris, Musée Carnavalet).

146. Alexandre Lenoir, *Musée des Monuments Français*, vol. v, Paris 1806: view of the Elysée.

147. C.W.
Eckersberg, *Woman
seated in the Elysée of
the Musée des
Monuments Français*,
1811, pen and ink with
wash (Copenhagen,
Statens Museum for
Kunst).

148. 'Tomb of Héloïse
and Abelard' in the
Elysée of the Musée des
Monuments Français
etched in outline with
added watercolours
(Paris, Louvre).

history worthy of being represented in the Elysée, and his museum soon became
an important source of patronage for sculptors.[44] Monuments were made not
only for Descartes, Molière and Pascal but also for Peiresc, Winckelmann and
Lenoir's mentor Montfaucon, whose memorial was appropriately composed of
'hieroglyphs, Egyptian figures, Greek reliefs, figures surviving from the late
Empire period and debris taken from monuments dating from the earliest ages of
the monarchy'.[45] Lenoir was always anxious to get hold of 'authentic' ashes and
bones of his heroes[46] – he also distributed specimens of them to enthusiastic
collectors[47] – and he organised special ceremonies to welcome them to the Elysée,
on the lines of those that were held to receive the remains of Voltaire and Rousseau
in the Panthéon.[48]

The concept, purpose and arrangement of the Elysée marks the most decisive of
Lenoir's breaks with his initial notion of neutralising the past, but we can observe
the same change at work in almost every aspect of the museum. We have seen
that, when applying in 1795 for permission to reconstruct the tomb of François Ier
he had chosen his words with the utmost caution. Yet, five years later, when
the task had been accomplished in a somewhat idiosyncratic manner and the
monument placed in an hexagonal room of its own, Lenoir endorsed the achievements of that monarch with an enthusiasm that would have done credit to any
courtier of the *ancien régime*: 'I see again on the mouth [of the statue] of François Ier
the touching farewell with which he honoured Leonardo da Vinci; I look once
more on that forehead which undoes the work of battles [*défait les batailles*] and on
that open hand so generous with the treasure that it graciously distributes to artists
and scientists.' These words of an anonymous writer (very probably Lenoir
himself) appear in the *avant-propos* of the 1800 edition of the official description of
the contents of the Musée des Monuments Français. Both the sentiment and the
tone are characteristic of the response that was inspired by the works on display.

Lenoir may have done more than any other single figure in history to rescue a
threatened heritage, but, like many fanatics, he became so blinded by the grandeur
of his cause and identified its promotion so closely with himself that he was liable
to forget what had been its *raison d'être*. Moreover, he was boastful and obstinate,
as keen on his own glory as on that of the artists and great men whose achievements he celebrated. He thought of the Musée National in the Louvre more as a
rival, perhaps an enemy, than as a partner, and did what he could to obstruct the
transfer to it of objects under his control, even when their presence in the Petits
Augustins was clearly inappropriate.[49] He was, however, very quick to point out
that the tomb of Charlemagne, removed from Aix-la-Chapelle, 'must undoubtedly
enter the collection of the Monuments Français, and it is no doubt only by
inadvertence that it has been deposited in the Musée Napoleon'.[50] Far worse was
the fact that he continued to 'rescue' art long after it no longer needed rescuing.[51]
If a tomb was not 'mediaeval' enough, he employed his craftsmen to make it more
so; if some famous character was missing from his survey of French history, he
would falsify the evidence of an existing identification[52] or run up a new memorial
created specially for him – just as seventeenth- and eighteenth-century antiquarians
had 'baptised' (and partially created) their 'Faustinas' and 'Pompeys'; if the marble

for such a memorial was in short supply, he was quite ready to break up a religious monument for the purpose.[53] In fact, after his early years in the museum he was probably making more antiquities than he was rescuing.[54] In addition to all this, his scholarship was careless and out-of-date when measured against the standards attained by contemporary students of earlier art, and its deficiencies were soon recognised.[55]

Leopoldo Cicognara (who found the museum too dark, damp and cold for serious study to be possible) commented that

one comes across strange compositions and monsters from Horace because separate fragments have been jumbled together so as to reconstruct monuments that never really existed. Even if one does not actually see young girls with the neck of a horse, there are other very strange couplings made for reasons of symmetry, size or proportion (assuming that other more fantastic reasons are not responsible) which present individual works composed of differing periods designed by differing artists for differing purposes.[56]

Yet the antagonism aroused by Lenoir was, for the most part, owing to other causes. Many observers deplored the fact (though some admittedly welcomed it) that the museum had falsely 'democratised' the character of French monuments by juxtaposing those that had been designed for monarchs with others (mostly fabricated by Lenoir's craftsmen) that were devoted to far humbler personages.[57] Critics argued that he had deformed the very nature of the arts by removing them from their true setting – the churches and palaces for which they had been created – and placing them in the artificial context of a historical museum. It is hardly surprising that Quatremère de Quincy chose this line of attack, for he had consistently objected to the displacement of paintings and sculptures from their original locations and their transfer to museums of any kind.[58] The similar onslaughts of the sculptor Deseine, who had at one time collaborated with Lenoir, may have come as more of a shock, even though he had not concealed his strongly royalist opinions.[59] But it was Chateaubriand who was the most eloquent enemy of the Musée des Monuments Français: 'Cramped within a small space, arranged by centuries, deprived of their harmony with the antiquity of temples and Christian worship, of use only for the history of art rather than the history of customs and religion, no longer retaining even their dust, these monuments have nothing any more to say to the imagination or the heart.'[60] The same point was made, somewhat more sympathetically, by another visitor: 'The very beauty of a tomb which, during his lifetime, had flattered the vanity of some great man is disastrous to his ashes. The columns, the statues, the reliefs with which he had had himself surrounded are dismantled and carefully taken away and no one cares what happens to his remains which are neglected and dispersed. It is only the tomb that is seen, and it is the name of the sculptor and not his own that is remembered.'[61] But Lenoir's many critics who argued in this way did not pause to consider that the elimination of associations was the price that he had had to pay to save the monuments themselves from being eliminated;[62] nor probably did they realise that, in theory at least, he himself agreed that such monuments were best left in the places for which they had been designed. He claimed only that when, as had obviously been the case, they were in danger of being violently dispersed, 'a historical collection can provide just as much interest combined with better protection against destruction'.[63]

Lenoir's enemies also failed to acknowledge that after its first year or two of existence the Musée des Monuments Français was no longer serving only the cause of art history, but was also evoking the very spirit of the nation's identity and giving visible, tangible, form to a past which had, for a short but terrible time, been on the verge of annihilation. It is doubtful whether even the rhapsodical writing of Chateaubriand (some of it, ironically, inspired by the Musée des Monuments Français)[64] was as potent in bringing back to life a feeling for the Middle Ages and the Renaissance as was Lenoir's flair for 'gloomy magic'. Scattered through the abbeys and churches of Paris for which they had been designed, tombs and stained glass windows and escutcheons had attracted the antiquarians and offended public taste. Many had been vandalised even before the Revolution, for they could leave little mark on the sensibilities of men educated to accept the principles of the Enlightenment. Now, broken-up and fancifully recomposed, crammed into the Petits Augustins and its surrounding gardens, they acquired a force that they had perhaps never previously had – and it was a force that owed little to the appeal of art. In itself, the notion of a historical museum (now so integral a feature of our culture), as distinct from a museum of the arts or of curiosities or of one designed to serve erudition or the education of young painters, was not entirely new when Lenoir planned the Musée des Monuments Français. In Arles tentative steps had been taken as early as the last years of the seventeenth century to preserve the city's surviving antiquities in one place, though it was not until the 1780s that these had been assembled within a battered convent to form the Musée Public d'Antiquités de la Ville d'Arles.[65] More than fifty years before that the city of Toulouse had created a historical museum, but this consisted chiefly of paintings that were specially commissioned to represent important events between the arrival of the Celts and the Wars of Religion.[66] And there were other examples of a similar kind. Above all, the role of Westminster Abbey as a shrine to the great men of British history was widely known throughout Europe and certainly exerted a significant influence on Lenoir.[67] But the impact of the Musée des Monuments Français was even greater, and it is hardly an exaggeration to suggest that as an evocation of a vanished world the ruins of Rome had at last found a rival in the redesigned rooms of the Petits Augustins.

It was not to survive for long. As Napoleon pursued his policy of reconciling France to the Church, demands to return monuments to Saint-Denis and elsewhere became ever more pressing. And with Napoleon's downfall and the return of the royal family and aristocratic émigrés, private property and ancestral tombs were also reclaimed. Quite soon critics and claimants had their way. At the end of 1816, shortly after Lenoir had been elected an Honorary Fellow of the Society of Antiquaries in London,[68] the museum was abolished with a stroke of the pen. Many monuments were reinstated in their churches of origin (where they were often subjected to further 'restoration'), and some of the other sculptures went to the Louvre where we shall come across them again in a different context. A few particularly desirable items, such as a group of portrait drawings by the Clouets and a small bronze equestrian figure believed to represent Charlemagne, remained in Lenoir's own possession, though it is not quite clear whether they had ever been exhibited.[69]

In much the same way as Lenoir had earlier claimed to welcome the revolution principally because it had allowed him to create the museum, so in retrospect its dismantling was described by his admirers as 'a blow of cold vengeance against our revolution'.[70] During its twenty years of legal existence Lenoir had fostered, enlarged and publicised it (through an interminable number of catalogues) with a frenetic zeal that even now has never been parallelled in the hardly reticent world of museum directors.

The legacy of the Musée des Monuments Français was lasting. Despite Lenoir's own taste and despite the great number of objects from the sixteenth and seventeenth centuries on view, it was the art of the Middle Ages that attracted most attention from art lovers and scholars. Although it was sometimes argued that its main purpose should be to indicate 'in the clearest manner what the arts, and especially sculpture, ought *not* to be',[71] many impressive and sometimes beautiful publications owe their existence to research carried out in the Petits Augustins.[72] Public and private collections were also stimulated by its example, and shortly before 1838 Alexandre du Sommerard, who formed the most famous of these, acknowledged how much the modern study of mediaeval art had been indebted to it:

> The creation, or rather the ever-to-be-regretted dispersal, of the Musée des Monuments Français – so picturesquely arranged and so well-described by Alexandre Le Noir – was needed to draw attention to the effect and the importance of these old things. It was their loss that made our riches appreciated and that, thanks to the successive efforts of MM Quatremère de Quincy, Alexandre de La Borde, Raoul-Rochette, Artaud, Willemin, Gilbert etc., gave really effective guidance to the new archaeological studies.[73]

The centre of those studies became Du Sommerard's own collection which, in 1843, the year after his death, was bought by the State, together with the Hôtel de Cluny, where he had been living for the previous year, and the adjoining Roman Baths. As early as 1833 the architect Albert Lenoir (son of Alexandre) had drawn up plans for the display of the collection which were closely based on the principles established by his father at the Musée des Monuments Français. The new Musée de Cluny was therefore everywhere thought of as the natural successor to the museum that Lenoir had devised at the height of the Revolution.[74]

Artists as well as scholars had flocked to the Musée des Monuments Français in its heyday, particularly those of royalist inclinations, and they had found in it sources for their so-called 'troubadour' pictures which represented some of the more informal episodes of French history.[75] These, in turn, encouraged the demand for those large-scale reconstructions of heroic events from the national past that dominated historical painting throughout Europe during much of the nineteenth century.[76] But although it is often simple to find particular details of furnishing or costume in troubadour pictures which were clearly derived (as Lenoir had hoped would be the case) from objects in the museum, perhaps the main artistic lesson to be drawn from it was another. The contents of the Petits Augustins had shown how few had been the principal events in French history that had actually been illustrated by artists contemporary with them. When, in 1837, Louis-Philippe decided to convert the palace of Versailles into a museum of French history, artists were commissioned to represent just those scenes – The Baptism of Clovis, The Entry of Charles VIII into Naples – that had *not* been recorded in earlier centuries.

Within the context of the present book, however, the real significance of Lenoir's achievement is different – and more important. As early as 1809 it was noted that as well as 'the painters, sculptors, architects and decorators who come to the museum to study the history of art and both military and civilian costumes', there could also be found there 'the austere historian who follows with an observant eye the ancient history of art so as to compare it with the monuments':[77] indeed, once the risks inherent in recalling the feudal past had been exorcised by the rapid changes in current French politics, Lenoir did all he could to encourage a historical, and not merely an artistic, approach to the monuments in his charge by sprinkling his catalogue entries with biographical anecdotes and summaries of colourful episodes. We are told that 'it was unusual for visitors to complete their day without attentively reading some chapters of our history'.[78] Another *habitué* of the museum recalled in old age that 'as children we had become intimately acquainted with all those marble personages: kings, warriors, prelates, writers, poets, artists. We could hardly read, but already we were familiar not only with their features but also with their histories . . . [Going to the Petits Augustins] was a good preparation for reading Augustin Thierry, Barante and all that cluster of historians who soon afterwards were to throw light on those parts of our national history that were still covered in darkness.'[79]

After the museum had been closed, so many historians of all kinds and beliefs acknowledged the great importance that it had had for their work that Guizot was hardly exaggerating when he described Lenoir as 'the founder of historical studies'.[80] It is true that Augustin Thierry claimed that it was through his reading of Chateaubriand that he had been converted to historical research; none the less, he deplored the dismantling of the Petits Augustins,[81] and a few years after his death it was said of him that 'Lenoir did not merely create, amidst the prevailing storms, a museum full of poetry, a refuge for early French art: he gave us Augustin Thierry; it was through visiting the Gothic rooms of this picturesque museum, so deserving of our regrets, that the eloquent, penetrating and patient interpreter of our old chroniclers conceived the idea of unravelling the chaos surrounding the origins of our history'.[82] Prosper de Barante, whose chronicles of Burgundy were regularly compared with the novels of Sir Walter Scott because of the 'local colour' with which he attempted to recreate the Middle Ages,[83] was another historian who said that it had been wrong to destroy the Musée des Monuments Français, though he hoped that the Musée de Cluny, founded by Alexandre du Sommerard, would

149. Léon-Mathieu Cochereau, *Artist drawing in Musée des Monuments Français* (Paris, Musée Carnavalet).

prove to be of comparable importance for scholars.[84] And yet another mediaevalist, the comte de Montalembert, who deplored the chaotic and renewed 'restoration' of the tombs that had been taken back from the museum to Saint-Denis and elsewhere, emphasised that 'the monuments of our past are essential auxiliaries to our historical studies; they are the still-living witnesses whom we must consult every day'.[85] But it is Jules Michelet who has left us the most vivid impression of what the Musée des Monuments Français could mean for a young historian, and it is in his work that we can see its impact at its most effective:

> Even now I can recall the feeling, still just the same and still stirring, that made my heart beat when, as a small child, I would enter beneath those dark vaults and gaze at the pale faces; and would then, keen, curious and timid, walk and look, room after room, epoch after epoch [pl. 149]. What was I looking for? I hardly know – the life of the time, no doubt, and the spirit of the ages. I was not altogether certain that they were not alive, all those marble sleepers, stretched out on their tombs. And when I moved from the sumptuous monuments of the sixteenth century, glowing with alabaster, to the low room of the Merovingians, in which was to be found the sword of Dagobert, I felt it possible that I would suddenly see Chilpéric and Fredégonde raise themselves and sit up.[86]

It was the Musée des Monuments Français, wrote Michelet on another occasion,[87] that gave him his first vivid sense of history, and, indeed, no student of the past had ever spoken of an artistic heritage in quite this way. But had Michelet been unable to deepen and develop responses of this kind he could have done no more than exploit the evocative and picturesque (not to say rhetorical) prose that has so often been held against him. Fortunately, however, he could also take more rewarding historical advantage of the visual images that meant so much to him by drawing on an intellectual discussion that, as we have seen, had been developing over the previous half century. He thus became the first great historian to attempt to reconstruct all aspects of the past – psychological and moral as much as narrative and political – to a significant extent on the basis of the visual evidence available to him.

Michelet

i

It was not until 1846, when he was aged forty-eight, that Michelet first recorded in print the overwhelming impression made on him as a child by the Musée des Monuments Français, and it was seven years later that he described with such eloquence the visits that he had paid there 'so many times' with his mother – visits to those low, dark rooms in which he had imagined that he might see the early monarchs of France suddenly rise from their tombs.[1] By then he himself had long been demonstrating, in a succession of books, that art of bringing the past to life which, together with so many of his admirers, he considered to be one of the principal tasks of the historian.[2] He had, however, been referring to the museum in lectures well before – ever since the first course he had given at the Collège de France in 1838 and, as he noted in his journal, the memories of it 'made me relive my childhood'.[3] It is, therefore, surprising that neither in the account of that childhood which he began to write when he was still only twenty-two nor in the diaries that he kept at the same period does he ever mention the Musée des Monuments Français which had been dismantled only a few years earlier.

Michelet's upbringing was bleak, marked by hunger and cold: his father, a printer, was arrested for debt; his mother died when he was seventeen. He describes his timidity in the face of the callousness and the coarseness that he saw all around him, and the solitude to which he felt himself driven as a result. But he describes also the compensations. It is true that the dawning of his own sensuality and the temporary appeal of religious beliefs were mixed blessings; but the deep affection he felt for his school friend Paul Poinsot (for whose benefit he wrote his early memoir, but who was to die before it was completed) brought him nothing but happiness. So also did his omnivorous reading – not only in French, but in Greek, Latin and English, and then in German and Italian. And he conceived ambitious literary plans. But in none of the accounts of his childhood and adolescence that he wrote when still a young man, do we hear anything of interest about the visual arts, which, as we shall see, were later to play so very important a role in his life and work. For two years he went to drawing classes with M. Mossa, an extreme royalist, 'assez bon petit homme, artiste sans talents et même jugeant mal, comme je m'en suis aperçu depuis, ne trouvant rien de plus beau que Vanloo et Boucher', but the experience proved to be of no value, 'à cause du mauvais ton des élèves'.[4] Eight years or so later, when he was aged twenty-two, he took his mistress, Pauline Rousseau (whom he was to marry in 1824), to see David's *Death of Socrates*, which was temporarily hanging in the Musée du Luxembourg. Once there he 'gave her a lecture on history and mythology', and while she admired David's *Leonidas* and above all Girodet's *Endymion*, 'I showed her in a visible manner, that the statue of Venus on a goat made an impression on me'.[5] And that is all.

In 1824 Michelet, who was by now teaching history at the Collège de Sainte-Barbe, 'discovered' Vico and soon set about translating extracts from the *Scienza Nuova* and other works. It was probably this exhilarating experience that aroused his interest in breaking down barriers between the various intellectual disciplines. In August 1825 he prepared the ground by choosing as the theme of the speech he gave at a prize-giving ceremony: 'l'unité de la science'. In this he argued that no single branch of learning – languages, literature, history, physics or mathematics – should be studied in isolation from the others.[6] Within three months he was dissatisfied with this ambition and noted in his journal that 'one could also make a sparkling speech on the "unité de l'histoire du genre humain"'.[7] He realised the difficulties involved: one problem that worried him was the chronological range that would have to be explored if the project was to be practicable – if too short a period was chosen, it would be impossible to establish a link between the various activities to be studied; if too long, the proposed task would be unmanageable.[8] None the less, he continued to be enthralled by the possibilities that were opening up before him, and it is now, between late 1825 and early 1826, that his ideas first become directly relevant to the theme of this book.

It has already been pointed out that Vico showed no interest in the visual arts; but Michelet appreciated at once that they would necessarily be required to play an important part in his scheme of things. On 12 February 1826 he made a number of proposals in his *journal des idées* about how to treat the history of sixteenth-century France, and in one of these he commented: 'One could begin with the political and literary history of the Ligue, then do the history of the sixteenth century, then the literary history of France. The illustrations [*la partie pittoresque*] could be very remarkable: 1. portraits of the great authors; 2. pictures painted at the same time as the principal scenes (processions, massacres), if there are any; 3. medals and coins; 4. emblems and heraldic devices of the great nobles; 5. monuments and architecture of the period; 6. a plan of Paris at the time; 7. a map of France. Are there any collections of sermons and songs of the period? Compare them with the speeches and songs of the Revolution'.[9]

Unfortunately, despite the journal he had written between 1820 and 1822 and despite the notes on his reading and ideas from which we have already quoted, it was only in 1830 that he began to keep a real diary – which he continued until the end of his life – though we have some very brief jottings dating from his visit to Germany in the summer of 1828. It was his first visit to Italy that inspired him to make much fuller records of his daily activities. Such records were by now traditional; but Michelet's journals strike a new note. From the first they are distinguished by an almost insatiable pursuit of monuments of all kinds: it is hard to believe that anyone before him had looked at so many churches and palaces, pictures and sculptures, and had then felt the need to make rapid, and sometimes telling, comments on them. But it is not only the quantity of his observations that surprises: it is also their nature and the uses to which he put them.

When Michelet went to Italy in 1830 neither the physical appearance of the land nor the aesthetic criteria by which its monuments were judged had changed in any fundamental way since the days of Montesquieu, Gibbon and other eighteenth-century travellers; much of his time was therefore devoted to cities that they had visited before him. But, unlike them, he was almost as interested in the humble and the unexpected as in the sublime and the consecrated, and – even more importantly – unlike them, he did not confine his views on architecture, sculpture and painting to his private journals, but introduced them directly into his major historical works. Thus, in his *Introduction à l'Histoire universelle* (which he published at the age of thirty-three and which, towards the end of his life he considered to have been his first really significant contribution to history[10]) he demonstrated the individualism that had characterised life in Italy, especially during the Middle Ages, by pointing to the apparent fact that

> The Italians alone possessed any civic architecture at the various times when the other nations knew only religious architecture. The word *pontifex* means builder of bridges. Etruscan buildings, unlike those of the East, all serve a practical purpose. They are town walls, aqueducts, tombs; one pays much less attention to their temples. Mediaeval Italy built many churches, but these were also used for political meetings. While Germany, England and France raised only religious edifices, Italy made roads and canals. Thus Germany was ahead of Italy in the production of prodigious cathedrals. Gian Galeazzo Sforza had to seek architects in Strasbourg in order to close the vaults of Milan cathedral.[11]

When writing this he must have been recalling monuments that he had seen in Italy some months earlier (though in this case he had not described them in his journals) and then backing up his memories (deforming them may explain the process more accurately) by some, surely unreliable, written hypothesis in order to establish a conclusion that he had probably reached independently.

Again and again, for Michelet the process of allegorising what he saw took place almost at the same moment as the act of vision itself. Thus three or four days after his arrival in Rome he looked down on the city from the Campidoglio and, remembering, perhaps, how vividly Herder had seen the essential spirit of ancient Rome reflected in its buildings, he noted that 'The Pantheon represents worship in antiquity, the Colosseum the struggle of the two religions, St Peter's the triumph of Christianity. Christianity conquered Rome from the Colosseum to St Peter's. The Aventine and the Capitol, political duality. All this can be seen from the Palace of the Senators on the Capitol.'[12] For his *Histoire romaine* (which he began a few months later and published almost immediately after the *Introduction à l'Histoire universelle*) he had only to give a little more colour to these insights in order to close the first chapter in an evocative manner that was to be characteristic of much of his historical writing: 'When one surveys them from the Capitol, the principal

150. *Dacian Captive*,
marble (Vatican Museum,
Braccio Nuovo).

monuments of this tragic city allow one to grasp, without difficulty, the progress
and unity of its history. The Forum shows you the Republic; the Pantheon of
Augustus and Agrippa displays the unification of all the peoples and all the gods of
the ancient world in the same empire, the same temple. This monument of the
central epoch of Roman history is situated at the very centre of Rome, while at its
two extremities you see, in the Colosseum, the first struggles of Christianity and,
in the church of St Peter's, its triumph and supremacy.'[13]

The travel notes that Michelet made during this first visit to Italy served him not
only for the *Introduction à l'Histoire universelle* and the *Histoire romaine*, both of
which were published within little more than a year of his return to Paris, but also
for the *Histoire de France* to which he was to devote much of the rest of his life. On
12 April 1830 he went to the Braccio Nuovo of the Vatican Museum and recorded,
among many other sculptures there, 'Les *Captifs daces nature brute*' (pl. 150).[14] In
the first volume of the *Histoire de France*, which was published in December 1833,

hè drew on these at much greater length in order to characterise the 'profound impersonality of the German genius', which had been admirably grasped by the ancient sculptor: 'With their enormous proportions and forests of unkempt hair, they do not in any way convey a notion of barbarian savagery but rather that of great brute force, that of an ox or an elephant, which has about it something curiously indecisive and vague . . . This indecision in their manner of looking has often struck me among the most eminent men in Germany.'[15]

From his earliest historical writing Michelet introduced his readers to what was then still a novel concept: both the actual structure of past societies and the defining characteristics of different nationalities could be directly visualised and interpreted by imaginative contemplation of the arts that those societies and nations had left behind them. 'Monuments of this kind', he wrote of the cathedrals of Paris, Saint-Denis and Reims, 'are great historical facts',[16] and he was very proud of his originality in drawing on such facts for his understanding of the past. 'Before me', he claimed in a letter written just as the first two volumes of his *Histoire de France* were published,[17] 'no one had spoken of geography from the standpoint of the historian, no one had attempted to write the history of art in the Middle Ages. I do not make an exception either for the Germans or for the author of *Notre-Dame de Paris*. He has walked around [*tourné autour*] the monuments, but I have explained how that vegetation of stone has sprouted and grown.'

'Walked around': these are the very words with which in the *Histoire* itself he describes the attitude of those who visit a church as they would a Gothic museum. They would be full of praise for the delicacy of its ornamentation, ignorantly impressed by some refined but laborious example of craftsmanship dating from the period of decadence; but deaf to its profound symbolism.[18] From the pages of his journal[19] we can follow Michelet as he himself had, two years earlier, 'walked around' the Gothic churches of Normandy and Brittany, prompted by just those motives of curiosity, that search for philosophical explanations or abstruse interpretations, which he was later to castigate in others – but at the same time always eager to penetrate the deeper mysteries which had now been almost irretrievably lost. We find him dismissing Victor Hugo's apparent notion that mediaeval architecture was capricious and, on the contrary, discerning in it a logical coherence – 'a superb dialectic in stone'; comparing the plans of the churches he was visiting in such numbers with those of England and Germany, not all of which he knew at first hand; calling on local antiquarians at six in the morning in order to be shown how the variety of window structures (wide or coupled or divided by columns; simple or flamboyant) could help determine the date of each building; reading the most up-to-date architectural treatises and visiting libraries so as to be able to run through the local journals; listening to current theories about the sources of the Gothic style – Lyon? Bâle? Cologne? Quick notes are jotted down in Rouen, in Saint-Ouen, in Caudebec, in Caen, in Morlaix and in many other towns of less importance; notes not only about architecture, but about the conditions of contemporary life, family matters, personal feelings; notes that are sometimes vivid, sometimes expressive, sometimes technical. It is these notes that constitute the raw material for page after page of sustained eloquence in the second volume of the published *Histoire* where he describes the significance of Christian beliefs for mediaeval France: a significance perceptible only to those who could understand how perfectly these beliefs had been expressed through the very structure of Gothic churches.

How often Michelet travels throughout Europe in this way, visiting not only churches, but also those small, local museums that were everywhere coming into being during the 1830s and 1840s: portraits of district worthies accumulated in the library of some provincial archbishopric, together, perhaps, with the odd treasure rescued from a looted country house in the neighbourhood, fragments of vandalised ecclesiastical furnishings and prizes of an amateur archaeological expedition – instruments as essential for the creation of a sense of history as were the illustrated books and journals that were appearing in increasing numbers. These, too, Michelet studied carefully: notably the *Annales Archéologiques* edited by the devoutly Catholic scholar Adolphe Didron (author of *L'Histoire de Dieu*), which, as from 1844, not only published innumerable engravings of objects of all kinds associated with Christian worship but explained how essential it was to be able to unravel their iconographical significance if mediaeval art was to have any serious meaning.[20]

Michelet himself (during the early stages of his life, before he turned away in disgust from the Middle Ages) claimed that only the pilgrim, and not the tourist, can genuinely understand the art of the period – 'we must touch these stones with care, tread lightly on these flagstones. All this still bleeds, still suffers'[21] – and it is not therefore surprising that one clerical reviewer should have found it difficult to reconcile the historian's passion with his lack of Christian faith.[22] Nevertheless, the great importance that Michelet ascribed to art and the novelty of his approach – 'monuments breathe, ogives in the cathedrals think, transepts meditate and dream', in the words of one reviewer[23] – were at once apparent to his contemporaries, even if the validity of his examples was not always accepted. In a long series of courteous but very critical articles, the baron d'Eckstein charged Michelet (who had sent him the book for review) with having misunderstood Hegel and with having wrongly interpreted the racial characteristics of the early French tribes.[24] Eckstein, who had been born at Altona (adjoining Hamburg) of a Lutheran family of German-Jewish origins and who had been converted to Catholicism as a result of living in Rome during the French occupation of the city, was an influential Indianist and student of Oriental religions (much derided by Heine as 'Baron Buddha').[25] He was very sensitive to the recklessness of Michelet's sweeping generalisations. How misleading, for instance, to define the Germans as 'profoundly impersonal' partly on the basis of two sculptures in the Braccio Nuovo of the Museo Pio-Clementino! 'And so we find M. Michelet's thoughts carved in the Vatican,' he mocked: 'it is German translated into stone. Let us accept what he says about those Dacians. When I was in Rome, many years ago, I didn't think of checking.' But what had the Dacians to do with the Goths, and hence the Germans? 'And as for the very undecided manner in which learned German writers look at M. Michelet, without focusing properly on him, that is certainly unfortunate... If [Kant and Lessing] had met him, they, I am sure, would have derived real pleasure from focusing their gaze on him; they would quickly have recognised in him a man of feeling and talent who is very well informed, but who sometimes chases after effect and goes in search of paradoxes.'[26]

Eckstein was equally sceptical of that Gaulish art of which Michelet (relying, incidentally, on textual rather than on visual sources) claimed that 'from its very birth it has something impetuous, exaggerated, tragic . . . something that was to drive it towards the gigantic and towards that striving for the infinite which later was to raise ever higher the vaults of our cathedrals.'[27] 'I confess', notes Eckstein,

> that I have difficulty in understanding this bringing together of such widely differing ideas. Was there a Gaulish art? No . . . the Gaulish art of which M. Michelet speaks is no more than a type of Roman art borrowed from Greek art: it is an imitation in no way different from the imitation that we find adopted by all the artists of the Roman Empire . . . And the colossal element in Graeco-Roman sculpture has nothing in common with that 'striving for the infinite' which M. Michelet attributes to the architecture of the mediaeval cathedrals. That striving for the infinite, if the expression is as exact as it is picturesque, is due exclusively to the inspiration of Christianity . . . And, in any case, it is a great mistake to denote as *French* the architecture of mediaeval cathedrals. The earliest groups of masons are found on the banks of the Rhine, at Strasbourg and Cologne.[28]

In fact, Michelet, who carefully included in his footnotes the result of his researches concerning the origins and nature of Gothic architecture,[29] was himself convinced of the primacy of the German masons, but he felt that in the process of being transported into France the style had changed radically.[30] In any case, criticisms of this kind in no way deterred him from continuing to explore visual sources as historical evidence and from asking of them questions about the past of a wholly different order from any previously put to them.

Michelet's responses to architecture, sculpture and painting were always of a far deeper, more personal, nature than were necessary for an adventurous historian keen to pursue new avenues of research. On a visit to Germany in 1842 he was able to discover in painting and in late mediaeval sculpture a kind of cure, or at least relief, for psychological problems that were, at that time, particularly worrying for him. It was he who was the first writer to see in Dürer's tense, frontally posed and half-length *Self-Portrait* in Munich (pl. 151) that analogy with hieratic images of Christ that has struck later historians as so obvious and also as so disturbing; but for Michelet this Christ was a man with a passion for art and yet, at the same time, a 'laborious, suffering, sublime workman'. And in Nuremberg he was struck by the stone self-portrait of Adam Kraft (pl. 152) in the church of St Lawrence who crouches in a half-kneeling position at the foot of the tabernacle and helps to support on his shoulder the gallery that runs around its base. Equally impressive was the small bronze self-portrait of Peter Vischer who stands, half-concealed in a niche of the saint's richly decorated shrine in St Sebald, clad in an apron and holding his hammer. These, and other works of a comparable nature, demonstrated to Michelet that there need be no rigid barrier between the skilled

workman and the artist. He himself had been tormented by the fear that he was too much of an artist (no critic had ever denied his mastery of style) and that his artistic temperament – remote, selfish and aristocratic – risked cutting him off from the people to whom he belonged by origin and whose cause he supported. Now he could see in the Gothic masterpieces of Germany that no such betrayal need be involved. 'The journey has helped me to understand myself,' he proclaimed in his diary; 'the workman who is incomplete everywhere else reaches full development only in Germany', and he repeatedly emphasised that he, too, was only a rough, laborious workman.[31]

ii

Feelings such as this may explain the intensity with which Michelet everywhere turned to the visual arts to help him in his task, but they throw only an oblique light on the actual use to which he put them. Even on his first visit to Italy he had shown an astonishing, not to say reckless, capacity to build generalisations on the basis of the monuments that he saw there; and although his knowledge of the arts

increased vastly as the years went by, his varied approaches to them as historical sources did not change in any fundamental way.

Coins and medals, which for so long had constituted the principal visual sources drawn upon by historians, seem to have held little interest for Michelet, but on one or two occasions he turned to mediaeval royal seals – which were frequently discussed in antiquarian journals – for visual evidence of a kind that can truly be described as historical rather than antiquarian. English seals were double-sided and showed, on the obverse, the ruler as King of England and therefore seated and, on the reverse, the king as Duke of Normandy and therefore on horseback, brandishing a sword. French seals, which were single-sided, showed the king only in the seated position. This difference sprang from the differing nature of the kingship of the two countries, but for Michelet it provided a vivid indication of the 'motionless majesty' of the French monarchy, although, in fact, those seals of the French king that portrayed him as Duke of Aquitaine represented him, too, on horseback, as a leader of men. Michelet considered that the seated position was not merely the embodiment of royal authority, but rather a symbol of ruthless power.[32] Later, he was to claim that Charles V of France was the first modern king of that country – cunning, learned, cold: 'a seated king, like the royal effigy on seals. Until then it had been believed that a king should be mounted. Philippe-le-Bel, with his chancellor Pierre Flotte, had himself gone to Courtrai to be defeated. Charles V fought better from his chair'.[33]

Mediaeval tombs had attracted the devoted attention of antiquarians ever since the sixteenth century and had frequently been illustrated in handsome folios published in England, France, Germany and elsewhere. To the scholar they could serve as manuals of costume, genealogy and heraldry, and they also constituted the most trustworthy and easily accessible source for establishing the dates of important events from an otherwise barely recorded past. Their value in supplying plausible portraits of famous men had been recognised ever since the time of Paolo Giovio. But Michelet, in a brief page or two, seems to have been the first historian to sense the potential significance of tombs as an index of changing attitudes to death – and thus to prepare the ground for much recent research. Taking as his point of departure the remarkable instructions given in his will by Louis duc d'Orléans (assassinated in 1407) for a tomb on which he was to be portrayed, lying in the attitude of death, 'dressed in the habit of the Celestine monks, with beneath my head, instead of a pillow, a rough stone in the manner of a rock and at my feet, instead of lions, another rough rock', Michelet suggested that 'in the first ages of Christianity, when faith was a living force, grief was patient; death seemed only a brief divorce; it separated, but so as to reunite.' He claimed that this strong faith in the soul and in the reunion of souls was demonstrated by the lack of attention paid to mortal remains and hence to the lack of magnificent tombs. Later, however, in the fifteenth century, faith and hope had almost imperceptibly diminished, and as a result, mortal remains had had to be embellished and glorified: the tomb became a chapel, even a church, of which the dead man was to be god.[34] By a natural train of thought Michelet then recalled the tombs of the Scaligeri in 'silent Verona' where two years earlier he had exclaimed in his journal: 'Art here is not art; it is history, the whole historical drama of the Middle Ages';[35] and (quite irrelevantly, as he acknowledged) he contrasted the heavy, simple anonymous structure whose owner – so he learned from Maffei's *Verona Illustrata*[36] – could not be identified, with the magnificent one adjoining it, made up of three storeys of statues of saints and prophets surmounted by a marble horseman. This was the tomb of Cansignorio (pl. 153), and the other must be – 'selon toute apparence' – that of the brother he had murdered...[37] But Michelet's most pungent response to the evidence provided by tomb sculpture was stimulated by Germain Pilon's famous marble group in the Louvre of *The Three Graces* (pl. 154) which had been carved in order to support an urn designed to contain the heart ('if there was one') of Catherine de Médicis next to that of her husband, Henri II, in whose honour she had commissioned the monument. There had from the first been controversy about these refined, half-draped figures, and the monks of the church of the Celestines in which they were placed had hoped to be able to convey the impression that they represented the theological virtues.[38] Some writers did indeed maintain this,[39] but when they were exhibited in the Musée des Monuments Français, Lenoir rightly insisted that the figures were those of the Three Graces.[40] Michelet,

153. Verona, tomb of Cansignorio.

154. Germain Pilon, *The Three Graces*, marble (Paris, Louvre).

however, who ignored the well-documented evidence to this effect and who went so far as to accept the discredited tradition[41] that 'these charming smooth figures were certainly portraits', came to the icy conclusion that 'these beauties have here been entrusted with the task of representing the three theological virtues which, as is well known, were in the heart of Catherine: Faith, Hope and Charity.'[42]

Michelet realised how misleading it could be to accept the flattery of funerary monuments as a source of impartial information about the achievements of the illustrious dead, but his perception rather faltered when he came to consider their portraits. He has, understandably, been criticised because of the naïvety with which he was prepared to read into the features of those depicted the very characteristics that he expected to find there.[43] The fallacy inherent in such an approach had, as we have seen, been apparent to Gibbon nearly a century earlier, and Michelet sometimes compounded his misjudgements by relying on incorrectly identified portraits which, none the less, continued to yield to his scrutiny those strengths or weaknesses of character he was looking for in some other historical personage. Discovering a wrongly labelled portrait at Ferney of the Habsburg Empress Maria Theresa, he believed that he was gazing at a representation of 'the odious Russian minotaur', Catherine the Great: a mediocre work, it was true, but one produced by some faithful Flemish artist who, incapable of lying or embellishing, had laboriously and pedantically painted only what he saw. How different was her hard, gloomy, inhuman expression here from that of the 'mawkish female Caesar' shown in so many insipid portraits! But this coarsening could be explained easily enough: by her association with murderers such as the Orloffs and the Potemkins; by her own connivance in murder; by her atrocious treachery and her mass slaughters in Poland and Turkey; and by 'the degrading brutality of the filthy torrent of purchased *amours* ceaselessly renewed by the old woman'. All this was visible in the portrait at Ferney which must have given Voltaire such a shock in 1770 when it revealed to him her body thickened by fat ('matière') and swollen with iniquity.[44] Michelet had not very much more sympathy for Maria Theresa – but her vices were utterly different: she was a hypocritical intriguer, a bigot encouraged to pursue the path of clerical reform only by the hope of laying her hands on Church property.[45] However, it seems likely that had he known that it was she who was shown in the portrait he was looking at, he would have discovered in it a merciless delineation of those very vices.

We can point to further weaknesses in Michelet's treatment of portraiture. When describing Charles IX's appearance on the eve of the Massacre of St Bartholomew, he draws on some vividly written testimony by contemporaries which reaches a climax with the words that the king had 'at times a little convulsive smile, while the eye, wholly at odds with the tautly pursed mouth, gave the appearance, with its sideways glance, of a merry half-wink'.[46] Michelet proceeds to point out that neither the drawing at the Bibliothèque Sainte-Geneviève[47] nor the fine bust in the Louvre (pl. 155)[48] has 'dared to do more than hint at this cruel feature' – as if he were unaware of the fact that an official royal bust is hardly the place where one might expect to find indications of so distressing a facial tic.[49] Such faults of method constitute the price paid by Michelet for pioneering an approach to portraiture that was as original as it was thorough.

155. Germain Pilon (workshop of), *Charles IX*, marble, variant of bust in the Louvre (New York, Metropolitan Museum of Art, Altman Bequest).

It was natural that Michelet's overwhelming urge to 'resurrect' the past should have made it necessary for him to bring before the eyes of his readers, and of himself, the precise physical appearance of the principal figures whose actions he recorded. But there was another reason for the special attention he paid to portraiture. Michelet looked upon the 'picturesque' approach to history as superficial,[50] for it left out far too much of importance, and it could only describe, not explain. Brought up in an age that owed much to theories that had been evolved by Lavater, Gall and others and that were being diffused in countless caricatures and 'physiognomical' manuals, both serious and humorous, he accepted the notion that mens' motives could be interpreted, at least in part, through a study of their features. One source appeared to provide him with particularly striking evidence of this.

Portrait drawings in coloured chalks of the leading figures of the French courts of the sixteenth century had long been well known to antiquarians and collectors. Even before the century was over André Thevet had had access to those belonging to Catherine de Médicis; later Roger de Gaignières had assembled a group of some 250 which was to enter the royal library in 1717,[51] and at much the same time Henry Howard, later fourth Earl of Carlisle, acquired in Florence a magnificent set of about 300 which languished, little appreciated, at the family residence of Castle Howard in Yorkshire.[52] It is not surprising that such drawings should have attracted the special attention of Alexandre Lenoir, that great preserver of the visual documentation of French history, and he obtained about 40 from a variety of sources that cannot now be traced. He kept these for himself, along with 200 painted portraits, even though the Musée des Monuments Français was still flourishing under his rapacious control at the time that he began to build up this parallel collection of his own. In 1838 all these portraits were bought by the Duke of Sutherland, who kept them at Stafford House in London,[53] but later in the century both they and the ones in Castle Howard came into the possession of the duc d'Aumale and returned to France.[54]

Early in the 1820s attempts had been made to bring some sort of order into the extremely vague arrangement and classification of the drawings from the Gaignières and other collections which were to be found in what eventually became known as the Bibliothèque Nationale. In 1822 Jean-Adrien Joly, director of its Cabinets des Estampes, had them bound into two volumes, and some thought was given to the authorship of the drawings, for as most of them were inscribed with the names of the sitters, there were no problems about identifying them. Joly seems to have accepted the traditional attribution of many of them to a certain mysterious 'Cornelio', among other artists who were believed to include King François Ier himself,[55] but when, in 1825, he acquired from a minor historical painter called Jacques-Joseph Lécurieux a further group of some fifty-six rather similar portrait drawings, he described them, anachronistically, as being of 'various persons from the reign of Henri III . . . attributed to Janet [i.e., Jean Clouet]'.[56] A few years later, Joly's successor, noting that one of these drawings was inscribed 'Fulonius', referred to the volume into which he bound them as being by 'Foulon and others', and some writers have maintained that Benjamin Foulon, a follower of the Clouets, was responsible for annotating the drawings.[57] Although it is now recognised that all these crayon portraits, scattered throughout Paris and other cities, vary considerably in quality, originality, purpose, period and authorship, a failure to realise this was of much significance for the conclusions that Michelet drew from them.

Ever since the first decade of the nineteenth century artists and art lovers had been making use of the extremely well-stocked print room of the Bibliothèque Nationale. It was open to the public on Tuesdays and Fridays, but the collections could also be consulted by registered visitors on other days. Curiously, Michelet's name does not appear in the records,[58] nor – even more curiously – does he refer in his journals to his researches there. And yet he must have worked assiduously both in the Cabinet des Estampes and also in the Bibliothèque Sainte-Geneviève, where there was another important group of sixteenth-century portrait drawings (which were transferred to the Bibliothèque Nationale in 1861),[59] for his published volumes contain enthusiastic accounts of the drawings (and also of many prints) in these two collections.

The 'Foulon' volume, which especially enthralled Michelet, though he seems to have used the name rather indiscriminately,[60] has most recently been considered to consist of drawings produced in the studio of François Clouet in about 1571 – and certainly before the Massacre of St Bartholomew in the following year, because of the presence in it of Admiral de Coligny. The portraits are mostly of persons belonging to the circle of Catherine de Médicis – a number of Protestants among them – and it has been suggested that the album was commissioned by her to be presented to the duchesse de Villeroy, whose family was well represented in it.[61] To the modern eye most of these drawings seem bland, elegant, flattering, a little vacuous and very carefully finished. In the early nineteenth century, however, they (and others like them) were believed to be preliminary studies made by artists in preparation for the many painted representations of the same persons which were to be found in a number of public and private collections: Holbein, whose example

156. Marc Du Val,
*The Three Coligny
Brothers*, black chalk
(Paris, Bibliothèque
Nationale).

may perhaps have inspired the Clouet dynasty, was known to have produced
most of his powerful and searching drawings for this very purpose.[62] Certainly,
Michelet took it for granted that these 'admirable drawings, terrible in their truth,
have preserved this court for us. In general they contradict the testimony both
of engravings and of memoirs, which are written portraits. These veracious
drawings, inexorable and accusing, sketched in red, black and white chalks, by
an awe-struck hand in the presence of the sitter have no need of inscriptions.
They name themselves. Here are Guise, the Cardinal of Lorraine, Coligny, the
connétable. Each makes us cry out "It is he!" '[63]

COLLIGNEI FRATRES.

O_ctus Cardinalis.   Gaspar thalassiarchus.   Franciscus ordinum pedestrium præfectus.

157. Marc Du Val, *The Three Coligny Brothers*, engraving (Paris, Bibliothèque Nationale).

Michelet felt that the circumstances under which these portraits had apparently been made gave them a quite special authority. Comparing the drawing in the Cabinet des Estampes, of the three Coligny brothers (pl. 156), which probably dates from before the murder of the admiral in 1572,[64] with the engraving made from it (pl. 157) and signed by Marc Du Val in 1579 (at a time when there was a recovery of the Huguenot position at court), he claims that the print wholly distorts the nature of the original by exaggerating the belligerence of the admiral's features: 'The author [of the print] was dreaming of the Massacre of St Bartholomew, and he has shown it in the face. He believed him to have been a man of

158. François Clouet, *Admiral Coligny*, red and black chalks (Paris, Bibliothèque Nationale).

war, this great and most peaceful of men.'[65] It is true that all the delicacy of the drawing has been lost in the rough version of it that has emerged from the copper plate; but to modern observers this will probably appear to be the result of the different medium rather than of any change in the interpretation of character.

On another occasion Michelet refers to portrait drawings of Coligny in the Cabinet des Estampes in an attempt to explain his strange behaviour before the massacre – that massacre whose likelihood had been predicted so often:

Why then did this ageing captain, prudent and full of experience, a man whose hair had turned grey in the conduct of affairs, why did he hand himself over to his enemies? Had he suddenly become a child, a silly little girl, this Admiral Coligny? Or will it be said that his second marriage (of which we shall shortly speak) had softened his heart and made him seek peace at any price? That, as a husband, he was too good and always allowed himself to be driven by his women – to war, by the first of them, and to peace, by the second? Such explanations will hardly suggest themselves once one has seen – among the excellent Foulon drawings – the face of the man, his firm and sad expression, the features of a judge in Israel, that astonishingly austere face [pl. 158].

And he then follows up this observation on the basis of other 'more certain' facts which provide further explanations of Coligny's behaviour.[66]

Michelet's use of artistic evidence was thus extremely adventurous even when he was working within traditional areas of scholarly research (such as ecclesiastical monuments and portraiture) and turning to them for answers to questions of a traditional nature (about the character, behaviour and achievements of important figures from the past). But he was also prepared to venture into quite unexplored territory. We have seen that from the first he had conceived of great historical movements taking visible and concrete shape in some of the monuments of sculpture and architecture that he explored in Rome. It was not long before he was ready to recognise in artistic creations of all kinds less precise but more telling indications of the spirit of an age or of a people. Many absurdities – in Michelet's own works and in those of later writers – were published as a consequence of such assumptions (which owe much to the theories of Hegel); but they should not blind us to the originality and the fascination of the tool that he now offered to historians.

In the remarkable 'Tableau de France' (published in 1833 as the opening chapter of the second volume of his history), Michelet sometimes adds impressions drawn from the arts to those that he based on geography and history, on law and custom and on the physical appearance and temperament of people whom he met. From these and many other sources he sought to characterise the rich regional variety of the country which had, none the less, been integrated into a harmonious unity. When, however, he came to 'notre bonne et forte Flandre'[67] (included, presumably, because, or in spite of, the fact that 'l'Histoire de France commence avec la langue française'[68]), he went much further and concluded that the vulgar and sensual temperament that distinguished its inhabitants could not find sufficient outlet in the accounts of written history, so that the visual arts had to be called upon at some length to complete the description. Thus the architecture of Flanders is made up of generous forms. The pointed arch softens into gentle curves and voluptuous swellings. Churches, carefully tended, washed and decorated like Flemish houses, dazzle the eye with their cleanliness and richness, the splendour of their brass ornaments, the abundance of their black-and-white marbles – even if the sculptures reveal themselves on close inspection to be of wood for reasons of economy. And from the towers high above can be heard the beautifully ordered chimes of the church bells, the honour and joy of the Flemish community. But even music and architecture are too abstract to indicate the special nature of the region. Colours (true, living colours) are required: pictures of hearty and vulgar festivals where red men and white women drink, smoke and clumsily dance together; but also pictures of atrocious tortures, of indecent and horrible martyrdoms and of enormous Madonnas, fresh, fat, scandalously beautiful. It is the brush of the 'terrible' Rubens – so different from the sober and serious painting of Rembrandt and Gerard Dou, living (like Erasmus and Grotius) surrounded by the melancholy marshes of Holland – who can illuminate for us the true character of Flanders: not the allegorical and official pictures in Paris commissioned by Marie de Médicis, but those to be seen in Antwerp and Brussels.

In later years Taine, Thoré, Fromentin and many others were to draw on the contrast between the political and religious conditions of Holland and Flanders in

order to 'explain' the differences between the styles of painting in those neighbouring regions. But although it may well have been Michelet who inspired their
theories, he himself approached the issue from the opposite angle. For him it was
the art that provided the evidence he needed in order to be able to understand the
temperament and, by implication, the history, of the inhabitants of Flanders – just
as the 'white, angular, razor-sharp rocks' and the fury of the sea ('English by
inclination and disliking France, for it smashes our ships and silts up our ports')
helped to explain the very different character of Brittany.[69]

Michelet often returned to the visual arts when trying to throw light on the
beliefs and circumstances of earlier societies: not only (as was already commonplace) to the religious solemnity of Gothic cathedrals, but also to less expected
images. 'Go to the library', he tells his readers, 'and take up the prints of Callot
and Rembrandt. What a ridiculous comparison, you will say, and you will be
right: it is like bringing the sand and the pebbles of some dry little stream into the
presence of an ocean. Never mind. Look, study, ask questions.'[70] And what he
sees in the contrasting works of the two men – their styles as well as the subject-
matter they depict – is the difference between the cruel oppression endured by the
peasantry of France and the freedom and pride of the Dutch.

Perhaps the most remarkable of all Michelet's often confused attempts to make
use of the arts as an indication of the temper of a particular society, and one that is
worth quoting at some length, occurs when he is discussing the problem of why
François Ier chose to idle away the winter of 1524 in the luxury of Northern Italy –
a misjudgement that was soon to lead to his disastrous defeat and capture at the
Battle of Pavia. Certainly, said Michelet,[71] the landscape appealed to the king, as
he was to show in some poems that he wrote later; and it is inconceivable that he
could have spent four months without indulging in some affair of the heart.
Nevertheless, historians have been wrong to try to identify any particular great
lady who could have made him forget those who remained in France. For the issue
was a different one: in Italy 'tout est dame'. Those whom Correggio copied so
often, whose forms are sometimes rather mean, badly fed, too thin are all the more
charming for that very reason. Their grace is entirely of the spirit.

> This was a time of a great revelation for Italy. The pure Florentine Madonnas to
> whom Raphael has already given life are still lacking in sparkle. But now a new
> race has emerged, revived by suffering and growing up in tears. A new tem-
> perament is stirring, delicate and charming, the sickly smile of a timid fear
> which smiles only so as not to weep. Who will be able to grasp this disposi-
> tion? . . . The Lombard peasant from the village of Correggio, the famished
> artist who is unable to feed his family: he records what he sees – this new Italy,
> still young, but ailing and nervous. Look at the little St Catherine in the *Mystic
> Marriage* [pl. 159] in the Louvre – a poor little creature who will not live, or who
> will remain small. She is more than sickly, she has no health; one can see this
> from the irregularity of the joints of her arms which he has copied so accurately.
> And yet, for all that, she has a painful grace, and the piercing thorn of her heart
> penetrates our innermost feelings and makes us tremble with pity, tenderness
> and a contagious shudder.

159. Correggio, *Mystic Marriage of St Catherine* (Paris, Louvre).

Such was Italy at this moment, enfeebled and pallid. Correggio had merely to copy it and draw inspiration from this new source, characterised by a strange smile quivering between suffering and grace. François Ier did not see Correggio, but he experienced and relished Correggio's Italy: 'And I have no doubt that this was the reason for his long period of inaction.'

No historian, or art historian, would today choose to write about Correggio or François Ier in this way; but art historians have commented at length on the changes that seem to have come over Italian painting towards the end of the second decade of the sixteenth century, and many have tried to see in these changes a reflection of some more profound crisis in the spiritual and political condition of Italy at this time. In drawing on a picture in order to characterise, however recklessly, the *mentalité* of Italy at a crucial moment in its history, Michelet was the first man to adopt an approach to the study of culture that is still in constant use.

iii

It is, however, Michelet's 'invention' of the Renaissance that has remained his most enduring achievement: his contention that the sixteenth century witnessed not just, as had long been acknowledged, 'the rebirth of art and letters', but – much more importantly – 'the discovery of the world, the discovery of man'.[72] That something of great and wide-ranging significance had occurred in this period had been recognised by many earlier historians (Roscoe among them), but it was Michelet

who first tried to explore the changes in some detail and to build up from them
that general synthesis which he described as the Renaissance. He began adopting
the term in his lecture course given at the Collège de France in 1840,[73] but it was
not until his use of it as the title of the seventh volume of his *Histoire de France*
which appeared in 1855 (twelve years after he had first thought of publishing it)[74]
that it entered into general circulation – and thus attracted the attention of Jacob
Burckhardt.

The background to this 'invention' has been much analysed, and an ingenious
psychological interpretation of its meaning for Michelet himself was suggested
more than a generation ago by Lucien Febvre,[75] one of his greatest disciples.
Febvre drew attention to the birth of a sudden passion in his life following his
guilt-ridden grief associated with the death of his first wife; his personal emancipation from the Church and Christianity itself; his growing dislike for the
Middle Ages. All this can be accepted. Yet other factors were also involved.
Michelet's broadening of the concept of the Renaissance from a movement that
had implied no more than the rebirth of arts and letters to one that embraced every
aspect of human existence was possible and took the form it did only because of
his sensitivity to the arts and his conviction of their extreme importance.

Like many people of his generation, Michelet had, in his youth, combined an
enthusiasm for the architecture of the Middle Ages with a traditional admiration
for the painting of the High Renaissance. But he also showed a great interest in
sculpture and was a frequent visitor[76] to the so-called 'Musée de la Renaissance'
which was created in 1824 but did not become accessible to the public until 1835,
and even then only with the greatest difficulty.[77] It was accommodated in a set of
rooms in the Louvre and was placed under the direction of the department of
classical antiquities. It contained a number of statues which had been transferred to
it from Lenoir's disbanded Musée des Monuments Français, as well as others
from a variety of different locations. Among the figures to be admired there
were Michelangelo's *Prisoners*, Germain Pilon's *Three Graces* (which so irritated
Michelet), Puget's *Milon de Crotone*, Bouchardon's *Cupid* and two groups by
Canova. It can thus be seen that the name of Renaissance, which had been given
to the museum, was applied in so broad a sense as to be almost devoid of meaning.
None the less, Michelet may well have been struck by the fact that the word was
used at all, though he was certainly familiar with Lenoir's catalogue of *his* museum
which, as early as 1802, had referred to 'the century universally known as regards
the arts of design, and even as regards letters, under the remarkable designation of
the *century of the Renaissance*'.[78]

Between 1849 and 1851 the fifteenth-, and especially the sixteenth-century
French and Italian sculptures in the Louvre were rearranged far more logically in
five galleries of their own, each one named after a prominent French master:[79]
Michelangelo's *Prisoners* and Benvenuto Cellini's *Diana* were placed in the 'Salle de
Jean de Douay, dit de Boulogne', in the company of various French portrait busts
of the period. The extreme nationalism flaunted by this installation led to some
criticism, and the room was soon renamed.[80] However, the artistic linking of
France and Italy on a level of equality surely encouraged Michelet to assign a

leading role to France in the creation of the Renaissance. He claimed that although the French had been barbarians on the eve of their first descent into Italy, only they had been capable of understanding the true achievements of Italian artists and of transmitting them to the rest of Europe and to posterity: 'The discovery of Italy made a much greater impact on the sixteenth century than did that of America. All other nations follow behind France, but they in their turn are initiated and begin to see clearly by the light of this new sun.'[81]

Michelet's sense of artistic chronology was somewhat vague, but like most Frenchmen of his time, except for a small number of extreme Catholic reactionaries of a kind he particularly hated (but whose works he studied), he had in general little feeling for Italian art of the fifteenth century, apart from the rare occasions when it appeared to be moving in the direction of realism.[82] This led him to visualise that century not, as has become customary for later historians, as a period of great revival and strength in the field of painting, sculpture and architecture, but, on the contrary, as a dead, oppressive era which crushed such talent as emerged. He believed, however, that it was only through art that man could escape from the detestable Middle Ages – 'ce terrible mourant qui ne pouvait mourir ni vivre, et devenait plus cruel en touchant à sa dernière heure'[83] – because art had not been persecuted as had science and technology. The great genius who might have achieved the needed breakthrough was Brunelleschi, 'the Christopher Columbus of this world',[84] who had designed the cupola of Florence cathedral in 1420 (pl. 160). But, astonishingly enough, Brunelleschi's example had barely been followed. 'In the face of this victory of the Renaissance, the dying Gothic comes back to life, and makes a final effort': the spire of Strasbourg cathedral is, however, followed by exhaustion and self-indulgence. The Gothic becomes even more fragile and increasingly surrounds itself with all the trivial arts of ornamentation, with the daintiness of the carver and the embroiderer, with little curls and lace-like effects – all of which are exemplified in the pretty church of Brou (pl. 161).[85]

It is true that it was more than eighty years after the acceptance of Brunelleschi's design for the cupola of Florence cathedral that, in 1506, Margaret of Austria laid the first stone for the church of Brou.[86] Nevertheless, Michelet's unexplained move from Tuscany to France is disconcerting and would remain inexplicable were it not for the fact that his intimate friend Edgar Quinet had as early as 1834 written a remarkable article – prose poem might be a more accurate description – called 'Des Arts de la Renaissance et de l'Eglise de Brou' which had made much the same point, though with far greater precision.[87] Quinet compared the modern Italy of Raphael and Michelangelo with that still primitive region of France covered by forests and marshes, 'which has retained until today the infinite melancholy of uninhabited places', where 'the Middle Ages came to seek shelter for the last time in the church of Brou', the final monument of an enfeebled architecture in which everything betrayed symptoms of weakness and exhaustion.

Michelet must have seized on Quinet's essay with particular satisfaction, because it appeared to support his claim that Brunelleschi had been an isolated giant, struggling in vain against the persistence and inertia of the Gothic. Only with the painting of Leonardo – and at this point Michelet openly acknowledges his debt to

160. L.-T. Turpin de Crissé, *View of Florence Cathedral* (London, Hazlitt, Gooden and Fox 1984).

161. Isidore Taylor, *Voyages Pittoresques* (Franche Comté), 1825: the church of Brou (lithograph from a drawing by Bonington, probably based on a sketch made on the spot by Taylor).

Quinet[88] – does the Renaissance make itself felt once more. But Leonardo suffers the same fate as Brunelleschi: he has no successors.[89] Even the placid and charming Raphael proves to be a disappointment because he cuts himself off with such determination, such selfishness, from the tragic life of his times: 'Do those impassive Madonnas know what their living sisters have suffered at the hands of Borgia at the sack of Forlì and of Capua? Can those philosophers of *The School of Athens* continue with their reasoning and their calculations on the day that Brescia is sacked and a violent [soldier] strikes a blow at the future restorer of mathematics [Niccolo Tartaglia] as he clings close to his mother? And, finally, that *Psyche*, twice painted by Raphael with such charm, has she not heard the terrible cry of Milan tortured by the Spaniards, who tomorrow will be at Rome?'[90] There was only one real man at this time: 'one heart, one true hero' – Michelangelo, whose art incorporates the very soul of Italy, and to him and his works Michelet devotes some twenty-five rapturous pages.[91]

Michelet could thus postpone the flowering of the artistic Renaissance until well into the sixteenth century, and because he was always so ready to interpret art as the embodiment of great movements of the human spirit, it was natural for him to associate the paintings of Michelangelo (and the sculptures he could see in the Musée de la Renaissance) with those geographical, religious, social and political changes that marked a watershed in the history of the world.

The emphasis that has here been placed on Michelet's responses to painting, sculpture and architecture may give the impression that it was entirely as a result of those responses that he was inspired to propose what was certainly one of the boldest historiographical concepts of the nineteenth century. Such an impression would be quite wrong. None the less, it would be almost equally mistaken not to appreciate how much his 'invention' of a Renaissance whose frontiers extended far beyond the confines of art owes to his feeling for art. Even more important than this, however, is the fact that Michelet had introduced the evidence to be derived from painting, sculpture and architecture into the very forefront of historical enquiry, thus both bringing to fruition what had hitherto been the over-ambitious and sterile dreams of antiquarians and, at the same time, opening the way to investigations of a kind that none of them had ever been remotely able to conceive.

162. Alexandre de Laborde, *Versailles Ancien et Moderne*, 1841: Versailles museum.

Museums, Illustrations and the Search for Authenticity

i

When Michelet recalled his childhood visits to the Musée des Monuments Français with its incomparable treasury of sculptures, which had emerged only recently from convents, palaces and churches to the powerful summons of the Revolution and which stood there awkwardly placed and deprived of their bases, he refused to think of them as having been confused or disorganised: 'On the contrary, for the first time a powerful order reigned among them, a true order, the only true order, one that reflected the sequence of the ages. The perpetuity of the nation was revealed by them.'[1] Such a reaction to Lenoir's talents as a decorator was natural enough, but it was the very opposite of what had been intended when, little more than a decade earlier, the storage depot of the Petits Augustins had been tentatively reorganised in the midst of a city that was doing all it could to destroy the very notion of continuity. The transformation of an institution that had ostensibly been designed only for the study of art into one that could evoke powerful sentiments about national history was not perhaps accidental, but it was certainly not inevitable. However, at almost exactly the same moment, a museum was being created at the other end of Europe with precisely this purpose in mind.

The Temple of Sibyl opened in Pulawy Park on the banks of the Vistula not far from Warsaw in 1801 (pl. 163).[2] Its name, and also its architecture, were taken from the round, early Roman temple picturesquely situated above the falls of Tivoli near Rome, and they give a thoroughly misleading impression of the contents of the building which had at first been called, much more appropriately, the Temple of Memory. Eighteen giant marble columns encircled it, and as the visitor walked up the steps leading to the double doors ahead of him he could see, inscribed above the entrance, the words THE PAST TO THE FUTURE. The upper of the two rounded halls was crowned by a dome, from the centre of which light streamed on to the exhibits. In the middle was an altar made of pink granite and on it stood the Royal Casket containing jewels that had belonged to the kings of Poland, as well as miniatures portraying them, fragments of their costumes and small objects taken form their tombs. In the apse facing the entrance were trophies from victorious wars – shields, swords and captured banners. This chaste neo-classical interior also

163. Jean-Pierre Norblin, *Temple of Sibyl at Pulawy*, 1803, wash drawing (Cracow, Czartoryski Museum).

contained booty seized from the Turks after King Jan Sobieski had relieved Vienna from the siege of 1683, and in two semi-circular cupboards, furnished with specially designed glass-covered drawers, were caskets, snuff-boxes, fans, watches, seals, coins, medals, costumes and other tokens of the kind. Around the walls of the lower hall, into which natural light could not penetrate, hung commemorative shields of gilded bronze.

The Temple of Sibyl, which had been conceived after the final dismemberment of Poland, was more a giant reliquary than a museum. Its contents were varied in character, but all had one feature in common: they provided tangible proof that a great Polish Kingdom had once existed. The purpose of the Temple was to display a coherent view of history in visual form.

Princess Czartoryski, on one of whose family's many estates the temple was built, had long been interested, like very many of her contemporaries throughout Europe, in buying up historical associations wherever she could lay her hands on them. At Stratford-upon-Avon she paid twenty guineas for a chair on which Shakespeare had sat, and in London she acquired mementoes of Henry VIII and Cromwell. All these, and countless more, were taken to the 'Gothic House', a garden pavilion on the same estate, which had at first been intended for the temple's caretaker, but which was soon radically transformed and expanded into a second museum. This, too, was historical in character. Princess Czartoryski hoped to insert into its walls bricks from the Bastille, stones from a castle of François Ier, and a capital or bas-relief from either the Pantheon or the Capitol in Rome. Above the entrance she had inscribed Virgil's most poignant line: SUNT LACRIMAE RERUM

ET MENTEM MORTALIA TANGUNT. The range, quality and authenticity of the objects displayed varied widely: Heloise and Abelard were represented by pieces of bone (Princess Czartoryski was in touch with Lenoir in Paris); Petrarch and Laura by fragments of costume; Ossian by framed grass gathered from the tomb of Fingal; Henri IV, Cromwell, Newton and Charles XII of Sweden by death masks; and François Ier's mistress, 'La Belle Ferronière', by Leonardo da Vinci's magnificent portrait, *A Lady with an Ermine*, which had been acquired in Italy by Adam George Czartoryski, son of the Princess, and suitably rechristened so as to be made eligible.

Historical collections of the kind to be seen in the Gothic House at Pulawy Park were by no means rare in Europe during the early years of the nineteenth century. However, the notion of putting what were taken to be authentic objects from past epochs to the service of an ideological cause, as was done at the Temple of Sibyl, was still unusual, although there were plenty of religious precedents. It was soon to be widely followed.[3]

In 1833, just three years after the contents of the temple had had to be hurriedly dismantled and concealed so as to escape the army of Grand Duke Constantine of Russia which had come to put down the Polish uprising, and just three years also after the duc d'Orléans's accession to the throne of France as King Louis-Philippe, in the wake of a dynastic revolution, it was decided to convert the abandoned palace of Versailles (the most potent symbol of Bourbon authoritarianism) into a vast museum to contain 'tous les souvenirs historiques nationaux qu'il appartient aux arts de perpetuer' (pl. 162). It was the new king's intention to celebrate 'la grandeur de la France et la splendour de la couronne'[4] – the same combination of nation and crown that, a generation or so earlier, had inspired the more touching and more fragile enterprise of Princess Czartoryski. Very large numbers of very large historical canvases were commissioned from painters of all kinds. After some years of neglect Pharamond was to be resurrected once again, and the artist to whom he was entrusted was told to take special care to distinguish the costumes of the Gauls from those of the Franks and to consult the portfolios of Roger de Gaignières, as well as various volumes of engravings and the *Monumens* of Mont-faucon.[5] It is the continuity of the visual sources used to record French history rather than the continuity of French history itself that is particularly striking.

The Versailles museum had, in the words of one of its conservators, been formed 'non pas au point de vue de l'art, mais au point du vue de l'histoire'. This sentiment cannot have been very encouraging for the many painters who were engaged in struggling with their canvases of 'The meeting between Philippe-Auguste and Henry VII at Gisors on 21 January 1188' or 'The treaty concluded between the Crusaders and the Venetians in the Church of St Mark in 1201' or other subjects of the kind; and it was recognised at the time, as it has been ever since, that the contribution of the museum to the arts was, with a few outstanding exceptions, not a distinguished one. What, however, of history? Extravagant claims were made. The museum was 'the largest and the most varied collection of works of art that any nation has ever dedicated to the memories of its history. Sieges and battles, conquests, crusades, historical facts, ceremonies, persons illustrious through blood, genius, courage, science or beauty; pictures, portraits, statues, tombs'.[6]

All this may well have been correct, and yet by standards that had been well understood ever since Montfaucon, the version of history presented by the museum was very deficient. Perhaps this was its intention. Certainly, if the word 'fantasies' is substituted for 'memories', what was to be seen at Versailles becomes much more comprehensible. For some periods, it is true, the imaginative efforts of modern painters could be supplemented by evidence intended to carry greater weight: contemporary busts, for instance, or – more usually – copies of busts, and casts of tombs that had been often arbitrarily reassembled both during and after their display in the Musée des Monuments Français. Moreover, Versailles itself, and what remained of its decoration by Lebrun and Coysevox, could clearly evoke a powerful image of the nature of the monarchy under Louis XIV – although depictions of many of the more important events that took place both then and during the eighteenth century were also commissioned from modern artists. Such extreme disparities of style in recording the same period must surely have disturbed any visitor hoping to be brought into direct visual contact with the past. Disparities – but also consistencies. However great the attention paid to changing costumes and weaponry, a victory won by the French over the English in 1745 can appear uncannily similar to a victory won by the French over the Russians in 1807 when both are painted by Horace Vernet between 1828 and 1836.[7]

It was, of course, recent history that offered potentially the richest and most authentic visual sources for the museum – but these were also the most controversial. It is true that, after being concealed during much of the Restoration, the great canvases that had been commissioned from David, Gros and Girodet to celebrate the triumphs of Napoleon could now be used to provide a powerful evocation of his regime. The Revolution itself, however, could be represented only by the victorious battles – yet more victorious battles! – that had been fought under its auspices. Danton and Robespierre might never have existed as far as the museum was concerned: they were not 'historical facts'.

The Temple of Sibyl had been intended to keep alive the memory of a nation that had been destroyed, and this was accomplished by displaying the visible relics of its glory within a building that epitomised all that was most admired in ancient architecture. The museum of Versailles had been intended to blur (if not to eradicate) the memories associated with one of the most celebrated buildings in France – memories of despotic and extravagant monarchs isolated from the subjects over whom they ruled – and to substitute a different set of memories altogether: more than a thousand years of monarchy and nation united in the common cause of defeating enemies and spreading civilisation. The Germanische Nationalmuseum, which opened in Nuremberg on 15 June 1853, was intended to create a history for a nation that did not yet exist.[8]

The site chosen for the museum was a deconsecrated Carthusian monastery which had belonged to the city since the Reformation. The nucleus of its first collections came from Hans von und zu Aufsess who had, for some twenty years, been trying to create an institution of the kind.[9] Many small provincial museums scattered throughout Europe had been born in this way, but – as was indicated by its name – the founders of the Nuremberg museum had been fired by an extra-ordinary ambition. They aimed to do nothing less than to exhibit German civi-lisation as a whole. Subscriptions for membership were sought for – and received – from individuals living in all the states where the German language was spoken.[10] Much help was also given by many of the rulers of those states who, before very long, would be swept away by that very German nationalism that had, from the first, been incarnated in the museum and its collections. But although, especially after the foundation of the Empire in 1871, the National Museum did indeed become the focus of an extreme patriotism which assumed extraordinary, and sometimes morbid, proportions,[11] such emotions are fortunately less dangerous when they lack the power to give them substance. The early years of the museum were marked by very high standards of scholarship and presentation. It was the intention of the founders to establish a 'well-arranged repertoire of the sources of German history, literature and art from the earliest periods until 1650', and the museum was to be intimately associated with archives and a library.[12] A few years later the policy was defined a little more clearly as 'to make known through its collections as true and as complete as possible a picture of the life and activities of our ancestors, and in its halls to recall to memory the most important moments of the history of the fatherland and to honour the memories of the most outstanding men and women of Germany'.[13]

These outstanding men and women were honoured in a special section of the museum in which their portraits were shown through the medium of coins, medals and tombs, as well as pictures and engravings. From the admirable monthly bulletins issued by the museum (illustrated with wood engravings of excellent quality) we can trace with interest and respect the acquisition, by purchase or gift, of prints, illuminated manuscripts, books and archives, and all kinds of furnishing; and we can also read about the development of every aspect of the museum and its holdings, and follow current literature on mediaeval German history through short and informative reviews.[14]

For visitors to the monastery itself the impact was of a different order and far more emotional. As the great vaulted halls began to fill with monuments (pl. 164) it became possible to walk along cloisters lined with up-turned tombstones and men in armour; to stand in the weapon room from whose walls hung swords and shields and banners; to see in the choir copies of the tombs of some of the great figures of German history (pl. 165); while in the former refectory were casts of the monumental bronze lion from Brunswick and the bronze doors and column from Hildesheim. Later would come stained-glass windows and Romanesque arches. Anachronisms and regional confusion served the purpose of enabling the visitor to experience the resonances of an 'histoire imaginaire' by wandering through a 'musée imaginaire'. And part of that history could be taken home in the form of bronze casts or copies in ivory or wood which were available from the very beginning.[15]

The Germanische Nationalmuseum of Nuremberg was certainly the greatest museum of its kind in Europe, but it was by no means the only one, nor was it the

165. Franz Hablitschek, *Church of the Carthusian Monastery forming Part of the Germanische Nationalmuseum*, *c*.1864, engraving (Nuremberg, Germanische Nationalmuseum).

164 (left). Ludwig Braun, *Selected Views of the Germanische Nationalmuseum*, after 1868, pencil with wash (Nuremberg, Germanische Nationalmuseum).

166. Wilhelm von Kaulbach, *Opening of the Tomb of Charlemagne on the Orders of Emperor Otho III*, 1859, fresco, now destroyed, formerly in the Germanische Nationalmuseum.

first; for many other peoples aspiring to become states tried to create a national identity for themselves by bringing together material remains from their past histories.[16] Towards the end of the century, however, we find a change of emphasis. The Italians, for instance, seemed to have acquired their national identity through a combination of politics and force, and many cities chose to celebrate this achievement through the creation of special museums. But as the history was so recent most of the great captains and epics by which it had been characterised could be represented either through photography or through large-scale depictions that were more or less contemporary – of a kind that had obviously not been available to the curators of Versailles hoping to portray 'The Baptism of Clovis' or 'Charlemagne crossing the Alps'. It is true that the paintings displayed in the various museums of the Risorgimento scattered throughout Italy were often painted a generation or so after the events themselves.[17] None the less, the artists had lived through, sometimes participated in, the struggle for independence, and this gave their pictures that same sort of authenticity that was, for instance, regularly attributed to the Bayeux Tapestry, however great the element of political propaganda to be discerned in it.

That authenticity was denied to the modern frescoes that were, at various times, commissioned to decorate the Nuremberg museum. The earliest of these, which faced the cast of the bronze Lion of Brunswick in the refectory, was Wilhelm von Kaulbach's melodramatic *Opening of the Tomb of Charlemagne on the Orders of the Emperor Otho III* (pl. 166). When this was unveiled in 1859 Hans von und zu Aufsess, founder of the museum, was overjoyed because he saw in the reverential and awe-struck gestures of Otho and his retinue, as they gaze at the majestic effigy of Charlemagne seated on his throne, the perfect symbol of his own endeavours to illuminate a distant and hidden past with the flaring torches of scholarship and thus take heart from the glories of the German nation.[18]

ii

This was an entirely logical response to a work that had never been intended as an accurate representation of an actual historical scene – although Otho had, in fact, taken Charlemagne's bones under his protection. Nevertheless, the artifice of Kaulbach's fresco did conflict with precisely those values of authenticity that formed the *raison d'être* of the museum and that were proclaimed by all the other exhibits in it, whether originals or replicas. And for at least a generation historians had been complaining about the wholly misleading effect produced on the public by such imaginative reconstructions of the past which, long before they had become indispensable as the basic ingredients of historical museums such as the one at Versailles, had been familiar – on a smaller scale – in the form of illustrations to history books. It is appropriate that the first sustained challenge to this convention seems to have been made by the leading exponent of a new kind of national history.

Augustin Thierry proclaimed again and again that to rely, as his predecessors had so often relied, on bland and well-composed narratives, produced by writers living long after the events they were recording, could lead only to a complete misunderstanding of the past. It was essential to return not merely to the original documentary sources, such as charters and contemporary chronicles, but to the very words from which those sources had been compiled. It was only by listening to our ancestors talking spontaneously in their own language that we could appreciate how different they had been from ourselves and could, therefore, begin to understand their world as they themselves had understood it. One of the aims of Thierry, as of many of his contemporaries, was to introduce into the writing of serious history that vivid sense of colour and actuality that Sir Walter Scott had brought to the historical novel and Chateaubriand to his rhapsodic evocations of an Age of Faith.[19] It was inevitable that Thierry, and the new generation of historians inspired by him, should look also to authentic pictorial sources and should complain about the deceptive impression of the past that was conveyed by modern illustrators. It was in 1827 that Thierry did just this.

'Many engravings', he wrote in his *Lettres sur l'Histoire de France*,[20] 'provide the most bizarre travesties of the principal scenes of our history. Flick through the most popular of those little works, which are so dear to mothers concerned for

167. Augustin Thierry, *Histoire de la Conquête d'Angleterre*, 5th edition, 1838: 'Edithe au cou de cygne, reconnaît le corps du roi Harold'.

the education of their children, and you will see the Franks and the Gauls shaking hands over their alliance to drive out the Romans, the coronation of Clovis at Reims, Charlemagne covered in fleurs de lys, and Philippe-Auguste, in steel armour after the fashion of the sixteenth century, placing his crown on an altar on the day of the battle of Bouvines.'[21]

Thierry's complaint was all the more poignant because, eleven years later, the fifth edition of his own major contribution to scholarship, the *Histoire de la Conquête d'Angleterre*, was published with a series of engravings taken not from the Bayeux Tapestry (to which he referred at important points in his discussion of the invasion) but from the most fanciful and romantic drawings specially devised by Tony Johannot and other modern artists (pl. 167): but by then he was blind and all this was invisible to him.

We have seen that much thought had been given to the accurate illustration of historical works ever since the fourteenth century when genuine antique coins had been reproduced for this purpose in accounts of the Roman Empire. Later it became quite common to introduce other evidence of the kind – ancient armour or mediaeval tombs – into editions of earlier writers as well as into antiquarian volumes. However, one supreme obstacle stood in the way of any more ample visualisation of the past that aimed to be as authentic as it was immediate. Remarkably few of the most celebrated or notorious events that could be read about in books appeared to have been recorded in images – or, at least, in images that had survived. Occasionally an enterprising writer or publisher might go to desperate lengths to remedy this omission. In his translation (at one remove) of a work that was itself a forgery from late antiquity (a supposedly eye-witness account of the Trojan war) Charles de Bourgueville wrote in 1572 that his woodcuts had been copied from the illustrations in a manuscript ('parroissant vieil à merveilles') that had been lent to him by a friend ('la modestie duquel ne me permet le nommer').[22] Relying on this manuscript, which in turn looked back to ancient effigies in bronze and marble, Charles de Bourgueville claimed to be able to show the true features of Achilles and Agammemnon and even the beheading of Polyxena and the rape of Helen. In fact, for all the protestations he made about the reliability of the sources used (there were, for instance, no gods or goddesses in this version of the war), De Bourgueville was here adopting a policy that, inevitably, was to become a standard one. Famous events from the past were reproduced in a style that was little, if at all, to be distinguished from that of the present.

During most of the seventeenth and eighteenth centuries the situation changed only very slowly. Readers and publishers alike accepted the convention whereby the ungainly costumes and monuments of the Middle Ages, which were constantly being brought to light by new research, would be juxtaposed to illustrated narratives of remote events drawn in a manner that suggested the modern boudoir. Thus a very handsome and posthumous edition of a translation into English of the *Histoire d'Angleterre* by Rapin-Thoyras was published in London between 1732 and 1747 with additional volumes to bring it up to date. For this edition the conscientious antiquarian and draughtsman George Vertue engraved, sometimes alone and sometimes in collaboration, careful and tolerably accurate reproductions of mediaeval royal tombs and documented portraits, and included, on the same plate, little representations of some episode dating from the same period as the monument which he treated in the most fanciful rococo idiom (pl. 168). Almost never, it would appear, has the 'principle of disjunction' proposed by Panofsky to describe the contrast, in the art of the Middle Ages, between contemporary styles and antique subject-matter (or the situation in reverse)[23] been so apparent as in these scholarly histories of the mid-eighteenth century.

The one concession that was frequently made to providing at least some illusion of distance between the past and the present was the adoption of a style that was loosely based on that of the Venetian High Renaissance – even when the subject-matter of the narrative being recorded dated back to very much earlier periods. This is well displayed in the attractive illustrations that were commissioned to decorate the twenty-eight fine folios of Muratori's *Rerum Italicarum Scriptores*, published between 1723 and 1751. Muratori was the greatest mediaevalist of the first half of the eighteenth century, and we have seen that he was, in theory, at least, fully aware of the support that could be given to the historian by objects as well as by texts. Indeed, among his editions of countless unpublished sources (written in barbaric Latin or Italian dialect) for the history of Italy between AD 500 and 1500 we very occasionally come across the reproduction of some important artefact, such as the iron crown of the emperors. But, as was natural for an enterprise that was promoted by the group of noblemen who made up the so-called Società Palatina and that was conducted on a day-to-day basis by the cultivated and ambitious publisher Filippo Angelati, there could be no question of matching the crudity and difficulty of the texts with illustrations of a similar nature. Moreover, it was Muratori himself who wrote that 'as much as possible must be done so that the work should appear thoroughly decorous; and I would be pleased if that engraver [Zucchi] could produce embellishments of a kind that

From a most Antient Original in the Quire, Westminster Abby.

Desig et Sculp G Vertu

RICARDVS II REX

168. George Vertue, *King Richard II*, with scroll representing 'this King's resignation of his crown to Henry of Bolingbroke [Henry IV]', engraving made to illustrate posthumous translation of Rapin-Thoynas, *Histoire d'Angleterre*.

ANDREÆ DANDULI CHRONICON.

INCIPIT LIBER QUARTUS CONTINENS CAPITULA XIV.

CAPITULUM PRIMUM.

De Pontificatu Sancti Marci Evangelistæ habens partes V.

Arcus Evangelista in Aquilegia primò Catholicam Ecclesiam fundavit Anno Christi Jesu Domini nostri XLVIII. Hic ex genere Levi Sacerdos, Evägelista Dei electus, & Petri Apostoli in baptismate filius, atque in divino sermone discipulus, prædicante Petro Romæ, ut quotidie audientibus nulla satietas fieret, rogatus est à fratribus, ut ea, quæ ille verbo prædicaret, ad perpetuam eorum commonitionem scripturæ commendaret. Petrus verò ut per Spiritum Sanctum se spoliatum comperit, furto delectatus, factum confirmavit, legendamq; Ecclesiis scripturam tradidit.

Pars Prima.

Marcus itaque, assumpto Evangelio, quod ipse consecrat, jussu Petri Aquilegiam vênit, & in quem primum egressus est locum, Murfiana vocatur, ubi Ecclesia sui nominis postea constructa est; & innumeros sua prædicatione, & doctrina, subsequentibus signis, ad Christi Fidem convertit. Nam (*) juvenem quemdam Athaulfum filium Ulfi lepræ morbo percussum in suburbanis Aquilegiæ sanitati restituit, & supplicantibus Neophytis Evangelium suum transcripsit, & observandum dedit, quod usque in hodiernum diem in eadem Ecclesia devotissimè veneratur.

Pars II.

Cum igitur Beatus Marcus hos cerneret in Fide roboratos, & jussu Petri Romam redire disposuisset, Hermacoram Civem Aquilejensem, quem ad regendum Populum acquisitum aptiorem cognoverat, in navicula secum assumpsit, & directò navigans in Paludes, ubi nunc Rivaltina Civitas constructa dignoscitur, tamdem pervênit, cui tunc Rivoaltus nomen erat; & urgente vento naviculam ad Tumbam ligavit; apparuitque ei in extasi posito Angelus Dei dicens: *Pax tibi, Marce. Hic requiescet corpus tuum.* Cui cùm se passurum illico naufragium hæsitaret, subintulit Angelus: *Ne timeas Evangelista Dei, quia adhuc tibi grandis via restat, multaque te pro Christi nomine oportet pati. Post verò passionem tuam circumvicinarum Regionum devoti & fideles Populi, Infidelium crebras persecutiones declinare volentes, hic mirificam Urbem fabricabunt, & corpus tuum denique habere merebuntur: quod summa veneratione colent: tuisque meritis & precibus plurima beneficia consecuturi sunt.* Tunc Beatus Marcus ex-

(*) *Desunt hæc in Codice Ambrosiano.*

169. L.A. Muratori, *Rerum Italicarum Scriptores*, vol. XII, 1728: chronicle of Andrea Dandolo, with vignette by Francesco Zucchi.

attracts the ignorant to buy books'.[24] And so about twenty artists in different towns of Italy were employed to produce, in a vaguely Renaissance style, small and delightful engravings to record – but surely also to disguise – some of the most obscure episodes of mediaeval history (pl. 169).

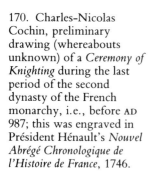

170. Charles-Nicolas Cochin, preliminary drawing (whereabouts unknown) of a *Ceremony of Knighting* during the last period of the second dynasty of the French monarchy, i.e., before AD 987; this was engraved in Président Hénault's *Nouvel Abrégé Chronologique de l'Histoire de France*, 1746.

Occasionally artists let us hear their own views about the illustrations they were required to supply for publications of this kind. In the 1740s the very popular, prolific and influential engraver Charles-Nicolas Cochin was commissioned to produce vignettes to adorn various editions of the President Hénault's *Nouvel abrégé chronologique de l'histoire de France*.[25] Cochin acknowledged that it could be useful for an artist to study medals, and we know that he not only looked at mediaeval tapestries in the hope that these would inform him about costume at the time of King Dagobert but also made notes (relying no doubt on the volumes of Montfaucon) on the sort of crowns worn by kings in the fourteenth century; but he went out of his way to declare that beauty should never be sacrificed to historical exactitude in book illustration, and he criticised men of letters who 'nearly always spend their time complaining about the inaccuracy of the costumes worn: that's what they are best at looking at. No doubt they are right enough, and what they say on the matter may be very useful . . .'. But it was not essential; and as he was of the opinion that Veronese offered a perfect example of a painter who was of the first rank despite the inaccuracy of his costumes, he decided to adopt a somewhat watered-down version of Veronese's style when recording scenes from the twelfth, thirteenth, fourteenth and most other centuries – including earlier ones (pl. 170). And the President Hénault himself was thoroughly satisfied and considered that these illustrations were all 'historical'.

As the eighteenth century drew to a close not everyone was prepared to take so relaxed a view, and in England especially a far more critical attitude to current methods of visualising the past becomes apparent. In 1773 Joseph Strutt, not a pedantic man of letters but a budding artist and engraver aged twenty-four, wrote of the inaccuracies to be found in pictorial representations of scenes from the Middle Ages (which were just beginning to become popular) and acknowledged that this was due to the inaccessibility of authentic sources. He therefore published a slim volume which, despite a slightly misleading title, reproduced sixty portraits of English kings from Edgar in 966 to Henry VIII, often found in 'delineations of the most remarkable passages of history'. These had been drawn and engraved by

171. Joseph Strutt, reproduction of a scene from a Flemish MS of Froissart's *Chronicles* (British Library, Royal MS 18.E.ii) showing Richard II handing over his crown and sceptre to the Duke of Lancaster (Henry IV), in *The Royal and Ecclesiastical Antiquities of England*, 1773.

himself from illuminated manuscripts in the British Museum, the King's Library, the Bodleian and elsewhere. Although it was the dress and the customs that had particularly fascinated him (and in his footnotes he included very full details of the colours of the originals as well as of the character of each manuscript), he realised that these works were not to be thought of merely as fashion plates. The appeal of such manuscripts to the wider historical imagination and to scholarship was a considerable one; but he was aware that some of them were 'not quite so ancient as the point of history they are designed to illustrate'. He acknowledged this when discussing 'an old transcript of Froissart's chronicle' which he dated (on stylistic grounds) to the end of the reign of Henry VI, but which represented the moment some sixty years earlier when Richard II, still in his royal robes, had handed over his crown and sceptre to the treacherous Duke of Lancaster who thus at once became King Henry IV but 'who received them with much pretended diffidence and humility' (pl. 171). Around these protagonists of a scene that remains haunting to all lovers of Shakespeare (though it is to Holinshead, Shakespeare's source, that Strutt refers) stand the leading spiritual and temporal lords of the realm.[26]

Strutt admired the 'good taste' of these illuminations, 'considering the poor state of the art at that time', but when, two years later, he devoted three volumes to a 'compleat view of the Manners, Customs, Arms, Habits, &c of the Inhabitants of England from the arrival of the Saxons, till the reign of Henry the Eighth', he found himself obliged to reproduce many early manuscripts whose ungainliness seemed shocking and whose apparent lack of understanding of 'anything more antient than the manners and customs of their own particular times' might be thought to render the whole laborious operation a pointless one. However, whether or not he was aware of the observations made some thirty years earlier by La Curne de Sainte-Palaye about this very issue, Strutt quickly recognised that such 'ignorant errors' could be extremely useful for the accurate light they threw on 'the customs of that period in which each illuminator or designer lived'. It might be argued, he admitted, that these designers had resorted to pure fantasy, but it was possible to show that this had not been the case. Many of the manuscripts portrayed in their frontispieces some king or nobleman, surrounded by a retinue of followers, receiving the book that had been made for him. It could be assumed that such men would be correctly dressed in contemporary costume, and this allowed checks to be made on the scenes depicted on later pages. Moreover, many different manuscripts from the same century could be compared, and an examination of this kind showed that they agreed with each other – and with descriptions 'collected from the old historians'.[27] Strutt therefore felt himself to be thoroughly justified in publishing careful and accurate reproductions of these highly unusual sources, though he admitted that he felt a sense of relief when he reached the far superior quality of the later works.[28]

In 1777 and 1778 Strutt followed up what had hitherto been essentially antiquarian books with two volumes of *The Chronicle of England*, 'a compleat history civil, military and ecclesiastical, of the ancient Britons and Saxons, from the landing of Julius Caesar in Britain to the Norman Conquest. With a compleat view of the Manners, Customs, Arts, Habits &c of those people'. It is clear that he felt that a serious history of this kind, intended for an educated but not an antiquarian readership, would only be disfigured by the crudity of authentic illustrations, were he to reproduce them as faithfully as he had done in his previous volumes. He explained that although the forty-two engravings in the book – copied from manuscript illuminations, 'buildings, earth-works, monuments or the like' – had been 'taken from the things themselves with the greatest exactness', he had decided to improve the figures with a better proportion and higher finish than the originals, though 'some will be given exactly copied, to display the taste of the times in which they were done'.

Strutt himself, like Montfaucon (whose works were familiar to him), recognised that the disproportion of figures in early manuscripts – 'where may be frequently seen, cities inhabited by people, whose heads rise above the tops of houses' – did not invalidate the essential accuracy of the depictions of the men, women and buildings shown in them. But he was anxious to make his Saxons as presentable as possible to the taste of his own day. And so on at least one occasion he seems to have designed a wholly imaginary pastoral scene of 'ancient Germans as described by Tacitus' in which, on the extreme left, an ancient Saxon folds his arms and

172. Joseph Strutt, *The Chronicle of England*, vol. I, 1779, showing ancient Germans and Saxons, as described by Tacitus, Sidonius Apollinaris, Paul the Deacon and others.

leans comfortably on his spear while crossing his legs in one of the most admired of eighteenth-century poses (pl. 172); at the right stands a bare-breasted girl in breeches talking to a venerably bearded and amiable warrior, and other figures also engage in conversation; the background consists of 'primitive' huts and trees of a kind that one might expect to find on some fashionable country estate. Elsewhere Strutt combines into one plate details taken from different manuscripts; and on yet another occasion he again takes figures from different manuscripts, but places them against a partly imaginary setting.[29] The resulting mixture of authentic crudity and contemporary artistic fashion looks curious to modern eyes, but (in more sophisticated forms) this sort of combination was to become very widely adopted and seems to have won credibility as an effective means of throwing light on the past. For although Strutt had realised that mediaeval illuminations could provide images that were narrative, as well as antiquarian, in character, neither he nor anyone else at the time seems to have suggested that these illuminations themselves should be reproduced to serve as illustrations for history books.

A bold attempt to make use of authentic sources in order to illustrate those episodes from English history that had been neglected by the artists who had actually lived through them was made by the publisher and engraver Valentine Green between 1786 and 1792. For his *Acta Historica Reginarum Angliae*, which opened with *Queen Matilda soliciting the Empress Maude for the Release of her Husband*

King Stephen from Imprisonment in 1161 and closed with *The Articles of the Union presented by the Commissioners to Queen Anne in 1706*, he commissioned twelve drawings from the German artist Johann Gerhard Huck, who had come to England from Düsseldorf. Green himself provided the designs and had the drawings engraved. The drawings and prints were then exhibited at his gallery and offered for sale. Purchasers of a complete set of the engravings were supplied with a book which contained an illustrated key to the sources on which he had based his figures and a well-documented (and fully annotated) historical account of the relevant events. Green went to great lengths to explain the principles behind his enterprise.[30] As no true portraits existed for the British, Roman, Saxon and Danish eras, but only 'the obscurity of monkish fiction', his history of the queens of England could not begin until after the Norman Conquest. Portraits of the queens, together with those of 'other distinguished persons who either actually were, or presumably might have been assisting in the several scenes in which they are represented', were taken from 'coins, seals, illuminated missals, and manuscripts, ancient paintings on glass, and sepulchral monuments'. These were not always trustworthy as sources, but they were all that was available, and it could be assumed that, if several of them showed similar peculiarities in the features of the same person, this was due to correct observation rather than to defective art. True portraits, Green insisted, were absolutely indispensable for historical scenes, for they were

> the surest and most authentic guides to facts; in fine . . . by them alone we can safely discriminate between one Subject and another. – To set this matter in a still stronger light: were we to amuse ourselves by taking away the titles from many Historical Compositions that might be selected, and which have been engraved, it would be curious to remark, to what a number of other stories those identical works might be made to apply, with nearly the same effect as to those on which they were originally formed. – On the other hand, introduce but one principal Portrait, in each of the subjects to which they respectively and properly belong, and those Subjects can never afterwards be either mistaken for, or transferred to, any other History, or be fixed to any other point of either time or place.

Rigid observance of facts was essential, and those facts were to be sought for in the 'ancient TALKATIVE Historians, as they are quaintly termed'.

What impression would a reader of the late eighteenth century have made of the versions of the past to be found in this book? The courtiers of *Queen Mary II reviewing the Militia of London and Westminster in Hyde Park in 1692* would surely have presented no problem. Each portrait was copied with tolerable fidelity from pictures (or prints after pictures) by Kneller, Riley and other painters whose styles could be assimilated without difficulty by contemporary taste while yet retaining some feeling of an earlier day. But anyone wondering about the appearance of Queen Matilda's attendants in 1161 (pl. 173) or Queen Eleanor's in 1284 would surely have felt that these ladies were remarkably similar to the figures to be seen in familiar Bolognese pictures of the seventeenth century. None the less, Valentine

QUEEN MATILDA.

Plate I.

DESIDERIUS ERASMUS.

173. J.G. Huck (engraved and published by Valentine Green), *Acta Historica Reginarum Angliae*, 1792: key to the sources used for 'Queen Matilda soliciting the Empress Maude for the release of her husband King Stephen from imprisonment'.

174. George Dyer, *Biographical Sketches*, 1819: Erasmus.

Green's long preface provides one of the most interesting accounts that have come down to us of how the new need for authenticity could be reconciled with a demand for historical representations which, by their very nature, could never be authentic.

Other English publishers and engravers were later to produce variants of Green's formula. The *Biographical Sketches of the Lives and Characters of Illustrious and Eminent Men* published by the print seller George Dyer in 1819 were illustrated with full-length portraits which range over many centuries and which, for the most part, look recognisable enough – and at the same time curiously unfamiliar. Authentic sources have been used, where possible, but they have then been adapted to show 'the person pourtrayed in his usual walk of life, and not placed in studied attitude, or habited in theatrical dress': Erasmus, whose features we know so well from the portraits of Holbein, now stands proudly in swelling robes

Mort de la duchesse d'Orléans.

175. Barante, *Ducs de Bourgogne*, 6th edition, 1842: 'Mort de la duchesse d'Orléans' (by Achille Devéria).

adorned with sagging fur-lined sleeves (pl. 174); Charles I has been removed from Van Dyck's great hunting portrait in the Louvre and gazes sadly at us; Lord Chesterfield sits and talks in an elegant rococo chair.[31]

Ventures such as those of Green and Dyer carried on into the nineteenth century an earlier tradition of trying to make the past appear as natural as possible to the modern reader. Another tendency soon came to the fore which was based on exactly the opposite premise. Here, too, the original sources had been carefully studied – the helmets and halberds, the censers and enamelled coffers to be seen in the newly created historical museums – but they were used in such a way as to suggest that the past had been remote, picturesque, exotic.

What, one wonder, did Prosper de Barante make of interpretations of this kind? In the preface to the first edition of his *Histoire des ducs de Bourgogne de la maison de Valois*, published, with no illustrations, in 1824–6, he suggested that it should be the aim of the historian to 'give back to history itself the appeal that the historical novel has borrowed from it', but he argued that this could be done successfully only if the historian omitted all his own opinions from the narrative he constructed on the basis of ancient chronicles. As far as possible, these should be allowed to speak for themselves, backed up by official documents such as state papers, for only in this way could the true 'colour' of mediaeval history be sensed.[32] Yet Barante, like Thierry, endured (or did he enjoy?) the price of success. The fifth edition of his *Histoire*, of 1837–8, was plentifully illustrated by most of the leading artists of the day – Delacroix, Delaroche, Boulanger, Devéria, Johannot, Roqueplan and so on – and in other editions we come across a strange jumble of authentic visual documentation (the seal, the arms and the tomb of Philippe le Hardi, for instance), of grotesquely gesticulating portraits which have been 'adapted' – at some remove – from original sources, and of completely imaginary compositions (such as Devéria's *Mort de la duchesse d'Orléans*; pl. 175), based on nothing other than the artist's caprice.[33]

It was engravings of just this kind that had, a year earlier, led the American historian of Spain and Spanish America, W.H. Prescott, to complain that 'I do not care for the sort of illustrations with which the French historical writers sometimes embellish their works, which seem to me better suited to romance than history. But authentic portraits of the great actors in the drama, I shall always try to get'.[34] Indeed, Prescott, who despite his near blindness took a real interest in the visual arts, went to much trouble and expense to make use of what he believed (sometimes rather optimistically) were accurate portraits in order to illustrate his histories. Thus for the *Reign of Philip the Second* he employed a Spanish artist to make copies in watercolour of pictures in public and private collections in Madrid and had them engraved in London. Although he himself had never seen the originals, he was satisfied enough with these rather unreliable adaptations to discover in Titian's Philip II 'something in the sinister look of the eye which is far from winning our confidence', just as 'the wiry lineaments of the countenance [of the Duke of Alva; pl. 176] seem to have the hardness of steel. One sees that it must be a true copy of the iron-hearted chief who trampled under foot the liberties of the Netherlands.'[35]

This kind of interpretation of portraits became popular in the middle years of the century, but it was not until 1859–60 that a decisive step was taken to draw extensively on contemporary visual sources for the illustration of every aspect of history over a long period. In their joint preface to the two volumes of the *Histoire de France depuis les temps les plus anciens jusqu'à nos jours d'après les documents originaux et les monuments de l'art de chaque époque* which they published in these years, Henri Bordier and Edouard Charton showed themselves to be fully aware of the novelty of their enterprise and of the problems that it posed; but they also acknowledged, perhaps over-generously, that they were filling a need that had already been widely felt. 'The study of history through monuments', they began, 'has made great progress over the last half-century. It is today unanimously recognised that the teaching of history needs to draw on two sources, that of texts and that of works of art which are contemporary with the events described.'[36] Imaginary and unfaithful· plates – in other words, the very kind of plates most popular with publishers – could produce only a false impression on the mind of the reader; they themselves had therefore gone to considerable lengths to make sure that the visual sources they reproduced were authentic and accurate. This necessarily meant that

176. W.H. Prescott, *Reign of Philip II*, London 1855, vol. II: portrait of the Duke of Alva.

the early parts of their work could be only sparsely illustrated, for 'we have not wished to make up for a shortage [of images] which is in itself significant. We have provided only what actually exists – or at least what we have found – and nothing more.' In the Middle Ages, of course, the number of works of art had greatly increased, and 'there comes a time when the history of France is sculpted, painted, drawn, engraved, almost scene by scene, day by day'.

Henri Bordier, an archivist of strong republican convictions, was deeply interested in the illuminated manuscripts in the Bibliothèque Nationale, of which he hoped to make an inventory, and it is not, therefore, surprising that this *Histoire de France* at last demonstrated how rich a source these could be for the illustration of mediaeval history. Edouard Charton also was wholly committed to public education. He was something of a mystic by temperament, and in his youth he had been converted to Saint-Simonism. He was much impressed by English periodicals of an improving kind, such as Charles Knight's *Penny Magazine*, and in 1833 he founded the enormously successful and influential *Magasin Pittoresque* which he continued to direct for fifty years. It was indeed from its offices that the *Histoire de France* was edited.[37]

The huge numbers of illustrations reproduce a great variety of objects which range in time and in character from prehistoric monuments to the Colonne de Juillet erected in the Place de la Bastille to commemorate the victims of the Revolution of 1830 – with which event the book closes on a note of triumph. To some extent, therefore, the carefully chosen prints reproduced in the two volumes of Bordier's and Charton's *Histoire de France* can be thought of as achieving the unattainable aims of Louis-Philippe's museum at Versailles. For the first time it became possible to see contemporary visual records of a comprehensive national history – though it must be admitted that the uniformly drab quality of the wood engravings somewhat diminishes the impact that one might expect to find made by the changing styles of artefacts separated by so many decades and centuries. The objects represented – an arrowhead, a coin, a bust, a bas-relief, a painting, an engraving, a church – were copied from many different sources (which are usually identified, though often somewhat vaguely as 'd'après une estampe du temps') (pl. 177); and each narrative and political section was followed by one devoted to the arts and letters in a way that was by now traditional – though it is curious that, with rare exceptions in the case of architecture, these are illustrated only by portraits of the artists and never by their works. Bordier and Charton, however, often referred to specific pictures, and they recognised, and cautiously endorsed, recent changes in aesthetic taste – such as the rehabilitation of Watteau and Boucher – but in their chapters on the arts they almost never related stylistic developments to wider cultural or political movements; and correspondingly in their discussions of political events (which rely ostentatiously on original documents) they do not look to the arts for evidence to support their narrative. Thus there are a number of reproductions of scenes from the Bayeux Tapestry, but they are not referred to in their account of the Norman Conquest – any more than portraits are examined for the psychological light that they might throw on the protagonists of more recent history. Bordier and Charton occasionally quoted

14 octobre 1614. — États généraux tenus dans la grande salle Bourbon, à Paris. — Estampe du temps.
(Collection Hennin.) — Voy. la légende ci-contre, p. 181.

177. Edouard Bordier and Edouard Charton, *Histoire de France*, 2nd edition, 1862, vol. II:
reproduction of an anonymous engraving (from the Hennin Collection) of the Meeting of the
States General in 1614.

from Michelet, but they showed no interest in the sort of parallels that he liked to draw between politics and the arts. On one level their *Histoire de France* provides an impressive combination of literary and visual sources – a literal combination because the engravings very often have no borders and merge into the text – but in a deeper sense the book constitutes no more than a richly and imaginatively illustrated narrative of a traditional kind.

A significant number of the prints in their two volumes were copied from the 15,000 drawings and engravings relating to the history of France which had been assembled in sixty-nine folios over a period of many years by Michel Hennin and which, on his death in 1863 at the age of eighty-six, he was to bequeath to the Bibliothèque Nationale.[38] Hennin was one of the last antiquarian collectors and scholars in a line that stretched back to Roger de Gaignières and Montfaucon – for whose achievements he expressed admiration qualified by reservations about their standards of accuracy.[39] He had been born in Switzerland and had spent much of his life in Italy (and then in Germany) in the service of Napoleon's brother-in-law Eugène de Beauharnais. In 1856 – three years before the appearance of Bordier's and Charton's history – he published the first of the ten volumes of his *Les Monuments de l'Histoire de France*, which drew in part on his own collection, but far more on works in the public domain. The compilation, which was itself unillustrated, was arranged as far as possible on chronological lines. Thus it was possible to consult any date from Childéric in AD 481 until the reign of Henri IV and to find under it brief descriptions of those figured monuments – a coin, a seal, a carved capital, an illuminated manuscript and so on – that appeared to represent some contemporary notability or event, and also the whereabouts (in a drawing in a public or private collection, an antiquarian journal or other publication) of a reproduction of the monument in question.

All this obviously constituted an invaluable tool for research, but of greater importance as a stimulus to Bordier and Charton must have been the four hundred pages of introduction in which Hennin set out his claims for the importance of the visual image as a source for the historian.[40] And, in fact, the strengths and weaknesses of this quasi-manifesto provide us with our clearest available insight into the manner in which those writers who accepted this premise tried to tackle the problems facing them. Hennin's essential point, which he repeated again and again, was that to have historical value an illustration must be contemporary with the event it recorded, and he lacked any feeling for those elaborate reconstructions of the past that had been so popular with the painters of his own day.[41] Like many writers and artists over the previous hundred years, he recognised that anachronistic images could be useful for the information that they supplied about the costumes and conventions of an artist's own times, but he felt, none the less, that it was a pity that so much religious art had been produced in the Middle Ages at the expense of scenes from contemporary life.[42] Matters had not even improved with the Renaissance, for painters had then taken to depicting important figures in antique dress – an absurd custom which had survived into the nineteenth century itself. Hennin's approach was thus entirely antiquarian, and he never discussed the problems of why such conventions had changed or whether these changes might not themselves have raised issues of real importance for historical studies. Still less was he concerned with artistic style as a phenomenon of historical interest, despite his criticisms of Montfaucon (who had, in fact, been aware of this very point) for having employed copyists who had misrepresented the style of those objects that they had aimed to reproduce faithfully. And, even within the limits that he himself imposed on his discussion of the arts as evidence for the scholar, his approach was sometimes lacking in perception: thus he failed to point out that even a contemporary representation of some significant episode could be historically misleading – perhaps deliberately so. 'En regardant les trois estampes de l'entrée de Henri IV à Paris, publiées par J. Le Clerc on croit être à cette entrée même':[43] the phrase sums up his whole attitude to the nature of such documents.

On the other hand, Hennin was more aware than most (if not all) previous writers of certain essential aspects of visual sources. He knew that, with the possible exception of etchings and engravings, they had all been crucially affected by the passing of time. War, iconoclasm, robbery, inadequate copies, unsatisfactory restoration, radical transformations carried out in the interests of changing taste – all these, and much more, had had a devastating effect on the raw materials available to the historian, which were thus extremely precarious: even daguerreotypes and photographs faded with the years and were not as reliable as they seemed.[44] And Hennin also raised, but did not solve, one other problem of outstanding significance: whereas it could be claimed that the production of a large number of illustrations of some historical episode provided testimony of its impact on public opinion, it had to be admitted that certain extremely important events had attracted almost no attention at all from artists or craftsmen: 'Pour des faits importants accomplis, le silence des écrivains est une faute; le silence des monuments est un enseignement.'[45] But Hennin was baffled by the meaning of that lesson – which indeed has continued to disconcert historians.

12

The Historical Significance of Style

i

In 1826, when he was aged thirty-one, Augustin Thierry went blind. Some years later he described a visit to the churches of Languedoc and Provence when he could no longer read even the clearest inscriptions and his sight was only just strong enough to make out the main features of the architecture itself:

> In the presence of these ruined buildings whose period and style I wished to determine, some strange inner sense came to the aid of my eyes. Enlivened by what I would gladly call the historical passion, I could see further and more clearly. None of the principal outlines, no characteristic feature, escaped me, and the readiness of my observation, so uncertain in ordinary circumstances, surprised the people who were accompanying me. Such were the last responses I derived from the sense of sight . . .[1]

Painful groping, flashes of vision, the descent of darkness: to how many historians writing of the arts could one not metaphorically apply Thierry's dreadful experience?

During the course of the nineteenth and early twentieth centuries many among the finest historians in Europe and America were well-informed lovers of painting, sculpture and architecture, and (as we shall see) this love is often reflected in their books. Ranke was probably the earliest and certainly the most eminent among them. He spent long hours in the picture galleries of Italy, and as a young man he wrote a *History of Italian Art* which, however, he did not publish until nearly fifty years after it had been completed.[2] In his first historical masterpiece, *Geschichten der romanischen und germanischen Völker von 1494 bis 1535*, which appeared in 1824, he followed the precedent of Gibbon (with none of Gibbon's hesitation) in turning to the portrait of Julius II by Raphael (pl. 129) – known to him from a copy in Berlin – so as to understand the mind of that pope with his 'strongly marked features, closed mouth, well-directed gaze and long white beard, as he sits and meditates in his armchair'.[3] And when he wrote the *History of the Popes* immediately afterwards he not only discussed, with great feeling, the creation of Baroque Rome with its palaces, gardens and collections, but also broke with the well-established tradition of merely adding a section on the arts to an essentially political narrative. Instead, he incorporated some pages on Italian painting between the Carracci and Guercino into the very structure of the book in order to illustrate the increasing part played by serious religious belief in the life of the period – with results that could sometimes be 'Baroque and forced' but that did not thereby imply any lack of sincerity.[4]

Mommsen, too, showed a keen interest in the arts, and among some of the other writers in German-speaking countries the relationship between art history and history was so close that these branches of study actually overlapped. Franz Kugler, for instance, one of the founders of art history and for many years the most widely read and influential scholar in the field anywhere in Europe, also published, in 1840, an extremely successful *History of Frederick the Great*. He chose the young and unknown Adolph Menzel to illustrate this with brilliantly conceived neo-rococo images, which are sometimes based on specific sources but which none the less reveal a view of eighteenth-century monarchy as transformed by romantic sensibilities as any episode from the Middle Ages illustrated at this period.[5] Of Kugler's disciple, Jacob Burckhardt, it would be difficult to decide whether he was greater as a historian or as an art historian; and among Burckhardt's many admirers Ferdinand Gregorovius wrote a *History of Rome in the Middle Ages* which not only relied heavily on the evidence of surviving (and destroyed) monuments for its reconstruction of the past but which also evoked a picture of the city that was based on the most acute visual sensitivity.[6] Karl Justi is yet another of the great German writers whose books – on Velázquez and on Winckelmann – are hard to characterise, so familiar does he seem to have been with every aspect of the art and life of the periods he discusses.

Ernst Curtius, however, is the German historian whose approach was most strikingly affected by an enthusiasm for art. The first volume of his *Griechische Geschichte* was published in Berlin in 1857 when he was aged forty-three, and soon became recognised, outside as well as inside Germany, as by far the most important contribution to the subject that had yet appeared anywhere. Curtius had spent some years in Greece, and he was later to direct the epoch-making excavations at Olympia. His knowledge of Greek archaeology and of the literary sources of Greek history was both profound and up-to-date – but in his approach to the golden age of Athens he can be thought of as a late, but faithful, inheritor of the ideas of Winckelmann. When he came to describe the rebuilding of the city after the defeat of the Persians he richly embroidered the account to be found in Plutarch's *Life of Pericles* and drew on his own emotional involvement with the city in order to produce an almost visionary picture of the creation of an earthly paradise:

> The Athenian people, partial both to work and to gain, took delight in the busy stir occasioned by the public works of Pericles. Materials of all kinds had to be brought to hand – metals, ivory, precious stones, and foreign kinds of wood. All classes took part in the public artistic activity, – from the artist, who in solitude matures his ideas and prepares his designs, through all classes of merchants, tradesmen, and artisans, down to the miners and road-builders, the

wheelwrights, rope-makers, and waggoners, whose business it was to transport the innumerable blocks of marble to the height of the citadel . . . A loftier patriotism communicated itself to the citizens, when they saw their native city adorned, before all other towns, with the noblest works of art: and as these works, notwithstanding their splendour, were characterised by a lofty simplicity, and one and all pervaded by elevating ideas, they could not but exercise an educating and refining influence upon the minds of those who witnessed their gradual completion, and who afterwards had them constantly before their eyes. For they exercise a power which raises man above the narrow limits of his personal circumstances, and obliges him to conceive highly and worthily of the state which can create such things, as well as of his own duties as a citizen. But even those who could not look upon the state with the love and admiration of an Attic citizen, even the subjects and the foreigners, could not withdraw themselves from the impression produced by the glories of Athens . . . ; so that whoever appreciated these, could not but take pride in Athens as the capital of Greece, and in a certain sense regard himself as an Athenian. This was the end which Pericles desired; Athens was to prove herself worthy to rule over Hellenes: and the employment of the public resources for this purpose was in truth no waste . . .[7]

It is tempting to think of this noble, but extraordinary, paean to Greek civilisation (in which there is no reference to slavery) as a deliberate riposte to Herder's equally intense response to the making of ancient Rome: perhaps more to the point are Rollin's strictures on the extravagance of Pericles and, above all, the many accounts, which had been popular during the first half of the nineteenth century, of the building of the great Gothic cathedrals during the 'Age of Faith'.

In France both Guizot and Thiers began their literary careers as art critics, although it is true that little, if any, evidence of this is to be found in the major historical works to which they then turned. However, Renan and Taine followed Michelet's example by writing at length about the visual arts and by drawing on them to supplement their more specifically historical researches.

It was for spiritual consolation in a world that he found vulgar and despicable that Renan turned to the art of Rome and especially of Athens. But his studies led him also to very different fields, and both the range of his appreciation and the intensity of his gaze were far more searching than those of Michelet whom he always looked upon as the most beloved of masters.[8] While writing his thesis on 'Averroes and Averroism in Scholastic Philosophy', when he was still in his twenties, he made extensive use of what was to be seen in paintings and frescoes attributed to Orcagna, Buffalmacco, Traini, Taddeo Gaddi, Benozzo Gozzoli and other artists in Pisa and Florence. To some of these his attention had been drawn by his familiarity with the texts and illustrations of a number of writers – Seroux d'Agincourt among them; others he discovered for himself. And he presented his evidence with none of Michelet's romantic intuition, but with a sureness of touch that was quite new to historical writing.[9]

Like all his contemporaries, Renan was, in theory, scornful of 'les minauderies du Bernin, les extravagances de Borromini', because they symbolised the trivial decadence into which Italy collapsed during the seventeenth century.[10] However, when he came to look at the art itself his denunciations faltered somewhat. In that 'little masterpiece of a church', the Martorana in Palermo, he was not shocked by 'ces petits guichets où les mosaïques primitives se mêlent aux enfantillages du rococo le plus effréné'. And surely we can hear the tones of the art lover and not only those of the historian and man of caution when he denounces any idea of 'restoring' the church: 'Laissez donc ce petit monument tel qu'il est'. After all, the Baroque, too, was expressive in its own way, and who could be sure that taste might not change? 'The seventeenth century slashed the Middle Ages without ever imagining that one day this barbaric, incorrect, often savage art would have its value. Nowadays the seventeenth century is destroyed as vacuous and without character. Who knows . . . whether the nineteenth century will not in turn be accused of vandalism?' And travellers to Italy today can only echo with anguish his painfully relevant complaint that 'under the pretext of bringing buildings back to what they once were the seventeenth and eighteenth centuries are being obliterated'.[11]

It is gratifying to find Renan (prompted by his brother-in-law Arnold Scheffer) among the earliest and most enthusiastic admirers of 'the sparkle, the vitality, the colour, the originality and the individualism' of Tiepolo's frescoes in the Palazzo Labia in Venice. 'Did Tiepolo', he wrote to Flaubert in 1874, 'wish to give a history lesson or a lesson in morality, a lesson in archaeology or a lesson in politics? Did he wish to exalt or to demean Anthony and Cleopatra? Was he accused of lacking in respect for a royal majesty that was compromising itself by taking part in a banquet of a somewhat equivocal nature? No. He was opening up a brilliant dream for the imagination. That is enough. Neither the archaeologist, nor the moralist, nor the historian, nor the politician can have any cause for complaint.'[12]

The sheer hedonism of his response to the magic of Tiepolo is unusual. Art was inclined to speak to Renan in more didactic terms. It is perhaps significant, in view of so many bizarre precedents, that it should have been when trying to explore the character of the apparently notorious Faustina that he turned with particular eagerness to the evidence provided by images of the empress[13] – for he wished to defend her against the calumnies of ancient writers. He was well aware that 'le témoignage des monuments figurés sera sûrement tenu pour suspect', but this, he claimed, was because it was entirely in the empress's favour. In any case, he made no mention whatsoever of the marble group of *Faustina and the Gladiator* in the Louvre (pl. 73), though it seems likely that he knew of the identification, and he mocked those authors who claimed to detect in Faustina's features 'l'air d'une franche cocotte'. It is to other sources that he turns in a spirit which, at first sight, appears alarmingly naïve: a bas-relief in the Villa Albani shows her surrounded by young girls and pouring corn into the folds of their robes; another relief portrays her as Abundance listening to a speech by her husband; a fine sculpture in the Capitoline Museum in Rome represents her apotheosis 'while the excellent emperor looks up at her with an expression full of love'; her medals render her sometimes as Pudicity, sometimes as Venus. And then Renan pounces. It will be said, he points out, that all these representations are merely expressions of official adulation or pious lies. But would it have been possible to select for her medals precisely those images that would most have lent themselves to ridicule if the scandals reported by later historians had even been suspected by her contemporaries? The argument may not be wholly convincing, but it does at least demonstrate how much more sophisticated the interpretation of images had become since the days of the Abbé Raguenet.

The range of the Goncourt brothers was very much narrower than that of Michelet, Renan or Taine (although their connoisseurship was very much deeper), but within their limits they drew copiously on the arts when composing their pioneering histories of French social life during the eighteenth century and the revolutionary period. Edmond, especially, was highly self-conscious about the novelty of their approach,[14] and their example was, in time, to encourage many other writers to follow in their footsteps.

In England, also, historians were looking to the arts with renewed interest and enthusiasm. Ruskin's *The Stones of Venice* was based on the assumption that the city's political, and above all its spiritual, development could best be understood by a careful consideration of its principal monuments. Ruskin's adulation of the Gothic was matched by that of the pedantic and cantankerous Edward Augustus Freeman, author of *The History of the Norman Conquest*, who began his scholarly career with a *History of Architecture* published in 1849. And Freeman's friend J.R. Green, author of the enormously popular *Short History of the English People*, showed a particular love of painting.[15] So, too, did W.H. Lecky, who – as we shall see in a later chapter – used his wide knowledge of Italian art to somewhat eccentric effect in his *History of the Rise and Influence of the Spirit of Rationalism in Europe*, while Mandell Creighton, the historian of the papacy, had originally planned to write a history of Italian art.[16] Although Macaulay himself had been little interested in painting, his editor C.H. Firth was not only a leading authority on the political and military history of seventeenth-century England but also a specialist on the prints and pictures of the period.[17] Froude was enthusiastic about the pictures in the Prado – 'the finest in the world, I suppose . . . Oh, the pictures at Madrid!'[18] And, above all, John Addington Symonds, the historian of the Italian Renaissance, wrote at length and with deep feeling about Italian art, not only in the *History* itself, but also in separate studies. It was, however, the American Henry Adams who tried, with more passion than any other historian except Ruskin, to penetrate to the very core of mediaeval civilisation, and to find there spiritual values applicable to his own times, by studying the architecture, sculpture and stained glass windows of the great French cathedrals and churches. 'We were a serious race,' he writes of the Normans at the beginning of *Mont Saint-Michel and Chartres*; 'If you want other proof of it besides our record in war and in politics, you have only to look at our art. Religious art is the measure of human depth and sincerity; any triviality, any weakness, cries aloud'.[19]

ii

Among all the many nineteenth-century historians who showed a true interest in the arts – and only a few of them have been mentioned here – three in particular wrestled with the issue of how to make systematic use of the evidence apparently provided by architecture, sculpture and painting for their studies of the past: John Ruskin, Jacob Burckhardt and Hippolyte Taine. It was Italian art, of different periods, that drew their attention to the problem, and all three paid very significant visits to Italy during the 1850s and 1860s. All three also made important contributions to a wide range of other topics, but it is the historical aspect of their researches that will alone be considered in the following pages.

To John Ruskin the idea of drawing on the arts as a source for understanding the past seems to have developed rapidly from a sudden intuition that occurred to him while looking at Veronese's *Wedding Feast at Cana* in the Louvre on 8 September 1849: 'the first distinct expression which fixed itself on one was that of the entire superiority of Painting to Literature as a test, expression, and record of human intellect, and of the enormously greater quantity of Intellect which might be forced into a picture – and read there – compared with that which might be expressed in words . . . I felt that painting had never yet been understood as it is, an Interpretation of Humanity.'[20] Looking back years after the publication, between 1851 and 1853, of the three volumes of *The Stones of Venice*, he claimed that in writing that book he had had 'no other aim than to show that the Gothic architecture of Venice had arisen out of, and indicated in all its features, a state of pure national faith, and of domestic virtue; and that its Renaissance architecture had arisen out of, and in all its features indicated, a state of concealed national infidelity, and of domestic corruption'.[21] And in 1884, by which time he was extremely critical of this early work and had utterly changed his mind about the nature of Venetian society,[22] he still maintained that the arts provided a uniquely valuable key for the understanding of history: 'Great nations write their autobiographies in three manuscripts; the book of their deeds, the book of their words, and the book of their art. Not one of these books can be understood unless we read the two others; but of the three, the only quite trustworthy one is the last.'[23]

When Ruskin came to Venice in November 1849[24] to work on the study of its Gothic monuments which he had had in mind for some time, he was aged thirty and already famous as the author of the first two volumes of *Modern Painters*. The beauty of his style was greatly admired, and his vehement advocacy of a succession of artistic causes – notably the paintings of Turner, of Tintoretto and of the early Italian masters – was beginning to convert his readers into disciples. The depth of his emotional response to certain favourite writers and, above all, to the Bible, as striking in the cadences of his prose as in the range of his quotations, was not concealed by the extreme self-assurance of what he was later to describe as his 'pert little Protestant mind';[25] but although he was reluctant to admit it to his parents, his prejudices were gradually disintegrating under the impact of those masterpieces of Catholic painting, sculpture and architecture with which he was becoming increasingly familiar. No work of Ruskin was ever confined to a single theme, and despite his claim that in *The Stones of Venice* he had had 'no other aim' than to indicate the moral implications of Gothic and Renaissance architecture, that book was in fact concerned with a very large variety of (more-or-less) related pre-occupations: among these was an interpretation of the city's history derived from a study of its changing artistic monuments.

Ruskin had first visited Venice briefly with his parents in 1835 as a boy of sixteen, and in 1841 he had been there for another eight days during which he had once again made careful drawings of St Mark's and other monuments. But it was the five weeks he spent there on his own in 1845, followed by another two weeks with his parents a year later,[26] that really enabled him to examine Venetian painting and architecture thoroughly and also to observe with horror the coming to Venice of railways, of gas lamps and – most devastating of all, more devastating indeed than even he could yet have guessed at – of large-scale 'restoration'. Now in 1849, as he settled in the Danieli hotel for this the most decisive of all his visits, the outward circumstances were very different in two ways, though neither seems to have made much of an impact on him: he was married, and, after just over a year as an independent republic, Venice had been compelled to surrender to its Austrian masters.[27]

That event was at least a reminder – but by then it was hardly needed – that Venice offered to the historian a theme of compelling interest: the irredeemable decline and fall of what had once been one of Europe's great empires. But, to sensitive observers, the city also appeared to offer clues as to how that theme might be approached. Nowhere else in the world was it possible to see a more conspicuous display of splendid monuments erected to the glory of God and of man which ranged in time from the early (although not the earliest) Christians until Napoleon: and to many art lovers and antiquarians of the middle of the nineteenth century the abundance of mediaeval architecture more than com-pensated for the lack of those ruins of classical antiquity, hitherto unchallenged in popular esteem, which still survived in Rome. Churches and private palaces and government offices in the closest proximity were decorated in a wide variety of styles, and because none of these dominated the others (as was the case in most Italian cities), a rich, but confused 'history of Venice based on examples of its arts drawn from every period' – to adapt the titles of so many books published in these years – could be visualised on the spot by anyone prepared to take the briefest of excursions in a gondola, or even a stroll round the Piazza S. Marco and its immediate surroundings. To claim that the city of Venice itself was an example – in stone and richly coloured marbles and paint – of the type of illustrated pub-lication on which Bordier and Charton were soon to embark hardly begins to do justice to its grandeur and beauty, let alone the life of its inhabitants, but does give some indication of at least part of its appeal to historians who, as we have seen, were becoming increasingly interested in visual documents.

In his search for such visual documents (in the narrowest sense of the term) Ruskin surprised his friends and even himself – and wholly astonished the local inhabitants – by the extent of his industry and enterprise during the next four months of often bitterly cold weather. He climbed up ladders to examine the most minute details of the capitals and mouldings of St Mark's and other buildings, and lay flat on the ground to study the bases of their columns.[28] He covered hundreds of pages with careful notes and with sketches that emphasised, with the most delicate precision, the particular features that interested him (pl. 178).[29] In fact, with the possible exception of Rome, no city had ever before been subjected to such loving and meticulous scrutiny. Much of Ruskin's material was never discussed in his published book;[30] but although his relentless copying was certainly inspired in large part by an almost sensual appetite for the surface beauty of Venetian architecture[31] and by his fear that it would soon be lost at the hands of the 'restorers', we should also consider it as being equivalent to the lengthy notes made in archives and libraries by more conventional historians of the city. Ruskin himself explains why this visual research was necessary. He had, he tells us, expected that the main chronological outlines of the development of Venetian architecture had been securely established by local antiquarians. He soon found, however, that this was absolutely not the case (he singled out Cicognara as being 'so inaccurate as hardly to deserve mention') and that enormous discrepancies – of up to a hundred years – were to be found in the various datings proposed for even so important a structure as the Doge's Palace.[32]

Quite early in the course of his enquiry into the nature of mediaeval architecture Ruskin came to the conclusion that this palace was 'the central building of the world' because it contained in almost equal proportions the three elements – the Roman, Lombard and Arab – that combined to make up the Gothic.[33] It

178. Ruskin, *South-west Portico of St Mark's from the Loggia of the Doge's Palace*, c.1849, pencil and watercolour, heightened with white (Private Collection).

was, however, only by the time of his second extended stay in the city, which took place after the publication of the first volume of *The Stones of Venice*, that he decided just how important a role he would have to assign to the Palazzo Ducale in his vision of the development of Venetian history. In a letter of April 1852, which reveals much about his conception of the kind of history he believed himself to be writing, he explained to his father that

> the fact is the whole book will be a kind of great 'moral of the Ducal Palace of Venice', and all its minor information will concentrate itself on the Ducal Palace and its meaning, as the History of Herodotus concentrates itself on the Battle of Salamis. He rambles all over the world and gives the History of Egypt and of Babylon and of Persia and of Scythia and of Phoenicia and of old Greece, and to a careless student the book appears a farrago of unconnected matter, but a careful one discovers that all in the eight first books are mere prefaces to the ninth, and that whatever is told, or investigated, is to show what the men were, who brought their ships beak to beak in the straits of Salamis. And so I shall give many a scattered description of a moulding here and an arch there, but they will be mere notes to the account of the Rise and Fall of the Ducal Palace, and that account itself will be subservient to the showing of the causes and consequences of the rise and fall of art in Europe.[34]

That rise and fall could be demonstrated only once the chronological development of Venetian architecture had been fully understood, and Ruskin quickly came to the conclusion that 'every date in question was determinable only by internal evidence; and it became necessary for me to examine not only every one of the older palaces, stone by stone, but every fragment throughout the city which afforded any clue to the formation of its styles'.[35] In fact, Ruskin could not, and did not, rely only on internal evidence. He was always ready to take advantage of the ideas and researches of local antiquarians (for whom he expressed the utmost contempt), and under the guidance of his friend the archivist Rawdon Brown, that most tolerant and delightful of authorities on Venice, he examined 'most of the written documents', both published and unpublished, concerned with the architecture of the city – and he made extensive use of them in his discussion of the Palazzo Ducale. But he claimed that, in his examination of that building, he also studied 'one document more, to which the Venetian antiquaries never thought of referring, – the masonry of the palace itself'.[36]

Thus in their early stages Ruskin's researches were in many ways similar to those of other connoisseurs such as Waagen and Cavalcaselle (both heartily scorned by him), whose written sources were usually inadequate and who therefore had to propose the authorship and dating of thousands of little-studied and often ruined pictures largely on the basis of their differing styles; indeed, Cavalcaselle was as assiduous as Ruskin in making drawings – admittedly of a more schematic and less elegant kind – for this very purpose.

Nevertheless, connoisseurship did not for Ruskin (as it did for Cavalcaselle) constitute an end in itself. He needed to draw on evidence apparently provided by the changing character of art in order to solve the quite specific historical problem (which had such crucial implications for the future of England) of how and why Venice had declined. He turned in the first place to the two most important books that had been concerned with the issue. He read – or, rather, he asked his wife to read and annotate for him – Sismondi's *Histoire des républiques italiennes du moyen âge*;[37] and, above all, he studied Pierre Daru's still authoritative *Histoire de la République de Venise*, which had first been published in 1819 and had been frequently re-edited since.[38] Indeed, it is only through a brief consideration of this work that we can appreciate in full the astonishing nature of *The Stones of Venice*.

The opening sentence is as arresting as any in historical literature: 'Une république fameuse, longtemps puissante, remarquable par la singularité de son origine, de son site et de ses institutions, a disparu de nos jours, sous nos yeux, en un moment.'[39] And, thereafter, the narrative proceeds with fluent efficiency – but without such cunning cadences and without much pathos or colour. Towards the end of many volumes filled with accounts of oppression, ruthlessness, violence and greed Daru comes to the sad conclusion that 'Although, like other nations, Venice had her periods of glory and prosperity, she did not have ages of heroism – those ages when noble passions and republican virtues raise a people above others: at no stage in her history, for instance, do we find a contempt for riches.'[40] It was, however, the documentation that gave the book its particular importance, for it was only after the fall of Venice that her hitherto secret archives became easily available, and Daru was the first historian to make telling use of these in a work that was, in fact, written exclusively in France (to which masses of Venetian papers had been removed and where printed sources were in good supply). For Daru had not himself ever set foot among the stones of Venice, though he corresponded with Venetian scholars and employed assistants there to copy documents for him. He devoted the years immediately following Waterloo to the production of his seven volumes (which were to attract attention all over Europe and to arouse the anger of Venetian patriots, Cicognara among them), during one of the very brief setbacks to a remarkable career of almost continuous success.

Pierre Daru had been born in Montpellier in 1767. He began to translate Latin poetry when still a schoolboy, and he continued to do so at various moments throughout his life. Although he supported the early stages of the Revolution, he soon ran into trouble and was imprisoned for a very short period. When in 1798 the sculptures and pictures that had been seized from Rome as a consequence of the Treaty of Tolentino reached Toulon, it was Daru's version of Horace's *Carmen Saeculare* that was sung on the occasion of their official reception. But his real triumph came with the Consulate and the Empire during which he served under (and in close contact with) Napoleon as his Intendant-général and thus had the enormous responsibility of keeping the armies well supplied from Italy to Moscow. Although he retained his early liberal sympathies, he obviously did not express them in too tactless a manner, and, in any case, his abilities made him indispensable: despite having rallied to the emperor during the Hundred Days, he had before the end of 1819 already been created a peer of the realm by Louis XVIII. It is perhaps not surprising that his young cousin Stendhal (who was, for a time, in love with his wife) found him dry, dogged, unimaginative, passionless.[41]

Daru approached Venetian history very much as an experienced man of the world, and although so much of his material was new, his attitude to the past was already somewhat old-fashioned. He was interested only in the military, economic and constitutional aspects of his subject, and his easy mastery of the vast number of documents he had investigated depended in part on the lack of critical expertise with which he studied them: he was prepared to give as much weight to a secondary and obviously prejudiced narrative as to original and reliable sources. He had no feeling whatsoever for the city's artistic achievements, and on the extremely rare occasions when he mentions the name of a specific painter, such as Titian, he never refers even to those of his works that he could have seen in Paris. Nor was he much more than conventionally shocked by the cruelties that so often confronted him. He alluded, from time to time, to 'l'illustre historien Voltaire'[42] and to Gibbon, and he enjoyed summing up some of the more sensational episodes in his narrative in a spirit that recalled theirs: 'Nous avons vu quatre doges de suite exilés avec les yeux crevés; nous venons d'en voir quatre qui abdiquent pour embrasser la vie religieuse: c'est l'esprit d'imitation qui presque toujours décide des actions des hommes'.[43]

Such dry, matter-of-fact irony is of itself sufficient to indicate how utterly, how – one would have thought – unbridgeably, remote in spirit was Daru's attitude to the past of Venice from that of Ruskin. And yet it is surely a judgement of Daru's that inspired Ruskin when, near the beginning of *The Stones of Venice*, he writes what is perhaps the single most important sentence in that book, for it is the sentence on which will depend all else: 'I date the commencement of the Fall of Venice from the death of Carlo Zeno, 8th May 1418.'[44]

That date has puzzled all commentators[45] – the more so as in this volume Ruskin makes only one other passing reference to Zeno. However, two years later, he explained (in a distinctly oblique manner) that he had indicated Zeno's death as a turning point because he considered 'that no state could be held as in decline which numbered such a man amongst its citizens';[46] and this estimate of Zeno's worth must have been conveyed to him by Daru. It is true that for Daru there had been many flaws in the character and many setbacks in the career of this great commander on land and on sea who, in the war of Chioggia between 1378 and 1381, had successfully and gallantly defended Venice against an overwhelming alliance of Italian and foreign states; and it is also true that it never occurred to him to see his death as an event of crucial historical moment. None the less, Daru had described Zeno as 'l'un des plus grands hommes dont la nation vénitienne puisse s'honorer',[47] and about no other figure in Venetian history did he ever speak with even comparable admiration.

It would thus appear that it was from conventional narrative history (however unconventionally interpreted) that Ruskin derived his initial ideas regarding the period when Venice began to decline; but when he came to consider the reasons for that decline he admitted to dissatisfaction with sources of this kind, which were invariably unconvincing or prejudiced. Had the fall of the city been prompted by the changes made to her constitution in 1297 when, after six hundred years of ducal authority, power in the Republic had been entrusted exclusively to the nobility? Or had these changes themselves merely been the consequence of national enervation? Or, 'as I rather think', might not the history of Venice be written 'almost without reference to the construction of her senate or the prerogatives of her Doge?' The problem could best be solved by making use of 'frequent and irrefragable' evidence drawn from the arts which demonstrated 'that the decline of her political prosperity was exactly coincident with that of domestic and individual religion'.[48]

'Irrefragable' hardly seems the appropriate adjective: but it is surely significant, for only two years earlier Pietro Selvatico had explained that his views on the dating of the Palazzo Ducale – views that Ruskin was determined to refute, despite a certain respect he felt for this writer on Venetian art[49] – had been reached on the basis of 'irrefragable written evidence [*irrefragibili carte*]'.[50] Although Ruskin used his very different evidence in a wide variety of often incompatible ways, it was almost exclusively from her arts that he derived his impression of Venice's past. And, in a precise reversal of the attitude of those historians who have been discussed earlier in this book, if the conclusions drawn from the arts appeared to conflict with those recorded in the literary sources, it was the latter, and not the former, that had to be amended. Thus, when he read in Daru that in 1382 Carlo Zeno had been passed over for the dogeship by Michele Morosini, 'who during the war had tripled his fortune by his speculations',[51] Ruskin was so convinced that the face of the statue on Morosini's tomb – 'resolute, thoughtful, serene, and full of beauty' (pl. 179) – provided an explicit contradiction of such calumnies that he wrote for more information to Count Carlo Morosini, the doge's descendant; and, not surprisingly, he found 'absolutely convincing' the count's indignant refutation of Daru's judgement.[52]

Ruskin, however, needed to make one small adjustment to his dates in order to render acceptable his interpretation of the artistic facts at his disposal. Although the fall of Venice had begun with the death in 1418 of Carlo Zeno, it was not until five years later with the death of 'another of her noblest and wisest children', Doge Tommaso Mocenigo, that there had occurred the *visible* commencement of that decline.[53]

For all his virtues, signs of that decline were to be seen – but only just – in Mocenigo's own tomb (pl. 180). Ruskin frequently changed his mind about this tomb in the church of SS Giovanni e Paolo, which was completed by two Tuscan sculptors in the year of Mocenigo's death but which has subsequently been altered. On a pedestal at the top of the monument stands the figure of Justice (believed by Ruskin to be the Virgin), and beneath this a great canopy, held open by two angels standing on the sarcophagus, stretches down to the base of the tomb. The doge lies on the sarcophagus on the front of which are figures of the Virtues with a Roman warrior at each side. On the wall behind the canopy are two tiers of niches, in the top ones of which stand six saints. In our day, as in Ruskin's, the monument has been recognised as marking the impact of the style of the Florentine Renaissance on traditional Venetian conventions: one of the two warriors, for instance, is taken directly from Donatello's St George, and the niches containing the Virtues and Saints are closed by rounded shell forms rather than by pointed Gothic arches.[54]

When Ruskin first saw this tomb, he noted: 'Insist on large curtain and pole – pushed aside by small angels. Much worse cut altogether than I thought: Madonna

180. Tomb of Doge Tommaso Mocenigo (died 1423), *c.*1423, signed by Pietro Lamberti and Giovanni di Martino of Fiesole (Venice, SS Giovanni e Paolo).

179 (left). Tomb of Doge Michele Morosini (died 1382), early fifteenth century (Venice, SS Giovanni e Paolo).

at top. Six figures in upper niches of shrine, I know not what virtues below;
figures in Roman armour at angles. Insist on violent crocketing all over, in Porta
della Carta style and entire Renaissance character . . . these plinths and luxuriant
crockets projecting at its vertical sides, and every Renaissance character in full
development'.[55] In his published book, however, Ruskin 'insisted' on none of
these defects and completely changed his emphasis by pointing out that 'the
classical element enters largely into its details, but the feeling of the whole is as yet
unaffected'. And he then wrote, with eloquence and beautiful observation, about
the

> faithful but tender portrait, wrought as far as it can be without painfulness, of
> the doge as he lay in death. He wears his Ducal robe and bonnet – his head is
> laid slightly aside upon his pillow – his hands are simply crossed as they fall. The
> face is emaciated, the features large, but so pure and lordly in their natural
> chiselling, that they must have looked like marble even in their animation. They
> are deeply worn away by thought and death; the veins on the temple branched
> and starting; the skin gathered in sharp folds; the brow high-arched and shaggy;
> the eyeball magnificently large; the curve of the lips just veiled by the light
> moustache at the side; the beard short, double, and sharp-pointed: all noble and
> quiet; the white sepulchral dust marking like light the stern angles of the cheek
> and brow.[56]

But when, two years later, he returned to the tomb, he was again disturbed by its
Renaissance features: 'the great conspicuousness' of the images of the Virtues
'marks the increase of the boastful feeling in the treatment of monuments. For the
rest, this tomb is the last in Venice which can be considered as belonging to the
Gothic period. Its mouldings are already rudely classical, and it has meaningless
figures in Roman armour at the angles; but its tabernacle above is still Gothic, and
the recumbent figure is very beautiful.'[57]

Ruskin's shifts of emphasis in his evaluation of Mocenigo's tomb were as
significant for his interpretation of the decline of Venice as the differing con-
structions placed on the archival documents of the *ancien régime* have proved to be
for historians of the French Revolution. For he was convinced that 'of all the
evidence . . . presented by the various art of the fifteenth century' which threw
light on the growth of that insolent pride which had played so decisive a role in the
fall of Venice, none was so interesting or so conclusive as that deduced from
its tombs. For this reason he devoted an important discussion – which he had
intended to make much longer – to some of the principal tombs of Venice and
Verona.[58]

We have seen that ten years earlier Michelet had discussed the significance of
tombs for the historian – and we know that Ruskin was acquainted with some of
the writings of Michelet, though it is not clear whether he read the *Histoire de
France*. Like Michelet, Ruskin believed that the magnificence of a tomb was usually
in inverse proportion to the virtue of its occupant, but – as one consequence of his
artistic convictions – Ruskin was inevitably driven to grant far less importance
than did Michelet to the role that could be played by individual heroes or villains

in shaping the destiny of a nation. It is not just that, despite his attentive research into the structure and decoration of Gothic cathedrals, Michelet wholly lacked Ruskin's powers of feeling and observation; it is rather that although Ruskin's conclusions may often have been mistaken and his deductions misguided, none the less, the thoroughness of his investigations into 'the stones of Venice', combined with the precision of his drawings, made it obvious to him, in a way that Michelet never wholly grasped, that broad changes in style and convention usually owe more to their period than to individual choice. For Michelet the very fact that the monument in Verona of 'l'assassin' Cansignorio (pl. 153) was particularly sumptuous had made it quite logical for him to deduce (on the basis of no evidence he found it necessary to declare) that the heavy anonymous tomb adjoining it must be that of his murdered brother.[59] Ruskin, also, was fully aware of Cansignorio's crimes, and he was prepared to acknowledge that it was in fact just these that might have been responsible for the sumptuousness – he, too, uses the word – of the monument erected to him (in his own lifetime), of the comparative coarseness of the carving and, above all, of the prominence on it given to figures of the Virtues. None the less, the monument was 'beautiful, for it still belongs to the noble time, the latter part of the fourteenth century'; for just the same reason the rather earlier monument of the 'feeble and wicked' Mastino II was an 'altogether exquisite work of art', whose composition 'would have been as perfect as its decoration is refined', were it not for the 'slight circumstance' of its being flawed by the presence of the thoroughly undeserved figure of Fortitude.[60] When discussing the historical and moral significance to be deduced from the evidence being examined by him, Ruskin always found it difficult to weigh up the relative importance that he felt he should attach to the sometimes conflicting messages signalled by the aesthetic quality and the sincerity of the image. Naturally, he was most at ease when there appeared to be no contradiction between the two – an ugly or dishonest project crudely executed or a pious one treated with imagination or refinement – but if a choice had to be made it was usually quality that won the day. And as, in his eyes, artistic style – that 'irrefragable' index of prevailing morality – deteriorated relentlessly the more it approached the Renaissance, so the sum of human wickedness, or weakness, responsible for the fall of Venice could be gauged on a timescale, almost irrespective of the activities of particular individuals, in whose behaviour Ruskin showed little interest.

It must have been gratifying that the sepulchre of Francesco Foscari in the Frari (pl. 181) should have struck him as vulgar and proud, for that doge (who succeeded Mocenigo and who died in 1457) had earned Ruskin's contempt for having destroyed the last surviving Byzantine part of the Palazzo Ducale in order to put up a Renaissance building in its place. However, although there was 'nothing in the history of Foscari which would lead us to expect anything particularly noble in his face', Ruskin was inclined to attribute to the 'despicable carver' and not to the doge himself the baseness of his portrait: 'a huge, gross, bony clown's face, with the peculiar sodden and sensual cunning in it which is seen so often in the countenances of the worst Romanist priests'.[61] Ruskin's attitude to the tomb in SS Giovanni e Paolo of Doge Andrea Vendramin (pl. 182) was broadly similar. The

181. Tomb of Doge
Franceso Foscari
(died 1457), *c.*1457,
attributed to Antonio
and Paolo Bregno
(Venice, Frari).

182 (facing page).
Tomb of Doge
Andrea Vendramin
(died 1478),
completed 1490s,
attributed to Pietro,
Antonio and Tullio
Lombardo (Venice,
SS Giovanni e
Paolo).

HIC REQUIESCIT
ANNO
MDCLXI

VIXIT
ANNOS
LXX

DEVIXIT
ANNO
MDCLIX

faults or sins of this doge, who had died in 1478 after a reign of two years 'leaving Venice disgraced by sea and land', are forgotten, almost forgiven, and it is the sculptor who is famously denounced for having failed to carve the side of the head which could not be seen from below: that 'utter coldness of feeling, as could only consist with an extreme of intellectual and moral degradation: Who, with a heart in his breast, could have stayed his hand as he drew the dim lines of the old man's countenance – unmajestic once, indeed, but at least sanctified by the solemnities of death – could have stayed his hand, as he reached the bend of the grey forehead, and measured out the last veins of it at so much the zecchin?'[62] It is the age that is chiefly to be blamed, and when Ruskin reached the monuments of the seventeenth century, which represented for him the total degradation of art, he did not even bother to discuss (as Michelet would certainly have done) the career of a doge such as Giovanni Pesaro, whose monument in the Frari was borne 'by four colossal negro caryatides, grinning and horrible, with faces of black marble and white eyes' (pl. 183).[63] Had that doge fought bravely against the Turks, had he advanced his family's fortunes at the expense of the State? It is of no consequence. The artistic evidence, as unforgiving as any Calvinist theologian, condemns him and all his contemporaries, irrespective of their virtues or vices as individuals. In the early pages of *The Stones of Venice* Ruskin had made a distinction between the greedy commercialisation of Venetian public life and the vitality of religion in private life;[64] but by now the individual had no chance of standing up against the spirit of the times, which was positively Hegelian in its intensity.

Daru, too, like all historians, had seen the decline and fall of Venice as a fairly continuous and probably inevitable process, though for him it had been punctuated by occasional and short-lived periods of recovery due to the valour or shrewdness of some military hero or statesman. The periods and events that he indicated as having marked the collapse – the stagnation of trade, the conquest of an empire on the mainland of Italy, the discovery of America, the overwhelming strength of the Ottomans, the eventual retreat into neutrality and the sloth that came from too prolonged a peace – were very different from those later to be insisted on by Ruskin, for whom the whole issue was a moral one, and thus much more fundamental. Yet wider forces were at work than the morality of any individual, and it was always on the basis of artistic evidence that Ruskin tried to establish this point.

In his discussion of the sculptures at the angles of the Palazzo Ducale (to which we shall return) Ruskin claimed that the *Fall of Man* (pl. 184) and the *Drunkenness of Noah*, at the corners of the façade facing the Lagoon, represented the Gothic spirit – that is, 'the frank confession of its own weakness' – while the *Judgement of Solomon* (pl. 185), carved in the fifteenth century, at the further end of the façade facing the Piazzetta, represented the Renaissance spirit – that is, 'firm confidence in its own wisdom'.[65] He acknowledged that the *Judgement of Solomon* was 'excellent in itself, so that it always strikes the eye of a careless observer more than the others', but he emphasised that it was 'of immeasurably inferior spirit in the workmanship' and that the leaves of the tree in it, which had in any case been partially copied from the fig tree in the *Fall of Man*, had none of the original's truth

183. Tomb of Doge Giovanni Pesaro (died 1659), 1669, by Longhena and Melchior Barthel (Venice, Frari).

184. Venice, Palazzo Ducale, corner of façades facing the Piazzetta and the Lagoon: Fall of Man; end of fourteenth century, Istrian stone.

185. Venice, Palazzo Ducale, angle of façade adjoining Porta della Carta: Justice of Solomon; late 1420s or early 1430s, Istrian stone.

to nature: 'they are ill set on the stems, bluntly defined on the edges, and their curves are not those of growing leaves, but of wrinkled drapery'.[66] Above all, Ruskin wondered whether what he admitted to be the 'very noble' capital beneath this sculpture, which represented 'examples of acts of justice or good government', ought to be visualised as 'nothing more than a cloak for consummate violence and guilt'. To this he replied:

> But in the main, I believe the expression of feeling to be genuine. I do not believe, of the majority of the leading Venetians of this period whose portraits have come down to us, that they were deliberately and everlastingly hypocrites. I see no hypocrisy in their countenances. Much capacity of it, much subtlety, much natural and acquired reserve; but no meanness. On the contrary, infinite grandeur, repose, courage, and the peculiar unity and tranquillity of expression which comes of sincerity or *wholeness* of heart, and which it would take much demonstration to make me believe could by any possibility be seen on the countenance of an insincere man.

On the basis of such portraits Ruskin was able to 'trust . . . that these Venetian nobles of the fifteenth century did, in the main, desire to do judgment and justice to all men'. Faced with the need to reconcile the sincere features to be seen in fifteenth-century portraiture with what he repeatedly denounced as the spirit of the Renaissance, Ruskin concluded that 'the whole system of morality had been by this time undermined by the teaching of the Romish Church, the idea of justice had become separated from that of truth, so that dissimulation in the interest of the state assumed the aspect of duty'.[67]

We cannot be certain what were the portraits that Ruskin had seen, but it seems very likely that, in addition to tomb sculpture, he had in mind the extremely stylised images of the doges which, as from the middle of the fourteenth-century, were systematically commissioned for the Palazzo Ducale and which, after the fire of 1577, were replaced by others painted by the Tintoretto workshop in a deliberately archaising style.[68] It need hardly be stressed that these official sets, as well as individual masterpieces such as Giovanni Bellini's *Doge Leonardo Loredano* (which had recently been acquired by the National Gallery in London), were designed to create precisely the impression experienced by Ruskin, and it is surprising to find him accepting them so naïvely at face value.

It was naturally painting that presented him with his most serious problem. If, as could be determined from 'the testimony of Art', the fall of Venice had commenced *visibly* in 1423, how was it possible that a century and a half later, at a time when architecture and sculpture had decayed beyond redemption, Tintoretto could still produce pictures that, like the *Crucifixion* in S. Rocco, were 'beyond all analysis, and above all praise'?[69] Only once did Ruskin try to tackle the issue in *The Stones of Venice*. Gentile and Giovanni Bellini, he explained, who were born in 1421 and 1423, 'close the line of sacred painters of Venice. But the most solemn spirit of religion animates their work to the last.' On the other hand, 'there is no religion in any work of Titian' whose 'larger sacred subjects are merely themes for the exhibition of pictorial rhetoric, – composition and colour'. And the same principle applied to Tintoretto, even though his mind, 'incomparably more deep and serious than that of Titian, casts the solemnity of its own tone over the sacred subjects which it approaches, and sometimes forgets itself into devotion'. But, argues Ruskin, such differences had nothing to do with the individual beliefs or characters of these artists – the fact, for instance, that Bellini was a religious man and Titian was not. The cause was at once more general and more profound: 'Bellini was brought up in faith; Titian in formalism. Between the years of their births the vital religion of Venice had expired.'[70]

It will at once be evident that, far from making use of the evidence of art to determine the date and nature of Venice's decline, Ruskin is here trying to explain the character of the art by what he claims to know of the decline – and doing so, moreover, in a manner quite inconsistent with the importance he attributed to quality of execution. And yet this circular argument provides one of the exceedingly rare occasions on which, when looking back nearly thirty years later at what he had written, he expresses not his usual ironical dismissal of youthful theories, but on the contrary extreme satisfaction with them: 'These two paragraphs are as true and sound as they are audacious. I am very proud of them, on re-reading.'[71] Be that as it may, he must surely have felt some relief when he turned to architecture as the principal 'document' required for an understanding of Venetian history.

186. Venice, Palazzo Ducale.

The two principal façades of the Palazzo Ducale – one facing the Lagoon and the other, the Piazzetta (pl. 186) – are virtually identical in conception and in style of execution. It was therefore natural to think of them as having been designed and built at the same time. However, written documents, which were known to nineteenth-century antiquarians, proved that this had not been the case. Work on the southern (Lagoon) façade and on the first part of the adjoining western one, which together formed the outer walls of a vast council chamber, had been fully under way in the 1340s and 1360s, even though the chamber itself was not finally ready for use until 1423; whereas the remainder of the western façade was added only after 1423 to replace an earlier building which was knocked down at that time.[72] Extreme care had evidently been taken to convey a uniform appearance, and apart from the fact that the point of juncture between old and new was marked by a supporting column that was thicker than the others, it was not at all easy to distinguish between the work of the fourteenth-century and the additions that had been made to it seventy years later.

Count Leopoldo Cicognara, who was among the many writers on the arts in Venice who tried to reconcile the apparent conflict of evidence between what could be seen and what could be read, detected the join but, after some hesitation, came to the conclusion that only one explanation could account for the homogeneity of the façades. The style of the fifteenth-century extension of the palace (from the twelfth arch of the Piazzetta façade until the Porta della Carta) must have been so much to the taste of the day that it had then been carried back to transform all the original, fourteenth-century, part of the building so as to impose an overall effect of absolute regularity.[73] In other words, all the external façades to be seen in Cicognara's day (as in our own) dated from the 1420s; and various authorities either accepted his explanation of how this had happened (which Cicognara could not back with any documentary support) or, like Selvatico, reached a similar conclusion on the basis of a rather different process of reasoning.[74] However, the question was by no means settled and it continues to give rise to controversy from time to time.[75]

These debates formed the background to the 'consternation' with which, in the autumn of 1849, Ruskin greeted the news that 'the Venetian antiquaries were not agreed within a century as to the date of the building of the façade of the Ducal Palace'.[76] He himself was already as convinced of the total superiority of the Gothic over the 'pestilent art of the Renaissance'[77] as Cicognara had been of the opposite; and faced by so important a monument it was essential for him to destroy the thesis that it could be a work of the fifteenth century. To do this he drew on the one document that, so he claimed, had been neglected by the Venetian antiquarians – the masonry. He noted that, after turning the corner from the southern to the western façade, the masonry suddenly changed, 'at the centre of the eighth arch from the sea angle on the Piazzetta side', from smaller to larger stones. This demonstrated that the first part of the façade, and the whole of the southern one, must date from an earlier period – the fourteenth century; and this was confirmed by the change in style of the capitals from purely Giottesque to Renaissance Classic.[78] The same observation was made at much the same time by a Venetian antiquarian,[79] but for Ruskin the change of style to be seen in the capitals was of supreme importance and was not merely a significant pointer to the correct dating of the façades. Most of the fifteenth-century capitals had been 'clumsily copied' from the older ones, and this – he arbitrarily asserted – was not because their sculptors had, like the architect, been obliged to follow the principal forms of the older palace, but because they 'had not the wit to invent new capitals'. And in one such copy – that of a capital incorporating the Virtues – the new version was tolerably accurate and complete, except that in the scene of Hope praying, '*The hand of God is gone.*'[80]

No symbol could explain more clearly why, for Ruskin, the hammer stroke, that had been lifted against what still survived of the old Byzantine palace in order to replace it with a 'Renaissance' structure, signified 'the knell of the architecture of Venice, – and of Venice herself'.[81] The act had been decreed in 1422 by the 'noble Doge Mocenigo',[82] whose tomb had aroused such mixed feelings in Ruskin, and it was carried out at the beginning of the reign of his successor, Francesco Foscari, in 1423, the date that marked the 'visible commencement' of the fall of Venice.

Indeed, in view of Ruskin's uncertainties about the quality of Mocenigo's tomb, it might be thought that it was just this phase in the reconstruction of the Palazzo Ducale that had originally encouraged him to choose the year 1423 as a cardinal date in his vision of the city's decline. But this is not the case. He was himself genuinely surprised by what, in a letter to his father, he described as the 'coincidence . . . that the first hammer should have been lifted against the *old* palace in the very year, from which I have dated the *visible* commencement of the fall of Venice, 1424'[83] – for, however dogmatic he was about the date of the decline itself, he was evidently prepared to allow himself a little latitude as regards the precise year of its visible manifestation.

Thereafter, Ruskin could draw on his fanatically precise and delicate observation, combined with a moral sensitivity which was constantly expanding the limits of his imagination, in order to analyse and denounce what he saw as the almost uninterrupted degradation of Venetian art: from the style of the Renaissance, which was heartless above all because it offered no satisfaction to the creative instincts of the craftsmen employed on it, to the 'grotesque' style of the seventeenth and eighteenth centuries which, unlike the mediaeval grotesques of Northern art, had no place for reverence, for the appreciation of beauty or for mercy.[84]

Fortunately, the 'testimony of Art'[85] could, on occasion, be more reassuring and could even allow Ruskin to absolve certain episodes in Venetian history from charges that had been accepted by earlier judges. Confronted with Daru's careful reasoning that the seizure of all power in the state by a limited number of aristocratic families between 1289 and about 1319 had been an injustice and an act of usurpation, whose consequences had been sinister,[86] Ruskin remembered only that this step had coincided with 'the commencement of a great architectural epoch, in which took place the first appliance of the energy of the aristocratic power, and of the Gothic style, to the works of the Ducal Palace'. He therefore had to explain that the constitutional changes, which had so disconcerted the liberal Daru, signalled in fact 'an expression, by the people, of respect for the families which had been chiefly instrumental in raising the commonwealth to such a height of prosperity', and he even went so far as to claim provocatively that the newly designed prison consisted of 'comfortable rooms with good flat roofs of larch, and carefully ventilated'.[87]

Ruskin, however, was by no means always consistent. Sometimes he would look upon forms of architecture, and of architectural decoration, as symbols of human needs and aspirations – so that the 'singular increase of simplicity in all architectural ornamentation' which occurred at the beginning of the thirteenth century reflected what 'I suppose [was] a singular simplicity in [Venice's] domestic life';[88] while at others he would dismiss, in terms of robust commonsense, German theories that Gothic spires in some way reflected the devotional spirit of the

Northern Middle Ages: 'the chances of damp in the cellar, or of loose tiles in the roof, have, unhappily, much more to do with the fashions of a man's house building than his ideas of celestial happiness or angelic virtue'.[89]

In fact, despite all the claims he made for the 'irrefragable' testimony of art and despite the power with which he explored the moral significance of architecture and sculpture, Ruskin only very rarely made use of such evidence to clarify the actual history of Venice. And when he did so he alternated between appeals to reason and assertions of dogma in a highly idiosyncratic manner.

The early chronicles were obscure and controversial, and the comparative rarity of reliable written documents made it natural to turn to the city's monuments in search of information about its distant past; but this search was complicated by the fact that those monuments could not themselves be easily dated. In the desolate, deserted island of Torcello – 'the mother of Venice'[90] – Ruskin looked at

187. Torcello cathedral: detail of ambo, reconstructed in the fourteenth century from much earlier fragments.

the undecorated walls of the cathedral, and at its side windows closed with massy stone shutters, and concluded that it must have been built by men in flight and distress – those men who in AD 641 had fled from the mainland in the wake of the Lombard invasions. And yet within the brilliantly luminous church (for the victims of fear and depression could not bear darkness) the capitals and certain other elements had been carved with intricate richness (pl. 187). This richness – and also the grandeur of the mosaics – testified to the piety of the first settlers and their reverence for God, and – through God – for Nature. Further evidence of the state of mind of the early worshippers in Torcello cathedral was provided by the raised ranks of rough seats and the episcopal throne in the curve of the apse, enabling the bishop and presbyters to 'watch as well as guide the devotions of the people, and discharge literally in the daily service the functions of bishops or *overseers* of the flock of God'.[91]

Years later Ruskin acknowledged that 'a great deal of this talk is flighty, and some of it fallacious',[92] and even at the time he recognised that a few of his interpretations presented difficulties. It was hard to reconcile the skilled craftsmanship to be found in some of the features of the interior decoration with the 'flight and distress' which were, apparently, responsible for the bareness of the rest, and – in an appendix – he agreed that the cathedral might, as some writers had maintained, have been built in the eleventh rather than in the seventh century. And there were other problems. Yet none of them really mattered, because the spirit of all these centuries in which 'the dominion of Venice was begun and she went forth conquering and to conquer' was marked by 'the strength of heart' so nobly expressed in Torcello cathedral.[93]

Whatever doubts we may have about the approach Ruskin adopted and the conclusions he reached in Torcello, we must surely feel that his interpretation of the artistic evidence is based, at least in theory, on observation and reason. The bare exterior of Torcello cathedral *could* be held to signify that it was built by men in flight and distress; the raised seats in the apse *could* indicate the pastoral commitments of the clergy. But when we move from the small island of Torcello to the great metropolis of Byzantine Venice the approach changes radically. For the city to be explored no longer existed. On the basis of St Mark's, of a small number of fragmentary and heavily restored palaces, and of the 'ghastly ruin' of the Fondaco dei Turchi,[94] Ruskin himself had to construct the very visual evidence that needed to be interpreted. And so he described, with the most imaginative eloquence, 'that first and fairest Venice which rose out of the barrenness of the lagoon, and the sorrow of her people; a city of graceful arcades and gleaming walls, veined with azure and warm with gold, and fretted with white sculpture like frost upon forest branches turned to marble . . .'; and he then proceeded to analyse this city for the light that it could throw on early Venetian history – but he based his conclusions on very different criteria from any that he had hitherto adopted. The argument turned principally on the 'nobleness and sacredness' of colour.[95] To this Ruskin returns again and again: 'I believe that from the beginning of the world there has never been a true or fine school of art in which colour was despised';[96] and 'the principal circumstance which marks the seriousness of the early Venetian mind is . . . that love of bright and pure colour which, in a modified form, was afterwards the root of all the triumph of the Venetian schools of painting, but which, in its utmost simplicity, was characteristic of the Byzantine period only'. However, the claim that colour signified seriousness and that 'all good colour is in some degree pensive, the loveliest is melancholy, and the purest and most thoughtful minds are those which love colour the most' is derived not from reasonable inferences of the kind that Ruskin had made from the architecture of Torcello cathedral, but from 'universal law' promulgated in the Bible, where 'it was not without meaning [that] the love of Israel to his chosen son [was] expressed by the coat "of many colours"' and where many other instances of this nature were to be found.[97]

Ruskin was to make further visits to Venice and was to change his mind about important aspects of the city and its art; he was also to write at length about monuments elsewhere in Europe and to intensify his views on the dominant role played by moral forces in shaping society. But he never again attempted to construct so (relatively) coherent a historical synthesis of a past civilisation as he had done in that work of youthful genius, *The Stones of Venice*, whose third and last volume appeared in 1853.

iii

It was in March of that year that Jacob Burckhardt set out for Rome, after having angrily resigned from the school at which he had been teaching in Basle. He was aged thirty-five. The long, wavy brown hair that swelled over his ears still indicated that he had grown up during the full tide of Romanticism, but the withdrawn eyes and the thick, slightly drooping though trim, moustache suggested that he had put that period well behind him (pl. 188). Such deductions, drawn from the few portraits and photographs that he reluctantly consented to have made of himself,[98] recall the interpretations of character so frequently to be found in the works of other historians in these years, and – like all such interpretations – they inevitably appear to correspond with other evidence we possess about his life at this time. He continued to write the occasional poem, but hints of passionate attachments were long since over. So, too, was his (brief) sympathy with political liberalism, and his once deep friendship with the left-wing poet and art historian Gottfried Kinkel. With hindsight we can see that he was already well on the way to becoming the figure who is so familiar to us from descriptions of his later years: solitary by instinct and devoid of all social ambition; disillusioned with almost every aspect of the modern world and still more apprehensive about the future; but obsessively devoted to his researches into art and history and also to his mission of communicating them, by word of mouth rather than through published books, to relatively small audiences. Only in Italy did he feel fully at ease.

He had already paid earlier visits there, and, as he had done in Belgium and Germany as well as in his native Switzerland, he had made extensive notes and many drawings to record his deeply felt impressions of churches and monuments of all kinds – drawings, however, that were wholly unlike the tense and delicate ones produced by his almost exact contemporary Ruskin: Burckhardt's are appealing, but lack authority – they are fragile, unemphatic, impersonal. And, unlike Ruskin, Burckhardt was already exceptionally well informed even about the art that he had not seen.

For Burckhardt had spent over a year in Berlin preparing new editions of two books by his teacher and friend Franz Kugler, the *Handbuch der Geschichte der Malerei seit Constantin der Grossen* and the *Handbuch der Kunstgeschichte*.[99] These two long, learned and enormously influential works embraced a far wider field of art history than had ever hitherto been explored or assembled. For the first of them, which Burckhardt extensively rewrote, he (as much as Kugler before him) had had to investigate not only the great names of the Italian Middle Ages and Renaissance, but such little-known – though already controversial – issues as the art of the catacombs, Byzantine mosaics, the formation of the Romanesque and the styles of mediaeval miniatures. For the second, to which he contributed rather less, he had to keep abreast of new research into the origins of *menhirs*, parallels between the pyramids of Egypt and of Central America, the relationship of Sassanian to Roman and Islamic art, the ground plans of Armenian churches and other problems of equal complexity. He had naturally had to rely on wholly inadequate illustrations, and his hasty alterations and additions to Kugler's text were not always accurate;

but his work on these books had not only given Burckhardt a breadth of art-historical understanding which makes Ruskin appear provincial by comparison, but had also provided him with a vast amount of knowledge on the basis of which he could assess the evidence provided by the visual arts for an understanding of history.

This issue had preoccupied him for some years, and he raised it again and again, not only in his writings but also in lectures that he gave to the general public and at the University of Basle, both before and after he was elected to an official post there. He was fascinated by the attempts of some recent historians to relate artistic styles to wider cultural (and even political) developments,[100] and at one point he claimed (in a manner that was by now quite common) that 'the most secret beliefs and ideals [of an age] are transmitted to posterity perhaps only through the medium of art, and this transmission is all the more trustworthy because it is unintended'.[101] But he insisted that interpretations should not be made in too narrow, too Hegelian a spirit,[102] and in a note that he added in 1851 to the script of some lectures delivered a few years earlier, he wrote categorically that 'Art is not the measure of History; its development or decline does not provide absolute evidence for or against a period or a nationality, but it is always one of the highest living elements of gifted peoples.'[103]

By then the matter had acquired new urgency for him. On 19 January 1848 during a visit to Rome, when he was absorbed in the art he saw all around him, he wrote to a friend that he had just conceived 'a great literary plan' of a 'Library of Cultural History', made up of 'small, clear, readable, cheap volumes', to be written partly by himself and partly by others and to be devoted to the 'Age of Pericles – the later Roman Empire – the Eighth Century – the Age of the Hohenstaufen – German life in the Fifteenth Century – The Age of Raphael, and so on'.[104]

Back in Basle, Burckhardt began to assemble large quantities of notes for a volume, obviously projected as one of the series, which in 1853 was to be published as *Die Zeit Constantins des Großen*.[105] And he thus found himself forced to confront the problem that (as we have seen) had faced artists and chroniclers ever since the fifteenth century: why had the arts of antiquity declined so drastically in quality even before the impact of the barbarian invasions?

When Burckhardt tried to draw conclusions from the Arch of Constantine itself and from the 'diseased, bloated, scrofulous' figures that he found on the tombs, coins, mosaics and bases of drinking-glasses of the period; from the mediocre style that characterised the colossal porphyri sarcophagi of Helena and Constantine in the Vatican; as well as from the architectural richness and the expensive and exotic marbles, whose use at Palmyra and Spalato had become 'proverbial', he was reluctant to turn – in the spirit of Hegel or, indeed, of Ruskin – to 'a general philosophic consideration of the period' from which some *a priori* answer might emerge. Instead, he looked to purely contingent reasons to account for a series of separate, even if related, weaknesses. Thus the arch was 'a hasty production, and this is enough to explain and excuse the great crudeness of the carving of the sculptures'. As for 'the ugliness of the figures and the meanness of expression', that

188. Hermine von Reck, *Jacob Burckhardt*, 1853 (Basle, Private Collection).

could be accounted for by the fact that artists had lost all contact with ideals of beauty in the surrounding world, for the human race had physically (though not morally) deteriorated due to disease, famine and anxiety. Moreover, the fashion for exotic and very intractable building materials – the mere restoration of the sarcophagus of Helena under Pius VI is said in the catalogue 'to have claimed the labour of twenty-five men for nine years, from which we can calculate the work needed for its original manufacture' – compelled artistic genius to take second place to the exertion of slaves who alone could undertake the slow abrasion of the porphyry that was required; and exactly the same effect was caused by the sub-stitution of mosaic for painting.[106]

Burckhardt's reluctance to produce any overall theory to account for the phenomenon of artistic decline – a reluctance that was so characteristic of him and so uncharacteristic of his contemporaries – is striking partly because he was forthcoming, indeed reckless, in his discussion of the political character of the age. Constantine was a 'genius whose ambition and love of power allowed him not a moment of peace . . . a murderous egoist',[107] surrounded by liars, hypocrites and sycophants (of whom the most notable was Eusebius, the Christian historian of his reign). Such tyrants were soon to re-appear in Burckhardt's studies, and they fascinated almost as much as they repelled him: 'no one', he conceded, 'has contested Constantine's right to the title "Great" '.[108] And although he commented coolly that 'we do not wish to deny the possibility that he allowed a kind of superstition in favour of Christ to develop within him',[109] the question of his religious sincerity was largely irrelevant, for 'a high historical necessity introduced Christianity into the world as a conclusion to the ancient world, as a break with it and yet in part to rescue it and transmit it to new peoples who, as pagans, might perhaps have utterly barbarised and destroyed a purely pagan Roman Empire'.[110]

Yet although Burckhardt usually rejected from his discussion of the arts any hint of that quasi-Hegelian determinism that (following so many historians of Christianity) he was prepared to accept in other fields, he seems to have felt uneasy about having acknowledged even the most limited relationship between art and politics during the reign of Constantine – a relationship that was seized upon by Kugler who, in reviewing the book, emphasised how important an under-standing of art could be for historical writing in general.[111] Certainly Burckhardt expressed a growing distaste for 'chatter about art':[112] the book that he was planning when he set out for Italy in March 1853 had as its essential aim the introduction to other travellers of that 'enjoyment' of art that he himself had so keenly experienced on previous journeys.

Unfortunately, few letters and no drawings survive from this voyage,[113] although we know which towns he visited. Some idea of how he spent his time in them can be derived from an account he wrote of the six energetic but exhilarating weeks he spent in Naples. Allowing for the appropriate adjustments, these are likely to have been similar to others he passed elsewhere, for he was already a man of regular habits. His explorations of the city would begin at six in the morning and would be punctuated by one cup of black and one of white coffee. At eleven he would take a glass of sweet wine, and before lunch he would go for a bathe in the sea. In the afternoon he would settle into his hotel room to make a fair copy of the notes he had scribbled in the morning. Towards evening he would ride a mule up to the hills outside the town.[114]

Such information is scanty enough, but the *Cicerone* itself (which was published two years later) gives a personal, even at times emotional, account of what was to be discovered in Italy. On the first page he calls attention to the sea which can be seen sparkling through the columns of the Temple of Neptune at Paestum and, on the last, he refers to his own homesickness (which only temporarily slumbers but never dies) for Rome the 'unforgettable'. Again and again he records his direct responses to the monuments at which he gazes, and he even makes the occasional joke about some of them: he, too, like other visitors to the Etruscan museum in the Vatican, has been reminded of the typical Englishman when looking at the 'long upper lip and strangely stiff chin' of many of the terracotta heads displayed in it.[115]

This artful spontaneity (which in no way conflicts with a range of detailed observation and knowledge extending from antiquity to the end of the eighteenth century and from candlesticks and gardens to churches and palaces) led Burckhardt to exclude as far as possible, or at least to minimise, any discussion of the historical background of the works he described – on the grounds that he did not wish to arouse distracting emotions. In looking at early Christian monuments we must judge them purely on the basis of their artistic quality and reject the 'elegiac impression' that may come to us from our awareness that in them the Church, 'which we visualise in our fantasies, even unconsciously, as being surrounded by a mysterious halo', was making use of the products of a wholly different civilisation;[116] and – in a passage that reads like a refutation of everything that Ruskin had just published on the Palazzo Ducale in Venice – he pointed out that if we can forget 'the historical and poetical preconceptions of all kinds which exert so strong an impression on our imaginations', we are forced to admit that, for all the beauty of the upper storey, the proportions of the building as a whole are unsatisfactory.[117] To this general approach, which he frequently reiterated,[118] Burckhardt allowed one exception. Works created in styles that he considered inferior (such as the Baroque) or utterly alien to the taste of his own times (such as that of Michelangelo) were to be looked at from the point of view of the historian rather than that of the art lover.[119] We shall see that this argument, which was (and still is) widely accepted, has been of great significance to the theme of this book.

None the less, despite his successful determination to make of the *Cicerone* a work concerned above all with the appreciation of artistic quality, Burckhardt derived from his own insights in the preparation and writing of it most of the key concepts that, five years later, were to inform his historical masterpiece, *The Civilisation of the Renaissance in Italy*.

As has long been recognised, a lack of any sustained attention to the visual arts is one of the most curious features of that book. Burckhardt himself declared that he planned to remedy 'the greatest gap [*der grössten Lucke*]' in it by writing 'a special work on the art of the Renaissance', but in his second edition, of 1869, he acknowledged that he had been able to fulfil this intention only in part.[120] Indeed, although a substantial amount of the material that he had collected was published either by himself or, after his death, by his executors,[121] neither this material nor Burckhardt's references to it are strictly relevant to the general nature of the *Civilisation*. For what is so conspicuously missing from this is not a general discussion of the art of the Italian Renaissance; it is, rather, any consideration of the evidence that could have been drawn from that art in order to throw light on the civilisation of the period. After all, Burckhardt frequently drew on evidence of this kind from the literature of the Renaissance, even though he never set out to discuss the literature for its own sake. The observations on Italian architecture, which appeared in 1867 as Volume IV of Kugler's general history of architecture and which Burckhardt himself specifically mentions in connection with the *Civilisation*, in fact read far more like a series of learned footnotes to the *Cicerone*.[122]

In the *Civilisation* Burckhardt often goes out of his way to avoid references to the arts even when they might have been to the point. Thus in writing about Can Grande della Scala in his section on 'Despots of the Fourteenth Century' he mentions his literary patronage, but not his tomb at Verona;[123] yet in the *Cicerone* of a few years earlier he had claimed of this tomb and of those of the other Scaligeri that they were 'as important from the point of view of cultural history as from the artistic standpoint'.[124] Similarly, when stressing the value attached by the Gonzagas to the breeding of racehorses he does not refer to Giulio Romano's frescoes of these in the Palazzo del Té in Mantua (which, admittedly, he was unable to visit when preparing the *Cicerone*, though he had been there on an earlier journey to Italy).[125] In an extended discussion on the Italian discovery of the beauty of landscape he devotes less than one line to Italian painting, and in an equally extended discussion on the Italian discovery of man he points to the evidence provided by literary portraiture, but hardly ever mentions painted portraits.[126]

On those rare occasions in the *Civilisation* when he does, briefly, touch on the visual arts, he tends to downgrade their significance for the cultural historian by pointing out that changes in them are always long preceded by those that occur in other forms of culture ('Bildung').[127] And he is also keen to distinguish his approach from the one he had adopted earlier in the *Cicerone*. Thus in his vivid account, filled with the most lurid details, of the factional struggles in Perugia during the late fifteenth century he describes how 'Simonetto Baglione, a lad of scarcely eighteen, fought in the square with a handful of followers against hundreds of the enemy: he fell at last with more than twenty wounds, but recovered himself when Astorre Baglione came to his help, and, mounting on horseback in gilded armour with a falcon on his helmet "like Mars in bearing and in deeds, plunged into the struggle"'. He then follows this with his first references to specific paintings: 'At that time Raphael, a boy of twelve years of age, was at school under Pietro Perugino. The impressions of these days are perhaps immortalised in the small, early pictures of St Michael and St George: something of them, it may be, lives eternally in the great painting of St Michael: and if Astorre Baglione has anywhere found his apotheosis, it is in the figure of the heavenly horseman in the Heliodorus.'[128] This passage would be far more convincing as the

189. Raphael, *Expulsion of Heliodorus*, fresco (Vatican Palace, Stanza dell'Eliodoro).

description of some small picture of historical genre devoted to the life of Raphael (of a kind popular during the Romantic period when Burckhardt had been young) than as a serious account of a likely source of artistic inspiration; and it is of interest precisely because it differs so radically from Burckhardt's account of Raphael's creative processes in the *Cicerone*. The *St George* and the two *St Michael*s were not mentioned in that book as they were not to be seen in Italy, but in his rapturous discussion of the fresco of Heliodorus in the Vatican (pl. 189), as in his analysis of the Stanze in general, Burckhardt had confined himself to evoking 'the marvellous movement of the group consisting of the divine figure on horseback, accompanied on each side by impetuous youths, and the sacrilegious criminal who has fallen together with his followers', and he stressed the superb composition and the foreshortening of the figures.[129] Indeed, he had frequently gone out of his way to insist that, in the treatment of his subjects and sometimes in their choice, Raphael had nearly always been motivated by 'purely artistic considerations'.[130]

It is therefore not in his discussions either of particular events or even of the general climate of belief that we must look for the concealed yet omnipresent impact on *The Civilisation of the Renaissance in Italy* of Burckhardt's direct and passionate study of art: that study provided him rather with a series of concepts which, when transmuted from the sphere of art to that of politics or culture in its widest sense, enabled him to approach all the central issues that most concerned him.

Burckhardt's notion of the Italian Renaissance was in one very important way opposed to those that had previously been offered by Voltaire, by Roscoe and by nearly all other writers who had discussed the subject since it had begun to arouse interest during the Enlightenment. However much they differed from each other, these predecessors had for the most part agreed that 'the revival of the arts and letters', which constituted the core of the movement, had been prompted essentially by the rediscovery of the ancient world and had taken place in the sixteenth century. And this dating had also been accepted by Michelet who, however, had assigned far wider and far deeper significance to the Renaissance than had any earlier historian. But for Burckhardt 'the decisive victory of the moderns'[131] had occurred in the fifteenth century – indeed, its roots could be traced back almost a hundred years before that – and it did not depend essentially on the new impact of classical antiquity, as had always 'one-sidedly' been maintained. On the contrary, 'most of the intellectual tendencies' that characterised it would have been perfectly possible without the influence of antiquity.[132] The real essence of the civilisation of the Renaissance in Italy (and Burckhardt did not share Michelet's unqualified enthusiasm that the Middle Ages had finally come to an end) was to be found in individualism and the cult of personality, often carried to extremes and often dangerous.

Despite the fact that *The Civilisation of the Renaissance in Italy* contains so few references to art, the name of Vasari appears frequently among the footnotes; and it can be claimed that each one of Burckhardt's revolutionary and epoch-making insights into the origins and nature of Renaissance civilisation had come to him as a result of those investigations into art and art-historical sources that he had used for the *Cicerone*.

Italian fifteenth-century painting had already attracted admiring attention well before Burckhardt began to plan the *Cicerone*; but (with few exceptions) recent writers had been drawn to it primarily because its values seemed to be so different from those of the High Renaissance of the sixteenth century which had traditionally been accepted as the culmination of European art as a whole – and which was still so accepted by Michelet. For Rio, for Lord Lindsay and, to a large extent, for Ruskin the painting of fifteenth-century Italy – or, rather, certain regions of fifteenth-century Italy – was marked by a child-like innocence and a humble devotion to spiritual values which still survived in the work of the young Raphael but which thereafter succumbed to academic pedantry, corruption and sensual materialism. Burckhardt was exceptional not so much because he appreciated fifteenth-century painting as because he saw it as continuously striving towards the still-higher perfection of the sixteenth century which culminated in the great late works of Raphael. His attitude owed far more to Vasari than it did to most of his immediate predecessors or contemporaries.

The new spirit had made itself felt in the first decades of the fifteenth century.

Although painting remained tied to the Church, it gave 'more than the Church required . . . a picture of the real world. Artists became absorbed in studying and representing the outer appearance of things and gradually took over every aspect of the human figure and its surroundings (Realism)'. Generic treatment of features and drapery gave way to exactitude and naturalism. And beauty, which had hitherto been thought of as the chief attribute of holiness, disappeared in this pursuit of accuracy or else became a form of beauty that is only of this world. In that sense art gave the Church *less* than it asked for, because the religious element can flourish, even survive, only if it retains absolute, undivided control: any concession, however, slight, to the secular must break the spell – even, for instance, the careful observation of a piece of drapery for its own sake or an interest in placing figures correctly in space.[133]

Some years earlier Burckhardt had attributed such developments to a relaxation by the Church of its authority over artists who, as a result, had begun to flaunt their ambitions and their individuality.[134] This idea was to reappear, in a very similar form but applied to politics, at the beginning of *The Civilisation of the Renaissance in Italy* where he emphasised that the rise of uninhibited despots in the fourteenth and fifteenth centuries had been made possible only by the relative weakness of the emperor and the pope.[135] Although in the *Cicerone* Burckhardt was always cautious about invoking historical circumstances to account for artistic change, it is clear that he believed that painters had been able to embark on the search for realism just because the Church no longer enjoyed a monopoly of power.

It was in Florence that these new developments had been most striking,[136] and – as Burckhardt pointed out – in his early days Perugino had belonged to the Florentine school. Later in life, however, he returned to Perugia and threw over what he had learned from the Florentines; and in order to satisfy public demand for a certain type of religious imagery he turned out an endless series of repetitive and mechanical figures.[137] None the less, when his apprentice Raphael was required to complete pictures by his master it was from Perugino's earlier and more sincere work that he sought his inspiration. Raphael, indeed, was never prepared to rest on his laurels, and throughout his life, urged on by considerations of morality even more than of aesthetics, he strove for ever new, and ever higher, forms of expression. 'This moral quality would have remained with him into old age. And if we consider the extraordinary creative force of his last years, we can appreciate how much we have lost forever though his premature death.'[138]

Burckhardt's approach to architecture was similar and just as unusual. Kugler, and German historians generally, had constantly downgraded the significance of Renaissance architecture of the fifteenth and sixteenth centuries alike, for – so they maintained – it was not a truly 'organic style', as was the architecture of ancient Greece and, still more, of mediaeval Germany; rather, it constituted an unsatisfactory attempt to combine certain features taken from varying buildings of antiquity, and it did not offer anything of value to contemporary designers. It took Burckhardt many years of Italian travel and study before he was able to break free from the limitations on appreciation imposed by ideas such as these, but when he did so his commitment to the new values was whole-hearted. He acknowledged that Italian Renaissance architecture had not been 'organic', but claimed that it did, none the less, provide an excellent model, and that, in any case, the issue of eclecticism was not of decisive significance.[139] 'We can', he wrote, 'distinguish two periods of the true Renaissance. The first period goes from 1420 to 1500 and can be looked upon as the period of research. The second period just reaches the year 1540, and it is the golden age of modern architecture which, in its greatest buildings, achieves a special harmony between those forms that are fundamental and those that are decorative and are confined to their true proportions.'[140]

Burckhardt could not accept Michelet's notion that Brunelleschi had been a solitary genius who had tried, but failed, to introduce the Renaissance into Italy so as to break the stranglehold of the Middle Ages. On the contrary, 'what had been begun by Brunelleschi was continued by Michelozzo . . . without whose Palazzo Riccardi Bernardino Rossellino and Benedetto da Maiano would not have been able to build their palaces'.[141] It was true that none of these architects had been of the stature of Brunelleschi, but their buildings showed that, in its first phase at least, the Renaissance was an achievement of the fifteenth century and one that came into being thanks to the varying talents of many men, of whom Brunelleschi happened to be the greatest.

In the spirit of Vasari Burckhardt tended to search for indications of the Renaissance wherever they were to be found and to greet them with enthusiasm. In this respect his attitude was exactly the opposite of that of Ruskin, even though their observations were often similar. Thus both men agreed that the late Gothic style of the Porta della Carta of the Palazzo Ducale in Venice was tending towards the Renaissance, but whereas for Ruskin its degraded and vicious nature was characterised by 'insipid confusion', Burckhardt found it to be 'very valuable and excellent'.[142]

There had, of course, been setbacks, but these had occurred not – as Michelet had thought – in the fifteenth century, but much earlier, and, in any case, they had fortunately been only temporary stumbles on the road that led to the Renaissance. This notion had first struck him on a visit to Florence in 1846. There he had studied the Baptistery and the church of SS Apostoli, whose eleventh-century structure had been drastically brought up to date in the fifteenth and sixteenth centuries. Burckhardt saw in the church 'a certain premature blooming [*Vorblüte*] of the Renaissance' which had then been suppressed 'by the German style until, in the fifteenth century, it once again broke through, this time irresistibly'.[143] Nine years later in the *Cicerone* he returned to this notion when considering the church of S. Miniato al Monte (see pl. 88), whose façade had been completed as early as the first years of the thirteenth century and whose classicising appearance had long puzzled historians: 'it combines all the artistic potentialities of the pre-Gothic period, and in so marvellous a way, that one almost feels regret to see that afterwards the Gothic style from the North was introduced [into Florence]'.[144]

Thus, both in painting and in architecture, the Renaissance had maintained itself, despite occasional threats, from the early fifteenth until the mid-sixteenth century. Despite Burckhardt's view that 'Art is not the measure of History; its develop-

190. Façade of Palazzo Pitti, Florence, originally designed by Brunelleschi *c*.1440, but vastly changed in character and increased in scale in the late sixteenth and early seventeenth centuries.

ment or decline does not provide absolute evidence for or against a period or a nationality',[145] it would have required doubts of exceptional force for a scholar, so steeped in the forms of cultural history being propagated by German writers of the early decades of the nineteenth century, not to have visualised the astonishing artistic developments that he had observed as in some ways indicative of a much wider spiritual process. The early chapters of *The Civilisation of the Renaissance in Italy* published five years later prove that Burckhardt did not feel such doubts.

When describing the solemn effect created by Brunelleschi's monumental façade of Palazzo Pitti (pl. 190), which was partly built and extended by later architects, Burckhardt commented that 'one wonders who was this man of power [*Gewaltmensch*] who scorned the world and who, thanks to the means at his disposal, tried to keep himself distant from anything pleasing or delicate'.[146] This curious phrase, which was subsequently to be of particular fascination to Nietzsche,[147] seems to be referring to Brunelleschi (although Burckhardt much admired the lightness of style of some of his other buildings) rather than to his patron (about whom it would have been wholly inappropriate). The reader of the

191. Donatello, *Mary Magdalen*, polychrome wood (Florence, Baptistery).

192. Francesco da Sangallo (attributed to), *St John the Baptist*, marble, 1520s(?) (Florence, Museo del Bargello).

193. Matteo Civitale, *Adoring Angel*, after 1477 (Lucca cathedral, Capella del Sacramento).

194. Matteo Civitale, *Adoring Angel*, after 1477 (Lucca cathedral, Capella del Sacramento).

Civilisation will at once detect in it some of the germs of Burckhardt's memorable descriptions in that book of the bloodthirsty but cultivated tyrants who so appalled and fascinated him. Although such men had not, in fact, ruled over Florence, it was in the works of Florentine artists that he discovered many of the attributes that he would later describe as characteristic of the Renaissance despot.

Burckhardt had first come across Donatello's *Magdalen* (pl. 191) in the Baptistery of Florence cathedral when travelling in Italy during the spring of 1846, and he had been repelled by the statue's extreme naturalism.[148] On his visit to Florence in 1853 this repulsion was transmuted into a combination of real dread and hatred, which was directed to other works by Donatello besides the startling *Magdalen*. Of the marble *St John the Baptist* (pl. 192), which is now believed to be an early work by Francesco da Sangallo dating from more than half a century after Donatello's death, he wrote that it was 'horrible! like a skeleton . . .; it is crude and topples forward and would fall down to the right if let go. The feet and hands look exactly as if they had been flayed.'[149] In the *Cicerone* Burckhardt's language is naturally more controlled, but his considered view of Donatello is of great significance for his later interpretation of Italian society.

'It frequently happens in the history of art that a new direction of style concentrates in one artist all the most extreme forms through which it seeks to make an

195. Donatello, *Annunciation* (Florence S. Croce).

inexorable challenge to earlier styles. But in such a change of style it is rare to find the novelty and the opposition to what has gone before so wholly and so one-sidedly incorporated in an artist as was the spirit of the fifteenth century in Donatello'. In the early *Annunciation* in S. Croce (pl. 195) there was still a fleeting acknowledgement of classical antiquity, though the boy-angels who cling to each other on the cornice to avoid giddiness (pl. 196) already look to the future and would never have been found in works of any previous age. In some of Donatello's later sculptures, also, there would be echoes of ancient sarcophagi and other antiquities, 'but these features stand out strangely amid the others'. Donatello, continued Burckhardt, 'was a naturalist of great talent, who recognised no limits to his art. Everything that existed seemed to him capable of being represented in sculpture by the very fact of its existence, and of its possession of a character of its own. To give life to this character at its most austere and its most harsh, and sometimes (when the subject allowed) also at its most powerful and most grandiose – this was for him the highest goal.'[150]

Burckhardt must have recalled these impressions when, four or five years afterwards, he found himself having to write about the 'appalling' *condottieri* who offer us 'some of the earliest instances of criminals deliberately repudiating every moral restraint' – men whose character exemplified 'the fundamental vice which was at the same time a condition of its greatness, namely, excessive individualism'.[151] The fascinated distrust of all forms of power, which we find here and elsewhere in the *Civilisation* and still more in his later writings, can already be discerned in his response to Donatello and certain other artists. Although his extremely ambiguous and often hostile feelings about Michelangelo are more apparent in his private notes than in his published works,[152] the summing-up of the artist which he gives in the *Cicerone* will be understood as a damning indictment by all those who are familiar with Burckhardt's views of his own times:

He was like a powerful personification of the destiny that lay ahead for art: his works and the successes they enjoyed contain all the elements needed for a definition of the fundamental nature of modern art. What is characteristic of the art of the last three centuries – i.e., subjectivity – makes its appearance in Michelangelo under the guise of a creative force freed from every external constraint – not unwillingly or unconsciously, as in so many of the great movements of the spirit that took place in the sixteenth century, but with weighty intent.[153]

In his attitude to Donatello and Michelangelo Burckhardt reveals both how much he was indebted to Vasari and at the same time how decisively he rejected Vasari's judgements. It was, for instance, Vasari who had made the observation (seized on by Burckhardt) that the pairs of angels on the cornice of the *Annunciation* in S. Croce are clinging together out of fear; but Vasari had admired Donatello with unqualified enthusiasm for 'the grace, design and excellence' that had both put him on a level with the ancients and, combined with his naturalism, had enabled him to encourage Florentine artists to take decisive steps towards the perfection of Michelangelo. Burckhardt, on the other hand, while acknowledging Donatello's 'enormous influence', felt that it had been partially dangerous: 'without that powerful inner tendency towards the beautiful, which again and again lifted art above naked realism and above the superficial imitation of antiquity – that is, without the powerful spirit of the Quattrocento, the fashion for Donatello's principles could have become a fatal one'.[154] Resort to a Hegelian movement of the spirit, almost independent of the abilities and wills of individual artists (which Burckhardt had already invoked when opening his discussion of Donatello), allowed him to hint that this unruly sculptor had been a marginal rather than a central figure in the evolution of the Renaissance. It was true that 'he had not lacked a feeling of beauty, but this had always had to make way for character when that was in question',[155] whereas 'the great Matteo Civitale' (who, many years earlier, had been singled out by Cicognara as under-appreciated)[156] had 'overcome Donatello's hard angularities' and in the adoring angels of Lucca cathedral (pls 193, 194) had been able to 'combine the noblest style of any that had been seen in the fifteenth century since the time of Ghiberti with an expression of devout fervour and youthful, aristocratic beauty'.[157] In a somewhat similar way the contrast proposed in the *Civilisation* between the rich development of human individuality in Florence and the individuality of despots elsewhere

196. Detail of pl. 195.

in Italy (which was granted only to themselves and their nearest dependants)[158] leaves open the question as to which of these two systems Burckhardt regarded as having been particularly characteristic of the Renaissance.

Burckhardt's rejection of the traditional view that the rebirth of antiquity had been primarily responsible for the Renaissance also seems to be a reflection, whether conscious or not, of his earlier investigations into Italian art. Although he had, in the *Cicerone*, agreed with Vasari that, in architecture, Brunelleschi had been 'the first to recall to life the forms of classical antiquity',[159] he had done little to develop this; and we have seen that when discussing the sculpture of Donatello he had gone out of his way to stress its anti-classical features.

In *The Civilisation of the Renaissance in Italy* Burckhardt claimed that although the Renaissance had not been dependent on antiquity, it had nevertheless been 'coloured in a thousand ways by the influence of the ancient world'. It might have been essentially the same without the classical revival, but it was only made manifest to us with and through that revival.[160] This conclusion emerges quite naturally from his perceptive and wide-ranging scrutiny of Italian architecture, sculpture and painting of the fifteenth century. And a similar process can be seen at work in many of Burckhardt's most influential judgements – not the least of which was that the Renaissance had been essentially an Italian rather than a universal movement of the spirit.

Thus although Burckhardt's greatest historical masterpiece barely refers to art, it is a book whose principal insights (as much as its overall form) are based directly on the love and study of art. Art served him as an inspiration and a shaping spirit rather than as a document in any strict sense, and it is in the *Civilisation* that those claims for the historical importance of the image, which had been made ever since the Renaissance itself, found their most sophisticated – but unexpected – vindication.

This view of Burckhardt's approach to the Italian Renaissance seems to be confirmed by the nature of his later achievements. He wrote, frequently and superbly, about the visual arts until the end of his life, and his enthusiasm for cultural history increased rather than diminished with the years. Yet he never combined them in a large-scale work as he had once hoped to do. If architecture and sculpture play only a marginal role in his posthumously published *Greek Cultural History*, that is surely because, although he was familiar with the antiquities in the museums of London, Berlin and Munich, he never visited Greece itself. Had he done so, and had he devoted a *Cicerone* to that country also, he would have been able to give a greater sense of form and more feeling for the actuality of the ancient world, to a book that is both subtle and profound but – by the standards he had set for himself and for his admirers – not wholly satisfying.

iv

The Civilisation of the Renaissance in Italy was published in 1860. It was not a success, but among the first to appreciate its true quality was Hippolyte Taine who, nine years later, when the second edition appeared, was to describe it as

'Livre admirable, le plus complet et le plus philosophique qu'on ait écrit sur la renaissance italienne'[161] – and Burckhardt in turn was to admire Taine's uncompleted *Les Origines de la France contemporaine* as a masterpiece of cultural history.[162]

In 1860 Taine came to England: he felt the need to confirm on the spot the impressions of English civilisation that he had already derived from his extensive reading.[163] In the four substantial volumes on English literature which he published three years later he wrote at length about Carlyle, but he never mentioned Ruskin, and it is by no means clear whether he had yet read *Modern Painters* and *The Stones of Venice*. However, he subsequently commented in passing on both books.[164] They stimulated thought, he wrote, but whereas he strongly disagreed with *Modern Painters*, he said nothing specific about *The Stones of Venice*. It is, however, very tempting to suggest that some of its descriptions and arguments may have strengthened in him the conviction that his visit to Italy in 1864 was to be thought of as 'un cours d'histoire italienne que je fais avec de la peinture pour documents au lieu de la faire avec de la littérature'.[165]

In another letter, sent from Venice, Taine wrote that 'j'ai trouvé dans les monuments, dans les tableaux, dans les statues une seconde littérature qui commente et complète l'autre':[166] and this was rather more accurate, for like Ruskin, and even more than Ruskin, he constantly turned to textual as well as to visual sources for his interpretation of the Italian past. None the less, he looked far more widely (though far less intensively) than Ruskin, and he drew very imaginatively on the architecture, sculpture and painting that he saw in Rome, Naples, Florence, Venice and elsewhere in order to understand the history of those cities. His decision to rely so much on evidence of this kind was a quite deliberate one, whose outlines had first come to him much earlier as a result of careful thought about the nature of historical research. It did not spring from any spontaneous feeling for the arts, nor did it lead to any great understanding of them.

In the 1840s Taine must have been one of the most brilliant and hard-working students in France, but although a younger sister toyed with the idea of becoming a painter, his own interests were exclusively literary, philosophical and scientific.[167] However, in 1846 he became very friendly with Emile-Marcelin-Isidore Planat, an enthusiastic lover of the arts, who years later, under the pseudonym Marcelin, was to found that most celebrated of weekly illustrated magazines, *La Vie Parisienne*.

More than four decades after their first meeting, Taine's obituary of Planat described the impact made on him by this gifted but impecunious contemporary.[168] Although the memories recorded in this article may well have been coloured by his own later researches, Taine's impressions are worth recording here because they are so perceptive and because they reveal so much about ideas and aims that the two men must have discussed on many occasions. Planat, he tells us, was a passionate collector of engravings (and he evidently encouraged Taine to join him on his expeditions),[169] of which he eventually accumulated some three hundred thousand – not in fine states or rare examples, but anything, however bad the quality, that was 'evocative' and that illustrated some aspect of the customs of past ages; anything that would bring him into direct touch with the people who had lived in those ages: a prince, a courtier, a woman of easy virtue, a soldier. Through studying prints of this kind Planat could transport himself into a wide variety of different periods: those of Louis-Philippe or the Restoration, of the Empire or the Republic, of Louis XVI or the early eighteenth century or Louis XIV – all the way back to sixteenth-century Italy. 'He would speak as if he had lived in those times'; he could see how people had dressed and how they had behaved on ceremonies or on visits; how they had greeted each other and flirted and danced. 'And so he had an entry into five or six worlds, each as complete as our own. Without any conscious effort of the will he would enter them . . . He felt at home and relaxed – more relaxed than in our own world.' But Taine had doubts about the morality of such dreaming and, more importantly, about the intellectual value of taking so visual an approach to the past. For art necessarily gave the impression that the world of the past was complete and at an end rather than in a state of constant change. Above all, art was misleading because in reality no one could ever have lived up to the images created by the great masters: 'the sitters of Hals or Rembrandt were certainly not worthy of their portraits; look at the Burgomaster Six or the *Syndics*; no Dutch administrator in 1650 could have conveyed such intensity of expression or of life – the people would have flocked around him in the street'. Whereas, 'when we leave the museum, especially under a grey sky, the passers-by seem to be like feeble sketches, badly drawn and emerging only weakly from grimy paper, works that are either tentative experiments or discarded rejects'.

Such were the dangers of approaching the past through its art. Nevertheless, Taine acknowledged, Planat had been a 'true historian', because what he instinctively and immediately looked for in engravings and pictures were the differences between men living at different times. He could see at a glance that the Frenchman of his day was 'an animal of a different kind' from a Frenchman living in 1780 or, still more, in 1680, let alone in 1580: 'an animal with different needs, appetites and revulsions; with different feelings, images and ideas'. Each had had its own particular concept of happiness and honour, its own emotions, and its own special attitude in the face of pleasure or danger or death. Merely by looking at engravings and without any preconceived system Planat had been able to distinguish those prevailing sentiments that, in any given epoch, had governed the actions of most men then alive and that therefore constituted the very essence of the social organisation.

However much some of these ideas may have been elaborated (and surely exaggerated) by Taine in later years, we know that Planat's views on the value of the arts as historical evidence made an immediate impact on him. For it was Planat who introduced him to what was to become one of the centres of his intellectual life: the Cabinet des Estampes; and once he had settled permanently in Paris he returned to it again and again. Over a period of some years in the 1850s he seems to have paid regular visits there twice a week, each one of an hour and a half, for he was determined to 'learn the language' of prints.[170] He soon found himself able 'to decipher it' fluently – 'un pli de vêtement est une trace de passion comme une epithète' – and despite some jaunty comments to a friend about the erotic nature of certain prints by Raphael ('un vigoureux et magnifique sultan'[171]) his approach always had about it something of the relentlessly methodical. It is not surprising that the exquisite Goncourt brothers (who were, however, also pioneers in the study of prints in order to throw light on social history) should have been dismayed by Taine's attitude when in 1863 he went to examine their engravings: 'il les regarde et nous voyons qu'il ne les voit pas', they commented, adding, in a phrase that tells us much about the importance that art was now beginning to acquire for historical research, 'However as one must give the impression of being able to see, and as art is now beginning to pass for something from which one can derive ideas, he spins out elaborate phrases in the style of a witty man who happens to be blind.'[172]

Taine's contacts with the other arts were, in these early years of his life, not very fruitful. He failed to write the books he seems to have conceived on Italian pictures in the Louvre or on painting in the Low Countries, but although the comparisons he enjoyed making in some of his letters between the *Last Judgement* of Michelangelo and the works of John Martin do not suggest that he could yet have produced anything of great interest or sensitivity,[173] he took every opportunity to widen his visual experiences when travelling in the French provinces. In 1863 he wrote with exceptional warmth and perception about *Le Nouveau-Né* by Georges de La Tour in Rennes which had been 'discovered' only two years earlier and which was then associated with the name of Le Nain.[174] He showed a certain fascination with modern painting and was particularly keen on Couture and Decamps, though he also expressed a cautious admiration for Delacroix.[175] His responses to architecture were not always conventional: Poitiers, which had struck him as ugly, indeed 'affreuse', in 1852, was described merely as 'amusante' twelve years later.[176] He expressed some interest in the 'vaste et curieuse' church of Saint-Sernin in Toulouse and in the cathedral of Reims, but he reserved his enthusiasm for the 'noble' city of Nancy which contained 'Rien de bourgeois: j'entends rien du petit bourgeois prud'homme.' He admired many Renaissance sculptures,[177] but only the antique attracted his whole-hearted commitment. Among the casts in the Louvre, he 'adored' three or four bodies: 'the Apollon Sauroctonus, the two young athletes, the handsome standing young man whose head is owned by Paradol'.[178] It seems somewhat surprising that in October 1864, on the basis presumably of these rather limited experiences, he should have been chosen to succeed Viollet-le-Duc as Professor of Aesthetics and of the History of Art at the École des Beaux-Arts. However, he had by then just returned from Italy and was about to publish the impressions of his travels there which, two years later, were to culminate in the two substantial volumes, largely devoted to art, of his *Voyage en Italie*.

Although the literature of travel to Italy had been subjected to many a metamorphosis over the centuries, it had long been commonplace to ridicule the genre as a whole on the grounds that nothing new could possibly be said about a land that had already been so thoroughly explored. It is, however, easy enough to understand why so many volumes on Italy continued to be published. It is not just that the central place occupied by Roman civilisation in European education, and the varied beauties of the landscape and art to be seen in so many regions and cities, attracted talented writers from many different countries. Almost as significant (as the very well-prepared Taine must certainly have realised when he set out on his journey) was the fact that as yet there existed so very few readable books devoted to the history of Italian art and that the flexible genre of travel literature offered one of the most convenient ways of satisfying an interest that was growing rapidly. Indeed, many of the great classics of art-historical research in the nineteenth century made little, if any, attempt to conceal the debt that they owed to a long tradition of travel writing in general – Rumohr's investigations into early Italian painting, for instance, in 1827–31; Passavant's and Waagen's recordings of Old Master collections in 1833, 1837–9 and 1854–7; Burckhardt's *Cicerone* of 1855; and articles by Thoré, Morelli and Fromentin in the next two decades. And for Taine, who had already formulated his theory about the decisive impact on artistic creation of 'race', 'milieu' and 'moment', the opportunity of seeing works of art in the very places where they had been created was particularly important. Despite his ambitious claims that he was trying to study Italian history through its visual rather than the more usual literary sources, he – like most of his predecessors (whose insights are frequently to be detected in his own observations) – often found himself looking at the art with eyes conditioned by what he knew of conventional historical narrative. None the less, the manner in which he combined these two approaches can sometimes be ingenious enough to make it difficult for us to be able to disentangle them, and he often raises stimulating issues of real importance.

Thin, a little stiff, with a small beard, bluish eyes visible behind his spectacles; dry by temperament but eager to please and witty in conversation – that was how the Goncourts saw Taine shortly before his departure for Italy.[179] He was already well known, chiefly for his fierce attacks on leading figures in the philosophical pantheon of nineteenth-century France and for his studies of English literature – well known, but not successful, for his unconventional views had led to repeated rebuffs in the academic world. He had worked himself into exhaustion and illness, and his austere, frustrated life with a crotchety mother and a younger sister inclined to mysticism was relieved only by infrequent visits to literary salons and to brothels.[180] Italy signified, above all, a sense of liberation. He felt awkward in his conventional clothes, and became intoxicated by the virile nude bodies he saw all around him – in the streets of Naples, in the museums of ancient art, and in those fragments of ancient literature to which he constantly alluded in order to emphasise the importance attributed by the Greeks to physical beauty and the cult of the body; alluded to, but also distorted and actually falsified, by omitting qualifications that had been essential to the writers from whom he claimed to be quoting.[181]

This passion, which is so often celebrated in his book, attracted a satirical comment from the Goncourts who pointed out that 'the greatest enthusiasm for the nude, for civilisations based on gymnastics, is to be found among badly built people. The idea of having a handsome nude body is a dream of Taine'.[182] But, however ridiculous it sometimes appeared to be, it was a dream that helped to condition his view of Italy as a country of youth, lacking inhibitions and prone to violence.

Such a view was not new. It had been extravagantly proclaimed by Stendhal, and it had influenced historians as sober as Burckhardt. Indeed, Stendhal (and many other writers after him) had assigned to the bloodthirsty violence and debauchery of the fifteenth and sixteenth centuries, which (oddly) were believed to have been the special privilege of the Italians, a relationship as integral to the art of the Renaissance as the Age of Faith had had to that of the Gothic cathedrals and the frescoes of Giotto: the Borgias, and later the Cenci family, had been as fertile in their influence on art as St Francis and Dante.

Taine's approach was usually more sophisticated and more cautious – he went out of his way to dissociate himself from Stendhal's cult of an energy that had benefited the individual at the expense of the State – but he agreed that the vendetta ('that word which has been almost erased from our spirit') provided the key to Italian history.[183] He responded keenly to the High Renaissance, but with even more warmth to that moment when art, in Florence especially, began to break free from Gothic conventions and to reveal just those seeds of change that Ruskin had looked upon with horror.[184] In general, Taine, for whom (in his own famous words) 'vice and virtue are products like vitriol and sugar', looked upon history as something to be studied dispassionately. Naturally, he had some personal enthusiasms, and he sometimes claimed to be surprised by these; yet his lack of any very individual taste and of much spontaneity of character, combined with the careful preparations he had made before travelling to Italy, suggest that (to take one example) his discovery of Tintoretto in Venice may have been prompted more by a reading of Ruskin than by any sudden conversion in the Scuola di San Rocco.[185] He appreciated art because it seemed to provide so uniquely powerful an impression of the morals, customs, beliefs and character of earlier centuries – usually, it has to be admitted, as he had learned about them from written sources. Thus, in what struck him as the endlessly repetitive mosaics of saints moving along the aisles of the church of S. Apollinare Nuovo in Ravenna (pl. 197), the figures themselves retained some traces of ancient dignity, but their features lacked all individuality and looked as if they had been barbarously drawn by some inexperienced child: 'there is not one among these people who is not a sottish, debased, sickly idiot'. They conveyed the appearance of well-built men whose ancestors had been of good stock but who themselves were now half-destroyed, dissolved as it were, by too much fasting, too many prayers. Far more vividly than the old chronicles or than Gibbon they conveyed the spectacle, unique in the history of humanity, of the thousand-year long decay of an ancient civilisation which, surrounded by Eastern influences, had dragged out its existence under a corrupt form of Christianity.[186] Similarly, the busts of the later Roman emperors in the Capitoline Museum could reveal more than could the feeble chronicles that had survived from that period. But what? Taine never tells us, and when he turns back to an earlier and better-documented period he finds – to take one among many examples – that the head of Nero showed that he had 'looked like an actor, a leading singer at the opera, stupid and vicious, a man unhealthy in imagination and

197. Martyr saints, mosaics, sixth century AD (Ravenna, S. Apollinare Nuovo).

brain'.[187] We have seen that such an approach had already been derided by Gibbon a century before; but occasionally Taine did try to test, with much more precision, his claim that he was making use of monuments to replace, or at the very least to supplement, written sources. Thus, characteristically acting on a principle put forward by naturalists early in the nineteenth century, that 'an animal can be very easily understood by looking at its shell', he set out quite programmatically to deduce what could be learned about Cardinal Albani from an examination of his villa (pl. 198).[188] It was clear that he must have been a 'grand seigneur homme de cour': that was obvious from the rigid planning of the gardens which recalled Versailles in the attempts that had been made to subordinate all aspects of nature to the convenience of human pastimes and to deprive them of any character of their own. The cardinal must also have been an antiquarian: the statues and ancient fragments to be seen everywhere in his villa, even embedded into the walls, varied enormously in quality, and many of them could have been acquired only out of a spirit of pedantry – that pedantry that diverted the mind from important questions and helped to fill the empty hours. A third point, 'non moins visible', was that he had been an Italian, a man of the South, for the lay-out of the buildings would have looked absurdly out of place in northern Europe. And as

Taine continues his exploration of the Villa Albani he evokes the abbés who look around and talk as they wait for their master: 'They raise their eyes to the *Parnassus* by Mengs and compare it with the one by Raphael, thus showing off their culture and good taste and at the same time avoiding any dangerously compromising conversations.'

Taine's attempt to evoke the life of a past society from the architecture created for it retains a certain interest as a sort of 'scientific' experiment inspired ultimately by the zoological demonstrations of Cuvier; but it can hardly be said to be very deep or convincing. On one occasion, however, some speculations by him of a rather similar kind proved to be exceedingly influential.

The church of the Gesù, which was built for the Jesuits in Rome during the second half of the sixteenth century and very sumptuously decorated a hundred years later, is now recognised as having been one of the most seminal as well as one of the most spectacular in the city. Its long, broad, hall-like nave designed by Giacomo Vignola between 1568 and 1573 became a model for churches all over

198. Percier and Fontaine, *Choix des plus célèbres maisons de plaisance de Rome et de ses environs*, Paris 1809: general view of Villa Albani.

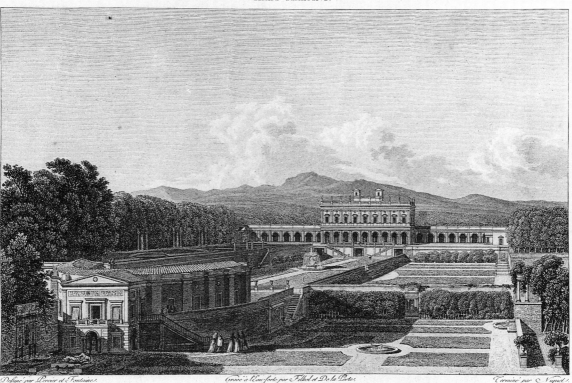

VILLA ALBANI.

Dessiné par Percier et Fontaine.   Gravé à l'eau-forte par Tilliol et De la Porte.   Terminé par Viquel.

VUE GÉNÉRALE DE LA MAISON DE PLAISANCE DU PRINCE ALBANI,

près la porte Salara hors les murs de Rome.

Europe, as, too, did its imposing but relatively restrained façade of two storeys connected by massive volutes; while the illusionistic effect of the ceiling fresco representing *The Triumph of the Name of Jesus*, which was painted by Giovanni Battista Gaulli between 1676 and 1679 probably under the inspiration of Bernini, was also widely imitated (although less in Rome than elsewhere) and represents one of the supreme masterpieces of Baroque design (pls 199 and 203). During the first half of the nineteenth century the sheer richness of the church fascinated most visitors to Rome, so that it was not ignored as were so many others of its period; but its history, and the very names of the artists and patrons associated with it, were almost as unfamiliar to any but the writer of guide books as had been those of mediaeval churches two centuries earlier. It was looked upon as an example of extreme bad taste. Taine shared this general view – as he shared most general views on aesthetic matters – but he did not, as was customary, attribute what he thought of as its vulgarity merely to the general decadence of art and society. For him its style was specifically related to the role of the Jesuits.

During these years it was becoming increasingly frequent to associate almost exclusively with the Jesuits all those churches that today would be described as Baroque – a term then little used. It is not clear when the notion originated, but in 1844 – before it acquired general currency – Burckhardt wrote an article on the 'Jesuitenstil' for the encyclopaedia then being published by the Brockhaus brothers. Clearly referring to the Baroque (although he does not use the word), he stressed the control exerted over the architecture of their buildings by the Jesuits of Germany. None the less, he distinguished between an early stage, when with 'affected respectability' they had been prepared to retain mediaeval styles for their churches and had confined their extremely lavish decoration to the interiors, and the period after about 1650 when they had built them in a degenerate Italian style which combined richness and magnificence with inner poverty.[189]

It was, however, the baroque decoration of the churches of Belgium that was to attract most attention. In the late 1840s the Antwerp print-seller Louis Granello published a series of lithographs illustrating once again some of the most extravagant pulpits in Antwerp, Brussels, Ghent and other Belgian cities, whose 'singularity' had already fascinated travellers nearly a century earlier.[190] It was to Belgium that many Frenchmen had fled after Napoleon III's *coup d'état* in December 1851, and this, too, must have played some part in spreading an awareness of the style. Thus in *Les Misérables*, published in 1862, M. Gillenormand tells Cosette that she and Marius should marry not in their parish church of Saint-Denis-du-Saint-Sacrement but in Saint-Paul: 'L'église est mieux. C'est bâti par les Jésuites. C'est plus coquet... Le chef d'oeuvre de l'architecture Jésuite est à Namur. Ça s'appelle Saint-Loup. Il faudra y aller quand vous serez mariés. Cela vaut le voyage.'[191] Saint-Loup, which had been built for the Society between 1621 and 1645 by the Jesuit architect Pierre Huyssens is very striking for its tall façade of three storeys which diminish in width as they rise and which are elaborately adorned with banded columns, and for its interior of red-and-black marble.[192] Two years after Victor Hugo, Baudelaire was to describe the church as a 'merveille sinistre et galante... un terrible et délicieux catafalque', which differed from all

199. Rome, Gesù: interior.

the other examples of Jesuit architecture known to him, and he, too, spoke appreciatively of the 'style Jesuitique' of the churches of Namur.[193] And in his *Du Principe de l'art et de sa destination sociale*, which was published posthumously in 1865, Proudhon, with characteristic assertiveness and characteristic lack of precision, referred to what he seems to imply is the established fact that 'the Jesuits gave us their architecture as well as their morality'.[194] However, it was Taine's visit to the Gesù in Rome on 15 March 1864 that proved to be decisive in spreading the notion that the Jesuits had 'a taste as well as a theology and a political aim; a new conception of the divine and the human always brings about a new way of conceiving beauty: man speaks in his decorations, in his capitals and in his cupolas sometimes more clearly and always more sincerely than in his actions and in his writings'.[195]

To Taine, what man appeared to be saying through the decoration of the capitals and the cupolas in the Gesù was clear enough.[196] The great 'pagan renaissance' of the sixteenth century had begun to change its nature so that the building resembled a magnificent banqueting hall decked out with objects of silver and crystal, all of which symbolised deference to the Church: 'Ancient Rome unified the universe into a single empire; I am renewing Rome and succeeding to that empire. What Rome did for peoples' bodies I shall do for their minds. By means of my missions, my seminaries, my hierarchy I shall establish the Church magnificently throughout the universe and for all time'. Such sentiments, explained Taine, were common to all the ecclesiastical edifices of the period, for they all aimed to glorify not Christianity but the Church. However, one had only to take a few steps in the Gesù to see that the Jesuits had made a distinctive contribution of their own to that policy: 'guided by their nimble, delicate hands religion has become worldly: she wants to please and she adorns her temple like a drawing room'. The little rotundas at the two sides of the nave were delightful marble chambers, fresh and softly lit like the boudoir or the bathroom of some beautiful woman. Everything was designed to dazzle the eye. Everywhere was the glitter of precious marbles and gilding, everywhere the elegant legs of pretty marble angels and ornaments of bronze and agate and lapis lazuli.

All this, continued Taine, had been devised as part of a deliberate system. He, too, had been impressed by the Jesuit art that he had seen in Belgium some years earlier – Saint-Charles Borromée, for instance, their church in Antwerp, the first major work built by Pierre Huyssens (in the second decade of the seventeenth century). Its interior, with all the paintings made for it by Rubens, had been burnt down in 1718, but it had been lavishly rebuilt and decorated in keeping with the rich façade which survived the fire. There was also the astonishingly elaborate wooden pulpit carved between 1696 and 1699 by Hendrik Frans Verbrugghen for the Jesuit church at Louvain but removed in 1776 to the Gothic cathedral of Brussels.[197] A lithograph of this was to be found in Granello's album (pl. 200), and Taine described it as 'a real garden, with trellises, greenery, a peacock, an eagle, all sorts of animals, the whole menagerie of paradise, Adam and Eve decently clothed and the angel who aims to be wrathful but who looks as if he is laughing'.[198] For him it revealed the same kind of genial and sugary art as was to be found in other

LA CHAIRE DE VÉRITÉ, | THE PULPIT,

SCULPTÉE PAR H. VERBRUGGEN DANS L'ÉGLISE DE ST GUDULE À BRUXELLES. | IN THE CHURCH OF ST GUDULE BRUSSELS.

200. H.F. Verbrugghen, pulpit carved between 1696–99 for Jesuit church in Louvain (Brussels cathedral), lithograph published in 1840s by Louis Granello of Antwerp.

Jesuit buildings – an art characterised also by the feeble verses in Latin and French, and by the illustrations, to be found in the *Imago primi seculi*, that superb book that had been designed in Flanders to celebrate the first centenary of the approval of the statutes of the Society of Jesus and which was, as it were, the manifesto of their taste.

This taste could be summed up in the phrase 'all the sweetmeats of pious confectionary' ('tous les bonbons de la confiserie dévote'). But such sweetmeats had been made with genius; for by relying on them the Jesuits had reconquered half of Europe. The seventeenth-century Church realised that some sort of accommodation would have to be made with the new world that had emerged from the Renaissance and that there was no possibility of returning to the Middle Ages. And so the Jesuits both attenuated the severe restrictions on human beliefs and behaviour that had once been demanded by the rigidity of the Fathers and the Councils and, at the same time, put limits on these newly granted freedoms by seeking methodical control of the imagination. It was a stroke of genius on their part to appreciate how much more basic was imagination than reason in conditioning our attitude to the world. And, once again, Taine resorted to an analogy from the natural sciences in order to explain the ways in which images directed to the senses lodge themselves in our brains. There they multiply and eventually, like some almost invisible seed which is transformed into vegetation, they become powerful enough to take over our wills. This had been the aim of the *Spiritual Exercises* of St Ignatius and it was the aim also of those responsible for the decoration to be seen in Jesuit churches.

Taine's suggestions, and the many controversies to which they gave rise, proved to be enormously influential,[199] and his pages on the Gesù certainly provide the most effective evidence of his declared intent to reconstruct history exclusively on the basis of the visual arts – even though he was obviously well informed about the Jesuits from written sources also. The most original feature of his analysis is his determination to discover a rational motive behind the creation of what was for him a thoroughly uncongenial style: he was not satisfied to attribute it merely to spiritual debasement. Taine accepted the notion that all civilisations decay and all artistic styles decline; and to illustrate the process of decline he chose the example of Tiepolo, 'a mannerist who seeks for melodrama in his religious paintings, and movement and effect in his allegorical ones . . .'[200] – but he did not associate the decay of civilisations with the decline of art as closely as was by now conventional. Like Ruskin, and so many other travellers, he tried to gauge the development of tomb sculpture in the Venetian church of SS Giovanni e Paolo, and (like Ruskin) he found the later works to be deplorable and castigated them vigorously.[201] But he did not point to them as an index of the degeneracy of the age, and he avoided what appear to us to be the simplistic conclusions of some of his later writing. At times, indeed, he went out of his way to refute easy parallels between aesthetic and spiritual values. 'What a contrast between art and morals!' he exclaims of the fifteenth-century Umbrian pictures he sees in Perugia,[202] and when he wrote that 'if one wishes to understand an art one must study the soul of the public to whom it was addressed',[203] he appeared to be touching on major issues of taste and patronage – though he did not follow them up as rewardingly as might have been hoped.

Ultimately, despite their novelty and some brilliant insights, even the pages on the Gesù fail to convince; and this is not just because modern scholars – with far more time and far more documented sources at their disposal than were available to Taine – have invalidated his notion of a politically motivated Jesuit art. More important is the fact that his visual evidence, and the selective use that he made of it, can be shown to be inadequate.

We have seen that Taine's feeling for art was mocked by the Goncourts before he went to Italy, and since then many other critics have been made uneasy by that mixture of brashness and the doctrinaire that sometimes characterises his responses to it. It is also curious that so very fine a descriptive writer and so perceptive a historian should have been so ready to accept some of the wilder fabrications told about the pictures he saw in the galleries of Rome and elsewhere. It is true that he appreciated the fact that even documentary engravings often had to be treated with caution because 'the artist has been unable to prevent himself being an artist';[204]

and that, much later, in his last book, *Les Origines de la France contemporaine*, he was to point out that eighteenth-century illustrators had, despite some attention to costume, failed to indicate any real differences between early Christians, German tribesmen, Arabs and other distant peoples: 'les mêmes corps, les mêmes visages et la même physiognomie, attenués, effacés, décents, accomodés aux bienséances'.[205] And yet when he visited the Palazzo Doria he had no hesitation in expressing apparently well-informed admiration for a portrait claimed to be by Veronese (who was born in 1528) of Lucrezia Borgia (who died in 1519) 'in black velvet, the breast a little uncovered . . . looking as she must have done when Bembo presented her with the carefully phrased protestations of his magniloquent letters' (pl. 201).[206]

The deficiencies of Taine's response to the decoration of the Gesù and other Jesuit churches were far less dramatic – but their consequences were far more telling. In the first place, he seems not to have noted – though earlier nineteenth-century travellers sometimes had[207] – that the extravagant stuccoing of the

201. Scipione Pulzone (attributed to), *Portrait of a Lady* (Rome, Palazzo Doria).

vault and also the rich ornamentation of silver, bronze, marble and lapis lazuli, which made so great an impression on him, did not belong to the original structure of the church, and indeed conflicted with its design. Most of it had been installed in the last decades of the seventeenth century, while the pilasters had been painted yellow only eight years before Taine's arrival in Rome. Thus all those 'sweetmeats of genius' had not been put in place until long *after* the Jesuits had reconquered half of Europe for the Church and could not, as he suggested, have formed part of some deeply conceived plan related to the *Spiritual Exercises* of St Ignatius. Further, had Taine given even a passing glance to the paintings in the side chapels, many of which were close in date to the building of the church itself and thus really did precede the great Catholic victories of the late sixteenth and early seventeenth centuries, he would have seen that, for the most part, they did not at all conform to his notion of a prettified style: among them, for instance, were many scenes of martyrdom, suffering and brutality. But this was an aspect of 'Jesuit art' to which Taine utterly closed his eyes. Thus he makes a passing reference to the marble groups (by Théodon and Legros) of the *Triumph of Faith over Paganism* and of *Religion overthrowing Heresy* which date from the very last years of the seventeenth century and which are placed on each side of the sumptuous altar of St Ignatius (pl. 202); but he says only that they 'proclaim the new spirit, that of orthodoxy and obedience', and he makes no attempt to describe the cowering and tortured personifications of the enemies of the Church which are being crushed into obedience (or annihilation) by Jesuit orthodoxy.

Taine had every personal reason to appreciate – and many occasions to lament – how powerful were the remaining weapons of clerical authority even in the France of his own day; but when looking at the Gesù he preferred to evoke the seductive appeal of the decoration rather than the equally ostentatious demonstrations of brute force. In fact, even the magnificent fresco on the vault (pl. 203), so radiant, so colourful, so warm, so welcoming at first sight – the most perfect incarnation, it would seem, of Taine's concept of Jesuit art – proves threatening enough when looked at more carefully: rays from the Name of Jesus do not merely illuminate the blessed, they also assail the damned. Naked, distorted bodies are hurled down by blinding light beyond the enclosing stucco frame, within which we are allowed our vision of Heaven, and appear to be crashing into the nave below. And had Taine looked at some of the other Jesuit churches in Rome – at S. Stefano Rotondo, for instance – he could have seen the most horrific series of frescoes that had ever been painted in the city: a cycle of atrocious scenes of torture, mostly enacted under the late Roman Empire, which showed, in as much detail as possible, the varieties of martyrdom suffered by early Christian saints.

Thus Taine's analysis of the tactics of the Jesuits was based on a very tendentious use of the visual documentation available to him. And he failed to follow the example that he attributed to his mentor Planat who, as a 'true historian', would immediately deduce from the study of art that men living at different times must have had 'different needs, appetites and revulsions; with different feelings, images and ideas'. His visit to Italy, however, was only spasmodically concerned with what could be learned about that country's history from a study of its art. Far

202. Rome, Gesù: altar of St Ignatius designed by Andrea Pozzo, *c.*1695, polychrome marble, bronze, silver and other precious materials: on left, Théodon's *Triumph of Faith over Paganism* and, on right, Legros's *Religion overthrowing Heresy*; both marble, 1695–9.

203. G.B. Gaulli (Baciccio), *Triumph of the Name of Jesus*, 1676–9, fresco on the vault of the nave of the Gesù in Rome.

more important for him was the project on which he embarked immediately after his return: the explanation of the country's art on the basis of its history. It was the lectures and articles that he devoted to this topic – and the extension of his method to other parts of Europe – that established his fame as a writer on aesthetics. But that achievement is not the concern of this book.

13

The Deceptive Evidence of Art

i

However much their approaches differed and however much (or however little) they chose to act on their beliefs, historians, art historians and antiquarians alike were agreed that, in principle, figurative art could provide some direct insight into the past, as long as it was authentic and as long as it had been created at the same time as the persons or events with which it was concerned. Occasional exceptions – the fact that the art of the catacombs, for instance, was more revealing for the light it shed on the early Christians than on the adventures of Jonah and the whale, or even on the appearance of the early martyrs – did not affect this rule. Moreover, feeble art might be as revealing as good art because of the information it offered either about the decline of civilisation or about the piety of the devout who did not wish to concern themselves with distracting embellishments. None the less, for obvious reasons, most cultural historians of the nineteenth century tended to devote themselves primarily to the art that they admired – or that they found important (as Burckhardt did that of Donatello and Michelangelo) even when they could not genuinely appreciate it.

It was, however, possible to argue that true insight into the past was not to be reached by studying the great and the exceptional: it was the commonplace, the average, the second-rate that constituted a far more reliable guide to the mentality of an epoch.

One reason for this depended on just that factor that had attracted the attention of historians to art in the first place. It was the very beauty of art that was bound to make it a deceptive, even a treacherous, guide. We have seen that this insight came fleetingly to Taine when he contrasted what must, in reality, have been the dinginess of Dutch seventeenth-century officials with the splendid images of them that survived in the portraits of Rembrandt and Hals; and at one moment, while writing *The Stones of Venice*, Ruskin himself was suddenly and briefly struck by the potential fallacy that lay behind the whole conception of his book. Recalling his visits to the city before the days of the railway he described the moment when the gondola at last 'darted forth upon the breadth of silver sea, across which the front of the Ducal Palace, flushed with its sanguine veins, look[ed] to the snowy dome of Our Lady of Salvation'. And he continued by warning (himself perhaps) that 'it was no marvel that the mind should be so deeply entranced by the visionary charm of a scene so beautiful and so strange, as to forget the darker truths of its history and its being. Well might it seem that such a city had owed her existence rather to the rod of the enchanter, than the fear of the fugitive'.[1]

Writers interested in such matters obviously knew that one of the claims constantly made on behalf of the arts was the very fact that their beauty did provide some solace from the pressing miseries of the world. Yet it seems to have been only towards the end of the eighteenth century that an awareness began to develop of just how misleading an impression of those miseries was liable to be conveyed to the historian by the more successful attempts that had been made to offset them. One of the most eloquent expressions of this view is to be found in the preface by the Abbés de La Chau and Le Blond to their two magnificent volumes, published in 1780 and 1784, cataloguing the engraved gems of the duc d'Orléans: 'What do we find in History except wars and the rise and fall of empires – the painful picture of the misfortunes of the servitude of the human species? The Arts, on the contrary, are emblems of the grandeur and power of humanity... those achievements of the arts that have come down to us have, through their sweet and innocent illusions, helped us to cheat the miseries of life.'[2] And other writers of the time made much the same point, even though they showed no interest in following up its implications for the historian.

One solution to the problem apparently created for the historian by the existence of such 'sweet and innocent illusions' was to deny that they were necessarily deceptive, and, in the wake of Stendhal, to suggest that the same spiritual energy responsible for the noblest art could also stimulate the most ferocious crimes: both Burckhardt and Taine were attracted by this notion, but neither was prepared to accept it whole-heartedly. However, another and much more ingenious, explanation was offered by Michelet's close friend Edgar Quinet whose visit to Italy long preceded those of Ruskin, Burckhardt and Taine, and whose investigations into the relationship between art and history proved to be almost as fruitful as theirs a generation later. Indeed, Quinet was among the first to recognise the nature of the difficulty which (as was later to occur with Ruskin) was brought to his attention by the particular magic of the Palazzo Ducale in Venice. Standing in 1832 in the Sala del Maggior Consiglio, whose ceiling and walls glowed with paintings by Veronese and Tintoretto, he was struck by the reflection that 'the Senate lived between two sets of torture: beneath its feet were subterranean dungeons, above its head the leads [piombi]'. From this he drew the much more general conclusion that 'the sombre severity of the political regime of Venice never extended to its painting. If you look only at the government you get the impression that the whole of Venetian society must have been administered by a ceaseless reign of terror and that the imaginations of its citizens must have been enveloped in a lugubrious veil. If, on the contrary, you examine its art, you assume that these men must have lived in a state of perpetual festivity, and that their ardent imaginations can only have flourished in a regime of excessive freedom.'[3]

It was not until some years later that Quinet attempted to explain more fully why Italian Renaissance art could provide only a thoroughly specious impression of Italian history – and he was able to do so just because both Italian art and Italian history meant so much to him. In an imaginary dialogue composed in Switzerland where he lived as an exile during the Second Empire he asked a friend who was about to visit France – which he himself refused to do until 1870 – not to pass on messages to the people he saw there but only to convey his farewell to a few ancient sculptures and some paintings by Leonardo, Raphael and Veronese in the Louvre. 'Tell them that my eyes often turn towards them, that I look for them, and call to them. They will accept this greeting from you because they know that I adored them when I had the chance to warm myself in their rays... Speak to them of my cult'.[4] But Quinet's response to art did not derive only from love and an appreciation of the solace it could offer. One of his earliest commitments to the study of history, made in 1824 when he was aged twenty-one, had been to translate Herder's *Outlines of a Philosophy of the History of Man*. From this he probably drew the conclusion that the arts of a nation can serve as a valuable source for the illumination of its innermost beliefs – though Herder's own interests had been essentially confined to the literary. Quinet tells us that when preparing the lectures on Italian history that he was to deliver with enormous success at the Collège de France in the 1840s, he found that no modern study was of any use to him. For a long time he felt trapped in a labyrinth of misleading facts and theories. 'To try to escape I travelled throughout Italy. The monuments of religious and political architecture and the aged frescoes began to open my eyes. The walls dazzled me: I seemed to be touching the true life of Italy in the Middle Ages.'[5]

His travels, which lasted for some fourteen months between May 1832 and July 1833, filled Quinet with rapture,[6] and among the places which specially fascinated him was Pisa, where 'along the walls of the cemetery the pale virgins of Giotto glide among the tombs like figures that have been resuscitated. The time has come when the angels of Gozzoli, Buffalmacco and Fiesole [Fra Angelico] have begun to blow their golden trumpets and to apply their curved bows to their viols.'[7] The allusion to any specific painting is vague and confused, but he was to recall the frescoes in the Campo Santo in the first volume (published in 1848) of *Les Révolutions d'Italie*, his important interpretation of Italian history.[8] Describing the endless civil strife that prevailed in the republics of the fourteenth and fifteenth centuries and the expulsions that followed from it, Quinet suddenly inserts into his narrative a curious, indeed inexplicable, passage: 'What became of the craftsmen driven from their cities? Art was the chief refuge of those who had been proscribed. Carvers in stone and wood sought refuge in the Campo Santo of Pisa. An entire population of exiles took up paint brushes and created on its walls that ideal fatherland which was denied them on earth.'[9]

Three years later, in the second volume of his book,[10] Quinet seems to have generalised the misleading historical gloss that he had put on his poignant impressions of the Campo Santo and, by transforming the notion of material into spiritual exile, he constructed a theory of great significance about the relationship – or absence of relationship – between the arts of a period and the circumstances surrounding their creation.

Like most historians of Italy at this time, Quinet was particularly concerned with the physical and spiritual decline of that formerly pre-eminent nation and the implications that it might have for other societies, and he made constant analogies with the France of his own day. The most sinister aspect of the decline was, he felt, the acquiescence with which Italians had, over many centuries, succumbed to tyrannies of all kinds, both domestic and foreign; and he illustrated his theory partly by examining in some detail the contributions made to the failure of Italian nerves by a limited number of representative men, all of the greatest fame. Quinet did not usually accuse them of direct moral corruption – though he was merciless with the historian Francesco Guicciardini – but he tried to show that, for all their genius, they had in different ways sapped the Italian will to resist oppression. Dante, for instance, had placed far too much faith in the mirage of salvation by the Holy Roman Emperor – but at least he had directly engaged himself with the main political issues of his time. Although Boccaccio had (almost) unconsciously helped to destroy the misconceptions of feudalism and chivalry, he had nevertheless treated clerical abuses with a tolerant smile rather than with the cry of rage that was required. In the fifteenth and sixteenth centuries Italians more and more gave up striving for national independence despite the efforts to awaken them which had been made by the great but flawed Machiavelli. By then it was in any case too late. The best Italians had abandoned the struggle: they were now cosmopolitan, concerned not with a nation but with the search for, and creation of, an ideal world designed to appeal to all humanity. This aspect of Italian history was incarnated in the work of her artists who were, by the very nature of their profession, more universal than writers and less tied to the courts and conventions of contemporary life. It is for this reason that the architecture, sculpture and painting that they conceived proves to be so unrevealing about the times in which they lived or about the troubles that afflicted their homeland.

In different ways Leonardo, Raphael and Benvenuto Cellini all cut themselves off from the contingencies of the world: Leonardo by identifying with the spirit of creation and nature; Raphael by aspiring to a serene and universal religion whose purpose was to reconcile paganism and Christianity; and Cellini by an absolute and unmoral commitment to self-fulfilment and to art itself. Yet the 'tyranny of beauty' to which artists submitted in their opposition to the oppressive and hostile world that surrounded them was ultimately ineffective. Even Raphael's sublime and all-embracing vision in the Vatican Stanze, 'which is more Catholic than Catholicism itself', could not actually change the nature of a Church that remained incapable of reaching up to his ideal. The revolution of the High Renaissance was thus purely an artistic one. The case of the tormented Michelangelo was a little different, for the tragic circumstances of contemporary Italy were reflected in a number of his works. None the less, he spent the last twenty years of his life lost among the curves of the dome of St Peter's, and he took leave of the city and the world: 'le front dans la rue, il entre dans le ciel des pures intelligences'.[11]

It is unlikely that many other writers would have wholly agreed with the specific reasons given by Quinet to account for the deceptiveness of High Renaissance art as a source of direct historical evidence; but it is almost certain that most of them would have acknowledged that it was deceptive. The problem lay not only in the obvious fact that the artists of the early sixteenth century tended to eschew 'local colour' in their depictions of history, myth, allegory and sacred imagery and to concentrate on the general rather than on the particular – for, as Quinet had recognised, this in itself constituted a historical issue of real significance. Almost as important was a psychological barrier of formidable power. Any style that was particularly admired was (and often still is) expected to rouse in the spectator a response of an entirely different nature from that induced by some other style of apparently less distinction: the first embodied perfect, and hence timeless values; the second was of essentially 'historical interest', either because its weaknesses provided a cautionary demonstration of how arduous was the road to the peak and how facile was the descent from it, or because those weaknesses encouraged the observer to look for other sources of satisfaction. Distinctions of this kind, which had perhaps first been enunciated by Vasari, became very marked towards the end of the eighteenth century; and both then and later they were little challenged even when pure observation might have suggested that they were hardly justified by the actual nature of the images in question. At the very time that Quinet was in Italy a second edition was published of Lasinio's illustrated folio on the Campo Santo in Pisa, in which a contrast was made between the early, crude frescoes that preserve for us the costumes and customs of those times and which are thus very useful for an understanding of Petrarch and Villani, and the 'sublime' scenes painted in the fifteenth century by Benozzo Gozzoli.[12]

However, historical curiosity about a style very often develops into heartfelt admiration for it, as can be observed in the change of attitude to the Gothic that occurred towards the end of the eighteenth century. In later years the Baroque, Mannerism and the Neo-classical were to be reappraised in a somewhat similar spirit. And as soon as they had been endowed by art lovers with genuine qualities of the highest order, these styles too were, so to speak, put beyond the reach of students interested essentially in their value as historical evidence. But no such inhibition has stood in the way of this kind of research into 'the minor arts', 'popular art' or what could be classified as merely bad or indifferent art.

ii

Ever since the second half of the eighteenth century the study of popular songs, ballads, folk tales, festivals and other such traditions had been attracting much attention in antiquarian circles, especially in England and Germany, both for their intrinsic pathos and apparently untutored energy and for their evocation of regional and national histories. It was not long before such attention reached a wider public. In Paris the Académie Celtique, whose inaugural meeting of 30 March 1805 took place appropriately enough under the presidency of Alexandre Lenoir in the Musée des Monuments Français, began a systematic investigation into the vanishing customs of France,[13] and, within a generation, the researches into folk tales of the brothers Grimm became famous throughout Europe. However, although antiquarians had relentlessly continued to excavate barrows and to write lengthy papers on coins and sherds, the visual arts aroused almost none of the intellectual excitement generated by the early stages of the new interest in folklore. Thus a questionnaire sent out by the Académie Celtique to prefects and local experts throughout France asked for information about rituals and superstitions surviving in the villages and about songs, dances, fairy tales and dialects, but the only enquiries about the arts and crafts concerned the nature and design of tombstones. And when in 1807, some three hundred variants of a popular print adorned with six crude and simplified illustrations to a 'cantique' dedicated to the 'Vie et Débauche de l'Enfant Prodigue' were collected for the Académie Celtique, it was the text, and not the illustrations, that attracted attention, for it was through the text that local dialects could be studied.[14]

This neglect of the visual was owing partly to the fact that popular imagery flourished long after the songs and stories handed down by generations of peasants were on the decline: indeed, the illustrations for the 'Enfant Prodigue' dated from much the same time as the investigations that were under way concerning it.

When in the 1840s and 1850s antiquarians did first begin to look with fresh eyes at popular images, what struck them above all was that such material constituted an alternative to the high art (or the strictly archaeological artefacts) that had hitherto engaged universal attention. This perception was so central to their researches that for at least a generation thereafter it is very rare to find any theoretical distinction being made between caricature and popular art. The confusion was, if anything, increased by the illustrations to be found in their books which were so insensitively reproduced that it can sometimes be difficult to differentiate between the technique, or even the style, of a wooden misericord, an etching by Callot and an antique onyx. Thus any image, whose execution appeared to be crude or simplified or which distorted conventional appearances in order to produce an effect of ribaldry or satire or grossness or obscenity, tended to be classified as caricature, whatever its date or nationality. Such images could often be admired for their rough vigour and they were sometimes included in the huge graphic collections of those seventeenth-century amateurs who were keen to own examples of all artists, all styles, all subjects. In the 1660s, for instance, the Abbé de Marolles was purchasing not only Dürers and Marcantonio Raimondis and Parmigianinos, but also hundreds of *bouffoneries*. He did this because, despite their 'trop de licence' and 'assez mauvaises railleries', they were of use for the light that they could throw 'aux connaissances de l'Histoire du temps'.[15] It was for exactly the same reason that, two centuries later, it was these *bouffoneries* that were to attract the attention of scholars who showed themselves to be much more fascinated by them than by Marolles's masterpieces:[16] none of the reverence due to a Raphael (or even a Teniers) disqualified 'popular art' from disinterested historical study.

In 1813 an American artist from Philadelphia produced one of the earliest books to dip into this newly enticing field. James Peller Malcolm had come to London in the 1780s, and he soon devoted himself to engraving and to topographical and antiquarian studies. His *Historical Sketch of the Art of Caricaturing* was impressively illustrated with what he considered to be grotesque figures which were drawn almost exclusively from the British Museum, but which ranged widely: from a Roman lamp in the form of a naked man who forces his head through his upturned legs (pl. 204) to a mediaeval manuscript which 'exhibits a fiend endeavouring to fix a three-pronged instrument into the head of a figure who ascends to an angel ready to receive him' (pl. 205); from Chinese bronzes to the social and political satires of his own day. He thus brought to light much unfamiliar material, and he provided much useful information about the background to the English political caricatures that he chose to discuss. But his commendable reluctance to hurt peoples' feelings made him an erratic guide to the later eighteenth century (the name of Gillray is never mentioned), and he draws no conclusions from his compilation, except to point out that the supremacy of England in this branch of art provided a telling indication of the extent of the freedom to be found there.[17]

The example of Malcolm's slim treatise may perhaps have encouraged the

204. J.P. Malcolm, *Art of Caricaturing*, 1813: fig. 1 reproduces an Elizabethan satirical engraving directed against the pope, and figs 2 and 3 show Roman lamps.

205. J.P. Malcolm, *Art of Caricaturing*, 1813: reproduction of a miniature from Harleian MS 603 (in British Library).

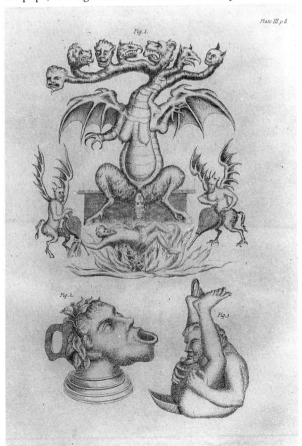

publication in France of an extensive series of fascicules, entitled *Musée de la Caricature*, which were assembled into two very handsome volumes in 1838.[18] The general editor – and an intermittent contributor – to the series was Pierre-Joseph Rousseau (known as E. Jaime), a prolific composer of light comedies; each fascicule contained three illustrations, many of them in excellent colour, and an explanatory essay of about four or five pages written by members of a team of authors associated with the Romantic movement, such as Charles Nodier, Jules Janin and Léon Gozlan. Although the illustrations were far more numerous than those that had been collected by Malcolm, the range was more limited. With only about two exceptions all the examples discussed were French and were confined to the graphic arts. The earliest ones were chosen from fourteenth-century manuscripts and the last dated from the end of the Napoleonic wars. Like Malcolm, Jaime and his team made no theoretical distinction between caricature and popular art: 'You have seen, on the portals of old churches, frightful gargoyles, sphinxes, chimaeras, demons with huge mouths and the legs of vipers, or tigers, or monkeys; all these sculptures are *caricatures* of the devil'.[19] And, like Malcolm, Jaime did not attempt to draw much in the way of conclusions from the nature of his material. His volumes were chiefly notable for the abundance of the visual sources that they made available, and they were used by many later writers on the subject.[20] But they were aimed mainly at those members of the public who bought other well-produced and well-illustrated anthologies compiled by groups of fashionable writers during the Romantic period. The stimulus for that systematic investigation of the grotesque, the comic and the popular that, a quarter of a century later, was to engage the attention of scholars in England, Germany and France came from a very different and much more circumscribed type of study.

In 1851 Theodor Panofka, whose inventive (and now much-derided) researches into the imagery of the ancient world had already won him fame throughout Europe and who was professor at the Kaiser Wilhelm University in Berlin, published a paper of twenty-five pages on *Parodien und Karikaturen auf Werken der Klassischen Kunst*. This was illustrated with three plates containing more than twenty small engravings which consisted for the most part of details taken from Greek vases (pl. 206). It was not long before some of these entered the repertoire of all scholars interested in the subject. Panofka discussed the meaning of the scenes which he reproduced and alluded to a number of others; in some of them, he suggested, the style of drawing was characterised by 'deliberate negligence [*absichtlichen Sorglosigkeit*]'.[21] He was fully aware of the novelty of his undertaking and of the new light that it could throw on the 'orientation and development of the Greek spirit'.[22] Although it had long been recognised that some figures to be seen on certain Greek vases and other artefacts must have been designed with satirical intent and although Pliny had drawn attention to the existence of comic genre painting in the ancient world, the idea that the Greeks had cultivated such low forms of art met with some resistance from a republic of letters that was still imbued with notions inherited from Winckelmann about the ideal beauty of Greek art. For this very reason, and also because of Panofka's

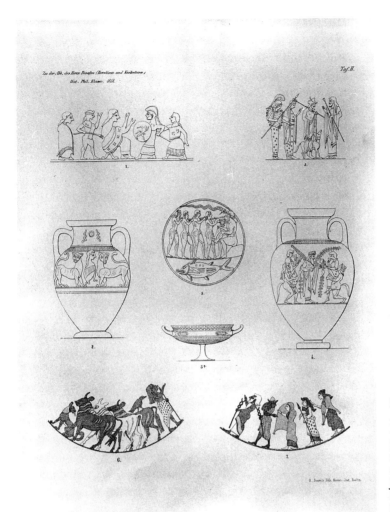

206. T. Panofka,
Parodieen und Karikaturen,
Berlin 1851: various
parodies of Greek myth
mostly to be seen on
archaic vases: fig. 1,
Judgement of Paris; fig.
5, Blinding of
Polyphemus, etc.

many contacts with France, his short essay attracted a good deal of attention among scholars throughout Europe.[23]

It was not until the 1860s, however, that isolated ventures of this kind were absorbed into popular volumes which began to transform the historical imagination. In 1862 Friedrich Ebeling, a student of political thought, published the first of a number of editions of a *Geschichte des Grotesk-Komischen*. This was a reworking of a book that had appeared three-quarters of a century earlier. The original version of 1788, by Karl Friedrich Vlögel, was adorned with just one illustration: it faced the title-page and showed two views of a battered terracotta figure of a Roman comic mime. The text, which was dedicated mostly to the stage and to burlesque processions of various kinds, formed a natural sequel to the same author's history of comic literature in four volumes that immediately preceded it. Ebeling was asked by his publisher to retain as much of the original book as possible but to bring it up to date and adapt it so that it would conform to the taste of his own times.[24] For this reason he added a substantial section on the visual arts and, more importantly, he inserted forty illustrations, many of them in colour. These ranged in time from antiquity to such recent French artists as Grandville and Tony Johannot; and among the objects represented were mediaeval coins, characters from the *commedia dell'arte* and the puppet theatre, playing-cards and satirical fashion plates of the eighteenth century. Ebeling's book thus put on display a significant amount of 'low art', and because he (or his publisher) decided to include a number of illustrations of quite surprising indecency he drew attention to an aspect of that art that was already causing some concern.

In England Thomas Wright avoided the topic as far as he possibly could; in France Champfleury referred to it often enough, but he explained that he would bring to 'the delicate task [of investigating it] all the prudence that would be necessary'.[25] It was the contemporary, and very extensive, researches of these two men, carried out at almost exactly the same time as the more limited and commonplace investigations of Ebeling, that lifted the subject of the 'alternative tradition' in art onto a new level.

Wright and Champfleury seem to have been working independently of each other,[26] though Wright's plentiful antiquarian researches were well known in France, and he had been elected a corresponding member of the Académie des Inscriptions et Belles-Lettres as early as 1842 when he was aged only thirty-two. He fell under the spell of Jacob Grimm,[27] and until his collapse into insanity thirty years later he poured out an unending stream of articles, books and scholarly (and not so scholarly) editions of early texts. Most of these were concerned with various aspects of popular life in the Middle Ages and were extensively illustrated with wood engravings very coarsely copied from illuminated manuscripts, church monuments and other figurative sources. His *History of Caricature and Grotesque in Literature and Art* appeared in 1865, the same year in which Champfleury published his *Histoire de la caricature antique* and *Histoire de la caricature moderne*.

There is a good deal in common between these works. This is partly due to the fact that, as we have seen, their authors were not strictly pioneers, but produced their books as the culmination of a long series of more casual studies into what could be thought of as the 'popular arts': for to both of them, as to their predecessors, any expressive deformation in painting or sculpture, from antiquity to their own day, served essentially the same purpose. In the words of Champfleury, caricature was 'le cri des citoyens . . . la foule'.[28] Even more important was the fact that both authors felt that they were examining a tradition that by now was virtually dead. 'There can hardly be said to be a school [of caricaturists] at the present day', claimed Wright in the concluding paragraph of his book; and Champfleury acknowledged that 'J'écris ces lignes à l'heure où la caricature, à peu près disparue en France, semble morte.'[29] At the same time the peasant had collaborated in his own corruption. Seduced by the art of the towns, he was abandoning 'his costumes, just as he forgets popular songs, legends and traditions so as to read adventure stories like *The Three Musketeers*, and prefers horrible lithographs to the wood engravings of naïf illustrators'.[30] Yet, despite the similarity of their assumptions, the approaches of the two men differed greatly.

Wright assembled a mass of texts and illustrations which extended, without interruption, from antiquity until his own day; but he had no feeling for the nature or quality of his material (apart from embarrassment at its all-too-frequent licentiousness) and no theory about its significance. Champfleury, however, opened his *Histoire de la caricature antique* with a resounding declaration of his beliefs: 'There are some men and women whose natures are so strangely constituted that they are more impressed by painting than by print, by a picture than by a book. A stroke of the pencil teaches them almost as much as history. Their first glimpse of the public and private life of some tribe or nation, of its morals and customs, come from a fresco, a statue, an engraved stone, a fragment of mosaic: only afterwards do they turn to books in their search for proof.'[31] And on another occasion he stressed that caricatures were becoming increasingly important to scholars who were now beginning 'to make use of visual sources [*monuments figurés*]' in order to study 'everything that can throw light on events and on man'.[32] Moreover, Champfleury had strong views about how such images should be interpreted, and he ridiculed the pedants for the excessively learned explanations they provided of crude and obvious representations which did not, in fact, require to be explained.[33] Above all, Champfleury was a crusader: crude and obvious the material might well be, he was later to insist, but it was just these characteristics that rendered it of such importance for the over-sophisticated and enervated painters of his own times.[34] What to other writers appeared to be defects in need of apology were for Champfleury virtues which ought to be propagated by anyone interested in the well-being of contemporary art. Champfleury reasserted these views until the end of his life. He produced expanded editions of his books on ancient and modern caricature (in 1867, 1872 and later), and he ventured much further into the field of what he considered to be undervalued arts and artefacts. He published volumes on ceramics of the revolutionary period (in 1867) and on popular imagery (in 1869), as well as on 'caricature' in the Middle Ages, the Renaissance and the seventeenth and eighteenth centuries (in 1871, 1874 and 1880).

Although he drew freely on Wright for some of his works, it was Champfleury who did more than any other writer of the nineteenth century to draw attention to the importance of the minor arts for an understanding of aspects of the past that had been largely neglected by historians. Indeed, the implications of his researches were not lost on a number of men of letters who were troubled by the fear that little visual evidence about the nature of contemporary France would be available to historians in the future. It must surely have been under the impact of Champfleury that in 1868 the critic Ernest Chesneau wrote in an anxious strain about the International Exhibition of that year:

Has it never occurred to you that the nineteenth century is progressing inevitably to its end and that, if nothing changes, it will reach that end without French art having left anything that will enable future generations to discover the France in which we have lived? Should France remain essentially as it has done for centuries, no doubt an authentic tradition will be established on the basis of our present customs: but it is certainly not in our modern pictures that our descendants will find the elements of that tradition – they will have to find them in our caricaturists, Gavarni, Daumier, our true 'peintres de moeurs', and in our illustrated periodicals.[35]

Champfleury's path to the popular arts seems, in retrospect at least, to have been a straightforward one. As a twenty-two year old provincial from Laon he had settled in Paris in 1843 and had quickly begun to make a name for himself as a journalist and writer of short stories. These often centred on the lives of artists, and soon he was writing directly about the arts themselves, both past and contemporary. His sympathies were chiefly with those painters who depicted the lives of simple people: Courbet, with whom he made friends, and the Le Nain brothers, about whom he wrote a number of pioneering studies. But local patriotism played as large a part as ideology in guiding his taste. The Le Nain brothers had come from his native town of Laon, and he also devoted an appreciative monograph to Quentin La Tour who had been born in the same part of France; for Champfleury this was more important than the fact that La Tour's ingratiating (though lively) pastel portraits of the most fashionable figures of the middle years of the eighteenth century were fundamentally antagonistic to just those values of naïvety and sincerity that he so often proclaimed on other occasions. Champfleury had, above all, been drawn to the pantomimes at the Théâtre des Funambules where the performances by the mime Jean-Gaspard Deburau had, for nearly twenty years, been exciting the younger generation of Romantic writers. Though Deburau himself died not long after Champfleury's arrival in Paris, his son carried on the tradition, and for him and other mimes Champfleury wrote a series of pantomimes which aimed to retain all the popular ingredients of the genre while at the same time giving to them a somewhat philosophical (though not didactic) character.

Like Courbet, Champfleury became identified with the controversies aroused by the advent of Realism during the early years of the Second Empire but, unlike Courbet, he was very reluctant indeed to be associated with left-wing opposition to the regime. The study of popular culture (which was in fact promoted by the government of Napoleon III) thus had a particular appeal for him partly because it enabled him to express a deep, sincere and defiantly expressed nostalgia for subversion and aberrations of all kinds as long as they were to be found in earlier societies. For all his commitment to realism it was the strange to which he was attracted. The most remarkable feature of his extensive researches is the lack of any sustained (or even much cursory) examination of those thousands of perfectly orthodox religious subjects – saints, above all – engraved from woodblocks, brightly coloured and often clearly derived from well-known compositions of the Old Masters, which constitute by far the largest proportion of the popular arts to have survived into the nineteenth century.

Although Champfleury discussed folk tales and assembled an anthology of 'Popular songs of the provinces of France', it was the visual arts that absorbed most of his erudition, and to the study of 'imagerie populaire' and caricature he transferred the commitment that he had once felt for his contemporary Courbet: it is this that justifies his reputation as a true pioneer of taste and scholarship. It was a change of emphasis rather than a change of direction that was required of him, for it was still, as always, the 'naïf' that engaged his sympathy. That very *naïveté*, however, raised certain issues that he never fully confronted, though they emerge sporadically from many of his books. How legitimate, for instance, was it to take it for granted that the imagery in question had been produced by, as well as, for 'the people?' And, above all, was *naïveté* to be thought of as a characteristic of 'the people' everywhere at all times, as he sometimes suggests, or was it part of the special heritage of France, providing an indication of 'son esprit gaulois, son sentiment amoureux'?[36] He was aware of the nationalist implications of his studies, and he commended the 'patriotic' motives that inspired the scholars of Scandinavia in their investigations into the popular arts,[37] and that led to the establishment in Stockholm in 1872 of the first museum in Europe for their display.[38] It was not long before folk art was to become the focus of a particularly vicious strain of chauvinism, but Champfleury's studies tended to encourage the development of another tendency latent in the study of popular woodcuts and ceramics: regionalism. He was, in any case, always more interested in looking at specific objects than in generalising from them.

During much of the nineteenth century a new and baffling world of images began to absorb the attention of people interested in the Middle Ages. In addition to the strained and glaring Christs, Kings and Apostles, enclosed and bisected within hard, black outlines, who dazzled the antiquarian with an almost barbaric intensity of blues and greens and reds as he gazed up at the stained-glass windows of cathedrals and churches; to the exquisitely refined and fashionably dressed saints, surrounded by borders decorated with exotic birds and butterflies and flowers, whose fragile poignancy enraptured him as he turned the vellum pages of fifteenth-century books of hours; to the grave, but sometimes smiling, Virgins, whose wooden robes with their calm heavy folds seemed to match in purity the finest pieces of Greek sculpture; and to the reclining marble bishops, hands clasped in devout prayer, who lay (as if asleep) enjoying in death the tranquillity they had earned through the virtue of their lives – in addition to all this, some very strange artefacts were emerging from the little-explored storehouse of ecclesiastical art (pl. 207).

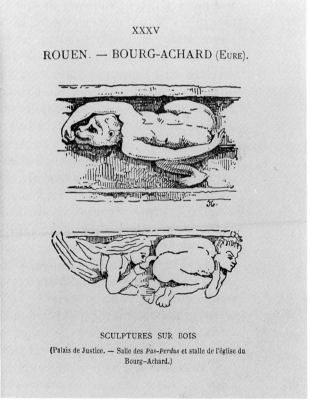

XXXV

ROUEN. — BOURG-ACHARD (Eure).

SCULPTURES SUR BOIS

(Palais de Justice. — Salle des *Pas-Perdus* et stalle de l'église du Bourg-Achard.)

207. Jules Adeline, *Les Sculptures grotesques*: wooden sculptures in Rouen (Salle des Pas-Perdus) and Bourg-Achard (stall in church).

Human bodies with animal heads, heads of the most doubtful character; devils straining their lungs in order to stoke up the flames beneath huge caldrons; figures of the damned being carried away by impetuous steeds; women whose sexual organs are being devoured by demons; animals preaching from the pulpit; mounted men dragging from the tails of their horses wretched victims whose entrails spill out from their torn bellies; dragons whose grimacing jaws spew out the water of the gutters; monkeys in clerical garb; heads of men who are half-mad, half-priests; large teeth and even larger mouths that swallow up entire human beings; animals playing the organ; grimacing fauns that jeer at the faithful; victims impaled on long skewers; donkeys that bray as they play the lyre.[39]

Such was some of the imagery, to be seen on the corbels and misericords, gargoyles and capitals, friezes and reliefs of countless churches and cathedrals, which over a period of many centuries had survived decay and iconoclasm, theft and even restoration. Its vigorous crudity delighted Victor Hugo, but dismayed the devout who found it difficult to reconcile such vivid records of mockery and farce, greed and lust, superstition and paganism, cruelty and freakishness with newly trumpeted notions concerning the Age of Faith. And so a stream of abbés and other writers employed by the Catholic press poured out article after article to explain that things were not as they seemed:[40] a painting of the Dance of Death might be hideous, but in it one could hear 'the heart-beats of France, the fatherland, but the fatherland laid low and discouraged, and which having lost its way can now count only on Death rather than on its own spirit';[41] obscenity was often not actually present at all, but only imagined by the beholder; and even when it really was there it might be quite unrelated to actual sexuality; grotesque figures looking like monks were probably intended to represent not the clergy but peasants or poor people who also wore tunics and cowls; above all, everything that appeared to the uninstructed onlooker as ridiculous or unnatural or offensive was, in fact, profoundly serious because all such images were symbolic and only to be interpreted with difficulty.[42]

Some of these attempts to challenge over-simplified assumptions were astute enough; and Thomas Wright made a valid point when he suggested that the exaggeration of gestures to be found in some early art may have served only to elucidate the narrative and did not necessarily carry any grotesque or satirical implications.[43] But Champfleury reacted to all such theories with ridicule; and he was equally scathing about those 'Voltairians' who claimed that the farcical nature of so much ecclesiastical art had been intended as satire. 'When I began these studies I had the idea that the stones of our cathedrals were speaking witnesses of the rebellious state of the people; I end them without believing that their eloquence is of so seditious a nature.' Champfleury, in fact, went out of his way to give the simplest, most straightforward explanation that he found compatible with the unusual imagery he set out to discuss. Thus the scenes of monkish lechery that were sometimes represented in illuminated manuscripts were much more likely to constitute warnings than true records of actual behaviour; and in any case, until very recently a great deal of public jollity did take place in churches. But, above all, what might appear to orthodox commentators as complex religious symbolism and to 'Voltairians' as bitter anti-clerical satire was, in fact, something very different: it was a '*naïf*, unselfconscious art, as innocent as the child who lifts up his chemise in public'.[44]

The theory that popular art was a reflection of the essentially naïve and good-humoured 'people' constituted both the starting point and the conclusion of all Champfleury's researches into the subject, and because of his assumption that these characteristics of 'the people' had remained constant over the centuries, he was unable to give any historical dimension to his study of popular art. He ridiculed second-hand Hegelian notions that every time the artist took up his palette or his chisel he would exclaim that 'the state of mind of my contemporaries will emerge from each stroke of my brush';[45] but this was because he rejected any elements of self-consciousness in the creation of popular art and also because such a proposition implied that the passage of time must be of significance. For Champfleury neither of these counted. Discussing the ostentatious but comic phallic imagery to be seen in a mosaic from Herculaneum he commented that even Aristophanes 'pretended to blush' at sights of this kind, whereas in India, Egypt, China, Japan and the Middle Ages they were turned into motifs of fantasy, caprice, oddity and satire.[46] Just as the carvers of crude decorations to be found in mediaeval town halls were like children who feel no embarrassment when urinating in public, so, too, in the eighteenth century the juxtaposition on popular ceramics of clashing colours may have shocked the bourgeois, but was perfectly congenial to children and savages – and also to the peasant who, in certain other of his tastes as well, had many of the same instincts as the Phoenician and the Etruscan, the Chinese and the Japanese.[47] From all this it would appear that despite the repeated claims made by Champfleury for the historical importance of popular imagery as a gauge of religious, political and other beliefs, such imagery could, in fact, reflect little more than an entirely stable sense of healthy values: indeed, when pointing out the similarities between devotional engravings of the fifteenth and the nineteenth centuries, Champfleury acknowledged that 'the stuttering of children is the same everywhere; despite the fact that progress came to a halt, such engravings present to us the charm of innocence, and the charm of modern image makers derives from the fact that they have remained children, that is to say that they have escaped from the progress made by urban art'.[48] Rightly interpreted, therefore, the popular arts can tell us nothing about historical change, and can at best serve as an index of the degree of sophistication attained by the society in which they are to be found. Thus in a country in which representations of the male organ arouse laughter and (as in Algiers or Constantinople today) can be shown to children of both sexes without fear of making them blush, civilisation must be in a backward state.[49] On one occasion, however, Champfleury made a serious attempt to move beyond this very restrictive viewpoint.

Nineteenth-century appreciation and classification of eighteenth-century ceramics went hand in hand with enthusiasm for the other arts of the *ancien régime*, and by the 1830s there was already widespread demand for the lustrous bowls and dishes

of Chantilly and Vincennes, and for all the luxurious and often fanciful products
of other leading French factories. But there was general agreement that with the
coming of the Revolution quality had declined precipitously.[50] In about 1850,
however, Champfleury began to collect the crude faience-ware that some factories
had been driven to make for a popular market after 1786 when the commercial
treaty with England had undercut prices for fine porcelain. He had few rivals.
These plates, whose ungainly decoration and gaudy colours repelled amateurs even
when they carried no political messages of a subversive kind, were still less
appealing when they were adorned with a Phrygian cap or an energetic peasant or
a slogan such as 'La République Française 1793'. To track down such objects
Champfleury and the dealer who acted for him[51] had to travel all over the French
countryside and to search through rat-infested barns, where, once the vogue for
them had passed, pieces had been stored alongside unwanted ancestral portraits, or
through the cottages of less fashion-conscious peasants who still proudly displayed
them on their sideboards. None was yet to be found in shops. Champfleury
realised that 'popular' images, whether engraved or painted on ceramics, were
actually produced on an industrial scale in towns that might be quite remote from
those markets whence they reached their humble customers. Yet the very fact that
they were still to be discovered in the surroundings for which they had been
intended must have strengthened his conviction that his growing collection was
bringing him into direct contact with an art 'made by the people working for the
people'.[52]

These ceramics could therefore provide unique evidence of the responses stirred
up by the quickly changing phases of the Revolution among those sections of
society unable to record them through the written word. 'In these works of
pottery one can follow the steps of the Revolution. The principles of 1789
reverberate in the heart of the people as on a bell. Weaknesses in drawing appear to
fade away in face of the strength of popular feeling. I can read this art as I can read
a book – even more clearly, in fact.'[53] Their testimony was essential because the
impact of the Revolution had been so radically distorted by later artists who had
chosen to depict it for the sentimental bourgeoisie. How many pictures of the
'Dernier banquet des Girondins', the 'Famille royale au Temple' and of Louis XVII
were to be seen at every exhibition! And hatred for the Revolution had led to scorn
and misunderstanding for the art that it had itself produced. It was Champfleury's
aim to make of that art 'the eloquent advocate of the Revolution'.[54] The intensity
of this battle of taste and style and politics emerges vividly from his contacts with
the leading connoisseurs of eighteenth-century art, who – like him – prided
themselves on their pioneering role in the launching of new artistic fashions. In
1860 he went to inspect the paintings and drawings that had been assembled with
such fastidious discrimination by the Goncourt brothers, and from their collection
and their desultory comments on the arts of the revolutionary period he concluded
that they were 'naïf Siamese twins' who allowed themselves to be enticed only by
'scintillating brushwork and delicate glazes'.[55] They in turn despised him and
considered him to be an 'enemy', and Edmond was later to write of his plates that
'I believe that of all the pottery of every civilisation since the beginning of the

world there has never been a product so ugly, so stupid and so indicative of the anti-artistic mind of a society'.[56]

Despite such outbursts the differences between them were not all-embracing. The Goncourt brothers were as keen as Champfleury to draw on the arts in order to illustrate the past, and at least one painter (Prud'hon) was equally loved by all three. Indeed, Champfleury occasionally made use of high, as well as of low, art in his exploration of the Revolutionary state of mind, though he did so in a somewhat perfunctory manner. Thus he claimed that Boilly's *Triomphe de Marat* 'proved that when taking part in celebrations the people were gay, relaxed and cleanly dressed' – even though he knew that this picture was said to have been painted under the Terror in order to atone for others that had been denounced as obscene.[57] On a more sophisticated level he argued that the sheer quality of much of the art produced by David and various other painters provided an indication of the moral seriousness of the Revolution that had inspired it. One painter exemplified this above all others: 'Jean Goujon personifies the Renaissance; Prud'hon the Revolution. It is Prud'hon whom posterity will seek in the Revolution, and so this much abused period will be represented by the most ideally beautiful figure in all French art.'[58]

It was, however, the use that he made of popular faience-ware that constituted Champfleury's real innovation in historical method. No longer was he content to rest his case on the naïve vigour and other distinctive qualities of the images concerned. He tried rather to pose serious questions about their significance. It is true that nearly all the plates that he examined were adorned with inscriptions – 'faïence parlante' was the name that he gave to the genre – and that, like the numismatists of earlier centuries, Champfleury paid special attention to the essential clues offered by these texts; none the less, he was far more responsive than they had ever been to the style and nature of the visual image itself. Thus in discussing how very rarely ceramics seemed to have been inscribed with the word 'sans-culottes', he pointed out that the only example known to him was a vase that was decorated with lively and colourful putti gathering roses in the manner of Fragonard, and he concluded, therefore, that the inscription must have been added later.[59]

By examining more than ten thousand 'patriotic ceramics' – he himself owned between five and six hundred which he was unable to sell at the price he hoped for[60] – Champfleury tried to discover just which were the revolutionary sentiments that had most affected people living in the country, far away from the main centres of political activity, and to what extent those sentiments had changed over the years. The survival of very large numbers of plates and bowls dedicated to Mirabeau (pl. 208) – the only personality of the whole period to be so honoured – was in itself an indication that this 'orator, although he was accused of lacking principles, none the less himself remained a principle as far as the people were concerned'.[61] In this case Champfleury's approach was almost entirely based on statistics – he did not, for instance, refer to the fact that it was only the dead, and never the living, Mirabeau who appealed to the potters. At other times, however, he took his clues from changes in the imagery. He claimed that the gradual

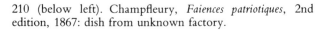

208. Champfleury, *Faiences patriotiques*, 2nd edition, 1867: salad bowl from Nevers.

209 (right). Champfleury, *Faiences patriotiques*, 2nd edition, 1867: cistern from Nevers.

210 (below left). Champfleury, *Faiences patriotiques*, 2nd edition, 1867: dish from unknown factory.

211 (below right). Champfleury, *Faiences patriotiques*, 2nd edition, 1867: dish from unknown factory.

radicalisation of the Revolution in rural areas was demonstrated by a large group of ceramics that celebrated the *tiers état*. In the earliest ones the sword of the aristocrat and the crozier of the clergy were harmoniously disposed around the crown or the fleur-de-lys, while the peasant with his spade seems to be supporting them – although he does not show any signs of discomfort (pl. 210); but soon the symbols of royalty disappeared, and by 1791 it was liberty (in the form of an open cage) rather than the monarchy that appeared to be sustained by the sword, crozier and spade as shown on a rare cistern inscribed with the words 'Vive la Réunion' (pl. 209).[62] In the same year more ominous signs were to be seen. A number of plates depicted a peasant either struggling under the heavy burden of the sword and the cross or laying them on the ground: in each case he proclaimed 'Je suis las de les porter' (pl. 211).[63] Sometimes, however, Champfleury showed himself to be aware of the dangers of assuming that every example of 'faïence parlante' must reflect popular sentiments. He pointed to the 'anomaly' of a plate inscribed 'Le tiers nuit' and assumed that so reactionary a pronouncement could only have been made in secret for some embittered aristocrat:[64] it is, therefore, surprising that he failed to suggest that the concord between the three estates, so elegantly proclaimed on the cistern, could well have been inspired by the aspirations of a bourgeois client, for so handsome an example of tableware is most unlikely to have been commissioned for a peasant.

Champfleury discussed and illustrated some of the themes most frequently depicted on popular ceramics, but he also devoted a number of pages to one that, so he insisted, was never to be found on them, despite widely held views to the contrary. The guillotine, he explained, 'was an instrument of the town and not of the village'. It might have been suitable for decorating fashionable earrings, but no such image of hatred or vengeance had ever been made for the plate of a peasant; and if one day an example should ever turn up, it would be a forgery intended to deceive some simple-minded collector.[65]

It was as important for Champfleury to investigate the centres of production of popular pottery as it was for the refined connoisseur to distinguish between the factories of Chantilly, Sèvres and Moustiers: 'step by step, thanks to a number of discoveries, I was able to expound the state of mind prevalent in certain provinces by examining the range of *faïences patriotiques* that had been manufactured in them.'[66] Nevers, placed at the very heart of France, was by far the most abundant source, and from Nevers huge stocks were carried along the Loire, and thence, through a close-knit network of canals, to such cities as Paris, Nantes, Orléans and Bordeaux. They were then distributed into the surrounding villages. Very large quantities of 'faïence parlante' could also be found in the region of Beauvais; but this town had been 'infected with royalism' and careful inspection showed that the pieces had not been made there but had been imported from Nevers, so that it was reasonable to claim that 'strong gusts of patriotism had blown throughout the country districts of the Oise and the Nièvre'.

Champfleury's analyses of the imagery and the production of 'faïences parlantes' during the revolutionary period, and the many questions he raised about them, constitute his most significant contribution to the study of the popular arts and of history – despite much confusion of thought and long irrelevant digressions. It is true that some of his other books – on caricature throughout the ages and, above all, on the illustrations of the Wandering Jew and other legends – also introduced a mass of unfamiliar (and rather more absorbing) imagery to the historian. It was, however, only when discussing a short period of less than two decades that he was able to break free from the temptation to succumb to a simplified notion of 'the people' as a uniform mass, sharing the same characteristics every-where and for all time, and to appreciate – briefly and timidly – that a kind of art that (for all his genuine admiration) he acknowledged to be of secondary quality could, for that very reason, be of real historical value, and not merely of antiquarian fascination.

iii

We have seen that for Champfleury, and most of his contemporaries, interest in popular imagery depended partly on the fact that it seemed to represent an alternative tradition, of undoubted power, to the high art of their own day and of the previous century, and that for this reason little distinction was at first made between 'popular', 'primitive' and 'caricature'. Champfleury would surely not have been surprised had he been able to read a report, written in 1865 when his studies were at their most intense, to the effect that Australian aboriginals were unable to recognise coloured engravings of themselves, whereas 'a rude drawing with all the latter parts exaggerated they can realise'.[67] It is therefore understand-able that he found it difficult to draw conclusions of a conventional historical nature from the kind of art to which, so unconventionally, he had chosen to devote himself; for, with the exception of the 'faïence parlante' of the Revolutionary period, most of it was not only anonymous but apparently timeless: if anything, it was of significance to the ethnologist and the psychologist rather than to the historian. And yet Champfleury's illustrated books drew attention to countless images that, just because they had not been consecrated by cultivated taste, demanded investigation rather than obeisance. Museums of popular European art came into existence at almost exactly the same moment as did museums of primitive art imported from the European colonies. But, as had happened some three centuries earlier with the cult of numismatics, the study of both these arts tended to become circumscribed and uncritical. Champfleury himself showed almost no interest in commenting on the similarities and differences between the objects that he collected and the refined porcelains and sculptures of the same period; and it was rare for any scholar to combine research into the popular, the conventional and the trivial with an interest in 'high art'. Indeed, until very recently, it has seemed repugnant to lovers of such art, rightly considered as among mankind's noblest achievements, to accept that an understanding of it might actually be increased by a consideration of the popular, the conventional and the trivial. It is one of the very many achievements of Aby Warburg that he was able to break through such ideological barriers and thereby give renewed vitality to the appreciation, as well as the study, of 'high' images and also to enhance their value for the historian.

The immediate steps leading to this insight can be traced quite clearly, but Ernst Gombrich has suggested that Warburg's readiness to embark on so adventurous a path also owed much to the general inspiration of Karl Lamprecht, whose lectures he attended in 1887 when he was a twenty-one year old student at the University of Bonn.[68]

Lamprecht was certainly the most influential – and by far the most controversial – cultural historian in Germany in the generation following that of Burckhardt.[69] He wrote extensively on the economic history of France and of Germany in the Middle Ages, but he had also studied art history in Munich, and this experience was to be fruitfully exploited in the twenty-odd volumes, some of them running to more than six hundred pages, of his *Deutsche Geschichte*.[70] This enormous work, underpinned by systematic theorising in a spirit utterly alien to that both of Burckhardt and of Warburg, discusses the development of the German spirit through a series of concepts (the symbolic, the typical, the conventional and the individual) derived from a consideration of the national culture. Lamprecht claimed that painting and sculpture were the best instruments for measuring ('die besten Gradmesser') movements of the spirit.[71] Many pages are therefore devoted to the visual arts which he obviously studied with some care. Pictures are often described and conclusions about the distinguishing character of successive ages are drawn from them. Indeed, Lamprecht's book, which was composed over many years, long after Warburg had left Bonn, must be the most ambitious attempt ever made to study a nation's history in the light of its culture; but, despite the space devoted to the arts, it can hardly be claimed that these volumes contributed much to the historical interpretation of images. Moreover, not one illustration is included among their thousands of pages.

In 1882, however, well before the *Deutsche Geschichte*, Lamprecht had published a slim, well-illustrated treatise which is likely to have been of greater interest to Warburg. It was devoted to the richly decorated initials to be found in German manuscripts, mostly from the Rhineland, dating between the eighth and the thirteenth centuries. Lamprecht explained that, although ornamentation of this kind had, for the most part, been overlooked by historians, it had survived in such large quantities that it offered uniquely copious material for studying continuity and change in the spiritual life of the period.[72] Moreover, we know from notes made by Warburg that, in his lectures, Lamprecht laid special emphasis on the 'prosaic' and 'conventional' aspects of Gothic art, and would also discuss the nature of symbolism, religious ritual, folk customs and ceremonies, as well as the expressive potential of gesture.

Whether or not it was from Lamprecht that Warburg was introduced to issues of this kind, they certainly remained of the utmost importance to him for the rest of his life. He himself experienced the impact of religious rituals and folk costumes when, in 1895, he travelled to the Indian settlements of Arizona, at first with the intention of investigating the ornamental patterns in use among local craftsmen and later in order to watch tribal dances and other ceremonies. The stimulus to take this surprising step, two years after having published his thesis on the mythological paintings of Botticelli, may – Gombrich has suggested – have come from the writings of Adolf Bastian, founder of the Berlin Museum of Ethnology. Like so many students of popular culture (not least Champfleury), Bastian feared that the arts and customs of primitive societies were on the verge of being extinguished by the modern world, and he insisted on the absolute necessity of studying and collecting what still remained before it was too late to do so. Within less than ten years Warburg himself was trying to organise a congress of folklorists in Hamburg. He had discovered that he needed to understand the nature of what could be thought of as 'popular art' in the fifteenth century and the reasons for its alarmingly long survival in the very sanctuary of the Florentine Renaissance: for, in this case, far from being an endangered species in need of preservation, the art in question had been more like a pest or a weed which threatened to stifle the spiritual development of modern man. From surviving inventories he had discovered that the Medici Villa Careggi, meeting place of the leading Florentine devotees of the thought of Plato and – so Warburg believed – the original home of Botticelli's *Primavera* (the principal theme of his dissertation), had been extensively decorated with cheap Burgundian hangings on which were painted erotic and coarsely humorous subjects. The nature of these would have been familiar enough to Champfleury and his followers, and from now on Warburg began to study the themes and the styles to be found in works of this kind with the same care that he devoted to the high art of the Florentine Renaissance, for whose achievements he had such profound admiration.

With these 'low' hangings he associated other artefacts that seemed to be at odds with conventional notions of that Renaissance: the unadorned realism of Flemish portraiture, for instance, which had evidently been far more welcome to Florentine patrons than traditional art history acknowledged, and also those colourful, mannered tapestries from the North which were eagerly collected by Italian lovers of antiquity despite the fact that they represented the heroes of Greece and Rome clothed in the latest and most extravagant styles of the Burgundian court.

But these Alexanders in their fashionable and colourful costumes (pl. 212) were not the charming products of a 'childish' imagination. On the contrary. The most trivial of images could carry the most portentous implications for this German scholar whose interpretation of Renaissance art (and hence society) was just as imbued with moral concerns as was that of Ruskin – but from a directly opposite standpoint. 'This realistic style of representing costumes in the French manner [*alla franzese*]', he warned in an article devoted to early Florentine engravings of scenes of amorous dalliance, 'which seems so ingenuous and so innocent was in fact the principal enemy of that new and expressive style that required the heroic aspiration of Antonio Pollaiuolo (pl. 213) in order to shake off these heavy and luxurious garments.'[73] Warburg, like Michelet, felt that civilisation had been threatened by the detestable Middle Ages – 'ce terrible mourant qui ne pouvait mourir ni vivre, et devenait plus cruel en touchant à sa dernière heure'. And the plates which illustrated his article told a similar story. Facing each other on opposite pages were two variants of *The Planet Venus* from the set of engravings of the planets asso-

212. Flemish fifteenth-century tapestry: scenes from the life of Alexander the Great (Rome, Palazzo Doria).

213 (below). Antonio Pollaiuolo, *Battle of the Nude Men*, engraving (Oxford, Ashmolean Museum).

sizione nello stile della pittura fiorentina profana, quando dalla pittura di mobili nuziali « alla franzese » essa tentava di assurgere all'arte

PARTICOLARE DALLA STAMPA « IL PIANETA DI VENERE ».

Così in questi modesti ornamenti di coperchi avremmo il prodotto, molto notevole come sintomo, di quella critica età di tran-

PARTICOLARE DALLA STAMPA « IL PIANETA DI VENERE ».

più ideale dello stile antico: Sandro, sempre occupato dagli scopi pratici della galanteria che vuol nascondere e manifestare i segreti nel tempo stesso, non ha trovato ancora una maniera di espressione decisa: anche perchè il suo mentore Poliziano non l'ha introdotto nel regno platonico della Venere celeste. Ma una diecina d'anni più

214. Details of earlier and later versions of an engraving (attributed to Baccio Baldini) of the planet Venus, published by Aby Warburg on adjoining pages to demonstrate the reform *all'antica* of the 'barbaric Northern costume' of the woman dancing.

ciated with Baccio Baldini (pl. 214). They are somewhat confused in design, and although there are major differences between them as regards arrangement, the direction of composition and the poses of the figures, the spirit of both is essentially similar: courtly young people make music and dance in a landscape strewn with flowers, while the behaviour of nude couples in the background emphasises the eroticism symbolised by Venus. But, points out Warburg, whereas the woman dancing in the first of the prints revealed the full uncouthness ('barbarie') of the Northern source from which they are both derived, in the second, the 'antique butterfly has emerged from the Burgundian larva, the drapery flutters victoriously and Medusa's wings have replaced the heavy bonnet. And thus we witness the archaising idealism which is brought to its highest expression in the work of Botticelli', who may therefore have been responsible for this print. In an analysis of this kind Warburg seems to have taken over and developed (far more acutely than its author was ever able to do) Taine's aphorism that 'un pli de vêtement est une trace de passion comme une epithète'.

Warburg was to change his mind about the disastrous impact of the late Gothic

style, but his researches were almost invariably characterised by the contrasts – if
not necessarily the conflicts – he brought to light between differing kinds of
images and by the implications of such contrasts for our understanding of the past.
Merely to glance at the illustrations on which his historical enquiries were so
solidly, but so untheoretically, based is to be confronted by a kind of experience
that is still very rare and must once have been unique. How often those illustrations
seem to have emerged from the volumes of a Flögel or a Wright or a Champfleury
or from the catalogue of some museum of folk art only to find themselves in the
exalted company of Botticelli and Dürer, Memling and Ghirlandajo!

For although Warburg (prompted no doubt by the terrible tensions that were for
some years to destroy his own mental stability) was always vividly aware of the
threats to high civilisation from crudity and violence as well as from the fashionable and the facile, he also recognised that the cultural world inhabited by Lorenzo
de' Medici and his contemporaries could embrace, without excessive strain, the
coexistence of apparently antagonistic sets of images. Indeed, it was perfectly
possible for that very art that incarnated humanity's noblest aspirations to draw for
its own ends on the resources that were sometimes offered by the second-rate, the
naïve and the superstitious. Thus, in an essay of 1901 on the fresco by Ghirlandajo
of *The Confirmation of the Rule of the Franciscan Order* (pl. 215), to be seen in the
Sassetti chapel of the church of S. Trinita in Florence,[74] Warburg explains that we

215. Domenico Ghirlandajo, *Confirmation of the Rule of the Franciscan Order by Pope Honorius III*, fresco (Florence, Santa
Trinita, Sassetti chapel).

can best understand the nature of this 'masterpiece . . . with its marvellous and insufficiently appreciated' portraits of Lorenzo de' Medici together with his family and friends in the company of Francesco Sassetti, the patron, if we realise that the painting had emerged from a 'solemn and barbaric custom'. Ever since late antiquity Christians of power and influence had done what they could to bring themselves as closely (and as visibly) as possible into contact with places of worship; and this eventually culminated in the privilege of being allowed to present to churches wax portrait-figures of themselves and their families. These were made with the most extreme realism and dressed in the donors' own clothes. By the early sixteenth century the church of the Annunziata in Florence was so crowded with hundreds of life-size wax figures that many of them had to be attached by cord to the beams of the roof high above ground level – from which they would crash down from time to time and disturb the prayers of the devout – and the walls had to be specially strengthened: 'the church must have ressembled a collection of wax-works'. In Lorenzo's day the display was not yet quite so grotesque, but it was none the less the survival into the Renaissance of this crass custom that helped to explain his intrusion, with that of so many of his contemporaries, into a solemn ceremony of momentous importance for the history of Christianity, which had taken place some two and a half centuries earlier. And their desire to put themselves under the protection of the saints explained also the realism with which their features were rendered. Ghirlandajo's fresco thus signified 'a relatively discreet substitute for fetishistic magic'; but Warburg was very mindful of the dangerous power of superstitious beliefs.

We have seen that it had always been agreed that the second-rate could be of 'historical interest' for the light that it was capable of throwing on the customs and fashions of earlier societies; and it was also a commonplace that it was worth studying art that was obviously crude and rudimentary in order to retrace the steps by which perfection had been attained in the masterpieces of Raphael. Warburg (whose vast achievement extends far beyond the few aspects of it that have been touched on here) accepted the hierarchy of values implied by this kind of approach. But he greatly enriched those values by demonstrating for the first time that an investigation of the demons and monsters, the astrological deformations and the triviality to be found sometimes in such dismaying proximity to the painting so much loved by Burckhardt, could transform our understanding of that painting without in any way impugning its quality. Renaissance art, which to earlier historians of culture had appeared to be timeless and detached from the world, could now be interpreted as an accomplishment that was essentially dynamic, the product of a difficult struggle. It did, after all, offer essential evidence about the nature of Italian history; the objections raised by Quinet had been answered.

Art as Prophecy

i

In 1573, a few years after a savagely destructive wave of iconoclasm had swept through the Southern Netherlands and at a time when the issue of ecclesiastical imagery was very acute, Bernhard Jobin, a Protestant publisher, issued a coloured woodcut by Tobias Stimmer of the capitals of two columns that were then to be seen in the nave of Strasbourg cathedral (pl. 216). This image was among the most curious of all the mediaeval 'caricatures' to attract the attention of Champfleury.[1]

The more important of the capitals displayed a procession of animals, led by a standing bear holding in his right hand a holy-water sprinkler and in his left one a bucket; he was followed by a wolf or a fox with a crucifix as tall as himself and by a hare with a large, flaring candle. Behind them a pig and a goat carried a litter on which reclined a sleeping fox, while below was a bitch apparently reaching out for the pig's tail. On the other capital were two, almost identical, donkeys reading the Mass.[2]

What exactly was meant by these carvings, which were destroyed in 1685, is still not certain. They probably portrayed some scene from Renard (the fox) or from one of the other popular tales which, despite tinges of anti-clerical satire, were frequently to be found represented in Gothic churches and cathedrals. By the late sixteenth century, however, the meaning must have been lost, and Jobin's broadsheet was entitled *Copies of some curious and instructive [wolbedenklicher] images of Romish idolatry.* To explain these images, which were reprinted on a number of occasions, Jobin invited his brother-in-law, Johann Fischart, to produce a verse commentary on them.

Fischart, a widely travelled, cultivated and virulent Protestant polemicist, who was soon to win fame as a satirist and as the translator of Rabelais's *Gargantua,* interpreted the procession as an exposure of the vices of the clergy which had been made by a perspicacious sculptor three hundred years earlier. The sleeping fox symbolised their hypocrisy; the pig and the goat, the greed and the lust of the priests and the monks; the bitch, their impudent concubines; and he continued in this spirit with all the other animals.[3]

Fifteen years later the Catholic apologist Johann Nass took it upon himself to provide a more satisfyingly orthodox explanation. Nass, who had frequently been

216. Tobias Stimmer, *Abzeichnis etlicher wolbedenklicher Bilder von Romischen abgotsdienst,* coloured woodcut of 1573 republished by Bernhard Jobin in 1576 (Zurich, Zentralbibliothek).

attacked by Fischart as 'an impudent lying monk' and ridiculed for his low birth (he had started life as a tailor), was a preacher and pamphleteer of great violence who, as a young man, had come very close to accepting the Lutheran faith. His long poem on the Strasbourg capitals was one of his last publications, for two years later, in 1590, he died at the age of fifty-six.[4]

For Nass, too, the animals symbolised various vices, but he saw the scene in general not as the depiction of life as it had been three hundred years earlier, but as a prophecy 'of the recent great apostasy from the true service of God and of the condition of the bestial sects and gangs'. The sleeping fox was faith, which, so the Lutherans claimed, could fulfil everything of itself without the need for good deeds; the pig and the goat denoted violation of the chastity that had once been demanded of those who served at the altar; and Nass, like Fischart before him, ran through the other animals in the same vein. But his task was a harder one, for he had to account for the presence in the cathedral of representations of Lutheran malpractices carved more than two hundred years before the birth of Luther. This had been made possible because of the authentic witness of prophecy,

> which announces such things in all countries where sects and gangs are found so that their deceptions should be brought to light for the good of the world. This is what I say of the sculptors who made these carvings at Strasbourg, in the cathedral, three hundred years ago; because there was then a people, and also teachers, who sought for God with true hearts and who fled from great sin and error. By the Holy Ghost they were told of the future when evil would come, and of the apostasy from the old faith, and all this they entrusted to books and also to stone, as you can see represented here.[5]

Nass's exegesis belongs to an age-old tradition about the nature of prophetic dreams, but it is unusual to find so specific, easily visible and carefully dated an image being credited with the power to foretell the future in this way. However, although discussion of the capital continued to cause trouble – as late as 1728, long after it had been destroyed, a Lutheran bookseller in Strasbourg was severely punished for reprinting Fischart's broadsheet[6] – Nass's explanation of how it came to be in the cathedral does not seem to have carried much weight. It is in the following century that we first come across an image (or series of images) that for long enjoyed the reputation of having been endowed with the gift of prophecy.

In 1635 Van Dyck was required to paint a picture of Charles I that would show his head from three different angles (pl. 217). Charles, whose authority was at its peak, had this triple portrait sent to Rome to serve as a model for Bernini who had been granted special permission by the pope to make a marble bust of the king. When Bernini looked at the picture 'he foretold something of funest and unhappy, which the countenance of that Excellent Prince fore-boded'. This is first recorded in print by John Evelyn who merely says that he has 'been told' it.[7] And as he himself had never seen the painting and was writing sixty years later, long after the Civil War and the execution of Charles I, his story is nowadays treated with the utmost scepticism.[8] But Bernini's supposed reaction need not be dismissed as wholly improbable. He could not, after all, have been familiar with the conventions of sensitive and aristocratic restraint adopted by Van Dyck for so many of his English portraits; and, even by the standard of those conventions, the features shown in the triple portrait convey a sense of melancholy which still strikes us as different in character from anything that can be detected in the recorded appearance of other sovereigns of the period. But whether or not there is any truth to Evelyn's story, its implications were weighty, for it was repeated and elaborated in the eighteenth and nineteenth centuries, and it gave birth to the notion that Van Dyck had, in some prophetic way, recorded for posterity the spirit of a court that he felt to be doomed. In fact, the context of Evelyn's comments suggests that it was the king's true physiognomy, rather than Van Dyck's perspicacious interpretation of it, that had so impressed Bernini, but the distinction would not have been an easy one to make at the time (any more than it is today); and, in any case, by recording the anecdote immediately after an almost identical one that referred to the legendary Apelles, Evelyn is implying that it is given to only the greatest painters to see so deeply into the future.

A very similar version of the story is recorded by Sir Richard Bulstrode, who had himself served under the king during the Civil War and who died in 1711 at the age of 101.[9] It may indeed have originated with him, because his *Memoirs and Reflections* were published only posthumously, and it is not clear when he wrote the manuscripts on which they were based.[10] Bulstrode's version is slightly, but significantly, different from Evelyn's, for he claims that when Bernini saw the painting by Van Dyck he did not know whose portrait it was. This is improbable, to say the least, but it certainly emphasises the role of the artist as oracle. By the early nineteenth century Bulstrode and Evelyn were held to reinforce each other, and it was reported that 'the well-known anecdote of the sculptor is authentic', and that 'there is no portrait of any other Sovereign, which awakens such powerful emotions as does the head of Charles the First'.[11]

It is true that not everyone could accept the idea that Van Dyck had shown prophetic insight in his portrait of the king. Looking in about 1715 at another portrait by him of Charles (pl. 218) – and one that to our eyes seems to be somewhat more robust – Jonathan Richardson must have had Evelyn's comment in mind when he emphasised that by putting in it 'something of sorrow' Van Dyck was merely being 'historical', because he had painted it when the king was 'entring into his Troubles'; in fact, this second portrait dated from much the same period as the one sent to Rome, long before there was the remotest hint of impending tribulations.[12] And in 1830 Isaac D'Israeli took the trouble to examine a 'fine and large' picture by Mytens, painted at the time of the king's accession, and a miniature copy of one said to be by Van Dyck, dating from the same period. In neither of these did he find any trace of the 'secret sorrow . . . deepened melancholy . . . painful thoughts' that had struck Bernini. He concluded that, 'had the physiognomical predicter examined the two portraits of the happier days of Charles, he might have augured a happier fate. It is therefore evident that what was peculiar in the countenance of Charles was not discoverable till after his thirtieth year.'[13]

The prophetic character of Van Dyck's portraits of Charles I and the Stuart court has remained legendary until our own day, despite all the objections of the

217 (above). Van Dyck, *Charles I in Three Positions* (The Royal Collection, Windsor Castle).

218. Van Dyck, *Charles I* (The Royal Collection, St James's Palace).

doubters. But it is also unique. No similar interpretations seem to have been put on the rare portraits believed to represent Mary Queen of Scots in her heyday which were either reproduced from original sources or manufactured *ex novo* during the eighteenth century.[14]

ii

None the less, even though few serious historians have ever tried to put it to the test, the idea that the earliest signs of impending changes – in politics, morals, society or religion – are to be detected in the arts has had (and continues to have) a powerful effect on the historical imagination. The origins and growth of this idea are not easy to investigate, because at different times it has embraced quite different concepts. It is, however, worth trying to separate some of these related strands and to indicate why and when they became particularly influential.

Towards the end of the eighteenth and the beginning of the nineteenth centuries a number of thinkers, especially in Germany (where there was much dissatisfaction with what were seen as French superficiality, rationalism and materialism), maintained that artists of all kinds were blessed with a prophetic insight that was denied not merely to ordinary people, but even to men of learning. And many of the Romantic poets, evoking with new conviction what was already an age-old tradition, sincerely believed that they had been endowed with this gift which harked back to the sacred origins of their calling, though they did not, of course, claim to be fortune-tellers in the conventional sense of the phrase.[15]

Particularly revealing light on the development of this concept is thrown by some discussions that preceded the publication in March 1789 of Schiller's rapturous poem, *Die Künstler*.[16] Schiller had from the first conceived of this as a sort of philosophical hymn dedicated to man's nobility and the moral heights he had reached in modern times – 'Wie schön, o Mensch, mit deinem Palmenzweige,/ Stehst du an das Jahrhunderts Neige/In edler stolzer Männlichkeit . . .' – and he had proclaimed that such progress had been made possible by culture in general and by art in particular. However, when he showed an early draft of the poem to Wieland, this new mentor claimed that the emphasis given to these two factors was unbalanced. Wieland was pained by Schiller's idea that art was only the serving-maid of higher culture: this was to subordinate spring to autumn. Such humility was very far from him: 'He places everything that is conceived of as science and scholarship below art and asserts that the former are the servants of the latter.'[17] In the light of these objections, in which he found much that was true, Schiller changed part of his poem so as to make it absolutely clear that it was art that prepared the way for learning and morality: 'Art reveals swiftly and easily truths which the speculative and scientific intellect discovers late and with difficulty', in the words of a recent writer on Schiller.[18]

Such generalised claims for the intuitive precedence of the arts became part of the accepted domain of German aesthetic thought and quickly spread throughout Europe. However, a generation or so later they were given a wholly new

219. Jacques-Louis David, *Oath of the Horatii* (Paris, Louvre).

dimension and began to impinge on the consciousness of historians also: for by then they seemed to have been reinforced by precise, empirical evidence of a kind that was far removed from anything that Schiller had had in mind.

Five years before Schiller had begun *Die Künstler* Jacques-Louis David exhibited in his studio in Rome a large painting which he had just completed there and which was devoted to an episode from the legendary history of the city: the three sons of the military commander Horatius vow to represent the kingdom in a combat with the three Curatii brothers from the neighbouring and hostile kingdom of Alba, despite the fact that the two families are intimately bound by ties of love and marriage (pl. 219). Such an evocation of 'those blessed times when luxury had not yet extended its powerful sway over the happy territories of Lazio, and when all the greatness of the Roman spirit was still manifest'[19] proved to be an enormous public success. But the antiquarians – including Seroux d'Agincourt – were worried: had the event actually taken place?[20] And if it had, was not what we know about it too vague to constitute a suitable subject for a major picture? Why were two of the brothers raising their *left* arms? Why did their swords look so different from each other? Why was there no altar? However, despite these and a few other objections, the triumph of the picture was complete.[21]

Some months afterwards, in September 1785, it hung in the Salon in Paris

where, preceded by its dazzling reputation, it had arrived at the last moment. Like
other pictures produced in response to a commission from the king, it was shown
high up,[22] but David had solicited support from influential backers to make sure
that it would be displayed to full advantage, and it was placed at the very centre of
the principal wall (pl. 220). Immediately above it, and projecting over part of the
adjoining pictures on each side, was a composition, somewhat in the manner of a
very horizontally expanded Poussin, of *The Extreme Unction* by Jean Bardin –
'long, long, long' commented a bored visitor who, like the other critics, treated it
with weary condescension.[23] Below, commissioned by the King of Sweden, was
Adolf Ulric Wertmuller's *The Queen with Monseigneur the Dauphin and Madame, the
King's Daughter, taking a walk in the English Garden of the Petit Trianon,* whose
desiccated charm quite failed to inspire even those critics who would have liked
to advertise their loyalty to the royal family.[24] The tense energy, the 'fierté
républicaine',[25] of the *Oath of the Horatii* crushed its neighbours and dominated the
entire Salon: almost all the remaining pictures, including a number of equal size
by established artists depicting impeccably noble themes chosen from antiquity,
seemed somewhat monotonous (however '*sage*') by comparison with the 'sublime
execution' of David's masterpiece, which showed up 'the old maxims and
superseded taste' prevailing in other high-minded scenes of the conflict between
love and duty.[26]

There were, it is true, many criticisms, but these were, for the most part,

220. P.A. Martini, *The Salon of 1785*, engraving.

Coup d'œil exact de l'arrangement des Peintures au Salon du Louvre, en 1785.
Gravé de mémoire, et terminé durant le temps de l'exposition.

A Paris, chez Bonet, Peintre en miniature, Rue Guénégaud N.º 24.

different in character from those that had been made in Rome. No one showed an interest in the subject, but in Paris, too, some writers objected to the raising, by two of the brothers, of their left instead of their right arms to take the oath; and there were a few other strictures of a similar kind. But stylistic considerations predominated, and two in particular aroused controversy: the excessive uniformity of the composition and colour, and the fact that by placing the principal figures or groups in three quite distinct areas of his canvas, separated by harsh intervals, David seemed to be ignoring all the rules of composition which required the eye to be led gently from one part of the picture to another.[27]

Despite David's defiance of academic conventions – indeed, partly because of it – enthusiasm easily submerged disapproval. Critics welcomed the 'absolutely new composition' which matched the 'patriotic and cruel system of morality of the earliest Romans', and 'the simplicity and energy of the arrangement worthy of those simple and heroic times'. For all its faults, it was 'undeniably, the finest picture of the Salon' and 'of all the modern pictures I have seen, the one that has struck me as the most assured [le plus décidé], the one that owes the least to familiar conventions and the customary style of our masters'.[28]

There was at least one prediction that any intelligent and observant art lover could safely have made even before the Salon closed: David (and the style with which he was identified) would henceforth enjoy an even greater success than had hitherto been the case. He had for some years been highly acclaimed; now he became by far the most admired painter of the time. Only with some members of the Academy itself – which, so he felt, had put obstacles in his way from the first and which continued to do so in the hour of his triumph – were his relations becoming increasingly difficult, even bitter. However, he was receiving commissions of all kinds, from the royal family and private patrons alike, and he was later to feel understandably proud of the successes achieved by his scenes of ancient history (The Death of Socrates, The Lictors bringing back to Brutus the Bodies of his Sons), by his venture into erotic mythology (The Loves of Paris and Helen) and by his portraits.[29]

When in 1789 and 1790 arbitrary power began to crumble and government seemed to be moving, very hesitantly and with many setbacks, in the direction of constitutional monarchy, David, like some of the more liberal-minded nobles and members of the wealthy and cultivated bourgeoisie in whose circles he moved, welcomed the process with keen satisfaction. He may even have witnessed for himself one of the principal steps (resolute, despite intimidation, and peaceful, despite provocation) that had been taken in that direction: the solemn oath sworn on 20 June 1789 by the representatives of the Third Estate of the States General, in a Versailles tennis court (to which they had gone after being driven from their usual meeting place in the palace), to the effect that they would continue their deliberations until a constitution had been drawn up that would, among other things, 'maintain the true principles of the monarchy'. Certainly David thought of painting this scene, perhaps on his own initiative, although it was not long before he was ardently campaigning to be given an official (and lucrative) commission to record it for posterity.[30]

It was, in fact, David himself who drafted the clumsy and declamatory speech made to the Jacobin Club by the deputy Edmond-Louis-Alexis Dubois-Crancy on 28 October 1790 which proposed that the Tennis Club should be preserved in good condition as a monument for all lovers of freedom, and that 'the most energetic of paint brushes and the most skilful of etching needles should transmit to our descendants what, after ten centuries of oppression, France has done for them'. That brush was to be his own, and in pressing his claim David made, for the first time, a statement that, in retrospect, we can see to have been of the utmost significance: 'Let us declare that to bring our thought to life on canvas we have chosen the author of Brutus and the Horatii, this patriot and Frenchman, whose genius anticipated the Revolution [*dont le génie a devancé la Revolution*].'[31]

What exactly did David mean by this pregnant phrase? Was he implying that when painting the *Horatii* and the *Brutus* he had, in fact, been intending to convey some 'pre-Revolutionary' political message? It is easy enough to understand why in 1790 he should have hinted that this was indeed the case – though it is a hint that he was reluctant to pursue much further, despite many opportunities to do so.[32] But it is also easy to understand how the oath that had recently been taken at a Versailles tennis court by (among others) friends and acquaintances of his could have genuinely struck him as being a natural sequel to the oath sworn by the Horatii in ancient Rome which he himself had imaginatively recreated only a few years earlier. Indeed, details from the *Oath of the Horatii* were constantly being adapted to give force to representations of current events.[33] Above all, it was becoming evident that the ruthlessly austere style that David (and a few others) had adopted for depicting public scenes of ancient virtue – at a time when public scenes of modern virtue seemed non-existent – was a highly appropriate one for recording contemporary developments now that, at last, these struck participants and onlookers as being worthy of the Greeks and Romans.

For all these reasons the notion that David's artistic genius 'had always foretold the Revolution [*sembla toujours prévoir la révolution*]'[34] was repeated by others, but it does not seem that either they or David himself believed that this was because of some innate power which could be tapped only by artists. Sometimes, indeed, David was given more direct credit for anticipating the future than merely being in touch with it, for the *Horatii* and *Brutus* were praised also for their part in actually bringing about the future by 'enflaming souls for liberty'.[35] To anyone who had suggested that David possessed powers of prediction it would have been tempting to reply that, whatever might have been the case in 1784–5 – when he had painted the *Horatii* – he had lost them by 1790–1, for he would not otherwise have given so much prominence in the *Oath of the Tennis Court* (pl. 221) to men who were soon to be denounced as traitors. It was this that forced him to abandon the picture, although by 1798 he was proposing to assign to himself a sort of retrospective insight by eliminating from his composition most of the deputies in it who were 'fort insignifiants pour la postérité' and substituting 'all those who have won renown for themselves since then and who, for this reason, are of far greater interest to our descendants'.[36]

Cautious and confused though such theories were, they gradually began to

221. Jacques-Louis David, preliminary drawing for the *Oath of the Tennis Court*, pencil, pen and ink with wash and heightening with white (Paris, Louvre, Cabinet des Dessins, on deposit in the Musée National of Versailles).

222. Jacques-Louis David, unfinished and cut-down painting of the *Oath of the Tennis Court*, oil with black chalk, white chalk, brown ink on canvas (Paris, Louvre, Cabinet des Dessins on deposit in the Musée National of Versailles).

convince. It was an erstwhile friend of David, the liberal-minded Italian Filippo
Mazzei, who, when writing his memoirs in about 1810, recalled a dinner that had
taken place in Paris more than twenty-one years earlier on the day after the royal
family had been forced to move there from Versailles. David had been present and
had launched into a ferocious attack on the queen who, he hoped, would be either
strangled or hacked to pieces. Afterwards, the Countess of Albany asked whether
he was not a little mad. 'It is certain', I answered, 'that painters and poets always
have a streak of madness, and also of the prophetic.'[37] The statement is a general
one, and as far as madness went, it was already a cliché with a very long tradition
behind it. Yet it seems likely that Mazzei was specifically alluding to the discussions that a few years earlier had linked the *Oath of the Horatii* to revolutionary
developments. It is, in any case, certain that the pictures painted by David between
1785 and 1789 have, more than any other single works of art, been responsible for
implanting into historical thought the idea that a major shift in artistic style can
indicate – must indicate? – a forthcoming upheaval in society in general or even in
the very stability of the world.[38]

iii

Thus, by the end of the eighteenth century, some of the principal issues that were
thereafter to be fundamental to any consideration of the artist as augur had already
emerged. On the one hand, the artist could be thought of as consciously (though
probably secretly) making use of his intuition in order to depict, through his
choice of style or subject-matter, an impression of the future which he either feared
or desired – whether or not he believed that future to be inevitable was irrelevant
as long as posterity was able to verify that it had in fact come to pass. On the
other hand, the artist could be envisaged as no more than a component, but an
absolutely essential component, of a sort of driving historical process in which the
individual played almost no part whatsoever. In these ways the supposedly
prophetic powers of the artist could be attributed to different causes that were not
identical but that could all too easily be seen as overlapping or even inextricably
associated.

A broad theoretical basis for accepting the latter of these two versions was
established by a number of differing, and often conflicting, left-wing thinkers in
France during the first two or three decades of the nineteenth century. It cannot be
said that any of the writers involved showed an interest in the visual arts, but all of
them were much concerned with the role in society of 'the artist' – taken in an
even wider sense than the traditional one of poets, painters and musicians. Some
argued that this should be essentially subordinate to that of industrialists and
intellectuals, whose ideas artists could help to propagate in attractive and accessible
forms; others maintained that the artists themselves could take the leading role in
guiding society towards a happier future. Saint-Simon, in whose circle these
discussions originated, was by no means consistent, and although he sometimes

seemed to advocate the second of these alternatives, he always believed that the part to be played by the artist must necessarily be circumscribed by the quite specific nature of the message he would be required to convey.[39]

The following generation was more supple. The religious, not to say mystical and sentimental, tone adopted by Pierre Leroux when speaking about the role of the arts was of itself enough to lift the artist on to a far higher plane than he had occupied in the thought of Saint-Simon; and – as so often happened in the controversies of the time – it was when reproaching the artists of his own day (for their neglect of contemporary issues) that Leroux assigned to those of the past a position of pre-eminent significance: 'Poet, whence has humanity come and whither is it going? You do not know; but all the great artists of the Middle Ages believed that they knew, and indeed they did know beneath a veil of prophecy. It is this that was known to the builders of cathedrals; that was known to Dante, Raphael, Michelangelo'.[40]

We have seen that half a century earlier Schiller had proclaimed in *Die Künstler* that the special powers inherent in creative artists enabled them to play a more direct role in furthering the spiritual progress of mankind than was possible for scientists or scholars. It is therefore interesting that this poem should in 1828 have been translated into French for publication in *Le Gymnase*, a Saint-Simonian journal (which lasted for only four months), even though the social advances that the Saint-Simonians had in mind were wholly different from Schiller's hopes for humanity as a whole. Moreover, in 1826, Philippe Buchez, a disciple of Saint-Simon but far more independent than most of them, had already drawn on both traditions and declared that the genius of arts and letters lay in their ability to 'envisage the future, to discover through inspiration what is taught by the sciences, and to indicate to the population at large the road to happiness and immortality'.[41]

The overwhelming majority of such generalisations tended to be vague and to avoid any reference to specific artists. However, the Saint-Simonians took a particular interest in the works of David, and their varying reactions to him naturally throw much light on the prophetic role that they assigned to the arts.

In reviewing the exhibition that, in 1826, accompanied the posthumous sale of the contents of David's studio, a writer in the Saint-Simonian journal *Le Producteur* produced an interpretation of his abandoned and cut-down painting of the *Oath of the Tennis Court* (pl. 222) which appeared to suggest that, in some cases, an artist might find himself representing the future whether or not he was conscious of doing so. Thus he writes of the group of three men ('the idea of which is even more profound than it is ingenious') standing closely linked together below Jean-Sylvain Bailly as he reads out the oath: 'they are the Abbé Grégoire, Don Gerle and the Protestant minister Rabaut, who draw close to each other and who, in place of the memory of their dissensions, offer the hope of a common future, which will be favourable to humanity. I do not know whether the painter saw in this group everything that we can see there; but it is certain that he presents us with the very image of the fall of theological power; we see the secular and regular clergy, the orthodox and the heretic, all submerged together by the same future destiny.'[42] What, one wonders, did the writer see in the composition of these three personages, who – like the other figures in the sketch – are portrayed nude, to justify the 'certainty' with which he interpreted them in this light?

On the other hand, when discussing the *Death of Marat*, the same writer felt inclined to reproach David for not having realised that 'we men of the nineteenth century would have liked to have seen in it Charlotte Corday, quite calm as she stands next to her victim. For us she would be a heroine . . . When looking at this picture everyone was asking where was Charlotte Corday.' And he concludes that David had not assigned to woman the role that would later be recognised as having been her due because he was 'too dominated by the spirit of the times in which he lived, however contradictory and sudden the changes between them, to be able to bring together the figures of Marat and Corday'.[43]

Sometimes we are offered hints that the artist is a sensitive instrument capable of registering experiences inaccessible to ordinary human beings. Concerning David's political behaviour we are asked to remember 'that in himself he was nothing; and imagination of the kind needed to produce his art has to search wherever it can for the wherewithal with which to nourish itself. Nothing is so variable as a great artist, because nothing is so susceptible as a great artist to the creative impulse provided by new impressions.' But although these hints are not exactly negated, their force is certainly weakened by the inferences drawn from a study of David's preliminary drawings: 'we find in them tangible proof that, in our civilisation, the artist actually invents very little, whether in painting or in literature. His creative genius consists above all in the capacity to reorganise in some new way the ideas of his predecessors; he is gratified if he can add one or two new ideas to the stock of those that make up the theory and practice of his art prevalent in his lifetime.' As for the impact of the artist on society, we see in these sketches the germ of all those reminiscences of the antique that subsequently submerged the costumes and furnishing of our theatres, museums and private houses.[44]

The relatively limited role allotted to David by the Saint-Simonians in the furtherance of human progress was owing partly to the fact that his work had been both conceived and created in a Critical rather than an Organic period – the terms will be discussed shortly – as was implied in a lecture republished in *L'Organisateur, Journal de la doctrine saint-simonienne*: 'Messieurs! si l'on dit le siècle de Phidias, le siècle de Raphaël, on se borne à dire l'école de David.'[45] However, four years later, in 1834 Balzac appears to make a direct challenge to these reservations. Balzac was generally full of scorn for the Saint-Simonians, but he admired Leroux, and he must in any case have been thinking of notions that emanated from their debates when he wrote that 'a man who can exert power over thought is a sovereign. Kings rule over nations for a limited period; the artist rules over centuries; he changes the very nature of things, he revolutionises the way by which we make our moral judgements, his weight is felt in the world, he moulds the world. So it was with Gutenberg, Columbus, Schwartz, Descartes, Raphael, Voltaire, David.'[46]

Juxtaposition of the names of Raphael and David is not as surprising as it may at first appear. On other occasions also we find them associated, sometimes because the supposed strength of their (very divergent) convictions appeared to make so vivid a contrast with the general flabbiness of the artists of the July Monarchy,[47] but more usually because the antithetical ages in which they had lived could be held to be responsible for the very different roles that were assigned to them as witnesses to the progress of humanity.

For many art lovers of the early and middle years of the nineteenth century the development of Raphael presented a serious problem. It was from his later works that there seemed to have sprung that Bolognese art of the seventeenth century that was considered to be cold, pedantic and heartless. His admirers were therefore much more keen to emphasise his traditional than his innovatory qualities. The Saint-Simonians were presumably aware of this, but their main concern was another: how was his art to be placed in relation to the alternating Organic and Critical epochs that constituted the main indications of the evolution of mankind? The Organic had been exemplified above all by the flowering of paganism and then of Christianity, periods when 'all men are enrolled under the same banner – that is to say, they obey the same affections and the same thoughts, and their actions are directed towards the same ends'. Critical phases were marked by a breakdown of this unity of purpose, and they were brought about by Greek Philosophers and Protestant Reformers. During Organic periods the arts all work together in harmony under the general guidance of the Temple and the Church. The Theatre, however (and to some extent the Novel), which, both in antiquity and in the Middle Ages, begins by conforming to this pattern (through perform- ances of the mystery plays, for instance) eventually helps to destroy it through the indirect presentation of potentially subversive opinions. This demonstrates that the role of the arts is an oblique one.

There is a further difficulty. Most perfect works of art appear exactly at the moment when Organic periods are disintegrating. 'Phidias', maintains the lecturer in *L'Organisateur*, in a statement of some chronological imprecision, 'is a con- temporary of Socrates; Michelangelo and Raphael of Luther'. But this gives a misleading impression: the real reason for the simultaneous appearance of such very different kinds of genius is that artistic perfection takes a very long time to reach fulfilment and that as (with the exception of ancient Egypt) Organic periods were short lived, it was inevitable that a perfect work of art (such as a picture by Raphael) conceived in an Organic period would only emerge in a Critical one. But there was more to it than this. Although both had been Organic, the pagan period had been exclusively materialistic and the Christian period exclusively spiritualist. Hence the Critical epochs that succeeded these Organic ones had been tinged by, respectively, 'idealism' and 'physicism'. In the Organic epoch of the future, how- ever, both the materialist and the spiritualist will be fused into an absolute and eternal harmony. Meanwhile, some temporary foretaste of what will eventually occur can be provided by those perfect works of art which are likely to have been conceived in an Organic age but reach fruition in a Critical one. Thus 'the [statue of] Olympian Jupiter expresses something other than material omnipotence: intellectual power is also present in a very high degree: thus it is no longer exclusively pagan, but carries within itself some element of a spiritualist reaction: in this sense one should not say that it has *re-animated* peoples' piety, because that would imply making them turn back to the past; one should say, rather, that it has

prepared, or *animated*, new piety. We can speak in analogous terms about the
famous picture of the 'Transfiguration' (pl. 223): its *forms* are so beautiful that,
although the picture is a product of Christian thought, it might be possible to
detect in it a seed of materialist protest. So it is that great artists, men whose
prophetic gaze is constantly straining towards the future, have been the first to
demonstrate the necessity of abandoning a doctrine that is incomplete by introducing into their works some elements opposed to that doctrine; and thereby, at
the same time, the more intimate harmony that is found in their compositions
between material and spiritual beauty.'[48]

Translated from theology into history this seems to imply that Raphael has, by
virtue of his genius and the age into which he has been born (but irrespective of his
conscious intentions), been able to foresee the next stage in the foreordained
development of humanity and to incorporate some elements of materialism into a
picture that had been designed by him (and by his patrons) to be spiritual in form
and content.

Notions of this kind, usually expressed in less metaphysical terminology, soon
spread so widely that there is no point in pursuing their origins much further.
Thus it is hardly surprising to find Thoré-Bürger, who in his younger days had
been an ardent disciple of the Saint-Simonians, writing in 1865 that 'The arts must
not be judged from the point of view of the past, but from the point of view of the
future. Art is always ahead of the idea; that is its characteristic, because art is the
spontaneous feeling which precedes thought.'[49] And much of his discussion of
seventeenth-century painting is based on this premiss. Ruskin went further and
suggested that such Protestant virtues as were to be found in the England of his
day – 'the habits of philosophical investigation, of accurate thought, of domestic
seclusion and independence, of stern self-reliance and sincere upright searching into
religious truth' – had been prefigured only in the distinctive features of the Gothic
schools – 'veined foliage, and thorny fretwork, and shadowy niche, and buttressed
pier, and fearless height of subtle pinnacle and crested tower'.[50] And he claimed
that 'the labour of the whole Geological Society, for the last fifty years, has but
now arrived at the ascertainment of those truths respecting mountain form which
Turner saw and expressed with a few strokes of a camel's hair pencil fifty years
ago when he was a boy'.[51] But he appears to be taking such assumptions for
granted and no longer feels the need to look for a theory with which to give them
some backing.

In 1865, however, W.H. Lecky, the Anglo-Irish historian, drew on some of
these vaguely expressed notions in order to give substance to a book that was to
bring him, at the age of only twenty-seven, immediate fame and was eventually to
be very widely translated – into Russian and Japanese as well as into German and
Dutch: *History of the Rise and Influence of the Spirit of Rationalism in Europe*.[52]
Lecky's great love and knowledge of art were acquired during his frequent travels
in France, Italy and Spain. By 1861 he could already boast that he was familiar not
only with the contents of the Prado, where he had 'an admirable opportunity of
mastering some of the minor Spanish painters who are hardly ever to be seen in
Italy or Germany', but also with 'every other school of painting in the world'.[53]

223. Raphael, *Transfiguration* (Vatican, Pinacoteca).

He formed a collection of his own and employed a Spanish painter to make copies of works by Velázquez, who was his particular favourite.[54] In 1862 he wrote, 'I am beginning to feel as if I know almost every picture in Florence and have been reading so much about them that I am quite sick of the subject and have reverted with great pleasure to history'.[55] But despite so much first-hand knowledge and despite the fact that he was later to regret that he had 'no subject susceptible of such brilliant colouring as what I wrote about art',[56] he drew far more on literary sources than on his own impressions when discussing art in his *History*; and of these sources some of the ones he most admired were the pioneering investigations of Christian iconography by Adolphe-Napoléon Didron,[57] whose earliest works had appeared in a journal edited by the Saint-Simonian Philippe Buchez.[58]

Lecky wished to discover why belief in witchcraft and miracles, which had been so profoundly rooted in the outlook of both Catholics and Protestants, had almost disappeared from the Europe of his day. Scientific arguments, new discoveries, reasoning – all these were largely irrelevant; and so too was intelligence: 'for many centuries the ablest men were not merely unwilling to repudiate the superstition; they often pressed forward earnestly, and with the most intense conviction, to defend it'. The main cause had to be sought for in 'a gradual, insensible, yet profound modification of the habits of thought prevailing in Europe'; and the best way of gauging this change in the 'climate of opinion' was through a study of the visual arts, for 'the more the subject is examined, the more evident it becomes that, before the invention of printing, painting was the most faithful mirror of the popular mind; and that there was scarcely an intellectual movement that it did not reflect'.[59]

We have seen that claims of this kind had already been made often enough by antiquarians, connoisseurs and art historians. Lecky, however, seems to have been the first historian who had no professional concern with the arts to take them seriously. But to be serious is not necessarily to be consistent or profound, and the use made of art by Lecky to interpret history can be confused and confusing – the more so as he never fully explains the principles that guided him in his attempts to demonstrate that 'before printing was invented . . . the true course of ecclesiastical history is to be sought much more in the works of the artists than of the theologians'.[60] The course of art, he seems to imply, moves between two sets of opposing polarities: the symbolic and the anthropomorphic, and the ugly and the beautiful. True religious feeling of the noblest sort manifests itself only through the first of the categories in each set. Thus the art of the catacombs, being purely symbolic, was 'singularly sublime', a 'fact of extreme importance in ecclesiastical history', even though the early Christians had incorporated into their art many images taken over directly from paganism. Indeed, it was because of the use they made of Orpheus and naked genii (as well as of such symbolical scenes from the Bible as Jonah rescued from the fish's mouth) that they had excluded 'all images of sorrow, suffering, and vengeance, at a time that seemed beyond all others most calculated to produce them'. On the other hand, from the thirteenth century onwards, one finds displayed in Catholic art every form of anthropomorphism of which 'there is probably none which a Protestant deems so repulsive as the portraits of the First Person of the Trinity that are now so common' and that are, as Lecky's mentor, Didron, had pointed out (with admiration and awe rather than with pained disgust) to be found in much painting between Raphael and John Martin. 'In a condition of thought in which the Deity was only realised in the form of man it was extremely natural that the number of divinities should be multiplied'. Hence all those Virgins and Saints which led to forms of polytheism and idolatry. When history takes a normal course, Lecky maintains, nations discard their images as they gradually move away from idolatry; but on two occasions they did not do this – once in ancient Greece and once in the Renaissance. In these two civilisations alone images were retained, but as they changed their nature, we can make use of them to trace successive stages in man's progress, 'for the aesthetic sentiment and a devotional feeling are so entirely different, that it is impossible for both to be at the same moment predominating over the mind, and very unusual for both to be concentrated upon the same object'.[61]

Mediaeval art, claimed Lecky, is generally ugly – and in asserting this he was explicitly looking back to the tradition (discussed in an earlier chapter of this book) that had been inaugurated by Filippo Buonarroti.[62] For that reason it gives a true reflection of the devout spirit of the time. However, the aesthetic gradually supersedes the devotional – and here Lecky seems to be reflecting some of the ideas of the Saint-Simonians. This was demonstrated by the later Raphael, who helped to secularise art, and above all by Michelangelo, of whom he wrote (in a phrase that he was later to modify) that he had reduced the *Last Judgement* 'to the province of artistic criticism' for 'scarcely another great painter so completely eliminated the religious sentiment from art'.[63]

A similar process was at work in architecture: 'Cologne Cathedral, the last of the great mediaeval works, remained unfinished', while the design of St Peter's 'was confided to Michael Angelo, who had been the chief agent in the secularisation of painting'. Indeed,

> of all the edifices that have been raised by the hand of man, there is none that presents to the historian of the human mind a deeper interest than St. Peter's, and there is certainly none that tells a sadder tale of the frustration of human efforts and the futility of human hopes... For it represents the conclusion of that impulse, growing out of the anthropomorphic habits of an early civilisation, which had led men for so many centuries to express their religious feelings by sensuous images of grandeur, of obscurity, and of terrorism. It represents the absorption of the religious by the aesthetic element, which was the sure sign that the religious function of architecture had terminated. The age of the cathedrals had passed. The age of the printing press had begun.[64]

The age had, of course, begun well before Michelangelo's birth, but Lecky was anxious to demonstrate that fundamental historical change could be charted more satisfactorily through images than through words. This was because the changes that we can perceive in history – such as a decline in the belief in witchcraft – are themselves the belated consequences of far more deeply rooted shifts in the climate of opinion, and it is these that find immediate reflection in the arts (of literature, sometimes, as well as of painting):

> the development of the imagination preceded, as it always does precede, the development of the reason. Men were entranced with the chaste beauty of Greek literature before they were imbued with the spirit of abstraction, of free criticism, and of elevated philosophy, which it breathes. They learned to admire a pure style or a graceful picture before they learned to appreciate a refined creed or an untramelled philosophy. All through Europe, the first effect of the revival of learning was to produce a general efflorescence of the beautiful. A general discontent with the existing forms of belief was not produced till much later.[65]

Throughout these pages, of which he was very proud, there are difficulties in seizing the precise meaning of Lecky's arguments, but – as befits the historian of the rise of rationalism – he does not seem to be offering the almost mystical explanations suggested by the Saint-Simonians to account for the guiding role of artists: artists did not literally anticipate the future, they merely appeared to be doing so because they could communicate ideas more immediately through the medium of architecture or painting or verse than moralists or philosophers or scientists could do through that of complex language. And so it was that those currents of feeling that would eventually lead to 'the free criticism, elevated philosophy and refined creed' of the Reformation had first manifested themselves through the 'chaste beauty of Greek literature' and a 'pure style or graceful picture'.

iv

Lecky claimed that 'in the ultimate results' the Reformation had contributed more than any movement in history, 'to the emancipation of the human mind from all superstitious terrors', but he was also forced to acknowledge that 'for a time it had aggravated the very evils it was intended to correct'.[66] It was this aggravation that, naturally enough, was of primary interest to historians who were struck by the supposed prophetic insight that had been granted to great artists. And, just as naturally, it was after the First World War that such investigations became especially popular, for the outbreak of that war also, like those of the Reformation and the French Revolution, appeared to have been presaged by mysterious new developments in the arts.

Early in the 1920s interpretations along those lines began to proliferate, especially in Germany where they ranged from the vaguely philosophical notions that had been popular with the Romantics to concepts that aimed to be far more historically precise. Thus in one chapter of the essay on Proust that he began in 1922 and published three years later, the great critic and cultural historian Ernst Robert Curtius (grandson of Ernst, the archaeologist and historian of Greece) rather optimistically analysed the birth of a new kind of positive and healthy relativism which, so he claimed, would overcome the false and sceptical relativism of the nineteenth century. And he continued:

Is it surprising that a work of literature should lead us to considerations of this nature? Yet it is just the sensitive organs of the artist that are always the first to register a new way of seeing. If historical prediction is possible; if, to put it more correctly and less pretentiously, we can envisage in advance the essential outlines of some future period, this can only be done by art, never by historical research, never by academic philosophy. 'Novels', said Friedrich Schlegel, 'are the Socratic dialogues of our time; human wisdom has escaped from the academy to this freer form.' Creative works of literature and art are milestones which enable us to trace the curve of the modern spirit. We should detect in the relativism of Proust, as in the representation of space to be seen in modern painting, indications of a change in consciousness whose importance it would be rash to underestimate.[67]

When Max J. Friedländer, director of the Print Room of the Kaiser Friedrich Museum in Berlin, read this he commented that an example of Curtius's theory that 'decisive cultural changes are to be traced earliest of all in works of art' was provided by Dürer's *Apocalypse* which had been 'a premonition of the Reformation'.[68] Friedländer's response to a passage that must have given him much pleasure was natural enough, for only a few years earlier he had written in his monograph on Dürer, published in Leipzig in 1921, that in creating the *Apocalypse* 'the sensitivity of that artist's spirit [*seine empfindliche Seele*] had 'felt the storm that was hovering in the air and that would burst with the spiritual upheaval of the Reformation'.[69]

Dürer's fifteen large wood engravings illustrating the Revelation, then attributed to St John the Evangelist, were published by him in 1498 in the form of a book which included the text itself in separate German and Latin translations. The confused and barbaric scenes described by the writer as he pours out the prophetic vision granted to him of the forthcoming battles between good and evil, leading to the destruction of Babylon and its replacement by the new Jerusalem, are given far more vivid reality in Dürer's plates than in the words he was trying to represent. The engravings quickly became famous, a second edition appeared in 1511 and they were widely imitated throughout Europe. Three centuries later certain images from the series – such as *The Four Horsemen of the Apocalypse* – entered deeply into the Romantic consciousness, and at much the same time art historians began to explore their style and significance.

Scenes from the Apocalypse had been illustrated very frequently in German art – but never on so complete a scale – and although Dürer's genius lifted his treatment of it on to a far higher plane than that of any of his predecessors, he had looked back to earlier versions of the subject for some of his ideas and images. All this was brought to light by scholars of the nineteenth and early twentieth centuries who also discussed other millenarial themes that were especially popular in German art: the very date of 1498 was significant in this respect. It was, of course, fully acknowledged that the feeling that the world has been betrayed by false spiritual leaders and is full of evil and corruption which can only be purged by fire and sword is a very old and frequently recurring one; but it was possible to argue, plausibly enough in the light of available evidence, that sentiments to this effect had rarely been expressed with such vehemence as they were towards the end of the fifteenth century. They were common enough in Italy as well as in Germany, but because the Revelation of St John could itself be interpreted as having been directed against Rome (though a Rome that was still pagan), there was naturally much speculation about Dürer's own attitude to Rome and the papacy when he embarked on the *Apocalypse*. Nothing whatsoever was (or is) known about this. None the less – in much the same way that David's commitment to the Revolution in 1789–90 encouraged historians to look for hidden evidence of his 'pre-Revolutionary politics' in the startling pictures painted by him five years earlier – the fact that, twenty years *after* the publication of the *Apocalypse*, Dürer was to side with Luther when he made his challenge to Rome, inevitably led some scholars to claim that in 1498 he 'already belonged to the younger generation of spirits in Germany, who placed their trust in a pure form of belief, and he belonged not so much among the humanists as already much more among the reformers'.[70]

It was, however, not until 1921 that this claim was seriously pursued and that renewed attempts were made to discover profound spiritual meanings in the woodcuts. And to a generation that had barely survived the destruction of civilisation new significance was to be discerned in Dürer's images. Over a period of four or five years events so unbelievably strange and awesome had been experienced that their very possibility could hardly have been imagined only a decade earlier. Men had seen ships torn apart by torpedoes fired from beneath the seas; cities battered by bombs dropped from above the clouds; soldiers choked by yellow clouds of poison gas or flattened by armour-plated tanks; kings and emperors fleeing into exile or being massacred with their families; revolutions threatening to turn the world upside down. And many witnesses (using the word in its widest sense) of such scenes believed that all this had been a consequence of that gross worship of materialist values that had prevailed before 1914, and that, after much-needed but terrible purification, the world was now ready for a new era of idealism. How poignant for such survivors must have been the sight of Dürer's visionary cavalry (pl. 224), mounted on lion-headed horses spitting fire and hurtling down towards earth at the sound of the archangel's trumpet, while below them four angels – their features seemingly exhausted by the strain of so much violence – swing their long swords in order to hack through the women and horses and crowned heads who cower at their feet; or of the overpowering invincible figure of St Michael who stands on the dragon as he pierces its throat with his lance while his companions perform similar butchery in the service of the true faith (pl. 225); or of the Four Horsemen of the Apocalypse (ancestors of so many subsequent representations of blind destruction) who charge over the world with relentless impetuosity, their eyes fixed on distant targets, indifferent to the fate of high born and low born alike who are trampled beneath the hooves of Death on his skeletal horse (pl. 226); or even of the quiet final scene in which the dragon of evil is driven by an angel into the bottomless pit within which it will be locked for a thousand years, while above, on a hill, another angel points out to the youthful St John the new Jerusalem, with its mediaeval towers and gables and steeples,

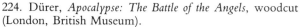

224. Dürer, *Apocalypse: The Battle of the Angels*, woodcut (London, British Museum).

225. Dürer, *Apocalypse: St Michael fighting the Dragon*, woodcut (London, British Museum).

which comes down from God out of heaven, 'prepared as a bride adorned for her husband' (pl. 227). Can we be surprised that it was in these years that Dürer's rendering of St John's Revelation was retrospectively accredited with prophetic powers extending to situations, in the sixteenth as in the twentieth century, that he could never have envisaged?

In 1921, a few months before his death, Max Dvořák, Professor of the History of Art at Vienna University, gave a lecture on 'Dürer's *Apocalypse*' which was published posthumously in Munich in 1924 in a volume of essays significantly entitled *Kunstgeschichte als Geistesgeschichte*.[71] Dvořák, who had succeeded Wickhoff and Riegl in the Chair and who was a friend of Kokoschka, had for some years been attracted to the new anti-naturalist art of Germany and Central Europe which he felt offered an alternative to the crass materialism of his surroundings. Inevitably, as a highly trained art historian, he found himself looking back at certain earlier unrealistic schools of painting – notably that of 'Mannerism' – in the light of his current enthusiasms; and because he believed that artistic styles expressed the deepest and innermost beliefs and aspirations of the times in which they were created, he assigned to the artists who practised them a role that he

226. Dürer, *Apocalypse: The Four Horsemen of the Apocalypse*, woodcut (London, British Museum).

227. Dürer, *Apocalypse: The Angel with the Key hurls the Dragon into the Abyss, and Another Angel shows St John the New Jerusalem*, woodcut (London, British Museum).

himself did not hesitate to describe as prophetic. His general standpoint is perhaps best indicated in the closing words of a lecture on El Greco which he delivered in 1920 and which was later published alongside the lecture on Dürer:

It is not difficult to see why, over the next two hundred years, El Greco was to become more and more neglected; these were years dominated by the natural sciences, by mathematical thought and a superstitious regard for causality, for technical development and the mechanisation of culture – years dominated by the eye and the mind but demonstrating an almost complete disregard for the heart. Today, this materialistic culture is approaching its end. I am thinking not so much of its external demise as of its inner collapse which, for over a generation now, we have been able to observe affecting every sphere of cultural life, especially our philosophical and scientific thinking, until today it is disciplines such as sociology and psychology which take precedence. Indeed, even in the natural sciences the old, positivist suppositions, once regarded as absolute, have been fundamentally shaken. We have seen how both in literature and art

228. Dürer, *Apocalypse: St John receiving his Commands from Heaven*, woodcut (London, British Museum).

229. Dürer, *Apocalypse: The Whore of Babylon*, woodcut (London, British Museum).

there has been a turning towards a spirituality freed from all dependence on naturalism, a tendency similar to that of the Middle Ages and the mannerist period. And, finally, one can observe in all cultural sectors a certain unity of events which is apparently directed, by some mysterious law of human destiny, towards a new, spiritual, anti-materialistic age. In the eternal rivalry between spirit and matter, the scales now seem to be balanced in favour of the spirit. It is thanks to this turn of events that we have come to recognise in El Greco a great artist and a prophetic spirit, one whose fame is assured for all time.[72]

Thus El Greco fulfilled the more mystical requirements of the prophetic role by almost unconsciously incarnating and expressing those aspects of the spirit of his time that – so Dvořák hoped (with the same sadly misplaced optimism shown by Curtius at much the same moment) – were about to prevail in the wake of the World War. The case of Dürer was rather different, even though Dvořák could not have defined it adequately without his belief in the powers of divination granted to supreme artists. For Dürer is credited with having produced in the *Apocalypse* not merely 'the first great German work of art of our era' but also 'a sermon as profound and eloquent as any by Luther but earlier in time [*eine Predigt von Luthers Tiefe und Beredsamkeit vor Luther*] in which spirit speaks to spirit'. The artist's prophetic role is confirmed in Dvořák's astonishing phrase that 'as late as 1521 he fulminates in his diaries against the Holy See, when on his journey through the Netherlands he hears an erroneous rumour of Luther's death'. The implication of this can be only that Dürer's hostility to the papacy can in some way be traced back to the time when he was working on the *Apocalypse*. But it is not, in fact, until the middle of 1519 that we have any hint of his views in this respect (for it is in that year that he is recorded as being preoccupied with the teachings of Luther). Dvořák's assessment of Dürer's sentiments twenty-one years earlier depends entirely on his analysis of the imagery and style that he finds in the wood engravings of the *Apocalypse*.

Dvořák concentrates essentially on two of the plates, from the first of which he deduces (in a not very comprehensible manner) what was the basis of Dürer's approach to visionary subjects in general, and from the second what was his attitude to specific issues of the day.[73]

In the print showing *St John receiving his Commands from Heaven* (pl. 228) Dvořák contrasts the peaceful landscape below, which Dürer could have depicted from his own personal observations, with the fantastic heavenly scene above: this could have come to the artist only through meditation on 'strange, yet long-familiar ideas of supranatural powers, shapes and images seen in churches and old manuscripts, things which live in the imagination only and are yet more real than anything else'. Dürer, however, is able to fuse the two spheres of his consciousness (the one based on experience of the senses, the other on supra-natural impressions) into a dreamlike unity. Such subjectivism would not have been possible in the Middle Ages when man's relationship to the universe had been conditioned exclusively by general theological explanations. However, Flemish and Italian artists had 'sought to remodel this relationship on the basis of observation and experience', and (unlike these artists themselves) the Germans had made use of their discoveries not in the interests of imitating nature and exploring her laws but so as to enrich the inner life of the imagination. It is for this reason that 'it would be quite wrong to explain the strange style of the *Apocalypse* as a last flicker of the spirit of the Middle Ages'.

Dvořák's notion that the *Apocalypse* was to be seen as a 'polemical pamphlet', and a 'revolutionary hymn directed against Rome' depended, above all, on his interpretation of the plate of *The Whore of Babylon* (pl. 229), and his approach to this is far more traditional than his treatment of *St John receiving his Commands from Heaven*. He suggests (as others had done before him) that by basing his image of the Babylonian whore on a drawing of a beautiful woman – perhaps a courtesan – which he had made in Venice three years earlier, Dürer clearly intended to equate her with the Rome of his own day (just as – so Dvořák assumes – St John's onslaught had been aimed at the pagan Rome of *his* times). Dvořák backs up his argument by proceeding to 'read' Dürer's mysterious language in much the same spirit that, over the previous two centuries, antiquarians had adopted when trying to understand the gestures and expressions to be found on Greek vases or mediaeval tapestries. Thus only one member of the crowd appears to be admiring the Whore: a little monk with wide open eyes and sensuously painted lips sinks to his knees and worships her. The faces of the other onlookers reflect anxiety and terror or revulsion. The young page and the woman cast timid glances. The eyes of the peasant farmer express defiance and contempt. The central figure which we may assume to represent Dürer himself stands with legs apart, arms akimbo, in an attitude of unshakeable rectitude, and regards the Whore with critical eyes . . .

The weaknesses of such an approach do not need to be emphasised here;[74] nor does the fact that an allegory disguised in so baffling a manner that it cannot be interpreted for more than four centuries hardly constitutes a very convincing 'polemical pamphlet' or 'revolutionary hymn'. What is of importance is the impulse that was given by Dvořák, at a particularly significant moment, to the notion of the artist as prophet. Dvořák's concept of that role is, it is true, very different from that of Friedländer (the coincidence of dates makes it unlikely that either knew of the other). For Dvořák the *Apocalypse* is 'almost a piece of autobiography' and represents Dürer's personal view regarding the major spiritual problems of his time. For Friedländer, the foreshadowing of the Reformation by the *Apocalypse* is much less the consequence of conscious deliberation than an instinctive response to a very early change in barometric pressure (to use his own climatic metaphor). Yet there seems little doubt that the inspiration for both men must have come from a contemplation of those artistic developments that, so it seemed, had so uncannily forecast the experiences that they themselves had lived through.

v

Talk of the Apocalypse was to be heard throughout Europe in the decades around 1900,[75] but it did not always betoken vengeful doom. 'Today', wrote Franz Marc in January 1912 in his subscription prospectus for the almanac of the *Blaue Reiter*,

art is moving in a direction of which our fathers would never even have dreamed. We stand before the new pictures as in a dream, and we hear the apocalyptic horsemen in the air. There is an artistic tension all over Europe. Everywhere new artists are greeting each other, a look, a handshake is enough for them to understand each other!

We know that the basic ideas of what we feel and create today have existed before us, and we are emphasising that in *essence* they are not new. But we must proclaim the fact that everywhere in Europe new forces are sprouting like a beautiful unexpected seed, and we must point out all the places where new things are originating.[76]

For some years before the outbreak of the First World War a number of painters in different European countries thought of themselves as creating forms of art that could be described as prophetic: art that aimed to influence human attitudes to the present and thus to foresee a world that could be very different in the future. The futures that they envisaged varied widely. So, too, did the artistic styles that they brought into being in order to express their visions, but both to themselves and to the public that first saw them, and even to art historians writing about them generations later, all these styles seemed to mark a very important break with representational traditions that stretched back to the Renaissance. Pictures by these painters still tend to hang in galleries specially designed for modern and contemporary art rather than in the great national museums built in the nineteenth century to house masterpieces of all periods; and their reputations are still often gauged more by their perceived contribution to the birth of modernism than by any reasoned attempt to analyse their intrinsic painterly achievements (just as, in a much-despised past, an artist's standing might be measured by the importance of the subjects that he painted rather than by a consideration of his actual gifts). So fundamental is this aspect of their work that it is not surprising to discover that from an early date they were credited by their admirers and detractors (but rarely by themselves) with having in some way 'anticipated' not only subsequent developments in the arts, but also the new world that came into being between the end of 1914 and the end of 1917. To some extent, however, the formation and later interpretation of all these artists can be associated with concepts that had first been formulated in Paris many years earlier.

It was there that artists ever since the time of David, followed by Courbet and Daumier and then Manet and the Impressionists, had been most forceful (though not always very precise) in claiming that new developments in the progress of humanity could only be recorded through new forms of creative expression. Towards the end of the nineteenth century Gauguin, Van Gogh and their contemporaries had, however, modified this line of thought by taking it a stage further, while at the same time narrowing its scope. These men, whose own talents were ignored, rather than derided, by the wider public, argued not so much that they would win recognition after their deaths as that it was their mission to determine the direction in which art was going to move so that they could themselves be on the side of the future. Never had speculation about the art of the future been so intense as it was in these years. For Van Gogh it became something of an obsession, and his conclusions gave him the courage to continue working under appalling strain: 'the painter of the *future*', he wrote in May 1888, '*will be a colourist such as has never yet existed*'[77] – words that well describe his own achievements at the time. Thus the notion of art as prophecy was already deeply enshrined in French thought well before Guillaume Apollinaire systematically set out to use this criterion as his gauge of quality and then summed up this phase of his life in the beautiful lines published less than nine months before his death:

> Pitié pour nous qui combattons toujours aux frontières
> De l'illimité et de l'avenir
> Pitié pour nos erreurs pour nos péchés.[78]

It must surely have been Picasso and his other friends among the Cubists whom he had chiefly in mind, for during the previous decade they appeared to have introduced into art novelties more daring than any that had been made for centuries.

Restrained, sombre colours – predominantly greys and ochres – evenly lit across the surface of the canvas and divided by strong verticals, horizontals, and a few diagonals and curves (pl. 230); geometric shapes hinting at squares and rectangles,

230. Picasso, *Violin and Grapes*, spring–summer 1912 (Collection, The Museum of Modern Art, New York).

but quite uneven in size and juxtaposed to no discernible end; a confused but static jigsaw puzzle in which none of the pieces fitted naturally so that they had had to be arbitrarily broken up in order to keep them in place: that is what was at first to be seen in Cubist pictures, and it resembled nothing that could be seen outside them. But a closer look – and recourse to a catalogue or the label attached to the frame – gradually revealed that these shapes were not, in fact, arbitrary and did not, as some critics claimed, amount to no more than abstract forms. Hard, solid objects emerged from the faceted background – and then seemed to merge back into it and disappear: a table, a guitar, a clarinet, a violin, a pipe, a newspaper, sometimes a portrait, occasionally a fragmented word. By clinging to such clues the spectator could begin to make out more; and what had at first seemed quite meaningless turned out to comprise fragmented objects visualised from different angles in a comprehensible framework.

Picasso and Braque, the joint creators of Cubism, did not at the time make any public statements about the motives that inspired the transformation of natural appearances to be seen in their works; but the clear impression we get from their contemporaries, and even from later statements made by the artists themselves, is that (whether or not they were, as is sometimes claimed, influenced by new developments in philosophy and the sciences) they were primarily concerned with problems of representation and form and with efforts to create a far more 'real reality' than the one that was accessible only to the eye. The criticism and re-generation of society were of no interest to them as artists. Nor, despite the fact that they were (according to their supporters) responding with enthusiasm to the new world that was coming into being around them, did they appear to revel in the fundamental break that their own art made with that of the past. On the contrary, the continuity between their paintings and those of Cézanne, Courbet and even David was frequently stressed by their advocates.[79]

In Holland and Italy, Germany and Russia there was no surviving tradition of this kind to support the more imaginative artists of the day. When, to very varying extents and in very different ways, they tried to adapt the new language being worked out in Paris they gloried in the novelty of their aims and achievements. The intense and still-living controversies that quickly developed about the extent – or even existence – of a debt owed by all these artists to French forerunners indicate how essential it had by now become to belong to the 'vanguard'. And, outside France, artistic change was often accompanied by much declamatory literature to explain and publicise the importance for art, and even mankind as a whole, of what was being designed.

Thus in the pictures that in 1913 Giacomo Balla dedicated to the theme of 'Speed', intersecting curves of clashing colours, which seem to deepen and recede in intensity as we look at them, sweep across the surface in both horizontal and vertical directions (pl. 231). Landscape is hinted at, but certainly not represented, and these paintings seem to carry to their most extreme a number of the ambitions of the Futurists as they had been set out by Balla and his friends three years earlier: 'ALL FORMS OF IMITATION MUST BE DESPISED, ALL FORMS OF ORIGINALITY GLORIFIED . . . ALL SUBJECTS PREVIOUSLY USED MUST BE SWEPT AWAY IN ORDER TO EXPRESS OUR

231. Giacomo Balla, *Abstract Speed – The Car has passed*, 1913 (London, Tate Gallery).

WHIRLING LIFE OF STEEL, OF PRIDE, OF FEVER AND OF SPEED . . . UNIVERSAL DYNAMISM
MUST BE RENDERED IN PAINTING AS A DYNAMIC SENSATION . . .'[80]

In the canvases that Piet Mondrian began to compose shortly afterwards all the movement and stridency so characteristic of Balla and the Futurists is utterly rejected. 'Futurism', he explained,

> although a great step beyond naturalism, is excessively concerned with human sensations. Cubism, which still relies for its subject-matter on earlier forms of beauty (and is therefore less of our time than Futurism), took the great step towards abstraction; it thus belongs both to our time and to the future: modern not in its content but in its effect. I think of myself as belonging to neither tendency, while recognising in myself the contemporary spirit of both.[81]

In his *Composition, No.* 7 of 1914 (pl. 232) no recognisable allusion to the outside world survives, whatever may have been the inspiration of the actual patterns we see. Straight black lines run vertically and horizontally up and along the canvas, becoming thinner and lighter as they approach the edges which they never quite reach. They are constantly being slightly dislocated from their course, and we are

232. Piet Mondrian, *Composition No. 7 (Façade)*, 1914 (Fort Worth, Kimbell Art Museum).

233. Kasimir Malevich, *Painterly Realism. Boy with Knapsack – Colour Masses in the Fourth Dimension*, 1914–15 (Collection, The Museum of Modern Art, New York).

thus presented with a kaleidoscope of rectangles and squares of different sizes which, in a few cases, terminate in semi-circles so as to resemble the plan of an apsed basilica. These lozenges are coloured in the most delicate dove grey and ochre and pale blue with touches of pink and mauve, sometimes thickened to produce an effect of creamy impasto, at others quite smooth. It was through pictures such as this that Mondrian strove for 'the spiritual, therefore, the divine, the universal'. This, he felt certain, was 'an art for the future'.

The aims that Kandinsky had set out a little earlier were not dissimilar and were just as mystical. They were also very ambitious, for he believed that painting was 'one of the most powerful agents of the spiritual life' and that its purpose was to 'serve the development and refinement of the human soul'. In his canvases dating from the last years of peace, figures and landscapes can barely be detected (or even imagined) in the patches and scrawls, the thrusts and explosions of vivid colour that burst upon us. For him the gradual eradication of recognisable subject-matter was a necessary step in his battle against the tainted materialism of the times, and it would eventually lead to the realm of pure spirituality.[82]

At much the same time Malevich took the most drastic step of all. In his *Colour Masses in the Fourth Dimension* (pl. 233), which was first exhibited in 1915, two squares of differing dimensions, one red and the other black, are spatially juxtaposed to each other and to the rectangular borders of the grey canvas on which they lie in such a way that the eye can discern no clear or logical relationship between them. Like Mondrian, and like many Russian artists, Malevich respected the Futurists as pioneers who had 'opened up the "new" in modern life: the beauty of speed'; none the less, he rejected Futurism and 'spat on the altar of its art'. For Futurism was still too tied to natural appearances, while the Suprematism that he advocated aimed to move one stage further in pursuit of the new, and thus convey the modern exclusively through geometrical shapes of pure colour.[83]

German painters also aimed to extend and then to defy the frontiers of modern art, but their attitude to it tended to be very different. Their pictures reflected the visible world clearly enough, but it was a reflection distorted by fear, violence and hatred. In Kirchner's Berlin street scenes of 1913 and 1914 tapering giantesses stride past us, arrogant and ostentatious in their harsh greens and blues and reds; their faces no more than masks into which painted eyes and lips have been brutally slashed, the garish feathers on their hats all but concealing the buildings just visible behind them. And what seem to us (in the light of subsequent events) to be the most remarkable German pictures of this time were painted by another artist working in Berlin, the Jewish Ludwig Meidner, who combined the Expressionism of Kirchner and his friends with distant echoes of Cubism and Futurism in order to produce his 'Apocalyptic Landscapes' of 1912 and 1913 (pl. 234). The collapse and destruction of great cities had been exultantly described in literature ever since the Bible and had been represented in luridly sensational pictures by many artists, including some who had made a speciality of the genre, such as 'Monsù Desiderio' in the seventeenth and John Martin in the nineteenth century. But the housefronts that lurch and topple to the ground in Meidner's stridently coloured canvases; the panic-stricken, bowler-hatted figures who attempt to flee over streets that seem to

234. Ludwig Meidner, *Apocalyptic Landscape*, 1913 (Los Angeles County Museum of Art).

have melted into jagged tracks through some decayed and disintegrating jungle; the naked and twisted corpses, their arms and legs outstretched, that sprawl amidst the rubbish of a town struck by a devastating earthquake; the very explosions that seem to burst in the sky and tear it to shreds – all these were too painfully ferocious and jarring to appeal to that craving for the picturesque and the exotic that had marked earlier ventures into scenes of ruin and terror.[84]

Modernity, not horror, was what Meidner claimed to be striving for, and when in 1914 he discussed his aims he gave no hint that he was gloating over some terrible destructive force which would one day be visited on Berlin, no indication that he shared Kirchner's revulsion for the anguished crowds that thronged the city's streets. On the contrary. He wished to do no more than 'paint our home, the great town for which we have an infinite love'.[85] Nevertheless, the violence and intensity of the language with which he described how this was to be done reveal much about the nature of the pictures that he had just completed. We must, he

explained, abandon those touches of rural sweetness that had characterised the
urban views of the Impressionists such as Monet and Pissarro in the seventies and
the eighties: 'A street does not consist of tonal values; it is rather a bombardment
of hissing rows of windows, of blustering cones of light between vehicles of all
kinds and thousands of leaping globes, human rags, advertising signboards and
masses of threatening, formless colours (pl. 235).' Three factors were of special
importance for the painter of urban scenes: light, viewpoint and use of the straight
line. Light must not be spread over the whole picture. On the contrary, its flow is
uneven. It breaks things up. 'We become dazzled by a chaos of light and dark
between rows of tall houses.' Light makes everything move so that towers and
houses and lanterns appear to be hanging or swaying. Light can be white or silver
or violet or blue.

Even more important is the artist's viewpoint.

If, for instance, we stand in the middle of the street, in front of us at the far end
all the houses are seen as vertical and their rows of windows seem to confirm
conventional perspective because they run along to the horizon. But the houses
near us – which we can see with only half an eye – appear to wobble and to
collapse. Here the lines, which in reality are parallel, shoot steeply upwards
and meet each other. Gables, chimneys, windows are dark, chaotic masses,
fantastically cut short and many-sided.

As for the straight line, whose use had been banned from painting, it alone could

235. Ludwig Meidner, *Wahnsee Bahnhof*, ink with white highlights, 1913 (Los Angeles County
Museum of Art).

render faithfully the forms of the modern town, and its beauty was becoming apparent to the contemporaries of modern engineers: 'Let it be said in passing that the modern Cubist movement also feels great sympathy for geometrical forms, and that their significance is even greater for us', for 'how many triangles, squares, polygons and circles assault us in the streets!' As regards colour, there was not much that needed to be said. To paint Berlin, black and white should be used, only a little ultramarine and ochre, but much umber.

Meidner concluded with words that appear to echo those to be found in the Futurist manifestoes to which he explicitly refers:

> Let us paint what is near to us, the town which is our universe, the streets full of tumult, the elegance of its iron bridges, its gasometers hanging in mountains of white clouds, the shrieking colours of its autobuses and the locomotives of its express trains, the swaying telegraph wires (are they not like a song?), the harlequinades of its advertisement columns, and then Night, the Night of the great town ... Would not the dramatic character of a well-painted factory chimney move us more deeply than all the 'Fires in the Borgo' and 'Battles of Constantine' by Raphael?

A few pictures (and a few concepts) chosen almost at random from very many more just as striking – pictures painted in Amsterdam and St Petersburg, Milan and Berlin; pictures that celebrate a new world changing with a speed (the speed of the automobile and the aeroplane) that appeared to grow more remorseless every year, and pictures that reject the growth of that world with horror; pictures that are sometimes related to each other in style and sometimes totally unconnected; yet pictures that all have two features in common. They were created by artists who were not only fully aware of the gulf that separated them from earlier art, but who rejoiced in the existence of that gulf. And they were painted only a few years before the world in which they had been created was violently blown away and irrevocably destroyed by war and revolution. Chance – or Prescience?

It was the painters of the avant-garde themselves who first began to discuss the issue of whether the momentous events of these years had in some strange way been foretold in their works and in those of their fellow artists. And their answers differed widely. What may be the earliest example of the matter being raised occurred within a few months of the outbreak of the war. When asked whether a large painting that he had completed shortly before Christmas 1913 – 'a non-representational picture, a free pattern of coloured arabesque, explosive and ballistic in its design'[86] – demonstrated that he had already then foreboded war, Kandinsky replied, 'Not this war. I had no premonition of that. But I knew that a terrible struggle was going on in the spiritual sphere, and that made me paint the picture'.[87] Meidner, on the other hand, was very much more specific when, in 1919, he declared that his pre-war pictures had been painted at a time when 'the great world storm was already baring its teeth and casting its harsh shadow over the whimpering hand which was carrying my brush'.[88] In the same year Malevich wrote that 'Cubism and Futurism were revolutionary movements in art, antici-pating the revolution in the economic and political life of 1917'.[89]

It may, however, be significant that Malevich should have indicated the two styles that he himself had self-consciously, even publicly, rejected when adopting Suprematism as the one that he looked upon as the most appropriate to the times. Certainly, some other members of the pre-war avant-garde were keen to disengage their own particular art from any direct association with the future which actually had come into being as opposed to the future for which they had been so ardently struggling before 1914. Thus Vlaminck – whose pioneering role as an admirer of African artefacts and as a painter of vigorous Fauve landscapes had been much praised by Guillame Apollinaire – went so far as to imply that it was the futility of the Cubists, and above all of their admirers, that had foreshadowed the inevitable devastation that was to follow their triumph. Writing in 1929 he described how

> towards the middle of June 1914 I went into a modern art gallery in the rue La Boétie. A few aesthetes were gazing fascinated at one of the latest Cubist lucubrations which hung above M. Paul Guillaume's desk, and they were talking about it in the tones of initiates or converts. The ground trembled beneath me. To see these members of the so-called élite – young intellectuals and grave figures with gold-rimmed spectacles – looking with respect at these geometrical and coloured shapes; to hear them ask for explanations from those who financed such mystifications, convinced that for a modest sum they would win their share of the Spanish treasure – all this gave me a premonition of a precipice. I saw no limits to human stupidity and realised that it was capable of the wildest lunacies. Suddenly, in a flash, I foresaw the war.[90]

Distinctions of this kind soon disappeared once the notion that the artists of the avant-garde had in some ways had a premonition of the coming new world was taken over by historians of culture: Fauvism, Cubism, Futurism, Suprematism, Neo-Plasticism, Expressionism – all, indiscriminately, were called upon to supply the necessary evidence.[91]

Kandinsky's denial that his 'explosive' picture of 1913 had been based on an intuition of the imminence of war was made in a letter to Michael Sadler to whom he had sent it as a gift. The denial produced a strong effect on Sadler, for nearly twenty years later he returned to the issue and proceeded to discuss it within a much wider context. Sadler, who had been born in 1861, was a well-known figure in the English educational world. He had become a discriminating collector of paintings and, in 1912, he was brought into contact with Kandinsky by his son, who, two years afterwards, was to translate *Über das Geistige in der Kunst* into English. Father and son visited the Kandinskys in Bavaria and were much impressed by the simplicity of their way of life and gentleness of character and by the small pictures on glass that hung on the walls of their country cottage, 'very brightly coloured, of religious subjects mostly – some 18th century Bavarian peasant work, some painted by a man in Murnau, the last who practises the old traditional art, and a few (mystic and primitive looking) by Kandinsky himself'.[92] Sadler bought some works on the spot, but the large picture, *Fragment 2* (pl. 236) for *Composition VII*, the most important of his pre-war paintings, which Kandinsky

236. Wassily Kandinsky, *Fragment 2 for Composition VII*, 1913 (Buffalo, Albright-Knox Art Gallery).

unexpectedly sent to him in England, may have come as something of a surprise. In any case, he nicknamed it 'War in the air' and it was 'a year later, by which time we had got only too familiar with bombs and fighting planes' that he asked the artist about its significance.[93]

In 1932 Sadler, who had by then been knighted and was Master of University College, Oxford, gave a lecture to the Liberal Summer School in that city, and he accompanied it with an exhibition, lasting two days and installed in the Hall and Library of his college, of 'nearly two hundred examples of modern art (pictures, drawings, lithographs, colour prints, sculpture, pottery and textiles)'. The title of his lecture was 'Modern Art and Revolution', and it was devoted to the question of 'whether the temper of mind and trend of feeling disclosed by the work of many modern artists portend economic and social revolution'.[94] It was immediately published by Leonard and Virginia Woolf for the Hogarth Press as one of their 'Day to Day' pamphlets.

Sadler's exploration of a theme that tends to attract the brash, the self-confident and the mystic is diffident and cautious with a predisposition to the rational. But he pays for these qualities by a reluctance to follow any argument very far or to come to any conclusion about specific cases. He circles round the main issue, draws quite near to it at times and then quickly moves on to other matters, such as the principal characteristics of modern art and, more rewardingly, the nature of the 'repugnance, anger and alarm' aroused by it. The pertinent comments he makes about this, often based on his own experiences, lead him to imply that it is in fact the prophetic powers of the innovating artist that make us feel uneasy with him. And yet he is not at all precise about the actual existence of such powers. Referring to the great changes in taste that have punctuated European art at irregular intervals he admits that 'it is hazardous to attempt an answer to the question whether, in these early transmutations of taste, the artist was adjusting himself to new conditions already in being or was a harbinger of startling changes still to come'. He is, at first, rather more confident in suggesting that 'in the aggressive modernism of much of the art of our own day there is something minatory, something that frightens those who are timid about the future. Do these new developments in art actually portend a drastic change in the way we now live and in the faiths which have power over our wills?' But then, characteristically, he retreats – for current movements in modern art 'are so various and disparate that they may point only to a future of confusion'.

There is, however, one short but amazing passage in Sadler's lecture in which he throws caution recklessly to the winds. He was unwilling to accept the full implications of Kandinsky's disclaimer of premonitory intuition and went so far as to suggest that not only he but Meryon also – in an etching of the Ministry of the Marine in Paris, dating from 1866 – had been able to prophesy the aerial onslaughts of the Great War: 'It was almost the last plate he etched before he died. In silhouette against storm-clouds which are bright with dawn or sunset, enemy aircraft fly to the attack. Some of the planes are shaped like fish or birds or horses, but others might pass for what we see today.'

Such a flight of fancy is quite uncharacteristic of a speaker who proclaimed that 'I do not want to say a shade more than I feel', and what appear to be his most considered reflections on the matter are far more muted:

A few men of genius practising the art of painting have had premonitions. These premonitions were vague, whether gloomy or sanguine. But some men of unusual sensibility do seem to have had an inkling of what was in the air, and of what was about to spring from causes which were still hidden from common observation. Nevertheless, we must allow for the fact that these causes, having long been in unnoticed operation, may be understood by a few men who have had special reason or facilities for studying them. And it is always possible that from such a source as this the painter may have caught hints of what was coming.

A conclusion as careful and rational as this may well appear to deflate the significance of the issue as a whole, and indeed, by the end of his lecture Sadler himself appears to have felt that the portents to which he had earlier drawn attention were very much less weighty than he had once thought. Tensions in modern art seem to adumbrate only 'deep changes in the existing economic order and in our form of government and, therefore, in our ways of education'. The new world 'may involve for some people, as Vigeland's simplified sculpture at Oslo suggests, a return to a life more primitive than we are at present wont to lead'. Thus 'to meet the needs of this age it seems inevitable that there should be a change in the formula of a liberal education. Something that will integrate body, mind and emotions is called for.'

A little more than a decade later it was all too apparent that such prophecies were pathetically tame (though it is true that the 'more primitive' life apparently foreshadowed by Vigeland's 'simplified sculpture' would presumably have involved total nudity). Looking back in 1946 on more than thirty years of unparalleled horror, which had none the less also witnessed much painting of the highest quality, the French art historian Germain Bazin was far more uncompromising than Sadler in trying to link these two phenomena. In a short book which he called *Le Crépuscule des images* he insisted that the artist 'is like a kind of magus gifted with second sight who from the palimpsest of an epoch can unravel its destiny and express it in the language of forms. For the artist is often a prophet whose vision is not so much the product of its own time as the augur of time to come. A work of art – at least when it is a work of genius – is an anticipation or a correspondence rather than a consequence.' The example he chose to illustrate this point is somewhat strange and was understandably described by him as very remarkable. Tintoretto's mural painting of *Paradise* in the Palazzo Ducale in Venice (which dates from about 1588) apparently provides a visual equivalent for the notion of universal gravity at the very moment when Copernicus had just discovered the principle of heliocentrism (which occurred in the first decade of the sixteenth century), of which Tintoretto certainly knew nothing.[95]

The intuitions of artists, claims Bazin, are often keener than those of thinkers, and the creative force of artists, which is not restrained by the logical mechanism of words, always anticipates and reaches further than written thought. Thus it was artists who preceded writers in apprehending the collapse of the world in the twentieth century. Just when 'douceur de vivre' was at its height and the world was becoming intoxicated by the whirl of Viennese waltzes, omens began to appear of what lay ahead: the bloody puppets of Rouault, the nightmare masks of Ensor; the gesticulations of the Fauves and the Cubists, 'those torturers of the human body, which for a thousand years had been worshipped as sacred'; the turbulent landscapes of Vlaminck, the joyless streets of Utrillo; above all, the despairing clowns of Picasso's blue period. Indeed, Picasso, 'the prophetic genius of our century', presaged all its disasters 'at the very moment when all humanity was dancing on a volcano and allowing itself to be mesmerised by promises of a golden age with which the ideologues, the sociologists and the democrats were dazzling the world'. And, well before the first crimes committed against civilisation by Germany, the torment that oppressed that country was revealed by the revival of Expressionism, while the portraits of civilised industrialists, architects, scholars and art lovers painted by the Austrian Kokoschka show that he had been able to discern 'the beast of prey that is to be found in every German'.[96]

No one will deny that an artist may, just as much as a writer or a politician, speculate about the future and may then try to express his vision of that future through making use of a particular style or a particular choice of imagery. And speculation about the possibilities of a war in Europe and a revolution in Russia was widespread during the early years of the twentieth century. But the prophetic power attributed to artists in cases of the kind considered in this chapter is related to their exceptional sensitivities rather than to their abilities at making clever guesses or to their faculties of reasoning; indeed, it is, as we have seen, very often believed to be a sort of mystical talent, of which the artist himself is unaware and which can, by definition, be detected only with hindsight. That hindsight inevitably has an effect on the way in which a painter is judged. Hubert Robert's views of the Louvre in ruins, inspired by the fragmentary palaces and temples of ancient Rome, were probably enjoyed as pleasing, somewhat titillating, *capricci* by the collectors of the *ancien régime*; by 1791, however, the German *philosophe* Grimm, the editor of Diderot's *Salons*, could write bitterly to Catherine the Great, that 'one can only assume that Robert, whose principal talent is to paint ruins, must find himself in his element just now. Wherever he turns, he can find his speciality thoroughly in vogue, and can see the most beautiful, freshest ruins in the world.'[97] And Robert himself may well have thought back somewhat ruefully to his early fantasies when, many years later, he found himself – surely to his utter astonishment – painting the demolition of some of the finest churches in Paris.

However, not all pictures of catastrophe and not all decisive stylistic changes have been quickly followed by dramatic events in the world outside art, as happened to the ruin fantasies of Hubert Robert or the apocalyptic townscapes of Ludwig Meidner. The case of Delacroix is revealing. His stylistic innovations startled his contemporaries, and his imagery still impresses us with its violence: we can understand why Baudelaire seized on the element of 'molochism' to be found in his work, and even why he credited Delacroix with a special intuition into the most genuine and most profound undercurrents of nineteenth-century 'modernity'.[98] But it is hardly surprising that Michael Sadler apparently went out of his way to select Delacroix as his example of a painter who adjusted himself 'to new conditions already in being' as distinct from others who foretold 'startling changes still to come'.[99] No one seems to have claimed that *La Mort de Sardanapale* 'anticipated' the Revolution of 1830, or *Attila et les Barbares foulant aux pieds l'Italie et les Arts* the catastrophes of the Franco-Prussian war and the Commune. The gift of divination has evidently been distributed in a somewhat arbitrary manner, and the historian would be unwise to rely with too much confidence on the evidence suggested by it.

Huizinga and the 'Flemish Renaissance'

i

In 1919, at a time when many people inclined to historical speculation were suggesting that major changes in the visual arts could provide valuable clues about more momentous changes which would become apparent only later in other areas of human activity, the Dutch historian Johan Huizinga published the book that, five years afterwards, was to be translated into English as *The Waning of the Middle Ages*. In it he argued that one very conspicuous artistic innovation – the apparent 'realism' introduced into fifteenth-century Flemish art by Jan van Eyck and his successors – had been wrongly interpreted. Far from heralding the birth of a new society, such paintings as the Ghent altarpiece should be thought of as the last reflection of a civilisation that was already in a state of final decay. In support of this view, and in subsequent reflections on some of the implications arising from it, Huizinga raised a number of brief, almost casual but profound, questions on the relationship between art and the historical imagination. Few of these have (as far as I am aware) been analysed with the attention that they demand, and Huizinga remains the last great historian to have made an outstanding contribution to the theme discussed in this book. The extent and nature of that contribution can be appreciated only if the background to the problem explored by him is first examined at some length.[1]

ii

Ever since the Renaissance, and indeed earlier, issues of nationalism – or at least of local patriotism – have been introduced into much historical writing on the arts. Vasari's assertion that the Florentine school reigned supreme over all others in Italy, provoked, within his own lifetime (and still more in the seventeenth and eighteenth centuries), powerful counter-attacks from the champions of other Italian cities; who, nevertheless, were unanimous in agreeing with him that the glories of art in Italy surpassed those of any other region of Europe. Their arguments were based sometimes on the precocity of past achievements, sometimes on the quality of contemporary ones, and occasionally on a combination of both – although the

French, who first entered the fray towards the end of the seventeenth century, could choose only the second of these alternatives as a basis for their own claims.

Many of the ensuing controversies served at least one useful purpose – the investigation of neglected works of art and unexplored archives; but in their earlier stages they tended to interest only those scholars who were actively involved in studying them. We have seen, however, that for the more philosophically minded writers of the eighteenth century the arts began to serve as an important gauge for measuring many other aspects of civilisation and that this tendency was greatly intensified during the Romantic period and later. In sixteenth-century Rome the weaknesses apparently to be found in the art of Titian, compared with that of Michelangelo, could be ascribed to the regrettable Venetian habit of not paying enough attention to drawing; but in nineteenth-century Berlin the lack of smooth professionalism apparently to be found in the art of Dürer, compared with that of his Italian contemporaries, could suggest far deeper and more wide-ranging implications. It constituted a 'faithful mirror of his noble, pure, genuine and truly German spirit'.[2] Such assumptions, whether explicit or implicit, lay behind most writing on the arts throughout Europe.

The opportunity to reach conclusions of this nature had been greatly stimulated by the artistic upheavals that accompanied the French Revolution. The removal to Paris of such legendary but little-known masterpieces from Northern Europe as panels from the Ghent altarpiece, and the throwing on to the market of unfamiliar mediaeval paintings from secularised churches and convents, could offer the most exhilarating visual impressions to those who, for varying reasons, were disposed to welcome a changed perspective. For a number of German connoisseurs and collectors in particular the discovery of such pictures (even before the names of their authors had been correctly identified) seemed to point to the existence of a cultural heritage that was as worthy of admiration, if not more so, than the traditional one based on antiquity and the Italian sixteenth century. It was not long before public museums and scholarly research took over the initiative from the enthusiasm of individuals.

In its early stages the rediscovery of the Flemish and German painters of the fifteenth and sixteenth centuries developed simultaneously, and not very much distinction was made between them.[3] In the first bays of the Grande Galerie in the Louvre a few Van Eycks and 'Hemmelincks' and 'Claissenses', removed from Bruges and Ghent, were exhibited alongside Dürers and Holbeins; they were arranged in chronological order and were generally classified as the 'École Flamande', although a distinction between the schools was acknowledged in the catalogue entries devoted to individual pictures.[4] They seem to have attracted little attention, and visitors no doubt hurried past them to marvel at the Van Dycks and Rembrandts and Dujardins that were hung in large quantities further down the gallery. However, in July and August 1802 they were examined with great care by Friedrich Schlegel. Schlegel was then aged thirty-two, and his interests had hitherto been concentrated mainly on antiquity and on contemporary literature. But just before visiting Paris he had spent four months in Dresden, where the masterpieces of the Italian Renaissance which he had seen in the gallery had made a

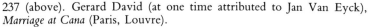

237 (above). Gerard David (at one time attributed to Jan Van Eyck), *Marriage at Cana* (Paris, Louvre).

238. Holbein (old copy after), *Madonna of the Burgomeister Meyer* (Dresden, Gemäldegalerie).

decisive impact on him, and where he had had long conversations about old German art with Wilhelm Tieck, who was a passionate admirer of Dürer. It was to Tieck that he addressed his impressions of the Louvre, which were first published between 1803 and 1805.[5]

As was to be expected, Schlegel was greatly struck by the Raphaels and the Correggios – artists who were represented by world-famous examples of their work in Dresden; but he declared that he was not attracted by later Italian art, and he decided to devote some pages to the few 'old German pictures' on view. These began with a series of excellent paintings attributed to Jan Van Eyck, in whose *Marriage at Cana* (pl. 237) the womens' heads recalled those in the celebrated *Madonna* by Holbein (pl. 238) that he had admired in Dresden.[6] In them was to be seen a similar combination of humility and divinity, more sincere than in Raphael's (Sistine) *Madonna*, where the representation of the divine was too general and would have been equally suitable for a Juno or even a Diana (a source from which it may well have been derived). Van Eyck – whose panels detached from the Ghent altarpiece Schlegel also greatly praised – ought in fact to be considered the founder of the German school which culminated in Holbein and Dürer.[7] Indeed, the principal achievements of German painting were all characterised by one or other of the styles to be found in these three exemplars.

Van Eyck, Holbein and Dürer had long been very well known by name,[8] but, Schlegel pointed out, the early days of German (and Italian) art had also given birth to other remarkable painters whose memory had quickly been eclipsed by

239. Memling, Moreel triptych (Bruges, Groeninge Museum).

these very famous masters. One such was 'the old painter Hemmerlinck' whose picture in the Louvre of some saints in a landscape was worthy of the most supreme achievements of the German school.

Memling's 'Moreel triptych' (pl. 239) had doubtless been taken by the French armies from the Hospice of Saint-Jean in Bruges, because an authoritative guide book of 1769 had admired its 'précieux fini et la plus belle couleur: c'est le plus beau Tableau de ce Maître, c'est même une curiosité'.[9] In the large central panel St Christopher in a blue tunic and red robe has just guided himself to dry land across the river behind him with the help of his long staff; on his shoulder sits the infant Christ in a golden halo, and on each side is a tonsured saint in black, one holding a crozier, the other stroking a deer. The lush, but mountainous, landscape stretches back into the distance under a darkening, cloudy sky. On the outer wings the donor and his wife kneel at their prayer stools, their sons and daughters behind them, and their name-saints, William and Barbara, protectively at their sides. In Paris the painting seems to have attracted no attention until it revealed to Schlegel the existence of a kind of artistic experience hitherto wholly unfamiliar to him. For it was the sentiment (and not the 'précieux fini') that struck him above all: the kindly expression on the face of St Christopher, the tranquillity, the simplicity, the peacefulness, the calm, the gentleness, the candour – he reiterates these and similar terms, as though mesmerised both by the vision he has seen and by his inability to convey the nature of its beauty to Tieck and his friends who knew nothing with which he could compare it. Except Dürer, perhaps; but Dürer without the element of caricature, an infinitely milder Dürer. Certainly the picture was quintessentially German in character.

In September 1803 three young art lovers from Cologne, Johann Baptist Bertram and the brothers, Sulpiz and Melchior, Boisserée, arrived in Paris and soon became close friends of Schlegel. He showed them the pictures he admired in the

Louvre, and they in turn introduced him to Gothic architecture; as yet he had not even visited Notre-Dame. In April 1804 they all went on an expedition to Cologne, stopping on the way in Brussels, Louvain, Aachen and other historic cities.[10] In the well-lit museum of Brussels, where they were able to see a further display of early Northern pictures, Schlegel again tried to distinguish the characteristics of the German and Flemish styles and to understand the relationship between them. It is not always easy to follow his reasoning, because many of the works he discussed can no longer be identified, but in general he considered Dürer an artist who had attempted to combine the qualities of both schools. However, he could still find no painter who moved him as much as Memling.

Cologne was under French occupation, church property had been secularised, and from the debris and confusion a few collectors, who were now joined by the Boisserée brothers, began to assemble wonderful paintings which demonstrated 'the unity and interconnection of the early German and early Netherlandish styles'.[11] Although these collections were enthusiastically admired by Schlegel, it was a large gold-ground triptych of the *Adoration of the Magi* (pl. 240) in the chapel of the town hall that offered him his second revelation of sublimity in these years.[12] Its excellence had inevitably led to its being attributed to Dürer, the greatest of German artists, but although Schlegel agreed that the bizarre stances and costumes of some of the attendants of the Magi faintly recalled his style, the attribution was not convincing. The soft flesh colours of the heads were far closer to Holbein – but they were more characteristic of the times in general than of any specific artist. The carpet-like dark-green foreground and the earnest expression of the faces were, however, very reminiscent of Van Eyck: in this way, the painting combined features to be found in all the best masters. But once again, as with Memling, it was the sentiment – its expression of spiritual love especially – that made the most telling impact on Schlegel, and in this respect it surpassed the three tutelary geniuses. After listing some of its special beauties, Schlegel described the tender grief with which St Ursula gazes at her young lover (in the left wing of the triptych); the peaceful attitudes and pale countenances of the martyrs beside her; and all those melancholy accessories that melt the joyous grandeur of the principal subject into an inner feeling of gentle love. He concluded that it was impossible to see anything more perfect made by the hand of man.

But who was the man who had created this masterpiece? He was unknown, as was the architect of Cologne cathedral, for they had both been prompted by love of work and not by vanity. However, Schlegel felt certain (without arguing the point) that it must have been completed by 1410, and this meant that it could only have been painted by Master Wilhelm, who had been named in a chronicle of the later fourteenth century as the most famous artist of the day. The chronology was a little uncertain – Schlegel referred in general terms to the flowering of the German school exemplified by Wilhelm of Cologne, Johann Van Eyck and Hemmelinck[13] – but it soon became accepted in Germany that the masters of the Cologne school had provided the stimulus required to give birth to panel painting in Flanders.[14] And within a dozen years the triptych of the *Adoration of the Magi* (which had not yet been attributed to Stefan Lochner) was described by Goethe as

240. Stefan Lochner, *Adoration of the Magi with Saints Ursula and Gereon* (Cologne, cathedral).

being 'the object of so much adulation that I am afraid it will soon be as obscured in the mind's eye by such rhapsodies as it was formerly to the physical eye by the soot of lamps and candles'.[15]

The exquisite tenderness and religious feeling of the Cologne school, whose newly discovered works were repeatedly compared with the masterpieces of Fra Angelico, continued to arouse passionate enthusiasm in Germany – and elsewhere in Europe, once the results of German scholarship became available in translation.[16] But it gradually became apparent that these 'childlike' paintings were significantly different in character from those to be seen in Flanders, as was first pointed out with absolute precision by Gustav Friedrich Waagen in 1822. In his small, but epoch-making, monograph on the brothers Van Eyck which appeared in Breslau in that year (illustrated with just one schematic diagram), Waagen, who was then aged twenty-eight, broke with the sentimental effusions that had hitherto typified discussions of the Northern primitives. He looked steadily at their achievements and explored such original written sources as survived, instead of repeating the untested traditions handed down by later historians. In so doing he broke also with the conventions of the circles in which he himself had grown up and, together with his mentor Carl Friedrich von Rumohr, he turned self-consciously to the techniques applied by Niebuhr to the early legends of Rome. With his *Ueber Hubert und Johann van Eyck*, and with Rumohr's *Italienische Forschungen* of a few years later, unknown epochs of art were brought to light and a new era of art-historical writing was born.[17]

It was true, Waagen pointed out, that there were certain parallels between the Cologne school of artists and the brothers Van Eyck. Indeed, if one compared the paintings of Jan Van Eyck (pl. 241) with the Cologne *Adoration*, which was charac-

241. Jan Van Eyck, Ghent altarpiece: central panel representing the *Adoration of the Lamb* (Ghent, cathedral of St Bavon).

terised by a symmetrical composition, a correct relationship between the figures, simple and noble draperies, as well as the beautiful, pure and tender expressions of the womens' features and the dignified ones of the men, the Flemish painter might even seem inferior in such respects.[18] But how much more life and individuality and variety were to be found in Van Eyck; and how different was his painterly technique – firm, strong outlines, for instance, rather than the softness that marked the Cologne school; true and bold local colours rather than German pallor. Van Eyck was the herald of a specifically Netherlandish school of art whose nature was moulded by precise social and political circumstances.

With some reservations, the distinction drawn by Waagen between the Cologne and Flemish schools came to be widely accepted,[19] although controversy about the relative importance of their contributions to European art was still rumbling more than half a century later.[20] Both Flemish and German artists could claim admiration from believers in progress (through their respective 'discoveries' of the techniques of oil painting and of engraving), but in an age in which mediaeval and Renaissance styles were looked upon as having been almost ideologically antagonistic, the exact status of the brothers Van Eyck remained somewhat uncertain.

There was general agreement that the 'successful representation of art and nature in all its truth' was to be found in their work.[21] The eye was carried far and wide into distant space, and 'the whole visible world around us – heaven and earth –

objects near and distant – the graceful line of a distant mountain – the green
meadow – trees laden with fruit – the conveniences and elegancies of the dwellings
of men, and the various implements and necessaries of life' were all reflected in
their pictures. And yet, although human figures 'stand in necessary relation to each
other, and form, together with the accessories, for the first time, one perfect and
significant whole', none the less, 'in single figures they still preserve the statue-like
solemnity and dignity of the early style, and have only combined more life with
the same traditional motives'. However, even though the (by now dismembered)
Ghent altarpiece demonstrated that the brothers 'stand on the frontier of two
different styles', their achievement must be thought of as marking a completely
new departure rather than 'as the last link of a connected chain of improvements
gradually unrolled'. Thus, very soon after the dawn of Van Eyck studies, we
already find, tentatively formulated, those crucial questions – realist or symbolist?
forward-looking or backward-looking? – that were, nearly a century later, to
colour the interpretation of a whole civilisation – the civilisation of fifteenth-
century Burgundy.

To the comte (later marquis) Léon de Laborde, the scholar who laid the
foundations for the modern analysis and elucidation of that civilisation, the art of
the Van Eycks posed no such ambiguities. After the greatest difficulties he had
in 1847 eventually been allowed to see the wings of the *Adoration of the Lamb* on
which the figures of Adam and of Eve had been depicted larger than life (pls 242,
243).[22] For reasons of decency these had, for more than half a century, been hidden
away by the bishops of Ghent and propped up against the walls of an attic with no
protection from extreme changes of temperature and humidity. To the comte de
Laborde these paintings, in which realism had been carried so far that traces of sun-
tan indicated which parts of the models' bodies were normally left uncovered,
represented nature itself. The Van Eycks, he claimed, had inscribed on their banner
the words 'Imitation of Nature', and once their own masterpieces had earned them
the right of conquest, they had enjoined this programme on the land as a whole.[23]
Nor was it surprising that it had remained dominant ever since. The principle had
borne fruit because it was sound. Not only was it backed up by a long tradition of
miniature painting which encouraged minutely detailed imitation, it was also more
suited than any other to the national character, so that, after a short interval of
looking to Italian models, the artists of the Low Countries returned in the seventeenth century to the road opened by the Van Eycks. The overriding importance
of this notion was soon to become apparent.

Even in an age when distinguished birth was not held to be incompatible with a
professional career devoted to scholarship, and when the meticulous investigation
of diminutive objects and detailed records could keep company with a lively and
well-informed curiosity about wide historical issues, the range of interests of
the well-connected, independent-minded and sometimes sharp-tongued Léon de
Laborde impressed his contemporaries, while at the same time arousing both in
them and in himself the fear that his energies would be fruitlessly dispersed. This
was a fear that was partly justified by the tentative, disjointed and fragmentary
nature of his researches which he would agree to publish only in very limited
editions.[24]

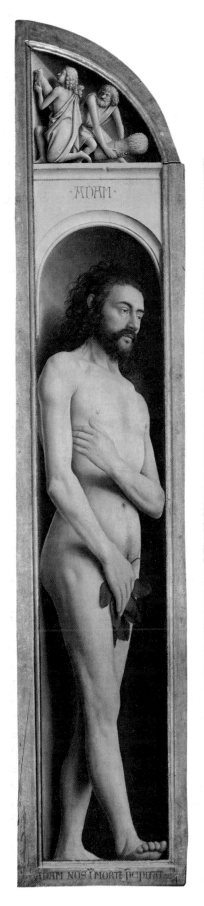

242 and 243. Jan Van
Eyck, Ghent
altarpiece: *Adam* and
Eve (Ghent, cathedral
of St Bavon).

Born in 1807, the son of Alexandre de Laborde, the traveller and archaeologist who, almost single-handedly, 'discovered' the architecture of Spain and presented it to Europe in splendid volumes, Léon accompanied his father to Petra, the Sinai desert and other remote sites in the Middle East at the age of eighteen. Five years later he published his impressions and often significant discoveries in a fine folio, illustrated for the most part by lithographs of the drawings he had made on the spot. The portrait of himself in his travelling robes as an 'Arabe du Désert' (reproduced by Achille Déveria from a drawing by Madame D.) presents us with an elegant and insouciant explorer of a type familiar from many English publications.[25]

In 1847 Léon de Laborde succeeded the comte de Clarac as Keeper of Sculpture in the Louvre, but he was also a conservative deputy, very closely attached to the Orléans family, and a year later he was driven from his post by the Revolution. Soon afterwards he returned to the Louvre, but his new position, which remained precarious for a time, was rather lower in status. Greek and Roman art was removed from his control, and he was left in charge of only the mediaeval, Renaissance and modern sculptures. A good deal of his energy was devoted to the recovery of those many objects from Lenoir's Musée des Monuments Français which still lay scattered and neglected in the École des Beaux-Arts, but (as well as many articles) he also wrote an extremely thorough, discerning and well-documented catalogue of the enamels in his department. In addition, he took a keen interest in the application of arts to industry and in the artistic education of children, who should, he felt, be taught to draw at the same time as they were taught to read and write.

It was, however, as an archivist that he was (rightly) considered to be not only an authoritative pioneer but also one of the four 'saints' of the French art-historical church.[26] It was immediately after his dismissal from the Louvre that Laborde began work on his selection of (mostly unpublished) documents relating to the dukes of Burgundy – and later to the Renaissance in France. Yet his was not to be a dry, pedantic, though useful, assortment of material of the kind that had been undertaken often enough since the time of Montfaucon and his Benedictine colleagues, to whom he (generously) attributed the aim of 'associating the serious nature of history with that anecdotal colour which provides it with charm and interest'.[27] Laborde's volumes were intended to form the basis, the 'pièces justificatives', for a cultural history which he projected but never composed, for his researches tended to be published in a fragmentary way. He certainly believed that 'documents would indeed be arid if one could not from time to time relate them to some work of art',[28] and the more attached he became to the arts of Northern Europe the more he applied to them his skills as a connoisseur. He travelled to English country houses as well as to Belgian churches in order to learn to distinguish between the authentic and the fictitious works by Van Eyck and Clouet which were attracting increasing intention and in order to be able to characterise the styles of Roger van der Weyden and Holbein: and he did so with an independence of judgement which is impressive but not always convincing.[29]

From the first, however, Laborde had realised that the devastation caused by wars and revolutions meant that it would be impossible to write a serious history of the arts in Burgundy based only on the evidence of the monuments that had survived. And so he explored the archives of Lille and Dijon, of Brussels, Ghent, Bruges and the other great centres of Flemish art in the former duchy. He derived special satisfaction from those that had not yet been too rigorously classified, 'because the kind of information which we need is not to be found in any special category but is intrinsic to every aspect of political, administrative, religious or civic life'.[30] By relying on such sources and on the researches of local scholars (whose discoveries he always scrupulously acknowledged) he was able to provide the background to, and occasionally the outlines of, the lives of a number of artists and craftsmen whose very names were as yet little known.

And yet, although Laborde never seems to have faced the issue directly, his attempt to combine 'research into unpublished documents with a critical examination of the original monuments' in order to lay the basis for a true history of the arts in Europe did not prove to be as helpful as might have been anticipated: it is even tempting to suggest that some faint awareness of this may have discouraged him from embarking on the narrative that he had intended to write.

Wherever he went Laborde naturally explored buildings and museums as well as archives; and on leaving his 'inn at Tournay, at Ghent, at all those Flemish and Dutch towns, but especially at Bruges', he would be overcome by 'a sort of vertigo', so great was the similarity between the art of the school of the fifteenth century and the scenes that now confronted him. Art and nature became so confused in his mind that he felt he was living in a picture by Van Eyck or in the pages of an illuminated manuscript – little houses with uniform façades, while their inhabitants, casting no shadow under the grey sky, stood isolated in wide streets lined with low buildings.[31] The fidelity of art to natural appearances was absolute.

But, back in the archives, the documents conjured up a very different world. Banners and escutcheons and jousting equipment; cloths of gold, and sheets of silk and white damask; silver dishes and goblets, richly gilded; golden necklaces elaborately worked and adorned with precious stones; chandeliers and rubies; lions and a dromedary as well as hunting dogs and falcons[32] – such were the items that filled page after page of the account books and that bring on a 'sort of vertigo' quite unlike that induced by the quiet, empty streets of Bruges. As he worked his way through so much direct, copious and awesome testimony in support of the already legendary account of the luxuries that had surrounded the dukes of Burgundy – 'those overgrown children, whose pleasure lay in the dazzle that they could produce by the richness and variety of their costumes and by the pomp and sparkle of their ceremonies'[33] – Laborde (himself an aristocrat whose fine art collection served to shield him from the ugliness of the modern world[34] and a man gifted with a strong visual imagination) must have seen in his mind's eye the evidence of a civilisation only very distantly, if at all, related to the sober realism that had struck him as characteristic of the Van Eycks and their successors. Could these conflicts of perception be reconciled?

It was left to Huizinga, more than three-quarters of a century later, to explore the possibility of doing just this. Meanwhile, however, Laborde went out of his way to reject any all-embracing synthesis. It was, he claimed, the existence rather than the nature of Flemish art that could be attributed to Burgundian patronage. Climate was irrelevant: England and Northern France were just as foggy. So, too, was national character – the Germans, and still more the Chinese, were just as patient and contemplative. So, too, were political conditions and industrial activity – what about the Hanseatic cities? – or issues of race and language. The luxury of the Burgundian court was evidence of its generosity,[35] and although Laborde was inclined to contradict himself about the extent and intelligence of its patronage – which was short-lived and not comparable to that of France[36] – none the less, it alone could account for the development of those seeds that God distributes at random but that can germinate only under specific conditions. And if realism was the path pursued by Flemish art, credit should be given not to the patrons but to the painters who, wearied of the servile derivation from Byzantine prototypes that was still prevalent, and lacking the stimulus of antiquity, could recognise that 'Imitation of Nature' was the only way forward.[37]

The significance of Van Eyck's 'realism' was universally acknowledged. Burckhardt, for instance, who had travelled in Belgium as a young man, retained the most unbounded admiration for the Ghent altarpiece.[38] Indeed, so great was the impact it made on him that when in 1855 he published the *Cicerone*, he seems to have hesitated for a moment in his conviction that only the Italians had had a true Renaissance. After all, the decisive changes that had marked their painting in the early fifteenth century were also to be seen in the 'immortal work of Jan Van Eyck whose solitary radiance inundated the whole century and the whole of German, French and Spanish art', and even fascinated the Italians themselves. But the word 'solitary' was crucial; for, whether or not Burckhardt was fully aware of the fact, he now applied to Flanders precisely the same argument that had been used by Michelet to explain the absence of any true Renaissance in Italy during the course of the fifteenth century. For Brunelleschi Burckhardt substituted Van Eyck as a lonely genius whose successors were not capable of keeping pace with him and who had therefore had to content themselves with a much more limited repertory of forms. And just as Michelet had claimed that it was not until Leonardo, many decades later, that effective blows could once again be struck at the Gothic which had tenaciously reasserted itself after the death of Brunelleschi, so Burckhardt insisted that 'a sort of paralysis affected the successors of Van Eyck so that Dürer, Matsys and Holbein came on to the scene too late and were compelled, as their first task, to free themselves from the burden of dead forms which constituted the legacy of the fifteenth century'.[39]

In the 1880s and 1890s the pioneering achievements of Laborde and Burckhardt were impetuously enrolled into supporting a cause with which they themselves would have had no sympathy: a decisive revival of the arts had occurred in the North before making itself felt in Italy – 'le dernier-né des fils de la Renaissance', as Louis Courajod provocatively characterised the nation that had been described by Burckhardt as 'the first-born of the sons of Europe'.[40]

Courajod was profoundly indebted to Burckhardt for whom he had the highest regard;[41] and the researches of Laborde constituted perhaps the single most important influence on his life as a scholar.[42] In 1874, at the age of thirty-four, he entered the department of sculpture in the Louvre which, a generation earlier, had been administered by Laborde, and, like him, he became deeply involved with the vestiges of Lenoir's disbanded Musée des Monuments Français and with the task of making up for its loss by creating a noble successor to it: this became so much of an obsession that his office served him also as a bedroom.[43] His archival work and his many brief but opinionated publications[44] were well known to his colleagues, but for nearly a decade from 1887 onwards he was given the chance to convey his ideas to a wider community: the students and ordinary members of the public who came to listen to his rousing lectures at the recently established École du Louvre – lectures that instinctively brought to mind the name of Michelet.[45] In a Second Empire room decorated in the style of the early eighteenth century, Courajod would sit at a green baize table on to which he would fling his sets of photographs as if they were exhibits in some important trial. The oil lamp was so placed that his face remained in darkness and only his hands were brightly lit. As his audience grew in numbers – the room could seat some 130 – he would project slides, which were then still a novelty. But, above all, he liked to talk in front of actual objects – casts and, when possible, the sculptures under his charge in the Louvre.[46]

Courajod was impetuous and intransigent, but he was also vulnerable and lonely. He never married, and the death of his mother when he was aged fifty-five broke his spirit and hastened his own death in the following year.[47] The emotional tone with which he sometimes sought to establish a 'paternal relationship and intellectual association' with the young people in his audience[48] must have played its part in reinforcing an influence that was in any case likely to be strong in a period of such intense nationalism as the 1890s. But, far from feeling any resentment against the Germans, Courajod directed his criticisms against traditional interpretations of the part played by Italy in the creation of modern art.

Burckhardt had maintained that the uncompromising realism of a sculptor such as Donatello had been far more significant than the revival of classical art and letters in inaugurating the modern spirit which he chose to define as the Renaissance. Courajod whole-heartedly endorsed this insight, but he insisted that it was in the North rather than in the South of Europe that artistic naturalism had first appeared and that it was in France and, above all, in Flanders that the origins of the Renaissance were to be sought – although he rather distrusted the word because of its implications of a 'rebirth' rather than of a new development.[49] He therefore quoted in full the pages in which Laborde had described the sort of vertigo that had overcome him when he suddenly realised the intimate kinship that existed between Flemish art and the appearance of Flemish towns and the conclusion to be drawn from this about the clearly expressed intention of the Van Eyck brothers to devote their genius to the imitation of nature.[50]

For Courajod himself, however, who was primarily interested in the history of sculpture, the whole process had begun a hundred years or so earlier. Between the second half of the twelfth century and the middle of the thirteenth it was the Gothic style of France that had reigned supreme in Europe: of that there could be no doubt. But it was widely held that thereafter there had been a decline.

This case had been powerfully argued by Ernest Renan in the most sustained of all his contributions to the history of art.[51] Renan claimed that despite some improvements in manuscript illumination and a few other fields, French art of the fourteenth century had, by retreating from classicism, become decadent: it was characterised by coarse tastelessness, by the pursuit of ugliness and vulgarity. Courajod wished to prove that, on the contrary, this advance of naturalism, following the idealism of High Gothic, had been an entirely progressive development. It was true that it was inspired, above all, by the art of Flanders; none the less, it was Paris (where many leading Flemish artists were at work) that was the main centre of attraction – 'nowhere was Flemish art practised more brilliantly than in Paris'[52] – and, when war devastated France itself, French art was able to survive in peaceful Burgundy. This Franco-Flemish art constituted a true Renaissance, characterised by individualism and realism, and it anticipated by some fifty years the naturalism of Donatello and Pisanello. The cult of antiquity, which was possible only in Italy and which eventually enabled that nation to overtake the movement in France (and thereafter to be given exclusive credit for its inauguration), had been 'un des heureux événements de la grande révolution... mais il n'en fut pas le point de départ'. Let us not forget, he exclaimed, 'that it was to the Flemish school, adopted by Northern France as early as the middle of the fourteenth century – it was to the Flemish school and to the new principles of emancipation that it personified and that it injected into Western Art that is due (I cannot repeat this often enough) the general movement from which was to emerge the definitive style of the Renaissance – and that includes the style of the Italian Renaissance'.[53]

Although it is unlikely that Courajod was aware of the fact, he appears in passages such as these – and there are many of them – to be taking over, but adapting, a type of argument that had earlier been used by Michelet in order to achieve much the same goal. Both men wished to give France a central (though not exclusive) role in the formation of the Renaissance. Michelet did this by placing the Renaissance in the sixteenth century on the grounds that only the French had been capable of refining, and then spreading, innovations that had first appeared in Italy: Courajod, on the other hand, dated the movement two hundred years earlier and stressed the intimate relationship between the powerfully organised Valois court and the artists it lured from Burgundy. Only towards the end of the fifteenth century had the impact of Italy made itself seriously felt: 'dès lors la cause est perdue pour l'ancienne forme purement française ou franco-flamande de la Renaissance'.[54]

Whatever his reservations about the importance usually attributed to the impact of the Italian Renaissance, Courajod responded deeply both to Italy itself and to Italian art.[55] As an enthusiast for the later mediaeval and Renaissance sculpture of Burgundy he obviously went on pilgrimages to Dijon and celebrated the pre-eminent significance of Claus Sluter; and we also know of the 'spiritual and archaeological intoxication that took hold of him when he fused his soul with that of the ancient stones which he interrogated one by one' in the other provinces of France.[56] But, surprisingly, there seems to be almost no evidence about his personal feelings for Belgium, and in the last years of his life he rarely if ever travelled abroad.

The lecture entitled 'Definition of the term "the Flemish style"' which he delivered in the École du Louvre on 26 December 1888 was indeed wholly impersonal in tone. It drew largely on the conclusions of others, and it contained none of the those poignant observations about the character of Bruges or Ghent that were coming to be almost obligatory for writers about the Flemish primitives – but this apparent reticence may be owing to the fact that his lectures have only come down to us in defective form.[57] This one is notable above all because it concentrated much more on painters than on sculptors, but a fortnight later Courajod explained this by insisting that Jan Van Eyck must have provided designs for statues, and that both he and Roger van der Weyden had certainly coloured those made by professional carvers.[58] But the lecture barely attempted to live up to the promise of its title and did little more than assert that 'for nearly a century the Flemish school, of the Van Eycks and of Claus Sluter, exercised an unchallenged dominion over the history of art in Europe, a truly tyrannical supremacy . . . Whether one likes it or not, Flemish art holds an enormous place in the history of civilisation.' The art of Northern Europe was, in general, violent and revolutionary by nature, and the influence of Flemish painting had been exerted entirely in the direction of realism. Nevertheless, Courajod concluded (in a rare concession to prevailing sentiment), 'there was certainly a treasure-house of tenderness in the soul of a Memling and a Quentin Matsys. The whole Flemish school had a heart so receptive to feeling and the emotions that it was destined to fall in love with nature above all and to aim to paint its soul and to give voice to the silent universe. It was the predestined mother of landscape and the portrait'. And Courajod urged his audience to consult photographs of the principal collections of Flemish primitives: those of London, Munich, Berlin, Madrid, Brussels and elsewhere, as well as some 'too rare but admirable panels in the Louvre, our Jan Van Eyck, our Memlings, the great altarpiece of the Hôpital of Beaune'.[59]

Flemish art had, because of its realism, been the motive force behind the whole European Renaissance, but its principal achievements were scattered and relatively unfamiliar: such must have been the two main conclusions drawn by the members of Courajod's audience as they tried to examine the inadequate evidence with which he had supplied them. A decade and half later an exhibition of the most decisive importance was to put the first of these conclusions to the test by remedying the drawbacks exemplified by the second.

iii

Early in 1900 Paul Wytsman, a Belgian writer on the arts, proposed that an exhibition of Flemish primitive paintings should be organised in Brussels. He was inspired by a series of nationally motivated exhibitions that had been held in many parts of Europe over the last few years, above all those devoted to

Rembrandt and Rubens in Amsterdam and Antwerp. A committee was set up, and letters were at once sent to the authorities in Bruges and in Ghent asking them to lend the major works by Memling and Van Eyck which were the pride of those cities. The speedy, but polite, refusals to do so were based on grounds soon to become universally familiar: potential damage to the pictures, on the one hand; certain damage to tourism, on the other. The sequel was more surprising. Why not, suggested the Brussels committee, transfer the proposed exhibition to Bruges itself? This was at once agreed – despite the fact that virtually all those who had conceived the project were now dropped from it[60] – and the organisation was eventually taken over by Baron Henri Kervyn de Lettenhove, son of the statesman and historian, and himself a fervent patriot, amateur artist and prolific writer on cultural topics.[61]

Vast difficulties remained. The original refusal by the municipality of Bruges to co-operate had created much ill feeling;[62] more was now added by its reluctance to offer any subsidy. Until it agreed to do so, the government declined to help. The new organisers sounded the patriotic note for all it was worth, and references were made to the studies of foreigners such as Laborde. Eventually, enough money was raised from a combination of public and private sources.

Almost as difficult as the financial problems was that of a suitable location. It had originally been thought that the Hôtel Gruuthuse (a handsome private mansion of the fifteenth century, adjoining the church of Notre-Dame, which had recently been acquired by the town) would make an ideal setting. But as the numbers of pictures promised for the exhibition grew ever larger, it was decided to use its rooms exclusively for the display of illuminated manuscripts and the decorative and even prehistoric arts. These were assembled in chaotic haste at the last moment, and although they included some magnificent objects which attracted enthusiastic crowds,[63] it was the impact of the pictures that proved to be of momentous importance. However, for many months the problem of where to hang these seemed to be insoluble. Only after endless bureaucratic objections was Kervyn at last able to persuade the municipal authorities, just six months before the exhibition was due to open, to transfer their meetings elsewhere and to let him make use of a set of eight offices and open spaces in the Palais Provincial. This imposing neo-Gothic edifice, built less than a generation earlier, occupied much of one side of the Grand Place, at the end of which stood the very symbol of mediaeval Bruges, its famous belfry. The emotional and patriotic implications of the exhibition could not have been demonstrated more clearly,[64] although it was widely acknowledged that in the small, dimly lit rooms allotted to them the pictures themselves were by no means seen to advantage.[65]

The process of selecting these took more than a year – Kervyn wrote later that three would have been desirable – and the actual requests for loans were sent out just one month before the opening date, so that a week before the inauguration only three out of more than four hundred promised had actually arrived.[66] Many details about the problems of negotiating the loans have been published (though far more remain unpublished),[67] and these provide information of great significance to the historian. The impact made by the Bruges exhibition took the particular form it did because of certain crucial presences and absences; and (as in all exhibitions) these were determined at least as much by accident as by choice.

It was their failure to obtain some major paintings from St Petersburg that taught Kervyn and his collaborators how important it was to make personal contacts in order to get hold of the pictures they needed.[68] They therefore visited many of the most prominent collectors in Europe. Their charm and tactical skills were evidently impressive, for from England alone they managed to borrow some seventy pictures, despite the fact that Belgian support for the Boers had aroused intense hostility in London and that the king refused to lend, partly because of the careless leniency with which the Belgian authorities had treated a youth who had tried to assassinate him in Brussels two years earlier.[69] And the French and Germans were also very generous. However, outside Belgium, where museums and churches had finally been persuaded to lend as freely as private collectors,[70] public institutions were hardly involved at all; thus nothing except photographs (which were displayed separately) came from the National Gallery in London or the Louvre, the Prado or the Kaiser Friedrich Museum – and much reliance had necessarily to be placed on the taste, whims and honesty of individual owners and dealers. Moreover, although some of the members of the organising committee were experts of the first order, it does not appear that more than a relatively small number of very well-known pictures had been specifically earmarked for the exhibition. We also get the impression from his reminiscences that Kervyn himself was so dazzled by the rich and elegant collectors whom he met in Paris, London and elsewhere, and whom he succeeded in enrolling into his advisory committees,[71] that he would have been happy to accept anything that they were ready to offer him. Inevitably, many minor and dubious works were given very optimistic labels.

Another problem (which has, often, seemed even more important to those involved in the preparation of exhibitions than the quality of the objects to be shown in them) was posed by the choice of title. Nor are such issues trivial, because the impact of an exhibition may well depend as much on the expectations that it arouses as on individual responses to its contents. Lengthy discussions were devoted to the topic from the day that the committee first met,[72] and they continued, at meetings and in the press, long after the crowds had been flocking into the Palais Provincial for weeks. Was it not absurd, even derogatory, to describe as 'primitive' artists of such great skill and sublime aspirations–artists, moreover, who had soared far above their precursors?[73] Everyone agreed that this term, which had been adopted from France, was irrelevant, even misleading, and the most passionate of its opponents was an exceedingly devout Belgian scholar, Jules Helbig, who had been interested in the Flemish masters for nearly forty years. It was true, he acknowledged, that 'their humility, their modest but inten-sive labour, their absence of charlatanism and bragging could perhaps be responsible for their still being classed among the "primitives", but it is not for us to leave them in a sort of antechamber of great art. When considering these masters we should remember the words of Pius IX of sacred memory: "One must give back to words their true value".'[74]

How the late pope would have solved the problem of the title Helbig does not reveal. What is clear is that he himself found it impossible to accept the notion of a 'Renaissance', which, despite all the arguments and rhetoric of Courajod, still retained too many Italian and pagan associations. When Kervyn asked him at a meeting if he could offer a suitable name, he came up with 'les maîtres antérieurs à la Renaissance'; to which the baron replied drily, 'We are looking for a word and not a phrase'.[75] And so 'primitives' was retained as a *pis aller*.

One reason why the question of the title raised such difficulties was that the organisers never made any direct public statement about the scope of the intended exhibition, nor does the evidence at present available suggest that the issue was much debated; and yet the choice of pictures, although at times illogical and even anti-historical, was certainly not fortuitous in its broad outlines. 'Primitive' was hardly a very suitable adjective for characterising Pieter Brueghel's *Adoration of the Magi*, *The Land of Cockaigne* (pl. 244) and the *Census at Bethlehem*,[76] but the reason for the inclusion of these three masterpieces, as for the exclusion of even a single work by Brueghel's slightly older Antwerp contemporary Franz Floris, is made absolutely clear by the closing words of a brief preliminary guide book which appeared a few days before the exhibition opened: 'Brueghel brings to a masterly conclusion the long list of national painters who resisted the growing influence of the Italian Renaissance . . . he is certainly among the most appealing and sympathetic figures of the Flemish sixteenth century. The list of Flemish primitives

244. Pieter Brueghel, *The Land of Cockaigne* (Munich, Alte Pinakothek).

assembled in Bruges could not close with more brio, good humour or delicate mockery.'[77] Indeed, the fact that Brueghel had actually gone to Italy and yet remained faithful to the art of his homeland earned him particular respect.[78]

In so doing he presented a noble contrast to Jan Gossaert (Mabuse) who, two generations earlier, had visited Italy 'and had been so captivated by the Renaissance that he had left behind all the traditions of his own school'.[79] Indeed, Gossaert had actually been praised by Italians of the sixteenth century for having been the first 'to take from Italy to those countries the practice of introducing nude figures into his scenes from history and poetry'.[80] Astonishingly enough, one (admittedly small and signed) demonstration of this – a robust and bearded Hercules, struggling with an Antaeus whose arms and legs flail the air – was to be seen in the exhibition,[81] but the remaining works attributed to him tended to be confined to uncontaminated portraits and religious scenes which in no way conflicted with the generally pious atmosphere of heavy-lidded Virgins and austere donors.

Gossaert's slight gesture in favour of nudity, paganism and Italy was, in fact, hardly noticed and certainly did not disturb the aim of commemorating the integrity of a vigorous national culture which lay at the heart of the enterprise. Of more concern was the fact that while Brueghel could exemplify the vigour that still remained even in the last beleaguered stages of that culture, unfortunate circumstances made it impossible for Baron Kervyn's team to celebrate its birth in a similarly robust manner. In 1816, only a year after the four central panels of the Ghent altarpiece had been returned to the city from their twenty years of exile in the Musée Napoléon in Paris, one of the canons of the cathedral kept the wings depicting *Adam* and *Eve* concealed and inaccessible, and sold off the remaining side wings. In 1821 these were acquired by the Berlin museum, and forty years later the panels of Adam and Eve were given to the Belgian state and displayed in the Royal Museum in Brussels. Thus by 1902 the supreme symbol of Flemish art had long been divided between three institutions. It was the dream of the organisers to reassemble the entire altarpiece for the Bruges exhibition – the literal dream, for Kervyn vividly described the sweet melodies that he heard at night after he had placed under his pillow a letter announcing the 'sensational news' that Berlin would lend the wings in its possession as long as Ghent sent the central panels.[82] This the local clergy (whose care for the masterpiece entrusted to them had hardly been very diligent over the previous hundred years) absolutely refused to countenance. In the end the entire Ghent altarpiece was represented only by the loan from Brussels of the *Adam* and the *Eve*.

Over a period of three and a half months, beginning in the middle of June 1902, some thirty-five thousand visitors walked through the immense entrance hall and vestibule of the Palais Provincial and up the monumental staircase, all of which had been decorated with mediaeval tapestries lent by the Rothschilds, the Somzées and other private and public owners.[83] The small, badly lit room that faced them on the first floor was devoted to the Van Eycks, their predecessors and their immediate successors;[84] and the two gaunt nudes lent from Brussels were thus among the first works to strike the crowds. The impact was overwhelming and set the tone for much later discussion on Flemish art. They had, it was claimed by one

245. Jan Van Eyck, *Virgin of Canon van der Paele* (Bruges, Groeninge Museum).

critic, been painted 'with a sincerity, indeed a brutality, which astounds even the most modern of our own realists'.[85] Facing them, in the place of honour was the *Virgin and Child in the Presence of Saints Donation and George and Canon G. van der Paele* (pl. 245): it was the 'grave, withdrawn' features of the prior, unsurpassable even by Dürer, that made the greatest impact in this richly coloured masterpiece,[86] and one critic felt inspired to write that it was 'the most realist picture that can be conceived, not, of course, through its choice of subject, but through its conception of art, which is the essential point. Courbet "who had never seen angels" is no more rigorous a realist than Jan Van Eyck who painted them'.[87]

Jan Van Eyck's austere rendering of his thin-lipped wife Margaret (pl. 257) hung in the same room, as did two pictures sent from England which were singled out in the preliminary brochure as being of quite particular importance. Of these the Duke of Devonshire's *Enthronement of St Thomas à Becket* (pl. 246) was inscribed with Jan Van Eyck's name and the date of 1421, which would have made it the earliest known work by the artist. This, and the obvious significance of the subject to English history, had led to its being much discussed; but, at least thirty years before the exhibition, its claims had been utterly discredited by Crowe and Cavalcaselle who declared that 'under no circumstances can we now accept it as a genuine work of Van Eyck in 1421'.[88] Even under the dirt and layers of thick repaint, it was evident that the style of the picture indicated a much later date, and that the repetitive, expressionless heads and rigidly crowded composition bore little relation to the work of Van Eyck. Its faltering reputation as one of his master-pieces did not survive the exhibition, although it was not until some years later that the inscription was shown to be false and the painting was recognised as one of a series devoted to the life of St Romold of Malines (who was, in fact, enthroned as Bishop of Dublin) produced at the end of the fifteenth century in the workshop of Colyn de Cooter.[89] A few acute observers noted that another fragment from the same set was also on view, but in a different room, under the name of Gerard David.

The other picture from England to be seen in the Van Eyck room was Sir Francis Cook's *Three Marys at the Sepulchre* (pl. 247), and this truly did cause the excitement that had been anticipated, not only because of its extraordinary appeal, but also because it appeared to be so different in character from the other works to be seen there. In the middle of a spacious and rocky landscape a white-robed angel with long golden hair kneels on the lid that has been laid, somewhat haphazardly, astride an empty coffin. To it the three mourning women, tall and slender in blue, green and red, have approached from the left, and against its sides sit or recline three armed and ungainly soldiers (farm labourers, perhaps, too hastily recruited) in bovine sleep. In the distance, figures on foot and on horseback make their way to a domed and turreted Jerusalem, while the dawn sky, dappled with fluffy pink clouds, begins to fill the whole painting with tender, but irregular light. The picture was described by Jules Helbig in the *Revue de l'Art Chrétien* as a work of 'exquisite charm and exceptional merit', and the name of Shakespeare was invoked to characterise its distinction;[90]

246. Master of the Youth of St Romold, '*Enthronement of St Thomas à Becket*' (Dublin, National Gallery of Ireland).

247. Hubert(?) Van Eyck *Three Marys at the Sepulchre* (Rotterdam, Boymans van Beuningen Museum).

and it is true that no other picture in the orbit of the Van Eycks appears quite so candid, so uncontrived – an effect which is, perhaps, due in part to certain weaknesses in the drawing and perspective.

Two years earlier the *Three Marys* had been attributed in the *Revue de l'Art Chrétien* to Jan Van Eyck's elder brother, Hubert, an artist of whom so little is known that his very existence has sometimes been doubted.[91] The attribution was widely (though not universally) accepted, and it was under his name that the picture was shown in Bruges. No doubt this was owing (at least in part) to the fact that James Weale, who had suggested the attribution, was also in charge of the catalogue.

James Weale, an Englishman, had long been the doyen of the historians of early Flemish painting.[92] He had been born in London in 1832, and at an early age he became interested in archaeology and mediaeval art. He was destined for the Church, but in 1849 – prompted in the first place by his enthusiasm for stained-glass windows and devotional pictures – he was converted to Catholicism and was forced to abandon the prospect of going to Oxford. Instead, he founded a school for poor children in Islington at which he taught until 1855 when he settled with his young family in Bruges, a city he had visited a few years earlier in the company of Nicholas Wiseman, the future cardinal.[93] There he wrote a guide book for travellers to Belgium and its neighbours, which made an outstanding contribution to the study of Northern art, and a series of articles which denounced the ubiquitous practice of 'restoration'. He also reconstructed the life and career of Gerard David and of other lesser painters whose work had barely been heard of at the time, and cleared away the misleading legends that surrounded such admired and popular masters as Memling. In 1867 he was entrusted by the Guild of St Thomas and St Luke with the task of cataloguing and partly organising an exhibition of early Flemish art in their principal hall.[94] He assembled more than two hundred pictures in all (most of them, admittedly, portraits of citizens of Bruges who had died before the eighteenth century), and his reputation was already sufficiently established for him to be able to borrow 'primitives' from many churches and religious institutions in Belgium, and even from leading private collectors in London and Paris.[95] Weale's approach to Flemish mediaeval art and the role it could still play was absolutely clear: in the first place, it was not Flemish at all, but derived essentially from the Rhineland school; in the second place, its Christian feeling could help to rescue modern art from the pit of realism into which it had sunk.

In 1878 Weale returned to England to embark on the perennial task of 'doing his utmost to reduce the chaotic state of things in the National Art Library at South Kensington into something like order, and to make the existence of treasures hidden away there known and accessible to students'.[96] He was always a difficult as well as a scholarly man, and his time in the museum was stormy; in 1897 he retired (though still beneath the age limit) and devoted himself to his researches. Some years later we hear of him as 'a lean, tall figure with wide yet stooping shoulders, clad in a grey coat of unfashionable cut, moving with shambling gait on out-turned feet; a full grey beard; and short-sighted eyes peering through spectacles from beneath the widest brim imaginable of a black felt hat . . . the very type of the antiquary in the mind's eye'.[97] Weale was aged nearly sixty-nine, and considered by the younger Germans to be the 'Nestor of early Netherlandish art history',[98] when, despite his 'great scepticism' and constantly worsening vision, he was persuaded by Kervyn de Lettenhove to take part in the proposed, but as yet uncertain, exhibition. Kervyn had barely met him, but had at once been astonished, amused and captivated by this eccentric Englishman 'who always seemed to be agitated by some kind of fever as he went to work in the archives', hurrying along, or rather running, absent-mindedly, with jerky steps, though he could not see more than two metres ahead of him, his legs knocking against each other in trousers that were much too wide. The two men engaged in a lengthy correspondence, of which only a fraction has been published,[99] and it is evident that Weale was not altogether happy about the arrangements that were being made. Although he was able to select a number of pictures on his own initiative, by no means all the others that were to be included met with his approval. He also disagreed strongly with his colleagues about the hanging. Above all, there were serious problems with the catalogue that he was expected to compile. He worked on his entries intermittently in England, but he arrived in Bruges only a few days before the exhibition was due to open, and not surprisingly there was a very long delay before the catalogue finally appeared.[100] Moreover, Weale (who was always more of an archivist than a connoisseur) was obliged to endorse in it all the attributions made by the lenders themselves, even when he was privately certain that they were not correct.[101] The records of the learned congress, which was held at Bruges two months after the exhibition opened in order to discuss some of the issues raised by it, suggest that he was in a distinctly tetchy mood, despite all the respect with which he was surrounded. An occasion that should have marked his apotheosis appeared rather to be indicating that his ascendancy was nearing its end and that a new taste and a new kind of scholarship were coming to the fore.[102]

The useful, well-informed but generally reticent preface to Weale's catalogue conveys no hint of the intensity with which he could react to certain of the artists about whom he was required to write (although the failure even to mention Brueghel signified strong disapproval[103]); no hint, either, of the fact that some of his views were coming to seem old-fashioned. Jan Van Eyck, he had written a year earlier,

> saw with his eyes, Memlinc with his soul. John studied, copied, and reproduced with marvellous accuracy the models he had before him. Memlinc, doubtless, studied and copied, but he did more; he meditated and reflected; his whole soul went into his work, and he idealised and glorified, and, so to say, transfigured the models which he had before him . . . many of the subjects he represented have never been so delicately and delightfully expressed by any other painter, with the exception, perhaps, of Fra Angelico. As compared with the other masters of the Netherlandish school, he is the most poetical and the most musical; many of his pictures are perfect little gems.

Van Eyck's Madonnas were 'always worldly, and at times even repulsive' and to the infant Christ he 'generally imparted a disagreeable look of old age, and Roger [van der Weyden] a thin and ungraceful form'; whereas in Memling's pictures 'a nobler and happier cast of countenance was to be seen'.[104] Nowhere were Van Eyck's limitations – 'his narrowness of vision, his want of religious, aye, even of poetical feeling' – revealed more clearly than in the Van der Paele panel (pl. 245).[105] Sometimes, it was true, Van Eyck could take advantage of his weaknesses to produce more individualised portraits, but

> Memlinc was a real artist, with far more sentiment than John van Eyck . . . It is easy to see by his paintings that he was indeed a man humble and pure of heart, who, when the arts were beginning to abdicate their position as handmaids of the Church in order to minister to the pleasures of men, preserved his love for the Christian tradition, and in earnest simplicity painted what he believed and venerated as he conceived and saw it in his meditations.[106]

In pages such as these Weale moves far beyond the purpose of Baron Kervyn de Lettenhove and his committee who had wished only to celebrate the 'Flemishness of Flemish art'. For Weale it was the godliness of early Flemish art that truly mattered, and he adapted to Memling and a few other painters some of the criteria that Rio and other Catholic writers had, three-quarters of a century earlier, formulated in relation to their contemporaries in Italy.

Memling had long been the most loved of all Flemish artists, and we have seen that his Moreel triptych was as much responsible as any single picture could be for the revival of interest in the Northern Primitives. By 1902, as Kervyn recognised, the success – indeed, the very existence – of an exhibition of the kind he was organising depended on an adequate representation of Memling,[107] nearly all of whose principal works were fortunately to be found in the hospices and churches of Bruges itself. When, therefore, the commission responsible for administering the relevant institutions refused to lend, as two years earlier they had refused to lend to Brussels, Kervyn threatened to resign, and it was only after the most extreme difficulties that all obstacles were overcome[108] and that the largest room of the exhibition was filled with some thirty-eight paintings attributed to the artist. It was claimed (rather too complacently) by the organisers that these amounted to more than half his total output and that of all his major paintings only three were missing: the *Crucifixion* from Lubeck, the *Last Judgement* from Danzig and the *Seven Griefs of the Virgin* from Munich.[109]

The most popular of all Memling's works – the ædicular shrine of St Ursula (pl. 248) – was placed under a glass case on a stand in the centre,[110] while around the walls hung some of his most celebrated religious masterpieces: from Chatsworth came the triptych showing in the central panel the Virgin and Child under a

248. Memling, *Shrine of St Ursula* (Bruges, Hospice of Saint-Jean).

249. Memling, *Donne Triptych* (London, National Gallery).

canopy in a palatial loggia opening on to a spacious landscape, with saints and angels presenting the kneeling figures of Sir John Donne and his daughter, while in each wing stands one of the St Johns (pl. 249); from Prince Doria in Rome, the unusually poignant and tender *Lamentation over the Dead Christ*; from Brussels, the *Martyrdom of St Sebastian*, whose appeal depended perhaps on the very absence of tension and violence with which the artist treated his subject; from Bruges itself came the Moreel triptych, the *Lamentation* and the beautiful *Mystic Marriage of St Catherine* – so motionless, silent and richly harmonious in colour – on one of whose wings the aftermath of the Baptist's beheading is represented with an apathy that verges on the perverse, while on the other an expressionless St John the Evangelist on Patmos records what appears to be an utterly prosaic Revelation.

Further altarpieces and devotional pictures arrived from private collections in London, Paris, Vienna, Munich and elsewhere, and although not all of them are today accepted as original works by Memling – and, indeed, some were rejected by Weale even at the time – the impact of so many sweet, gracious, idealised Madonnas, of so many gentle, well-behaved infant Christs and of so many grave, impassive saints and donors was over-whelming on those many visitors who came to the exhibition in order to find consolation in a godless world: 'without wishing to elevate him to the rank of one of the four or five geniuses at the very summit of humanity', wrote a correspondent for *La Quinzaine*, 'we can say that his soul, far more than any modern soul, was capable of understanding the joys of Paradise . . . He is the great Primitive, who represents the highest religious achievement of Flemish painting, the greatest name before Rubens.'[111]

A fine group of Memling's portraits had also been assembled – most notably the very striking *Man holding a Roman Coin*, lent by the Brussels museum – and these, too, were much admired. But whether as a result of deliberate policy or because the small, bust-length portraits had been more widely dispersed and were less accessible, it was the religious paintings that dominated the room devoted to him. And, with a few outstanding exceptions to be discussed shortly, visitors were inclined to endorse the traditional view that he was not only the 'King of the Exhibition' but also the 'doux génie', the Flemish equivalent of Fra Angelico, even 'the Raphael of the North, who made visible in his figures of saints and angels his own inner dreams composed of grace and tenderness'.[112]

The third painter to whom particular attention was paid at the exhibition was Gerard David. Weale had written of him a few years earlier that 'it was reserved to me to restore the name of this great artist to its proper place in the history of Low Country art',[113] and the presence of so many of his pictures came as something of a revelation. Some twenty attributed to him were on display, and the impression that they made was of a gentle follower of the gentle Memling, with whom he was sometimes confused[114] and whose values of calmness and piety he carried into the following generation while adding to them a very individual sense of colour.[115] His noble and solemn *Baptism of Christ with an Angel* from the Bruges museum was felt to be a picture 'of indescribable beauty' (pl. 250),[116] and it is hardly surprising that Weale should have been captivated by its wonderfully lyrical landscape, than which 'nothing can well be finer'.[117] But it was above all the *Virgin and Child with Saints and Angels*, (described by Kervyn as 'the most exquisite, if not the most

250. Gerard David, *Baptism of Christ with an Angel* (Bruges, Groeninge Museum).

251. Gerard David, *Virgin and Child with Saints and Angels* (Rouen, Musée des Beaux-Arts).

beautiful, work of this rare painter') which Weale especially insisted must be borrowed at all costs (pl. 251). It belonged to the museum of Rouen, and the problems involved in organising the loan were probably the greatest of all those encountered by the organisers.[118]

Beautiful pictures (and, indeed, pictures that are not beautiful) can inspire differing levels of emotion at different periods. It is not too difficult to suggest why the picture in Rouen should have been such a particular favourite of Weale and other nineteenth-century art lovers. That it had been presented by Gerard David himself (whose portrait and that of his wife are to be seen in the background at each end) to the Carmelite monastery of Sion, where it remained until it was sold off in 1783, and that it was one of the only three pictures by him which were quite securely documented certainly contributed to its reputation;[119] but more significant surely is the fact that in no other work did David (or perhaps any other Flemish artist) combine so movingly two qualities that were specially appreciated at the time: the devout 'innocence' of mediaeval art and the harmonious balance of the Renaissance. The Virgin and Child (who holds a bunch of grapes) are posed frontally at the centre of the long horizontal composition and are framed by two winged, music-making angels. On each side are five female saints, dressed in gowns of red and green and orange, who give the impression of being handmaidens, so unobtrusive are the attributes that indicate their martyrdoms and blessed status: the eyes delicately held by St Lucy, for instance, are barely distinguishable from precious jewels. And the subtle variations in their poses and the tender expressions of their faces, which extend from the very young to the mature, offset any effect of rigidity or contrived sophistication.

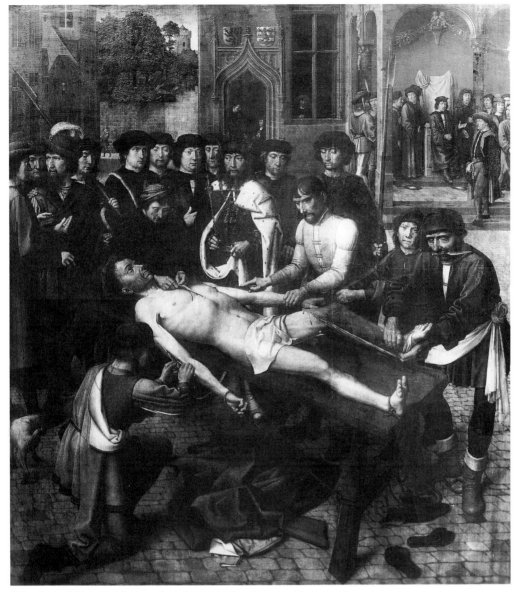

252. Gerard David, *Flaying of the Unjust Judge Sisamnes* (Bruges, Groeninge Museum).

But for lovers of the quiet, pious, gentle tradition of Memling, apparently reincarnated in David, the exhibition presented at least one serious problem: the large, horrifying *Flaying of the Unjust Judge Sisamnes* (pl. 252) which, together with *King Cambyses ordering the Arrest of Sisamnes*, David had painted for the magistrates of Bruges to hang in the justice room of their town hall as a warning against venality. In this picture 'the painter has produced with extraordinary calmness and serenity, the most realistic, the bloodiest of all tortures, that has ever been painted with such minuteness upon canvas'.[120] That Weale himself had felt uneasy about so uncharacteristic a work by the master whom he had discovered is revealed by the jarring tone of the comments to be found in his book of seven years earlier: 'the flaying of a man is doubtless by no means a pleasant thing to look at'. But he emphasised that 'it was not the painter who chose the subject . . . [and] we cannot hesitate in saying that Gerard executed perfectly the picture entrusted to him'.[121] Tortures when painted by the idiosyncratic Dieric Bouts, an artist of 'high and inflexible conscience'[122] were fearful in content, but not offensive in their impact; however, that Gerard David, of all artists, should have indulged in a scene of this kind was evidently so disturbing that a number of critics either failed to mention the matter at all or else dismissed it in a few anodyne words.[123]

Van Eyck, Memling and Gerard David were widely acknowledged to be the supreme masters of the exhibition, and, indeed, they were the only ones whose works seem to have been systematically pursued for it. Although seventeen pictures were attributed to Roger van der Weyden in the catalogue, elsewhere Weale acknowledged that of none of them 'can the authenticity be said to be established'.[124] Present-day scholarship is rather more generous about the selection that was made, but the obvious impossibility of exhibiting most of his greatest pictures meant that he did not emerge as strikingly as might otherwise have been expected. It is true that, even so, he had some passionate admirers;[125] but it is impossible not to wonder whether the whole balance of the exhibition might not have been decisively altered had his sublime *Seven Sacraments* been borrowed from the Antwerp Museum – to which it (together with two Van Eycks and many other masterpieces of the Flemish and German schools) had been bequeathed as early as 1841 by Florent van Ertborn, one of the first and greatest of all collectors in the field. Difficulties also stood in the way of an adequate display of Hugo van der Goes, whose works, commented one writer, were among those 'which deserve no more than the hasty acknowledgment granted in the Salons of our times to artists who have been included out of kindness or to fill up space'.[126] Bosch was represented by six pictures, at least two of which were authentic, but he did not attract the attention that would be given to him by later generations.[127]

The success of the exhibition (which had been opened by the king) surpassed all expectations. It duration was extended by three weeks, and a German scholar was reminded of Bayreuth during the festival season.[128] Some of those involved in the organisation felt that the ghost of *Bruges-la-morte* had at last been laid[129] – an allusion to the novel of that title published a few years earlier by the symbolist poet Georges Rodenbach which described the (rather melodramatic) events that befell a man who had chosen to live in the city because its melancholy matched the grief he felt for his recently deceased young wife. Foreign visitors, however, were enchanted to see how little Bruges seemed to have changed over the centuries.[130] Around the neo-Gothic Palais Provincial itself, gabled buildings of red brick, which had mostly been converted into inns and cafés, brought to the district an atmosphere of lively informality.[131] A little further off, narrow streets lined with small houses (some of them looking distinctly more mediaeval than they had done in the Middle Ages) were reflected in the quiet canals; deserted squares mottled with sparse clumps of grass and weeds; the steeples of Gothic churches – everything seemed to make of the city a perfect and entirely natural setting for the sincere, ingenuous, touching art of the Flemish primitives.[132] It is not surprising that remarkably few of the very many visitors to the exhibition who wrote of

Bruges in this spirit bothered to mention the fact that, among its most valuable possessions, was a marble Madonna and Child by almost the only man known to have spoken of the early Flemish painters with utter contempt: Michelangelo.[133]

Connoisseurs were naturally excited by the problems of attribution raised by so many undocumented and anonymous pictures. One of the most admired paintings on view – a small panel from Glasgow portraying a warrior and his protective saint – was at one time or another ascribed to Mabuse, Memling, Van Eyck, Hugo van der Goes, Gerard David, the Maître de Moulins or some other artist of the French school:[134] the catalogue prudently described the author as 'unknown'. And a few writers tried to penetrate the endlessly repeated and conventional platitudes about 'faith' and 'sincerity' in order to discover in the pictures on display a more complex and subtle indication of the spirit of the Middle Ages. It was doubtless gratifying to the devout that 'the religious idea dominates . . . there are only mysteries, miracles, and realistic scenes of martyrdom . . . the mystic idealism of supremely impassable beauty deifies all these hagio-iconographical scenes'; but it could be dismaying to discover that the price for this lay in the fact that

> all these old masters seem to have ignored pity, the emotion which acts upon the facial muscles or sharpens and discolours the features . . . The middle ages had not only harnessed the bodies of the heroes, the souls as well were closed, serene, cold, and deprived of tearful and soft pity. The mediaeval chroniclers and painters could and knew how to reproduce with the same candour and superior dryness carnage, human sacrifices, and murder. In all the pictures of martyrdom the victims appear to be under chloroform, and the torturers work calmly, with their eyes hardly illumined by attentive curiosity, just like chirurgians during an anatomy lesson'.[135]

iv

The exhibition *Les Primitifs flamands et l'Art ancien* held in Bruges for three and a half months in the summer and early autumn of 1902 must surely be unique in having decisively affected the lives of four major scholars.

As the weeks went by and the official catalogue still failed to appear, scathing comments in the press and angry recriminations among the organisers hardly suggested the likelihood of so remarkable an outcome. And when the catalogue was eventually published Weale's terse disclaimer of responsibility for any of the attributions in it (which had all been imposed by the owners)[136] demonstrated that its only use would be as an indication of what was on view. Because it had been preceded by a hastily produced compilation riddled with mistakes, Kervyn professed himself entirely satisfied. But not everyone agreed, and on 4 August he was dismayed by the appearance in Ghent of a 'Catalogue critique' of the paintings in the exhibition which had been deliberately designed in the same format as the official publication so that the two could be easily bound together.[137]

The 'Catalogue critique' was the work of a forty-year-old university professor,

Georges Hulin de Loo, who had hitherto specialised in social history and law.[138] But he was deeply interested in art and was therefore asked to join the organising committee of the Bruges exhibition and to travel to London and Vienna to secure some of the loans requested from collectors.[139] Despite the tone of respectful courtesy with which he always alluded to the opinions of Weale and his other colleagues, the polemical content of his pamphlet aroused a good deal of surprise.

Hulin de Loo began with a series of short essays – often related only marginally, if at all, to the exhibition itself – on anonymous masters whose achievements he tried to reconstruct on the basis of documentary sources and stylistic criticism. He then ran through each item in the official catalogue, sometimes silently endorsing its contents, sometimes adding to them and sometimes flatly contradicting them. Weale had acknowledged that Number 8 – the Duke of Devonshire's signed Van Eyck of the *Enthronement of St Thomas à Becket* – had been entirely repainted at the end of the fifteenth century; Hulin de Loo pointed out that it provided 'an excellent example of the powerlessness of signatures and documents to guarantee the authenticity of a picture. It is not a retouched Van Eyck. Neither the original design nor the composition are by him; the costumes do not belong to his period'. Number 55 – a Dieric Bouts, borrowed from Hofstede de Groot, the Dutch free-lance scholar and expert adviser to collectors and the trade – was listed by Hulin as merely 'École de Louvain'. On a single page, a Master of Flémalle, a Roger van der Weyden, two Memlings and a Gerard David (nos 213–17) all became 'Unknown' or, at best, 'School of Memling'.

The 'Catalogue critique' made the reputation of Hulin de Loo who, for the remaining forty-three years of his life, consolidated his position as one of the two leading authorities in the world on early Flemish painting.

The other – of whom he wrote with great admiration – was his almost exact contemporary, Max J. Friedländer.

Unlike Hulin de Loo, Friedländer had already published a large number of contributions to art history before 1902. After working for a short period as a volunteer in the print room of the Berlin museum, he spent a few years at the Wallraf-Richartz Museum in Cologne before returning to Berlin in 1896. There, under the directorship of Bode, he was first employed as a curator in the picture gallery of the newly established Kaiser Friedrich Museum. He became director of the print room in 1908, and of the whole museum less than twenty years later: this was the post he held when, as a Jew, he was dismissed in 1933.[140]

The first fifteen years of Friedländer's extremely productive career were largely devoted to the graphic works of the early German artists – Altdorfer, Cranach and Dürer above all. Only some four or five articles, amounting to less than a dozen pages, on Van Eyck and Quentin Matsys made apparent to the world of scholarship how great was his expertise in this field also.[141] His advice was constantly sought in the organisation of the Bruges exhibition,[142] and his long, authoritative review of it (followed, shortly afterwards, by a handsomely illustrated folio recording some of the leading pictures shown) marked a turning point in his career.[143] Thereafter, until his death in 1957, he dedicated ever more of his time and intellectual energy to the infinitely complex problems of connoisseurship raised by the early Flemish painters – a branch of study that seems to have promoted longevity in those who practised it – and the fourteen volumes of his *Altniederländische Malerei*, first published between 1924 and 1937, remain the most important contribution ever made to the subject and the basis for all subsequent research.

Like Hulin de Loo – to whom he confessed his great indebtedness,[144] although he did not accept all the views, let along the ruthless tone, of the 'Catalogue critique' – Friedländer was, in 1902, essentially concerned with the authorship of the pictures shown at Bruges and their similarity to others which it had not, unfortunately, been possible to present. Whereas the organisers had aimed to stress the autonomy and also the cultural unity revealed by so many examples of Flemish painting, for rigorous connoisseurs the importance of the exhibition lay precisely in the diversity of what had been brought to light. Friedländer showed no interest in the realism or piety or psychology of the artists concerned; or in the light thrown by their works on the civilisation of Northern Europe and its possible relationship to that of the South; or in the question of whether or not they were rightly described as 'primitives' as opposed to having pioneered a new approach to art and hence, perhaps, to historical change in general.

These, and other issues, were all raised in what was certainly the liveliest and most original among early critical responses to the exhibition although we will see that, in retrospect, its main importance lies in the masterly denial that it provoked of the very point that it tried so firmly to establish. The author was Hippolyte Fierens-Gevaert, an ambitious thirty-two year old critic, who had hitherto devoted himself principally to theories of contemporary art, about which he wrote rather nebulously with repeated invocations to the need for spirituality and to the lessons of Nietzsche and Tolstoy.[145] He had, however, also published an extended essay on Flemish painting 'de Van Eyck à Van Dyck' which, in 1901, he incorporated with amendments into a book on the 'psychology of Bruges' dedicated to the memory of Georges Rodenbach.[146] In this he aimed to set 'the golden age of Flemish art' into an international context, and he paid special attention to the importance that it had had for the Italians. Many of his comments are as fresh as they are perceptive, and they make it clear that he had already studied fifteenth-century art with great care. None the less, the impact of what he saw at the Palais Provincial turned out to be decisive, for the extraordinary assemblage of works on view led him not just to heighten his tone but to change some of his opinions and develop others to an extent that would hardly otherwise have been possible. Soon afterwards he was to produce very influential, though flawed, volumes on the painters of Flanders, and he ended his days in 1926 as director of the Brussels museum, Professor of the History of Art at the University of Liège and a leading figure in the international circuit of art-historical luminaries.[147]

Warning signals that Fierens-Gevaert's approach was likely to be unusual appeared quite early in the three articles he devoted to the exhibition, but it was only when he reached Memling that the full extent of his heterodoxy became clear. 'It is compulsory to respond with ecstasy to the pictures of this charming master, and on this occasion ecstasy has turned to frenzy. Alas, I have been unable to share

in this premeditated enthusiasm. The great artist struck me as mawkish compared
with Van Eyck, artificial compared with van der Weyden, lacking in vigour
compared with Thierry Bouts, lacking in self-control compared with Gerard
David . . .' Such a judgement shook the very foundations on which the exhibition
had been constructed. For a moment Fierens-Gevaert hesitated: perhaps his reaction was only a temporary one, provoked by the crowds and by the removal of the
artist's altarpieces and portraits from the small, private, silent rooms of the Hôpital
Saint-Jean where he, too, had once loved them so much. But then he resumed his
argument, although he hardly dared to confess to himself that already for some
years he had experienced a weakening in the religious passion that one was
expected to feel for Memling. 'Today I admit that he no longer seems to me to
have the exceptional importance and prolific grandeur not just of a Van Eyck, but
even of a Roger van der Weyden or a Gerard David or a Quentin Matsys'.
Naturally some of Memling's portraits were of exceptional merit, and he had been
able to convey 'not without preciosity' the ecstasies of mysticism. He had done
this without the theological power of the brothers Van Eyck and without the
human and tragic depth of van der Weyden, 'but certainly with elegance, and a
very subtle awareness of worldly refinement'. However, he had allowed himself to
rely too much on studio collaborators and had become rich and had bought
property in Bruges – 'not that I will have the bad taste to reproach him for that'.
He was, to sum up, the Benozzo Gozzoli of the Flemish school, and although
Benozzo was a great painter, he was not of the stature of Angelico or Botticelli or
Piero della Francesca or Mantegna or Ghirlandaio.[148]

In view of this judgement it is not surprising that Fierens-Gevaert saw Gerard
David also in a new light. He was the only artist whose standing had been
enhanced by the exhibition, and it was clear that he was on a level with the greatest
Flemish geniuses. No relationship to Memling is now acknowledged, but David is
compared favourably to Van Eyck and van der Weyden and he is implicitly sent on
a visit to Italy, and – perhaps under the influence of some works he had specially
admired there – he is credited with having taught the Flemish how to paint great
historical compositions: 'It is with this profoundly original and wilful creative
personality that the admirable Burgundian epoch comes to a close. Bruges is about
to die; the fifteenth century is ending; the Renaissance is in sight – and already the
grand figures of Gerard David, conceived with no concern for the constraints of
asceticism, foreshadow a revolution in art'.[149]

That revolution was to be pursued by Quentin Matsys – the greatest of the
Flemish artists after Van Eyck and Rubens – and also by Barendt van Orley, for
Fierens-Gevaert was not at all alarmed by Italian influences as long as they served
the cause of progress and as long as they were ultimately subordinated to the
native savour of Flanders, as was demonstrated, for instance, in the 'sublime
naïvety' of the portraits of Pourbus the Elder. It was true that the art of Brueghel,
which incorporated 'all the joy of Flanders . . . all the ingenuous, grotesque and
formidable gaiety of Flanders', constituted a great roar of laughter in the face of the
Italianisers; nevertheless, renewed Italianising was necessary before a new genius
was born who would be capable of combining, in a definitive form, those qualities

that had been assimilated from abroad and those innate gifts that were natural to the race. It fell to Rubens to accomplish this.[150]

Although Fierens-Gevaert ended his articles with a conventional tribute to the fifteenth-century masters 'who are dearer to me than all others' and to the city of Bruges which has remained for all Flemings 'the sacred reliquary of the Faith, the Fatherland and of Beauty', his interpretation of the exhibition directly challenged the notion, cherished by Weale and pilgrims to Bruges, that the finest Flemish art was essentially static in character. For him the pictures in the Palais Provincial demonstrated that, on the contrary, Flanders had, like Italy, experienced a Renaissance. When, three years later, he returned to the lessons of the exhibition, he did so with a patriotic fervour that was just as pronounced, but with an emphasis that was distinctly different. For by then another challenge had arisen.

The reaction against many aspects of modern life – because of its association with the cult of progress and materialism – which was so conspicuous a feature of much modern culture in the late nineteenth and early twentieth centuries profoundly affected attitudes to the artistic achievements of the past; widespread distaste for Gauguin or Picasso did not extend to the under-explored 'archaic' or 'naïf' painting and sculpture championed by them. 'Love of the Primitives', wrote one critic in 1904,[151] 'has for some years now made an appeal both to our blasé spirits and to our scholarly curiosity as historians'. And so, whether early art was interpreted (as it was by Courajod and Fierens-Gevaert) as having constituted a vanguard leading towards the Renaissance or whether it was seen as having pursued altogether different and higher values, it acquired a new and more pertinent status in current consciousness. Throughout Europe nationalist sentiment was as keen to bring to light distant ancestors as it was to promote contemporary practitioners. The year 1902 witnessed an exhibition of 'ancient art' in Barcelona as well as in Bruges, and two years later exhibitions of primitive paintings were held in Düsseldorf, Siena and Paris. The crude and vigorous painters and sculptors of Romanesque and Gothic Catalonia;[152] the 'bitter energy' to be found in the altarpieces of the 'master of St Bartholomew' (which some people were now beginning to prefer to the excessively pretty Madonnas by more familiar artists of the Cologne school);[153] the figures in polychrome wood attributed to Jacopo della Quercia, Vecchietta and other sculptors temporarily removed from the abbeys and churches of central Tuscany and installed in the Palazzo Pubblico[154] – everywhere the rediscovered heritage of impressive forefathers served to bolster the national pride of their living descendants. In words that must have made Weale wince, Kervyn proclaimed that the principal result of the exhibitions organised elsewhere in Europe had been 'to raise still higher the success of the one held in Bruges and the glory of our school ... Our painters dominated their rivals and reigned supreme! Flanders showed herself to be the richest and most powerful of nations through the genius of her children.'[155] And then he referred back to the speech he had made at the closing ceremony of 5 October 1902: 'Rarely have the glories of the past shed a more vivid light, and the legitimate pride we have all taken in this has made us more proud of our awareness of being Flemish, more proud of our name of Belgians. It has both increased our faith in the future and our love for the soil that covers the ashes of our fathers'.[156]

Words such as these must have struck a particularly sensitive nerve in France. For many years the French had been dismayed that while Italy had had a Renaissance and Flanders had had its primitives, they seemed to have had nothing of their own in the field of early painting which could be compared with these phenomena. However, in his 'Catalogue critique' Hulin de Loo had gone out of his way to taunt French scholars for their utter neglect of what had in fact been a significant heritage. Little can he have anticipated the over-compensation for this neglect that was to follow in 1904, when an exhibition devoted to 'Les Primitifs Français' was organised in Paris, divided between the Louvre and the Bibliothèque Nationale. It was entrusted to Henri Bouchot, Keeper of the Print Room at the Bibliothèque Nationale, an authority on French drawings and engravings of the sixteenth century – and a veteran of the Franco-Prussian war. A number of beautiful and important pictures were included, and some which had been exhibited two years earlier in Bruges were shown again in Paris. Certain painters, hitherto considered to be Flemish – such as the still mysterious Maître de Flemalle – now turned out to have been French. Attributions to names that were already famous, such as Jean Fouquet, were made with reckless abandon, and it was suddenly discovered that fifteenth-century France had seen the birth of a large number of regional schools of painting of the utmost importance. This exhibition proved to be a spectacular success, and it is agreed that it constituted a significant landmark in the scholarly study of French art. But the motives behind its organisation had not been scholarly, and the tone of the book that Bouchot wrote to accompany the exhibition was (fortunately) much ridiculed at the time, and still makes painful reading today. In the first few pages he attacked on all fronts. As the inhabitants of Bruges spoke French, their painters could (at least until the middle of the fifteenth century) be included in the French school, and it was in any case only posthumously that Roger de la Pasture had been annexed by the Flemings as Roger van der Weyden. As for the 'legend of an Italian "Renaissance"', this had hypnotised many generations of very sincere men: in fact 'our old French art' had been characterised by 'natural, human and true tendencies, at a time when our [Italian] neighbours long remained frozen in their Byzantine and traditional decorations'. The Italian painters who had come to Fontainebleau under François Ier had deformed the course of French art. There was no doubt, Bouchot conceded generously, that the brothers Van Eyck had in fact existed, but he then devoted a whole chapter to raising just such doubts. The Arnolfini portrait in London was 'one of the most probable pictures' to have been painted by Jan Van Eyck, although it certainly did not represent the Arnolfini and certainly did nothing to strengthen the attribution to him of the Virgin with the 'prétendu chancellier Rolin' in the Louvre (pl. 260) and the Virgin with van der Paele in Bruges (pl. 245). The very notion that the Van Eycks had made an important impact on European art was absurd; the painters of Bruges had invented nothing; and the current of influences between Flanders and France ran entirely in the opposite direction.[157]

It was with such issues in mind that Fierens-Gevaert returned to the question of the Flemish primitives. He was no longer concerned to prove that these fifteenth-century masters had, partly under the impulse of Gerard David, developed a momentum that would eventually lead to a true Renaissance. What was now at stake was the positive role played by the art of Flanders in promoting the European Renaissance as a whole, and Fierens-Gevaert's decided views on this were expressed in the very title of his book (which, however, hardly prepares the reader for its tone): *La Renaissance Septentrionale et les Premiers Maîtres des Flandres.*

To establish his theory Fierens-Gevaert began by accepting the principal assumption of Courajod's lectures on the origins of the Renaissance which had first been published in 1901, but which had been strangely neglected by Belgian art historians. The Renaissance had been characterised by the search for realism, and the earliest steps in this direction had been taken by the Italians at the dawn of the fourteenth century. But Giotto, and above all his followers, had not been able to go far enough, and help was therefore needed from the North. In the middle of the fourteenth century French art, inspired by immigrant painters from Flanders, had taken up the challenge – and at this point in his argument Fierens-Gevaert some-what diverged from Courajod by denying that Flemish art was, of its very nature, realist at all times: it merely happened to be so at this particular historical moment because of the relatively democratic conditions that prevailed in Flanders ('avant d'être dans l'art, le naturalisme fut dans les coeurs'). However, Flanders – just like modern Belgium – had not been big or powerful enough to maintain all its artists, many of whom had been attracted to the opulent court at Paris, where they had carried out their reforming mission. With the collapse of France, following English domination, Flemish artists had been forced to emigrate back to their homes and to Burgundy, and there they had inaugurated the Renaissance. By far the most important personalities had been the brothers Van Eyck, although their role had been obscured by French attempts to annex for themselves all those Flemish artists who had worked in France and by exaggerated – and puerile – claims made by the Dutch for the supremacy of the admittedly great sculptor Claus Sluter. In fact, the importance of the brothers Van Eyck had been international and had converted even the Italians. Despite Michelangelo's professed scorn for Flemish achieve-ments, neither he nor Raphael nor Leonardo ever abandoned the study of nature, and to that extent they could be considered followers of the Van Eycks. Indeed, ultimately Velázquez, Frans Hals, Giorgione, 'tous les impressionistes de la Renaissance, tous les maîtres du XVIIᵉ, puis du XVIIIᵉ siècle', all aspects of modern beauty were 'born of the principles inaugurated by the masters of the North. The fourteenth century was a solemn moment in the history of art and among our great ancestors those whom we must cherish with a particularly tender and respectful love are those who gave definitive resolution to the Northern conquests, the masters of the *Adoration*, the evangelists of our art and of modern art, the brothers Van Eyck'.

In his closing sentences Fierens-Gevaert forsakes art history altogether and strides into the realm of dogma and mysticism. 'The altarpiece of the Lamb is more than the masterpiece of a school and a race; it is the greatest act of faith known to the history of art. It incorporates all the international currents of beauty at the beginning of modern times, but at the same time it establishes our religious doctrines. If, as Hegel claims, painting is the centre of Christian art, the Ghent

polyptych is the centre of Christian painting . . . Thus by bringing back an epoch
to life [we can see that] the altarpiece of the Lamb reveals for us the face of God;
and thus Art, with the support of Faith, makes Heaven descend to Earth.' His
book was concluded, Fierens-Gevaert tells us, on Easter Sunday 1905.[158]

v

In 1943 Johan Huizinga (pl. 253),[159] who, at the age of seventy-one, had recently
been released from enforced detention in German-occupied Holland, recalled that
the Bruges exhibition of more than forty years earlier had been 'an experience of
the highest significance' in launching him on his career as a mediaeval historian.
It is true that 'a vague, fantastic longing for direct contact (with the period),
nourished chiefly by impressions derived from the visual arts', had never left him
since, as a seven-year-old schoolboy, he had witnessed a student pageant representing the entry of Edzard, Count of East Friesland, into the city of Groningen in
1505:[160] none the less, until he went to see the Flemish primitives displayed in the
Palais Provincial, he had devoted himself almost exclusively to the study of
comparative linguistics and Oriental religions. Now he embarked on the researches
for his earliest book, *The Origins of Haarlem*, and soon afterwards he conceived the
first sketchy outlines of his masterpiece, *The Waning of the Middle Ages*,[161] which
was based on the attempt 'to arrive at a genuine understanding of the art of the
brothers van Eyck and their contemporaries, that is to say, to grasp its meaning by
seeing it in connexion with the entire life of their times'.[162]

Huizinga had been born into a family of long-established Mennonites in
Groningen in 1872.[163] Although many of his ancestors had been pastors, his father
had eschewed a clerical life and had turned instead to medicine and to natural
history, eventually becoming Professor of Physiology at the local university. His
interests were inherited by his eldest son Jacob, but Johan, the second born,
showed no inclination for technical matters of any kind. At primary school the
love of history that had been awakened in him by the colourful costumes and
glittering metal armour of the student procession was encouraged by a gifted
woman teacher to whose lessons he remained indebted until the end of his life. At
the gymnasium, however, his studies changed direction, and his historical interests
were kept alive only by two hobbies, both of which he shared with his brother: a
passion for heraldry and an enthusiasm for collecting coins.[164] From Petrarch to
Burckhardt the very process of handling and examining the tangible vestiges of a
world that seemed to have slipped by for ever had helped to foster the belief that
the past had not been irredeemably lost but could somehow be recalled and
summoned back to life. Huizinga was perhaps the last great historian to succumb
to the apparently magical power of such relics.

Meanwhile, although his heart belonged to the Middle Ages, he began
to learn Hebrew and mastered Arabic; he also studied theories of mythology and histories of linguistics, and he dabbled in Middle High German
and Old Norse. In Leipzig he attended lectures on Lithuanian, Sanskrit

253. Johan Huizinga.

and Old Irish, and began to read Russian. On his return to Groningen he planned to write his thesis on 'The expression of perceptions of light and sound in the Indogermanic languages'. The topic, however, proved to be unmanageable, and he eventually obtained his doctorate in 1897 with a dissertation on the court jester in Sanskrit drama. A few months later he was driven (in the absence of anything more suitable) to seek a job as history master in the secondary school of Haarlem. He remained there for eight years, and although he continued to publish articles on Indian religion and literature, his teaching – in a school that valued the sciences far more highly than the humanities and to boys who were primarily interested in football – was confined to more conventional subjects: Egypt and the Ancient East, Greece and Rome, and the French Revolution. He was later to describe these lessons in terms that will not altogether surprise some admirers of his historical writings: 'I did not trouble myself much with the critical underpinning of what I was saying: I wanted above all to tell a living, invigorating story.'[165] In 1903 Huizinga took on the additional burden of becoming an unsalaried lecturer in Ancient Indian Culture and Literature at the University of Amsterdam; but by now he had already begun his researches into the origins of Haarlem, and in August 1905, at the age of thirty-three, he was appointed Professor of History at Groningen University.

Shortly before his death Huizinga was to write of the early period of his life (which will surely strike any modern reader as having been almost alarmingly industrious) with disappointment and self-reproach. Of his time in Germany he recorded that 'in these years I was really a very bad youth as far as my studies went . . . although I did not lack keenness',[166] and he also pointed out how limited was the extent of his reading: 'some Shakespeare, but not much yet; some German literature, but nothing out of the ordinary, Schiller, a bit of Goethe, Heine, a few lyrics, and just about nothing French at all. I was not a great reader, and have never been one'.[167] Above all, so he said, he had been a fantasist, a dreamer – prone to solitary wandering in the countryside, 'not exactly thinking, but my spirit roaming above the bounds of day-to-day existence in a kind of ethereal bliss . . .'.[168] His moods would sometimes alternate between phases of almost manic excitement and bouts of depression which might last for weeks at a time, although to outsiders they would convey no more than an impression of increased taciturnity. Marriage in 1902 brought an end to these symptoms – but, with hindsight, we can see (as perhaps the old and isolated Huizinga himself could not) the productive use to which the historian of later mediaeval Europe was subsequently to put such tense experiences. Did they not play some part in suggesting to him 'that perpetual oscillation between despair and distracted joy . . . that characterised life in the Middle Ages'?[169]

Although in terms of strictly scholarly results he might feel some cause for dissatisfaction about the progress of his life before he obtained the chair at Groningen, outside the lecture room and his textbooks he had acquired two sources of happiness which were also to prove of decisive benefit to his work: a love of music and a love of art. The subtle and profound claims that he was to make for these as guides to an understanding of the past were only formulated a little later; but even the most cursory reading of *The Waning of the Middle Ages* will surely reveal that no serious historical masterpiece (as distinct from romantic novel) has ever responded so spontaneously to the sights and sounds of earlier human societies. Within the very first pages we are introduced to 'cries and processions, songs and music', to 'the lover who wore the colours of his lady, companions the emblem of their confraternity, parties and servants the badges and blazon of their lords'; and, above all, to the one sound that 'rose ceaselessly above the noises of busy life and lifted all things unto a sphere of order and serenity: the sound of bells'.

Huizinga developed and deepened his love of music over the years, his tastes changing with the circumstances in which he heard it. First came Brahms and Grieg sung to him by the sister of one of his closest friends, who was gifted with 'an attractive mezzo-soprano voice and a delivery as full of feeling as it was natural'; then, frustrated by the course of his studies in Leipzig, he would go to concerts, church recitals and the opera – but only to performances of Wagner; finally his wife passed on to him her enthusiasm for Bach and Mozart, Schubert and Beethoven. But he never learnt to play an instrument, and 'as far as music was concerned, I always remained completely illiterate'.[170] His commitment to art was far more binding.

Huizinga was himself an extremely able and lively draughtsman. Early in life he made a set of humorous illustrations of significant and trivial episodes ranging over

254. Johan Huizinga, *1444: In Dodewaard werd een bloeiende appelboom gezien in Maart* (*1444: In Dodeward a flowering apple-tree is seen in March*), from Huizinga, *Keur van gedenkwaardige tafereelen*, Amsterdam 1950.

many centuries of Dutch history which were not published until after his death and which reveal a vein of good-natured satire hardly to be found in his written work (pl. 254).[171] Less surprising perhaps is the fact that he produced numerous sketches of dream sequences (though these, too, were generally comic in tone) and that he seems to have accompanied his lectures with drawings, made on the blackboard, of costumes and other accessories copied from illuminated manuscripts and from pictures.[172] But despite these gifts and despite the fact that much later he was to claim that he had passionately yearned for knowledge of the visual arts,[173] there does not seem to be any evidence that, during his early student years, Huizinga showed any special feeling for painting, either of the past or of his contemporaries. It was through literature (and certainly not through politics – for he never read a newspaper) that he absorbed new developments in thought and perception: Dutch writers, naturally, but also Rémy de Gourmont, Pierre Louys and Alfred Jarry, men whose 'extremely one-sided' view of the world seems to have been somewhat modified by the impact on him of Edgar Allan Poe, Rossetti and Robert Louis Stevenson.

This situation, however, changed in 1895 when Huizinga became involved with modern art, an involvement that was later to strike him as having been closely related to his own very different researches.[174] In that year he made contact with some medical students who agreed to get together from time to time to organise exhibitions of contemporary painters in Groningen. He himself had to miss the first two occasions (one of which was devoted to Van Gogh) because of his brief residence in Leipzig, but he played a prominent part in arranging the important exhibition of works by Jan Toorop in 1896.[175] This made a powerful impact on him. A representative group of pictures was assembled, and as Toorop, who was then nearly forty and well travelled, had been influenced by most of the styles he had encountered – those of Turner and of Manet, as well as of the Realists, the Impressionists and the Pointillists – the exhibition must have offered a startling introduction to the varied currents of modern art, which were as unfamiliar to Huizinga himself as they were to the other inhabitants of isolated Groningen. But the pictures whose presence he remembered till the end of his life were Toorop's most recent, most startling, ventures into Symbolism – *The Three Brides*, *The Garden of Sorrows*, *La Nouvelle Génération* and a few more: barely comprehensible allegories of innocence and sexual corruption in which large, expressionless eyes stare out at the spectator in fear or hatred, while across the congested surface of the canvas writhe boneless, elongated female bodies and the emaciated, grasping, palsied branches of battered tree stumps. That Toorop's pictures – 'modern' though they were – represented an end rather than a beginning must surely have struck even those who were fascinated by them; although, when asked to explain, the artist himself, who looked like an Oriental prince (he had been born in Java of a mother who was half Chinese), would only point to the dunes that formed the horizon in many of his more conventional works and mumble in his bewitching voice: 'the dunes, the mystery'.

The remaining exhibitions seem to have been something of an anti-climax. They certainly made little appeal to the public: on one Sunday afternoon Huizinga and his brother removed an ancient fireman's helmet and bugle from the museum and stood on the steps blowing it as hard as they could in the vain hope of bringing in a single visitor. The series came to an end in the spring of 1897 with an illustrated lecture based on photographs of works of art to be seen in Italy.

Among Toorop's friends and admirers was the critic, art historian and portrait painter Jan Veth[176] whose work is characterised by the most subdued and gentle realism. It was probably not long after the Groningen exhibition that he and Huizinga met and initiated an intimate friendship which ended only with the painter's death in 1925.[177] Their interests were complementary in the most remarkable way, and Huizinga looked upon his friend's house as a second home. Although the biography that he wrote of him contained little about Veth's paintings,[178] so close a contact with a man whose life was devoted to the practice and study of art must obviously have been of the greatest importance in stimulating Huizinga's own appreciation of painting. And this was strengthened still further by the Bruges exhibition of 1902 and by his (first) marriage in the same year, following which – so he wrote – his spirit lived not only in music, but 'in everything that was available to us of the visual arts'. Indeed, so strongly was he affected by such feelings that at one stage he thought of giving up his job as a schoolmaster in order to work in the Royal Museum of Antiquities – but he was deterred from pursuing this ambition when he realised that he would have to concern himself extensively with Greek sherds.[179]

In the light of these intense and recent experiences it is not wholly surprising that Huizinga should have chosen as the title for the inaugural lecture which he delivered at Groningen University on 4 November 1905 'The Aesthetic Element in Historical Thought'.[180]

With this lecture Huizinga plunged into a series of historiographical issues that, for several decades, had been keenly debated in many parts of Europe, although he referred almost exclusively to the contributions that had been made to them by German writers of the previous few years. To what extent had historical inquiry been changed by developments in the natural sciences, and, if it could not hope to provide equally convincing solutions, should it not either adopt wholly new methods (such as those offered by sociology) or abandon any claim to scientific credentials? How far should historians be concerned with individuals and how far with groups or wider social forces? Do the actions of great men determine the course of history or are great men themselves moulded by their environment and circumstances?

Huizinga trod carefully through these and other controversies, aware that 'every step is perilous, and to none more so than the neutral who wanders into No Man's Land'. It was Lamprecht's ambitious attempt to subordinate the significance of political change to the great driving forces of cultural history that chiefly pre-occupied him, and to it he frequently returned, sometimes with partial and qualified approval, sometimes sharply dismissive: 'We must beware', he insists, 'of assuming that great thinkers were of greater historical importance than kings, warriors and diplomats. "What are Pericles or Augustus today," Lamprecht exclaimed, "but mere names; labels of a great age?" What presumptuous exaggeration of the importance of literature! Have art and literature then so lifted us into the clouds that we can afford to be bored with mere courage and determination?'[181] History itself could not be considered an art and no marriage between the two was possible, and yet the issue of art was central: for the study of history and the creation of art had in common a mode of forming images. Indeed, for many years before he tried to work out these ideas in his lecture Huizinga had become convinced that 'historical perception can best be described as a vision, or (perhaps better) as an evocation of images'.[182] It was true that this visual analogy only applied decisively to the preliminary stages of historical investigation. However, its implications for the subject as a whole were of the utmost importance, for what precisely can one see? Only 'the life of men, and moreover of individual men rather than of groups and classes'. And Huizinga derided 'the dogma that only human societies, groups and associations form the subject of history . . . For in that case I would be allowed to take an interest in monasticism – in the Benedictines, the order of Friars Minor, or even of the Franciscan Spirituals – but not in St Francis himself, either as a representative of his order or as a man.'[183] Naturally, the historian had to think in wider categories also, but even major developments could often not be understood without reference to the individual, and to illustrate this Huizinga singled out a wonderful story told by Michelet. Long after the Revolution a young man asked the aged Merlin de Thionville how he had brought himself to condemn Robespierre. The old man seemed to be regretting his actions, and then he suddenly arose brusquely: 'Robespierre', he said, 'Robespierre. If you had seen *his green eyes*, you, too, would have condemned him as I did.'[184] Huizinga quotes with approval Michelet's notion of history as resurrection, but his claims for the role that can be played by the aesthetic element in stimulating the historical imagination extend far beyond anything maintained by Michelet. A new breadth of sensitivity, characteristic of the early twentieth century and demonstrated by the fact that 'we can enjoy Van Eyck as well as Rembrandt, the Rococo as well as Millet', allows us to combine 'the highest attainable objectivity with a highly subjective feeling'. Indeed, Huizinga implies that it is only through such subjective feelings that the historian can decide how many facts he will need in order to resurrect an historical personage.[185]

It is by no means always easy to follow Huizinga's sometimes defensive and convoluted arguments as he tries to back up his case with references to current psychological and philosophical theories. He was later to write that the lecture turned out to be 'very long and ponderous and prodigiously bored most of my audience'.[186] But that audience could not know how vividly he was to draw on his feeling for art when, little more than a decade afterwards, he published *The Waning of the Middle Ages*. It is, however, not only the hindsight available to us that makes the closing section of his lecture read so inspiringly, and movingly, today. There is also the fact that the claims being made for the visual arts by this young historian, in a university which hardly ranked among the famous European centres of learning, were as bold and self-confident as they were new. Huizinga did not yet appreciate the specific problems that they would raise for him – still less the fact that towards the end of his life he would have the most serious doubts about their validity. These will have to be considered in due course, but first it is worth trying to follow the advice he gave to his audience and to spend a few moments visualising Huizinga himself as he emphasised that 'the share of aesthetic intuition in the formation of a general historical picture is particularly important. Take your own general picture of Egyptian culture. Is it not almost entirely made up of notions based on Egyptian art? And how strongly is the general picture of the Middle Ages dominated by Gothic art! Or reverse the question and say: how much do we know about the thirteenth century when we read all the papal bulls but do not know the *Dies irae*?'

Similarly, a visit to Ravenna – a visit he himself had made three years before – could provide the best introduction to comprehending the fall of the ancient world, whose 'splendour survives in the flecks of green and gold in San Vitale and in the hue of nocturnal blue in the mausoleum of Galla Placidia'. It was true that art could not be the only key to an understanding of the mental climate of an age, and that we must 'see everything else we know about that age reflected in or illuminated by it'. However, it could not seriously be objected that heightened aesthetic receptivity could lead to misleading impressions of the past on the grounds that different people responded in different ways to the same art. This, after all, could also occur with any other kind of evidence: 'Our picture of the Middle Ages may differ vastly from that of the Romantics; but there is no doubt that their aesthetic enthusiasm helped to clarify our view of mediaeval history.' And similar changes in perception were likely to lead to equally impressive results in the future. 'How recently were our eyes opened to the breath-taking beauty of the work of Brueghel the Elder!', exclaimed Huizinga, recalling surely the *Census at Bethlehem*, the *Adoration of the Magi* and *The Land of Cockaigne* which the organisers had included in the Bruges exhibition of just three years earlier (but only with some reluctance, and as a rebuke to the pretensions of his Italianising contemporaries). 'With astonishment we now realise that it is something more than bawdry that he has to offer – that his work ranks with the greatest and most profound. This deeper understanding has not sprung from a systematic study of sixteenth-century cultural history. Yet it will lead us into seeing sixteenth-century Dutch history more lucidly, more sharply and more colourfully – in short, more historically.' And although Huizinga's conclusion somewhat attenuated this claim by insisting that there need to be no conflict between the demands of science and a preoccupation with aesthetics, which after all constituted only one facet of historical investigation and which would always require in addition the humble spadework of critical research, two points emerge forcefully from the lecture: the image comes first, and through the image we can see the past 'more lucidly, more sharply and more colourfully – *in short, more historically*'.[187]

Images – we have seen – had engrossed Huizinga over the previous decade or so, but it was only a year or two after his inaugural lecture that they assumed sufficient intensity to illuminate the past in the manner that he had advocated: and, despite his prediction, it was not the recently 'discovered' Brueghel who encouraged him to embark on his investigations, but the long appreciated 'primitives' – the primitives, however, seen in a very unusual light. He himself has described the immediate inspiration for *The Waning of the Middle Ages*:

I was from the first entirely conscious of the moment of its conception, and I have remained so ever since, even though it has not taken the form of a detailed and precise memory which can be summoned up before me. In particular, I cannot recall the exact timing of the intellectual process which I could best describe as a spark flashing from a transmitter. It must have been between 1906 and 1909, probably 1907. During the afternoon when my wife's time was taken up by looking after the young children I would sometimes walk alone for a bit outside the town which in those days still led directly on all sides to the broad, fresh Groningen countryside. On one such walk along the Damsterdiep or nearby, on a Sunday I think, the notion came to me that the late Middle Ages were not the herald of something that was to come, but the fading away of something that had already passed. This thought, if one can speak of it as a thought, revolved above all around the art of the Van Eycks and their con-temporaries, which considerably occupied my mind at that time. It was just in those years that it was usual to follow in the footsteps of Courajod and to agree with Fierens-Gevaert and Karl Volz in interpreting old Netherlandish art as the dawn of a Northern Renaissance. My perception was directly opposed to this. Some years passed, however, before I began to work it out. In 1909 . . . I held a course of lectures which I called 'Burgundian culture'. While my own notion of what I would give constantly changed, I began in 1910 to read as much as possible of the Burgundian and French historians of the period, Chastellain above all.[188]

vi

Just what it was that had struck Huizinga in the early Flemish pictures which he had seen in Bruges (and, later, elsewhere) can to a large extent be inferred from his discussions of them in a long essay, *The Art of the Van Eycks in the Life of their Times*, which he published in 1916 and then incorporated into *The Waning of the Middle Ages* three years afterwards – a book that he originally planned to call *In the Mirror of Van Eyck*. It is legitimate to look to these later works when analysing the early stages of his thought, because he quite specifically stated that it was the character of its art that had drawn his attention to the nature of mediaeval Burgundy long before he began to study other aspects of its civilisation; none the less it has to be acknowledged that, as his ideas developed, his eye must gradually have lost some of its original 'innocence' in order to see what was needed to strengthen his case.[189]

Like most sensitive observers, Huizinga sometimes changed his mind and was not entirely consistent in summing up his overall impressions; but this inconsistency matched an inconsistency that, so he claimed, was to be found in the creations of the fifteenth-century masters themselves. Was it 'sweet and tranquil serenity' that was reflected in their works or an 'element of splendour and pomp', which we barely notice because we are interested only in looking for beauty?[190] In fact, he implied, both sets of features were characteristic of Van Eyck and his contemporaries, whose achievements always tremble on the brink of exaggeration and the inharmonious. Take the case of Claus Sluter. All sculptural masterpieces, from the busts of imperial Rome to the eighteenth century, necessarily have much in common, particularly that 'optimum of purity and simplicity which we call classic'. At first sight this applies to Sluter, but when we look more closely at the prophets who surround the well of the Chartreuse de Champmol we can see that their features are too expressive and too personal (pl. 255): they strain too hard to communicate their poignancy to the spectator and so they risk losing that effect of stoical indifference (*ataraxia*) which is a privilege unique to great sculpture. And how much more disturbing would be the effect of Sluter's monument if it still remained intact, brilliantly coloured and gilded as it had originally been! Yet in the small 'pleurants' around the tomb of Philip the Bold the genius of Sluter and his school created 'the most profound expression of mourning, a funeral march in stone' (pl. 256).[191]

In Van Eyck, whose art will always remain as fresh as it was when first made, similar disjunctions are to be seen. Where can we find a purer form of fifteenth-century painting than in the Arnolfini marriage group in the National Gallery in London or a profounder analysis of character than in his portraits in general – 'the somewhat pointed and pinched face of his wife [pl. 257]; the aristocratic, impassive and morose head of Baudouin de Lannoy; the suffering and refined visage of

255. Claus Sluter, well (Chartreuse de Champmol, Dijon).

256 (below). Claus Sluter, tomb of Philip the Bold: detail showing procession of 'pleurants' (Dijon, Musée des Beaux-Arts).

257. Jan Van Eyck,
*Portrait of his Wife
Margaret* (Bruges,
Groeninge Museum).

Arnolfini in Berlin; the enigmatic candour of "Leal Souvenir"; the horrible, hermetic face of Canon van der Paele [pl. 245]'?[192] And yet the same artist can succumb (sometimes in the same pictures) to what can only be described as rhetoric: note, for instance, the grandiloquence of the St George who presents van der Paele to the Virgin, with his magnificent helmet, his gilt armour hinting at antiquity, and his theatrical gesture;[193] or the group of singing angels in the Ghent altarpiece with their 'heavy dresses of red and gold brocade, loaded with precious stones, those too expressive grimaces, the somewhat puerile decoration of the lectern' (pl. 258).[194] Similarly, Van Eyck was prepared to distort his naturalism, 'which is at the same time very naïve and very refined', in order to impart an element of eroticism ('ingenuous, however, and with no intention of pleasing') to Eve (pl. 243), whose breasts are shown too small and too high, whose arms are long and thin and whose belly is prominent in accordance with the taste in feminine beauty of his day.[195] This was the panel from the Ghent altarpiece that, when shown in Bruges in 1902, had struck visitors as characterised by an uncompromising realism worthy of Courbet.

258. Jan Van Eyck, Ghent altarpiece: panel with *Angel Choir* (Ghent, cathedral of St Bavon).

Some artists seemed to Huizinga to be immune to the temptations of sumptuous elegance or exaggerated refinement: Dieric Bouts, for instance, whose pictures were marked by a restraint and simplicity 'which can be thought of as the true expression of the bourgeoisie';[196] and, perhaps, Gerard David, who is mentioned only in passing but in terms that would have satisfied Weale, though certainly not Fierens-Gevaert, as the painter 'who carries on most directly the tradition of the primitive school', although with a more refined feeling for colour.[197] But David's 'primitive' character was also responsible for his principle weakness: that inability to compose that he shared with nearly all the Flemish artists of the fifteenth century, from the illustrators of small-scale manuscripts to painters of large public decorations.

Sometimes this problem could be solved by falling back on established formulas. Pietàs, Descents from the Cross, Adorations of the Shepherds – such venerable religious themes imposed on the artist a rhythmic pattern from which he could hardly escape. A very few painters, such as Roger van der Weyden, made deliberate attempts to discover new formal designs for themselves. And in certain other cases (such as the processions moving towards the altar in the central panel of the Ghent altarpiece (pl. 241)) Van Eyck managed to create an effect of rhythm by means of a 'purely arithmetical co-ordination'. But, in general, where movement was required and there were no precedents to provide authoritative guidance, the results could be disturbingly awkward, as in the Martyrdoms in Bruges and Brussels painted by Gerard David and Dieric Bouts, or downright ridiculous as in certain manuscript illuminations by Jean Miélot.[198] For what impaired Northern art of the fifteenth century more than anything else was the lack of any true sense of harmony.

To this issue Huizinga returned again and again. Decoration and ornament, he insisted, had been used not to enhance what was naturally beautiful but to rival it through extravagance and elaboration. What particularly struck him, for instance, in the two double panels by Melchior Broederlam of scenes from the Life of the Virgin and of Christ from the Chartreuse de Champmol which had been taken to the museum of Dijon, was the discord between the simplicity and sobriety of the paintings themselves and the overloaded sculptural framework which surrounded them.[199] And excess of a similar kind was also to be found in tapestries of the period which (unlike paintings) were used only for decorative purposes. But it was the art of Van Eyck that presented the greatest challenge to his perception. He concentrated on two pictures especially: the *Virgin of the Chancellor Rolin* in the Louvre (pl. 260), and the *Annunciation* then in the Hermitage (which he must have seen in 1907 when, on the personal instructions of the Tsar and against the wishes of the Director, it was sent to Bruges for the Exhibition of the Golden Fleece) (pl. 259).[200]

To judge from his description of the picture in Paris, Huizinga would appear to have been standing alarmingly close and examining it through a small but power-ful magnifying glass. No overall view is conveyed of the sheer bulk both of the praying chancellor, with his bull-like neck and brutal but handsome features, and of the Virgin enveloped in a billowing red robe who holds out the blessing Child

260. Jan Van Eyck, *Virgin of the Chancellor Rolin* (Paris, Louvre).

259. Jan Van Eyck, *Annunciation* (Washington, National Gallery of Art: Mellon Collection).

towards him. But all the details emerge with crystalline clarity, and Huizinga observes that in the work 'of any other artist the laborious exactness with which the materials of the dresses are painted, also the marbles of the tiles and the columns, the reflections of the window-panes, and the chancellor's breviary, would give an impression of pedantry. And even in him the exaggerated finish of the details, such as the ornaments of the capitals, on which a whole series of biblical scenes is represented, is hurtful to the general effect. But it is especially in the marvellous perspective opened up behind the figures of the Virgin and the donor that Van Eyck's passion for detail is given rein.' And Huizinga then quotes at length from a finely precise and evocative description of these details given by Durand-Gréville, a writer on Flemish art who had played a prominent part in the conference organised by the Bruges exhibition committee in 1902. But, concludes

Huizinga, despite all the ornaments, all the finish, all the tiny figures and objects just discernible in the distance, the unity and the harmony are not lost. And then he changes his mind. 'Having recently seen the picture again', he writes in a later edition, 'I can no longer deny it [the loss of harmony], as I formerly did on the strength of recollections many years old.'[201]

In the Hermitage *Annunciation* (which is set in a church) Van Eyck 'developed all the virtuosity of a master conscious of his power to overcome all difficulties', and in this, 'the most hieratic and at the same time the most refined of all his works', he was able to subordinate the accumulation of details to the unity of the whole.[202] However, for all his genius, Van Eyck was for Huizinga essentially a most painstaking recorder of minutiae – of the glitter of pearls and of gold and of precious stones; of the brilliance of red and gold brocade; of the patterns made by peacock feathers and ornamental tiles. He was also a master of anecdote. In no sense, except the purely chronological, was his art primitive.[203] On the contrary, despite the claims of Fierens-Gevaert and his followers, 'the scrupulous realism, the aspiration to give an exact rendering of every natural detail' represented the end of an old development rather than the beginning of a new one.[204]

vii

In his inaugural lecture Huizinga had urged that images (of the late Roman Empire, for instance, or of the Netherlands in the sixteenth century) should provide the initial stimulus to historical study; but he had not claimed that such images could be made to serve as the basis for a more sustained analysis. It is true that on his walk in the countryside outside Groningen he had, in a sudden flash, become convinced that his (very idiosyncratic) interpretation of fifteenth-century Flemish art demonstrated that the society in which it had been produced must also have been backward-looking and in decline; but he seems to have let the matter drop for some years. It was in *The Waning of the Middle Ages* of 1919 that he set out to explore to the full the implications of his intuition. By now, however, intuition had been fortified by an attentive reading of the writers of the period, and we shall see that among the most remarkable features of his book are precisely the powerful arguments advanced in it for treating evidence offered by the visual arts alone with extreme caution, not to say suspicion. None the less, Huizinga's personal response to art shaped the very nature of his creative achievement, and this is only one of the many respects in which *The Waning of the Middle Ages* recalls *The Civilisation of the Renaissance in Italy*.

The impact – both positive and negative – of Burckhardt's 'Essay' on Huizinga has always been stressed – not least by Huizinga himself, who fully understood that its indebtedness to art was far more pervasive than was apparent on the surface. 'The structure of this matchless example of cultural-historical synthesis', he wrote of *The Civilisation*, 'is as sturdy and harmonic as any Renaissance work of art.'[205] And, inspired by this ideal, he attached such importance to the formal design of his own masterpiece that he was on occasion prepared to sacrifice significant but potentially disruptive content. Thus he acknowledged, in a few brief words that have greatly irritated his critics, that Joan of Arc was almost entirely excluded because 'I knew that she would have torn the book I visualised in my mind completely out of balance. What kept me from introducing her in it was a sense of harmony – that and a vast and reverent humility.'[206]

It was a lack of true harmony that Huizinga found so disturbing in the pictures of fifteenth-century Flemish primitives. Yet there may have been another reason for his 'considered, deliberate' omission of Joan of Arc. It was not just because she was 'one of the few figures in history who cannot be anything but protagonists, who are never subordinate, always an end and never a means' that she could not be satisfactorily fitted into the composition of *The Waning of the Middle Ages*. More important surely was the fact that (as Huizinga pointed out in the separate essay that he devoted to her) nothing in her beliefs or behaviour corresponded to the image of the period that he wished to convey.[207]

Indications that Burckhardt had sometimes circumvented inconvenient evidence in order to present a more coherent historical pattern could certainly be found in *The Civilisation of the Renaissance in Italy*: it was, indeed, one of the most telling criticisms that Huizinga made of that book.[208] For, despite all the admiration that he felt for 'the wisest man of the nineteenth century',[209] Huizinga's *The Waning of the Middle Ages* constitutes a challenge as much as a tribute to Burckhardt's 'matchless example' – a challenge that is sounded in its very first words: 'To the world when it was half a thousand years younger, the outlines of all things seemed more clearly marked than to us.' This phrase cannot but recall Burckhardt's celebrated (and, to Huizinga, misleading) prelude to his section on 'The Development of the Individual': 'In the Middle Ages both sides of human consciousness – that which was turned within as that which was turned without – lay dreaming or half-awake beneath a common veil. The veil was woven of faith, illusion and childish prepossession, through which the world and history were seen clad in strange hues . . .'.

Huizinga fundamentally rejected the clear distinction that Burckhardt had drawn between the mediaeval world and the Renaissance: the veil, he suggested ironically, may have been caused by a flaw in Burckhardt's own camera.[210] Yet it soon becomes apparent that in *his* Middle Ages also dreams and strange hues and faith and illusion and childish prepossessions were by no means lacking. How far did he turn to evidence to be found in the visual arts to depict, with such powerful immediacy, a civilisation that alternated between wild lust and cruelty on the one hand and exaggerated piety on the other, between hard-headed avarice and fantastic dreams of out-dated chivalry? That he looked constantly at pictures and manuscripts in order to visualise the past, to experience it as if he were himself present at the scenes represented in them, seems obvious enough both from his book and from an almost contemporary essay in which he stressed how essential it was for historical museums to acquire for their collections true works of art just as much as artefacts and documents.[211] But it is at first sight surprising to discover how very rarely he draws on specific images to give substance to specific aspects of the mediaeval society he wishes to paint for us. Only once does he do so at all directly. His chapter on 'The Vision of Death' is by far the most visual in the book.[212] It relies to a significant extent on the evidence provided by monuments, such as the churchyard of the Innocents in Paris, and also by tomb sculpture, by frescoes, by pictures and by woodcuts in order to establish the point that the macabre feelings aroused by death were 'self-seeking and earthly' – indifferent to pity or resignation, longing or consolation. The exceptional character of this passage can best be appreciated by considering some of Huizinga's more striking omissions.

For many generations of art lovers the soberly dressed donors and their wives who kneel in the wings of Memling's altarpieces had of themselves been enough to indicate the presence in fifteenth-century Flanders of a devout, hard-working, prosperous bourgeois community. Huizinga barely mentions them. It would seem that, like the contemporary narrators on whom he self-consciously draws in order to discover the flavour rather than the realities of mediaeval life, he was essentially interested not in the actuality of day-to-day existence but in the dreams and illusions that society likes to foster. 'The chroniclers of the fifteenth century', he writes,

> have, nearly all, been the dupes of an absolute misappreciation of their times, of which the real moving forces escaped their attention... The extraordinary fortune of the Burgundian branch of the Valois transported to Flanders was in reality based on the wealth of the Flemish and Brabant towns. Nevertheless, dazzled by the splendour and magnificence of an extravagant court, [the chronicler] Chastellain imagined that the power of the house of Burgundy was especially due to the heroism and the devotion of knighthood.[213]

It is tempting to comment that by neglecting one class of visual evidence and (as we shall see) by emphasising another Huizinga has – perhaps deliberately – echoed the same misapprehension. The so-called 'Master of Flémalle', for instance, offered a much more solid, prosaic and less refined vision of the world than did Van Eyck. Huizinga recognised this, but by mentioning only one picture attributed to him (the Mérode altarpiece) and belittling its quality in some three or four lines devoted to its elements of genre and perhaps comedy,[214] he fails to point out the significance of an attitude to life that is far removed from the preciosities of court culture which lie at the heart of his theory of decadence.[215]

Some omissions are less easily explicable. It is odd that Gerard David's *Flaying of the Unjust Judge* (pl. 252), which had struck at least one visitor to the Bruges exhibition as being 'the most realistic, the bloodiest of all tortures that has ever been painted with such minuteness upon canvas',[216] was not singled out for attention by Huizinga who himself emphasised the important public role assumed by the savagery of public executions; but the picture is not even referred to in this context. It is true that in order to illustrate the 'dangerous association of religious with amatory sentiments' he described at some length[217] the 'decadent impiety' and 'blasphemous boldness' of Fouquet's *Virgin and Child* (pl. 261), which was among the finest works bequeathed to the Antwerp museum by Florent Van Ertborn in 1841. It had been painted for Etienne Chevalier, treasurer of Charles

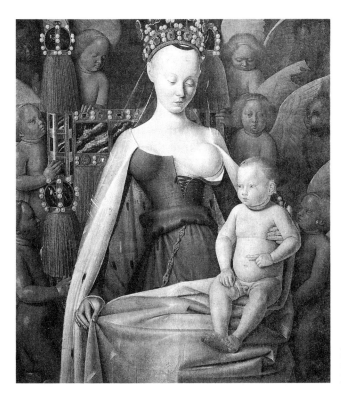

261. Jean Fouquet, *Virgin and Child* (Antwerp, Musée des Beaux-Arts).

VII, and (according to a tradition that dates back only to the seventeenth century, but that may be correct) the delicate, stylised and ivory-pale features of the Virgin, one of whose globe-like breasts is exposed, were those of Agnes Sorel, the royal mistress.[218] However, when discussing licentiousness in general, Huizinga alludes only to a small picture in the museum of Leipzig, 'which is sometimes attributed to the school of Van Eyck' and which depicted a naked girl in a room using witchcraft to force her lover to show himself – but he does so partly to make the point that paintings of this kind were very rare.[219]

Despite the paucity of examples in this particular area Huizinga could, of course, have drawn very much more extensively than he did on a plentiful supply of panel paintings and manuscript illuminations in order to enable the reader to visualise some of the principal aspects of mediaeval life that he wished to emphasise. It is, for instance, amazing that a writer so interested in dreams and so keen to explore the 'psycho-pathology' of the late Middle Ages should barely have alluded to Hieronymous Bosch, even when a number of his pictures seem directly relevant to some of the states of mind under discussion.[220] Huizinga was apparently reluctant here, and elsewhere, to venture on to territory that he felt had already attracted too much attention. In a cautious review, a few years later, of the relevant volume of Friedländer's *Altniederländische Malerei* he showed how suspicious he was of current interpretations of the artist and how reluctant to make any of his own. He congratulated Friedländer on his restraint in dealing with such matters and although he agreed that 'the need for psychological interpretation urges itself more here than in the case of any other master' he dismissed all suggestions as 'dangerous speculation'.[221]

In fact, for all the vividly evocative power of his descriptive writing, the revelations that Huizinga sought from art depended less on the apparently first-hand information to be found in images than on the more arcane evidence inadvertently supplied by their stylistic incongruities. To interpret such evidence he had both to be aware of these incongruities – and by no means all art lovers shared his views in this respect – and at the same time to discard as potentially misleading judgements based on modern taste. Thus we may be offended by Sluter's over-emotional prophets who stand round the well of the Chartreuse de Champmol, and still more by what they had once looked like before time had (fortunately) chastened their gaudy vulgarity: the green pedestals; the gilt mantels of the prophets and their red and azure tunics covered with golden stars; the spectacles of gilded brass fitted on to the nose of Jeremiah; and, above, the Cross (also gilded) with its arms shaped like capitals, bearing the heraldic devices of Flanders and Burgundy. Was all this the result of the duke's bad taste? Ought we to imagine Sluter struggling to escape from it in order to be able to create those monumentally simple 'pleurants' which still appeal so much to us? Surely not. Is it not much more likely that the sculptor shared the views of his patron and agreed with him that the bizarre was to be appreciated as much as the beautiful and that religious awe could be conveyed through the rare and the brilliant?[222]

Huizinga goes a stage further, and doubts whether the notion of aesthetic quality could have had much meaning in fifteenth-century Flanders; but in doing this he naturally has to fall back on his own standards of judgement. When describing courtly festivals, such as the one held at Lille in 1454 at which the guests took an oath to commit themselves to a crusade, Huizinga is horrified by 'these barbarous manifestations of arrogant pomp' which make so startling a contrast with pictures by 'the brothers Van Eyck, Dieric Bouts and Rogier van der Weyden, with their sweet and tranquil serenity . . . We find it difficult to regard these entertainments as something more than exhibitions of almost incredibly bad taste.'[223] And yet there was a straightforward explanation of why these festivals failed (more perhaps in his eyes than in the eyes of those for whom they were designed) 'to make visible in its entirety the dream of the heroic life'. Chivalry was itself no longer anything other than a vain convention and mere literature. Lacking any essential social function it could be given an illusion of validity only by using the most ponderous rhetoric.[224] And when he discusses (on the basis, incidentally, of written sources rather than of illuminated manuscripts) the bright and clashing colours of the costumes worn in these festivals and tournaments, Huizinga gives more precise reasons for the absence in them of any true feeling for beauty. Thus he singles out with particular distaste the appearance of a lady on one such occasion, dressed 'in violet-coloured silk on a hackney covered with a canopy of blue silk, led by three men in vermilion-tinted silk and in hoods of green silk', and claims that such colours were usually chosen more for their symbolic than for their aesthetic value. Blue and green tended to be relatively rare because they came to be associated with hypocrisy, infidelity and foolishness. Similar considerations may have led to a dislike of brown and yellow. Huizinga acknowledges, however, that 'aesthetic' aversion could have been responsible for the avoidance of these colours, though he seems to have felt some surprise that among the first artists to have developed a new refinement in the handling of colour should have been Gerard David whom (as we have seen) he looked upon as having been essentially a late upholder of the tradition of the primitives. Was one to conclude from this that aesthetic sentiment was gaining ground over an obsession with symbolism? And if so, why? 'Here is a domain in which the history of art and that of civilisation have still a great deal to learn from each other.'[225]

The issue was an important one, because an obsession with hollow symbolism was for Huizinga one of the most telling indications that the later Middle Ages were indeed in a state of terminal decline. Symbolism, like chivalry, had once served a true purpose. Through symbolism man had been able to make sense of an apparently inexplicable universe and impose on it 'impeccable order, architectonic structure, hieratic subordination'. But, like chivalry, symbolism had with time become 'a meaningless intellectual pastime'.[226] As soon as everything could be seen in terms of something else all true relationships and any sense of hierarchy became distorted. Moreover, the abuse of symbolism had led to a puerile form of allegory, as was clearly shown in miniature paintings by all but the most gifted artists, who were competent enough in the straightforward depiction of a shepherd and his flock but who failed to cope with the absurdity of having to represent Temperance by placing a clock on a woman's head.[227]

Sterility of the imagination lies at the heart of Huizinga's conception of the waning Middle Ages. It was manifested by the need 'to give concrete shape to every conception. Every thought seeks expression in an image, but in this image it solidifies and becomes rigid'.[228] And he reached this conclusion not so much on the basis of his study of garish festival costumes or second-rate illuminated manuscripts as from his observation of 'the naïve, and at the same time refined, naturalism of the brothers Van Eyck'. We have already seen that (apparently in the light of the Bruges exhibition and his subsequent explorations) Huizinga had discerned in their art an absence of true harmony and an overloading of detail; and that on his walk outside Groningen on a Sunday afternoon in 1907 it had suddenly struck him that these were features characteristic of decline rather than of renewal. Now, after his intense study of the written sources of Burgundian history, he at last felt able to explain in detail that the naturalism of the Van Eycks was not a matter of interest only to the art historian. Its significance was very much greater, for it represented 'one of the ultimate forms of development of the mediaeval mind'.[229]

The meticulous treatment of each individual detail that seems to characterise their works; their refusal to distinguish in scale or gravity between the serious and the trivial so that, in place of the majesty and rigour of sacred figures in earlier times, the celestial was now treated in a spirit of mundane reality and pious fancy, and every sacred being was given a minutely elaborate shape; their tendency to drape their angels and divine personages with ponderous and stiff brocades, glittering with gold and precious stones so that mysticism and materialism were placed on an equal footing[230] – all this, and much more, corresponds perfectly to the painstaking but cold futility that underlines an ageing set of beliefs, in which 'all holy concepts are constantly exposed to the danger of hardening into mere externalism'.[231] And this spiritual aridity is demonstrated also in the buildings of the time, which shared the same tendency 'to leave nothing without form, without figure, without ornament. The flamboyant style of architecture is like the postlude of an organist who cannot conclude. It decomposes all the formal elements endlessly; it interlaces all the details; there is not a line that has not its counterline. The form develops at the expense of the idea, the ornament grows rank, hiding all the line and all the surfaces. A *horror vacui* reigns, always a symptom of artistic decline.'[232] This sort of approach to fifteenth-century architecture had already been familiar to Laborde some seventy years earlier;[233] but both he and subsequent visitors to Flanders would have been amazed to discover that those very paintings by Van Eyck and his contemporaries that had struck them as bold and healthy alternatives to 'excessively elaborate, finicky and over-ingenious' town halls would be seen by Huizinga as characteristic of precisely the same state of mind: 'but another manifestation of the crystallising tendency of thought which we noticed in all the aspects of the mentality of the declining Middle Ages'.

viii

Huizinga's response to fifteenth-century Flemish art was original, and the ingenuity with which he drew on his impressions of it in order to interpret the character of a whole civilisation remains as stimulating as it was certainly sophisticated – and perhaps misguided; but what turns his achievement into a landmark in historical method is the explicitness with which he raises fundamental questions concerning the validity of his approach. His analysis also bears on the strengths and weaknesses of many of the arguments advanced earlier in this book; and because it has not been adequately examined, most later explorations of the impact of art on the historical imagination have been disappointing. For this reason *The Waning of the Middle Ages*, like the topic with which it is concerned, stands at the end rather than at the beginning of a voyage of discovery. Huizinga himself felt that this voyage, with which he is so closely associated, had got under way quite recently:

> If a man of culture of 1840 had been asked to characterise French civilisation of the fifteenth century in a few words, his answer would probably have been largely inspired by impressions from Barante's *Histoire des Ducs de Bourgogne* and Hugo's *Notre-Dame de Paris* . . . The experiment repeated today would yield a very different result. People would now refer . . . above all to works of art. The so-called primitive Flemish and French masters – Van Eyck, Rogier van der Weyden, Foucquet, Memling, with Claus Sluter, the sculptor, and the great musicians – would dominate their general idea of the epoch . . . Our perception of former times, our historical organ, so to say, is more and more becoming visual. Most educated people of today owe their conception of Egypt, Greece,

or the Middle Ages, much more to the sight of their monuments, either in the original or by reproductions, than to reading. The change of our ideas about the Middle Ages is due less to a weakening of the romantic sense than to the substitution of artistic for intellectual appreciation.[234]

What are the consequences of such a change in 'our historical organ'? In the first place, we are compelled to rely on very incomplete evidence. 'Outside ecclesiastical art very little remains. Profane art and applied art have only been preserved in rare specimens.'[235] What we can see and try to understand today – some tombs, some altarpieces and portraits, numerous miniatures, also a certain number of objects of industrial art, comprising vessels used in religious worship, sacerdotal dress and church furniture – is there purely because of the accidents of survival.[236] But whole departments of the fine and applied arts have irretrievably vanished – the bathing and hunting scenes of Roger van de Weyden and Jan Van Eyck, for instance,[237] and (above all) those court costumes 'with their precious stones and tiny bells'[238] and other sumptuous decorations that we know to have played so central a role in the life style of the fifteenth century. Literary tradition, on the other hand, 'reflects the whole life of the epoch. Written tradition, moreover, is not confined to literature: official records, in infinite number, enable us to augment almost indefinitely the accuracy of our picture.'[239]

The effect of the culling of monuments by time, accident and human destruction is, however, insidious not merely because the surviving evidence is so fragmentary. Just as important is the fact that this very scarcity has led to its being wrongly interpreted. We try to find in mediaeval art 'a means to step out of the routine of everyday life to pass some moments in contemplation', and we thus fail to understand 'the paradox that the Middle Ages knew only applied art'.[240] Whether designed to intensify worship, to preserve the memory of donors or to overwhelm the spectator through a display of extravagant pomp, art always had a practical purpose, and its aptitude for that purpose was always far more important than the issue of its beauty. A taste for art itself was an accidental by-product of excessive production, and it was only developed consciously in the Renaissance.

The most original (though not always the most convincing) contribution made by Huizinga to the challenge raised by his own approach – and by that of the long but discontinuous and unsystematic tradition of which it was the culmination – did, however, spring directly from his own feeling for beauty. Why is it, he asked, that, as a rule, the art of the fifteenth century can still move us whereas the literature of the period has lost most of its power to do so? In seeking to answer this question Huizinga was driven to explore the varying degrees of expressive potential inherent in the written and the visual form of communication. Such differences, he showed, depended on the emotion or the idea that had to be conveyed. Love, for instance, and some of its components (such as frivolity, sentimentality and eroticism) could not be convincingly represented in fifteenth-century painting. 'In the miniatures of that time the posture of lovers embracing remains hieratic and solemn', and even on a larger scale the means available for depicting affection or infatuation were still inadequate. Thus the portrait of a lovelorn woman (who could be identified as such by means of an inscription) had been interpreted by a recent scholar as the likeness of a devout donor. But that it would mistaken to conclude from the nature of such visual evidence that the sentiment itself did not then exist is clearly demonstrated by contemporary literature, which could draw to great effect on a varied tradition of amatory eloquence stemming from Plato and Ovid.[241] On the other hand, it is from the pictures of Geertgen tot sint Jans and the miniatures of the *Cuer d'amours éspris*, the *Heures d'Ailly* and the *Très Riches Heures de Chantilly*, and not from the forced, conventional poetry of the period, that we can learn of the delight with which some people at least responded to the effects of light breaking through darkness or the fresh beauty of the countryside in spring.[242]

Failure to take careful account of such issues, which were of basic importance to art historians and literary critics, risked undermining the analyses of all those whose 'historical organ' had, in Huizinga's phrase, been 'becoming more and more visual' in recent decades. Nowhere was this more important than in the changing interpretations made of the fundamental tenor of life in mediaeval France and Burgundy. To the reader, in 1840, of Barante and Hugo the age would have seemed 'grim and dark, scarcely illuminated by any ray of serenity and beauty'. To the student of Flemish painting 'the picture would altogether have changed its colour and tone. The aspect of mere cruelty and misery as conceived by romanticism, which derived its information chiefly from the chronicles, would have made room for a vision of pure and naïve beauty, of religious fervour and profound mystic peace.'[243]

The reason for this lay in the

> general phenomenon that the idea which works of art give us of an epoch is far more serene and happy than that which we glean in reading its chronicles, documents, or even literature. Plastic art does not lament. Even when giving expression to sorrow or pain it transports them to an elegiac sphere, where the bitter taste of suffering has passed away, whereas the poets and historians, voicing the endless griefs of life, always keep their immediate pungency and revive the harsh realities of bygone misery ... [Hence] the vision of an epoch resulting from the contemplation of works of art is always incomplete, always too favourable, and therefore fallacious.[244]

Huizinga's chapter on 'The Vision of Death' suggests that he himself did not accept without reservations a conclusion that (as we have seen) had already been apprehended, in part and intuitively, by Quinet and Ruskin when contemplating the cruel past of so radiant a city as Venice. It is, in any case, surprising that he should have based it on untested general laws rather than on a variety of contingent circumstances for which historical explanations were possible – the nature of patronage, for instance, or the difference between public and private spheres of expression.

It is once again to general principles that Huizinga turns in his examination of what the historian can, and cannot, learn from portraiture. Because he admires Jan Van Eyck for 'the profoundest character-drawing possible',[245] he wonders whether, in that artist's famous painting in the Louvre (pl. 260), there may not be a 'hypocritical expression' in the face of the devoutly kneeling Rolin, in view of the fact that contemporaries emphasised the chancellor's avarice, pride and lack of spirituality.[246] Before condemning him, however, we should remember that 'many other men of his time . . . also combined rigid piety with excesses of pride, of avarice and of lust. The depths of these natures of a past age are not easily sounded.' In comments such as these Huizinga may have been influenced by the views of his friend Jan Veth who, inspired by the example of Degas (to whom his own art owed so much), probably believed that disclosure had always been the principle aim of the portraitist. It seems unlikely that either Rolin or Van Eyck would have thought of portraiture in such terms or would have imagined that anything other than a devout expression was conceivable in the depiction of any donor in the presence of the Virgin and Child.

262. Roger van der Weyden (follower of), *Philip the Good* (Madrid, Royal Palace).

To have acknowledged this would perhaps have led Huizinga further along the road of doubt in his evaluation of imagery than he wished to go at this stage. However, when (several years later) he once again discussed – at far greater length – the conclusions that could be drawn from painted portraiture, his tone was notably more sceptical. It is true that he insisted that the value of such images was of the very highest – but only as long as we do not confuse the process of seeing with that of interpreting.[247] 'The fantasies of those who claim to be able to read in a picture the complete character of some individual, in all its mysterious depths and in all its most subtle psychological nuances, are well enough known. This is dangerous rhetoric of no use to history'.[248] The fallacy of the method lay in the fact that different portraits of a particular individual (sometimes indeed different versions of the same portrait) often looked very different. Huizinga illustrated his point by turning to Friedländer's *Die Altniederländische Malerei* in order to compare the various portraits, mostly derived from a prototype by Roger van der Weyden, of Philip the Good, Duke of Burgundy (pl. 262).

If the duke's appearance and expression vary significantly from image to image, can we not arrive at the truth by checking the evidence against contemporary written accounts of his character and actions? Huizinga considers some of these, notably the chronicle of his official historian, Georges Chastellain, and (not very surprisingly) discovers that the only point where the literary and the visual source are able to reinforce each other directly is in their treatment of the duke's features: 'his nose not aquiline, but long . . . his lips wide and strongly coloured', and so on. In every other respect the written records are naturally very much more informative, and when at the end of his article, Huizinga asks to what extent they can be shown to have confirmed the painted likeness, he can reply only: 'There is no answer to this question. No method exists that would enable us to verify these two methods of expression'. And then, in his very last sentences, he mentions – but in passing only – what the reader may feel could have been the most stimulating rather than (as he claims) the most impenetrable, of problems: what if someone should claim that the Philip of Chastellain is not to be recognised in the Philip of Roger van der Weyden? Huizinga concerns himself only with the general issue of the different means of description available to the writer and the artist and does not even raise the possibility that, within the limits imposed by those means, Roger and Chastellain might have wished to convey a wholly different impression of the duke's character. It is true that this is most unlikely to have been the case, as both men were in his service; but we have seen how often apparent conflicts of evidence between the visual and the written have depended on considerations of this kind, and it is curious that Huizinga should not have discussed an issue of such importance for his whole historical method.

It is evident, none the less, that Huizinga's doubts about the value of artistic evidence had already emerged in *The Waning of the Middle Ages*, which first appeared in 1919, and that those doubts became stronger with the passing of time. In a lecture on 'Renaissance and Realism', delivered in 1920 and completely revised for publication six years later,[249] even he himself does not seem to have appreciated quite how much his critique of Burckhardt's views of the Renaissance could also have been applied to his own interpretation of the Middle Ages. In denying that there was any necessary connection between the Renaissance and Realism (as had been claimed by Burckhardt and then by Courajod, who had 'found a hearing straight down to the present day') Huizinga emphasised that 'an age can produce realistic works of art without its spirit being markedly realistic'.[250] And he insisted that although 'the Van Eycks were utter realists as far as form is concerned, we know as good as nothing about their spirit. Everything that modern, aestheticising art criticism concludes from their works regarding their spirit is fantasy and paraphrase.'[251] But, if this is the case, should we not also be inhibited from drawing those conclusions about the relationship between their meticulous detail or lack of harmony and the decaying, autumnal nature of their society which constituted the starting point of Huizinga's masterpiece? Is not that masterpiece itself, as some of his critics have asserted, an example of the fantasy that springs from 'modern, aestheticising art criticism'?[252] Huizinga acknowledges the danger by making what amounts to a silent refutation (or at least modification) of the insight that had come to him some twenty years earlier during his walk in the countryside outside Groningen: 'literary products', he now claims, 'offer one criterion more than the visual arts: they make it possible for us to appraise the spirit as well as the form'.[253]

ix

'Tramway lines, concrete, asphalt and modern traffic destroyed the ancient face of the Netherlands', whose distinctive civilisation Huizinga set out to describe in a long essay devoted to 'Dutch Civilisation in the Seventeenth Century', which was begun at a time when 'the younger generation does not, indeed cannot ever, know the kind of beauty of which their elders only just managed to catch a glimpse'[254] and was revised under a German tyranny that was annihilating everything that had given distinction to that civilisation. Although contemporary art now disgusted him in all its forms,[255] his feeling for the visual remained as acute and informed as ever: on a visit to Oxford a few years earlier he had surprised his host by the knowledgeable way in which he had discussed the significance and the style of even the less familiar monuments in the city and by the impression he gave of combining 'an artist's perceptiveness . . . with a determination to search for historical truth'.[256] And now once again, in this last major work, he pointed out, as he had done in *The Waning of the Middle Ages*, that awareness of the past had been transformed by the new attention paid to images. The very words with which his essay opens reflect the ideas that he had first proclaimed in his inaugural lecture nearly forty years earlier:

> Were we to test the average Dutchman's knowledge of life in the Netherlands during the seventeenth century, we should probably find that it is largely confined to odd stray notions gleaned from paintings . . . Had we applied the same test a century ago . . . the results would have been quite different: in 1840, knowledge of history, in the ordinary political sense of the word, was far greater than it is today. Literature, too, was much better known, if only by its greatest works. Art, on the other hand, played a far less important part in nineteenth-century man's historical vista than it does in ours.[257]

This change in preception, Huizinga continued (without mentioning the extent to which he himself had been responsible for it), was not confined to the Netherlands; and by now he deplored it – not because it gave too serene an impression of earlier civilisations, but because it actually discouraged serious thought about them: 'As more and more visual material for the appreciation of the past became quite generally available, so thinking and writing about the past fell into increasing neglect.' And the irresistible spell cast over our spirit by the visible beauty of a picture led to the regrettable but inevitable result that 'when it comes to political and social history the great majority [of our people] is completely at sea'.[258] In his essay, therefore, Huizinga proposed to eschew the 'one-sided aesthetic view' of history prevalent in his own day, which had replaced the 'one-sided political approach' of a century earlier, in order to 'look at civilisation in the widest possible context'.[259]

He therefore devoted much of his attention to religion and politics,[260] literature and science; but he naturally also discussed the achievements of the great painters, and indeed some of his concise observations were to be followed up by art historians only many years after his death. Seventeenth-century pictures, he writes, are 'full of arcane allusions, and many of these we cannot hope to fathom even after the most careful research. Thus every bloom in every flower piece is a symbol, and the subject of every still life has emblematic as well as a natural significance. The same is true of many undecipherable details in the bearing of a market stall-keeper, servant or musician'.[261] And it is gratifying to read that 'it may be rather bold of me to say that Vermeer fails precisely when he depicts holy scenes, for instance Christ at Emmaus', in view of the fact that the famous picture of this subject, which had recently been acclaimed by Bredius and bought for the Boymans Museum, was detected as a forgery only in 1945.[262]

In *Dutch Civilisation in the Seventeenth Century* Huizinga follows a more conventional approach to the relationship between art and society than he had done in *The Waning of the Middle Ages*, though he does so with a sensitivity and an undisguised partiality that are far from conventional. Only once does he turn to painting as a source for gauging the nature of the beliefs or customs or circumstances of the time – and then in so tentative and facile a spirit that it is clear that he no longer has much trust in this method. Evidently forgetting his own maxim that 'the vision of an epoch resulting from the contemplation of works of art is always incomplete, always too favourable, and therefore fallacious', he asks rhetorically whether 'Ostade was very far wrong when he represented the Dutch peasant as a happy-go-lucky and well-fed fellow'.[263] And a similar venture into the implications of architectural form seems just as forced, and rather more surprising. The towers of the town halls, Huizinga writes, 'were graceful to the point of whimsy, in complete harmony with the carillon inside, the embodiment, as it were, of everything that is gay and light, delicate and graceful in the Dutch character . . .'[264] It is true that he had suggested that similar features were apparent in the lyricism of Hooft and Vondel, but it has to be said that – to judge from the tone and contents of his essay – these towers provide our only indication of the gaiety and lightness, delicacy and grace to be found among the inhabitants of the Netherlands in the seventeenth century.

Architects lost their note of happy fantasy and began to hanker after rigid forms; Rembrandt entered the twilight of his later years and the great age of Dutch painting was about to pass away; Dutch civilisation was in rapid decline.[265] But, asked Huizinga, was the concept of decline applicable to a society that was more tolerant, more tranquil, more prosperous than it had ever been and that, even as he wrote (in 1941), had not lost those qualities – 'vigour, determination, justice and fair play, charity, piety and faith in God' – that had made it great in the seventeenth century? To this question, he seems to imply, there was probably no answer. Could it be that it was only Dutch art (and poetry) that had declined, and not Dutch civilisation as a whole? Or should he have widened – and thereby distorted – one of the basic concepts that had lain behind *The Waning of the Middle Ages* so as to make it read: 'it is a general phenomenon that the idea which works of art give us of an epoch are *more ambiguous* [as distinct from 'more serene and happy'] than that which we glean in reading its chronicles, documents, or even literature'? Either acknowledgement would have solved his immediate problem; and either would have undermined the theoretical basis of what he had always maintained – and of what, before him, had been maintained by Ruskin and Burckhardt, Hegel and Winckelmann, Vasari and Raphael. So subtle, so various, so undogmatic a historian as Huizinga might not have been too dismayed. Nor would our own feelings about the impact of art on the historical imagination necessarily have been impoverished.[266]

Notes

Introduction

1. Herodotus, I, 24; II, 131.
2. Procopius, VIII, xxii, 5. This was to be derided by Scipione Maffei in his *Verona Illustrata*: see Maffei, 1731–2, III, p. 206.
3. Momigliano, 1950; Cochrane, 1985, pp. 423 ff.
4. Vasari, 1906, I, p. 229.
5. Hegel, 1975, I, p. 599.
6. This is demonstrated very clearly in the kind of material to be found in the historical and commemorative museums which are so very common these days; their origins are discussed below in Chapter 11. People who deny the existence of Nazi concentration camps are presumably impervious to any kind of evidence; but it is certainly through images rather than through words that the attempt would be made to convince them.
7. See the most interesting analysis of the fabrication by Eugène Appert of composite photographs purporting to report events that took place during the Paris Commune: English. I am grateful to M. André Jammes for drawing my attention to this article.
8. See Jaubert.
9. See the entertaining analysis of an (imaginary) nineteenth-century photograph in Burn, pp. 26–9.
10. Trachtenberg, p. 1.
11. Lacroix (Préface), pp. ii–iii.
12. Momigliano, 1950.
13. Huizinga, 1968, p. 10; and see below, Chapter 15.
14. Gombrich, 1963, p. 108 (*Art and Scholarship*).
15. Defoe, I, p. 182.
16. Colvin, p. 3.
17. Aston.
18. By using the phrase 'aesthetic discrimination' in this context I do not, of course, mean that the values we hold today must be accepted for all time, but only that judgements concerning quality have to be taken into account in assessing significance.
19. Baxandall, pp. 66–78.
20. Thus because I have written at some length about Michelet's use of painting to define the character of an age, I have (with great regret) omitted any discussion of a particularly sensitive example of an approach similar to his which can be found where one might least expect it – in a book by Bernard Berenson. The last pages of his monograph on Lorenzo Lotto, first published in 1895, suggest that the work of this artist bears 'witness to an attitude of mind in Italy which, although not dominant, could have been by no means rare. For the dominant tendencies of an epoch are never so predominant as to give a complete idea of it. To know the sixteenth century well, it is almost as important to study Lotto as Titian. Titian only embodies in art-forms what we already know about the ripe Renaissance, but Lotto supplements and even modifies our idea of this period.'
21. Such calls do not, of course, always imply that the visual arts can throw light on more traditional approaches to the past. The most systematic – indeed hectoring – solicitations of historians to widen the range of their sources have come from their colleagues of the so-called '*Annales* school'. But although that journal has published some art-historical articles (and book reviews) it cannot be said that its own closest collaborators have offered very rewarding examples of how the arts should be treated as historical evidence. Neither Lucien Febvre nor Marc Bloch drew significantly on the visual arts in their major works; and although Fernand Braudel describes the arts as 'ces grands témoins de toute histoire valable', his own references to them are so perfunctory that they could be removed without affecting his inspiring *La Méditerranée et le Monde Méditerranéen à l'Époque de Philippe II*: see I, p. 15 (Préface de la première édition) and II, pp. 156–63. In fact, of the *Annales* historians only Georges Duby has accorded a major role to impressions derived from the visual arts in order to interpret the civilisation of the Middle Ages, though it has been objected that in this interpretation 'an edifice's true value is calculated in terms of its ability to embody a particular theological or intellectual system . . . In the final analysis, the reader is left with the feeling that the arts are used only as an elaborate back-drop for the main intellectual and theological developments of mediaeval Europe': M.T. Davis, 1982. Philippe

Ariès was far more aware than any of the *Annales* historians of the significance of figurative sources – see his pioneering essay of 1951 'L'attitude devant l'histoire: le XVIIe siècle', reprinted in *Le Temps de l'Histoire* and many subsequent (and more influential) works.

22. See, in particular, a special issue of the *Journal of Interdisciplinary History* (XVII, no. 1, summer 1986) devoted to 'The Evidence of Art: Images and Meaning in History'. This contains a number of interesting articles, some of which are directly relevant to the theme of this book. One of the editors is Theodore K. Rabb, whose own *The Struggle for Stability in Early Modern Europe* proposes a bold (though, in my view, flawed) attempt to utilise the evidence of art for historical purposes. For another valuable collection of essays on the same theme see Freedberg and de Vries. By far the most ambitious recent book known to me that makes use of visual sources for the study of an earlier civilisation is Simon Schama's *The Embarrassment of Riches*.

23. See Haskell, 1977, and Haskell, 1988.
24. Such a title would, however, have required me to include an extensive discussion of the impact of the arts on fictional as well as on historical reconstructions of the past.

1 The Early Numismatists

1. Weiss, 1988, pp. 35–6.
2. Magnaguti; Billanovich, pp. 49–50.
3. Weiss, 1976 – but see Cunnally, pp. 4, 89. For general surveys, see E. Babelon, and Giard.
4. For Annius of Viterbo, see Ligota.
5. E.g., Erizzo, p. 64.
6. Baudrier, IX, pp. 205–7.
7. Strada; see, above all, Von Busch, pp. 193–219; also Jansen; Fučiková.
8. Varille, pp. 453–69; Baudrier, IX, pp. 229–30.
9. Guillaume du Choul: *Des Antiquités romaines* – this is in the Royal Library in Turin. It was drawn to my attention by Richard Cooper who very kindly supplied me with a photocopy of it, and who is now preparing a critical edition of this manuscript.
10. Du Choul (*Antiquités*): see the last page of the manuscript, 'Au Roy'.
11. There is a manuscript of Guillaume du Choul's *Des Bains et de la Palestre* in the Bibliothèque Nationale in Paris, and this, too, was made known to me by Richard Cooper.
12. Vico, 1548.
13. Campori, 1874.
14. Goltz, 1557. A number of portraits are missing and the roundels are left blank. I have used the Latin edition in the library of St John's College, Oxford. See, above all, Dekesel, 1988; also the cyclostyled notes by Paul Quarrie to accompany an exhibition in Eton College Library, 1985. For the portrait, see Campbell, pp. 165–6: both the portrait and the inscribed copy of Goltz's book are in the Musées Royaux des Beaux-Arts, Brussels.

15. Goltz, 1563: unpaginated at end of volume. See, above all, Palumbo-Fossati.
16. For Caro, see Castellani; Ligorio's numismatic researches were much discussed by his contemporaries: see, for example, Agustín, 1592, pp. 177 and 299. Other contemporary publications include those of Landi and Simeoni.
17. See E. Babelon, p. 100 – and the comments of Le Pois, p. 3v. For Strada's opinion of the work of Lazius, see Von Busch, pp. 199–201. For possible 'portraits' of him by Arcimboldo, see Hulten, pp. 86 and 87.
18. See for instance, Le Pois, Lazius, Occo, Patin, Vaillant and many others recorded by Renauldin.
19. Vico, 1555, p. 11.
20. Erizzo, pp. 1–3.
21. E. Babelon, p. 101.
22. Vico, 1555, pp. 50–1; Vico's source is Suetonius, *Tiberius*, 58.
23. Patin, 1674, p. 178.
24. E. Babelon, p. 96: Genesis 4: 22.
25. E. Babelon, p. 92, n. 1. The coin, whose obverse is indeed copied from the *denarii* of M. Junius Brutus of 54 BC commemorating his famous ancestor, is now thought to have been minted by a Scythian king called Koson or Kotison who died in 29 BC: see Burnett and others, p. 312.
26. Agustín, 1772.
27. Agustín, 1592, Dialogue IX.
28. Spon, 1673 (1974), Preface.
29. See, for instance, Grant.
30. Vico, 1555, pp. 109–10.
31. Patin, 1667 (2nd edition), pp. 7–8. For Patin, see Biasuz, Waquet, and Dekesel, 1990.
32. Spanheim: last two pages of the unpaginated Preface.
33. The question remains controversial: see Wallace-Hadrill.
34. Jobert, 1739, I, pp. 149 and 215.
35. Addison, p. 263.

2 Portraits from the Past

1. Wardman.
2. Schmitt, pp. 190 ff.; Fittschen; Cunnally, pp. 87–9.
3. Schmitt, pp. 194 ff.
4. Parlato, pp. 73ff; Wardrop, pp. 19–33.
5. Mortoft, p. 68.
6. Fittschen, figs 334 and 335.
7. Fulvio; Weiss, 1959, and for a very useful survey of sixteenth-century books illustrated with medallic portraits, see Rave, 1959.
8. Hill, 1930, no. 1091.
9. Baudrier, IX, pp. 38–9.
10. Müntz, p. 254; Rave, 1959, p. 123.
11. See Vico, 1555, pp. 92 and 99, and the comments of Diethelm Keller in 1558 quoted by Rave, 1959, p. 132.
12. Agustín, 1592, p. 19; Hill, 1920, p. 11: see Reiskius.
13. Du Choul, *Des Antiquités romaines* (see Chapter

1, n. 9 above), unpaginated, in the section devoted to Octavian.

14. This was suggested by Antoine Le Pois, p.162r.
15. For the elusive Corneille, see Groër.
16. See, for instance, Antoine du Verdier (Au lecteur).
17. Antoine du Verdier, p. 288.
18. Vico, 1555, p. 53.
19. Torsellino.
20. [Jean de Bussières].
21. Antoine du Verdier (Au lecteur).
22. Plutarch, 1575: referred to in Harvard College Library catalogue of French sixteenth-century books, ii, p. 549, no. 443.
23. Plutarch, 1695, p. xiv.
24. Dekesel, 1988, p. 101; De Bie, *Vrais portraits* (Le graveur au lecteur): unpaginated.
25. De Bie, *Vrais portraits* (Le graveur au lecteur): unpaginated.
26. De Bie, *La France métallique*, pp. 4–5.
27. See Schnapper, 1988, p. 132.
28. Patin, 1674, p. 54.
29. Weiss, 1988, pp. 72, 80; Rome, Musei Capitolini, 1988, p. 221, no. 67.
30. Addison, p. 264.
31. Von Busch, pp. 108–219.
32. Von Busch, p. 149.
33. See Von Busch, pp. 111–12 for Strada's account of his activities written in 1575. Strada includes in this his work on behalf of Hans Jacob Fugger whose example was followed, and whose collections were acquired, by the duke. See also the many other purchases recorded by Von Busch, and also Frosien-Leinz in Weski and Frosien-Leinz, i, pp. 46 ff.
34. Von Busch, pp. 149–50.
35. See, e.g., Frosien-Leinz in Weski and Frosien-Leinz, i, pp. 41, and Von Busch, p. 140.
36. Von Busch, p. 146.
37. See the inscriptions recorded in Von Busch, pp. 220–5.
38. See Weski and Frosien-Leinz, ii, pls 1–23.
39. It is not entirely clear whether (as Frosien-Leinz claims in Weski and Frosien-Leinz, i, p. 35) Strada actually met Orsini himself when he visited Rome in 1554; it may be significant that Von Busch does not include Orsini's name among the antiquarians personally known to Strada: Von Busch, p. 197.
40. Nolhac, 1884, p. 145; Nolhac, 1887, p. 31.
41. Nolhac, 1887, p. 112.
42. Jongkees, p. 5.
43. Jongkees, pp. 6–9.
44. Jongkees, p. 44.
45. Ladner, iii, pp. 176–9, and for the 'Pope Joan', Lusini, ii, pp. 149–50 (with documents).
46. Ladner, iii, pp. 39–51, and ii, pp. 160–3; De Bruyne.
47. De Bruyne, pp. 2–3.
48. Ladner, iii, pp. 198–211.
49. Passamani.
50. For Paolo Giovio I have made very extensive use of the unpublished thesis, 'The portrait collection of Paolo Giovio' by Dr Linda Klinger, and I

am extremely grateful to her for allowing me to do so.

51. Klinger, i, pp. 23, 26–7, 39–40.
52. Müntz, p. 257.
53. Müntz, p. 276.
54. Klinger, i, p. 157.
55. Klinger, i, pp. 116 and 147, n. 106.
56. Klinger, i, p. 166.
57. Klinger and Raby.
58. Klinger, i, pp. 67–73.
59. Rave, 1961; Klinger, i, pp. 68–72.
60. Klinger, i, p. 69.
61. De Vecchi, p. 89; Klinger, i, pp. 72 and 147, n. 106.
62. Klinger, i, pp. 71 and 204.
63. Müntz, p. 273.
64. Müntz, pp. 299–300.
65. Klinger, ii (catalogue); Scullard.
66. Klinger, ii (catalogue).
67. Klinger, i, pp. 92–3.
68. Klinger, ii (catalogue).
69. Müntz, p. 301.
70. Klinger, i, pp. 173 and 210, and ii (catalogue).
71. Müntz, p. 276.
72. Klinger and Raby, p. 48.
73. Müntz, p. 264 n.
74. De Vecchi, p. 90.
75. Müntz, p. 264.
76. Rave, 1959, p. 150.
77. Klinger, i, pp. 77 ff.
78. Klinger, i, pp. 205–8.
79. Müntz, p. 271.
80. Klinger, i, pp. 227, n. 2, and 247.
81. Klinger, i, p. 219.
82. Vasari, 1906, vii, p. 681.
83. Linda Klinger has, however, pointed out to me (letter of 18 March 1991) that there is no evidence that Vasari had access to Giovio's portraits once they had been sent from Rome. Dr Klinger thinks that the principal reason why Perna omitted the portraits of artists from his volumes is that Giovio had not written the *Elogia* for them.
84. For the portraiture used by Vasari, see Prinz, and Hope.
85. Adhémar, 1942–3.
86. The 'Codex Mendoza', now in the Bodleian Library, Oxford: see Joppien. Further information about Thevet's life and tra · is to be found in Baudry.
87. Thevet, p. 44, n. 1.
88. Thevet, p. 613.
89. Globe, no. 239, pl. 108.
90. See, for instance, the entry for the *Epitome des gestes* of 1546 in the Harvard College Library catalogue of sixteenth-century French books, i, p. 256, no. 208, and Rave, 1959, pp. 158–9.
91. De Bie, *Vrais portraits*, p. 7 (blank roundel).
92. *Ordo et effigies*.
93. This is how he appears in the *Cronica Breve* of 1588, pl. 1, in which the engraved portraits (attributed to Francesco Franca) are copied from woodcuts by François Des Prez published in 1567: Zappella, i, pp. 95–6.

94. [Hofmann], using engravings previously published by Boissevin.
95. Larmessin, 1679, pl. 1, and 1714, pl. 1.
96. Schnapper, 1988, p. 132.
97. For an explicit statement to this effect, dating from the first half of the century, see Mascardi, pp. 98–9.
98. Mézeray, I, p. 188.
99. Daniel, I, pp. i–xi; and see Montfaucon, 1729–33, I, p. ix.
100. Velly, Villaret et Garnier, fig. 1.
101. Le Petit.
102. Berni, Cariola, Sardi.
103. There is no correspondence at all between the portraits of Tebaldo I in the two books.
104. Klinger, I, p. 175.
105. See Coffin, and Lodi (with references to earlier literature).
106. Lodi, p. 152.
107. Lodi, pp. 159–62.
108. Palazzi: unpaginated address to the 'erudito lectore'.
109. Duchesne, I, p. 377.
110. Tabourot. I am very grateful to M. André Jammes for drawing my attention to this book.
111. De Piles, pp. 82–3; for other comments about the importance of portrait collections, by Félibien and Saint-Simon (who in 1719 suggested that the singular features and costumes of the royal personages represented in the Gagnières collection should be drawn to the attention of the four-year-old Louis XV as an enticing way of introducing him to the serious study of history), see Schnapper, 1981.
112. Sansovino, p. 63.
113. Le Pois, p. 19r.
114. Du Choul, Discours, p. 76 (I have used the reprint of 1567).
115. Orsini, 1606, p. 14 and fig. 23: the notes for this posthumous edition were written by Orsini himself, but this comment may well have been made by the editor.
116. Clubb, pp. 3–56.
117. For a convenient summary of Della Porta's theories, see Baltrusaitis, pp. 12–19.
118. Della Porta, 1622, p. 17v.
119. Della Porta, 1622, pp. 25r and 144v; Fulco, pp. 120 and 132.
120. Fulco, p. 112.
121. Fulco, pp. 125–9.
122. Compare Giovio, 1575, p. 103, with Della Porta, 1622, p. 123v (Tamerlane); Giovio, 1575, p. 41, with Della Porta, 1622, p. 48v (Ezzelino); Giovio, 1577, p. 73, with Della Porta, 1622, p. 54r (Poliziano); Giovio, 1577, p. 76, with Della Porta, 1622, pp. 172v and 180r (Pico); Giovio, 1575, p. 201, with Della Porta, 1622, p. 123v (Cesare Borgia).
123. Della Porta, 1622, p. 191v: cf. the portraits in Jacopo da Bergamo, De plurimis claris sceletisque mulieribus, Ferrara, 1497, reproduced in Rave, 1959, p. 125.
124. Clubb, pp. 15 ff.
125. Spon, 1683, pp. 357–8.

126. Tristan, 1635, p. 508. This is repeated in the expanded editions of his book published in 1644 and 1657.
127. Evelyn, p. 339.
128. Genebrier, p. 92.
129. Klinger, I, p. 212.
130. Klinger, I, pp. 215–16.
131. Klinger, I, p. 217.
132. Klinger, I, p. 219.
133. Klinger, I, pp. 208, 211.
134. Klinger, I, p. 221.
135. Giovio, 1555, p. 1r.
136. Chabod, pp. 259–62.
137. Giovio, 1555, p. 48r.
138. Kinser, p. 80.
139. De Thou, 1713. The authenticity of De Thou's Memoires, which has sometimes been challenged, is reaffirmed by Kinser (p. 169), who, however, stresses that the French translations are all incorrect and incomplete (p. 188).
140. De Thou, 1713, p. 24.
141. I am grateful to M. Antoine Coron for this and other information about De Thou.
142. De Thou, 1713, p. 125.
143. De Thou, 1713, p. 58.
144. De Thou, 1713, p. 106. This is the picture now in the National Gallery in London.
145. De Thou, 1713, p. 32; Kinser, p. 18, who points out that he did record this in an anonymous, secretly published volume.
146. De Thou, 1713, p. 43.
147. De Thou, 1740, pp. vi, 545 (under the year 1585).
148. De Thou, 1713, p. 49.
149. De Thou, 1713, p. 67.
150. See Quesnel, II, pp. 351 ff. and 531–5. Peiresc was interested in having copies made of some of the portraits in it: see Jaffé.
151. Gibson; and see Harris, pp. 374–5.
152. Gibson, pp. viii and 138.
153. Harris, p. 393.
154. Richardson, 1715, pp. 12–13.
155. Hearne, p. 211.
156. Hearne, p. 367.
157. Vertue, I, p. 71.
158. Morton.
159. See Pinkerton (though Clarendon is not included among the authors discussed).
160. Sutherland Collection, catalogue.
161. W.H. Evans.
162. Mézeray, I (Préface): unpaginated, see last page.
163. Globe, p. 56, no. 70; and p. 61, no. 104.
164. Leti, unpaginated Istruttione e dilucidattione dell'Autore per quei che leggono. The portrait of Charles I appears as in I, p. 202. I am most grateful to Jonathan Franklin of the National Portrait Gallery, London, for pointing out to me that it was adapted from a print of Archduke Ernest of Austria (1553–95).
165. Hearne, p. 188 (13 August 1717). I am grateful to Lucy Whitaker of the Christ Church Picture Gallery, Oxford, for the information that this statue was removed in the nineteenth century to the gardens of Nuneham Park. I was fortunate

enough to track it down there early in 1992, somewhat battered and obscured by undergrowth, but corresponding well enough to Hearne's description–see pl. 59.
166. Evelyn, p. 46.
167. Defoe, II, p. 719 (1726).

3   Historical Narrative and Reportage

1. Hinks, p. 101.
2. *English Romanesque Art*, p. 126, no. 72.
3. See, e.g., Gaspar and Lyna, pl. LVIII; Guenée; Sherman.
4. Magnani.
5. See below, Chapter 5.
6. See pl. 60. For the tapestries (designed by Barendt van Orley) of the Battle of Pavia, in the Museo di Capodimonte in Naples, see Hale, 1990, pp. 145 and 191. The tapestries of the defeat of the Armada, commissioned in 1592 by Admiral Lord Howard of Effingham from Cornelis de Vroom of Haarlem and woven by François Spierincx of Delft, were completed in 1596 and destroyed when the House of Lords was burned down in 1834.
7. See Maccari, pp. 100–1 (with illustration).
8. For a discussion of this issue, see Chastel, pp. 41 ff.
9. For this section, see Wolters, especially pp. 164–81; P.F. Brown, 1984; P.F. Brown, 1988, pp. 79 ff. Of the mosaics depicting the transfer of the relics from Alexandria to Venice the only ones that survive are those above the Porta S. Alippio.
10. See Smith, and Pastor, XXIX, pp. 182–4; also Nani, I, pp. 648–9 (Libro X, Anno 1635).
11. See the classic article by Momigliano, 1950.
12. Evelyn, p. 48.
13. Evelyn, p. 158.
14. Schnapper, 1988, p. 295, quoting from the *Histoire de l'Académie royale des inscriptions*.
15. *Médailles*, p. 2.
16. Cunnally, pp. 150 and 153, no. 5. The silver coin in question, which was struck by Marcus Junius Brutus, in fact showed his ancestor, the first Consul (the elder Brutus), marching with his lictors. See above, Chapter 1, n. 25.
17. Erizzo, II, pp. 110 ff. I am very grateful to Dr Cathy King of the Ashmolean Museum, Oxford, for pointing out to me that Erizzo was referring to a contorniate: see A. and E. Alföldi, part 1, cat. nos 132 and 135; part 2, pl. 44, no. 12; pl. 45, nos 10–12. A very similar reverse is found on a contorniate portraying Alexander the Great: see Tocci, tav. LXI, no. 6.
18. Erizzo, II, pp. 77–8; and for *spintriae*, Simonetta and Riva. Ironically enough, it has recently been suggested that it was perhaps the very existence of these still mysterious *spintriae* (which can be dated to between *c.*37 and 22 BC) that gave rise to Suetonius's scandalous stories about Tiberius: Buttrey, p. 58.
19. Suetonius, see Sutherland, 1987, pp. 92–3; Griffin, p. 120; and Le Pois, p. 19r.

20. Rushforth; and Master Gregorius, pp. 32 and 83–5.
21. Frugoni, pp. 12, 20–2.
22. See the discussion of the letter from Lucius Verus to Fronto of AD 165 in Settis, 1988, pp. 104–5.
23. Baxandall, p. 81.
24. Farinella, pp. 209–37.
25. Cavallero.
26. Vasari, quoted by Venturoli, p. 433.
27. Haskell and Penny, pp. 46–7. Raffaello Fabretti's volume on the column published in 1683 criticises earlier works on the subject and refers to its importance as an historical source; but – despite the ambitious claims he makes for his own researches – his approach also is essentially antiquarian.
28. These were drawn to my attention by a member of the audience who attended a course of lectures I gave at the Scuola Normale, Pisa, in 1985.
29. Mascardi, p. 287.
30. Mascardi, pp. 403 ff.
31. Mascardi, pp. 9–10.
32. Mascardi, p. 177.
33. Mascardi, p. 11.
34. Mascardi, pp. 190–1.
35. For the interpretations of this statue, see (with references to earlier literature) Haskell and Penny, pp. 188–9.
36. Settis, 1981.
37. Erizzo, II, p. 519; Cohen, II, p. 156; Mattingly, IV (1940), p. 543 and pl. 74, no. 11.
38. For all this, see Haskell, 1987 ('Scholars and Images'), which has been extensively modified here.
39. Tristan, 1635, pp. 509–11.
40. Perrier, pl. 21.
41. Buiatti.
42. Angeloni, p. 157 and italicised commentary to pl. 43; Scipione Maffei (1825–6, IV, p. 326) made the same point as Bellori, but rather more energetically: 'non si sarebbe figurata in tal guisa un' Imperadrice . . .'. However, as late as 1807 it was still possible for visitors to Rome to believe that the figures perhaps represented 'Faustina with her favourite Gladiator Carinus': d'Uklanski, II, pp. 63.
43. [Raguenet], pp. 30–1.
44. See Henfrey.
45. Pliny, *Natural History*, XXXV, 140.
46. A.B. Gardiner, and the corrections by Scharloo.
47. Jones, pp. 13–18.
48. *Tiziano*, pp. 196–208; Haskell, 1987 ('Scholars and Images'), p. 515.
49. Mommsen, p. 111.
50. Pastor, XIX, p. 262.
51. Pastor, XIX, p. 268.
52. Scavizzi.
53. Pastor, XIX, p. 265.
54. Pastor, XIX, pp. 268–9.
55. Prudentius, *Peristephanon*, Hymnus XI, ll. 183–8 (in *Oeuvres*, IV, p. 171).
56. Kelly, p. 22; I, 12, *In Ezech*, ch. 401; Montes-

quieu, II, p. 725 (Le Spicilège).

57. Molanus, ch. v, pp. 20–1.
58. [Bottari], I, p. 137 and pl. XXXIV.
59. Baronius (Rinaldi), I, p. 28: St Luke, 8. Baronius also comments on portraits of St Peter and St Paul said to have been made in their lifetimes: I, p. 132.
60. Gibbon (1896–8), v, p. 247.
61. For all this, see Cicognara, I, p. 116.
62. Baronio (Rinaldi), I, p. 21; Scavizzi, p. 197; Sosti; Scala; Zen.
63. Scoto, II, p. 53v.
64. Baronius (Rinaldi), I, p. 184.
65. Baronius (Rinaldi), I, p. 454: I am very grateful to Dr Cathy King of the Ashmolean Museum, Oxford, for pointing out to me that Baronius was probably looking at the Alexandrian coinage of (for instance) Antoninus Pius: see Dattari, II, tav. XVII, no. 2643, and ibid., no. 925 for a similar reverse on a coin of Trajan.
66. Scavizzi, p. 45.
67. Meyer, pp. 292–3.
68. Gaston, pp. 150–1.
69. For the opinions of the Huguenot Maximilien Misson, whose travel book to Italy was first translated into English in 1691 and frequently reprinted, see Gaston, p. 152.
70. Wilpert, pp. 22–3, 49 (and pl. XII), 78 (and pls XXI–XXII).
71. Bosio, pp. 627–9.
72. Du Choul, p. 29.
73. Du Choul, p. 69.
74. Du Choul, p. 248.

4 The Issue of Quality

1. Cunnally; Schnapper, 1988, pp. 119–79.
2. Strada (Au lecteur): unpaginated.
3. Vico, 1555, p. 53.
4. Agustín, p. 13.
5. Panofsky, 1972, pp. 13–14.
6. Krautheimer, p. 307.
7. Krautheimer, pp. 159–68.
8. Krautheimer, pp. 357–8.
9. Bober and Rubinstein, nos 98 and 94, (pp. 130–1 and 127).
10. Krautheimer, pp. 227–8.
11. Buddensieg.
12. For an early reference to the role of Sylvester, see Master Gregorius, p. 51.
13. Settis, 1986, pp. 379–80 and fig. 349. See also Rubin, pp. 106–7 for references (in Eusebius) to Constantine's destruction of the idols, and sixteenth-century frescoes of the scene; Borsook, pp. 38–42, especially n. 18.
14. Ghiberti, I, p. 35.
15. Filarete, I, p. xix.
16. Pope-Hennessy, pp. 77 and 332.
17. Bober and Rubinstein, no. 176 (pp. 206–8); Nesselrath, 1988, p. 235.
18. Parlato, p. 115.
19. Filarete, I, p. 176.
20. Ibid.
21. Manetti, pp. 10 ff.
22. Manetti, pp. 61, 63. Both SS Apostoli and S Piero Scheraggio have been fundamentally changed since Manetti's day (Paatz, I, pp. 226–63 and Sanpaolesi), but San Miniato al Monte, which was built at much the same time, the middle of the eleventh century, has the same 'proto-Renaissance' features as they once did and has raised the same problems for architectural historians.
23. See Weiss, 1988, p. 74, for the passionate admiration for the mosaics expressed by Giovanni Rucellai in 1450. This is specially notable because Rucellai gave no indication that he believed them to be pagan. For more usual responses, see Amadio.
24. Golzio, pp. 82–92.
25. Nesselrath, 1986, pp. 357–69.
26. Golzio, p. 85.
27. Bober and Rubinstein, no. 182 (pp. 214–16).
28. Nesselrath 1986, p. 365. It is hardly necessary to add that it never occurred to Raphael (or to anyone else before the end of the nineteenth century) that late antique art might have constituted a change rather than a decline from the norms established in the early Empire.
29. Jones and Penny, pp. 199–205 for Raphael's archaeological investigations.
30. Bober and Rubinstein, no. 176 (pp. 206–8).
31. Wazbinski.
32. Although Vasari develops his theories fully only in the second edition, Fehl seems to me to be mistaken in stating categorically that there are basic differences between the first and second editions as regards his treatment of the Arch of Constantine: Fehl, p. 27.
33. Vasari, 1906, I (Proemio), pp. 224–5.
34. Vasari, 1906, I (Proemio), pp. 226–8.
35. Vasari, 1906, I (Proemio), p. 230.
36. Vasari, 1906, I (Proemio), p. 232.
37. Vasari, 1906, I, (Proemio), pp. 232–3; De Beer.
38. Buddensieg, p. 60.
39. Herklotz, especially pp. 60 ff.
40. Baronius, III, pp. 86–7 (Christi, 312).
41. Gilio, p. 111.
42. Pintard, pp. 261–2.
43. Mancini, I, pp. 48–9.
44. Rubens to Peiresc, 4 September 1636 (Rubens, p. 405): I am grateful to Elizabeth McGrath for this reference.
45. The late Giovanni Previtali seems to have been the first scholar to draw attention to the significance of Buonarroti's comments: Previtali, pp. 31–2.
46. See Gallo.
47. Quoted by Gallo, p. 20.
48. Cristofani, pp. 16–31.
49. [Buonarroti], 1698, p. 314.
50. Buonarroti, 1716, pp. 84–5.
51. For a general discussion of this theme, see Gombrich, 1971.
52. Marangoni, pp. 77–8 with reference also to the views of P. Lodovico Marocci.
53. Bottari, I, p. 62; II, pp. v, vi – and many similar passages.

5 Problems of Interpretation

1. Montfaucon, 1722, I (Préface), p. iv. I have used this second edition throughout.
2. Montfaucon, 1722, I (Préface), pp. i–iii.
3. Montfaucon's *Diarium Italicum* of 1702 was criticised (mostly on points of detail) by Francesco Ficoroni in 1709, and this criticism in turn attracted further polemics.
4. Montfaucon, 1722, I (Préface), pp. iii–vii.
5. E. de Broglie, I, pp. 357–8.
6. Montfaucon, 1722, I (Préface), p. xiv.
7. E. de Broglie, I, p. 370.
8. Johnson, II, p. 856.
9. Montfaucon, 1722, I (Préface), p. x.
10. Montfaucon, 1722, I (Préface), p. xiii.
11. Rostand, p. 105.
12. Montfaucon, 1722, I (Préface), pp. xv ff.
13. Montfaucon, 1729–33, I (Préface), pp. i–ii.
14. Montfaucon, 1729–33, I (Préface), p. ii.
15. Montfaucon, 1729–33, I (Préface), p. vi.
16. Duplessis, 1870; Schnapper, 1988, pp. 291–6. Philippe Ariès was the first to draw attention, in 1951, to the importance for historical methodology of Gaignières's collection of illustrated material in general: see Ariès, pp. 178 ff.
17. Hugues-Adrien Joly writing to Karl Heinrich von Heinecken in July 1782 about the visit to the Cabinet des Estampes of the comte et comtesse du Nord (the future Tsar Paul I of Russia and his wife): Joly, p. 112.
18. Montfaucon, 1729–33, I, p. 55.
19. Vanuxem, 1957, pp. 45–7.
20. *Ibid.*, pp. 47 ff.
21. Montfaucon, 1729–33, I (Préface), p. xi.
22. Montfaucon, 1729–33, v (Au lecteur): unpaginated.
23. Montfaucon, 1729–33, I, p. 371; *Dictionnaire de Biographie Française*, XIV, pp. 594–5; Schnapper, 1988, pp. 297–301.
24. Lancelot, 1729 (publishing his contribution of 1724), pp. 739–55; and see the obituary of Lancelot, who died in 1740 at the age of sixty-five, in *Memoires de litterature tirez des Registres de l'Académie Royale des Inscriptions et Belles-Lettres*, tome XVI, Paris 1751, pp. 257–68.
25. Huard, 1913, p. 360.
26. Montfaucon, 1729–33, II, p. 2.
27. *Ibid.*
28. Montfaucon, 1729–33, I, p. 375 (wrongly printed as 735).
29. Werckmeister, pp. 535–48.
30. Montfaucon, 1729–33, I, p. 375 (wrongly printed as 735).
31. Lancelot, 1729, p. 740.
32. Wilson, p. 197, suggests only that Edward is 'apparently giving orders to Harold', and agrees that 'the Tapestry gives no indication of the reason for the journey'. Other modern authorities have been just as non-committal, if not more so.
33. Montfaucon, 1729–33, II, p. 3. His description of the scene in I, p. 373 is a little more hesitant.
34. Lancelot, 1729, p. 747.
35. Montfaucon, 1729–33, II, p. 10.
36. Lancelot, 1733, p. 605.
37. For the most thorough survey of the literature on the tapestry, see S.A. Brown.
38. Hume's cursory allusion (I, pp. 127–8 n) of five years earlier is not relevant in this context.
39. Lyttelton, I, pp. 353–5.
40. Abbé de la Rue.
41. Amyot, 1819, p. 197.
42. Amyot, 1819, p. 205.
43. Freeman, III, p. 575.
44. Freeman, III, p. 572.
45. Amyot, 1818, p. 92.
46. Freeman, III, p. 676, referring to the opinion of Dr Collingwood Bruce in 1856.
47. Lomazzo, p. 154 (wrongly printed as 146), 165–6, 168.
48. L.B. Alberti, pp. 80–1 (para. 42).
49. Vasari, 1550 (1986), pp. 891–2.
50. Lomazzo, p. 162.
51. Reynolds, pp. 221–2 (Discourse XII).
52. Bulwer, *Chirologia*, p. 91.
53. Bulwer, *Chiromania*, p. 21.
54. Bulwer, *Chiromania*, pp. 80–1.
55. See, for instance, Gombrich, 1972, and the very extensive bibliography attached to the volume.
56. Buonarroti, 1698, pp. viii–ix.
57. Roy, pp. 102–3, also refers to the similarity of structure between the treatises of Lamazzo and Lairesse.
58. Lairesse, 1707, facing p. 54, and 1738, pp. 38–9 (pl. XII, examples 1 and 2). This is the text that I have used.
59. Lairesse, 1707, facing p. 68, and 1738, pp. 50–1 (pl. XIII, example 2, and pl. XIV, example 3).
60. Lairesse, 1707, facing p. 67, and 1738, pp. 51–2 (pl. XIV, example 4, and pl. XV, examples 5 and 6).
61. Lairesse, 1738, p. 45.
62. Lairesse, 1738, pp. 46–7, and see 1787, I, pp. 134–5.
63. For Du Bos's discussion of the so-called *Papirius*, see Haskell and Penny, pp. 288–91.
64. Du Bos, I, p. 86 ff (1967 reprint, pp. 29–30).
65. Richardson, 1722, pp. 161–2.
66. Walpole, IV, p. 72.
67. Lichtenberg, p. 102; Paulson, I, pp. 271 ff.
68. Graham, p. 85.
69. Graham, pp. 87–101.
70. Lavater, 1775, 1776, 1777, 1778.
71. Lavater, 1781, 1783, 1786, 1803.
72. Lavater, 1781–1803, I, p. 119.
73. Lavater, 1781–1803, I, pp. 167–82.
74. Lavater, 1781–1803, IV, p. 186.
75. See, for instance, the different approaches to the features of Diomedes and Ulysses (reproduced from the dedicatory page of Winckelmann, 1764) in Lavater, 1775–8, III, p. 57, and 1781–1803, II, p. 341. And many other examples could be given.
76. Lavater, 1781–1803, III, p. 261. This passage and the illustration are not to be found in the earlier Lavater, 1775–8; see Winckelmann, 1783–4, II, pp. 351–2.
77. Lavater, 1781–1803, II, pp. 98 ff.
78. Lavater, 1781–1803, II, p. 368.
79. Lavater, 1781–1803, II, p. 80.

80. Lavater, 1781–1803, II, p. 24.
81. Lavater, 1781–1803, III, pp. 186–7.
82. De Jorio, 1832, p. 63. But, as he frequently emphasises, the main influence on De Jorio was Engel's *Ideen zu einer Mimik* of 1785–6, which was translated into Italian in 1820.
83. De Jorio, 1832, pp. ix–x.
84. Navarro.
85. *Annali Civili*, p. 25.
86. De Jorio, 1825, p. 45.
87. De Jorio, 1832, p, xii.
88. Croce, p. 280.
89. De Jorio, 1832, pp. vi–vii.
90. De Jorio, 1832, pp. 322–4 and pl. II.
91. De Jorio, 1832, p. xi.
92. De Jorio, 1832, pp. 363–6 and pl. XVII.
93. *Annali Civili*, p. 25.

6   The Dialogue between Antiquarians and Historians

1. See, for instance, a number of references to Montfaucon in Vertue; and for Strutt, see below, Chapter 11.
2. See Lelong, 1719 and 1768–78. The Appendix is published in volume IV, 1775; and see, at the beginning of the same volume, the *Éloges* of Fevret de Fontette by MM Perret and Dupuy of the Académie Royale des Inscriptions et Belles-Lettres.
3. *Ibid.* Many years later Fevret de Fontette's collection (which was sold in 1770 to the Royal Library, where it joined the portfolios of Gaignières's drawings as well as some forty thousand drawn and engraved portraits of 'françois et françoises illustres', all carefully annotated) was to attract the special attention of Michel Hennin, for whom see below, Chapter 11.
4. For La Curne de Sainte-Palaye, see Gossman.
5. Sainte-Palaye, VIII, 1733, p. 528.
6. See Gossman for some stimulating ideas about the appeal of Gothic art to figures of the Enlightenment.
7. Sainte-Palaye, XIII, 1740, p. 574; XV, 1743, p. 615.
8. Sainte-Palaye, XIII, 1740, p. 574. For Montfaucon's illustrations and commentary see Montfaucon (1729–33), II, pp. 234 and 296; and for a recent scholarly opinion, Dogaer, p. 112. The manuscript in the Bibliothèque Nationale is Fonds Français, nos 2643–4.
9. Sainte-Palaye, XVII, 1751, p. 794, quoted Gossman, p. 250.
10. E. de Broglie, II, pp. 218–19.
11. I am very grateful to Carlo Ginzburg for showing me an advance copy of his article on Jean Chapelain's dialogue of 1646, *De la lecture des vieux romans*, in which Chapelain discusses mediaeval romances in much the same spirit as Sainte-Palaye was to refer to mediaeval art in the following century. In his article Ginzburg also points to some precedents for this approach.
12. Lalande, I, p. 98.
13. Gibbon, 1961, p. 21 (5 May 1764).
14. *Turin*, I, pp. 42–3.
15. Gibbon, 1961, p. 22.
16. *Turin*, III, pp. 1397–8.
17. *Turin*, I, pp. 42–9, Romagnini; Maffei (1955), I, pp. 469 ff. (1724); Caylus, III, p. 271; Franzoni, 1982.
18. See the frequent references to Montfaucon in Maffei, 1731–2.
19. *Turin*, I, pp. 42–3.
20. E. Wright, II, p. 396 ff.
21. Heikamp, pp. 466 and 492 ff.
22. E. Wright, II, plan facing p. 397.
23. Montesquieu, II, p. 29 (*Pensées*).
24. Montesquieu, II, p. lii for the dating of the *Pensées*.
25. Montesquieu, II, pp. 1316–17 (*Voyage en Italie*), referring to the article of the Abbé Nadal.
26. Montesquieu, II, p. 1315 (*Voyage en Italie*).
27. Montesquieu, II, pp. 278–9 (*Pensées*).
28. Montesquieu, II, p. 1315 (*Voyage en Italie*).
29. Montesquieu, II, pp. 1313 ff. (*Voyage en Italie*).
30. For an interesting discussion of the impact of his Italian travels on Montesquieu's political thought, see Harder, pp. 121 ff.
31. Giannone, 1971, pp. 24–5, and for d'Aulisio, see Liotta.
32. Giannone, 1753, I, p. xxv.
33. *Ibid.*
34. Giannone, 1753, I, pp. 367 ff.
35. Blunt, 1975, p. 48 (with references); *Napoli, Città d'Arte*, I, pp. 39–41.
36. Blunt, 1975, p. 36; *Napoli, Città d'Arte*, II, p. 296.
37. Giannone, 1753, IV, p. 306.
38. Giannone, 1753, I, pp. 349, 367.
39. Giannone, 1971, p. 25.
40. Breventano.
41. Impellizzeri and Rotta.
42. Bandur.
43. *Biographie Universelle* (Michaud), XXVIII, p. 183.
44. Giannone, 1753, I, p. 166.
45. Bertelli, pp. 407–16.
46. Muratori, 1901–22, I, p. 324 (25 June 1698; to Magliabechi).
47. Muratori, 1901–22, I, pp. 126 and 129 (18 and 25 January 1696).
48. Muratori, 1901–22, II, pp. 376 (1699) and 668 (1704).
49. Muratori, 1901–22, XI, p. 5117 (6 December 1747; to Mazzucchelli).
50. Muratori, 1901–22, IX, pp. 3844–5 (27 January 1739; to Giuseppe Bianchini).
51. Muratori, 1901–22, III, p. 1101 (12 July 1709; to Vallisnieri).
52. McCuiag, p. 256, n. 14; and pp. 251–90 for the amazing story of his difficulties with censorship.
53. Muratori, 1901–22, III, p. 1207 (24 October 1710; to Filippo del Torre).
54. Muratori, 1901–22, V, pp. 1829–30 (14 August 1716).
55. Bertelli, pp. 286–8.
56. Bertelli, pp. 100–258.
57. Bertelli, p. 89, n. 161 (quoting from *Riflessioni sul Buon Gusto*).

58. Muratori, 1901–22, VII, pp. 2808–11 (5 November 1728).
59. Muratori, 1901–22, I, p. 333 (10 September 1698; to Magliabechi).
60. F. Bianchini.
61. Muratori, 1901–22, II, p. 482 (25 November 1700).
62. Campori, 1866, pp. 154 ff. for letters from Vleughels to the Abate Grassetti of 1710 with friendly messages to Muratori, and pp. 556–7 for Crespi's letter of 1744.
63. Campori, 1866, pp. 517–49 (1703–9).
64. Bertelli, p. 249.
65. See Lazius, p. 784, and Muratori, 1901–22, XI, p. 5217 (1748).
66. Muratori, 1751, I (Prefazione): unpaginated.
67. Muratori, 1751, I, p. 351 (*Delle Arti de gl'Italiani dopo la declinazione dell'Imperio Romano*: Dissertazione ventesimaquarta).
68. Muratori, 1751, I, p. 353 (*Delle Arti de gl'Italiani*).
69. Muratori, 1751, I, pp. 351–2 (*Delle Arti de gl'Italiani*).
70. Muratori, 1901–22, p. 324 (25 June 1698).
71. Grassi Fiorentino.
72. Ciampini, I, pp. 63–4 (pl. XXV).
73. Ciampini, II, pp. 65–101 (with plates).
74. Bevilacqua, 1975.
75. Vasari, 1568, I, pp. 232–4.
76. Leandro Alberti, 1553, p. 278r.
77. Vasari, 1906, I (Proemio), p. 232.
78. Maffei, 1731–2, III, p. 74.
79. Maffei, 1731–2, III, pp. 73–4.
80. Maffei, 1955, *passim*; and Barbieri.
81. Maffei, 1825–6, II, p. 501: in the 1731–2 edition (I, p. 294), Giannone is not named as the author of the opinion dismissed by Maffei.
82. Maffei, 1731–2, I, pp. 69–71.
83. Maffei, 1955, I, pp. 507–8 (15 December 1725).
84. Maffei, 1731–2, I, p. 338.
85. Franzoni, 1982 (*L'Accademia Filarmonica*).
86. Franzoni, 1982; 1985.
87. Franzoni, 1974–5, p. 562 (quoting from Maffei, *Dittico Quiriniano*, 1754).
88. Maffei, 1731–2, III, p. 59.
89. Bevilacqua.
90. Maffei, 1731–2, III, p. 57.
91. Maffei, 1731–2, III, pp. 188–9.
92. Maffei, 1731–2, III, pp. 101–2.
93. Maffei, 1731–2, III, p. 74.
94. See Pomian, 1987, for all this section.
95. Caylus, III, pp. x–xi, xxxiii, 42.
96. Caylus, VI, p. viii.
97. Caylus, I, pp. iii–iv; II, p. 22; IV, p. 19.
98. Caylus, II, p. ii.
99. Caylus, I, pp. 37–8; II, pp. 379–80.
100. Haskell, 1987 (*The Painful Birth of the Art Book*).
101. Caylus, II, p. 56.
102. Caylus, I, p. 251; IV, p. 144.
103. Caylus, VII, p. xv.
104. Caylus, III, p. 23; VI, p. 29.
105. Caylus, I, pp. v–vii.
106. Caylus, III, p. vi; V, pp. vi–vii.
107. Caylus, I, pp. xi, 282; II, p. 126. See also Vickers for later claims to this effect by D'Hancarville.

108. Caylus, II, p. 313.
109. Caylus, I, pp. 81, 95; II, p. 85; III, pp. 72–3.
110. Caylus, IV, p. 301; VI, p. 323 and pl. CIII, no. 1. See *Pièces d'Echecs*, p. 25, no. 31 and fig. 17.
111. Caylus, III, p. 225; IV, p. 75.
112. Caylus, I, pp. 159, 181–2.
113. Caylus, III, pp. 14, 33.
114. Caylus, II, p. 305.
115. Caylus, III, p. xi.
116. Caylus, II, p. 316 and pl. XC, nos iii–iv; IV, pp. 104–5. A century later Champfleury (for whom see below, Chapter 13) was to refer to Caylus's opinions on such matters when he, too, came to very similar conclusions: *Caricature antique*, pp. 87–8.
117. Caylus, II, p. 304 and pl. LXXXVI.
118. Caylus, I, p. 92.
119. Caylus, I, p. 12.
120. Caylus, III, pp. 167–8 and pl. XLIV, no. 1.
121. Caylus, IV, p. 69; V, pp. viii–ix; VI, pp. 102, 151–2.
122. Caylus, VI, pp. 219–28. Cicognara (1813–18, I, p. 135) was later to develop this idea and to point out that in antiquity, as in his own day, artists must have treated costume in a stylised manner so as to avoid the merely fashionable; what we see, therefore, may not be reliable.
123. Caylus, II, pp. 313–14 and pl. XC.
124. Caylus, I, p. 171; II, pp. 23–4; IV, p. 61; VI, p. 100.
125. Caylus, I, pp. 3, 117–18; II, p. 43; III, p. 2; V, pp. 90, 127; VI, p. 119; VII, pp. 150–1.
126. Caylus, II, pp. 398–9; III, pp. 34, 69; IV, p. 106; VI, p. ix.
127. Caylus, I, p. 101.
128. Caylus, V, pp. v–xiv.
129. Caylus, V, p. 198 and pl. LXX, no. iii.
130. Caylus, II, p. 1.
131. Seroux d'Agincourt, II (Sculpture, Renouvellement), p. 85.
132. Baridon, p. 84 (with references).
133. Gibbon, 1984, p. 117.
134. Gibbon, 1984, p. 113; Momigliano, 1969.
135. Gibbon, 1796, II, pp. 25–6.
136. Gibbon, 1952, p. 104 (*Le Séjour de Gibbon à Paris, 1763*).
137. Keynes; Gibbon, 1945, p. 259 (Montfaucon).
138. Gibbon, 1961, p. 122. Gibbon is here referring specifically to Muratori's discussion of the first century AD.
139. Gibbon, 1896–8, IV, p. 181, n. 34. Despite this *boutade*, Gibbon warmly admired Muratori's historical researches.
140. Gibbon, 1984, p. 100.
141. Gibbon, 1952, pp. 30–1 (*Journal de mon voyage dans quelques endroits de la Suisse, 1755*).
142. Gibbon, 1984, p. 101.
143. Gibbon, 1961, p. 179.
144. For all this section see Haskell, 1987 (*Gibbon and the History of Art*), pp. 16–29.
145. Gibbon, 1961, pp. 74–5 and 83. The Domenichino cannot now be traced; the Veronese is in the Palazzo Rosso, Genoa.
146. Gibbon, 1961, p. 228.

147. Gibbon, 1961, p. 166. Gibbon had, of course, not seen Montesquieu's notes.
148. Gibbon, 1952, p. 98 (*Le Séjour de Gibbon à Paris, 1763*).
149. Gibbon, 1961, p. 167.
150. Mansuelli, I, pp. 37–8, no. 11.
151. Gibbon, 1961, pp. 177–8.
152. *Ibid.*
153. Gibbon, 1945, pp. 211–14, 254–7.
154. Gibbon, 1961, pp. 166–7.
155. Gibbon, 1961, p. 112.
156. Gibbon, 1961, p. 168.
157. Gibbon, 1961, p. 138. This picture is now generally accepted as a copy of the original in the National Gallery, London.
158. Gibbon, 1961, p. 168.
159. Gibbon, 1961, p. 169.
160. Haskell and Penny, pp. 172–3.
161. Gibbon, 1961, p. 170.
162. Gibbon, 1945, p. 168.
163. Gibbon, 1984, p. 143 ('musing in the Church of the Zoccolanti').
164. Gibbon, 1896–8, VII, p. 301.
165. Gibbon, 1945, pp. 82–3 (Petri Angeli Bargaei, *De Privatorum Publicorumque Aedificiorum Urbis Romae Eversoribus Epistola*).
166. Haskell and Penny, pp. 296–300.
167. Gibbon, 1896–8, VII, p. 323.
168. Gibbon, 1961, p. 251.
169. Gibbon, 1896–8, I, p. 391.
170. Adam, p. 2.
171. Wilkes, pp. 23, 40.
172. Adam, p. 3.
173. Adam, p. 4.
174. Adam, p. 2.
175. Winckelmann, 1764, II, p. 423; 1783–4, II, pp. 412–13; also for Winckelmann's great admiration for Adam, Winckelmann, 1766, pp. 201–2.
176. Winckelmann, 1764, II, p. 423; 1783–4, II, p. 411.
177. Gibbon, 1896–8, I, p. 391.
178. *Ibid.*, n. 130.
179. Quoted by Haskell, 1987 (*Gibbon and the History of Art*), pp. 24–5.
180. Cicognara, 1813–18, I, pp. 69–70.
181. Seroux d'Agincourt, I (Discours Préliminaire), p. i.
182. Seroux d'Agincourt, I (Discours Préliminaire), p. iii.
183. Where no other reference is given, see Haskell, 1987 (*Gibbon and the History of Art*), pp. 16–29.
184. Loyrette, however, claims (p. 41) that the project was developed between 1774 and 1777.
185. Seroux d'Agincourt, I (Tableau Historique), ch. III, p. 5.
186. Seroux d'Agincourt, I (Préface), p. 1.
187. Seroux d'Agincourt, IV, pl. II (Architecture); V, pl. XIV (Peinture).
188. Seroux d'Agincourt, II (Sculpture, Introduction), p. 16.
189. Seroux d'Agincourt, I (Tableau Historique), chs VI and VII, pp. 16, 22.
190. Seroux d'Agincourt, I (Tableau Historique),

ch. X, p. 34.
191. De Rossi, I, pp. 61–2.
192. Seroux d'Agincourt, II (Peinture, Décadence), p. 22.
193. Seroux d'Agincourt, I (Architecture, Décadence), pp. 21–3.
194. Seroux d'Agincourt, I (Tableau Historique), p. 36.
195. Seroux d'Agincourt, II (Peinture, Décadence), p. 23.
196. Malamani, I, pp. 27–8.
197. Cicognara, 1973, p. 179 (as he described him on hearing of his death in 1814).
198. Malamani, II, p. 398.
199. Malamani, II, pp. 397 and 399; Haskell, 1982 (*Cicognara eretico*).
200. See Chapter 4 for the statue; Malamani, II, p. 399.
201. Malamani, II, p. 149.
202. Cicognara, 1813–18, I, p. 92.
203. Cicognara, 1813–18, I, p. 97.
204. Cicognara, 1813–18, I, p. 94.
205. Cicognara, 1813–18, I, p. 97; Malamani, II, p. 398.
206. Cicognara, 1813–18, I, p. 99.
207. Malamani, II, p. 398.
208. Cicognara, 1813–18, I, pp. 101–2.

7   The Birth of Cultural History

1. Robertson, I, p. 166.
2. Voltaire, 1947, I, p. 2 (ch. 1).
3. Ferté, pp. 56–61.
4. Rollin, 1740.
5. Ferté, p. 338; and p. 347 (for a more favourable opinion by Voltaire).
6. Ferté, pp. 346–7 for Sainte-Beuve; Michelet, 1959, p. 211 (*Mémorial*).
7. Rollin, 1740, I, p. vii.
8. Ferté, p. 371.
9. Bossuet, pp. 948–52; and see the references to Prudentius in the sixteenth century: Rubin, p. 106.
10. Rollin, 1740, V, pp. 543–4.
11. Rollin, 1740, V, p. 543.
12. Rollin, 1740, IV, p. 3.
13. Rollin, 1740, I, pp. 13–16, 52–4, etc.
14. Rollin, 1768 (The Author to the Reader): unpaginated.
15. Rollin, 1768.
16. Fraser.
17. See, for instance, Rollin, 1740, V, pp. 626–7.
18. Rollin, 1740, V, p. 565.
19. Rollin, 1740, V, p. 617.
20. Rollin, 1740, II, p. 308.
21. Saint-Pierre, pp. iv, vii–viii.
22. Brumfitt, p. 48.
23. Saint-Pierre, pp. xxxii–xxxvi.
24. Saint-Pierre, p. 283.
25. Saint-Pierre, pp. 5, 41–2.
26. Saint-Pierre, p. 28.
27. Saint-Pierre, pp. 96–7.
28. Voltaire, 1947, II, p. 71 n. (ch. XXIX).

29. Seznec, 1957, p. 138, n. 23.
30. Voltaire, 1968, pp. 41–2 (*Remarques sur l'histoire*, 1742).
31. Voltaire, 1947, II, p. 131 (ch. XXXII); Du Bos, however, had claimed that neither poetry nor painting exhausted the subjects that they treated (Du Bos, II, section XXIII).
32. Voltaire, 1947, II, p. 324 (*Catalogue des écrivains*).
33. Brumfitt, p. 48.
34. Voltaire, 1947, I, p. 23 (ch. II).
35. Souchal, I, pp. 253–5.
36. Voltaire, 1947, II, p. 59 (ch. XXVIII).
37. Voltaire, 1968–77, XII, pp. 381–2 (D 4761) and XIII, pp. 124–5 (D 4963) and 168–70 (D 4997) for the relevant letters between Voltaire and Hénault, written in 1752. I am grateful to Christian Michel for bringing these to my attention.
38. Brumfitt, p. 49, n. 6.
39. Voltaire, 1963, II, pp. 818–56 (*Chapitre des Arts*): the manuscripts are in St Petersburg.
40. Galluzzi: see Cochrane, 1973, pp. 459–62.
41. In Chandler, pp. xviii–xix, Sherman writes that 'quite early in life Roscoe conceived a desire to write a biography of Lorenzo. I suspect it was about 1773...'.
42. Roscoe, 1797, I, p. xix.
43. Sellers, p. 45.
44. See, for instance, Washington Irving, quoted in Chandler, p. xviii.
45. Roscoe, 1797, I, pp. xiv–xv.
46. Chandler, pp. 59–60.
47. Sellers, pp. 45–53.
48. Roscoe, 1797, I, pp. i–ii.
49. Roscoe, 1797, I, p. ii.
50. Roscoe, 1797, II, p. 175.
51. Roscoe, 1797, I, p. iii.
52. Roscoe, 1797, II, p. 182.
53. Roscoe, 1816.
54. G. Bianchini, p. vi.
55. Meloni Trkulja.
56. Gibbon, 1961, pp. 137–8.
57. Zacchiroli, pp. 99–108 gives the fullest list of the pictures on view.
58. Lanzi, pp. 67–8.
59. Compton.
60. Fuseli, 1982, p. 82 (letter to Roscoe of 29 May 1792).
61. Although, later, Roscoe did own at least two paintings by Fuseli of episodes taken from the life of Lorenzo, both of which are now lost (Schiff, I, p. 648, no. 22, and p. 653, no. 77). See the letters from Fuseli to Roscoe of 5 May and 27 June 1795, in Fuseli, 1982, pp. 133–6.
62. Fuseli, 1982, p. 125 (Fuseli to Roscoe, 15 June 1795).
63. Fuseli, 1982, p. 77 (Fuseli to Roscoe, 28 November 1791).
64. Fuseli, 1982, p. 319 (Roscoe to Fuseli, 17 June 1805).
65. Fuseli, 1982, pp. 325–41 (Fuseli to Roscoe, between 27 September 1805 and 22 February 1806).
66. Knowles, I, pp. 110–57.
67. Fuseli, 1982, p. 157 (Fuseli to Roscoe, 11 August 1796).
68. Roscoe, 1797, p. 190. It is true that Roscoe gave perfunctory praise to Pollaiuolo's 'great knowledge of muscular action' in this picture and that he was more generous about the artist's *Hercules and Antaeus*. But this is because he had to rely only on Vasari's account of it and did not have access to a reproduction. He is not the only historian who has found it easier to draw on written testimony than on direct observation when describing a work of art.
69. Knowles, I, p. 149.
70. *L'Etruria Pittrice*.
71. Fuseli, 1982, p. 91 (Fuseli to Roscoe, 26 February 1794).
72. Lloyd, pp. 73–5, no. 24.
73. Lanzi, pp. xvi–xvii.
74. Hale, 1963, p. 88.
75. Sismondi, VII, p. 290, n. 1.
76. De Salis, p. 83.
77. De Salis, p. 137.
78. Sismondi, VII, pp. 327–9.

8   The Arts as an Index of Society

1. W.M. Davis, pp. 123–4, referring to Plato's *The Laws*, II, 256.
2. E.g., Molière, quoted by Frankl, p. 338.
3. Turnbull, p. 44 (I owe this reference to Alex Potts).
4. Shaftesbury, I, p. 143.
5. Shaftesbury, I, pp. 144–5. As Ernst Gombrich has pointed out to me, Tacitus had made the same (very logical) point about the decline of eloquence in his *Dialogue on Oratory*.
6. Winckelmann, 1764, I, p. 248; 1783–4, II, p. 139.
7. Wickelmann, 1764, I, p. 25; 1783–4, I, p. 54.
8. Winckelmann, 1764, I, pp. 83–4; 1783–4, I, pp. 169–71.
9. Winckelmann, 1783–4, II, pp. 98–9: this passage is not found in the first, German, edition.
10. Winckelmann, 1764, II, pp. 315–16; 1783–4, II, pp. 163–4.
11. See, for instance, the criticisms of Heyne included in Winckelmann, 1783–4, II, pp. 299–303, n. 1.
12. Winckelmann, 1764, I, p. 28; 1783–4, I, p. 57.
13. See the comments by Plutarch recorded in Winckelmann, 1783–4, II, p. 237, note. a.
14. Winckelmann, 1764, II, p. 345; 1783–4, II, p. 237.
15. Winckelmann, 1764, II, pp. 368–71; 1783–4, II, pp. 281–4. I am grateful to Alex Potts for drawing my attention to the significance of this passage.
16. Winckelmann, 1764, II, p. 410; 1783–4, II, p. 386.
17. Winckelmann, 1764, II, p. 404; 1783–4, II, p. 376.
18. E. Pommier, 1989; and see Haskell, 1991, p. 90

for the twist given to Winckelmann's words.

19. Gillies, I, pp. 505–9.
20. Berlin, pp. 145–216.
21. Herder (ed. Rouché), pp. 144–6.
22. Herder, 1977–88, I, p. 116: letter of 22 November 1768, kindly brought to my attention by Pascal Griener.
23. Herder, 1803, II, pp. 96–106. I have used this for all the translations of Herder's work in my text; 1877–1913, XIV, pp. 75–83.
24. Herder, 1803, II, p. 195; 1877–1913, XIV, p. 151.
25. Herder, 1803, II, pp. 253–5; 1877–1913, XIV, pp. 196–8.
26. Robert T. Clark, pp. 308, 348, 356–7.
27. Herder, 1803, II, pp. 612–13; 1877–1913, XIV, pp. 488–9.
28. E.g., Frankl, pp. 418 ff.; Rouché in Herder (ed. Rouché), p. 20.
29. Potts, 1978.
30. Goethe, 1981, XII, pp. 14, 12: I have used the translation by John Gage in Goethe, 1980, pp. 103–12.
31. See below, Chapter 15, and Francastel.
32. Frankl, pp. 481–2.
33. Pugin, 1836; 1841.
34. Hegel, 1975, II, pp. 719–20.
35. Pater, p. 175 (*Winckelmann*).
36. Hegel, 1975, I, pp. 360–1.
37. Hegel, 1975, II, pp. 652 and 875–81.
38. Hegel, 1975, II, p. 724.
39. Hegel, 1975, II, p. 684.
40. Hegel, 1975, I, p. 170.
41. Hegel, 1975, II, pp. 886–7.
42. Hegel, 1985, p. 111. I am very grateful to Michael Inwood for bringing this to my attention.
43. Gombrich, 1969, p. 9 (with references). It will be obvious how deeply I have been influenced by Gombrich's classic article, and by other writings by him on this matter.
44. Tronchon, p. 4.
45. Haac, pp. 97–101.
46. Viallaneix, pp. 151–2.

9 The Musée des Monuments Français

1. *Mercure de France*, 1803, XIII, pp. 208–9, quoted by Poirier, p. 98.
2. Chateaubriand, 1978, p. 882.
3. Réau, 1959, I, p. 230.
4. Réau, 1959, I, p. 13; Vidler, p. 136.
5. See above, Chapter 7; and E. Pommier, 1988, pp. 175–6.
6. Stein, pp. 20–6.
7. Sandoz, p. 44, no. 36 (*Death of St Louis*); p. 46, no. 41 (*Louis XVI after his Coronation*).
8. Sandoz, p. 36, no. 28; J.-P. Babelon, 1972, pp. 47 ff.
9. Huard, 1940, p. 189, n. 1.
10. Huard, 1940, p. 189; Poulot, p. 503. And see Lenoir, 1800–6, I, p. 4.
11. Hermant, p. 711; Vidler, p. 132.
12. Chateaubriand, 1978, pp. 1198, 1200.
13. E.A.R. Brown, p. 8.
14. *Inventaire Général*, II, pp. 102 and 148.
15. Huard, 1940, pp. 198–201.
16. Lenoir, 1806 (Avant-Propos), p. v.
17. Huard, 1940, p. 201.
18. Lenoir, 1803 (Avant-Propos), p. 3.
19. Poulot, p. 504.
20. Lenoir, 1806, p. 65; Kennedy, p. 89.
21. Lenoir, 1806, p. 206.
22. Vidler, p. 137.
23. Mellon, pp. 78–9.
24. Lenoir in his report of late 1795 to the Comité de l'instruction publique, in *Inventaire Général*, I, p. 26.
25. Lenoir, 1806 (Avant-Propos), p. ix.
26. E. Pommier, 1989, p. 15.
27. Huard, 1925, p. 113.
28. Biet, pp. 2–12, plates I–XII.
29. Lenoir, 1806, p. 65.
30. Lenoir, 1806, p. 12.
31. Lenoir, 1806, p. 96; Erlande-Brandenburg, pp. 50–1; Poulot, p. 504.
32. Biet, plates XIII–XVI; Lenoir, 1806, pp. 96–7; Huard, 1925, pp. 114, 118.
33. Vanuxem, 1971, pp. 146–7.
34. Lenoir, 1803, p. 129; Foucart, p. 228.
35. Greatheed, pp. 23, 119.
36. Kotzebue, p. 149.
37. Lenoir, 1806, pp. 96–7, n. 1. Lenoir sometimes claimed that Bonaparte made this comment in the 'Salle du 14ème siècle': see Foucart, p. 228.
38. Huard, 1925, pp. 115–19; Vanuxem, 1971, p. 147.
39. Erlande-Brandenburg, p. 51.
40. Lenoir, 1800–6, I, pp. 19–20.
41. Poulot, p. 509. Many years later the imagination of Burckhardt was to be struck by this monument: Kaegi, II, pp. 266–7.
42. 'Gothique' retrouvé, p. 84.
43. Lenoir, 1806, pp. 86–8.
44. Poulot, p. 507.
45. Lenoir, 1800–6, V, p. 45.
46. Lenoir to the Minister of the Interior, 8 November 1805: *Inventaire Général*, I, p. 323–4.
47. Greene, p. 216.
48. 'Gothique' retrouvé, p. 77.
49. Huard, 1940, *passim*.
50. Lenoir, 1806, p. 84.
51. Foucart, p. 225; Greene, p. 218.
52. Huard, 1932, pp. 171–2. 'Gothique' retrouvé, p. 77; E.A.R. Brown, pp. 15 ff.
53. Vanuxem, cited by Foucart, p. 225.
54. Some indication of the scale of Lenoir's operations can be gauged from his 'Observations sur l'Elysée', with accompanying illustrations, in Lenoir, 1800–6, V, pp. 171–204.
55. Vanuxem, 1971, pp. 145 and 147; Foucart, p. 228; Poulot, p. 499.
56. Cicognara, 1813–18, II, p. 198.
57. Poulot, pp. 512–14.
58. Schneider.
59. Deseine.
60. Chateaubriand, 1978, p. 936, note A.
61. Poulot, p. 514.

62. Haskell, 1983.
63. Lenoir in a reported conversation: see Poulot, p. 515.
64. Poirier, pp. 102–3.
65. E. Pommier, 1986, p. 454.
66. E. Pommier, 1986, p. 459.
67. Poulot, p. 516.
68. J. Evans, p. 225.
69. For the bronze 'Charlemagne', which is now in the Louvre, see *Karl der Grosse*, pp. 42–3. For the portrait drawings, see below, Chapter 10.
70. Laviron et Galbaccio, p. 275.
71. Schlegel, 1959, p. 104. Schlegel did, however, admire the stained glass and a few pictures, especially a Russian Madonna 'which seems to be from the earliest times' and which rather incongruously remained in the museum even after Lenoir had sent most of the non-French objects to other institutions.
72. Despite his criticism, Cicognara found it essential to work *aux Augustins*: see his letter to Canova of 9 August 1813 in Cicognara, 1973, p. 48.
73. A. du Sommerard, I, 1838, p. v. The words come from the *annonce* for the book and must therefore have been published earlier than this date. Much later Courajod was to make the same point: Courajod, 1899–1903, II, pp. 1–18.
74. Although Stephen Bann has emphasised what he considers to be basic differences between the concepts of the two collections: Bann, pp. 77–92.
75. Delécluze, pp. 242–5.
76. Pupil.
77. 'Observations sur l'état actuel du Musée des Monuments français' sent to the Minister of the Interior, 1809: *Inventaire Général*, I, p. 390.
78. Arago, quoted by Poulot, p. 511.
79. Quoted in Poulot, pp. 520–1.
80. Mellon, p. 76.
81. Thierry, 1840, I, p. 230.
82. Ernest Vinet, quoted by Poulot, p. 531, n. 62.
83. Reizov, pp. 243–4.
84. *'Gothique' retrouvé*, p. 78; Poulot, p. 524.
85. Montalembert, pp. 289–93.
86. Michelet, 1952, II, pp. 538–9 n. (book XII, ch. 7).
87. Michelet, 1965, p. 65 (à M. Edgar Quinet).

10 Michelet

1. Michelet, 1952, II, pp. 538–9.
2. Preface to 1866 edition of *Histoire romaine* (*Oeuvres Complètes*, II, p. 335); and see letter of Victor Duruy to Madame Michelet, 28 April 1884, quoted in Michelet, *Oeuvres Complètes*, I, p. 64.
3. Michelet, 1959–76, I, p. 501 (25 March 1843); also I, pp. 489 and 492 (29 December 1842, and 5 and 7 January 1843).
4. Michelet, 1959, p. 194 (*Mémorial*).
5. Michelet, 1959, p. 109 (*Journal*, 1 September 1820). These pictures are recorded (and illustrated) in Landon, pls 8, 12, 26; David's *Socrates*

was apparently lent to the Luxembourg by the marquis de Vérac: see Sterling, 1955, pp. 192–6. Pauline also admired an unidentified *Romulus*. The sculpture of 'Venus on a goat' which attracted Michelet was Pierre Julien's *La Baigneuse*: Landon, pl. 58.
6. See Michelet, *Discours sur l'Unité de la Science* (*Oeuvres Complètes*, I, pp. 249–55).
7. Michelet, 1959, p. 235 (*Journal des idées*, November 1825).
8. Michelet, 1959, p. 236 (*Journal des idées*, December 1825).
9. Michelet, 1959, pp. 238–9 (*Journal des idées*, 12 February 1826).
10. Michelet's comment to this effect was made in 1871 (Michelet, *Oeuvres Complètes*, II, p. 217).
11. Michelet, *Introduction à l'Histoire universelle* (*Oeuvres Complètes*, II, p. 242).
12. Michelet, 1959–76, I, p. 62 (7 April 1830).
13. Michelet, *Histoire romaine*, ch. 1 (*Oeuvres Complètes*, II, p. 349).
14. Michelet, 1959–76, p. 64 (12 April 1830). These two heads are still in the Braccio Nuovo of the Vatican Museum.
15. Michelet, 1833–67, I (1833), pp. 171–2.
16. Michelet, 1833–67, II (1833), p. 663.
17. Michelet, letter to Lenormand of December 1833, quoted in *Oeuvres Complètes*, IV, p. 7.
18. Michelet, 1833–67, II (1833), pp. 659–60.
19. Michelet, 1959–76, I, pp. 79–102 (August 1831).
20. Brisac and Léniaud.
21. Michelet, 1833–67, II (1833), p. 661.
22. The Abbé Douhaire (in *L'Univers*, 1 January 1834): see Michelet, *Oeuvres Complètes*, IV, pp. 728–32.
23. Désiré Nisard (in *Le National*, 31 January 1834): see Michelet, *Oeuvres Complètes*, IV, p. 750.
24. Baron d'Eckstein (in *Revue Européenne*, August 1834): see Michelet, *Oeuvres Complètes*, IV, p. 843.
25. See Burtin.
26. Baron d'Eckstein (in *Revue Européenne*, March 1834): see Michelet, *Oeuvres Complètes*, IV, pp. 784–5.
27. Michelet, 1833–67, I (1833), p. 87.
28. Baron d'Eckstein (in *Revue Européenne*, February 1834): see Michelet, *Oeuvres Complètes*, IV, p. 761.
29. Michelet, 1833–67, II (1833), pp. 673–4, 677, 679, 692, etc.
30. Michelet, 1833–67, II (1833), p. 682.
31. Seznec, 1977; Białostocki, p. 101; Michelet, 1959–76, I, pp. 441, and 457–8 (21 July 1842).
32. Michelet, 1833–67, II (1833), pp. 305–6.
33. Michelet, 1833–67, III (1837), pp. 443–4.
34. Michelet, 1833–67, IV (1840), pp. 155–6.
35. Michelet, 1959–76, I, p. 265 (24 July 1838).
36. Maffei, 1731–2, III, p. 78.
37. Michelet, 1833–67, IV (1840), pp. 158–9. Michelet was almost certainly correct that the tomb in question was that of Cangrande II murdered by his brother in 1359.
38. J. Babelon, 1927, pp. 17–18 and 58–9.

39. Watelet, for instance, as recorded in Lenoir, 1800–6, III, p. 134.
40. *Ibid.*
41. J. Babelon, 1927, p. 58.
42. Michelet, 1833–67, X, (1856), p. 306.
43. See Jean Pommier, 1961, who has much of interest to say about Michelet's use of portraiture but who does not identify the sources of his quotations.
44. Jean Pommier, 1961, p. 11; Michelet, 1833–67, XVII (1867), pp. 115–17.
45. Michelet, 1833–67, XVI (1866), p. 333, and XVII (1867), pp. xi–xii.
46. Michelet, 1833–67, X (1856), p. 18.
47. See below, n. 59.
48. J. Babelon, 1927, p. 63, no. 14 (pl. XL).
49. For another example of his biased interpretation of royal portraiture, see Michelet 1833–67, IX (1856), p. 182.
50. Monod, I, p. 265.
51. Moreau-Nélaton, 1924, II, pp. 30–1.
52. Moreau-Nélaton, 1924, II, p. 8.
53. Raoul de Broglie, 1970: unpaginated.
54. Moreau-Nélaton, 1924, II, p. 8; and Raoul de Broglie, 1970: unpaginated.
55. Moreau-Nélaton, 1924, II, pp. 33–5.
56. Moreau-Nélaton, 1924, II, pp. 43–9.
57. *Les Clouet*, p. 33.
58. Lethève, in his discussion of these records, mentions that before 1860 Taine's name is not found among them, although we know that he was a regular visitor: Lethève, p. 108. Perhaps both Michelet and Taine went only on the 'open days' of Tuesday and Friday.
59. Moreau-Nélaton, 1924, II, pp. 49–50.
60. Michelet, 1833–67, X (1856), p. 472, and elsewhere.
61. *Les Clouet*, pp. 10 and 33; and for its contents and those of the other albums, see Adhémar, 1973.
62. *Les Clouet*, p. 9; Ainsworth.
63. Michelet, 1833–67, IX (1856), pp. 180–1.
64. *Les Clouet*, p. 47, no. 88 (pl. XIX).
65. Michelet, 1833–67, X (1856), p. 472.
66. Michelet, 1833–67, IX (1856), p. 380.
67. Michelet, 1833–67, II (1833), p. 103.
68. Michelet, 1833–67, II (1833), p. 3.
69. Michelet, 1833–67, II (1833), pp. 10–15.
70. Michelet, 1833–67, XI (1857), pp. 454–5.
71. Michelet, 1833–67, VIII (1855), pp. 228–33.
72. Michelet, 1833–67, VII (1855), p. ii.
73. Febvre, pp. 719–20.
74. Monod, II, p. 153.
75. Febvre, pp. 722–9.
76. Michelet, 1959–76, I, pp. 480, 489 etc. (October, December 1842).
77. *L'Artiste*, 1835 (2), 1ère série, tome X, pp. 66–7.
78. Lenoir, 1800–6, III, p. 29.
79. Aulanier, pp. 95–7.
80. De Ghilhermy.
81. Michelet, 1833–67, VII (1855), pp. 57–8.
82. Monod, II, pp. 49–50.
83. Michelet, 1833–67, VII (1855), p. lxiii.
84. Michelet, 1833–67, VII (1855), p. lxxxi.
85. Michelet, 1833–67, VII (1855), p. lxxxvii.
86. Angoulvert.
87. Quinet, 1857–8, VI, pp. 351–63.
88. Michelet, 1833–67, VII (1855), pp. lviii–xci.
89. Michelet, 1833–67, VII (1855), p. xcii.
90. Michelet, 1833–67, VII (1855), pp. 216–17.
91. Michelet, 1833–67, VII (1855), pp. 218–42.

11   Museums, Illustrations and the Search for Authenticity

1. Michelet, 1952, pp. 538–9.
2. For all this section, see Zygulski.
3. The most curious imitation of Princess Czartoryski's museum was also created by a Polish aristocrat – Count Wladyslaw Broel-Plater. It opened in 1870, and as it, too, was designed to be a 'museum of Polish historical memories', the nature of its contents was very similar to those formerly to be seen at Pulawy (many of which had by now been removed to Paris). However, this 'refuge for the native gods of Poland' was located in a castle near Zurich, because its founder had been forced to leave his country after the insurrection of 1830: Pomian, 1991, pp. 171–3.
4. Gaehtgens, pp. 61–2.
5. Gaehtgens, pp. 79 and 382.
6. Soulié, I (Avertissement), pp. vii and x.
7. Gaehtgens, pp. 206 and 229.
8. Veit, p. 19.
9. Burian, p. 127.
10. Veit, p. 15.
11. Kahsnitz, 1977, pp. 161–2.
12. Kahsnitz, 1978, p. 951.
13. Burian, p. 128.
14. See the *Anzeiger für Kunde der Deutschen Vorseit – Organ des Germanischen Museums*, published monthly in Nuremberg from July 1853. Moreover, the curator of antiquities at the museum and its secretary also edited the *Zeitschrifft für deutsche Kulturgeschichte*.
15. Veit, p. 25.
16. See many of the contributions to Deneke and Kahsnitz, 1977.
17. Fusco, p. 456. It is true that among the great figures of Italian culture commemorated by memorials in Santa Croce in Florence were a few who were not particularly associated with the city, and that Canova's famous monument to Alfieri portrayed the figure of Italy mourning over him. None the less, this church was not intended (at least until the Risorgimento itself) to be a national Italian shrine with political implications to be compared with those of the museums in Pulawy Park, Versailles or Nuremberg.
18. Kahsnitz, 1977, p. 168 and fig. 74.
19. Thierry, 1935, pp. 13–73; and for his special admiration for Chateaubriand see Thierry, 1835, pp. xiii–xiv and 124–33; and 1840, I, pp. 18–22. Scott's genius at evoking–for himself and for his readers (many serious historians among

them)–a most compelling awareness of the palpable appearance of life in earlier centuries can hardly be exaggerated; but (despite the relics of all kinds that he accumulated at Abbotsford) his own historical imagination seems to have been stimulated much more by literary than by visual sources.

20. Thierry, 1935, pp. 21–2 (letter 1).
21. A year before this Michelet had argued that history books should be illustrated only with visual documents that were contemporary with the events discussed, such as medals, costumes and architecture: Monod, I, p. 24.
22. Dares: I have used the facsimile edition in the British Library of this exceedingly rare book (only two copies are known) which is discussed in the Harvard College Library catalogue, I, pp. 205–6, no. 164.
23. Panofsky, 1972, p. 84.
24. Samek Ludovici.
25. For all this see C. Michel, especially pp. 55, 121–3.
26. Strutt, 1773, pp. iii and 21, and pl. 32. I am very grateful to Miss Janet Backhouse of the British Library for telling me that this Flemish manuscript was ordered for Edward IV: thus Strutt's dating of it to the time of Henry VI who was deposed in 1461 (but resumed the throne for a year in 1470–1 before being deposed again and murdered) was remarkably accurate.
27. Strutt, 1775–6, I (Preface), pp. i–ii.
28. Strutt, 1775–6, III (Preface): unpaginated.
29. Strutt, 1777–8, I, p. iv; II, p. 227; I, pl. xviii.
30. Huck and Green, pp. 2, 4, 6, 8. There is a full set of the prints in the British Museum. I am most grateful to David Alexander and Timothy Clayton for the help that they have given me in this matter.
31. Dyer, p. vi.
32. Barante, 1826, I, pp. 1–99.
33. Barante, 1842. See Bann, pp. 43ff. for a discussion of these issues.
34. Prescott, 1964, pp. 178–9 (letter of 27 October 1841 to Pascual de Gayangos).
35. C.H. Gardiner, pp. 41, 116, 151, 165, 246, 309. The engraving of a half-length portrait of Philip II used as a frontispiece to vol. I of the *History of the Reign of Philip the Second, King of Spain,* 2 vols, London 1855, must almost certainly have been taken from the (full-length) painting by Titian in the Prado (Wethey, II, no. 78), even though there are notable differences between them. Similarly, the portrait of the Duke of Alva (in vol. II, facing p. 137) may have been derived, even more loosely, from a picture in the family palace, now believed to be by a Flemish painter, Titian's portrait of the duke having been destroyed in a fire in 1604: Wethey, II, nos. X3 and L1. Prescott's discussion of the portraits used by him does not correspond precisely to what is actually to be seen in the two volumes. The frontispiece of the *History of the Reign of Ferdinand and Isabella, The Catholic, of Spain,* 2 vols, London 1854, reproduces

Parmigianino's portrait of Bartolomeo Sanvitale (Naples, Museo di Capodimonte) which was then believed to represent Christopher Columbus.

36. Bordier and Charton, I, (Avant-Propos), pp. v–vi.
37. Simon.
38. Duplessis, 1877–84, V, pp. i–vi.
39. Hennin, I, pp. 269–74.
40. Hennin's first volume was published in 1856, and the second, a year later.
41. Hennin, I, pp. 10–11 and 344–9.
42. Hennin, I, pp. 45–6.
43. Hennin, I, p. 12.
44. Hennin, I, pp. 88–90.
45. Hennin, I, p. 411.

12   The Historical Significance of Style

1. Thierry, 1835, pp. xxvii–xxviii.
2. Krieger, pp. 89–94; see also the notes made on art in his journals: Ranke, 1964, pp. 190–231.
3. Ranke, 1869–90, XXXIII, p. 214.
4. Ranke, 1869–90, XXXVII, pp. 322–4.
5. Paret, pp. 11–60.
6. For further evidence of that sensitivity, see his *Journals.*
7. E. Curtius, II, pp. 586–7.
8. It is true that he uses the phrase in letters to Mme Michelet, in 1881 and 1885 (Renan, X, pp. 853 and 933), but there is every reason to believe that he did greatly admire Michelet.
9. Renan, III, pp. 233–43; see also Renan, X, pp. 66 (letter to Victor Cousin of 17 February 1850) and 73 (letter to Charles Daremberg of 3 March 1850).
10. Renan, III, p. 311.
11. Renan, II, pp. 378–9 (*Vingt Jours en Sicile*).
12. Renan, II, p. 1134. It is, of course, true that this interpretation of Tiepolo's art was inspired by his wish to give support to the similar 'amoralism' that he found in Flaubert's *La Tentation de Saint Antoine.*
13. Renan, II, pp. 440–60 (*Examen de quelques faits relatifs à l'Impératrice Faustine femme de Marc-Aurèle*): see, especially, pp. 445–7.
14. Launay, pp. 111–14.
15. Stephens, I, p. 83; and Leslie Stephen, p. 216.
16. Creighton, I, pp. 135–6.
17. Kenyon, p. 223.
18. Dunn, II, pp. 290–5.
19. Henry Adams, p. 346.
20. Ruskin, 1956–9, II, p. 437 (8 September 1849).
21. Ruskin, 1903–12, IX, p. xxi.
22. Clegg, pp. 171–80.
23. Ruskin, 1903–12, XXIV, p. 203 (Preface to *St. Mark's Rest*).
24. Clegg, p. 75.
25. Ruskin, 1903–12, XXIV, p. 277.
26. Ruskin, 1903–12, IX, p. 3, n. 3. See also Clegg.
27. Ruskin, 1903–12, XI, pp. 254–5.
28. Ruskin, 1903–12, IX, p. 4; Unrau, p. 29.
29. Unrau, *passim.*; Hewison, *passim.*
30. Unrau, p. 30.

31. See the remarkable letter to his father of 2 June 1852: Ruskin, 1955, p. 293.
32. Ruskin, 1903–12, IX, pp. 3–5.
33. Ruskin, 1903–12, IX, p. 38.
34. Ruskin, 1903–12, X, p. 327, n. 1; Ruskin, 1955, pp. 261–3 (letter to his father of 26 April 1852).
35. Ruskin, 1903–12, IX, p. 4.
36. Ruskin, 1903–12, IX, p. 53.
37. Clegg, p. 73.
38. Ruskin, 1903–12, IX, p. 21, n. 5; Luciani, p. 110. This was a book that particularly infuriated Cicognara: Malamani, II, p. 225.
39. Daru, I, p. 5.
40. Daru, VI, p. 194.
41. For all this, see the 'Notice sur M. Daru' by M. Viennet, reprinted in vol. I of the fourth, 1853, edition of the *Histoire*; also frequent references in Stendhal, *Oeuvres intimes*; Luciani.
42. Daru, I, p. 211.
43. Daru, I, p. 116.
44. Ruskin, 1903–12, IX, p. 21.
45. Clegg, pp. 86–7.
46. Ruskin, 1903–12, IX, p. 98.
47. Daru, II, p. 270.
48. Ruskin, 1903–12, IX, pp. 22–3.
49. Ruskin, 1903–12, IX, p. 4.
50. Selvatico, p. 108.
51. Ruskin, 1903–12, XI, p. 99; Daru, II, p. 164.
52. Ruskin, 1903–12, XI, pp. 100 and 257.
53. Ruskin, 1903–12, IX, p. 21.
54. Selvatico, pp. 147–8; Da Mosto, pp. 107–8; Lorenzetti, p. 348.
55. Ruskin, 1903–12, IX, p. 48, n. 1.
56. Ruskin, 1903–12, IX, p. 48.
57. Ruskin, 1903–12, XI, p. 102.
58. Ruskin, 1903–12, XI, pp. 81 and 289–307.
59. Michelet, 1833–67, IV, pp. 158–9.
60. Ruskin, 1903–12, XI, pp. 89–90.
61. Ruskin, 1903–12, XI, pp. 103–5.
62. Ruskin, 1903–12, IX, pp. 49–52.
63. Ruskin, 1903–12, XI, p. 111.
64. Ruskin, 1903–12, IX, p. 24.
65. Ruskin, 1903–12, X, p. 359.
66. Ruskin, 1903–12, X, p. 363.
67. Ruskin, 1903–12, X, pp. 425–8.
68. Romanelli.
69. Ruskin, 1903–12, XI, p. 428.
70. Ruskin, 1903–12, IX, pp. 31–2.
71. Ruskin, 1903–12, IX, p. 31, n. *.
72. Ruskin, 1903–12, X, pp. 345–6.
73. It is extremely difficult to understand the exact implications of Cicognara's observations, which were not always consistent. I have here followed the interpretation of them made by Arslan, p. 138.
74. Selvatico, p. 109.
75. Arslan, pp. 138–9.
76. Ruskin, 1903–12, IX, p. 3.
77. Ruskin, 1903–12, IX, p. 47.
78. Ruskin, 1903–12, IX, p. 53.
79. Zanotto, I, p. 66: see Arslan, p. 169, n. 25, where, however, 1835 is wrongly printed for 1853. The editions of Zanotto that I have seen have two title pages, one dated 1842 and one

1853 and sometimes refer to Ruskin. It is difficult, therefore, to say precisely when he first noted the stylistic differences between the two sets of capitals.
80. Ruskin, 1903–12, IX, pp. 54–5.
81. Ruskin, 1903–12, X, p. 352.
82. Ruskin, 1903–12, IX, p. 58.
83. Ruskin, 1903–12, X, p. 352, n. 1.
84. Ruskin, 1903–12, XI, pp. 145 ff.
85. Ruskin, 1903–12, IX, p. 30.
86. Daru, I, pp. 521–4.
87. Ruskin, 1903–12, X, pp. 340–3.
88. Ruskin, 1903–12, X, pp. 307–8.
89. Ruskin, 1903–12, IX, pp. 185–6.
90. Ruskin, 1903–12, X, p. 18.
91. Ruskin, 1903–12, X, p. 25.
92. Ruskin, 1903–12, X, p. 20, n. †.
93. For all this see Ruskin, 1903–12, X, pp. 17–35, and the useful critique in Clegg, pp. 107–11.
94. Ruskin, 1903–12, X, p. 145.
95. Ruskin, 1903–12, X, pp. 171–2.
96. Ruskin, 1903–12, X, p. 109.
97. Ruskin, 1903–12, X, pp. 172–5.
98. Kaegi, 1947–82, III, pl. 1 and p. XVII.
99. Kaegi, 1947–82, III, pp. 49–138.
100. Kaegi, 1947–82, II, pp. 475–6.
101. Kaegi, 1947–82, III, p. 347.
102. Kaegi, 1947–82, II, p. 501.
103. Kaegi, 1947–82, II, p. 465.
104. Kaegi, 1947–82, III, pp. 169–70.
105. Kaegi, 1947–82, III, pp. 287–8.
106. Burckhardt, 1929–33, II, pp. 211–20.
107. Burckhardt, 1929–33, II, pp. 286–7.
108. Burckhardt, 1929–33, II, p. 332.
109. Burckhardt, 1929–33, II, p. 289.
110. Burckhardt, 1929–33, II, p. 113.
111. Kaegi, 1947–82, III, p. 419.
112. Kaegi, 1947–82, III, p. 426.
113. Kaegi, 1947–82, III, p. 452.
114. Kaegi, 1947–82, III, pp. 458–9.
115. Burckhardt, 1855, p. 417, n. 1.
116. Burckhardt, 1855, pp. 94–5.
117. Burckhardt, 1855, p. 155.
118. Burckhardt, 1855, p.124.
119. Burckhardt, 1855, pp. 366 and 676.
120. Burckhardt, 1860, p. 2; 1869, p. 2; 1990, p. 19.
121. Burckhardt, 1987, pp. xv–xviii (Introduction by Peter Murray).
122. Burckhardt, 1869, p.2.
123. Burckhardt, 1860, p. 7; 1990, p. 23.
124. Burckhardt, 1855, p. 167.
125. Burckhardt, 1860, pp. 290–1; 1855, p. 311; 1990, p. 191.
126. Burckhardt, 1860, pp. 327–47; 1990, pp. 213–25.
127. Burckhardt, 1860, pp. 310–11, 353; 1990, pp. 203, 229.
128. Burckhardt, 1860, pp. 29–30; 1990, pp. 36–7.
129. Burckhardt, 1855, p. 919.
130. Burckhardt, 1855, p. 916.
131. Burckhardt, 1860, p. 402; 1990, p. 257.
132. Burckhardt, 1860, p. 171; 1990, p. 120.
133. Burckhardt, 1855, pp. 793–4.
134. Kaegi, 1947–82, III, pp. 82–3.

135. Burckhardt, 1860, pp. 2–3; 1990, pp. 19–20.
136. Burckhardt, 1855, p. 796.
137. Burckhardt, 1855, p. 833.
138. Burckhardt, 1855, p. 935.
139. Burckhardt, 1855, pp. 169–70 and 180, n. 1. See also Kaegi, 1947–82, III, pp. 126 and 128–31.
140. Burckhardt, 1855, p. 169.
141. Burckhardt, 1855, p. 178.
142. Ruskin, 1903–12, IX, p. 44, and XI, p. 14; Burckhardt, 1855, p. 155.
143. Kaegi, 1947–82, III, p. 35.
144. Burckhardt, 1855, pp. 109–10.
145. See above, n. 102.
146. Burckhardt, 1855, p. 177.
147. Ghelardi, p. 5. In fact, on other occasions Burckhardt used the expression *Gewaltmensch* to describe such differing artists as Alberti, Murillo and Guido Reni; see Kaegi, 1947–82, III, p. 273.
148. Kaegi, 1947–82, III, p. 35.
149. Kaegi, 1947–82, III, p. 465; Burckhardt, 1855, pp. 596–7; and *Donatello*, pp. 348–62.
150. Burckhardt, 1855, pp. 596–7.
151. Burckhardt, 1860, pp. 453–5; 1990, pp. 288–9.
152. Kaegi, 1947–82, III, pp. 35 and 459; Burckhardt, 1855, pp. 670–1.
153. Burckhardt, 1855, p. 676.
154. Burckhardt, 1855, p. 601.
155. Burckhardt, 1855, p. 596.
156. Cicognara, 1813–18, II, pp. 77–80.
157. Burckhardt, 1855, p. 605.
158. Burckhardt, 1860, p. 10; 1990, p. 25.
159. Burckhardt, 1855, p. 174.
160. Burckhardt, 1860, p. 171; 1990, p. 120.
161. Kaegi, 1947–82, III, p. 763.
162. Kaegi, 1947–82, V, pp. 352, 583 and elsewhere.
163. Roe, p. 10.
164. Roe, p. 49; Taine, 1872, pp. 355–61.
165. Taine, 1902–7, II, pp. 293–7 (letter to his mother, 19 April 1864).
166. Taine, 1902–7, II, pp. 296–302 (letter of 29 April 1864).
167. Leger.
168. Taine, 1894, pp. 213–33 (the essay itself dates from 1888).
169. For references to Taine's own collections, see Taine, 1902–7, II, pp. 282 and 333–4.
170. Taine, 1902–7, II, pp. 25–6, 32, 126–7. Adhémar, 1981, p. 54 discusses the importance of prints for Taine and other historians.
171. Taine, 1902–7, II, pp. 126–7 (letter to Edouard de Suckau, 23 November 1855).
172. Goncourt, I, p. 1255 (29 March 1863).
173. Taine, 1902–7, II, pp. 36–42 (letter to Edouard de Suckau, 8 May 1854), 106–10 (letter to Guillaume Guizot, 5 August 1855), 153, 171. Léger, p. 270.
174. *Georges de La Tour*, pp. 95–6 and 198–203; Taine, 1897, pp. 51–3.
175. Taine, 1902–7, I, pp. 323–4; II, pp. 43, 113–14; Léger pp. 289, 306.
176. Léger, p. 160.
177. Taine, 1897, pp. 30, 90, 220, 229–31.
178. Taine, 1902–7, II, p. 31 (letter to Edouard de Suckau, 30 January 1854).
179. Goncourt, I, pp. 1242, 1247 (1 and 14 March 1863). Edmond was later to turn against him with great savagery.
180. Goncourt, II, p. 13 (18 January 1864).
181. Taine, 1965, I, pp. 58, 133–4, 159 ff.; Arnould, pp. 37, 39–40.
182. Goncourt, II, p. 247 (21 February 1866).
183. Taine, 1965, I, p. 28; II, p. 90.
184. Taine, 1965, II, pp. 12, 133.
185. Lepschy (pp. 111–20) discusses Taine's response to Tintoretto, but does not suggest that it was influenced by his possible reading of Ruskin.
186. Taine, 1965, II, pp. 186 ff.
187. Taine, 1965, I, pp. 128–30.
188. Taine, 1965, I, pp. 207–18.
189. Kaegi, 1947–82, II, p. 529.
190. The copy of this album that I have seen (Oxford, Department of the History of Art, Hope VI J) is untitled and contains forty-four lithographs of views in Antwerp, Brussels and elsewhere in Belgium, each one indicated in English and French. They are all published by L. Granello. Many of the pulpits had previously been engraved in Descamps's celebrated guidebook of 1769. His comment on their 'singularité' occurs on p. xvii.
191. Victor Hugo, p. 1369.
192. *Patrimoine . . . de la Belgique*, V, pt. 2, pp. 520–3.
193. Baudelaire, II, pp. 951–2 (*Pauvre Belgique*).
194. Proudhon, pp. 92–3.
195. Taine, 1965, I, p. 248.
196. Taine, 1965, I, pp. 248–58 for his comments on the Gesù.
197. Plantenga, pp. 83–91, and *La Sculpture au siècle de Rubens*, p. 277 (with references).
198. Taine, 1965, I, pp. 253–4. Not long before going to Italy Taine had referred to the 'goût jésuite' of the churches in Besançon, 'avec des façades en consoles, de gros saint-sacraments dorés, des colonnes emphatiques à l'intérieur': Taine, 1897, p. 143.
199. Galassi Paluzzi.
200. Taine, 1965, II, p. 267.
201. Taine, 1965, II, p. 253.
202. Taine, 1965, II, pp. 14–15.
203. Taine, 1965, I, p. 182.
204. Taine, 1965, I, p. 112.
205. Taine, 1876–94, I, p. 260.
206. Taine, 1965, I, p. 237. It seems likely that Taine was looking either at no. 30, now called 'Portrait of a lady by an anonymous Venetian artist of the 16th century', or – more probably, because of the partly uncovered breast – at no. 225, which is now attributed to Scipione Pulzone, although the sitter is unknown: see Safarik. The *Catalogo dei quadri esistenti nella Galleria del Principe Doria Pamphili* of 1851 (tipografia di Clemento Puccinelli) mentions a 'Ritratto di Lucrezia Borgia di Paolo Veronese', but fails to describe it.
207. Valery, III, p. 72.

13   The Deceptive Evidence of Art

1. Ruskin, 1903–12, X, p. 6.
2. La Chau and Le Blond, I (Preface). I am very

grateful to Pascal Griener for this reference.

3. Quinet, 1857–8, VI, p. 300 (*Allemagne et Italie*, published 1836).
4. Quinet, 1875, pp. 27–8 (IX: *Départ d'un Proscrit*).
5. Quinet, 1857–8, IV, p. 5 (*Les Révolutions d'Italie*: Avertissement, dated 27 September 1857).
6. Guerrini, pp. 4 ff.
7. Quinet, 1839, I, pp. 169–70.
8. Guerrini, p. 58.
9. Quinet, 1857–8, IV, p. 192 (*Les Révolutions d'Italie*).
10. Guerrini, p. 58.
11. Quinet, 1857–8, IV, pp. 348–75 (*Les Révolutions d'Italie*).
12. Lasinio, 1833, pp. 25–6.
13. Gluck, p. 65.
14. Van Gennep, III, pp. 14–18; Gluck, p. 66, no. 111.
15. Marolles, 1672, p. 57, nos cxxvii–cxxviii.
16. Champfleury, [1872], p. 138, n. 1.
17. Malcolm, pp. 13, 40, 54, 89, 158 and pls III (fig. 3) and X.
18. Jaime.
19. Jaime, 1st fascicule, p. 1 (by P. Paris).
20. E.g., Ebeling, and T. Wright.
21. Panofka, p. 6.
22. Panofka, p. 1; and see Champfleury, [1879], pp. 195–8.
23. Champfleury, [1879] (Preface to 1st edition of 1865), pp. xiii–xvii. In fact, Winckelmann himself had reproduced an obscene vase painting (attributed by him to an Etruscan artist) which, in a ruthlessly bowdlerised version, was popular with later writers on the grotesque: see Winckelmann, 1764, I, p. 116, and 1767, I, fig. 190, and II, pp. 254–5, and Champfleury, [1879], p. 112. I am grateful to Claire Lyons for informing me that the phylax vase on which the scene occurs is in the Vatican Museum and is now attributed to the painter Asteas (*c*.350–340 BC): Trendall, p. 46, no. 65.
24. Flögel, 1862, p. vii.
25. Champfleury, [1879], p. 136.
26. T. Wright, [1866?], pp. xxxii–xxxiii (note by Amédée Pichot).
27. Dorson, I, pp. 41–51.
28. Champfleury, [1872], pp. vii–viii.
29. Champfleury, [1872], p. viii.
30. Champfleury, 1867, p. 400.
31. Champfleury, [1879] (Preface to 1st edition of 1865), pp. xi–xii.
32. Champfleury, [1872], p. vii.
33. Champfleury, [1879], pp. 87–9, 187–90.
34. Champfleury, 1869, pp. xi–xii.
35. Chesnau, pp. 3–4.
36. Champfleury, 1869, p. xiii.
37. Champfleury, 1869, p. 58.
38. Noël, p. 146.
39. Champfleury, [1876], pp. 24–5.
40. Adeline, pp. 265–402 (Bibliography) and 138–41 (quotation from *Notre-Dame de Paris*).
41. See Champfleury's mockery of this commentary: Champfleury [1876], pp. 119–21.
42. Adeline, p. 302; Champfleury, [1876], *passim*.
43. T. Wright, 1865, pp. 56–60.

44. Champfleury, [1876], pp. 60, 174, 72, 83, 231.
45. Champfleury, [1879], p. 191.
46. Champfleury, [1879], pp. 150–1.
47. Champfleury, 1867, p. 10.
48. Champfleury, 1869, pp. xiii, xxiii.
49. Champfleury, [1879], p. 151.
50. See quotations in Champfleury, 1867, pp. 22–3.
51. Asfour, p. 182. For a recent, well-illustrated survey, see Garnier.
52. Champfleury, 1867, pp. 5, vi.
53. Champfleury, 1867, p. ix.
54. Champfleury, 1867, pp. 26, 34.
55. Champfleury, 1867, pp. 42, n. 2, and 37.
56. Goncourt, I, p. 849 (16 December 1860), and III, p. 997 (30 June 1889).
57. Champfleury, 1867, pp. 40, 43; *Boilly*, pp. 6–13, nos 13 and 14.
58. Champfleury, 1867, p. 58.
59. Champfleury, 1867, pp. 10, 256–8.
60. Champfleury, 1867, p. 316; Asfour, p. 181.
61. Champfleury, 1867, pp. 102–5.
62. Champfleury, 1867, pp. 133–5, 194–6.
63. Champfleury, 1867, pp. 117, 137.
64. Champfleury, 1867, pp. 136–9.
65. Champfleury, 1867, pp. 313–18; Asfour, p. 183. One such plate is to be found in the Gruthuus Museum in Bruges.
66. Champfleury, 1867, pp. 321–31.
67. Quoted in Goldwater, p. 43, n. 7.
68. All information about Warburg's ideas and development in this section, when not otherwise indicated, is taken from Gombrich 1970.
69. As well as Gombrich, 1970, pp. 30–7, see Popper, and Weintraub, pp. 161–207.
70. For Lamprecht's career and publications see Bücher.
71. Weintraub, p. 186, note 76.
72. Lamprecht, 1882, pp. 1–2.
73. Warburg, 1905, pp. 3 and 10–13.
74. Warburg, 1932, I, pp. 93–126 (*Bildniskunst und Florentinisches Bürgertum*, 1902). For the passages I have quoted from this article see pp. 96, 101, 100, 118, 100.

14 Art as Prophecy

1. Champfleury, [1876], pp. 157–63; Besson, pp. 205–7; Weber; *Tobias Stimmer*, pp. 263–4, nos 157, 157a.
2. See the reproduction in Strauss, I, p. 183, and III, p. 991.
3. Fischart, pp. 423–8.
4. Besson, pp. 193 ff.
5. For Nass's refutation of Fischart, see Scheible, pp. 1178–84. I am extremely grateful to Pascal Griener for his help with all these texts.
6. Champfleury, [1876], pp. 164–8.
7. Evelyn, p. 335. The triple portrait is now in the Royal Collection.
8. Strong, pp. 32–43. If Bernini did make the comment attributed to him by Evelyn, it is tempting to surmise (as Nicholas Penny has suggested to me) that he did so during the long discussion he had about his bust of Charles I with Nicholas Stone the Younger on 22 October

1638, and that it was through Stone that the story began to circulate after his return to England five years later. On the other hand, nothing in the record that he made of this discussion even hints at any reaction of this kind from Bernini. Stone died in 1646 before the king had been executed but after he had suffered much that was 'funest and unhappy': see Stone, p. 170.

9. Bulstrode, p. 66.

10. As Bulstrode was aged eighty-seven when Evelyn's *Numismata* was published, it might seem reasonable to assume that he had by then already completed his *Memoirs* and that he was therefore the first to record this very significant story. On the other hand, we know that when these *Memoirs* appeared posthumously in 1721 they included material – including episodes from Clarendon's *History* of 1702–4 – which was probably added by his publisher (see Firth). It is therefore not possible to be sure when Bernini's supposed response to Van Dyck's portrait was first noted.

11. D'Israeli, III, pp. 112, 116.

12. Richardson, 1715, pp. 174–5. This portrait is now at Windsor: see Millar, I, pp. 95–6, no. 145. I am most grateful to Sir Oliver Millar for his help about this painting.

13. D'Israeli, III, pp. 111–13.

14. See *The Queen's Image*.

15. Wiedmann, 1986, pp. 83–4.

16. Schiller, 1943, pp. 201–14.

17. Schiller, 1979, pp. 199–200 (letter to Körner, 9 February 1789).

18. Garland, p. 133.

19. Wildenstein, p. 18.

20. *Jacques-Louis David*, p. 167.

21. Wildenstein, p. 21.

22. For the arrangement of the pictures in the Salon of 1785 see the engraving by P.-A. Martini, *Coup-d'oeil exact de l'arrangement des Peintures au Salon du Louvre, en 1785* (pl. 220, above).

23. *Espion*, p. 41 (Deloynes, XIV, no. 337).

24. *Espion*, p. 39 (Deloynes, XIV, no. 337). The picture is now in Stockholm.

25. *Aristarque*, p. 16 (Deloynes, XIV, no. 340).

26. *Supplément du peintre anglais*, p. 2 (Deloynes, XIV, no. 328); *Frondeur*, p. 17 (Deloynes, XIV, no 329) of Berthélémy's *Manlius Torquatus*, now in Musée des Beaux-Arts, Tours.

27. *Supplément du peintre anglais*, p. 3 (Deloynes, XIV, no. 328); *Frondeur*, p. 67 (Deloynes, XIV, no. 329); 'Critès', *Troisième Promenade*, pp. 36–40 (Deloynes, XIV, no. 335); *Observations sur le Sallon*, p. 5 (Deloynes XIV, no. 339); *Avis Important*, p. 30 (Deloynes, XIV, no. 344).

28. *Avis Important*, p. 29 (Deloynes, XIV, no. 344); *Observations sur le Sallon*, p. 4 (Deloynes, XIV, no. 339); *Aristarque*, p. 15 (Deloynes, XIV, no. 340); *Avis Important*, p. 31 (Deloynes, XIV, no. 344).

29. See his Autobiography of 1793 in Bordes, pp. 174–5.

30. Bordes, pp. 26, 27, 30.

31. Bordes, pp. 48, 148–51.

32. See his Autobiography of 1793 and his statement of 1794 in Bordes, pp. 174–5 and 107, n. 182. The endlessly debated question of whether he had in fact had such intentions is (fortunately) irrelevant here.

33. Bordes, p. 100, n. 86.

34. Bordes, p. 53, at n. 180.

35. Bordes, p. 53, at n. 181.

36. Bordes, p. 178.

37. Bordes, p. 28 (and p. 192 for the date of his memoirs).

38. David was not the only artist to benefit from a reputation for prophecy during these turbulent years. In 1798 an official report claimed of Joseph-Benoît Suvée's bleak *Cornélie, mère des Gracques* (now in the Louvre) that 'exécuté sous l'ancien régime, [c]'est un tableau républicain'. This had, in fact, been commissioned by Louis XVI's younger brother, the comte d'Artois, before he emigrated (soon after the fall of the Bastille), but it was not completed until shortly before being exhibited in 1795: see *De David à Delacroix*, pp. 613–14, no. 170, and Montaiglon (edited), XVII, p. 168.

39. Hunt, pp. 11–20; Bénichou, p. 288.

40. D.O. Evans, pp. 137, 166.

41. Hunt, pp. 24, 83 ff; Bénichou, p. 289; for *Le Gymnase*, see Guyon.

42. *Le Producteur*, III, 1826, pp. 252–64 (see, especially, pp. 254–5, 258). The author signs himself J.A. Antoine Schnapper has kindly pointed out to me that the reference can only be to the unfinished picture now in Versailles.

43. *Le Producteur*, III, 1826, p. 258.

44. *Le Producteur*, III, 1826, pp. 260–1, 263.

45. *L'Organisateur*, 25 December 1830, no. 19, 2ème année, pp. 145–50 (see especially p. 148).

46. D.O. Evans, p. 44; and see the article by Balzac in *La Silhouette* of 25 February 1830 (referred to by Verbraeken, p. 126, n. 24) reprinted in Balzac, XXVI, p. 218.

47. *L'Artiste*, 1837, 1ère série, tome XIII, p. 14.

48. *L'Organisateur*, 25 December 1830, no. 19, 2ème année, pp. 145–50 (see especially p. 147).

49. Bürger, pp. 320–1.

50. Ruskin, 1903–11, X, pp. 242–3.

51. Ruskin, 1903–11, XI, p. 50.

52. Mrs Lecky, pp. 84, 105, 174.

53. Hyde, p. 42 (letter of 11 November 1861).

54. Auchmuty, p. 41.

55. Hyde, p. 49.

56. Hyde, p. 72 (letter of 2 September 1868).

57. Lecky, 1865, I, p. 223, n. 1.

58. Brisac and Léniaud, p. 37.

59. Lecky, 1865, I, pp. 72, 10–11, 122, and p. 56, n. 1.

60. Lecky, 1865, I, p. 284.

61. Lecky, 1865, I, pp. 218–27, 235–6, 253, 249.

62. Lecky, 1865, I, p. 249, n. 1.

63. Lecky, 1865, I, p. 277; cf. Lecky, 1904, I, p. 252.

64. Lecky, 1865, I, pp. 282–3.

65. Lecky, 1865, I, p. 260.

66. Lecky, 1865, I, p. 62.

67. E.R. Curtius, pp. 274–355 (see p. 345 for the passage quoted here).

68. Friedländer, 1969, p. 78.
69. Friedländer, 1921, p. 44.
70. Thausing, p. 198.
71. Białostocki, pp. 267–75.
72. Dvořák, 1984, p. 108.
73. See Białostocki, pp. 267–75 for an English translation of the lecture, which is published in Dvořák, 1928, pp. 193–202.
74. See Gombrich quoted in Białostocki, pp. 285–7.
75. In 1899 Vollard published Odilon Redon's album of lithographs of *L'Apocalypse*; and for Rudolf Steiner's lectures on the subject given in Nuremberg in 1908, Andrey Bely's essay on 'The Apocalypse in Russian Poetry' published in 1905 and Kandinsky's many depictions of the theme, see Washton-Long, pp. 28–35, 82–5.
76. Lankheit, p. 252.
77. Van Gogh, II, p. 559 (letter to Theo of 5 May 1888).
78. Apollinaire, pp. 313–14, 'La jolie rousse'.
79. Roskill.
80. Chipp, pp. 292–3.
81. Mondrian, pp. 14–15.
82. Washton-Long, p. 13.
83. Bowlt, pp. 124, 126. See *Malevich*, p. 70, pl. 42.
84. See, most recently, Eliel.
85. See Ludwig Meidner, 'Anleitung zum Malen von Grossstadtbildern', in Grochowiak, pp. 78–80.
86. Roethel and Benjamin, I, pp. 473–4 (where, however, the father is mistakenly credited with the translation of Kandinsky's *Über das Geistige in der Kunst*, which was, in fact, carried out by the son).
87. Sadler, p. 19.
88. Grochowiak, p. 65.
89. Quoted by Bowlt, p. xxxiii.
90. *Paris-Berlin*, p. 48.
91. For a curt dismissal of this notion, see Wiedmann, 1979, pp. 213–14.
92. Sadleir, pp. 237–9.
93. Sadler, p. 19.
94. Sadler, p. 5.
95. Bazin, p. 12. It is true that Bazin refers, in the vaguest of ways, to Tintoretto's paintings in the Palazzo Ducale (most of which date from after the fire of 1577) rather than to any specific work; but it seems likely that he had the *Paradise* in mind.
96. Bazin, pp. 29–32.
97. Réau, 1932, p. 185 (letter 151).
98. Baudelaire, pp. 760 (*L'Oeuvre et la Vie d'Eugène Delacroix*) and 440–1 (*Salon de 1846*).
99. Sadler, p. 7: 'apparently', because the sentence is so cryptic that it could mean just the opposite to this.

15 Huizinga and the 'Flemish Renaissance'

1. For a full discussion of Huizinga, see sections v–viii of this chapter.
2. Waagen, quoted Białostocki, p. 223.
3. Sulzberger.
4. *Notice des tableaux des écoles française et flamande,*

Exposés dans la grande Gallerie du Musée Central des Arts . . . , Paris An VII [1799], pp. 43–111. The two scenes from the *Judgement of Cambyses* attributed to Claissens (nos 206 and 207) are the paintings by Gerard David at Bruges.
5. See Schlegel, 1959, pp. xi–xxii, and Schlegel, 1984, pp. 207–8.
6. Schlegel, 1959, pp. 42–3. The 'Van Eyck' was, in fact, a Gerard David, from the French Royal Collection, and the 'Holbein' was the 'Meyer Madonna', later identified as a copy of the version in Darmstadt (Schlegel, 1984, p. 188).
7. Schlegel's discussion of this issue is not wholly consistent and can be somewhat confusing.
8. Naturally, attributions were often uncertain. Schlegel discusses, at length and with enthusiasm, a 'Dürer' *Crucifixion* in the Louvre, now attributed to a Flemish painter of the sixteenth century working in France (Schlegel, 1984, pp. 48–9 and 189).
9. Descamps, p. 301.
10. Schlegel, 1959, pp. xx–xxi.
11. Schlegel, 1959, p. 137.
12. Schlegel, 1959, pp. 139–43.
13. Schlegel, 1959, p. 152.
14. Sulzberger, I, p. 74.
15. Goethe, 1981, XII, p. 156 (from *Kunst und Altertum am Rhein und Main*, 1816), quoted Goethe (ed. Gage), p. 140.
16. Kugler, 1847, I, pp. 228 ff.; and see the English translation 'by a lady' of parts of an earlier edition of Kugler, published in London in 1846, II, p. 41.
17. Bickendorf.
18. Waagen, pp. 169–72. The second edition of two years later takes into account the inscription referring to Hubert which, in the meantime, had been discovered on the Ghent altarpiece.
19. See, for instance, Crowe and Cavalcaselle, 1857, pp. 311–12; Crowe and Cavalcaselle, 1872, pp. 345–60.
20. See the discussion in Dehaisnes, pp. 585–98.
21. Kugler, 1847, II, pp. 92–4; and Kugler, 1846, II, pp. 54–7.
22. Laborde, 1849, I, pp. cxii–cxiii.
23. Laborde, 1849, I, p. xcix.
24. See Chennevières, IV, ch. II, pp. 42–68; Laborde, 1849, I, p. cxxxvii; Laborde, 1855, pp. v–vi and unpaginated *Avis* at end of volume.
25. Laborde, 1830.
26. Chennevières, pp. 57–8.
27. Laborde, 1849, I, p. lxxi.
28. Laborde, 1855, p. vii.
29. Laborde, 1855, pp. 596–607, 645 ff.
30. Laborde, 1849, I, pp. lxxiii–lxxv.
31. Laborde, 1849, I, pp. xcv–xcviii.
32. Laborde, 1849, I, pp. 153, 336, 330, 163, 328, 217, 249, 482.
33. Laborde, 1849, I, p. xvii.
34. Chennevières, pp. 47, 55.
35. Laborde, 1849, I, pp. xcviii–xcix.
36. Laborde, 1849, I, pp. xlvi–xlvii.
37. Laborde, 1849, I, pp. xcviii–xcix.
38. Kaegi, 1947–82, VI, pp. 468 ff.
39. Burckhardt, 1855, p. 795. Michelet had himself

written of this period of Flemish art that 'La peinture a ses rechutes', and that the energetic Van Eyck had been succeeded by 'the woman', Hemling.

40. Courajod, 1899–1903, II, p. 23 (*Les Origines de la Renaissance en France*).
41. Courajod, 1884, p. 62; Courajod, 1899–1903, II, pp. 213 ff. and elsewhere.
42. A. Michel, 1896, p. 208; and many references in Courajod, 1899–1903.
43. A. Michel, 1896, pp. 211, 209. See, above all, the three volumes that he devoted to Lenoir between 1878 and 1887.
44. For a list of his publications, see Courajod, 1899–1903, III, pp. xx–xxxv.
45. A. Michel, 1896, p. 204; Courajod, 1899–1903, III, p. viii.
46. Vitry, pp. 62–5; Verne, p. 12; Vaudoyer, p. 72: I am most grateful to MM Dominique Ponnau and Bertrand Meyrab for these references.
47. A. Michel, 1896, pp. 207, 215–17.
48. Courajod, 1899–1903, II, p. 30.
49. Courajod, 1899–1903, II, p. 136.
50. Courajod, 1899–1903, II, pp. 303–5.
51. Renan, VIII, pp. 595–783 (*Discours sur l'état des Beaux-Arts en France au quatorzième siècle*).
52. Courajod, 1899–1903, II, p. 289.
53. Courajod, 1899–1903, II, p. 12.
54. Courajod, 1899–1903, II, p. 26.
55. A. Michel, 1896, p. 216.
56. A. Michel, 1896, p. 213.
57. Vitry, p. 62.
58. Courajod, 1899–1903, II, pp. 307–13.
59. Courajod, 1899–1903, II, pp. 289–305.
60. Wytsman; Kervyn, 1906, p. 11.
61. Académie Royale de Belgique, *Biographie Nationale*, XXXIX, supplément XI, 1976, pp. 522–31 (Nicolas N. Huyghebaert: 'Kervyn de Lettenhove').
62. Kervyn, 1906, p. 15.
63. Kervyn, 1902, p. 6; Kervyn, 1906, pp. 73–83, 115.
64. Kervyn, 1902, p. 11; Kervyn, 1906, pp. 69–71.
65. See, for instance, Germiny, p. 99; Weale, 1903, p. 42; Uzanne, p. 173; Dülberg, p. 50.
66. Kervyn, 1906, pp. 14, 29, 85.
67. Kervyn, 1906, pp. 23–4.
68. Kervyn, 1906, pp. 24–5.
69. Kervyn, 1906, pp. 37–41; *Dictionary of National Biography*, 2nd supplement, I, 1920, pp. 586–7 (Edward VII).
70. Kervyn, 1906, pp. 61–8.
71. Kervyn, 1906, pp. 27–34.
72. Bruges: *Compte Rendu*, 1902, p. 51.
73. Bruges: *Compte Rendu*, 1902, pp. 46–52.
74. Helbig, p. 370.
75. Bruges: *Compte Rendu*, 1902, p. 48.
76. The first two, which are in the National Gallery in London and the Alte Pinakothek in Munich, were lent by private collectors; the third already belonged to the Royal Museum in Brussels.
77. Wauters, p. 30.
78. See, for instance, Buschmann, pp. 352–3.
79. [Weale], 1902 (Catalogue), p. xxvi.

80. Guicciardini, quoted in Friedländer, 1967–76, VIII (*Jan Gossaert and Bernart van Orley*), p. 11.
81. [Weale], 1902 (Catalogue), no. 225; Friedländer, 1967–76, VIII (*Jan Gossaert and Bernart van Orley*), plate 40, no. 49 (private collection).
82. Kervyn, 1906, pp. 45–6.
83. Kervyn, 1906, pp. 71–3.
84. See the plan in Wauters.
85. Buschmann, p. 333.
86. Deprez, p. 350.
87. Bricon, p. 692.
88. Crowe and Cavalcaselle, 1872, p. 90; already in 1857, pp. 109–13, they had had the most serious doubts about it.
89. Vogelaar, pp. 53–62, nos 1380 and 1381. I am very grateful to Dr Lorne Campbell for his help over these pictures.
90. Helbig, p. 371.
91. Weale, 1900, p. 253.
92. Académie Royale de Belgique, *Biographie Nationale*, XXX, supplément 2, 1959, pp. 809–18 (O. De Sloovere: 'Weale'); Kervyn, 1926.
93. Tal.
94. Weale, 1867, pp. v–viii; Galichon.
95. The 'Memlings' he borrowed from the Fuller Russell and Moreau-Wolsey collections (Weale, 1867, nos 15 and 9) were both products of the studio of Roger van der Weyden – the *Diptych of the Crucifixion with Jeanne de France as the Donatrix* (Musée Condé, Chantilly) and the so-called 'Sforza triptych' (Royal Museum, Brussels): see Friedländer, 1967–76, II (*Rogier van der Weyden and the Master of Flemalle*), pls 107 and 109. I am most grateful to Mr Burton Frederickson of the Getty Provenance Index for this information.
96. Weale, 1901, p. vi.
97. H.P.M., p. 241; and for Kervyn's description, see Kervyn, 1926, p. 520.
98. Tschudi, p. 229.
99. Huyghebaert, p. 188.
100. Huyghebaert, p. 199 (letter from Weale in London of 15 May 1902 announcing his arrival in Bruges in the following week); Kervyn, 1906, pp. 90, 112–13; Kervyn, 1926, p. 520.
101. See some of the comments on some of the exhibited pictures in Weale, 1903.
102. Bruges: *Compte Rendu*, 1902.
103. This is confirmed by Weale, 1903, p. 42.
104. Weale, 1901, pp. 79–82.
105. Weale, 1903, p. 48.
106. Weale, 1901, p. 90.
107. Kervyn, 1906, p. 56.
108. Kervyn, 1906, pp. 55–60, 87–8.
109. Kervyn, 1902, p. 9; Kervyn, 1906, p. 89; Wauters, p. 16.
110. See the photograph in [Weale], 1902 (Catalogue).
111. Rouvre, pp. 110–11.
112. Durand-Gréville, p. 15.
113. Weale, 1895, p. 7.
114. Hymans, pp. 294–5.
115. Frantz, p. 30; Helbig, p. 368.
116. Uzanne, p. 177.
117. Weale, 1895, p. 23.

118. Kervyn, 1906, pp. 34–6.
119. Friedländer, 1967–76, VI, b (*Hans Memlinc and Gerard David*), pp. 79–80.
120. Uzanne, p. 177.
121. Weale, 1895, p. 13.
122. Hymans, p. 285.
123. Buschmann, for instance, who mentions the titles of the paintings (p. 348) refers to them only to make the point that David has by now 'thrown off his Italianising tendencies', while Forceville (p. 83) merely enthuses over David's 'finesse d'observation' in these pictures and his success in achieving the aim of all his school: to reveal the life of the soul in the features. Bricon (p. 701) devotes two lines to these scenes, and although he acknowledges that the executioners are the cruellest figures in the exhibition, he adds that 'they are executing someone who is guilty'. Uzanne (pp. 79–80) describes what is happening in gruesome detail, but concludes that 'nothing deranges the beautiful attitudes, the harmony, the clarity, the minute neatness of the painting, which remains superhuman, above suffering and fright'.
124. Weale, 1903, p. 202.
125. Durand-Gréville, pp. 6–9.
126. Rouvre, p. 102.
127. See, e.g. Durand-Gréville, p. 16; but Deprez, pp. 356–7, writes with some enthusiasm of both Bosch and Brueghel.
128. Dülberg, p. 49.
129. Kervyn, 1902, p. 14; Kervyn, 1906, p. 128; and see Germiny, p. 101 and Buschmann, p. 331.
130. See the references in Kervyn, 1902, pp. 12–14.
131. Fierens-Gevaert, 1902, p. 105.
132. Durand-Gréville, p. 1; Frantz, p. 27; Bricon, pp. 689–90, 705; Le Brun, p. 145; Buschmann, p. 331; Deprez, pp. 348–9; Forceville, pp. 76–7; Germiny, pp. 100–01.
133. See, however, Bricon, p. 690.
134. Buschmann, p. 336; Hymans, p. 281; Helbig, p. 367; Fierens-Gevaert, 1902, p. 116.
135. Uzanne, p. 179.
136. [Weale], 1902 (Catalogue), p. xxx.
137. Kervyn, 1906, pp. 111–15 (who appears to suggest, erroneously, that this appeared *before* Weale's catalogue); Hulin de Loo, p. iii.
138. Académie Royale de Belgique: *Bibliographie Nationale*, tome XXXII, supplément, tome IV, pp. 310–12 (Jacques Lavalleye: 'Hulin de Loo').
139. Kervyn, 1902, p. 5; Kervyn, 1906, p. 42.
140. Winkler.
141. Blumenreich.
142. Kervyn, 1906, p. 23.
143. Friedländer, 1903; Friedländer, 1903 (*Meister-werke*).
144. Friedländer, 1903 ('Die Brügger Leihausstellung'), p. 66.
145. Fierens-Gevaert, 1903 (1st edition 1897).
146. Fierens-Gevaert, 1901, pp. 1–111. He explains that some years earlier he had been asked by Rodenbach to collaborate on a large illustrated publication on Bruges (which never appeared): his own contribution was to be devoted to Memling. The chapter on Flemish painting in *Psychologie d'une Ville* began life as a lecture given in Brussels in November 1899 and then appeared, in a modified form, in the *Revue des Deux-Mondes* of June 1900.
147. Bautier, 1927; Bautier, 1928; Puyvelde.
148. Fierens-Gevaert, 1902, pp. 177–80.
149. Fierens-Gevaert, 1902, pp. 181–2.
150. Fierens-Gevaert, 1902, pp. 435–44.
151. Marguillier, p. 265.
152. For the contents of this exhibition see the catalogue edited by Don Carlos de Bofarull y Sans, and for its importance for Picasso, see Richardson, 1991, pp. 246–7. I am grateful to Enriqueta Harris for locating a copy in the library of the Victoria and Albert Museum.
153. Marguillier, pp. 268, 270.
154. Mason Perkins; Logan.
155. Kervyn, 1906, pp. 131–2.
156. Kervyn, 1902, p. 12.
157. Bouchot. See, especially, pp. 6, 10, 17, 240.
158. Fierens-Gevaert, 1905, pp. 2, 3, 10, 11, 12, 15, 16, 17, 173–5, 214–15.
159. Huizinga's collected works (*Verzamelde Werken*) were published in nine volumes in Haarlem between 1948 and 1953, and it is to this edition that scholars usually refer when discussing his books and articles. This is sadly not possible for those who, like myself, do not read Dutch, although (thanks to the help of Marion Koninck and Raymond Klumper) I have been able to do so in the case of some material that has never been translated. Elsewhere I have indicated the various translations on which I have had to rely. I am particularly grateful to Dr Anton van der Lem for guidance in this matter.
160. Huizinga (trs. Kaegi), 1947, pp. 45–46, 10–11.
161. The text of *Herfstij der Middeleeuwen* (which was first published in 1919) presents particular problems to the non-Dutch reader, who has, of course, also to forego any appreciation of the apparently superb style of the original. I have (unless otherwise indicated) used the English version of F. Hopman which appeared in London in 1924 under the title of *The Waning of the Middle Ages*. This is described (in the Preface) by Huizinga himself as a work of 'adaptation, reduction, and consolidation under the author's directions'. However, Weintraub's claim (p. 212, n. 13) that it is 'a very inferior, crippled version of the Dutch original' obviously carries much weight, as can be seen by comparing it with the French translation by J. Bastin, on which I have also drawn when necessary. In addition, Raymond Klumper has kindly checked for me a number of passages in the English version against the second Dutch edition of 1921.

I have been much less worried than many people by the use of the word 'Waning' (as distinct from the original 'Autumnal Season'). Despite what is very often said (see, for a recent example, Mettra and Le Goff in Huizinga, trs. Bastin, p. ii), it seems to me absolutely evident that Huizinga did look upon the period as one of decline: indeed, he occasionally writes of it with an intensity of hatred and scorn (e.g., Huizinga (trs. Hopman), p. 243) that recalls Michelet.

162. Huizinga (trs. Hopman), p. 7.
163. See Köster for all references to Huizinga's biography, unless otherwise indicated; and see also Kaegi, 1946.
164. Huizinga (trs. Kaegi), 1947, pp. 11–15.
165. Huizinga (trs. Kaegi), 1947, p. 39.
166. Huizinga (trs. Kaegi), 1947, p. 29.
167. Huizinga (trs. Kaegi), 1947, p. 20.
168. Huizinga (trs. Kaegi), 1947, pp. 29, 23–4.
169. Huizinga (trs. Kaegi), p. 10.
170. Huizinga (trs. Kaegi), 1947, pp. 24, 28, 43; Köster, p. 17.
171. Huizinga 1950; see also Valkenburg.
172. A number of these drawings are reproduced in the catalogue of the exhibition devoted to Huizinga which was held at Leiden in 1991–2. Others, belonging to his family, were kindly shown to me by Anton van der Lem. Köster, p. 18 also refers to anatomical drawings by him.
173. Huizinga (trs. Kaegi), 1947, p. 23.
174. Huizinga (trs. Kaegi), 1947, pp. 31–5.
175. Toorop, 1989, p. 150. See this catalogue, and also Toorop, 1977, for reproductions of many of the pictures exhibited in 1896, in which year the artist was aged nearly forty and not (as Huizinga said) thirty-six.
176. Toorop, 1989, pp. 17, 149.
177. Huizinga (trs. Kaegi), 1947, pp. 54–5: Huizinga says that they had then been friends for more than twenty-five years.
178. Köster, p. 33. I am grateful to Anton van der Lem for confirming this judgement.
179. Huizinga (trs. Kaegi), 1947, pp. 43, 46.
180. I have used the English translation of this which was published in Huizinga, 1968, pp. 219–43, and I have also benefited greatly from the discussion of the lecture by Oestreich.
181. Huizinga, 1968, pp. 220, 224, 233.
182. Huizinga (trs. Kaegi), 1947, p. 50.
183. Huizinga, 1968, pp. 231, 232.
184. Huizinga, 1968, p. 233; Michelet, 1952, II, p. 60 n.
185. Huizinga, 1968, pp. 237, 238.
186. Huizinga (trs. Kaegi), 1947, p. 51.
187. Huizinga, 1968, pp. 240–3 (my italics).
188. Huizinga (trs. Kaegi), 1947, pp. 55–6.
189. Gombrich, 1969, pp. 28–31, implies that Huizinga had responded in this way from the first: 'he simply knew too many facts about the age of van Eyck to find it easy to square his impression of his pictures with the voice of the documents. He felt he had rather to re-interpret the style of the painter to make it fit with what he knew of the culture'. But this view is surely tenable only if it can be shown that Huizinga was deliberately or inadvertently misleading his readers when he claimed that it was the pictures that had coloured his view of the age long before he knew anything about its culture.
190. Huizinga (trs. Hopman), pp. 151, 150. Admittedly, it is not quite clear whether he is referring to the same sort of works in both cases.

191. Huizinga (trs. Bastin), pp. 269–71; this is more complete than the English version.
192. Huizinga (trs. Bastin), p. 291. Van Eyck's portrait of his wife is in the Groeninge Museum, Bruges; Baudouin de Lannoy is in Berlin; 'Leal Souvenir' is in the National Gallery, London.
193. Huizinga (trs. Hopman), p. 297.
194. Huizinga (trs. Hopman), p. 286.
195. Huizinga (trs. Hopman), pp. 265, 313–14.
196. Huizinga (trs. Bastin), p. 276.
197. Huizinga (trs. Hopman), p. 274.
198. Huizinga (trs. Hopman), p. 317. For the particular manuscript referred to by Huizinga, see below, n. 227. For the Lille workshop of Jean Miélot, who was employed by Philip the Good, see Siècle d'Or de la Miniature Flamande, pp. 76–9.
199. For the relationship between the carved altarpiece by Jacques de Baerze and the panels painted for it by Broederlam, see Panofsky, 1953, I, pp. 78–9 and 86–8.
200. Kervyn, 1926, pp. 527–8.
201. Huizinga (trs. Hopman), pp. 279–80.
202. Huizinga (trs. Hopman), pp. 280–1.
203. Huizinga (trs. Hopman), p. 264.
204. Huizinga (trs. Bastin), pp. 289–90; (trs. Hopman), pp. 275–6.
205. Huizinga, 1960 ('The Problem of the Renaissance', first published 1920), p. 256.
206. Huizinga, 1960 ('Bernard Shaw's Saint', first published 1925), p. 239.
207. Huizinga, 1960, pp. 207–39, especially, p. 221.
208. Huizinga, 1960, pp. 260–1.
209. Huizinga, 1948–53, VII, p. 486.
210. Huizinga, 1960, p. 260.
211. Huizinga, 1948–53, II, pp. 559–69 (Het Historisch Museum). I am very grateful to Marion Koninck for translating this for me. See also the comments by Gerson, p. 209.
212. Huizinga (trs. Hopman), pp. 140–52.
213. Huizinga (trs. Hopman), p. 58.
214. Huizinga (trs. Hopman), p. 303.
215. Gerson, p. 212, reproaches Huizinga for failing to appreciate the true stature of this artist in his review of the relevant volume of Friedländer's Altniederländische Malerei (see Huizinga, 1948–53, III, pp. 492–3, kindly translated for me by Raymond Klumper). In fact, Friedländer himself, like almost all art historians at the time, was so obsessed with trying to discover the identity of this master (who is usually assumed to be the same as Robert Campin) that he hardly bothered to discuss any wider questions arising out of his style and vision.
216. Uzanne, p. 177.
217. Huizinga (trs. Hopman), pp. 159–60.
218. Reynaud, pp. 18–22.
219. Huizinga (trs. Hopman), p. 314. The picture is reproduced in the 1967 catalogue of paintings in the Leipzig Museum (plate 6) and is attributed to an artist of the Lower Rhine school. Huizinga, incidentally, stresses that the nude occupied a large place in tableaux vivants.
220. See, for instance, the reference (Huizinga (trs. Hopman), p. 200) to the 'hideous actuality' of the visions of Alain de la Roche, in which

animals representing the various sins are equipped with horrible genitals and emit torrents of fire which obscure the earth with their smoke . . .

221. Huizinga, 1948–53, III, pp. 501–3, (kindly translated by Raymond Klumper).
222. Huizinga (trs. Hopman), pp. 257–8.
223. Huizinga (trs. Hopman), pp. 251–2.
224. Huizinga (trs. Hopman), p. 253.
225. Huizinga (trs. Hopman), pp. 272–4.
226. Huizinga (trs. Hopman), pp. 207, 210.
227. Huizinga (trs. Hopman), p. 317. Huizinga is referring to the miniatures by Jean Miélot for Christine de Pisan's *Epitre d'Othéa à Hector* (and see Huizinga (trs. Hopman), p. 326, n. 1).
228. Huizinga (trs. Hopman), p. 153.
229. Huizinga (trs. Hopman), p. 265.
230. Huizinga (trs. Hopman), pp. 264, 263.
231. Huizinga (trs. Hopman), p. 153.
232. Huizinga (trs. Hopman), p. 250.
233. Laborde, 1849, I, pp. cxvii–cxviii.
234. Huizinga (trs. Hopman), pp. 244–5.
235. Huizinga (trs. Hopman), pp. 245.
236. Huizinga (trs. Hopman), p. 249. It is curious that Huizinga refers so little to tapestry.
237. Huizinga (trs. Hopman), p. 278.
238. Huizinga (trs. Hopman), p. 249.
239. Huizinga (trs. Hopman), p. 245.
240. Huizinga (trs. Hopman), p. 246.
241. Huizinga (trs. Hopman), p. 313.
242. Huizinga (trs. Hopman), p. 242.
243. Huizinga (trs. Hopman), p. 244.
244. Huizinga (trs. Hopman), pp. 244–5.
245. Huizinga (trs. Hopman), p. 277.
246. Huizinga (trs. Hopman), p. 263.
247. Huizinga, 1948–53, II, pp. 216–37 (*La physionomie morale de Philippe le Bon*, 1932).
248. Huizinga, 1948–53, II, p. 219.
249. Huizinga, 1948–53, p. 288.
250. Huizinga, 1960, p. 290.
251. Huizinga, 1960, p. 297.
252. See, for instance, the distinctly hostile preface by Garin to the Italian translation of 1940, and also the comment by Jacques Le Goff in Huizinga (trs. Bastin), p. xi.
253. Huizinga, 1960, p. 297.
254. Huizinga, 1968, p. 38.
255. See the pained comments by Gerson, pp. 219–20.
256. Huizinga, 1952, pp. vii–x (Preface by G.N. Clark).
257. Huizinga, 1968, p. 9.
258. Huizinga, 1968, p. 46.
259. Huizinga, 1968, p. 10.
260. Colie is one of Huizinga's many critics who insist that he did not in fact pay sufficient attention to political issues.
261. Huizinga, 1968, p. 80. However, had he foreseen the extent to which such concepts would have been adopted (and abused) he might have been more cautious, for – on the same page – he warns 'the modern art-lover' against 'the temptation of looking at the painter's ideas or subjects in the light of his own views and hence seeing more in them than was there'.
262. In private Huizinga apparently told his friends that he did not believe the 'Vermeer' to be a seventeenth-century picture: this is recorded by Gerson (p. 207, and n. 3) who, in general, is very critical of his approach as being too much that of a cultural historian.
263. Huizinga, 1968, p. 18.
264. Huizinga, 1968, p. 95.
265. Huizinga, 1968, pp. 97–104.
266. Since completing my chapter on Huizinga I have received from Professor Bram Kempers of Amsterdam his article (see Bibliography), whose title he has freely translated as 'The seduction of the image. The visual as a permanent source of inspiration in the work of Huizinga'. Professor Kempers has been kind enough to provide me with an English summary of this extremely interesting article, and it has caused me great satisfaction to find that the general outline of what I have written appears to correspond with his own conclusions which (unlike mine) are based on great knowledge of the original sources.

Works Cited in the Text and Notes

Adam, Robert, *Ruins of the Palace of the Emperor Diocletian at Spalatro in Dalmatia*, London 1764.

Adams, Henry, *Novels: Mont Saint-Michel. The Education*, The Library of America, New York 1983.

Addison, Joseph, 'Dialogues upon the Usefulness of Ancient Medals. Especially in relation to the Latin and Greek poets' (1726), I, pp. 253–355, in *The Works of Joseph Addison*, with notes by Richard Hurd, 6 vols, London 1901.

Adeline, Jules, *Les Sculptures grotesques et symboliques (Rouen et Environs)*, Préface par Champfleury, Rouen, n.d.

Adhémar, Jean, 'André Thevet – Collectionneur de portraits', *Revue Archéologique*, sixième série, XX (July–December), 1942–3, pp. 41–54.

Adhémar, Jean, 'Les portraits dessinés du XVIᵉ siècle au Cabinet des Estampes', *Gazette des Beaux-Arts*, 1973, II, pp. 121–98, 327–50.

Adhémar, Jean, 'Enseignement par l'image – II', *Gazette des Beaux-Arts*, September 1981, pp. 49–60.

Agustín, Antonio, *Dialoghi intorno alle medaglie inscrittioni et altre antichità tradotti di lingua spagnuola in italiana da Dionigi Ottaviano Sada*, Rome 1592.

Agustín, Antonio [Antonii Augustini], *Opera Omnia*, vol. VII, pp. 231–63: *Lettere italiane di Antonio Agostini a Fulvio Orsini*, Lucca 1772.

Ainsworth, Maryan, '"Paternes for phisioneamyes": Holbein's portraiture reconsidered', *Burlington Magazine*, CXXXII, 1990, pp. 173–86.

Alberti, Leandro, *Descrittione di tutta Italia*, Venice 1553.

Alberti, Leon Battista, *On Painting and On Sculpture. The Latin Texts of De Pictura and De Statua*, edited with translations, introduction and notes by Cecil Grayson, London 1972.

Alföldi, A. and E., *Die Kontorniat – Medaillons*, 2 vols, Berlin 1976.

Amadio, Adele Anna, *I Mosaici di S. Costanza*, Rome (*Xenia* Quaderni, 7), 1986.

Amyot, Thomas, 'Observations on an Historical Fact supposed to be established by the Bayeux Tapestry', read 26 February 1818. *Archaeologia*, XIX, 1821, pp. 88–95.

Amyot, Thomas, 'A Defence of the early Antiquity of the Bayeux Tapestry', read 11 March 1819. *Archaeologia*, XIX, 1821, pp. 192–208.

Angeloni, Francesco, *L'Historia Augusta da Giulio Cesare a Costantino il Magno* [this reprints Angeloni's text of 1641 with a commentary by Bellori], Rome 1685.

Angoulvert, P.-J., *L'église de Brou*, Paris, n.d.

Annali Civili del Regno delle due Sicilie, Cenni Necrologici: Canonico Andrea Jorio, LIII, January–April, 1855, pp. 24–8.

Antoni, Carlo, *Dallo Storicismo alla sociologia*, Florence 1940.

Apollinaire, Guillaume, *Oeuvres Poètiques*, Paris (Pléiade) 1956.

Ariès, Philippe, *Le Temps de l'Histoire*, Préface de Roger Chartier (2nd edition), Paris 1986.

L'Aristarque moderne au Sallon (Deloynes, XIV, no. 340), Paris 1785.

Arnould, Louis, *Un Voyage à Rome: Le Paganisme d'Hippolyte Taine en 1864*, Poitiers 1927.

Arslan, Edoardo, *Venezia Gotica*, Milan 1970.

Asfour, Amal, 'Champfleury, 1821–1889: A Collection of Ceramics from the Revolution of 1789', *Journal of the History of Collections*, I, no. 2, 1989, pp. 179–85.

Aston, Margaret, 'English Ruins and English History: The Dissolution and the sense of the past', *Journal of the Warburg and Courtauld Institutes*, XXXVI, 1973, pp. 231–55.

Auchmuty, James Johnston, *Lecky: A biographical and critical essay*, Dublin and London 1945.

Aulanier, Christiane, *Histoire du Palais et du Musée du Louvre*, VIII: *Le Musée Charles X*,

Paris, 1961.

Avis important d'une femme sur le Sallon de 1785 par madame E.A.R.T.L.A.D.C.S. (Deloynes, XIV, no. 344), Paris 1785.

Babelon, Ernest, *Traité des Monnaies Grecques et Romaines*, I: *Théorie et Doctrine*, Paris 1901.

Babelon, Jean, *Germain Pilon*, Paris 1927.

Babelon, Jean-Pierre, *L'église Saint-Roch à Paris*, Paris 1972.

Baltrusaitis, Jurgis, *Aberrations: quatre essais sur la légende des formes*, Paris 1957.

Balzac, Honoré de, *Oeuvres Complètes*, ed. La Société des Études Balzaciennes, 27 vols, Paris 1956–62.

Bandur, Matteo, *Numismata imperatorum Romanorum*, 2 vols, Paris 1718.

Bann, Stephen, *The Clothing of Clio: A study in the representation of history in nineteenth-century Britain and France*, Cambridge 1984.

Barante, Prosper de, *Histoire des ducs de Bourgogne de la maison de Valois 1364–1477* (4th edition), 2 vols, Paris 1826.

Barante, Prosper de, *Histoire des ducs de Bourgogne de la maison de Valois 1364–1477* (6th edition), 6 vols, Paris 1842.

Barbieri, Franco, 'Scipione Maffei storico dell'arte', in *Miscellanea Maffeiana*, Verona 1955.

Baridon, Michel, *Edward Gibbon et le mythe de Rome: Histoire et Idéologie au Siècle des Lumières*, Paris 1977.

Baronius, C., *Annales Ecclesiastici*, III (new edition), Antwerp 1598.

Baronius, C., *Annales Ecclesiastici tratti da quelli del Cardinal Baronio per Odorico Rinaldi*, 2 vols, Rome 1683.

Baronio e l'arte: Atti del Convegno Internazionale di Studi, Sora 10–13 ottobre 1984, a cura di Romeo de Maio, Agostino Borromeo, Luigi Gulia, Georg Lutz, Aldo Mazzacane, Sora (Centro di Studi Sorani 'Vincenzo Patriarca') 1985.

Baudelaire *Oeuvres Complètes*, ed. Claude Pichois, 2 vols, Paris (Pléiade) 1975–6.

Baudrier [Le Président] *Bibliographie Lyonnaise*, 12 vols, Paris, 1895–1921 (reprinted 1964).

Baudry, Jean, *Documents inédits sur André Thevet, cosmographe du roi*, Paris 1982.

Bautier, Pierre, 'Hippolyte Fierens-Gevaert (1870–1926)', *Gazette des Beaux-Arts*, 1927, 1er semestre, pp. 121–4.

Bautier, Pierre, 'Notice biographique sur Fierens-Gevaert (1870–1926)', *Bulletin de l'Académie Royale d'Archéologie de Belgique*, 1927 fascicule unique, 1928, pp. 117–19.

Baxandall, Michael, *Giotto and the Orators*, Oxford 1971.

Bazin, Germain, *Le Crépuscule des images* (2nd edition), Paris 1946.

Beer, E.S. de, 'Gothic: Origin and Diffusion of the Term; The Idea of Style in Architecture', *Journal of the Warburg and Courtauld Institutes*, XI, 1948, pp. 143–62.

Bénichou, Paul, *Le Temps des prophètes: Doctrines de l'âge romantique*, Paris 1977.

Berenson, Bernard, *Lorenzo Lotto* (2nd edition), London 1956.

Berlin, Isaiah, *Vico and Herder: Two studies in the History of Ideas*, London 1976.

Berni, Francesco, *De gli eroi della serenissima casa d'Este, ch'ebbero il dominio in Ferrara, Memorie di Francesco Berni, al serenissimo signor duca Francesco d'Este, duca di Modona, Reggio, etc.*, [Ferrara 1640].

Bertelli, Sergio, *Erudizione e Storia in Ludovico Antonio Muratori*, Naples 1960.

Bertheroy, Jean, 'Les Primitifs flamands à Bruges', *Revue Hebdomadaire*, 27 September 1902, pp. 414–29.

Besson, P., *Étude sur Jean Fischart*, Paris 1889.

Bevilacqua, A., 'Scipione Maffei, Storico e Critico d'Arte', *Archivio Veneto*, CVI, no. 139, 1975, pp. 95–138.

Białostocki, Jan, *Dürer and his Critics, 1500–1971: Chapters in the History of Ideas, including a Collection of Texts*, Baden-Baden 1986.

Bianchini, Francesco, *La Istoria Universale provata con monumenti, e figurata con simbolo de gli antichi*, Rome 1697.

Bianchini, Giuseppe, *Dei Granduchi di Toscana della reale casa de' Medici Protettori delle Lettere, e delle Belle Arti, Ragionamenti Istorici*, Venice 1741.

Biasuz, Giuseppe, 'Carlo Patin medico e numismatico', *Bollettino dei Musei Civici di Padova*, 1957–8, pp. 67–116.

Bickendorf, Gabriele, *Der Beginn der Kunstgeschichtsschreibung unter dem paradigma 'Geschichte': Gustav Friedrich Waagens Frühschrift 'Ueber Hubert und Johann van Eyck'*, Worms 1985.

Bie, Jacques de, *Explication ou description sommaire des medailles contenuës en l'oeuvre de La France metallique*, Paris 1636.

Bie, Jacques de, *Les Vrais portraits des Rois de France tirez de ce qui nous reste de leurs Monumens, Sceaux, Médailles, ou autres Effigies, conservées dans les plus rares & plus curieux Cabinets du Royaume – seconde Edition – Augmentée de nouveaux Portraits, & enrichie des Vies des Rois, par le R.P.H. de Coste, Paris Relig. de l'Ordre des Peres Minimes*, Paris 1636.

Biet, J.-E., *Souvenirs du Musée des Monumens Français* (text by J.-P. Brès), Paris 1821–6.

Billanovich, Giuseppe, 'Nella Biblioteca del

Petrarca', *Italia Medioevale e Umanistica*, III, 1960, pp. 1–58.

Biographie Universelle Ancienne et Moderne (Michaud), 42 vols, Paris, 1842–65.

Blumenreich, Leo, *Verzeichnis der Schriften Max J. Friedländers*, Berlin 1927.

Blunt, Anthony, *Neapolitan Baroque and Rococo Architecture*, London 1975.

Bober, Phyllis Pray and Ruth Rubinstein, *Renaissance Artists and Antique Sculpture*, Oxford 1986.

Bofarull y Sans, Don Cárlos de, *Catalogo de la Exposición de Arte Antiguo, publicado por la junta municipal de Museos y Bellas Artes. Redactado por Don Cárlos de Bofarull y Sans, Director del Museo Arqueológico Municipal*, Barcelona 1902.

Boilly, 1761–1845: Un grand peintre français de la Révolution à la Restauration, Musée des Beaux-Arts, Lille 1988–9.

Bordes, Philippe, *Le Serment du Jeu de Paume de Jacques-Louis David*, Paris 1983.

Bordier, Henri et Edouard Charton, *Histoire de France depuis les temps les plus anciens jusqu'à nos jours d'après les documents originaux et les monuments de l'art de chaque époque*, 2 vols, Paris 1859–60.

Borsook, Eve, *The Mural Painters of Tuscany from Cimabue to Andrea del Sarto* (2nd edition), Oxford 1980.

Bos, Abbé Du, *Réflexions critiques sur la poësie et sur la peinture* (7th edition), 3 vols, Paris 1770 (reprinted Geneva 1967).

Bosio, Antonio, *Roma Sotterranea: opera postuma . . . compita, disposta, & accresciuta dal M.R.P. Giovanni Severani da S. Severino*, Rome 1634 [despite date of 1632 on title-page].

Bossuet, 'Discours sur l'histoire universelle', in *Oeuvres*, ed. l'Abbé Velat and Yvonne Champailler, Paris (Pléiade) 1961, pp. 665–1027.

[Bottari] *Sculture e pitture sagre estratte dai cimiterj di Roma pubblicate già dagli autori della Roma sotterranea ed ora nuovamente date in luce colle spiegazioni per ordine di N.S. Clemente XII felicemente regnante*, 3 vols, Rome 1737, 1746, 1754.

Bouchot, Henri, *Les Primitifs Français 1292–1500. Complément documentaire au catalogue officiel de l'Exposition*, Paris 1904.

Bowlt, John (ed. and trans.), *Russian Art of the Avant-Garde: Theory and Criticism 1902–1934*, New York 1976.

Braudel, Fernand, *La Méditerranée et le Monde Méditerranéen à l'Époque de Philippe II* (seconde edition revue et augmentée), 2 vols, Paris 1966.

Breventano, Angelo, *De Langobardorum Origine ac Regibus compendiosa narratio*, [Rome] 1593.

Bricon, Etienne, 'Bruges et l'art primitif flamand', *La Grande Revue*, 1 September 1902, pp. 689–705.

Brisac, Catherine, and Jean-Michel Léniaud, 'Adolphe-Napoléon Didron, ou les media au service de l'art chrétien', *Revue de l'Art*, LXXVII, 1987, pp. 33–42.

Broglie, Emmanuel de, *Bernard de Montfaucon et les Bernardins 1715–1750*, 2 vols, Paris 1891.

Broglie, Raoul de, *Inventaire des Collections Publiques Françaises – Institut de France*, 1: *Chantilly, Musée Condé, Peintures de l'École Française, XVe–XVIIe siècle*, unpaginated introduction, Paris 1970.

Brown, Elizabeth A.R., 'The Oxford collection of the drawings of Roger de Gaignières and the royal tombs of Saint-Denis', *Transactions of the American Philosophical Society*, LXXVIII, part 5, 1988, pp. 1–74.

Brown, Patricia Fortini, 'Painting and History in Renaissance Venice', *Art History*, VII, no. 3, September 1984, pp. 263–94.

Brown, Patricia Fortini, *Venetian Narrative Painting in the Age of Carpaccio*, New Haven and London 1988.

Brown, Shirley Ann, (with a contribution by Michael W. Herren), *The Bayeux Tapestry: History and Bibliography*, Bury St Edmunds (The Boydell Press) 1988.

Bruges: Compte Rendu des Travaux de la Quatrième Section du XVIe Congrés de la Fédération, Archéologique et Historique, Tenu à Bruges du 10 au 14 Août 1902: Les Primitifs de l'Exposition et le Congrés de Bruges, Bruges 1902.

Brumfitt, J.H., *Voltaire Historian*, Oxford 1958 (reprinted 1970).

Bruyne, Luciano De, *L'Antica Serie di Ritratti Papali della Basilica di S. Paolo fuori le Mura*, Rome 1934.

Buddensieg, Tilmann, 'Gregory the Great, the destroyer of pagan idols', *Journal of the Warburg and Courtauld Institutes*, XXVIII, 1965, pp. 44–65.

Bücher, Karl, 'Worte zum Gedächtnis an Karl Lamprecht', *Berichte über die Verhandlung der Königl. Sächsischen Gesellschaft der Wissenschaften su Leipzig: Philologisch-historische Klasse*, 67 Band, 1915, 3. Helf, Leipzig 1916, pp. 93–119.

Bürger, W., *Trésors d'Art en Angleterre* (3rd edition), Paris 1865.

Buiatti, A., 'Francesco Angeloni', in *Dizionario Biografico degli Italiani*, III (1961), pp. 241–2.

Bulstrode, Sir Richard, *Memoirs and Reflections upon the Reign and Government of King Charles the Ist and King Charles the II^d*, London 1721.

Bulwer, John, *Chirologia: or the Natural Language of the Hand* and *Chironomia: or the Art of Manual Rhetoricke*, London 1644.

[Buonarroti, Filippo], *Osservazioni istoriche sopra alcuni medaglioni antichi*, Rome 1698.

Buonarroti, Filippo, *Osservazioni sopra alcuni frammenti di vasi antichi di vetro ornati di figure trovati ne' cimiteri di Roma*, Florence 1716.

Burckhardt, Jacob, *Der Cicerone: Eine Anleitung zum Genuss der Kunstwerke Italiens*, Basel 1855.

Burckhardt, Jacob, *Die Cultur der Renaissance in Italien: Ein Versuch*, Basel 1860.

Burckhardt, Jacob, *Die Cultur der Renaissance in Italien* (zweite durchgeschene Auflage), Leipzig 1869.

Burckhardt, Jacob, *Gesamtausgabe*, 14 vols, Berlin and Leipzig 1929–33.

Burckhardt, Jacob, *The Architecture of the Italian Renaissance*, ed. Peter Murray, Harmondsworth 1987.

Burckhardt, Jacob, *The Civilization of the Renaissance in Italy*, trans. S.G.C. Middlemore, Harmondsworth 1990.

Burian, Peter, 'Das Germanische National-museum und die deutsche Nation', in Bernard Deneke and Rainer Kahsnitz (ed.), *Der Germanische Nationalmuseum Nürnberg 1852–1977*, Munich and Berlin 1978, pp. 127–262.

Burn, W.L., *The Age of Equipoise*, London 1964 (reprinted 1968).

Burnett, Andrew, Michel Amandry and Père Pau Ripolles, *Roman Provincial Coinage*, London and Paris, I, 1992.

Burtin, P.-M., Nicolas, *Un semeur d'idées au temps de la Restauration: le Baron d'Eckstein*, Paris 1931.

Busch, Renate von, *Studien zu deutschen Antiken-sammlungen des 16 Jahrhunderts*, Tübingen 1973.

Buschmann, P., Juniore, 'L'esposizione dei pri-mitivi fiaminghi a Bruggia', *Emporium*, November 1902, pp. 331–58.

[Bussières, Jean de], *Flosculi historici delibati nunc delibatiores redditi, sive Historia Universalis . . .* (2nd edition), Cologne 1656 [the first edition was published in Lyons in 1649].

Buttrey, T.V., 'The *Spintriae* as a Historical Source', *The Numismatic Chronicle*, 1973, pp. 52–63.

Campbell, Lorne, *Renaissance Portraits: European Portrait-Painting in the 14th, 15th and 16th Centuries*, New Haven and London 1990.

Campori, Giuseppe, *Lettere artistiche inedite*, Modena 1866 (anastatic reprint, Bologna 1975).

Campori, Giuseppe, 'Enea Vico e l'antico

museo estense delle medaglie', *Atti e Memorie delle RR Deputazioni di Storia patria per le provincie modenesi e parmensi*, VII, 1874, pp. 37–45.

Cariola, Antonio, *Ritratti de Ser^mi Principi d'Este Sig^ri di Ferrara – con l'aggiunta de loro fatti più memorabili. Ridotti in sommario dal Sr Antonio Cariola. Al Ser^mo Alfonso IV Principe di Modona*. Ferrara 1641.

Castellani, Giuseppe, 'Annibale Caro numis-matico', *Rivista italiano di numismatica*, XV, 1907, pp. 311–31.

Cavallero, Anna, 'Gli affreschi delle "historie di Traiano" nel palazzo Santorio presso S. Maria in Via Lata – Precisazioni sulle fonti', *Storia dell' Arte*, 1983, pp. 163–7.

Caylus, comte de, *Recueil d'Antiquités Egyp-tiennes, Etrusques, Grecques et Romaines*, 7 vols, Paris 1752, 1756, 1759, 1761, 1762, 1764, 1767.

Chabod, Federico, 'Paolo Giovio', in *Scritti sul Rinascimento*, Turin 1974, pp. 241–67.

Champfleury, *Histoire des faiences patriotiques sous la Révolution*, (2nd edition), Paris 1867.

Champfleury, *Histoire de l'imagerie populaire*, Paris 1869.

Champfleury, *Histoire de la caricature moderne* (2ème edition, très-augmentée), Paris [1872].

Champfleury, *Histoire de la caricature au moyen âge et sous la renaissance* (2ème edition, très-augmentée), Paris [1876].

Champfleury, *Histoire de la caricature antique* (3ème edition, très-augmentée), Paris [1879].

Chandler, George, *William Roscoe of Liverpool*, introduction by Sir Alfred Sherman, London 1953.

Chastel, André, *The Sack of Rome, 1527*, Prince-ton 1983.

Chateaubriand, *Génie du Christianisme*, ed. Maurice Regard, Paris (Pléiade) 1978.

Chennevieres, Philippe de, 'Le Comte Léon de Laborde', in *Souvenirs d'un Directeur des Beaux-Arts*, IV, pp. 42–68 reprinted Paris (Arthena) 1979.

Chesneau, Ernest, *Les Nations Rivales dans l'Art*, Paris 1868.

Chipp, Herchel B., *Theories of Modern Art*, Uni-versity of California Press 1968.

Choul, Guillaume du, *Discours de la religion des anciens romains . . . illustré de médailles & figures retirées des marbres antiques qui se treuvent à Rome, & par nostre Gaule*, Lyon 1567.

Choul, Guillaume du, *Des Antiquités romaines. Premier Livre faict par le commandement du Roy par M. Guillaume Choul, Lionnoys Conseiller du dict Seigneur et Bailly des Mōtagnes du Daulphine*, MS Biblioteca Reale, Turin.

Choul, Guillaume du, *Des Bains et de la Palestre*,

MS in Bibliothèque Nationale, Paris.

Ciampini, Giovanni, *Vetera Monimenta in quibus paecipuè musiva opera sacrarum, profanarumque aedium structura, ac nonnulli antiqui Ritus, Dissertationibus Iconibusque illustrantur*, 2 vols, Rome 1690, 1699.

Cicognara, Leopoldo, *Storia della Scultura dal suo risorgimento in Italia*, 3 vols, Venice (1813, 1816, 1818).

Cicognara, Leopoldo, *Lettere ad Antonio Canova*, ed. Gianni Venturi, Urbino 1973.

Clark, Robert T., Jr., *Herder – His Life and Thought*, Berkeley and Los Angeles, 1955.

Clegg, Jeanne, *Ruskin and Venice*, London 1981.

Les Clouet & la Cour des Rois de France, exhibition catalogue, Paris (Bibliothèque Nationale) 1970.

Clubb, Louise George, *Giambattista Della Porta Dramatist*, Princeton 1965.

Cochrane, Eric, *Florence in the forgotten centuries, 1527–1800*, Chicago and London 1973.

Cochrane, Eric, *Historians and Historiography in the Italian Renaissance*, Chicago and London 1985.

Coffin, David R., 'Pirro Ligorio and decoration of the late sixteenth century at Ferrara', *Art Bulletin*, XXXVII, 1955, pp. 167–85.

Cohen, Henry, *Description historique des monnaies frappées sous l'Empire Romain*, 8 vols, Paris and London, 1880–92.

Colie, R.L., 'Johan Huizinga and the Task of Cultural History', *The American Historical Review*, LXIX, no. 3, April 1964, pp. 607–30.

Colvin, H.M., 'Aubrey's *Chronologia Architectonica*', in *Concerning Architecture: Essays presented to Nikolaus Pevsner*, ed. John Summerson, London 1968, pp. 1–12.

Compton, Michael, 'William Roscoe and Early Collectors of Italian Primitives', *The Liverpool Libraries, Museums and Arts Committee Bulletin*, Walker Art Gallery, IX, 1960–1, pp. 27–51.

Courajod, Louis, *Alexandre Lenoir – Son Journal et le Musée des Monuments Français*, 3 vols, Paris 1878–1887; II, pp. 1–18: 'L'influence du Musée des Monuments français sur le développement de l'art et des études historiques pendant la première moitié du dix-neuvième siècle'.

Courajod, Louis, review of Burckhardt's *Cicerone*, *La Chronique des Arts*, 1884, p. 62.

Courajod, Louis, *Leçons professées à l'École du Louvre (1887–1896)* publiées sous la direction de M.M. Henry Lemonnier et André Michel, 3 vols, Paris 1899, 1901, 1903.

Creighton, Mrs, *Life and Letters of Mandell Creighton*, 2 vols, London 1904.

Cristofani, Mauro, *La Scoperta degli Etruschi – Archeologia e Antiquaria nel '700*, Rome 1983.

'Critès', *Troisième Promenade de Critès au Sallon* (Deloynes, XIV, no. 335), Paris 1785.

Croce, Benedetto, 'Il "Linguaggio dei Gesti"', in *Varietà di Storia Letteraria e Civile*, serie prima, Bari 1935, pp. 271–80.

Cronica Breve de i fatti illustri de' Re di Francia, con le loro Effigie dal naturale, cominciando da Faramondo..., Venice 1588.

Crowe, J.A., and G.B. Cavalcaselle, *The Early Flemish Painters: Notices of Their Lives and Works*, London 1857.

Crowe, J.A., and G.B. Cavalcaselle, *The Early Flemish Painters: Notices of Their Lives and Works* (2nd edition), London 1872.

Cunnally, John, *The Role of Greek and Roman Coins in the Art of the Italian Renaissance, 1984*, U.M.I. 1988.

Curtius, Ernst, *The History of Greece*, trs. A.W. Ward, 5 vols, London 1868–73.

Curtius, Ernst Robert, *Französischer Geist in zwanzigsten Jahrhundert*, Berne 1952.

Daniel, Père G., *Histoire de France depuis l'établissement de la monarchie françoise dans les Gaules*, 3 vols, Paris 1713.

Dares Phrygius, *L'Histoire veritable de la guerre des Grecs, et des Troyens*, tr. C. de Bourgueville from the Latin of C. Nepos, Caen 1572.

Daru, P., *Histoire de la République de Venise* (seconde édition, revue et corrigée), 8 vols, Paris 1821.

Dattari, G., *Monete Imperiali Greche – Numi Augg. Alexandrini*, 2 vols, Cairo 1901.

David, Jacques-Louis, exhibition catalogue by Antoine Schnapper, Paris (Grand Palais) 1989–90.

De David à Delacroix – La peinture française de 1774 à 1830, exhibition catalogue, Paris (Grand Palais) 1974–5.

Davis, Miles T., review of English translation of Georges Duby, 'The Age of the Cathedrals: Art and Society, 980–1420', *Journal of the Society of Architectural Historians*, XLI, no. 2, May 1982, pp. 156–8.

Davis, Whitney M., 'Plato on Egyptian Art', *The Journal of Egyptian Archaeology*, 1979, pp. 121–7.

Defoe, Daniel, *A Tour thro' the whole Island of Great Britain*, ed. with an introduction by G.D.H. Cole, 2 vols, London 1927 (I: 1724, II: 1725, III: 1727).

Dehaisnes, M. le Chanoine, *Histoire de l'Art dans la Flandre, l'Artois & le Hainaut avant le XVe siècle*, Lille 1886.

Dekesel, C.E., *Hubertus Goltzius – The father of ancient numismatics*, Ghent 1988.

Dekesel, C.E., *Charles Patin – A man without a*

country (an annotated and illustrated bibliography), Ghent 1990.

Delécluze, E-J., *Louis David, son école et son temps*, Paris 1855.

Deloynes, *Catalogue de la collection de pièces sur les Beaux-Arts . . . recueillie par . . . M. Deloynes*, ed. Georges Duplessis, Paris 1881.

Deneke, Bernward, and Rainer Kahsnitz (eds), *Das Kunst – und Kulturgeschichtliche Museum im 19. Jahrhundert – Vorträge des Symposions im Germanischen National Museum, Nürnberg*, Munich 1977.

Deneke, Bernward, and Rainer Kahsnitz (eds), *Das Germanische Nationalmuseum Nürnberg 1852–1977*, Munich and Berlin 1978.

Deprez, Eugène, 'L'Exposition des Primitifs Flamands à Bruges', *Le Correspondant*, 25 July 1902, pp. 348–58.

Descamps, J.B., *Voyage pittoresque de la Flandre et du Brabant, Avec des Réflexions relativement aux Arts et quelques Gravures*, Paris 1769.

Deseine, *Opinion sur les Musées où se trouvent retenus tous les objets d'arts qui sont la propriété des temples consacrés à la religion catholique*, Paris 1801; republished in Deseine, *Notices Historiques sur les anciennes académies royales de peinture, sculpture de Paris, et celle d'architecture*, Paris 1814, pp. 233–312.

D'Israeli, Isaac, *Commentaries on the Life and Reign of Charles the First, King of England*, 3 vols, London 1830.

Dogaer, Georges, *Flemish miniature painting in the 15th and 16th centuries*, Amsterdam 1987.

Donatello, *Omagio a Donatello, 1386–1986: Donatello e la Storia del Museo*, Florence (Museo Nazionale del Bargello) 1985.

Dorbec, Prosper, 'De l'École de Droit à l'École du Louvre vers 1895', *1882–1932 l'École du Louvre*, ed. Henri Verne and others, Paris 1932, pp. 81–4.

Dorson, Richard M., *Peasant Customs and Savage Myths*, 2 vols, London 1968.

Duchesne, François, *Histoire de tous les Cardinaux Français de naissance . . . enrichie de leurs armes et de leurs portraits*, 2 vols, Paris 1660.

Dülberg, Franz, 'Die Ausstellung Altniederländischer Meister in Brügge', *Zeitschrift für bildende Kunst, mit dem Beiblatt Kunstchronik*, 1903, pp. 49–57, 135–42; 1904, pp. 187–94.

Dunn, W.H., *James Anthony Froude – A biography*, 2 vols, Oxford 1963.

Duplessis, Georges, 'Roger de Gaignières et ses collections iconographiques', *Gazette des Beaux-Arts*, 1870, I, pp. 468–88.

Duplessis, Georges, *Inventaire de la collection d'estampes relatives à l'histoire de France léguée en 1863 à la Bibliothèque Nationale par M. Michel Hennin*, 5 vols, Paris 1877–84.

Durand-Greville, E., 'L'Exposition des Primitifs Flamands à Bruges', *Journal de St. Petersbourg*, 1902, pp. 1–17.

Dvořák, Max, *Kunstgeschichte als Geistesgeschichte*, Munich 1928.

Dvořák, Max, *The History of Art as the History of Ideas*, trs. John Harvey, London 1984.

Dyer, Charles George, *Biographical Sketches of the Lives and Characters of Illustrious and Eminent Men, Illustrated with whole length portraits*, London 1819.

Ebeling, Friedrich W., see Flögel, Karl Friedrich.

Effigies regum francorum omnium, a Pharamundo, ad Ludovicum XIII, usque, ad vivum, quantum fieri potuit, expressae, Francofurti, In Bibliopolio Jacobi de Zetter, Anno 1622.

Eliel, Carol, *The Apocalyptic Landscapes of Ludwig Meidner*, Los Angeles County Museum of Art 1989.

English, Donald E., 'Political Photography and the Paris Commune of 1871: the Photographs of Eugène Appert', *History of Photography*, VII, no. 1, January 1983, pp. 31–42.

English Romanesque Art 1066–1200, exhibition catalogue, London (Hayward Gallery) 1984.

Epitome des Gestes de cinquante huict roys de France, depuis Pharamonde iusque au present très Chrestien François de Valoys, A. Lyon, par Balthazar Arnoullet, 1546.

Erizzo, Sebastiano, *Discorso sopra le medaglie de gli antichi* (Di nuovo in questa quarta Editione dall' istesso Authore revisto, et ampliato), Venice, n.d.

Erlande-Brandenburg, Alain, 'Le Musée des Monuments français et les origines du Musée de Cluny' in Deneker, Bernward, and Rainer Kahsnitz (eds), *Das Kunst-und Kulturgeschichtliche Museum im 19 Jahrhundert*, Munich 1977, pp. 49–58.

L'espion des peintres de l'Académie royale Année 1785 (Deloynes, XIV, no. 337), Paris 1785.

L'Etruria Pittrice ovvero storia della pittura toscana dedotta dai suoi monumenti che si esibiscono in Stampa dal secolo X fino al presente, 2 vols, Florence 1791 and 1795.

Evans, David Owen, *Le Socialisme Romantique – Pierre Leroux et ses Contemporains*, Paris 1948.

Evans, Joan, *A History of the Society of Antiquaries*, Oxford 1956.

Evans, Wilfred Hugo, *L'Historien Mézeray et la conception de l'Histoire en France au XVIIᵉ siècle*, Paris 1930.

Evelyn, John, *Numismata*, London 1697.

Fabretti, R., *De Columna Traiani Syntagma*, Rome 1683.

Farinella, Vincenzo, 'Jacopo Ripanda a Palazzo Santoro – un ciclo di storia romana e le sue fonti classiche', *Studi Classici e Orientali*,

XXXVI, Università degli Studi di Pisa 1986.

Febvre, Lucien, 'Comment Jules Michelet inventa la Renaissance', 1950, reprinted in *Pour une Histoire 'à part entière'*, Paris 1962, pp. 717–29.

Fehl, Philipp P., 'Vasari and the Arch of Constantine', *Giorgio Vasari – tra decorazione ambientale e storiografia artistica*, convegno di studi (ed. G.C. Garfagnini), 1985, pp. 27–44.

Ferté, H., *Rollin – Sa vie, ses œuvres et l'université de son temps*, Paris 1902.

Ficoroni, F., *Osservazioni di Francesco de' Ficoroni sopra l'Antichità di Roma; descritte nel Diario Italico Publicato in Parigi l'anno 1702 Dal M. Rev. padre D. Bernardo de Montfaucon, nel fine delle quali s'aggiungono molte cose antiche singolari scoperte ultimamente tra le rovine dell' antichità*. In Roma Nella Stamperia di Antonio de' Rossi alla Piazza di Ceri, 1709.

Fierens-Gevaert, H., *Psychologie d'Une Ville – Essai sur Bruges*, Paris 1901.

Fierens-Gevaert, H., 'L'exposition des Primitifs Flamands à Bruges', *Revue de l'Art Ancien et Moderne*, 1902, pp. 105–16, pp. 173–82, pp. 435–44.

Fierens-Gevaert, H., *Essai sur l'Art Contemporain* (2ème édition revue (1st edition 1897)), Paris 1903.

Fierens-Gevaert, H., *Études sur l'Art Flamand. La Renaissance Septentrionale et les premiers maîtres des Flandres*, Brussels 1905.

Filarete, *Treatise on Architecture*, trs. with an introduction and notes by John R. Spencer, 2 vols, New Haven and London, 1965.

Firth, C.H., 'The "Memoirs" of Sir Richard Bulstrode', *English Historical Review*, 1895, pp. 266–75.

Fischart, Johann, *Werke – eine Auswahl*, ed. Adolf Hauffen, 3 vols, Stuttgart 1895.

Fittschen, Klaus, 'Sul ruolo del ritratto antico nell'arte italiana', in Settis, *Memoria*, II, pp. 383–412.

Fleming, John, *Robert Adam and his Circle in Edinburgh and Rome*, London 1962.

Flögel, Karl Friedrich, *Geschichte des Grotesk-Komischen* (Neu bearbeitet und erweitert von Dr. Friedrich W. Ebeling), Leipzig 1862.

Forceville, E. de, 'Les Primitifs Flamands à Bruges', *Études – revue fondée en 1856 par des Pères de la Compagnie de Jésus*, 5 October 1902, pp. 76–84.

Foucart, Bruno, 'La fortune critique d'Alexandre Lenoir et du premier Musée des Monuments Français', *L'Information d'Histoire de l'Art*, November–December 1969, pp. 223–32.

Francastel, Pierre, *Frontières du Gothique* (2nd edition), Paris 1971.

Frankl, Paul, *The Gothic – Literary Sources and Interpretations through Eight Centuries*, Princeton 1960.

Frantz, Henri, 'L'Exposition des Primitifs Flamands à Bruges', *Les Arts*, August 1902, pp. 27–34.

Franzoni, Lanfranco, 'Il Diomede in metallo corinzio già nel museo maffeiano di Verona', *Aquileia Nostra*, XLV–XLVI, 1974–5, pp. 552–64.

Franzoni, Lanfranco, 'Le origini della raccolta epigrafica dell'Accademia Filarmonica', in *L'Accademia Filarmonica di Verona e il suo teatro*, Verona 1982, pp. 63–88.

Franzoni, Lanfranco, 'Origine e storia del Museo Lapidario Maffeiano', *Il Museo Maffeiano riaperto al pubblico*, 1982, pp. 29–72.

Franzoni, Lanfranco, 'Il Museo Maffeiano secondo l'ordinamento di Scipione Maffei', *Atti del Convegno Scipione Maffei e il Museo Maffeiano*, (Verona 1983), Verona 1985, pp. 207–32.

Fraser, T.L., *Ancient Greek Painting – being a Translation from Rollin's Ancient History*, London 1901.

Freedberg, David, and Jan de Vries (eds) *Art in History – History in Art – Studies in Seventeenth-Century Dutch Culture*, Getty Center for the Arts and Humanities 1991.

Freeman, Edward A., *The History of the Norman Conquest of England, its causes and results*, 6 vols, Oxford 1867–79 (III, pp. 563–75: 'The authority of the Bayeux Tapestry').

Friedländer, Max J., 'Die Brügger Leihausstellung von 1902', *Repertorium für Kunstwissenschaft*, XXVI, 1903, pp. 66–91, 147–75.

Friedländer, Max J., *Meisterwerke der Niederländischen Malerei des XV u XVI Jahrhunderts auf der Ausstellung zu Brügge 1902*, Munich 1903.

Friedländer, Max J., *Albrecht Dürer*, Leipzig 1921.

Friedländer, Max J., *Early Netherlandish Painting*, trs. Heinz Norden, Leyden–Brussels, 14 vols, 1967–76.

Friedländer, Max J., *Reminiscences and Reflections*, London 1969.

Le Frondeur ou Dialogues sur le Sallon par l'auteur du Coup-de-patte et du Triumvirat – 1785, (Deloynes, XIV, no. 329), Paris 1785.

Frugoni, Chiara, 'L'antichità: dai *Mirabilia* all propaganda politica', in Settis, *Memoria*, I, pp. 5–72.

Fučiková, Eliška, 'Einige Erwägungen zum Werk des Jacopo und Ottavio Strada', *Leids Kunsthistorisch Jaarboek*, 1982, pp. 339–53.

Fulco, Giorgio, 'Per il "Museo" dei Fratelli della Porta', in *Rinascimento Meridionale e altri Studi: raccolta di studi pubblicata in onore di*

Mario Santoro, ed. M.C. Cafisse, Naples 1987, pp. 105–75.

Fulvio, Andrea, *Illustrium Imagines*, Roma G. Mazzocchi 1517; reprinted and ed. Roberto Pelli, with preface by Roberto Weiss, Rome 1967.

Fusco, Maria Antonella, 'I musei della storia', *Prospettive Settanta*, IV, 1984, pp. 454–9.

Fuseli, Henry, *The Collected English Letters*, ed. David H. Weinglass, New York, London, Liechtenstein 1982.

Gaehtgens, Thomas W., *Versailles – de la Résidence Royale au Musée Historique: La Galerie des Batailles dans le Musée Historique de Louis-Philippe*, Antwerp 1984.

Galassi Paluzzi, C., *Storia Segreta dello Stile dei Gesuiti*, Rome 1951.

Galichon, Emile, 'Exposition de Tableaux Primitifs à Bruges', *Gazette des Beaux-Arts*, 1867 (2), pp. 483–8.

Gallo, Daniela (ed.), *Filippo Buonarroti e la cultura antiquaria sotto gli ultimi Medici*, exhibition catalogue (Casa Buonarroti), Florence 1986.

Galluzzi, Jacopo Riguccio, *Istoria del granducato di Toscana sotto il governo dela casa Medici*, 5 vols, Florence 1781.

Gardiner, Anne Barbeau, 'The Medal that provoked a War – Charles II's lasting indignation over Adolfzoon's Breda Medal', *The Medal*, no. 17, 1990, pp. 11–15.

Gardiner, C. Harvey, *W.H. Prescott – A biography*, Austin and London, 1969.

Garland, H.B., *Schiller*, London 1949.

Garnier, Jacques, *Faïences patriotiques* (vol. II of *Rue de la Révolution: Images populaires de la Révolution française. Faïences et Estampes*), exhibition catalogue, Nevers 1989.

Gaspar, Camille, and Frédéric Lyna, *Les principaux manuscrits à peinture de la Bibliothèque Royale de Belgique*, 2 vols, Paris 1937.

Gaston, Robert W., 'British Travellers and Scholars in the Roman Catacombs', *Journal of the Warburg and Courtauld Institutes*, XLVI, 1983, pp. 144–65.

Genebrier, Claude, *Histoire de Carausius, Empereur de la Grande-Bretagne, collègue de Dioclétien et de Maximien. Prouvée par les Médailles*, Paris 1740.

Gennep, Arnold van, *Manuel de folklore francais contemporain*, 4 vols in 9, Paris 1937–58.

Germiny, L. de, 'Une visite à l'exposition de Bruges', *Les Echos de Sta. Chiara*, no. 20, 1902, pp. 93–102.

Gerson, H., 'Huizinga und die Kunstgeschichte', in *Johan Huizinga 1872–1972*, pp. 206–22.

Ghelardi, Maurizio, *La scoperta del Rinascimento: L' 'Età di Raffaello' di Jacob Burckhardt*, Turin 1991.

Ghiberti, Lorenzo, *Denkwürdigkeiten (I Commentarii)*, ed. Julius von Schlosser, 2 vols, Berlin 1912.

Ghilhermy, Ferdinand de, 'Musée du Sculpture au Louvre', *Annales Archéologiques*, XII, 1852, pp. 14–23, 84–96, 239–49; 294–9; XIII, 1853, pp. 125–33, 249–56; XIV, 1854, pp. 17–24, 88–94, 249–62, 316–28, 353–60.

Giannone, Pietro, *Istoria Civilie del regno di Napoli . . . Con accrescimento di Note, Riflessioni, Medaglie, e moltissime Correzioni, date e fatte dall' Autore, e che non si trovano nella Prima Edizione*, 4 vols, The Hague 1753.

Giannone, Pietro, 'Vita di Pietro Giannone scritta in Savoia nel castello di Miolans da lui medesimo e continuata nella Liguria nel castello di Ceva', in *Opere di Pietro Giannone*, ed. Sergio Bertelli and Giuseppe Ricuperati, Milan–Naples, 1971, pp. 3–346.

Giard, Jean-Baptiste, 'Critique de la Science des Monnaies Antiques', *Journal des Savants*, 1980, pp. 225–45.

Gibbon, Edward, *Miscellaneous Works*, ed. Lord Sheffield, 2 vols, London 1796.

Gibbon, Edward, *History of the Decline and Fall of the Roman Empire*, ed. J.B. Bury, 7 vols, London 1896–8.

Gibbon, Edward, *Le journal de Gibbon à Lausanne, 17 Août 1763–19 Avril 1764*, ed. Georges Bonnard, Lausanne 1945.

Gibbon, Edward, *Miscellanea Gibboniana* ['Journal de mon voyage dans quelques endroits de la Suisse', 1755 – publié d'après le manuscrit original inédit par G.R. de Beer & G.A. Bonnard. 'Le Séjour de Gibbon à Paris du 28 Janvier au 9 Mai 1763' – trois morceaux en fin du quatrième cahier de son journal publiés par George A. Bonnard. 'La Lettre de Gibbon sur le gouvernement de Berne', publiée par Louis Junod], Lausanne 1952.

Gibbon, Edward, *Journey from Geneva to Rome: His Journal from 20 April to 2 October 1764*, ed. Georges A. Bonnard, London 1961.

Gibbon, Edward, *Memoirs of my Life*, ed. with an introduction by Betty Radice, Harmondsworth (Penguin Books) 1984.

Gibson, Robin, *Catalogue of Portraits in the collection of the Earl of Clarendon*, published privately by the Paul Mellon Centre for Studies in British Art, London 1977.

Gilio, Giovanni Andrea, *Degli errori e degli abusi de' pittori circa l'istorie*, Camerino 1564, in Paola Barocchi (ed.) *Trattati d'Arte del Cinquecento*, Bari 1961, pp. 1–115.

Gillies, John, *The History of Ancient Greece, its colonies, and conquests; From the Earliest Ac-*

counts till the Division of the Macedonian Empire in the East. Including the History of Literature, Philosophy, and the Fine Arts, 2 vols, London 1786.

Ginzburg, Carlo, 'Fiction as Historical Evidence: A Dialogue in Paris, 1646', *Yale Journal of Criticism*, v, no. 2, 1992, pp. 165–78.

Giovio, Paolo, *La prima parte delle historie del suo tempo, Tradotte per M. Lodovico Domenichi*, Venice 1555.

Giovio, Paolo, *Pauli Jovii Novocomensis Episcopi Nucerini, Elogia Virorum bellica virtute illustrium, Septem libris jam olim ab Authore comprehensa, Et nunc ex eiusdem Musaeo ad vivum expressis Imaginibus exornata*, Basel 1575.

Giovio, Paolo, *Pauli Jovii Novocomensis Episcopi Nucerini, Elogia Virorum literis illustrium, quotquot vel nostra vel avorum memoria vixere. Ex eiusdem Musaeo (cuius descriptionem unà exhibemus) ad vivum expressis Imaginibus exornata*, Basel 1577.

Globe, Alexander, *Peter Stent – London Printseller circa 1642–1665*, Vancouver 1985.

Gluck, Denise, 'L'Académie Celtique et le Musée des Monuments Français: l'idée de sauvegarde', in *Hier pour demain – Arts, Traditions et Patrimoine*, exhibition catalogue, Paris (Grand Palais) 1980, pp. 65–6.

Goethe, *Von deutscher Baukunst (1772). Goethes Werke*, ed. Eric Trunz, 14 vols, Munich 1981: xii, pp. 7–15.

Goethe, *On Art*, sel. ed. and trs. John Gage, London 1980.

Gogh, Vincent Van, *The Complete Letters*, 3 vols, London 1958.

Goldwater, Robert, *Primitivism in Modern Art* (revised edition), New York 1967.

Goltz, Hubert, *Vivae Omnium fere Imperatorum Imagines, a C. Julio Caes. usque ad Carolum V et Ferdinandum eius fratrem, ex antiquis veterum numismatis . . . adumbratae*, Antwerp 1557.

Goltz, Hubert, *C. Julius Caesar sive historiae Imperatorum Caesarumque Romanorum ex antiquis numismatibus restitutae*, Bruges 1563.

Golzio, Vincenzo, *Raffaello nei documenti, nelle testimonianze dei contemporanei e nella letteratura del suo secolo*, Vatican City 1936.

Gombrich, E.H., *Meditations on a Hobby Horse and Other Essays on the Theory of Art*, London 1963.

Gombrich, E.H., *In Search of Cultural History*, Oxford 1969.

Gombrich, E.H., *Aby Warburg – An intellectual biography*, London 1970.

Gombrich, E.H., *The Ideas of Progress and their Impact on Art*, New York 1971.

Gombrich, E.H., 'Action and Expression in Western Art', in *Non-Verbal Communication*,

ed. R.A. Hinde, Cambridge 1972, pp. 373–93.

Goncourt, Edmond and Jules de, *Journal – Mémoires de la vie littéraire*, 4 vols, Paris 1956.

Gossman, Lionel, *Medievalism and the Ideologies of the Enlightenment. The World and Work of La Curne de Sainte-Palaye*, Baltimore 1968.

Le 'Gothique' retrouvé avant Viollet-le-Duc, exhibition at Hôtel de Sully, Paris 1979–80.

Graham, John, *Lavater's Essays on Physiognomy – A Study in the History of Ideas*, Berne 1979.

Grant, Michael, *Roman History from Coins – some uses of the Imperial Coinage to the Historian*, Cambridge 1968.

Grassi Fiorentino, S., 'Giovanni Giustino Ciampini', in *Dizionario Biografico degli Italiani*, xxv, 1981, pp. 136–43.

Greatheed, Bertie, *An Englishman in Paris: 1803*, ed. J.P.T. Bury and J.C. Barry, London 1953.

Greene, Christopher M., 'Alexandre Lenoir and the Musée des monuments français during the French Revolution', *French Historical Studies*, xii, spring 1981, pp. 200–22.

Gregorius, Master, *The Marvels of Rome*, trs. with an introduction and commentary by John Osborne, Toronto 1987. (See also Rushforth.)

Griffin, Miriam T., *Nero: The End of a Dynasty*, London 1984.

Grochowiak, Thomas, *Ludwig Meidner*, Recklinghausen 1966.

Groër, Anne de, 'Nouvelles recherches sur Corneille, à la lumière du Portrait de Pierre Aymeric', *La Revue du Louvre*, 1978, pp. 36–42.

Guenée, Bernard, 'Les grandes chroniques de France: le Roman aux roys (1274–1518)', in Pierre Nora (ed.), *Les Lieux de Mémoire*, ii (La Nation*), Paris 1986, pp. 189–214.

Guerrini, Isa Angrisani, *Quinet e l'Italia*, Geneva-Paris 1981.

Guyon, B., 'Une revue romantique inconnue: *Le Gymnase*', *Revue de Littérature Comparée*, 1931, pp. 314–21.

Haac, Oscar A., *Les principes inspirateurs de Michelet*, Paris 1951.

Hale, J.R., *England and the Italian Renaissance* (revised edition), London 1963.

Hale, J.R., *Artists and Warfare in the Renaissance*, New Haven and London 1990.

Harder, Hermann, *Le President de Brosses et le voyage en Italie au dix-huitième siècle*, Geneva 1981.

Harris, R.W., *Clarendon and the English Revolution*, London 1983.

Harvard College Library, Department of Painting and Graphic Arts, *Catalogue of Books and Manuscripts, part 1: French 16th-Century Books*, compiled by Ruth Mortimer, under the supervision of Philip Hofer and William A. Jackson, 2 vols, Cambridge, Mass. 1964.

Haskell, Francis, 'The Uses and Abuses of Art History', *The New York Review of Books*, 17 March 1977, pp. 6–10.

Haskell, Francis, 'Cicognara eretico' in *Jappelli e il suo tempo: Atti del Convegno Internazionale di Studi*, 1977, ed. Giuliana Mazzi, 2 vols, Padua 1982, pp. 217–25.

Haskell, Francis, 'Les musées et leurs ennemis', *Actes de la Recherche en sciences sociales*, XLIX, September 1983, pp. 103–6.

Haskell, Francis, *The Painful Birth of the Art Book*, London 1987.

Haskell, Francis, 'Scholars and images in France and Italy', in *'Il se rendit en Italie': études offertes à André Chastel*, Rome and Paris 1987, pp. 515–19.

Haskell, Francis, 'Gibbon and the History of Art', reprinted in *Past and Present in Art and Taste*, New Haven and London, 1987, pp. 16–29.

Haskell, Francis, 'Visual Sources and *The Embarrassment of Riches*', *Past and Present*, no. 120, August 1988, pp. 216–26.

Haskell, Francis, 'Winckelmann et son influence sur les historiens', in *Winckelmann: la naissance de l'histoire de l'art à l'époque des lumières*, ed. Edouard Pommier, cycle de conférences . . . au Louvre, Paris 1991, pp. 85–99.

Haskell, Francis, and Nicholas Penny, *Taste and the Antique* (2nd printing with corrections), New Haven and London 1982.

Hearne, Thomas, *The Remains of Thomas Hearne – Reliquae Hearnianae. Being extracts from his MS diaries*, compiled by Dr. John Bliss (revised by John Buchanan-Brown), London 1966.

Hegel, G.W.F., *Aesthetics – Lectures on Fine Art*, trs. T.M. Knox, 2 vols, Oxford 1975 (reprinted 1988).

Hegel, G.W.F., *Introduction to the Lectures on the History of Philosophy* trs. T.M. Knox and A.V. Miller, Oxford 1985.

Heikamp, Detlef, 'La Galleria degli Uffizi descritta e disegnata', in *Gli Uffizi – quattro secoli di una galleria: Atti del Convegno Internazionale di Studi*, 1982, ed. Paola Barocchi and Giovanna Ragionieri, 2 vols, Florence 1983, II, pp. 461–541.

Helbig, Jules, 'Les anciens maîtres flamands à l'Exposition de Bruges', *Revue de l'Art Chrétien*, September 1902, pp. 365–73.

Henfrey, Henry William, *Numismata Cromwelliana: or, The Medallic Illustrations of Oliver Cromwell*, London 1877.

Hennin, M., *Les Monuments de l'Histoire de France – catalogue des productions de la sculpture, de la peinture et de la gravure relatives à l'histoire de la France et des Français*, 10 vols, Paris 1856–63.

Herder, John Godfrey [Johann Gottfried von], *Outlines of a Philosophy of the History of Man*, trs. from the German by T. Churchill (2nd edition), 2 vols, London 1803.

Herder, Johann Gottfried von, *Sämmtliche Werke*, 33 vols, Berlin 1877–1913.

Herder, Johann Gottfried von, *Briefe*, ed. William Dobbek and Gunther Arnold, 9 vols, Weimar 1977–88.

Herder, Johann Gottfried von, *Auch eine Philosophie der Geschichte. Une autre philosophie de l'Histoire pour contribuer à l'éducation de l'Humanité – contribution a beaucoup de contributions du siècle* [German and French texts], trs. with notes and introduction by Max Rouché, Collection Bilingue, Aubrer n.d.

Herklotz, Ingo, '*Historia Sacra*' und mittelalterliche Kunst während der zweitern Hälfte des 16. Jahrhunderts in Rom in *Baronio e l'Arte*, pp. 21–74.

Hermant, Daniel, 'Destructions et Vandalisme pendant la Révolution Française', *Annales*, July–August 1978, no. 4, pp. 703–19.

Hewison, Robert, *Ruskin and Venice*, London 1978.

Hill, George Francis, *The Medallic Portraits of Christ – the false shekels – the thirty pieces of silver*, Oxford 1920.

Hill, George Francis, *A Corpus of Italian Medals of the Renaissance before Cellini*, 2 vols, London 1930.

Hinks, Roger, *Carolingian Art*, Ann Arbor 1962.

[Hofmann], *Der Könige in Frankreich, Leben, Regierung und Absterben: aus bewehrten Franzozischen Geschicht=Schreiben ubersezet und bis auf instehendes 1671 Jahr continuirt und samst ihren Bildissen nach Boissevins Conterfaten, zu finden bey Johann Hofmann Kunst-Handlern, Nürnberg 1671.*

Hope, Charles, 'Historical Portraits in the "Lives" and in the frescoes of Giorgio Vasari', in *Giorgio Vasari tra decorazione ambientale e storiografia artistica: Atti del Convegno di Studi*, Arezzo 1981, Florence 1985, pp. 321–38.

Huard, Georges, 'Quelques Lettres de Bénédictins Normands à Dom Bernard de Montfaucon pour la documentation des *Monumens de la Monarchie Françoise*', *Bulletin de la Société des Antiquaires de Normandie*, XXVIII, Caen 1913, pp. 343–75.

Huard, Georges, 'La Salle du XIIIe siècle du Musée des Monuments Français à l'École des Beaux-Arts', *Revue de l'Art Ancien et Moderne*, 1925, pp. 113–26.

Huard, Georges, 'Le tombeau de Gabrielle d'Estrées au Musée des Monuments Français', *Bulletin de la Société de l'Histoire de l'Art Français*, 1932, pp. 166–74.

Huard, Georges, 'Alexandre Lenoir et le Muséum Du mois de Décembre 1792 à la fin de l'an II', *Bulletin de la Société de l'Histoire de l'Art Français*, 1940, pp. 188–206.

Huck, J.G., and Valentine Green, *Acta Historica Reginarum Angliae. Twelve original drawings, formed on the History of the Queens of England, Executed by J.G. Huck, and engraved by Valentine Green . . . with an historical account, illustrating each subject, in English and French*, London 1792.

Hugo, Victor, *Les Misérables*, ed. Maurice Allen, Paris (Pléiade) 1951.

Huizinga, Johan, *Herfsttif der Middeleeuwen* (2nd edition), Haarlem 1921.

Huizinga, Johan, *L'Autunno del Medio Evo*, with an introduction by E. Garin, Florence 1940.

Huizinga, Johan, *Mein Weg zur Geschichte*, trs. into German by Werner Kaegi, Basel 1947.

Huizinga, Johan, *Verzamelde Werken*, 9 vols, Haarlem 1948–53.

Huizinga, Johan, *Keur van gedenkwaardige tafereelen uit de vaderlandsche historien. Volgens de beste bronnen bewerkt en naar tifdsorde gerangschikt*, Amsterdam 1950.

Huizinga, Johan, *Erasmus of Rotterdam*, trs. F. Hopman, London 1952.

Huizinga, Johan, *The Waning of the Middle Ages*, trs. F. Hopman (1st edition 1924), Harmond-sworth (Penguin Books) 1955.

Huizinga, Johan, *Men and Ideas – History, the Middle Ages, the Renaissance*, trs. James S. Holmes and Hans van Marle, London 1960.

Huizinga, Johan, *Dutch Civilisation in the seventeenth Century and Other Essays*, London 1968.

Huizinga, Johan, *L'Automne du Moyen Age*, trs. J. Bastin, with an introduction by Jacques le Goff, Paris 1980.

Johan Huizinga, 1872–1972, Papers delivered to the Johan Huizinga conference, Groningen 11–15 December 1972, ed. W.R.H. Koops, E.H. Kossmann and Gees van der Plaat, The Hague 1973.

Johan Huizinga. Een zweven over de tuinen van den geest: Leven en werk van Johan Huizinga. Catalogus van de tentoonstelling gehouden in het Academisch Historisch Museum te Leiden (exhibition catalogue), 1991–2.

Hulin de Loo, Georges, *Bruges 1902 – Exposition de Tableaux Flamands des XIVᵉ, XVᵉ et XVIᵉ siècles. Catalogue Critique – Précédé d'une introduction sur l'identité de certains Maitres Anonymes*, Ghent 1902.

Hulten, Pontus, and others, *The Arcimboldo Effect – Transformations of the face from the sixteenth to the twentieth century*, Milan 1987.

Hume, David, *The History of England from the Invasion of Julius Caesar to the Accession of Henry VII*, 2 vols, London 1762.

Hunt, H.J., *Le Socialisme et le Romantisme en France*, Oxford 1935.

Huyghebaert, N. 'Quelques lettres de James Weale relatives à l'Exposition des Primitifs Flamands de 1902', *Annales de la Société d'Emulation*, 1977, pp. 187–206.

Hyde, Montgomery (ed.), *A Victorian Historian: Private letters of W.E.H. Lecky 1859–78*, London 1947.

Hymans, Henri, 'L'Exposition des Primitifs Flamands à Bruges', *Gazette des Beaux-Arts*, 1902 (2), pp. 89–100, 189–207, 280–306.

Impellizzeri, S. and Rotta, S., 'Matteo Bandur', in *Dizionario Biografico degli Italiani*, v, 1963, pp. 739–50.

Inventaire Général des Richesses d'Art de la France, 'Archives du Musée des Monuments Français', 3 vols, Paris 1883–97.

Jaffé, David, 'Peiresc's Famous Men Picture Gallery', *L'Été Peiresc – Les Fioretti, II, Nouveaux mélanges*, pp. 132–42.

Jaime, E., *Musée de la Caricature ou recueil de caricatures les plus remarquables publiées en France depuis le XIV siècle jusqu'à nos jours avec un texte historique et descriptif*, 2 vols, Paris 1838.

Jansen, Dirk Jacob, 'Jacopo Strada (1515–1588): Antiquario della Sacra Cesarea Maestà', *Leids Kunsthistorisch Jaarboek*, 1982, pp. 57–69.

Jaubert, Alain, *Le Commissariat aux Archives: les photos qui falsifient l'Histoire*, Paris (Musée d'Art Moderne de la Ville de Paris) 1986–7.

[Jobert, Louis], *La Science des Medailles – nouvelle edition, avec des remarques historiques et critiques [by M. Bimard Baron de La Bastie]* [first, much smaller, edition is dated 1692], 2 vols, Paris 1739.

Johnson, Edgar, *Sir Walter Scott*, 2 vols, London 1970.

Joly, Hugues-Adrien, *Lettres à Karl-Heinrich von Heinecken, 1772–1789*, ed. W. McAllister Johnson, Paris 1988.

Jones, Marc, *Medals of the Sun King*, London (British Museum) n.d.

Jones, Roger and Nicholas Penny, *Raphael*, New Haven and London 1983.

Jongkees, J.H., *Fulvio Orsini's Imagines and the Portrait of Aristotle*, Groningen 1960.

Joppien, Rüdiger, 'Étude de quelques portraits ethnologiques dans l'oeuvre d'André Thevet', *Gazette des Beaux-Arts*, April 1978, pp. 125–35.

Jorio, Andrea de, *Description de quelques peintures antiques qui existent au Cabinet du Royal Musée-Bourbon*, Naples 1825.

Jorio, Andrea de, *La mimica degli antichi investigata nel gestire napoletano*, Naples 1832.

Kaegi, Werner, *Historische Meditationen*, II, Zurich 1946 (pp. 7–42: 'Johan Huizinga zum Gedächtnis'; pp. 243–86: 'Das historische Werk Johan Huizinga').

Kaegi, Werner, *Jacob Burckhardt – eine Biographie*, 8 vols in 7, Basel 1947–82.

Kahsnitz, Rainer, 'Museum und Denkmal', in Bernard Deneke and Rainer Kahsnitz (eds), *Das Kunst-und Kulturgeschichtliche Museum im 19 Jahrhundert*, Munich 1977, pp. 152–75.

Kahsnitz, Rainer (ed.), 'Texte zur Geschichte des Museums', in Bernard Deneke and Rainer Kahsnitz (eds), *Der Germanische Nationalmuseum Nürnberg 1852–1977*, Munich and Berlin 1978, pp. 951 ff.

Karl der Grosse, Werk und Wirtung, exhibition catalogue, Aachen 1965.

Kelly, J.N.D., *Jerome – His Life, Writings and Controversies*, London 1975.

Kempers, Bram, 'Der verleiding van het beeld. Het visuele als blijvende bron van inspiratie in het werk van Huizinga', *Tijdschrift voor Geschiedenis*, CV (1992), pp. 30–50.

Kennedy, Emmet, 'Remarks on Stanley Mellon's "Alexandre Lenoir: The Museum versus the Revolution"', *The Consortium on Revolutionary Europe – Proceedings*, Athens, Georgia 1979, pp. 89–91.

Kenyon, John, *The History Men*, London 1983.

Kervyn de Lettenhove, Baron H., *Discours prononcé . . . à la Séance de clôture de l'Exposition, 5 Octobre 1902*, Bruges 1902.

Kervyn de Lettenhove, Baron H., 'Des Primitifs à Bruges, en 1902', Bruges, 1906, Extrait des *Annales de la Société d'Emulation* (revue trimestrielle), 2nd fascicule, 1906.

Kervyn de Lettenhove, Baron H., 'W.H. James Weale, Esq., "Souvenirs"', *La Revue Belge*, 15 June 1926, pp. 518–34.

Keynes, Geoffrey, *The Library of Edward Gibbon*, London 1940.

Kinser, Samuel, *The Works of Jacques-Auguste de Thou*, The Hague 1966.

Klinger, Linda Susan, 'The Portrait Collection of Paolo Giovio', disertation presented to the faculty of Princeton University in candidacy for the degree of doctor of philosophy, unpublished typescript, 2 vols, 1991.

Klinger, Linda and Julian Raby, 'Barbarossa and Sinan: a portrait of two Ottoman corsairs from the collection of Paolo Giovio', in *Venezia e l'Oriente Vicino (a cura di Ernst J. Grube), Arte Veneziana e Arte Islamica*, Venice 1989, pp. 47–59.

Knowles, John, *The Life and Writings of Henry Fuseli, Esq., M.A.R.A.*, 3 vols, London 1831.

Köster, Kurt, *Johan Huizinga, 1872–1945*, Taunus 1947.

Kotzebue, August von, *Erinnerungen aus Paris im Jahre 1804*, Berlin 1804, reprinted as vol. XL of Kotzebue's *Ausgewählte Prosaische Schriften*, Vienna 1843.

Krautheimer, Richard, *Lorenzo Ghiberti*, Princeton 1956.

Krieger, Leonard, *Ranke – The Meaning of History*, Chicago 1977.

Kugler, Franz, *A Handbook of the History of Painting – Part II: The German, Flemish, and Dutch schools of Painting*, trs. from the German by a Lady; ed., with notes, by Sir Edmund Head, Bart., London 1846.

Kugler, Franz, *Handbuch der Geschichte der Malerei seit Constantin dem Grossen*. Zweite Auflage unter Mitwirkung des Verfassers umgearbeitet und vermehrt von Dr. Jacob Burckhardt, 2 vols, Berlin 1847.

Kunst der Reformationszeit, exhibition catalogue, Berlin (DDR) 1983.

Laborde, Léon de, *Voyage de l'Arabie Pétrée par Léon de Laborde et Linant*, Paris 1830.

Laborde, Léon de, *Les Ducs de Bourgogne – études sur Les Lettres, Les Arts et l'Industrie pendant le XVe siècle et plus particulièrement dans les Pays-Bas et le Duché de Bourgogne*, seconde partie, I, Preuves, Paris 1849.

Laborde, Léon de, *La Renaissance des Arts à la cour de France, Études sur le seizième siècle*, additions au tome premier, Paris 1855.

La Chau, Abbé de, and Abbé Le Blond, *Description des principales pierres gravées du cabinet de S.A.S. Monseigneur le Duc d'Orléans, premier prince du sang*, 2 vols, Paris 1780 and 1784.

Lacroix, Paul, *Les Arts au Moyen Age et à l'époque de la Renaissance . . . Ouvrage illustré de dix-neuf planches chromolithographiques . . . et de quatre cent gravures en bois* (3rd edition), Paris 1871.

Ladner, Gerhart B., *Die Papstbildnisse des Altertums und des Mittelalters*, 3 vols, Vatican City 1941–84.

Lairesse, Gerard de, *Het Groot Schilderboek*, Amsterdam 1707.

Lairesse, Gerard de, *The Art of Painting in all its branches, methodically demonstrated by discourses and plates, and exemplified by remarks on the Paintings of the best Masters; and their Per-*

fections and Oversights laid open, trs. John Frederick Fritsch, London 1738.

Lairesse, Gerard de, *Le Grand Livre des Peintres, ou l'Art de la Peinture, considéré dans toutes ses parties, & démontré par principes; avec des Réflexions sur les Ouvrages de quelques bons Maîtres, & sur les défauts qui s'y trouvent. Auquel on a joint les Principes du Dessein du même Autour.* Traduit du Hollandois sur la seconde Edition, 2 vols, Paris 1787.

La Lande, Jérôme de, *Voyage en Italie* (seconde édition, revue, corrigée), 7 vols, Yverdon 1787–8.

Lamprecht, Karl, *Initial – Ornamentik des VIII bis XIII Jahrhunderts,* vierundvierzig Steindruck-Tafeln, meist nach rheinischen Handschriften nebst erläuterndem Text, Leipzig 1882.

Lamprecht, Karl, *Deutsche Geschichte,* 15 vols, Berlin 1909–21.

Lancelot, [Antoine], 'Explication d'un monument de Guillaume le Conquérant' (21 July 1724), *Memoires de littérature tirez des Registres de l'Académie Royale des Inscriptions et Belles Lettres,* VI, Paris 1729, pp. 739–55.

Lancelot, [Antoine], 'Suite de l'Explication d'un Monument de Guillaume le Conquérant' (9 May 1730), *Memoires de littérature tirez des Registres de l'Académie Royale des Inscriptions et Belles-Lettres,* VIII, Paris 1733, pp. 602–68.

Landi, Costantino, *In veterum numismatum romanorum miscellanea explicationes,* Lyon 1560.

Landon, C.P., *Musée Royal du Luxembourg, recrée en 1822, et composé des principales productions des artistes vivans,* Paris 1823.

Lankheit, Klaus (editor), *The Blaue Reiter Almanac. Edited by Wassily Kandinsky and Franz Marc,* London 1974.

Lanzi, Luigi, *La Real Galleria di Firenze accresciuta e riordinata per comando di S.A.R. l'Arciduca Granduca di Toscana,* Pisa 1782 (reprinted Florence 1982).

Larmessin, Nicolas de, *Les Augustes Representations de tous les Roys de France depuis Pharamond, jusqu'a Louis XIIII, dit le grand, a present regnant,* Paris 1679 (later edition 1714).

La Rue, Abbé de, 'Memoir on the celebrated Tapestry of Bayeux. Communicated [to the Socety of Antiquaries] by the Translator, Francis Douce, Esq. F.A.S., with a letter to the Secretary, Nicholas Carlisle, Esq., read 12th November 1812', *Archaeologia,* XVII, 1814, pp. 85–109.

Lasinio, J.P., *Peintures à fresque du Camposanto de Pise, dessinées par Joseph Rossi et gravées par le Prof.r Chev.r J.P. Lasinio fils,* Florence 1833.

La Tour, Georges de, exhibition catalogue, Paris (Orangerie) 1972.

Launay, Élizabeth, *Les frères Goncourt collectionneurs de dessins,* Paris (Arthena) 1991.

Lavater, Johann Caspar, *Physiognomische Fragmente, zur Beförderung der Menschenkenntniss und Menschenliebe,* 4 vols, Leipzig and Winterthur: I: 1775); II: 1776); III: 1777); IV: 1778.

Lavater, Jean Gaspard, *Essai sur la Physiognomie destiné à faire Connoitre l'Homme & à le faire Aimer,* 4 vols, The Hague: I: 1781; II: 1783; III: 1786; IV: 1803.

Laviron, G., and B. Galbaccio, *Le Salon de 1833,* Paris 1833.

Lazius, Wolfgang, *De aliquot gentium migrationibus,* Basel 1572.

Le Brun, Giorgio, 'L'esposizione dei primitivi fiamminghi', *Rassegna d'Arte,* October 1902, pp.145–7.

Lecky, W.E.H., *History of the Rise and Influence of the Spirit of Rationalism in Europe,* 2 vols, London 1865 (new impression 1904).

Lecky, Mrs, *A Memoir of the Right Hon. William Edward Hartpole Lecky by his Wife,* London 1909.

Leger, François, *La Jeunesse d'Hippolyte Taine,* Paris 1980.

Lelong, Jacques, *Bibliothèque historique de la France,* Paris 1719.

Lelong, Jacques, *Bibliothèque historique de la France, contenant le Catalogue des Ouvrages, imprimés & manuscrits, qui traitent de l'Histoire de ce Royaume, ou qui y ont rapport; avec des notes critiques et historiques:* par feu Jacques Lelong, Prêtre de l'Oratoire, Bibliothèque de la Maison de Paris. (Nouvelle Édition, revue, corrigée & considérablement augmentée par M. Fevret de Fontette, Conseiller au Parlement de Dijon), 5 vols, Paris 1768–78.

Lenoir, Alexandre, *Musée des Monumens Français,* 5 vols, Paris 1800–6.

Lenoir, Alexandre, *Description historique et chronologique des Monumens de Sculpture, réunis au Musée des Monumens Français* (7th edition), Paris 1803.

Lenoir, Alexandre, *Description historique et chronologique des Monumens de Sculpture réunis au Musée des Monumens Français* (huitième édition revue et augmentée), Paris 1806.

Le Petit, Jean-François, *La Grande Chronique ancienne et moderne, de Hollande, Zelande, Westfrise, Utrecht, Frise, Overyssel & Groeningen, jusques à la fin de l'An 1600.* Receüillee tant des histoires desdites Provinces, que de divers autres Auteurs, par Jean François le Petit, Greffier de Bethune en Artois, 2 vols, Dordrecht 1601.

Le Pois, Antoine, *Discours sur les médailles et*

graveures antiques, principalement Romaines, Paris 1579.

Lepschy, Anna Laura, *Tintoretto Observed. A documentary survey of critical reactions from the 16th to the 20th century*, Ravenna 1983.

Lethève, Jacques, 'Le public du Cabinet des Estampes au dix-neuvième siècle', in *Humanisme actif – Mélanges d'Art et de Littérature offerts à Julien Cain*, 2 vols, Paris 1968, II, pp. 101–111.

Leti, Gregorio, *Teatro Belgico o vero ritratti historici, chronologici, politici, e geografici delle sette Provincie Unite*, 2 vols, Amsterdam 1690.

Lichtenberg, Georg Christoph, *The World of Hogarth – Lichtenberg's Commentaries on Hogarth's Engravings*, trs. from the German and with an introduction by Innes and Gustav Herdan, Boston 1966.

Ligota, C.R., 'Annius of Viterbo and Historical Method', *Journal of the Warburg and Courtauld Institutes*, L, 1987, pp. 44–56.

Liotta, F., 'Domenico d'Aulisio', in *Dizionario Biografico degli Italiani*, IV, 1962, pp. 584–7.

Lloyd, C.H., *Art and Its Images*, an exhibition of printed books containing engraved illustrations after Italian Painting, Oxford 1975.

Lodi, Letizia, 'Immagini della genealogia estense', in *L'Impresa di Alfonso II*, Saggi e documenti sulla produzione artistica a Ferrara nel secondo Cinquecento, Bologna 1987, pp. 151–62.

Logan, Mary, 'L'Exposition de l'ancien art siennois', *Gazette des Beaux-Arts*, 1904 (2), pp. 200–14.

Lomazzo, Gio. Paolo, *Trattato dell' Arte de la Pittura*, Milan 1584.

Lorenzetti, Giulio, *Venezia e il suo estuario – Guida Storico-artistica*, Rome 1956.

Loyrette, Henri, 'Séroux d'Agincourt et les origines de l'histoire de l'art médiéval', *Revue de l'Art*, XLVIII, 1980, pp. 40–56.

Luciani, G., 'Un complément inédit à l'*Histoire de la République de Venise* de Daru: la correspondance de P. Daru avec l'Abbé Moschini', *Revue des Études Italiennes*, 1959, pp. 105–48.

Lusini, V., *Il Duomo di Siena*, 2 vols, Siena 1939.

Lyttelton, George Lord, *The History of the Life of King Henry the Second, and of the Age in which he lived, in five books: to which is prefixed, A History of the Revolutions of England from the Death of Edward the Confessor to the Birth of Henry the Second* (3rd edition), 5 vols, London 1769.

M, H.P., 'The late Mr. W.H. James Weale', *Burlington Magazine*, XXX, 1917, pp. 241–3.

Maccari, Patrizia Giusti, *Pietro Paolini pittore lucchese 1603–1681*, Lucca 1987.

Maffei, Scipione, *Verona Illustrata*, 4 parts in one, Verona 1731–2 (fascimile reprint, Bologna 1974 with index volume 1975).

Maffei, Scipione, *Verona Illustrata*, con giunte, note e correzioni inedite dell'autore, 5 vols, Milan 1825–6.

Maffei, Scipione, *Epistolario (1700–1755)*, ed. Celestino Garibotto, 2 vols, Milan 1955.

Magnaguti, Alessandro, 'Il Petrarca numismatico', *Rivista italiana di numismatica*, XX, 1907, pp. 155–7.

Magnani, Luigi, *La Cronaca Figurata di Giovanni Villani*, Vatican City 1936.

Malamani, Vittorio, *Memorie del Conte Leopoldo Cicognara*, 2 vols, Venice 1888.

Malcolm, J.P., *An Historical Sketch of the Art of Caricaturing*, with graphic illustrations, London 1813.

Malevich, Kazimir, exhibition catalogue, Washington, D.C., Los Angeles and New York, 1990–1.

Mancini, Giulio, *Considerazioni sulla Pittura*, ed. Adriana Marucchi, 2 vols, Rome 1957.

Manetti, Antonio di Tuccio, *The Life of Brunelleschi*. Introduction, notes and critical text edition by Howard Saalman, University Park and London 1970.

Mansuelli, Guido A., *Galleria degli Uffizi – Le Sculture*, 2 vols, Rome 1958.

Marangoni, Giovanni, *Istoria della Cappella di Sancta Sanctorum di Roma*, Rome 1747.

Marguillier, Auguste, 'L'Exposition des Maîtres Anciens à Düsseldorf', *Gazette des Beaux-Arts*, 1904 (2), pp. 265–86.

Marolles, M. de, *Catalogue de Livres d'Estampes et de figures en taille-douce*, Paris 1672.

Mascardi, Agostino, *Dell' Arte Istorica – trattati cinque*, pubblicate per cura di Adolfo Bartoli, Florence 1859.

Mason Perkins, F., 'The Sienese Exhibition of Ancient Art', *Burlington Magazine*, V, April-September 1904, pp. 581–7.

Mattingly, Harold, *Coins of the Roman Empire in the British Museum*, 7 vols, London 1923–62.

McCuaig, William, *Carlo Sigonio – The changing world of the late Renaissance*, Princeton 1989.

Médailles sur les principaux événements du règne de Louis le Grand avec des explications historiques, Paris 1702.

Mellon, Stanley, 'Alexandre Lenoir: The Museum versus the Revolution', in *The Consortium on Revolutionary Europe – Proceedings*, Athens, Georgia 1979, pp. 75–88.

Meloni Trkulja, Silvia, 'Istituzioni Artistiche Fiorentine 1765–1825: Dalla Reggenza al Granducato di Petro Leopoldo', in *Saloni*,

Gallerie, Musei e loro influenza sullo sviluppo dell'arte dei secoli XIX e XX, ed. Francis Haskell, Bologna 1979, pp. 9–13.

Meyer, Wendel W., 'The Variable Climate of Rome: British Travellers to the Roman Catacombs in the Seventeenth Century', *Studi Secenteschi*, 1985, pp. 279–96.

Mézeray, F. de, *Histoire de France, depuis Faramond jusqu'au regne de Louis le Juste. Enrichie, de plusieurs belles & rares Antiquitez, & de la vie des Reynes. Des portraits au naturel des Rois, des Reines, & des Dauphins, tirez de leur Chartes, Effigies, & autres Originaux. Et d'un recueil des medailles qui ont esté fabriquées sous chaque Regne; & de leur explication servant d'éclaircissment à l'Histoire* (new edition), 3 vols, Paris 1685.

Michel, André, 'Louis Courajod', *Gazette des Beaux-Arts*, 1896 (2), pp. 203–17.

Michel, Christian, *Charles-Nicolas Cochin et le livre illustré au XVIIIᵉ siècle*, Geneva 1987.

Michelet, Jules, *Histoire de France*, 17 vols, Paris (I and II: 1833; III: 1837; IV: 1840; V: 1841; VI: 1844; VII and VIII: 1855; IX and X: 1856; XI: 1857; XII: 1858; XIII: 1860; XIV: 1862; XV: 1863; XVI: 1866; XVII: 1867).

Michelet, Jules, *Histoire de la Révolution française*, 2 vols, Paris (Pléiade) 1952.

Michelet, Jules, *Écrits de Jeunesse – Journal (1820– 1823) – Mémorial – Journal des idées*, ed. Paul Viallaneix (3rd edition), Paris 1959.

Michelet, Jules, *Journal*, ed. Paul Viallaneix and Claude Digeon, 4 vols, Paris 1959–76.

Michelet, Jules, *Le Peuple*, ed. Robert Casanova, Paris 1965.

Michelet, Jules, *Œuvres Complètes*, ed. Paul Viallaneix, Paris 1971–.

Millar, Oliver, *The Tudor, Stuart and Early Georgian Pictures in the Collection of Her Majesty the Queen*, 2 vols, London 1963.

Molanus, *De picturis et imaginibus sacris, liber unus: tractans de vitandis circa eas abusibus, & de earundem significationibus*. Authore Joanne Molanus Lovaniensi, Sacrae Theologiae Licentiato, & Lovanij ordinario Professore, Louvain 1570.

Momigliano, Arnaldo, 'Ancient History and the Antiquarian', *Journal of the Warburg and Courtauld Institutes*, nos 3–4, July – December 1950, pp. 285–315, reprinted in *Studies in Historiography*, London 1969, pp. 1–39.

Momigliano, A.D., *Gibbon's Contribution to Historical Method* (1954), reprinted in *Studies in Historiography*, 1969, pp. 40–55.

Mommsen, Theodor, *Tagebuch der französisch-italienischen Reise 1844/1845; nach dem Manuskript herausgegeben von G. und B. Walsen*, Bern and Frankfurt 1976.

Mondrian, Piet, *The New Art – The New Life: Collected Writings*, ed. and trs. Henry Holtzman and Martin S. James, London 1987.

Monod, G., *La Vie et la Pensée de Jules Michelet (1798–1852)*, 2 vols, Paris 1923.

Montaiglon, Anatole de (ed.), *Correspondance des directeurs de l'Académie de France à Rome avec les Surintendants des Bâtiments*, 18 vols, Paris 1887–1912 (VI–XVII ed. with Jules Guiffrey).

Montalembert, Le comte de, *Mélanges d'Art et de Littérature*, Paris 1861.

Montesquieu, *Œuvres Complètes*, ed. André Masson, 3 vols, Paris 1950–5.

Montfaucon, Bernard de, *Diarium Italicum sive Monumentorum Veterum, Bibliothecarum, Musæorum, & c. Notitiae singulares in Itinerario Italico collectae. Additis schematibus ac figuris*, Paris 1702.

Montfaucon, Bernard de, *L'Antiquité expliquée et représentée en figures* (seconde édition, revue et corrigée), 10 vols, Paris 1722 and 5 vols, of Supplément, 1724.

Montfaucon, Bernard de, *Les monumens de la Monarchie françoise, qui comprennent l'Histoire de France, avec les figures de chaque regne que l'injure des tems a epargnées*, 5 vols, Paris 1729, 1730, 1731, 1732, 1733.

Moreau-Nélaton, Étienne, *Les Clouet et leurs émules*, 3 vols, Paris 1924.

Mortoft, Francis, *His Book – being his travels through France and Italy 1658–1659*, ed. Malcolm Letts, works issued by the Hakluyt Society, 2nd series, no. 57, issued for 1925.

Morton, Morris, 'The case of the missing Woodcuts', *Print Quarterly*, IV, no. 4, December 1987, p. 352.

Mosto, Andrea da, *I Dogi di Venezia con particolare riguardo alle loro tombe*, Venice 1939.

Müntz, Eugène, 'Le Musée de Portraits de Paul Jove', *Memoires de l'Académie des Inscriptions et Belles-Lettres*, 36, II, 1900–1, pp. 249–343.

Muratori, Lodovico Antonio, *Dissertazioni sopra le antichità italiane, già composte e pubblicate in Latino dal proposto Lodovico Antonio Muratori, e da esso poscia compendiate e trasportate nell' Italiana favella. Opera postuma data in luce dal Proposto Gian-Francesco Soli Muratori suo nipote*, 3 vols, Milan 1751.

Muratori, Ludovico Antonio, *Epistolario*, ed. Matteo Campori, 14 vols, in 7, Modena 1901–22.

Nadal, Abbé, 'Du Luxe des Dames Romaines', *Memoires de littérature tirez des Registres de l'Académie Royale des Inscriptions et Belles-Lettres*, IV, Paris 1723, pp. 227–63.

Nani, Battista, *Historia della Republica Veneta*, 2 vols, Venice 1662.

Navarro, Gaetano, *Biografia del Canonico della Metropolitana di Napoli D. Andrea de Jorio*, Naples 1853.

Napoli – città d'arte, 2 vols, Naples 1986.

Nesselrath, Arnold, 'Raphael's archaeological method', in *Raeffaello a Roma – Il Convegno del 1983*, Rome 1986, pp. 357–71.

Nesselrath, Arnold, 'Simboli di Roma' and various entries to exhibition catalogue, *Da Pisanello alla nascita dei Musei Capitolini – L'Antico a Roma alla vigilia del Rinascimento*, Rome 1988.

Noël, M.-F., 'Les premiers musées d'ethnographie', in *Hier pour Demain: Arts, Traditions et Patrimoine*, exhibition catalogue, Paris (Grand Palais), 1980, pp. 146–8.

Nolhac, Pierre de, 'Les collections d'antiquités de Fulvio Orsini', in *Mélanges d'Archéologie et d'Histoire*, École Française de Rome, IVe année, 1884, pp. 139–231.

Nolhac, Pierre de, *La Bibliothèque de Fulvio Orsini*, Paris 1887.

Observations sur le Sallon de 1785: extraits du *Journal général de la France* ...(Deloynes, XIV, no. 339), Paris 1785.

Oestreich, Gerhard, 'Huizinga, Lamprecht und die deutsche Geschichtsphilosophie: Huizingas Groningen Antrittsvorlesung von 1905', in *Johan Huizinga, 1872–1972*, pp. 1–28.

Ordo et effigies regum Franciae cum numero annorum quibus singuli regnaverunt. Serie e ritratti de gli Re di francia col numero degli anni che chiascheduno ha regnato, n.d. [c.1600].

[Orsini Fulvio] *Imagines et Elogia Virorum Illustrium et Eruditor ex Antiquis Lapidibus et nomismatib. expressa cum annotationib. ex Biblioteca Fulvi Ursini*, Rome 1570.

Orsini, Fulvio, *Joannis Fabri Bambergensis, Medici Romani in Imagines Illustrium ex Fulvii Ursini Bibliotheca, Antwerpiae a' Theodoro Gallœo expressas, Commentarius*, Antwerp 1606.

Paatz, Walter und Elizabeth, *Die Kirchen von Florenz*, 6 vols, Frankfurt 1940–54.

[Palazzi, Giovanni], *Aquila Saxonica sub qua Imperatores Saxones ab Henrico Aucupe, Usque ad Henricum sanctum Occidentis Imperatorem XV. Elogiis, Hieroglyphicis, Numismatibus, Insignibus, Symbolis, Imaginibus Antiquis ad vivum exhibentur exculpti, & longa historiarum serie exarati* ..., Venice 1673.

Palumbo-Fossati, Isabella, 'Il collezionista Sebastiano Erizzo e l'inventario dei suoi beni', *Ateneo Veneto*, 1984, pp. 201–18.

Panofka, Theodor, *Parodieen und Karikaturen auf Werken der Klassischen Kunst*, Berlin 1851.

Panofsky, Erwin, *Early Netherlandish Painting: Its origins and character*, 2 vols, Cambridge, Mass. 1953.

Panofsky, Erwin, *Renaissance and Renascences in Western Art*, New York and London 1972.

Paret, Peter, *Art as History*, Princeton 1988.

Paris-Berlin, Rapports et Contrastes, France-Allemagne 1900–1933, exhibition catalogue, Paris (Centre Pompidou) 1978.

Parlato, Enrico, 'Il gusto all'antica di Filarete scultore', in *Da Pisanello alla nascita dei Musei Capitolini – L'Antico a Roma alla vigilia del Rinascimento*, exhibition catalogue, Rome 1988, pp. 114–34.

Parlato, Enrico, 'L'iconografia imperiale', in *Da Pisanello alla nascita dei Musei Capitolini – L'Antico a Roma alla vigilia del Rinascimento*, exhibition catalogue, Rome 1988, pp. 73–9.

Passamani, B., 'Giovanni Battista Cavalieri', in *Dizionario Biografico degli Italiani*, XXII, pp. 673–5.

Pastor, Ludwig, *The History of the Popes, from the close of the Middle Ages*, 40 vols, London 1938–53.

Pater, Walter, *The Renaissance: Studies in Art and Poetry*, the 1893 text, ed. with textual and explanatory notes by Donald L. Hill, Berkeley and Los Angeles, 1980.

Patin, Charles, *Introduction à la Connoissance des Médailles* (seconde édition, reveüe et augmentée), Paris 1667.

Patin, Charles, *Relations historiques et curieuses de voyages, en Allemagne, Angleterre, Hollande, Boheme, Suisse, etc.*, Lyon 1674.

Le Patrimoine monumental de la Belgique, V (in two parts): Province de Namur, Liège 1975.

Paulson, Ronald, *Hogarth's Graphic Works* (1st complete edition), 2 vols, New Haven and London 1965.

Penny, Nicholas, see Haskell and Penny; and see Jones and Penny.

Perrier, François, *Segmenta nobilium signorum et statuarum* ..., Rome and Paris 1638.

Pièces d'Échecs, exhibition catalogue, Paris (Bibliothèque Nationale: Cabinet des médailles et antiques) 1990.

[Piles, Roger de], *De L'idée du Peintre Parfait*, published as vol. VI of André Félibien, *Entretiens*, Trevoux 1725 (anastatic reprint 1966).

Pinkerton, John M., 'Richard Bull of Ongar, Sussex', *The Book Collector*, XXVII, spring 1978, pp. 41–59.

Pintard, René, *Le Libertinage Érudit dans la première moitié du XVIIe siècle* (2nd edition), Geneva and Paris 1983.

Plantenga, J.H., *L'Architecture religieuse dans l'ancien duché de Brabant depuis le règne des Archiducs jusqu'au Gouvernement Autrichien (1598–1713)*, The Hague 1925.

Pliny the Elder, *Natural History*, 10 vols, London and Cambridge, Mass. (Loeb) 1938–63.

Plutarch, *Plutarchus: Les vies des hommes illustres grecs et romains*, Lausanne 1575 [see reference in Harvard College Library, *French 16th-Century Books*, II, p. 549, no. 443].

Plutarch, *Les Vies des hommes illustres de Plutarque traduites en François avec des remarques par M^r et Me Dacier*, Paris 1695.

Poirier, Alice, *Les Idées artistiques de Chateaubriand*, Paris 1930.

Pomian, Krzysztof, 'Maffei et Caylus', reprinted in *Collectioneurs, amateurs et curieux, Paris, Venise: XVI–XVIII siècle*, Paris 1987, pp. 195–211.

Pomian, Krzysztof, 'Musée, nation, musée national', *Le Débat*, no. 65, May–August 1991, pp. 166–75.

Pommier, Edouard, 'Naissance des Musées de province', in Pierre Nora (ed), *Les Lieux de Mémoire*, II, (La Nation★★), Paris 1986, pp. 451–95.

Pommier, Edouard, 'La Théorie des Arts', in *Aux Armes & Aux Arts! Les Arts de la Révolution 1789–1799*, ed. Philippe Bordes and Régis Michel, Paris 1988, pp. 165–99.

Pommier, Edouard, 'Winckelmann et la vision de l'Antiquité classique dans la France des Lumières et de la Révolution', *Revue de l'Art*, no. 83, 1989, pp. 9–20.

Pommier, Jean, *Michelet interprète de la figure humaine*, London 1961.

Pope-Hennessy, John, *Italian Renaissance Sculpture*, London 1958.

Popper, Annie M., 'Karl Gotthard Lamprecht', in *Some Historians of Modern Europe*, ed. Bernadotte Schmitt, Chicago 1962, pp. 217–39.

Porta, Giovanni Battista della, *De humana physiognomia*, Vico Equense 1586 (anastatic reprint, Naples 1986).

Porta, Giovanni Battista della, *Della Fisonomia dell' Huomo – Libri Sei tradotti di Latino in Volgare, e dall' istesso Auttore accresciuti di figure, & di passi necessarij à diverse parti dell' opera: Et hora in questa Terza, & ultima Editione migliorati in più di mille luoghi, che nella stampa di Napoli si leggevano scorrettissimi . . .*, Padua 1622.

Potts, Alex, 'Political attitudes and the rise of historicism in art theory', *Art History*, I, no. 2, June 1978, pp. 191–213.

Poulot, Dominique, 'Alexandre Lenoir et les Musées des Monuments Français' in Pierre Nora (ed.), *Les Lieux de Mémoire*, II, (La Nation★★), Paris 1986, pp. 497–531.

Prescott, William H., *History of the Reign of Philip the Second, King of Spain*, 2 vols, London 1855.

Prescott, William Hickling, *The Papers*, sel. and ed. C. Harvey Gardiner, Urbana 1964.

Previtali, Giovanni, *La Fortuna dei Primitivi dal Vasari ai Neoclassici*, Turin 1964.

Prinz, Wolfram, 'Vasaris Sammlung von Künstlerbildnissen – mit einem kritischen Verzeichnis der 144 Vitenbildnisse in der zweiten Ausgabe der Lebenbeschreibungen von 1568', *Mitteilungen des Kunsthistorischen Institutes in Florenz-Beiheft zu Band XII*, 1966.

Procopius, *History of the Wars*, trs. H.B. Dewing, 5 vols, Cambridge, Mass. (Loeb) 1961–2.

Proudhon, P.-J., *Du Principe de l'art et de sa destination sociale*, Paris 1865.

Prudentius, *Œuvres*, ed. and trs. M. Lavarenne, 4 vols, Paris 1943–51.

Pugin, A. Welby, *Contrasts; or, A parallel between the noble edifices of the fourteenth and fifteenth centuries, and similar buildings of the present day; shewing the present decay of taste: Accompanied by appropriate text*, London 1836 (2nd edition, 1841).

Pupil, François, *Le style Troubadour*, Nancy 1982.

Puyvelde, Leo van, 'Hippolyte Fierens-Gevaert', in *Liber Memorialis – L'Université de Liège de 1867 à 1935*, Notices Biographiques publiées par les soins de Léon Halkin, I, Faculté de Philosophie et Lettres, Faculté de Droit, Liège 1936, pp. 44–5.

The Queen's Image, A Celebration of Mary, Queen of Scots, by Helen Smailes and Duncan Thomson, exhibition catalogue, Edinburgh (Scottish National Portrait Gallery) 1987.

Quesnel, Joseph, *Catalogus Bibliothecae Thuanae*, 2 vols in 1, Paris 1679, II, pp. 531–5: Portraits de differentes grandeurs, peints par d'habiles Maistres servant d'ornement au dessus des tablettes de la Bibliothèque.

Quinet, Edgar, *Allemagne et Italie. Philosophie et poesie*, 2 vols in 1, Paris 1839.

Quinet, Edgar, 'Des Arts de la Renaissance et de l'Eglise de Brou', 4 December 1834, in *Mélanges*, published in *Œuvres Complètes*, VI, pp. 351–63.

Quinet, Edgar, *Œuvres Complètes*, 10 vols, Paris 1857–8.

Quinet, Edgar, *Le Livre de l'Exilé, 1851–1870*, Paris 1875.

Rabb, Theodore K., *The Struggle for Stability in Early Modern Europe*, Oxford 1977.

Rabb, Theodore K., and Jonathan Brown (eds), 'The Evidence of Art: Images and Meaning in History', *The Journal of Interdisciplinary History*, XVII, no. 1, summer 1986.

[Raguenet], *Les Monumens de Rome, ou descriptions des plus beaux ouvrages . . . qui se voyent à Rome*, Rome 1700.

Ranke, Leopold von, *Sämmtliche Werke*, 54 vols

in 44, Leipzig 1869–90.

Ranke, Leopold von, *Tagebücher*, ed. Walther Peter Fuchs, Munich-Vienna 1964.

Rapin de Thoyras, Mr, *The History of England*, trs. from the French (and greatly extended) by N. Tindal (2nd edition), 4 vols in 5, London (1732, 1733, 1744, 1745, 1747).

Rave, P.O., 'Paolo Giovio und die Bildnisvitenbücher des Humanismus', *Jahrbuch der Berliner Museen*, I, 1959, pp. 119–54.

Rave, P.O., 'Das Museo Giovio zu Como', *Miscellanea Bibliothecae Hertzianae zu Ehren Leo Bruhns, Franz Graf Wolff Metternich, Ludwig Schudt*, Munich 1961, pp. 275–84.

Réau, Louis, *Correspondance artistique de Grimm avec Catherine II*, Paris 1932.

Réau, Louis, *Histoire du Vandalisme – Les monuments détruits de l'art français*, 2 vols, Paris 1959.

Reiskius, Joannes, *Exertitationes historicae de imaginibus Jesu Christi*, Jena 1685.

Réizov, B., *L'Historiographie Romantique Française*, Moscow n.d.

Renan, Ernest, *Œuvres Complètes*, ed. Henriette Psichari, 10 vols, Paris 1947–61.

Renauldin, L.J., *Études historiques et critiques sur les médecins numismatistes, contenant leur biographie et l'analyse de leurs écrits*, Paris [n.d., but 1852].

Reynaud, Nicole, *Jean Fouquet*, exhibition catalogue, Paris (Louvre) 1981.

Reynolds, Sir Joshua, *Discourses on Art*, ed. Robert A. Wark, New Haven and London 1975.

Richardson, Jonathan, *An Essay on the Theory of Painting*, London 1715.

Richardson, Mr, Sen. and Jun., *An Account of Some of the Statues, Bas-reliefs, Drawings and Pictures in Italy, etc.*, London 1722.

Richardson, John, *A Life of Picasso*, I: *1881–1906*, New York 1991.

Robertson, William, *The Works* (to which is prefixed an account of his life and writings, by Dugald Stewart), a new edition, 12 vols, London, 1817.

Rodenbach, Georges, *Bruges-la-Morte* (texte établi d'après l'édition originale de 1892), Brussels 1986.

Roe, F.C., *Taine et l'Angleterre*, Paris 1923.

Roethel, Hans K., and Jean K. Benjamin, *Kandinsky*, catalogue raisonné of the oil paintings, I: *1900–1915*, New York 1982.

Rollin, Charles, *Histoire ancienne des Egyptiens, des Carthaginois, des Assyriens, des Babyloniens, des Medes et des Perses, des Macédoniens, des Grecs*, 6 vols, Paris 1740.

Rollin, Charles, *The History of the Arts and Sciences of the Antient*, translated from the French (2nd edition), 3 vols, illustrated with fifty-two Copper Plates, London 1768 (vol. I: *Agriculture, Sculpture, Painting, Music, the Art Military*).

Romagnini, Gian Paolo, 'Il "parere" di Maffei per l'Università di Torino e la sua opera per il lapidario', in *Nuovi Studi Maffeiani, Atti del Convegno Scipione Maffei e il Museo Maffeiano*, Verona 1983, pp. 311–29.

Romanelli, Giandomenico, 'Ritrattistica dogale: ombre, immagini e volti', in *I Dogi*, ed. G. Benzoni, Banca Cattolica del Veneto, 1982, pp. 125–61.

Rome, Musei Capitolini, *Da Pisanello alla nascita dei Musei Capitolini – L'Antico a Roma alla vigilia del Rinascimento*, exhibition catalogue, Rome 1988.

Roscoe, William, *The Life of Lorenzo de' Medici, called the Magnificent* (3rd edition, corrected), 2 vols, London 1797.

Roscoe, William, *Catalogue of the Very select and valuable library of William Roscoe, Esq. which will be sold by auction, by Mr. Winstanley, at his rooms in Marble Street, Liverpool, on Monday the 19th of August*, London 1816.

Rosenberg, John D., *The Darkening Glass: A portrait of Ruskin's genius*, New York and London 1961.

Roskill, Mark, *The Interpretation of Cubism*, Philadelphia 1985.

Rossi, G.B. de, *La Roma Sotterranea*, 3 vols, Rome 1864–77.

Rostand, André, 'La documentation iconographique des *Monumens de la Monarchie Françoise* de Bernard de Montfaucon', *Bulletin de la Société de l'Histoire de l'Art Français*, 1932, pp. 104–49.

Rouillé, Guillaume, *La Première partie du Promptuaire des médailles des plus renommées personnes qui ont esté depuis le commencement du monde*, Lyon 1553.

Rouvre, Charles de, 'Bruges et les Primitifs', *La Quinzaine*, 1 November 1902, pp. 95–111.

Roy, Alain, *Gérard de Lairesse (1640–1711)*, Paris 1992.

Rubens, Peter Paul, *The Letters*, trs. and ed. Ruth Saunders Magurn, Cambridge, Mass. 1955.

Rubin, Patricia, 'The Private Chapel of Cardinal Alessandro Farnese in the Cancelleria, Rome', *Journal of the Warburg and Courtauld Institutes*, L, 1987, pp. 82–112.

Rushforth, G. McN., 'Magister Gregorius De Mirabilibus Urbis Romae: A New Description of Rome in the twelfth century', *Journal of Roman Studies*, IX, 1919, pp. 14–58.

Ruskin, John, *The Works*, ed. E.T. Cook and Alexander Wedderburn (The Library Edition), 39 vols, London 1903–12.

Ruskin, John, *Letters from Venice*, ed. John Lewis Bradley, New Haven 1955.

Ruskin, John, *Diaries*, sel. and annotated by Joan Evans and John Howard Whitehouse, 3 vols, Oxford 1956–9.

Sadleir, Michael, *Michael Ernst Sadler (Sir Michael Sadler K.C.S.I.) 1861–1943: A Memoir by his Son*, London 1949.

Sadler, Michael, *Modern Art and Revolution*, London 1932.

Safarik, Eduard A., *Breve guida della Galleria Doria Pamphilj in Roma*, Rome 1988.

Saint-Pierre, L'Abbé de, *Annales politiques (1658–1740)* (nouvelle édition, collationnée sur les exemplaires manuscrits et imprimés avec une introduction et des notes par Joseph Drouet), Paris 1912.

Sainte-Palaye, J.-B. de La Curne de, 'Memoires Concernant la Vie & les ourvrages de Rigord & de Guillaume le Breton' (12 December 1727), *Memoires de litterature tirez des Registres de l'Académie Royale des Inscriptions et Belles-Lettres*, VIII, Paris 1733, pp. 528–48.

Sainte-Palaye, J.-B. de La Curne de, 'Jugement de l'Histoire de Froissart' (1 July 1735), *Memoires de litterature tirez des Registres de l'Académie Royale des Inscriptions et Belles-Lettres*, XIII, Paris 1740, pp. 555–79.

Sainte-Palaye, J.-B. de La Curne de, 'Memoire concernant les premiers monumens de l'Histoire de France, avec la Notice & l'Histoire des Chroniques de Saint-Denys' (15 April 1738), *Memoires de litterature tirez des Registres de l'Académie Royale des Inscriptions et Belles-Lettres*, XV, Paris 1743, pp. 580–616.

Sainte-Palaye, J.-B. de La Curne de, 'Memoire concernant la lecture des anciens Romans de Chevalerie' (13 December 1743), *Memoires de litterature tirez des Registres de l'Académie Royale des Inscriptions et Belles-Lettres*, XVII, Paris 1751, pp. 787–99.

Salis, Jean-R. de, *Sismondi, 1773–1842: La vie et l'œuvre d'un cosmopolite philosophe*, Paris 1932.

Samek Ludovisi, Sergio, 'Gli illustratori dei "Rerum Italicarum Scriptores"', in *L.A. Muratori Storiografo: Atti del Convegno Internazionale di Studi Muratoriani*, Modena 1972, Florence 1975, pp. 139–50.

Sandoz, Marc, *Gabriel François Doyen, 1726–1806*, Paris 1975.

Sanpaolesi, Piero, 'San Piero Scheraggio – I', *Rivista d'Arte*, 1933, pp. 129–50.

Sansovino, Francesco, *L'Historia di Casa Orsina*, Venice 1565.

Sardi, Gasparo, *Libro delle historie ferraresi*, Ferrara 1646.

Scala, Mirella, 'Aspetti teorici della committenza negli *Annales Ecclesiastici* di Cesare Baronio', in *Baronio e l'arte*, pp. 261–87.

Scavizzi, Giuseppe, *Arte e architettura sacra – Cronache e documenti sulla controversia tra riformati e cattolici (1500–1550)*, Reggio Calabria 1981.

Schama, Simon, *The Embarrassment of Riches: An Interpretation of Dutch Culture in the Golden Age*, New York 1987.

Scharloo, Marjan (with an additional comment by Peter Barber), 'A peace medal that caused a war?', *The Medal*, no. 18, spring 1991, pp. 10–22.

Scheible, J., *Das Kloster*, X, part 2: *Fischart und Murner*, Stuttgart and Leipzig 1848

Schiff, Gert, *Johann Heinrich Füssli, 1741–1825*, 2 vols, Zurich and Munich 1973.

Schiller, *Gedichte, 1776–99*, ed. Julius Petersen and Friedrich Beissner, in *Schillers Werke*, Nationalausgabe, I, Weimar 1943.

Schiller, *Briefe, 1788–1790*, ed. Eberhard Haufe, in *Schillers Werke*, Nationalausgabe, XXV, Weimar 1979.

Schlegel, Friedrich, 'Gemäldeschreibungen aus Paris und den Niederlanden', in *Kritische Friedrich-Schlegel-Ausgabe*, IV, Munich and elsewhere, 1959, pp. 3–152.

Schlegel, Friedrich, *Gemälde Alter Meister*, mit Kommentar und Nachwort von Hans Eichner und Norma Lelless, Darmstadt 1984.

Schmitt, A., 'Zur Wiederbelebung der Antike im Trecento', *Mitteilungen des Kunsthistorischen Institutes in Florenz*, XVIII, (1974), pp. 167–218.

Schnapper, Antoine, 'The Position of the Portrait in France at the End of the Reign of Louis XIV (1680–1715)', in *Largilliere and the Eighteenth-Century Portrait*, exhibition catalogue, Montreal Museum of Fine Arts, 1981.

Schnapper, Antoine, *Le géant, la licorne et la tulipe – collections et collectionneurs dans la France du XVIIᵉ siècle – 1: Histoire et histoire naturelle*, Paris 1988.

Schneider, R., 'Un ennemi du Musée des Monuments Français', *Gazette des Beaux-Arts*, 1909 (2), pp. 353–70.

Scoto, Andrea, *Itinerario overo nova descrittione de' Viaggi principali d'Italia . . .*, Venice 1610.

Scullard, H.H., 'Hadrian's Elephants', *Numismatic Chronicle and Journal of the Royal Numismatic Society*, 6th series, VIII, 1948, pp. 158–68.

La Sculpture au Siècle de Rubens, dans les Pays-Bas méridienaux et la principauté de Liège, exhibition catalogue, Brussels (Musée d'Art Ancien) 1977.

Sellers, Ian, 'William Roscoe, the Roscoe circle and Radical Politics in Liverpool, 1787–1807', *Transactions of the Historic Society of Lancashire and Cheshire*, CXX, 1968, pp. 45–62.

Selvatico, P., *Sulla architettura e sulla scultura in Venezia dal medio evo sino ai nostri giorni – studi di P. Selvatico per servire di Guida estetica*, Venice 1847.

Seroux d'Agincourt, J.-B.-L.-G., *Histoire de l'art par les monumens, depuis sa décadence au IVe siècle jusqu'à son renouvellement au XVIe*, 6 vols, Paris 1823.

Settis, Salvatore, 'Roma 1513: Il gioco delle parti', in *Storia d'Italia* (Annali 4: *Intellectuali e Potere*), Turin 1981, pp. 701–8.

Settis, Salvatore (ed.), *Memoria dell'antico nell'arte italiana*, 3 vols, Turin 1985–6.

Settis, Salvatore, 'Continuità, distanza conoscenza. Tre usi dell' antico', in Settis, *Memoria*, III, pp. 375–486.

Settis, Salvatore, 'La Colonna', in Settis and others, *La Colonna Traiana*, Turin, 1988, pp. 45–255.

Seznec, Jean, *Essais sur Diderot et l'Antiquité*, Oxford 1957.

Seznec, Jean, 'Michelet in Germany: a journey in self-discovery', *History and Theory*, XVI, no. 1, 1977, pp. 1–10.

Shaftesbury, Anthony Earl of, *Characteristics of Men, Manners, Opinions, Times*, ed., with notes, by John M. Robertson with an introduction by Stanley Green, 2 vols in 1, Indianapolis and New York 1964.

Sherman, Claire Richter, *The Portraits of Charles V of France (1338–1380)*, New York 1969.

Le Siècle d'Or de la Miniature Flamande – Le mécénat de Philippe le Bon, exhibition catalogue, Brussels and Amsterdam 1959.

Simeoni, Gabriele, *Illustratione de gli epitaffi et medaglie antiche*, Lyon 1558.

Simon, Jules, 'Notice sur la vie et les travaux de M. E. Charton', in *Memoires de l'Académie des Sciences Morales et Politiques de l'Institut de France*, XVIII, 1894, pp. 73–119.

Simonetta, Bono, and Renzo Riva, *Le tessere erotiche romane*, Lugano 1981.

Sismondi, J.C.L. Simonde de, *Histoire des républiques italiennes du moyen âge* (new edition), 10 vols, Paris 1840.

Smith, Graham, 'A Drawing for the Sala Regia', *Burlington Magazine*, CXVIII, 1976, pp. 102–6.

Sommerard, M. du, *Les Arts au moyen âge en ce qui concerne principalement le Palais Romain de Paris, l'Hotel de Cluny issu de ses ruines et les objets d'art de la collection classée dans cet hôtel*, 5 vols, Paris 1838–46.

Sosti, Stefano, 'Le fonti per l'arte negli *Annales Ecclesiastici* di Cesare Baronio', in *Baronio e l'arte*, pp. 247–60.

Souchal, François, *French Sculptors of the 17th and 18th Centuries–The Reign of Louis XIV*, 3 vols, Oxford 1977–87.

Soulié, Eud., *Notice du Musée Impérial de Versailles* (2nd edition), 3 vols, Paris 1859–61.

[Spanheim, Ezekiel], *Les Césars de l'Empereur Julien, traduits du Grec, avec des Remarques & des Preuves illustrées par les Médailles, & autres anciens Monumens*, Paris 1683.

Spon, Jacob, *Recherche des antiquités et curiosités de la ville de Lyon*, Lyon 1673 (Minkoff reprint, Geneva 1974).

Spon, Jacob, 'De l'utilité des médailles pour l'étude de la physionomie', in *Recherches curieuses d'antiquité contenues en plusieurs dissertations, sur des Medailles, Bas-reliefs, Statües, Mosaïques, & Inscriptions antiques; enrichies d'un grand nombre de Figures en Taille douce*, Lyon 1683, pp. 353–96.

Stein, Henri, *Le peintre G.F. Doyen et l'origine du Musée des Monuments Français*, Paris 1888.

Stephen, Leslie, *Letters of John Richard Green*, London 1901.

Stephens, W.R.W., *The Life and Letters of Edward A. Freeman*, 2 vols, London 1895.

Sterling, Charles, *The Metropolitan Museum of Art: A Catalogue of French Paintings, XV–XVIII centuries*, New York 1955.

Tobias Stimmer, 1539–1584, exhibition catalogue, Kunstmuseum Basel 1984.

Stone, Nicholas (the Younger), *Diary*, published by the Walpole Society, VII, London 1918–19, pp. 158–200.

Strada, J., *Epitome du Thrésor des Antiquitez, c'est à dire, Pourtraits des vrayes Medailles des Empp. tant d'Orient que d'Occident. De l'estude de Jacques de Strada Mantuan Antiquaire* traduit par Jean Louueau d'Orléans, Lyon, 1553.

Strauss, Walter L., *The German Single-Leaf Woodcut 1550–1600*, 3 vols, New York 1975.

Strong, Roy, *Van Dyck: Charles I on Horseback*, London 1972.

Strutt, Joseph, *The Regal and Ecclesiastical Antiquities of England: containing, in a compleat series The Representations of all the English Monarchs, from Edward the Confessor to Henry the Eighth . . . The Whole carefully collected from Antient Illuminated Manuscripts*, London 1773.

Strutt, Joseph, *Horda, Angel-cynnan: or, A compleat view of the Manners, Customs, Arms, Habits, &c of the Inhabitants of England from the arrival of the Saxons, till the reign of Henry the Eighth*, 3 vols, London 1775–6.

Strutt, Joseph, *The Chronicle of England or, a*

compleat history civil, military and ecclesiastical, of the ancient Britons and Saxons, from the landing of Julius Caesar in Britain to the Norman Conquest. With a compleat view of the Manners, Customs, Arts, Habits &c of those people, 2 vols, London 1777–8.

Sulzberger, Suzanne, La réhabilitation des Primitifs Flamands, 1802–1867, 2 vols, Brussels 1961.

Supplément du peintre anglais au Salon 1785, (Deloynes, XIV, no. 328), Paris 1785.

Sutherland, Humphrey, Roman History and Coinage 44 BC–AD 69, Oxford 1987.

Sutherland Collection, catalogue, 2 vols, London 1837.

[Tabourot, Etienne], Icones et epitaphia quatuor postremorum Ducum Burgundiae ex augustissima Valesiorium familia – Les Pourtraits des quatre derniers Ducs de Bourgogne de la Royale maison de Valois, Paris 1587.

Taine, H., Histoire de la Littérature Anglaise, 4 vols, Paris 1863–4.

Taine, H., Notes sur l'Angleterre (2ème édition, revue et corrigée), Paris 1872.

Taine, H., Les Origines de la France contemporaine, 6 vols, Paris 1876–94.

Taine, H., Derniers Essais de Critique et d'Histoire, Paris 1894.

Taine, H., Carnets de Voyage – Notes sur la Province, 1863–1865, Paris 1897.

Taine, H., Sa Vie et sa Correspondance, 4 vols, Paris 1902–7.

Taine, Hippolyte, Voyage en Italie (1866), 2 vols, Paris (Julliard) 1965.

Tal, 'James Weale', Revue de l'Art Chrétien, 1902, pp. 519–21.

Taylor, Gerald, 'The Siege and Battle of Pavia'. Appendix I to Tradescant's Rarities – Essays on the Foundation of the Ashmolean Museum, 1683, with a catalogue of the surviving early collections, Oxford 1983, pp. 318–26.

Thausing, Moriz, Dürer, Geschichte seines Lebens und seiner Kunst, Leipzig 1876.

Thevet, André, Pourtraits et vies des hommes illustres grecz, latins, et payens recueilliz de leurs tableaux, livres, medailles antiques et modernes, Paris 1584.

Thierry, Augustin, Lettres sur l'Histoire de France (2nd edition 1827), reprinted Paris 1935.

Thierry, Augustin, Dix ans d'études historiques, Paris 1835.

Thierry, Augustin, Récits des Temps Mérovingiens précédés de Considerations sur l'Histoire de France, 3 vols in 1, Brussels 1840.

Thou, Jacques-Auguste de, Memoires de la vie de Jacques-Auguste de Thou . . . (nouvelle édition enrichie de Portraits, & d'une Pyramide fort curieuse), Amsterdam 1713.

Thou, Jacques-Auguste de, Histoire Universelle

(avec la suite par Nicolas Rigault), 11 vols, The Hague 1740.

Tiziano nelle Gallerie Fiorentine (presentazione di Mina Gregori), exhibition catalogue, Florence (Palazzo Pitti) 1978–9.

Tocci, Luigi Michelini, I Medaglioni romani e i Contorniati del Medagliere Vaticano, Vatican City 1965.

Toorop, Jan, 1858–1928, Impressioniste, Symboliste, Pointilliste, exhibition catalogue, Paris (Institut Néerlandais) 1977.

Toorop, Jan, exhibition catalogue by Victoria Hefting, The Hague 1989.

Torsellino, Orazio, Ristretto dell'historie del mondo, Rome 1634.

Trachtenberg, Alan, 'Albums of War: On Reading Civil War Photographs', Representations, no. 9, winter 1985, pp. 1–32.

Trendall, A.D., Phylax Vases (2nd edition), London 1967.

Tristan [Jean], Commentaires historiques, contenants en abregé les vies, éloges et censures des Empereurs, Imperatrices, Césars et Tyrans de l'Empire Romain, iusques à Pertinax, & diverses observations sur leur noms, familles & naissances. Le Tout illustré de l'exacte explication des revers enigmatiques de plusieurs centaines de medailles . . . le tout representé en dix-huit planches de tailles douces, Paris 1635 (later editions published in 1644 and 1657).

Tronchon, Henri, Le Jeune Edgar Quinet ou L'Aventure d'un Enthousiaste, Paris 1937.

Tschudi, Hugo von, 'Brügge. Ausstellung altniederländischer Gemälde', Repertorium für Kunswissenschaft, XXV, 1902, pp. 228–32.

Turin: Cultura figurativa e architettonica negli Stati del Re di Sardegna, 1773–1861. exhibition catalogue, ed. Enrico Castelnuovo and Marco Rosci, 3 vols, Turin 1980.

Turnbull, George, A Treatise on Ancient Painting, containing Observations on the Rise, Progress and Decline of that Art amongst the Greeks and Romans, London 1740.

Uklanski, Baron d', Travels in Upper Italy, Tuscany, and the Ecclesiastical State, in a series of letters, written to a friend in the years 1807 and 1808: to which are added, a few occasional poems, 2 vols, London 1816.

Unrau, John, Ruskin and St. Mark's, London 1984.

Uzanne, Octave, 'The Exhibition of Primitive Art at Bruges', The Connoisseur, 1902, pp. 172–80.

Valery, M., Voyages historiques, littéraires et artistiques en Italie (2ème édition, entièrement revue), 3 vols, Paris 1838.

Valkenburg, C.T. van, J. Huizinga: zijn leven en

zijn persoonlijkheid, Amsterdam–Antwerp 1946.

Vanuxem, Jacques, 'The Theories of Mabillon and Montfaucon on French Sculpture of the 12th Century', *Journal of the Courtauld and Warburg Institutes*, XX, 1957, pp. 45–58.

Vanuxem, Jacques, 'Aperçus sur quelques tableaux représentant le Musée des Monuments Français de Lenoir', *Bulletin de la Société de l'Histoire de l'Art Français*, 1971, pp. 145–51.

Varille, Mathieu, 'Antiquaires Lyonnais de la Renaissance', *Revue du Lyonnais*, 1923, pp. 420–69.

Vasari, Giorgio, *Le Vite de' più eccellenti architetti, pittori, et scultori italiani, da Cimabue insino à tempi nostri* (1550), ed. Lucio Bellosi and Aldo Rossi, Turin 1986.

Vasari, Giorgio, *Le Vite de' più eccellenti pittori scultori ed architetti* (1568), in *Le Opere,* ed. G. Milanesi, 9 vols, Florence 1906 (reprinted 1973).

Vaudoyer, Jean-Louis, 'Souvenirs d'un "auditeur"', in *1882–1932: L'École du Louvre,* ed. Henri Verne and others, Paris (Bibliothèque du Louvre) 1932, pp. 71–6.

Vecchi, Pier Luigi De, 'Il Museo Gioviano e le "Verae Imagines" degli Uomini Illustri', in *Omaggio a Tiziano – La cultura artistica milanese nell' età di Carlo V,* Milan 1977, pp. 87–93.

Veit, Ludwig, 'Chronik der Germanischen Nationalmuseums', in Bernward Deneke and Rainer Kahsnitz (eds), *Der Germanische Nationalmuseum, Nürnberg 1852–1977,* Munich and Berlin 1978, pp. 11–124.

Velly, Villaret et Garnier, *Histoire de France depuis l'établissement de la monarchie jusqu'au règne de Louis XIV – Tome treizième, seconde partie, contenant les Portraits gravés de la plus grande partie des Hommes Illustres, dont il est fait mention dans cette Histoire, depuis Pharamond, jusqu'au Roi Jean,* Paris 1778.

Venturoli, 'Nota su Jacopo Ripanda e il giovane Baldassare Peruzzi', *Storia dell'Arte,* IV, 1969, pp. 432–9.

Verbraeken, René, *Jacques-Louis David jugé par ses contemporains et par la postérité,* Paris 1973.

Verdier, Antoine du, *La Prosopographie des personnes insignes, enrichies de plusieurs effigies, & reduite en quatre livres,* Lyon 1573.

Verne, Henri, 'L'école du Louvre: De 1882 à 1932', in *1882–1932: L'École du Louvre,* ed. Henri Verne and others, Paris (Bibliothèque du Louvre) 1932, pp. 1–39.

Vertue, George, *The Notebooks* , published by the Walpole Society, 7 vols (XVIII, XX, XXII, XXIV, XXVI, XXIX, XXX), London 1930–55.

Viallaneix, Paul, *La voie royale: Essai sur l'idée de peuple dans l'œuvre de Michelet,* Paris 1959.

Vickers, Michael, 'Value and Simplicity: Eighteenth-century taste and the study of Greek vases', *Past and Present,* CXVI, 1987, pp. 98–137.

Vico, Enea, *Le Imagini con tutti i riversi trovati et le vite de gli Imperatori tratte dalle medaglie et dalle historie de gli antichi,* Venice 1548.

Vico, Enea, *Discorsi sopra le medaglie de gli antichi,* Venice 1555.

Vidler, Anthony, 'Grégoire, Lenoir et les "monuments parlants"', in Jean-Claude Bonnet (ed.), *La Carmagnole des Muses: L'homme de lettres et l'artiste dans la Révolution,* Paris 1989, pp. 131–54.

Vitry, Paul, 'Louis Courajod et André Michel', in *1882–1932: L'École du Louvre,* ed. Henri Verne and others, Paris (Bibliothèque du Louvre) 1932, pp. 61–70.

Vogelaar, Christiaan, *Netherlandish fifteenth- and sixteenth-century paintings in The National Gallery of Ireland – a complete catalogue,* Dublin 1987.

Voltaire, *Le Siècle de Louis XIV,* ed. René Groos, 2 vols, Paris 1947.

Voltaire, *Essai sur les mœurs et l'esprit des nations,* ed. René Pomeau, 2 vols, Paris 1963.

Voltaire, *Oeuvres historiques,* ed. René Pomeau, Paris (Pléiade) 1968.

Voltaire, *Correspondance and Related Documents,* ed. Theodore Besterman, 51 vols, Geneva and Oxford 1968–1977.

Waagen, Gustav Friedrich, *Ueber Hubert and Johann van Eyck,* Breslau 1822.

Wallace-Hadrill, Andrew, 'Image and Authority in the coinage of Augustus', *Journal of Roman Studies,* LXXVI, 1986, pp. 66–87.

Walpole, Horace, *Anecdotes of Painting in England,* 4 vols, Strawberry Hill, 1762–71.

Waquet, Françoise, 'Guy et Charles Patin, père et fils, et la contrabande du livre à Paris au XVIIᵉ siècle', *Journal des Savants,* 1979, pp. 125–48.

Warburg, A., 'Delle "Imprese Amorose" nelle più antiche incisioni fiorentine', *Rivista d'Arte,* VII–VIII, 1905, Appendix.

Warburg, A., *Gesammelte Schriften,* ed. Gertrud Bing, 2 vols, Leipzig and Berlin 1932.

Wardman, A.E., 'Description of personal appearance in Plutarch and Suetonius: the use of statues as evidence', *Classical Quarterly,* XVII, 1967, pp. 414–20.

Wardrop, James, *The Script of Humanism,* Oxford 1963.

Washton-Long, Rose-Carol, *Kandinsky: The Development of an Abstract Style,* Oxford 1980.

Wauters, A.-J., *Exposition des primitifs flamands à Bruges: 15 juin-15 septembre 1902. Première Section: Tableaux – coup d'oeil historique et énumération chronologique des principales œuvres exposées*, Brussels 1902.

Wazbinski, Zygmunt, 'L'Idée de l'Histoire dans la première et la séconde édition des Vies de Vasari', in *Il Vasari Storiografo e Artista: Atti del Congresso Internazionale del IV Centenario della Morte*, Florence 1976, pp. 1–25.

Weale, W.H. James, *Gilde de Saint Thomas & Saint Luc – Tableaux de l'Ancienne École Néerlandaise exposés a Bruges dans la Grande Salle des Halles, Septembre 1867*, exhibition catalogue, Bruges 1867.

Weale, W.H. James, *Gerard David – Painter and Illuminator*, London 1895.

Weale, W.H. James, 'Exposition de peintures des maîtres néerlandais antérieurs à la Renaissance à la New Gallery de Londres', *Revue de l'Art Chrétien*, 1900, pp. 252–8.

Weale, W.H. James, *Hans Memlinc*, London 1901.

[Weale, W.H. James], *Exposition des Primitifs flamands et d'Art ancien, Bruges – Première section: Tableaux*, exhibition catalogue, Bruges 1902.

Weale, W.H. James, 'The Early Painters of the Netherlands as illustrated by the Bruges Exhibition of 1902', *Burlington Magazine*, I, 1903, pp. 41–52, 206–17, 329–36.

Weber, Bruno, '"Die Welt begeret allezeit Wunder" – Versuch einer bibliographie der Einblatt-drucke von Bernhard Jobin in Strassburg', *Gutenberg Jahrbuch*, 1976, pp. 270–90.

Weintraub, Karl J., *Visions of Culture*, Chicago and London 1966.

Weiss, Roberto, 'Andrea Fulvio Antiquario Romano (c.1470–1527)', *Annali della Scuola Normale Superiore di Pisa – Lettere, Storia e Filosofia*, series 2, XXVIII (1959), fasc. I–IV, pp. 1–44.

Weiss, Roberto, 'The Study of ancient numismatics during the Renaissance (1313–1517)', *Numismatic Chronicle*, 1976, pp. 177–87.

Weiss, Roberto, *The Renaissance Discovery of Classical Antiquity* (2nd edition), Oxford (Blackwell) 1988.

Werckmeister, O.K., 'The political ideology of the Bayeux Tapestry', *Studi Medievali*, series 3, XVII, ii, 1976, pp. 535–95.

Weski, Ellen and Frozien-Leinz, Heike (ed.), *Das Antiquarium der Münchner Residenz: Katalog der Skulpturen*, 2 vols, Munich 1987.

Wethey, Harold E., *The Paintings of Titian*, 3 vols, London 1969–75.

Wiedmann, August, *Romantic Roots in Modern Art*, Old Woking 1979.

Wiedmann, August, *Romantic Art Theories*, Henley-on-Thames 1986.

Wildenstein, Daniel and Guy, *Documents complémentaires au Catalogue de l'œuvre de Louis David*, Paris 1973.

Wilkes, J.J., *Diocletian's Palace, Split: residence of a retired Roman Emperor*, Sheffield 1986.

Wilpert, Joseph, *Die Katakombengemälde und ihren alten Copien*, Freiburg 1891.

Wilson, David M., *The Bayeux Tapestry*, London 1985.

Winckelmann, Johann, *Geschichte der Kunst des Alterthums*, 2 vols, Dresden 1764.

Winckelmann, Johann, *Monumenti Antichi Inediti*, 3 vols, Rome 1767.

Winckelmann, Johann, *Storia delle Arti del Disegno presso gli antichi*. Tradotta dal Tedesco e in questa edizione corretta e aumentata dall' abate Carlo Fea, 3 vols, Rome 1783–4.

Winckelmann, Johann, 'Versuch einer Allegorie, besonders für die Kunst', 1766, reprinted in Johann Winckelmann, *Sämtliche Werke*, 12 vols, 1825–9 (1965 reprint), IX, pp. 3–270.

Winkler, Friedrich, 'Max J. Friedländer 5.6.1867–11.10.58', *Jahrbuch der Berliner Museen*, I, 1959, pp. 161–7.

Wolters, Wolfgang, *Der Bilderschmuck des Dogenpalastes*, Wiesbaden 1983.

Wright, Edward, *Some Observations made in travelling through France, Italy, etc. in the years 1720, 1721, and 1722*, 2 vols, London 1730.

Wright, Thomas, *A History of Caricature and Grotesque in Literature and Art*, London 1865.

Wright, Thomas, *Histoire de la Caricature et du Grotesque dans la littérature et dans l'Art*, traduite avec l'approbation de l'auteur par Octave Sachot, précédée d'une notice par Amédée Pichot (nouvelle édition revue et corrigée), Paris n.d.

Wytsman, P., *A propos de l'Exposition d'Œuvres des Ecoles primitives de peinture en Belgique et aux Pay-Bas, à Bruges*, Brussels 1902.

Zacchiroli, François, *Description de la Galerie Royale de Florence*, Florence 1783.

Zanotto, Francesco, *Il Palazzo Ducale di Venezia*, 4 vols, Venice: I: 1853 or 1842; II: 1858; III: 1853 or 1859; IV: 1861.

Zappella, Giuseppina, *Il ritratto nel libro italiano del Cinquecento*, 2 vols, Milan 1988.

Zen, Stefano, 'Civiltà cristiana e committenza eroica', in *Baronio e l'arte*, pp. 289–327.

Zygulski, Zdzislaw, *The National Museum in Cracow – The Czartoryski Collection. A Historical Outline and Selected Objects*, Warsaw 1978.

Illustrations

Unless otherwise indicated, photographs have been supplied by the owners of the works concerned.

Frontispiece. Joachim von Sandrart, frontispiece to his *Iconologia Deorum* of 1680.
1. *Aureus* of the Emperor Gordian III (AD 238–44) (Oxford, Ashmolean Museum).
2. Titian, *Jacopo Strada* (Vienna, Kunsthistorisches Museum).
3. Jacopo Strada, *Epitome Thesauri Antiquitatum* (Lyon 1553; reprinted Zurich 1557).
4. Guillaume du Choul, *The Author presenting* Des Antiquités romaines *to François 1ᵉʳ* (MS, Turin Royal Library).
5. Enea Vico, *Discorsi sopra le medaglie de gli antichi*, Venice 1555: dedicatory page to Cosimo I of Florence (Oxford, Bodleian Library, Douce VV 65).
6. Hubert Goltz, *Vivae Omnium fere Imperatorum Imagines*, Antwerp 1557 (Oxford, St John's College Library; reproduced by permission of the President and Fellows of St John's College, Oxford): Nero.
7. Hubert Goltz, *Sicilia, et Magna Graecia*, Bruges 1576: engraving of the painted portrait of Goltz by Antonis Mor, now in the Musée des Beaux-Arts, Brussels.
8. Gold *stater*, Olbia, last third of first century BC, obverse (Oxford, Ashmolean Museum).
9. Gold *stater*, Olbia, last third of first century BC, reverse of coin illustrated in pl. 8 (Oxford, Ashmolean Museum).
10. Ezekiel Spanheim, *Dissertationes de praestantia, et usu numismatum Antiquorum*, London 1706: portrait of Spanheim.
11a and b. Giovanni Mansionario, *Historia Imperialis*, c.1320 (Vatican MS Chig. 1. VII, 259, f. 24v): head of the Emperor Aurelian (270–5) derived from coin.
12a and b. Suetonius, *De Vita Caesarum*, c.1350 (Fermo, Bibl. Comunale, MS 81, f. 40v): half-length 'portrait' of the Emperor Galba, adapted from coin.
13. Suetonius, *De Vita Caesarum*, c.1470, MS by Bartolomeo Sanvito: Emperor Vitellius.
14. Andrea Fulvio, *Illustrium Imagines*, Rome 1517: Antonia Augusta.
15. Guillaume Rouillé, *Prontuario de le Medaglie*, 2nd edition, Lyon 1577: 'portraits' of Adam and Eve.
16. Guillaume Rouillé, *Prontuario de le Medaglie*, 2nd edition, Lyon 1577: 'portrait' of Jesus Christ.
17. *Solidus* of the Byzantine Emperor Justinian II (AD 685–95), with head of Christ as obverse (Oxford, Ashmolean Museum).
18. Padre Torsellino, *Ristretto dell'historie del mondo*, Rome 1634: Moses.
19. [Jean de Bussières], *Flosculi historici delibati*, Cologne 1656: Moses and other figures from the Old Testament and ancient history and myth.
20. Jacques de Bie, *La France métallique*, 1636: reverses of coins supposedly minted by Pharamond and other early French monarchs.
21. Munich, Antiquarium (photo: Peter Krückmann).
22. Munich, Antiquarium (photo: Peter Krückmann).
23. Fulvio Orsini, *Imagines et Elogia Virorum Illustrium*, Rome 1570: Hesiod.
24. Siena cathedral, details of wall of nave with terracotta busts of the popes made in the late fifteenth century (photo: Lensini Fabio, Siena).
25. Giovanni Battista de' Cavalieri, *Omnium Romanorum Pontificum Icones*, Rome 1595: St Marcellus.
26. Francesco da Sangallo, medal of Paolo Giovio (London, British Museum).
27. Detail of pl. 29, showing Bartolomeo Platina.
28. Paolo Giovio, *Elogia Virorum literis illustrium*, Basle 1577: Bartolomeo Platina.
29. Melozzo da Forlì, *Pope Sixtus IV with his four nephews, and his librarian Bartolomeo Platina kneeling*, c.1480, fresco transferred to canvas (Vatican, Pinacoteca).
30. Detail of pl. 32.
31. Paolo Giovio, *Elogia Virorum bellica virtute illustrium*, Basle 1575: Farinata degli Uberti.
32. Andrea del Castagno, *Farinata degli Uberti*, c.1449, fresco transferred to plaster ground (Florence, S. Apollonia – with the other 'Uomini Famosi', all of which were until 1847 to be seen in the Villa Carducci, Legnaia).
33. Silver *tetradrachma*, Carthago Nova, third century BC (Fitzwilliam Museum, Cambridge): man on an elephant – believed, in the Renaissance, to represent Hannibal.
34. Paolo Giovio, *Elogia Virorum bellica virtute illustrium*, Basle 1575: Hannibal.
35. André Thevet, *Pourtraits et vies des hommes illustres*, Paris 1584: Pliny the Younger.
36. Peter Stent, '*Thomas More*' (London, British Museum).

37. *Ordo et effigies regum Franciae*, n.pl., n.d. (*c*.1600): Pharamond.

38. *Cronica Breve de i fatti illustri de' Re di Francia*, Venice 1588: Pharamond.

39. *Der Könige in Frankreich, Leben, Regierung und Absterben*, Nuremberg 1671: Pharamond.

40. Nicolas de Larmessin, *Les Augustes Representations de tous les Roys de France*, Paris 1679: Pharamond.

41. Jean-François Le Petit, *La Grande Chronique ancienne et moderne de Hollande etc.*, Dordrecht 1601: 'Thierri, premier comte de Hollande et de Zeelande, l'an 863 regna 40 ans'.

42. [Etienne Tabourot], *Les Pourtraits des quatre derniers Ducs de Bourgogne*, Paris 1587: Philip the Bold.

43. Francesco Berni, *De gli eroi della serenissima casa d'Este*, Ferrara 1640: Almerico I, Marquess of Ferrara.

44. Antonio Cariola, *Ritratti de Ser^{mi} Principi d'Este Sig^{ri} de Ferrara*, Ferrara 1641: Almerico I and Tebaldo I, Marquesses of Ferrara.

45. Pirro Ligorio, drawing (pen, brown wash over black chalk) made for an illustrated genealogy of the house of Este (Oxford, Ashmolean Museum).

46. Giovanni Battista della Porta, *De Humana Physiognomia*, Vico Equense 1586: frontispiece with portrait of the author.

47. Giovanni Battista della Porta, *Della Fisionomia dell' Huomo*, Padua 1622: Cesare Borgia and Tamerlane.

48. Giovanni Battista della Porta, *Della Fisionomia dell' Huomo*, Padua 1622: Ezzelino, Tyrant of Padua.

49. Paolo Giovio, *Elogia Virorum bellica virtute illustrium*, Basle 1575: Tamerlane.

50. Paolo Giovio, *Elogia Virorum bellica virtute illustrium*, Basle 1575: Ezzelino, Tyrant of Padua.

51. Giovanni Battista della Porta, *Della Fisionomia dell' Huomo*, Padua 1622: Pico della Mirandola.

52. Giovanni Battista della Porta, *Della Fisionomia dell' Huomo*, Padua 1622: Messalina and Faustina.

53. Claude Genebrier, *Histoire de Carausius . . . Prouvée par les Médailles*, Paris 1740 (Oxford, Bodleian Library, Arch. Numm. X, 5, pl. 1): coins of the Emperor Carausius.

54. François de Mézeray, *Histoire de France*, Paris 1685, vol. I: 'Portrait of Charlemagne'.

55. François de Mézeray, *Histoire de France*, Paris 1685, vol. I: 'Reverses of medals of Charlemagne'.

56. Gregorio Leti, *Teatro Belgico*, Amsterdam 1690: Charles I.

57. Peter Stent, *Richard Cromwell*.

58. Peter Stent, *Charles II*.

59. Statue of Bishop Fell in the grounds of Nuneham Park, Oxfordshire.

60. Peter Heymanns, tapestry (446 × 690 cm) showing Martin Luther preaching in the presence of princes of the houses of Saxony and Pomerania, 1554 (Greifswald, Ernst-Moritz-Arndt-Universität).

61. Earliest-known representation of the murder – in 1170 – of Thomas à Becket, *c*.1180 (British Library, MS Cotton, Claudius B 11, f. 341).

62. Pietro Paolini, *Murder [in 1634] of General Wallenstein*, *c*.1634 (Lucca, Palazzo Orsetti).

63. *Reception [in ninth century] of the Relics of St Mark in Venice*, thirteenth-century mosaic above Porta di Sant' Alippio, basilica of S. Marco, Venice (photo: Alinari).

64. Illumination from Venetian manuscript of the mid-fourteenth century showing the emperor and the pope making peace in front of S. Marco in 1177 (Venice, Museo Correr, Cod. Correr 1, 383).

65. Giuseppe Porta (Salviati): 'The Peace of Venice', fresco in Sala Regia of Vatican Palace.

66. Jean Perrissin, *Premier volume contenant quarante tableaux ou histoires diverses qui sont memorables touchant les guerres, massacres, & troubles advenus en France en ces dernières années*, [Geneva] 1570 (Oxford, Bodleian Library, Antiq. b.v. 1): massacre at Tours in 1562.

67. Sebastiano Erizzo, *Discorso sopra le Medaglie*, 4th edition, n.d.: 'Reverse of a medal of Nero'.

68. Roman spintria (Oxford, Ashmolean Museum).

69. Pietro Santi Bartoli, engraving (in G.P. Bellori, *Columna Antoniniana Marci Aurelii*, Rome n.d.) of a relief from the column of Marcus Aurelius in Rome in which high-ranking barbarian men and women are shown giving themselves up to the emperor.

70. Pietro Santi Bartoli, engraving (in G.P. Bellori, *Colonna Traiana*, Rome n.d.) of a scene from Trajan's Column, in which the head of Decebalus, king of the Dacians, is being displayed by the victorious Roman army to Roman and Dacian soldiers.

71. Marble statue believed in the Renaissance to represent the Emperor Commodus as Hercules (Vatican Museum).

72a and b. Roman *as* of Faustina II with reverse, inscribed *Veneri Victrici*, portraying Mars and Venus (Oxford, Ashmolean Museum).

73. Marble group of Mars and Venus in the guise of an imperial couple, formerly known as 'Faustina and the Gladiator' (Paris, Louvre; photo: RMN).

74a and b. Bronze medal issued to celebrate Louis XIV's second conquest of the Franche-Comté in 1674 (London, British Museum).

75a and b. Dutch medal, dated 1693, parodying the victorious issues of Louis XIV (London, British Museum).

76. Titian, *A Concert* (Florence, Palazzo Pitti; photo: Alinari).

77. Giovanni Bottari, *Sculture e pitture sagre estratte dai cimiterj di Roma*, I, 1737: sarcophagus.

78. Detail of pl. 77, showing two figures once believed to reflect a bronze group commissioned by the woman whose issue of blood was staunched by Christ.

79. Baronius, *Annales*, II: relief from column of Marcus Aurelius showing Jupiter as the god of rain assuaging the thirst of the Roman army.

80. Antonio Bosio, title-page of *Roma Sotterranea*.

81 and 82. Painting in the catacomb of Domitilla in Rome depicting the Adoration of the (four) Magi, and the late sixteenth-century copy of the painting, interpreted as the martyrdom of a saint (photographed from Wilpert).

83 and 84. Painting in the catacomb in the cemetery of Novella (Via Salaria) in Rome depicting Noah in the Ark, and the late sixteenth-century copy of a similar painting, interpreted as St Marcellus preaching (photographed from Wilpert).

85. Maso di Banco, *St Sylvester Performing Miracles in the Roman Forum*, *c*.1335–40, fresco in the Bardi di Vernio chapel in Santa Croce, Florence.

86. Filarete, bronze reduction, dated 1465 (Dresden, Staatliche Kunstsammlungen), of the equestrian statue of Marcus Aurelius, at that time installed in front of

the Lateran palace; on the top surface of the base, Filarete identifies the emperor as Commodus.

87. Venice, façade of St Mark's (detail; photo: Alinari).

88. Florence, S. Miniato al Monte, façade (photo: Alinari).

89. Rome, Santa Costanza, detail of mosaic decoration of mid-fourth century AD, showing scenes of wine harvesting and bust of an unknown figure (photo: Scala).

90. Rome, Arch of Constantine, AD 315 (photo: Alinari).

91. Rome, Arch of Constantine, detail showing the horizontal relief of the emperor addressing the citizens, carved in the early fourth century, and, above it, circular medallions showing a hunting scene and the sacrifice to Diana after the hunt, dating from the period of Hadrian (117–38) (photo: Alinari).

92. Filippo Buonarroti, *Osservazioni sopra alcuni frammenti di vasi antichi*, 1716: bases of glass bowls of fourth century AD showing the Apostles Peter and Paul.

93. J.-B. Oudry, *Composition aux livres* (Montpellier, Musée Fabre; photo: O'Sughrue).

94. Roger de Gaignières, copy of wall painting in Sainte-Chapelle showing an artist presenting a diptych to Pope Innocent VI in the presence of Jean II, King of France, pen and brown ink with body colour and gold paint on vellum (Paris, Bibliothèque Nationale).

95. Roger de Gaignières, *Jean le Bon, Roy de France*, pen and brown ink with body colour and gold paint on vellum (Paris, Bibliothèque Nationale).

96. Montfaucon, *Monumens*, vol. I, Paris 1729, pl. vii: porch of Saint-Germain-des-Prés, Paris (now destroyed) showing 'Clovis et ses fils'.

97. Montfaucon, *Monumens*, vol. I, Paris 1729, pl. xxxv: reproduction of a part of the painted copy, made for M. Foucault, of the Bayeux Tapestry.

98. Montfaucon, *Monumens*, vol. II, Paris 1730, pl. i: reproduction of a part of the drawing, made for Montfaucon, of the Bayeux Tapestry.

99. Montfaucon, *Monumens*, vol. I, Paris 1729, pl. xxxviii: Harold and a courtier in the church at Bosham (from the reproduction of the painted copy, made for M. Foucault, of the Bayeux Tapestry).

100. Montfaucon, *Monumens*, vol. I, Paris 1729, pl. xxxvi: Edward the Confessor with Harold and a courtier (from the reproduction of the painted copy, made for M. Foucault, of the Bayeux Tapestry).

101. John Bulwer, *Chirologia*, 1644 (Oxford, Bodleian Library, 8° B 49, Art Seld., opp. p. 9): examples of gestures illustrating 'the natural language of the hand'.

102. John Bulwer, *Chironomia*, 1644 (Oxford, Bodleian Library, 8° B 49, Art Seld., opp. p. 150): examples of gestures illustrating 'the art of manual rhetoric'.

103. Gerard de Lairesse, *Het Groot Schilderboek*, Amsterdam 1707: illustration of variations in social status revealed by gestures of hands.

104. Gerard de Lairesse, *Het Groot Schilderboek*, Amsterdam 1707: illustrations of 'Liberality' (no. 3) and 'Voluntary Submission' (no. 2).

105. Gerard de Lairesse, *Het Groot Schilderboek*, Amsterdam 1707: nos 4, 5, 6 illustrate gestures representing different ways of giving.

106. Poussin, *Death of Germanicus* (Minneapolis Institute of Arts).

107. Hogarth, *Marriage à la Mode: Visit to the Doctor*.

108. J.G. Lavater, *Essai sur la Physiognomie*, vol. III, The Hague 1786 (Oxford, Bodleian Library, 165593, c. 3, vol. III, p. 194): 'Laquelle de ces deux attitudes préférez-vous? laquelle trouvez-vous la plus décente, la plus noble, la plus digne d'un caractère mâle et résolu, la plus propre à vous inspirer de l'intérêt et de la confiance?'

109. J.G. Lavater, *Essai sur la Physiognomie*, vol. III, The Hague 1786 (Oxford, Bodleian Library, 165593, c. 3, vol. III, p. 191): 'Deux femmes qui ont toute la foiblesse de leur sexe. La première a l'air d'être aux écoutes, ou plutôt de s'être égarée dans quelque rêverie; la seconde est nonchalammant assise, pour se délasser à son aise . . .'.

110. J.G. Lavater, *Essai sur la Physiognomie*, vol. III, The Hague 1786 (Oxford, Bodleian Library; 165593, c. 3, vol. III, p. 186): 'Cette attitude indique une prétention ridicule, qui exerce son empire sur un caractère humble et timide'.

111. J.G. Lavater, *Essai sur la Physiognomie*, vol. III, The Hague 1786 (Oxford, Bodleian Library; 165593, c. 3, vol. III, p. 187): 'Cinq attitudes de la même personne, représentée dans des situations différentes'.

112. Andrea de Jorio, *Mimica*, Naples 1832: gestures indicating silence (fig. 1), contempt for a dupe or a coarse figure (fig. 5) or for an imbecile (fig. 7), etc. etc.

113. Andrea de Jorio, *Mimica*, Naples 1832: 'Nè? Ch'aggio da scrivere?'

114. Andrea de Jorio, *Mimica*, Naples 1832: painting on a Greek vase showing Minerva holding a council of war.

115. Montfaucon, *Monumens*, vol. II, Paris 1730 reproduction of miniature illustrating a mid-fifteenth-century manuscript of Froissart, showing the arrival in Paris in 1324 of Isabelle, Queen of England.

116. Montfaucon, *Monumens*, vol. II, Paris 1730: reproduction of miniature illustrating a mid-fifteenth-century manuscript of Froissart, showing the capture in 1356 of the King of Navarre on the orders of Jean le Bon, King of France.

117. *Raccolta degli Imperatori Romani*, 1780: bust of the Emperor Gallienus in the Uffizi.

118. Naples, façade of the church of the Gerolimini (photo: Alinari).

119. Wolfgang Lazius, *De aliquot gentium migrationibus*, Basle, 1572 (Oxford, Bodleian Library, G. 3.2, Art, p. 784): a Lombard and an Herulian.

120. Ciampini, *Vetera Monimenta*, vol. I, Rome 1690: mosaics, said to date from the fifth or sixth century AD, in the Basilica Siciniana, Rome, depicting the martyrdoms of Saints Peter and Paul.

121. Ciampini, *Vetera Monimenta*, vol. II, Rome 1699: mosaics in S. Vitale, Ravenna.

122. G.B. Piranesi, 'Tempio di Ravenna', pen and bistre (London, Courtauld Institute Galleries).

123. Ravenna, mausoleum of Theodoric.

124. 'Conclamatio' – Italian marble relief of the fifteenth century (Paris, Louvre; photo: RMN).

125. Caylus, *Recueil*, vol. VI, Paris 1764: piece from a twelfth-century chess set from southern Italy (Paris, Bibliothèque Nationale).

126. Caylus, *Recueil*, vol. II, Paris 1756: gold plaque (late antique?) of figure holding a cornucopia.

127. Caylus, *Recueil*, vol. III, Paris 1759: Roman figures in lead and bronze.

128. Caylus, *Recueil*, vol. VI, Paris 1764: reproduction of details from the frescoes found in Herculaneum.

129. Raphael, *Pope Julius II* (London, National Gallery).

130. Head of Agrippa on bronze *as* issued by Caligula (Oxford, Ashmolean Museum).

131. Robert Adam, *Ruins of the Palace of the Emperor Diocletian*, 1764: view of the peristyle of the palace.

132. Seroux d'Agincourt, *Histoire de l'art par les monumens*, Paris 1823, vol. III, pl. ix: Seroux d'Agincourt meditating in the catacombs.

133. Paris, view of the Place des Victoires in the early eighteenth century with the marble statue by Martin Desjardins of Louis XIV. Engraving (photo courtesy of Peter Burke).

134. Desjardins's statue of Louis XIV, engraving from Northleigh, *Topographical Descriptions*, 1702 (photo courtesy of Peter Burke).

135. Desjardins, bronze figure of a bound 'slave' representing Turkey (now in the Place des Sceaux). This was removed in 1790 from the base of the marble statue of Louis XIV which was originally in the Place des Victoires and was subsequently destroyed (photo courtesy of François Souchal).

136. *L'Etruria Pittrice*, vol. I, 1791: engraving of detail of Pollaiuolo, *Martyrdom of St Sebastian*.

137. Antonio and Piero del Pollaiuolo (ascribed to), *Martyrdom of St Sebastian* (London, National Gallery).

138. *Belvedere Torso*, marble (Vatican Museum).

139. *Head of Antinous*, marble (Paris, Louvre; photo: RMN).

140. G.B. Piranesi, *Vedute di Roma*: Campo Vaccino.

141. Pugin, *Contrasts*, 2nd edition, 1846: contrasted residences for the poor.

142. Destruction in 1792 of the statues of Louis XIV in the Place Vendôme and Place des Victoires in Paris, pen and ink with wash, Soulavie Collection (Paris, Louvre: coll. Edmond de Rothschild; photo: RMN).

143. Hubert Robert: *Desecration of the Tombs at St Denis* (Paris, Musée Carnavalet).

144. Alexandre Lenoir trying to prevent the destruction of the monuments in Saint-Denis, pen and ink with wash, Soulavie Collection (Paris Louvre: coll. Edmond de Rothschild; photo: RMN).

145. J.-L. Vauzelle (engraving after), 'Salle du 13ème siècle' in the Musée des Monuments Français (Paris, Musée Carnavalet).

146. Alexandre Lenoir, *Musée des Monuments Français*, vol. v, Paris 1806: view of the Elysée.

147. C.W. Eckersberg, *Woman seated in the Elysée of the Musée des Monuments Français*, 1811, pen and ink with wash (Copenhagen, Statens Museum for Kunst).

148. 'Tomb of Héloïse and Abelard' in the Elysée of the Musée des Monuments Français etched in outline with added watercolours (Paris, Louvre; photo: RMN).

149. Léon-Mathieu Cochereau, *Artist drawing in Musée des Monuments Français* (Paris, Musée Carnavalet; photo: Bulloz).

150. *Dacian Captive*, marble (Vatican Museum, Braccio Nuovo; photo: Renan Pollès).

151. Dürer, *Self-Portrait* (Munich, Alte Pinakothek).

152. Adam Kraft, *Self-Portrait, supporting the Tabernacle* (Nuremberg, church of St Lawrence; photo: Lala Aufsberg).

153. Verona, tomb of Cansignorio (photo: Alinari).

154. Germain Pilon, *The Three Graces*, marble (Paris, Louvre; photo: RMN).

155. Germain Pilon (workshop of), *Charles IX*, marble – variant of the bust in the Louvre (New York, Metropolitan Museum of Art, Altman Bequest).

156. Marc Du Val, *The Three Coligny Brothers*, black chalk (Paris, Bibliothèque Nationale).

157. Marc Du Val, *The Three Coligny Brothers*, engraving (Paris, Bibliothèque Nationale).

158. François Clouet, *Admiral Coligny*, red and black chalks (Paris, Bibliothèque Nationale).

159. Correggio, *Mystic Marriage of St Catherine* (Paris, Louvre; photo: RMN).

160. L.-T. Turpin de Crissé, *View of Florence Cathedral* (London, Hazlitt, Gooden and Fox 1984).

161. Isidore Taylor, *Voyages Pittoresques* (Franche Comté), 1825: the church of Brou (lithograph from a drawing by Bonington, probably based on a sketch made on the spot by Taylor).

162. Alexandre de Laborde, *Versailles Ancien et Moderne*, 1841: Versailles museum.

163. Jean-Pierre Norblin, *Temple of Sibyl at Pulawy*, 1803, wash drawing (Cracow, Czartoryski Museum).

164. Ludwig Braun, *Selected Views of the Germanische Nationalmuseum*, after 1868, pencil with wash (Nuremberg, Germanische Nationalmuseum).

165. Franz Hablitschek, *Church of the Carthusian Monastery forming Part of the Germanische National-museum*, c.1864, engraving (Nuremberg, Germanische Nationalmuseum).

166. Wilhelm von Kaulbach, *Opening of the Tomb of Charlemagne on the Orders of Emperor Otho III*, 1859, fresco, now destroyed, formerly in the Germanische Nationalmuseum (photo: Germanische National-museum, Nuremberg).

167. Augustin Thierry, *Histoire de la Conquête d'Angleterre*, 5th edition, 1838: 'Edithe au cou de cygne, reconnaît le corps du roi Harold'.

168. George Vertue, *King Richard II*, with scroll representing 'this King's resignation of his crown to Henry of Bolingbroke [Henry IV]', engraving made to illustrate posthumous translation of Rapin-Thoynas, *Histoire d'Angleterre*.

169. L.A. Muratori, *Rerum Italicarum Scriptores*, vol. XII, 1728: chronicle of Andrea Dandolo, with vignette by Francesco Zucchi.

170. Charles-Nicolas Cochin, preliminary drawing (whereabouts unknown; photo courtesy of Christian Michel) of a *Ceremony of Knighting* during the last period of the second dynasty of the French monarchy, i.e., before AD 987; this was engraved in Président Hénault's *Nouvel Abrégé Chronologique de l'Histoire de France*, 1746 (see Michel, p. 231, no. 62h).

171. Joseph Strutt, reproduction of a scene from a Flemish MS of Froissart's *Chronicles* (British Library, Royal MS 18.E.ii) showing Richard II handing over his crown and sceptre to the Duke of Lancaster (Henry IV), in *The Royal and Ecclesiastical Antiquities of England*, 1773 (Oxford, Bodleian Library, PP 23, Th. Subt., pl. XXXII).

172. Joseph Strutt, *The Chronicle of England*, vol. I, 1779, showing ancient Germans and Saxons, as

described by Tacitus, Sidonius Apollinaris, Paul the Deacon and others.

173. J.G. Huck (engraved and published by Valentine Green), *Acta Historica Reginarum Angliae*, 1792: key to the sources used for 'Queen Matilda soliciting the Empress Maude for the release of her husband King Stephen from imprisonment'.

174. George Dyer, *Biographical Sketches*, 1819: Erasmus.

175. Barante, *Ducs de Bourgogne*, 6th edition, 1842: 'Mort de la duchesse d'Orléans' (by Achille Devéria).

176. W.H. Prescott, *Reign of Philip II*, London 1855, vol. II: portrait of the Duke of Alva.

177. Edouard Bordier and Edouard Charton, *Histoire de France*, 2nd edition, 1862, vol. II: reproduction of an anonymous engraving (from the Hennin Collection) of the Meeting of the States General in 1614.

178. Ruskin, *South-west Portico of St Mark's from the Loggia of the Doge's Palace*, c.1849, pencil and watercolour, heightened with white (Private Collection).

179. Tomb of Doge Michele Morosini (died 1382), early fifteenth century (Venice, SS Giovanni e Paolo; photo: Osvaldo Böhm).

180. Tomb of Doge Tommaso Mocenigo (died 1423), c.1423, signed by Pietro Lamberti and Giovanni di Martino di Fiesole (Venice, SS Giovanni e Paolo; photo: Osvaldo Böhm).

181. Tomb of Doge Franceso Foscari (died 1457), c.1457, attributed to Antonio and Paolo Bregno (Venice, Frari; photo: Osvaldo Böhm).

182. Tomb of Doge Andrea Vendramin (died 1478), completed 1490s, attributed to Pietro, Antonio and Tullio Lombardo (Venice, SS Giovanni e Paolo; photo: Osvaldo Böhm).

183. Tomb of Doge Giovanni Pesaro (died 1659), 1669, by Longhena and Melchior Barthel (Venice, Frari; photo: Osvaldo Böhm).

184. Venice, Palazzo Ducale, corner of façades facing the Piazzetta and the Lagoon: Fall of Man; end of fourteenth century, Istrian stone (photo: Alinari).

185. Venice, Palazzo Ducale, angle of façade adjoining Porta della Carta: Justice of Solomon; late 1420s or early 1430s, Istrian stone (photo: Alinari).

186. Venice, Palazzo Ducale (photo: Alinari).

187. Torcello cathedral: detail of ambo, reconstructed in the fourteenth century from much earlier fragments (photo: Alinari).

188. Hermine von Reck, *Jacob Burckhardt*, 1853 (Basle, Private Collection; photo: Universitäts-Bibliothek, Basel).

189. Raphael, *Expulsion of Heliodorus*, fresco (Vatican Palace, Stanza dell'Eliodoro; photo: Alinari).

190. Façade of Palazzo Pitti, Florence, originally designed by Brunelleschi c.1440, but vastly changed in character and increased in scale in late sixteenth and early seventeenth centuries (photo: Alinari).

191. Donatello, *Mary Magdalen*, polychrome wood (Florence, Baptistery; photo: Alinari).

192. Francesco da Sangallo (attributed to), *St John the Baptist*, marble, 1520s(?) (Florence, Museo del Bargello; photo: Alinari).

193. Matteo Civitale, *Adoring Angel*, after 1477 (Lucca cathedral, Capella del Sacramento; photo: Alinari).

194. Matteo Civitale, *Adoring Angel*, after 1477 (Lucca cathedral, Capella del Sacramento; photo: Alinari).

195. Donatello, *Annunciation* (Florence S. Croce; photo: Alinari).

196. Detail of pl. 195.

197. Martyr saints, mosaics, sixth century AD (Ravenna, S. Apollinare Nuovo; photo: Alinari).

198. Percier and Fontaine, *Choix des plus célèbres maisons de plaisance de Rome et de ses environs*, Paris 1809: general view of Villa Albani.

199. Rome, Gesù: interior (photo: Scala).

200. H.F. Verbrugghen, pulpit carved between 1696 and 1699 for Jesuit church in Louvain (Brussels cathedral), lithograph published in 1840s by Louis Granello of Antwerp.

201. Scipione Pulzone (attributed to), *Portrait of a Lady* (Rome, Palazzo Doria; photo: Alinari).

202. Rome, Gesù: altar of St Ignatius designed by Andrea Pozzo, c.1695, polychrome marble, bronze, silver and other precious materials: on left, Théodon's *Triumph of Faith over Paganism* and, on right, Legros's *Religion overthrowing Heresy*; both marble, 1695–9 (photo: Scala).

203. G.B. Gaulli (Baciccio), *Triumph of the Name of Jesus*, 1676–9, fresco on the vault of the nave of the Gesù in Rome (photo: Scala).

204. J.P. Malcolm, *Art of Caricaturing*, 1813: fig. 1 reproduces an Elizabethan satirical engraving directed against the pope, and figs 2 and 3 show Roman lamps.

205. J.P. Malcolm, *Art of Caricaturing*, 1813: reproduction of a miniature from Harleian MS 603 (in British Library).

206. T. Panofka, *Parodieen und Karikaturen*, Berlin 1851: various parodies of Greek myth mostly to be seen on archaic vases.

207. Jules Adeline, *Les Sculptures grotesques*: wooden sculptures in Rouen (Salle des Pas-Perdus) and Bourg-Achard (stall in church).

208. Champfleury, *Faiences patriotiques*, 2nd edition, 1867: salad bowl from Nevers.

209. Champfleury, *Faiences patriotiques*, 2nd edition, 1867: cistern from Nevers.

210. Champfleury, *Faiences patriotiques*, 2nd edition, 1867: dish from unknown factory.

211. Champfleury, *Faiences patriotiques*, 2nd edition, 1867: dish from unknown factory.

212. Flemish fifteenth-century tapestry: scenes from the life of Alexander the Great (Rome, Palazzo Doria; photo: Alinari).

213. Antonio Pollaiuolo, *Battle of the Nude Men*, engraving (Oxford, Ashmolean Museum).

214. Details of earlier and later versions of an engraving (attributed to Baccio Baldini) of the planet Venus, published by Aby Warburg on adjoining pages to demonstrate the reform *all'antica* of the 'barbaric Northern costume' of the woman dancing.

215. Domenico Ghirlandajo, *Confirmation of the Rule of the Franciscan Order by Pope Honorius III*, fresco (Florence, Santa Trinita, Sassetti chapel; photo: Alinari).

216. Tobias Stimmer, *Abzeichnis etlicher wolbedenklicher Bilder von Romischen abgotsdienst*, coloured woodcut of 1573 republished by Bernhard Jobin in 1576 (Zurich, Zentralbibliothek).

217. Van Dyck, *Charles I in Three Positions* (The Royal Collection, Windsor Castle. © Her Majesty the Queen; photo: Alinari).

218. Van Dyck, *Charles I* (The Royal Collection, St James's Palace. © Her Majesty the Queen; photo: A.C. Cooper).

219. Jacques-Louis David, *Oath of the Horatii* (Paris, Louvre; photo: RMN).

220. P.A. Martini, *The Salon of 1785*, engraving.

221. Jacques-Louis David, preliminary drawing for the *Oath of the Tennis Court*, pencil, pen and ink with wash and heightening with white (Paris, Louvre, Cabinet des Dessins, on deposit in the Musée National of Versailles; photo: RMN).

222. Jacques-Louis David, unfinished and cut-down painting for the *Oath of the Tennis Court*, oil with black chalk, white chalk, brown ink on canvas (Paris, Louvre, Cabinet des Dessins on deposit in the Musée National of Versailles; photo: RMN).

223. Raphael, *Transfiguration* (Vatican, Pinacoteca).

224. Dürer, *Apocalypse: The Battle of the Angels*, woodcut (London, British Museum).

225. Dürer, *Apocalypse: St Michael fighting the Dragon*, woodcut (London, British Museum).

226. Dürer, *Apocalypse: The Four Horsemen of the Apocalypse*, woodcut (London, British Museum).

227. Dürer, *Apocalypse: The Angel with the Key hurls the Dragon into the Abyss, and Another Angel shows St John the New Jerusalem*, woodcut (London, British Museum).

228. Dürer, *Apocalypse: St John receiving his Commands from Heaven*, woodcut (London, British Museum).

229. Dürer, *Apocalypse: The Whore of Babylon*, woodcut (London, British Museum).

230. Picasso, *Violin and Grapes*, spring–summer 1912, oil on canvas, 50.6 × 61 cm (Collection, The Museum of Modern Art, New York. Mrs. David M. Levy Bequest).

231. Giacomo Balla, *Abstract Speed – The Car has passed*, 1913 (London, Tate Gallery).

232. Piet Mondrian, *Composition No. 7 (Façade)*, 1914, oil on canvas, 120.3 × 101.3 cm (Fort Worth, Kimbell Art Museum, Gift of the Anne Burnett and Charles Tandy Foundation of Fort Worth in memory of Anne Burnett Tandy, 1983).

233. Kasimir Malevich, *Painterly Realism. Boy with Knapsack – Colour Masses in the Fourth Dimension*, 1914–15, oil on canvas, 71.1 × 44.5 cm (Collection, The Museum of Modern Art, New York).

234. Ludwig Meidner, *Apocalyptic Landscape*, 1913, oil on canvas, 95.2 × 80 cm (Los Angeles County Museum of Art, gift of Clifford Odets).

235. Ludwig Meidner, *Wahnsee Bahnhof*, ink with white highlights, 1913 (Los Angeles County Museum of Art, The Robert Gore Rifkind Center for German Expressionist Studies).

236. Wassily Kandinsky, *Fragment 2 for Composition VII*, 1913, oil on canvas, 87.6 × 89.7 cm (Buffalo, New York, Albright-Knox Art Gallery, Room of Contemporary Art Fund, 1947).

237. Gerard David (at one time attributed to Jan Van Eyck), *Marriage at Cana* (Paris, Louvre; photo: RMN).

238. Holbein (old copy after), *Madonna of the Burgomeister Meyer* (Dresden, Gemäldegalerie).

239. Memling, Moreel triptych (Bruges, Groeninge Museum).

240. Stefan Lochner, *Adoration of the Magi with Saints Ursula and Gereon* (Cologne, cathedral; photo: © Rheinisches Bildarchiv, Cologne).

241. Jan Van Eyck, Ghent altarpiece: central panel representing the *Adoration of the Lamb* (Ghent, cathedral of St Bavon; photo: Scala).

242. Jan Van Eyck, Ghent altarpiece: *Adam* (Ghent, cathedral of St Bavon; photo: Scala).

243. Jan Van Eyck, Ghent altarpiece: *Eve* (Ghent, cathedral of St Bavon; photo: Scala).

244. Pieter Brueghel, *The Land of Cockaigne* (Munich, Alte Pinakothek).

245. Jan Van Eyck, *Virgin of Canon van der Paele* (Bruges, Groeninge Museum; photo: Institut Royal, Brussels).

246. Master of the Youth of St Romold, '*Enthronement of St Thomas à Becket*' (Dublin, National Gallery of Ireland).

247. Hubert(?) Van Eyck *Three Marys at the Sepulchre* (Rotterdam, Boymans van Beuningen Museum; photo: Tom Haartsen).

248. Memling, *Shrine of St Ursula* (Bruges, Hospice of Saint-Jean; photo: Institut Royal, Brussels).

249. Memling, *Donne Triptych* (London, National Gallery).

250. Gerard David, *Baptism of Christ with an Angel* (Bruges, Groeninge Museum; photo: Scala).

251. Gerard David, *Virgin and Child with Saints and Angels* (Rouen, Musée des Beaux-Arts).

252. Gerard David, *Flaying of the Unjust Judge Sisamnes* (Bruges, Groeninge Museum; photo: Institut Royal, Brussels).

253. Johan Huizinga (photo courtesy of Anton van der Lem).

254. Johan Huizinga, *1444: In Dodeward werdt een blofiende appelboom gezien in Maart (1444: In Dodeward a flowering apple-tree is seen in March)*, from Huizinga, *Keur van gedenkwaardige tafereelen*, Amsterdam 1950.

255. Claus Sluter, well (Chartreuse de Champmol, Dijon; photo: David Finn).

256. Claus Sluter, tomb of Philip the Bold: detail showing procession of 'pleurants' (Dijon, Musée des Beaux-Arts; photo: David Finn).

257. Jan Van Eyck, *Portrait of his Wife Margaret* (Bruges, Groeninge Museum; photo: Institut Royal, Brussels).

258. Jan Van Eyck, Ghent altarpiece: panel with *Angel Choir* (Ghent, cathedral of St Bavon; photo: Scala).

259. Jan Van Eyck, *Annunciation* (Washington, National Gallery of Art: Mellon Collection).

260. Jan Van Eyck, *Virgin of the Chancellor Rolin* (Paris, Louvre; photo: Institut Royal, Brussels).

261. Jean Fouquet, *Virgin and Child* (Antwerp, Musée des Beaux-Arts).

262. Roger van der Weyden (follower of), *Philip the Good* (Madrid, Royal Palace; photo: MAS).

Index